Understanding
Secured Transactions

CAROLINA ACADEMIC PRESS

Understanding Series

UNDERSTANDING
ADMINISTRATIVE LAW
Seventh Edition
Kristin E. Hickman

UNDERSTANDING ALTERNATIVE
DISPUTE RESOLUTION,
Second Edition
Kristen M. Blankley and
Maureen A. Weston

UNDERSTANDING ANIMAL LAW
Adam Karp

UNDERSTANDING
ANTITRUST AND ITS ECONOMIC
IMPLICATIONS
Seventh Edition
E. Thomas Sullivan and Jeffrey L. Harrison

UNDERSTANDING
BANKRUPTCY
Fourth Edition
Jeffrey Ferriell and Edward J. Janger

UNDERSTANDING
CALIFORNIA COMMUNITY
PROPERTY LAW
Second Edition
Jo Carrillo

UNDERSTANDING
CAPITAL PUNISHMENT LAW
Fifth Edition
Linda E. Carter, Ellen S. Kreitzberg,
Scott W. Howe, and
Celestine Richards McConville

UNDERSTANDING CIVIL PROCEDURE
Seventh Edition
Gene R. Shreve, Peter Raven-Hansen,
and Charles Gardner Geyh

UNDERSTANDING CIVIL PROCEDURE
The California Edition
Walter W. Heiser,
Gene R. Shreve, Peter Raven-Hansen,
and Charles Gardner Geyh

UNDERSTANDING
CIVIL RIGHTS LITIGATION
Third Edition
Howard M. Wasserman

UNDERSTANDING
CONFLICT OF LAWS
Fourth Edition
William M. Richman, William L. Reynolds,
and Chris A. Whytock

UNDERSTANDING
CONSTITUTIONAL LAW
Fifth Edition
William D. Araiza

UNDERSTANDING CONTRACTS
Fifth Edition
Jeffrey Ferriell

UNDERSTANDING
COPYRIGHT LAW
Eighth Edition
Marshall A. Leaffer

UNDERSTANDING
CORPORATE LAW
Sixth Edition
Arthur R. Pinto and
James A. Fanto

UNDERSTANDING
CORPORATE TAXATION
Fourth Edition
Leandra Lederman and Michelle Kwon

UNDERSTANDING CRIMINAL LAW
Ninth Edition
Joshua Dressler

UNDERSTANDING CRIMINAL
PROCEDURE VOL. 1:
INVESTIGATION
Eighth Edition
Joshua Dressler, Alan C. Michaels
and Ric Simmons

UNDERSTANDING
CRIMINAL PROCEDURE VOL. 2:
ADJUDICATION
Fifth Edition
Joshua Dressler, Alan C. Michaels.
and Ric Simmons

UNDERSTANDING
DISABILITY LAW
Fourth Edition
Mark C. Weber

Understanding
Secured Transactions

SIXTH EDITION

William H. Henning
EXECUTIVE PROFESSOR OF LAW
TEXAS A&M UNIVERSITY SCHOOL OF LAW

R. Wilson Freyermuth
ROBERT L. HAWKINS, JR./DALE A. WHITMAN CHAIR IN LAW
CURATORS' DISTINGUISHED TEACHING PROFESSOR
UNIVERSITY OF MISSOURI SCHOOL OF LAW

Brook E. Gotberg
PROFESSOR OF LAW
BRIGHAM YOUNG UNIVERSITY J. REUBEN CLARK LAW SCHOOL

CAROLINA ACADEMIC PRESS
Durham, North Carolina

LIBRARY OF CONGRESS CATALOGING-IN-PUBLICATION DATA

Names: Henning, William H., 1947- author. | Freyermuth, R. Wilson, 1962-
author. | Gotberg, Brook E., author. |
Title: Understanding secured transactions / William H. Henning, R. Wilson
Freyermuth, Brook E. Gotberg.
Description: Sixth edition. | Durham : Carolina Academic Press, 2024. |
Series: Understanding series | Revised edition of: Understanding secured
transactions / William H. Lawrence, William H. Henning, R. Wilson
Freyermuth. 5th ed. c2012. | Includes bibliographical references and
index.
Identifiers: LCCN 2024022059 | ISBN 9781531027551 (paperback) | ISBN
9781531027568 (ebook)
Subjects: LCSH: Security (Law)—United States.
Classification: LCC KF1050 .L39 2024 | DDC 346.7307/4—dc23
LC record available at https://lccn.loc.gov/2024022059

Carolina Academic Press
700 Kent Street
Durham, North Carolina 27701
(919) 489-7486
www.cap-press.com

Printed in the United States of America

For my wonderful wife, Sandra, with all my love and gratitude.
W.H.H.

For my wife, Shari, with love and gratitude.
R.W.F.

For Mom and Dad—my best teachers.
B.E.G.

Contents

PART III · PERFECTION OF SECURITY INTERESTS

PART IV · PRIORITIES

PART V · DEFAULT

Chapter 17 · Default and Its Consequences

CONTENTS

Acknowledgment

This is the first edition of this book without Bill Lawrence (whom we referred to occasionally as "Jayhawk Bill" from his years teaching at the University of Kansas) as a co-author. The series began in 1997, before revised Article 9 became effective in 2001, when Bill Lawrence, Bill Henning, and Wilson Freyermuth teamed up for the first time. The book evolved as the law evolved. The second edition was transitional—the text focused primarily on pre-revision Article 9, and the revision's provisions were interspersed in bold. A third edition followed soon thereafter and shifted the focus to the revision. The Bankruptcy Code was amended by BAPCPA in 2005, and the fourth edition came out the next year. After that there was a hiatus, but the 2010 amendments to Article 9 spurred the team into action again. Jayhawk Bill's fifth and last edition came out in 2012.

This edition was needed after the 2022 amendments brought the U.C.C. into the digital age. Sadly, Bill passed away just as the amendments were being approved. He was our senior partner and a dear friend. We miss him.

Brook Gotberg joins us for this edition, and she's been a wonderful partner. All three authors acknowledge the enormous contributions Bill Lawrence made to this book, many of which still remain apparent in this edition. His name should be on the cover with ours, but he insisted otherwise before his death. That was Bill—brilliant and hard-working but humble. We're proud of this new edition but wish Bill had been along for the ride.

William H. Henning
R. Wilson Freyermuth
Brook E. Gotberg
June 2024

Preface

Like the other books in the *Understanding* series, this book is designed as a student text. Our approach is to aid students' understanding of secured transactions by informing them about both the law and the nature of the transactions to which the law applies.

The primary sources of law are Article 9 of the Uniform Commercial Code (U.C.C., or Code) and selected provisions of the Bankruptcy Code. Beyond a focus on the text of the statutes, an analysis of their underlying rationales is critical to an in-depth understanding of the codified provisions. The Official Comments to the U.C.C. and the Historical and Revision Notes to the Bankruptcy Code are helpful but often lack sufficient insights or clarity to provide adequate guidance. Learning the essence of each statutory section in isolation is difficult and insufficient; students must learn to interrelate multiple sections in a sophisticated manner in order to solve problems in this complex area of the law.

When the first edition of this book was published, the 1972 text of Article 9, as amended from time to time, was in effect. In 1998, the U.C.C.'s sponsoring bodies, the Uniform Law Commission and the American Law Institute, adopted a revised version of Article 9.[1] The revision represented a comprehensive modernization and reformulation of the law governing secured transactions. It was not in effect in any state as of the publication date of the second edition of this book, which was designed as a transitional work. The primary emphasis of the second edition was the 1972 Official Text, but it also provided a discussion of the revision and explained how its provisions would change existing law.

The 1998 revision was a remarkable success. It was promulgated with a delayed effective date of July 1, 2001, and by that date it was in effect in virtually every state, with the other states coming along within a few months thereafter. This universal adoption compelled the third edition, which focused on the revision and discussed former law only to the extent necessary to shed light on particular provisions of the revision.

The fourth edition incorporated significant revisions to bankruptcy law resulting from the Bankruptcy Abuse Prevention and Consumer Protection Act of 2005, and the fifth edition was necessitated by a significant set of amendments to Article 9

---

1. The sponsors approved minor amendments to the 1998 Official Text in 1999, 2000, and 2001.

promulgated by the sponsors in 2012. As with the 1998 revision, a deferred effective date (July 1, 2013) was selected, and again the amendments were universally adopted.

In 2019, the sponsors began a three-year drafting process that resulted in the promulgation of a sweeping set of amendments to the entire U.C.C. The purpose of the amendments is to adapt the Code to emerging technologies, such as artificial intelligence, distributed ledger technology, and virtual currency. They include a new Article 12 governing the holding and transfer of digital assets and a set of conforming amendments to Article 9 that facilitate the leveraging of those assets. At this time only 21 states have enacted the amendments, but as with previous major revisions, universal adoption is anticipated. This sixth edition thoroughly explains the 2022 amendments.

The law of secured transactions reflects business practices with which many students are unfamiliar. An understanding of the essential aspects of the transactions is crucial for any student who seeks to comprehend the law that governs them. This book explains different types of secured transactions. For example, it describes the structure and use of financing arrangements that are made possible through such techniques as asset-based securitization, mortgage warehouse lending, terminal and field warehousing, financing of accounts, factoring of accounts, and floor planning, as well as other methods of transacting business. The discussion of each financing arrangement is integrated into the place in the text in which the relevant substantive concepts are covered.

Much of the practice in the area of secured transactions involves preventative law, in which the practitioner advises the client on alternative methods of structuring transactions and the risks associated with each option. The book integrates and develops significant aspects of these considerations, going beyond the text of the U.C.C. by explaining the practical constraints that ultimately shape decision-making in this field.

The organization of the text's subject matter is largely based upon the traditional five-part approach to the law of secured transactions: (1) scope of the article, (2) attachment (creation) of security interests, (3) perfection of security interests, (4) priorities among competing claimants to collateral (i.e., the effects of being perfected or unperfected), and (5) enforcement of security interests. This organizational scheme is emphasized by designating each of these five concepts as a separate Part of the book.

Entries in the Table of Contents include a descriptive word or phrase, along with relevant section numbers of the U.C.C. and the Bankruptcy Code. It does not cite all the provisions that might be relevant, but only the most fundamental provisions relating to a particular topic. This approach should aid students using the book as a supplemental text by enabling them to find the relevant discussion based on either the subject or the basic statutory section numbers. The Table of Statutes and Index enable a more detailed search.

Understanding
Secured Transactions

Part I

Scope

<hr>

Synopsis

[A] The Security Concept
[B] An Organizational Overview of Article 9
[C] The Revised and Amended Uniform Commercial Code

[A] The Security Concept

The concept of a secured obligation developed to encourage lending, and thus promote commercial activity, by reducing the risk borne by lenders. Absent security, a borrower's promise to repay money, albeit legally enforceable, might not suffice to induce a prospective lender to proceed with a transaction—and even if the lender agreed to proceed, the terms, especially the interest rate, would inevitably reflect the level of risk. Similarly, a seller might be reluctant to give a prospective buyer current possession of property based solely on the buyer's promise to make installment payments. Lenders and credit sellers inevitably, whether secured or not, run the risk that an obligor will prove unable or unwilling to make the agreed payments. An unsecured creditor of either type that wishes to enforce its rights following a breach must proceed by judicial action. The process can be long and expensive, requiring a lawsuit to reduce the claim to judgment and then perhaps an execution on the judgment. To execute on a judgment, the successful litigant must procure a writ of execution, which empowers the sheriff to levy on property of the judgment debtor. Statutorily based exemption provisions will likely shield some or all of the debtor's property from the execution process. The sheriff will conduct an auction sale (which often yields a low price) for property reached and will distribute the proceeds to the judgment creditor in full or partial satisfaction of the judgment. The expense and delay associated with these procedures leaves lenders and credit sellers reluctant to rely solely on their rights under debt or sales law.

Lenders and credit sellers can enhance their positions in two major ways. They can insist that their obligor obtain a promise from a third person to act as surety and pay the obligation in the event of default. They can also insist that their obligor grant them an interest in real or personal property as security. The latter technique gives the creditor a special property interest in the identified property. One of the great advantages of this enhanced position is that, in the event of default, the creditor can proceed directly against the collateral without first reducing its claim to judgment. Secured creditors thus can reduce significantly the costs and delays associated with enforcement of their rights.

Although mortgage financing and secured financing are analogous with regard to real and personal property, respectively, separate bodies of law govern them. The focus of this book is on secured personal-property financing, with Article 9 of the Uniform Commercial Code (U.C.C., or the Code) as the predominant applicable law. The book discusses some overlaps between the bodies of law, the most important being the treatment of fixtures.[1]

In Article 9 terminology, the creditor's special property interest is a "security interest,"[2] and it is created through the consent of the debtor. Absent a security interest, a creditor does not have a property interest in any particular asset of its debtor. An unsecured credit seller of goods does not retain a property interest even in the goods sold;[3] in the event of a breach, the seller's basic remedy is its Article 2 claim for the unpaid balance of the purchase price.[4] Acquiring a consensual security interest adds to the rights available to secured parties under Article 9.

Although a security interest gives a secured party a property interest in identified assets of the debtor, the interest is unique, with two primary features defining its essential nature. First, a secured party does not have any right to foreclose on collateral unless a default occurs.[5] Because the secured party's property interest does not allow it to proceed against the property absent default, such action would constitute conversion. Second, even following a default, the secured party's disposition of the collateral is only for the purpose of satisfying the outstanding indebtedness. Generally, the secured party will dispose of the collateral by sale and apply the proceeds of the sale to the amount of the debt still owed.[6] A security interest thus allows a creditor, after default and without judicial process, to sell specific assets of the debtor to satisfy the outstanding indebtedness.

---

1. Chapter 15 discusses fixtures. *See also* § 1.06[C], *infra* (discussion of secondary financing transactions involving real estate).

2. U.C.C. § 1-201(b)(35).

3. A "sale" involves the passage of title to goods for a price. U.C.C. § 2-106(1). Unless the seller and buyer agree otherwise, the goods belong to the buyer, and the seller receives in exchange only a legally enforceable right to the purchase price. U.C.C. §§ 2-607(1), 2-709(1).

4. A credit seller may also have a right to reclaim the goods themselves from the buyer, but such a right is extremely limited. The seller must ascertain that the buyer received the goods while insolvent, and even then the seller generally must notify the buyer of its intent to reclaim them within ten days following their receipt. *See* U.C.C. § 2-702(2).

5. "*After default*, a secured party has the rights provided in this [Part 6 governing enforcement of security interest]...." U.C.C. § 9-601(a) (emphasis supplied). For a discussion of this provision, see § 17.02, *infra*.

6. U.C.C. § 9-615(a). The secured party cannot retain any surplus realized from the sale but rather must account for it to the debtor. U.C.C. § 9-615(d). For discussion of the disposition of collateral after default, see § 18.02, *infra*.

[B] An Organizational Overview of Article 9

The content of Article 9 is organized around five major concepts: (1) the scope of the article, (2) attachment of security interests, (3) perfection of security interests, (4) priorities among competing claimants to collateral, and (5) enforcement of security interests. These concepts are so logical and basic that they constitute the subjects of the five parts of this book.

Scope questions focus on whether Article 9 governs a particular transaction. The applicability of Article 9 is one of the most litigated areas under the U.C.C. A transaction may be labeled as something other than a security interest by the parties (e.g., a lease or consignment) yet be the functional equivalent of an Article 9 secured transaction and thus within the article's scope.[7] In addition, certain transactions involving the outright sale of payment rights also fall within the scope of the article.[8]

Attachment of a security interest addresses the creation of security interests. The process is contractual because Article 9 security interests are consensual in nature. The essential requirements are quite simple, although troublesome questions inevitably arise in specific contexts.

While the relationship between a secured party and a debtor is established by agreement, a secured party must also be concerned about the possibility of competing third-party claims to the collateral. In particular, courts are sympathetic with third parties that enter into relationships with the debtor on the mistaken belief that the debtor holds unencumbered ownership of assets in its possession. This problem is sometimes referred to as an "ostensible ownership" problem. To enhance its position against such claimants, a secured party must ordinarily "perfect" its security interest, generally by taking steps designed to give public notice of the interest (although some security interests are perfected automatically without public notice). The most effective mechanism for overcoming the ostensible-ownership problem is for the secured party to take possession of the collateral, and thus possession is an accepted method of perfection for assets capable of being physically possessed. Possession is impossible with certain intangible types of collateral and often impractical with others, however, and the most commonly used method of perfection is the public filing of a financing statement.[9] Several additional methods of perfection are available in limited circumstances. The discussion of perfection in this book focuses on the applicable methods and the policy choices that the drafters made in devising the perfection process.

If multiple persons claim competing interests in the same property, the law must have rules by which it can prioritize the competing interests. If one of the competing claimants is a secured party, Article 9 provides most of the priority rules. Federal bankruptcy law is also important with respect to secured claims asserted in a bankruptcy

---

7. See § 1.03[B], *infra.*
8. See § 1.05, *infra.*
9. Filing is the default method of perfection under Article 9. U.C.C. § 9-310(a). An overview of the various methods is provided in Chapter 4, *infra.*

proceeding. Some of the third-party claimants with which a secured party might have to compete include a bankruptcy trustee; another secured party; an unsecured creditor that causes the sheriff to levy on the collateral; a person that buys, leases, or licenses the collateral from the debtor; a person that stores or repairs the collateral and thereby acquires a claim to it based on state law other than Article 9; and a person with an interest in real estate to which a fixture that is collateral is affixed. This list by no means exhausts the potential claimants.

Default is a pivotal concept because it permits the secured party to enforce its security interest against the collateral. The enforcement phase of a transaction is sometimes referred to as the "foreclosure process." The issues associated with default include a determination of the events that constitute a default, the rights and duties of the parties following a default, the method chosen for the disposition of the collateral, and the provisions dealing with misbehavior by the secured party.

[C] The Revised and Amended Uniform Commercial Code

The Uniform Commercial Code is the product of a partnership between two organizations: the Uniform Law Commission[10] and the American Law Institute. After approval of an Official Text by the sponsors, it is introduced in the legislatures of the various states[11] and only becomes law to the extent of its adoptions.

The 1962 Official Text of the Uniform Commercial Code was the first to be widely enacted, and the approach to secured transactions in Article 9 of that text departed radically from pre-Code security laws.[12] Article 9 was extensively revised in 1972 and again in 1998. The 1998 Official Text has been amended several times, most recently in 2022. The 2022 amendments will not have been enacted by all the states by the time this edition is published, but universal enactment is anticipated, and thus a citation to Article 9 in this book that does not designate an official text is to the 2022 Official Text. When the book refers to the intent of the original drafters, it cites to the 1962 Official Text. When it refers to the law in effect immediately before the 2022 amendments, it cites to the 1998 Official Text or the 1998 revision. Unless otherwise stated, all citations to other articles of the Code are to the latest Official Text of those articles.

As part of the Uniform Commercial Code, Article 9 is a statutory model that has no force of law until it is enacted by an appropriate legislative body. Congress has never enacted any of the Code as federal law. State legislatures generally have been the enacting bodies.[13] The states are free to make changes and frequently do, thus the term

---

10. The formal name of the Uniform Law Commission is the National Conference of Commissioners on Uniform State Laws.

11. As used in the U.C.C., the term "state" means "a State of the United States, the District of Columbia, Puerto Rico, the United States Virgin Islands, or any territory or insular possession subject to the jurisdiction of the United States." U.C.C. § 9-102(a)(77).

12. *See* § 1.02, *infra*. There were largely unsuccessful versions of the Code published prior to 1962.

13. Article 9 has been adopted by certain Native American tribes, and there is reason to expect that this will occur more frequently in the future since the Uniform Law Commission has drafted a version

"uniform" isn't literally correct. Perhaps it would be better to say the states harmonize their laws. A lawyer researching an issue should consult the applicable state's version of the Code.

Although one of the underlying objectives of the Uniform Commercial Code is to promote uniformity of law among the various jurisdictions,[14] state legislatures can and frequently do deviate from the Code model. As a result, readers of this book should be mindful of the fact that the book discusses the uniform provisions found in the Official Text of Article 9 as promulgated by its sponsors and that a particular jurisdiction may have adopted a variation of a uniform provision.

---

of revised Article 9 titled the Model Tribal Secured Transactions Act (MTSTA) that is specifically adapted to tribal needs. The MTSTA was originally promulgated in 2005 and a revised version was promulgated in 2017. The revised MTSTA may be accessed at https://www.uniformlaws.org/committees/community-home?CommunityKey=1f31aa7f-74be-457e-904b-ba3b6d7d3646.

14. U.C.C. § 1-103(a)(3).

Chapter 1

Transactions within Article 9

Synopsis

§ 1.01 The Pre-Code Disarray of Secured Transactions Law

The law governing the use of personal property as collateral prior to the promulgation of the U.C.C. was inefficient, unduly complicated, and inadequate. It consisted of a patchwork quilt of common-law rules and statutes governing each of the security devices that states chose to recognize. Some of the traditional security devices included the pledge (in which the lender took possession of the collateral pending default or repayment), chattel mortgage (in which the debtor retained possession pending default), conditional sale (in which the seller delivered goods to the buyer but retained title pending payment), trust receipt (a three-party arrangement by which a lender financed a dealer's acquisition of new inventory from a supplier), and factor's lien (in which the debtor obtained financing on the strength of its existing inventory).[15]

Because each security device was the subject of a separate rule or statute, differences in formal requirements were common. For example, failure to file public notice of a chattel mortgage generally voided the mortgage against all third parties, whereas filing was not needed for a conditional sale or, at most, was required only for the seller to prevail over lien creditors. States maintained multiple filing systems to accommodate the different security devices, and inconsistencies in formalities, rights, and filing requirements abounded. Most of the differences lacked functional justifications. Errors attributable to the undue complexity of the overall system were frequent and had a serious impact on affected parties. Despite the multiplicity of security devices, the overall system was inadequate. The economy constantly evolves, thereby necessitating the creation of new types of transactions that are responsive to unique business conditions. Some desirable secured financing transactions could not go forward because they did not fall squarely within the parameters of any of the existing security devices. For example, despite increased interest in using inventory and intangible assets as collateral, lenders struggled for years to develop devices that would be effective for these

---

15. Other devices, usually authorized by statute, permitted the use of accounts receivable as collateral, facilitated the establishment of corporate trust indentures, and authorized the use of field warehouses. Article 9 originally provided a laundry list of pre-Code security devices. *See* U.C.C. § 9-102(2) (1962 Official Text). By the time of the 1998 revision, the list was no longer considered necessary.

kinds of assets. Some states eventually solved these problems with new, statutorily sanctioned security devices, but ultimately this approach proved unpalatable as each device added new wrinkles to an already overly complex system. The state of the law imposed unacceptable delay, cost, and uncertainty.

§ 1.02 The Unitary Approach of Article 9; Terminology Describing Parties

The promulgation of Article 9 of the U.C.C. represented a significant milestone in the law of secured financing. Article 9 provides the basis for a single, comprehensive statutory framework for the governance of secured transactions in personal property and fixtures. The original drafters stated their objective succinctly in the Comments: "The aim of this Article is to provide a simple and unified structure within which the immense variety of present-day secured financing transactions can go forward with less cost and with greater certainty."[16]

Article 9 achieved this objective by adopting a unitary approach to secured transactions. It did not abolish the previously existing security devices[17]—even today, terms like "pledge" and "conditional sale" are occasionally used—but it did repeal prior statutes governing the devices, bringing them all within its scope. Unless specifically excluded,[18] Article 9 applies to all transactions that create security interests in personal property or fixtures by contract, and neither the form of the transaction nor the terminology used by the parties is controlling. In other words, all consensual transactions that created security interests in personal property or fixtures were swept into the article.[19]

In addition to overcoming the disarray associated with prior secured-financing law, the enactment of Article 9, with its comprehensive, unitary approach, facilitated the use of new financing methods. The benefits of such flexibility were touted as among the basic objectives of the article. The original Comments stated,

> The Article's flexibility and simplified formalities should make it possible for new forms of secured financing, as they develop, to fit comfortably under its provisions, thus avoiding the necessity, so apparent in recent years, of year by year passing new statutes and tinkering with the old ones to allow legitimate business transactions to go forward.[20]

The simplification achieved by Article 9's unitary approach is readily demonstrated through the terms used to describe secured transactions and their participants. Irre-

---

16. U.C.C. §9-101, Comment (1962 Official Text). Despite the promulgation of earlier Official Texts, the U.C.C. was not widely adopted until the promulgation of the 1962 Official Text.

17. U.C.C. §9-102(2) and Comment 1 (1962 Official Text).

18. See §1.05, infra.

19. U.C.C. §9-102(1)(a) (1962 Official Text); U.C.C. §9-109(a)(1).

20. U.C.C. §9-101, Comment (1962 Official Text).

spective of the nature of the transaction or the terminology employed by the parties, Article 9 applies a consistent set of terms. The underlying "security agreement"[21] creates a "security interest"[22] in favor of a "secured party."[23] The property that is subject to the security interest is the "collateral."[24] The person that provides the collateral is the "debtor."[25] The term "obligor" describes the person that owes payment or performance of the secured obligation.[26] If the transaction is a consumer transaction,[27] the terms "consumer debtor"[28] and "consumer obligor"[29] apply.

Article 9 also contains certain provisions that apply to parties that are secondarily obligated[30] (such as sureties), and such parties are known as "secondary obligors."[31]

To illustrate the terminology, suppose A needs to borrow money but has insufficient collateral. A's friend, B, allows A to use her car as collateral but refuses to become personally obligated, meaning that she will not be personally liable for the deficiency if A defaults and foreclosure on the car yields less than the amount of the secured obligation. Even this security is not enough for the secured party, and another friend, C, incurs personal liability for the debt, either by co-signing A's promissory note for accommodation[32] or by signing a separate guaranty agreement.[33] On these facts, A is an obligor but not a debtor, B is a debtor but not an obligor, and C is both an obligor and a secondary obligor but not a debtor. For another example, assume A borrows money

---

21. U.C.C. § 9-102(a)(74). Chapter 2 discusses security agreements.

22. U.C.C. § 1-201(b)(35). The next subsection of the text discusses this term.

23. U.C.C. § 9-102(a)(73).

24. U.C.C. § 9-102(a)(12). For a discussion of the different types of collateral, see § 1.04, *infra*.

25. U.C.C. § 9-102(a)(28). The term can be a bit confusing because it has nothing to do with indebtedness.

26. U.C.C. § 9-102(a)(59). The debtor and the obligor are usually the same person, but that is not always the case. In the original article, the person that owed payment or other performance of the secured obligation was also a "debtor" (U.C.C. § 9-105(1)(d) (1962 Official Text)), but use of the same term to describe parties with different functions caused confusion.

27. *See* U.C.C. § 9-102(a)(26); § 1.04[A][1], *infra*. Article 9 includes a number of protective provisions applicable to consumer transactions.

28. U.C.C. § 9-102(a)(22).

29. U.C.C. § 9-102(a)(25).

30. For example, most of the rights and duties with regard to the foreclosure process affect secondary obligors but not other obligors. *See, e.g.,* U.C.C. § 9-611(c) (requiring secured party to send notice of disposition to secondary obligors but not other obligors). The major exception is Section 9-616(b), which gives any consumer obligor, whether secondary or otherwise, a right in some circumstances to an explanation of the method of calculation of a surplus or deficiency.

31. U.C.C. § 9-102(a)(72). "Secondary obligor" is a subset of "obligor," and a provision applicable to obligors also applies to secondary obligors. A provision applicable to secondary obligors is not applicable to an obligor that is not a secondary obligor.

32. *See* U.C.C. § 3-419(a) (accommodation party is a person that, without benefitting directly, signs a negotiable instrument in order to accommodate another party to the instrument). An accommodation party's obligation might be stated in primary (i.e., unconditional) terms, but such a party would have a right of recourse against the accommodated party and thus would qualify as a secondary obligor. U.C.C. § 3-419(e).

33. Article 3 governs the obligations of an accommodation party, whereas law other than the U.C.C. governs the obligations of a surety.

and uses his car as collateral. To accommodate A, B co-signs A's note for accommodation and grants a security interest in her car as collateral for her obligation as co-signer. If the secured party enforces its security interest in A's car, A is both a debtor and an obligor; B is both an obligor and a secondary obligor but not a debtor. If the secured party enforces its security interest in B's car, A is an obligor but not a debtor; B is a debtor, an obligor, and a secondary obligor.

The definition of "debtor" includes any person other than a secured party or lienholder with an interest in the collateral.[34] This can be the person that created the security interest or a subsequent transferee that acquires an interest in the collateral subject to the secured party's security interest under Article 9's priority rules. For example, suppose A borrows money and grants the lender a security interest in goods that she owns. A is both a debtor and an obligor. If A then sells the goods to B, who takes the goods subject to the security interest but does not assume the indebtedness, B owns the goods and is a debtor but not an obligor, and A, who no longer has an interest in the goods, is an obligor but not a debtor. The person referred to in a particular provision is generally clear from the context.

Subject to exceptions discussed elsewhere in this book, an ordinary transferee of collateral will take it subject to the secured party's security interest but beyond that will not be bound by the terms of the security agreement that created the interest. In certain situations, however, a transferee does become so bound,[35] and, to differentiate that transferee from others, the Code uses the term "new debtor."[36] In this latter context, the debtor that entered into the security agreement to which the new debtor is bound is referred to as the "original debtor."[37]

§ 1.03 General Applicability of Article 9

[A] Consensual Security Interests — § 9-109(a)(1)

Article 1 defines "security interest" broadly, the key part of the definition for current purposes being "an interest in personal property or fixtures which secures payment or performance of an obligation."[38] Article 9's basic scope provision, however, makes it applicable to "a transaction, regardless of its form, that creates a security interest

---

34. U.C.C. § 9-102(a)(28)(A).

35. *See* U.C.C. §§ 9-203(d), (e) (when person becomes bound by another person's security agreement and effect of becoming bound); 9-508 (effectiveness of financing statement filed in the name of the original debtor after new debtor becomes bound).

36. U.C.C. § 9-102(a)(56) (new debtor is "a person that becomes bound as debtor under Section 9-203(d) by a security agreement previously entered into by another person."). The person that previously entered into the security agreement is the "original debtor." U.C.C. § 9-102(a)(60). A new debtor is not necessarily a transferee. New debtors are discussed in § 5.02[C][2], *infra*.

37. U.C.C. § 9-102(a)(60).

38. U.C.C. § 1-201(b)(35). The definition is part of Article 1 rather than Article 9 because multiple Code articles use it. The definition is not limited to security interests created by contract.

in personal property or fixtures *by contract.*"[39] Article 9 thus applies to consensual encumbrances, as distinct from encumbrances that arise by operation of law (such as judicial, common-law, or statutory liens). Excluding for now certain designated exceptions from its scope,[40] Article 9 governs all consensual transactions that create security interests in personal property and fixtures.

The scope of Article 9 is based on substance rather than form. With parties sometimes disposed to disguise the true nature of their transactions, courts cannot simply accept their expressions of intention as controlling. As will be demonstrated below,[41] parties sometimes characterize a transaction as a consignment or lease when, at a functional level, the transaction operates like a secured transaction. Thus, Article 9's basic scope provision does not refer to contracts intended to create security interests but rather to contracts that actually create such interests.[42]

[B] Leases and Consignments

[1] Disguised Leases

One of the primary areas of difficulty with the scope of Article 9 has been distinguishing secured transactions involving goods as collateral from leases of goods. With the promulgation in 1990 of Article 2A on leases of goods, the drafters made corresponding amendments to Article 1 to address the problem. They replaced the previous test, which had relied on intent,[43] with a test that focuses on a transaction's economic nature.[44] The essential characteristics of secured transactions and leases are easy to distinguish. A credit seller that retains a security interest in goods delivered

---

39. U.C.C. §9-109(a)(1) (emphasis supplied). The article also governs an agricultural lien as defined by the article; a consignment as defined by the article; security interests arising automatically under certain provisions of Articles 2, 2A, 4, and 5; and outright sales of certain rights to payment. U.C.C. §9-109(a)(2)-(6). The book discusses these aspects of Article 9 elsewhere.

40. *See* §1.06, *infra.*

41. *See* §1.03[B], *infra.*

42. U.C.C. §9-109(a)(1). The original version of Article 9 referred to contracts intended to create a security interest (U.C.C. §9-102(a)(1) (1962 Official Text)), but this led to undue confusion. Although the word was retained in the 1972 Official Text, a comment was added reinforcing the basic proposition that Article 9 security interests arise by contract and that, in using "intended," the drafters did not mean to suggest that the parties' subjective intent was relevant to the proper legal categorization of their transaction. U.C.C. §9-109, Comment 2 (1972 Official Text). The drafters finally deleted the word in the 1998 Official Text to further emphasize the point. To make clear that the omission of the word did not represent a change in the law, the 2010 amendments added the following language at the end of Comment 2: "Likewise, the subjective intention of the parties with respect to the legal characterization of their transaction is irrelevant to whether this Article applies, as it was to the application of former Article 9 under the proper interpretation of former Section 9-102."

43. U.C.C. §1-201(37) (1962 Official Text).

44. The provision was initially part of a revised definition of security interest but was moved as part of the 2001 revision of Article 1 to a separate section. *See* U.C.C. §1-203.

to a buyer passes title to the goods.[45] The retained security interest gives the seller the right to repossess the goods in the event of default by the buyer.[46] Upon repossession, the seller/secured party disposes of the goods[47] and applies the proceeds to the outstanding indebtedness.[48] Any surplus proceeds belong to the buyer/debtor.[49] A lessor also retains an interest in goods delivered to another person, in this case the lessee. Like a secured party, a lessor has a right to repossess the goods following a default.[50] Unlike the secured party, however, the lessor need not dispose of the goods following repossession.[51] The lessor at all times retains title and thus owns the residual interest.

Distinguishing leases and secured transactions in actual practice has proved difficult and has led to some of the most pervasive litigation under the Code.[52] The similarity of some of the attributes of the transactions contributes to the problem. An even more significant factor is that, for a variety of reasons related to taxes, accounting, or bankruptcy, parties sometimes disguise a secured transaction by calling it a lease. For example, suppose a dealer delivers a piece of equipment to a user pursuant to a written contract binding the user to make twenty-four equal monthly payments of $1,000 each. The contract, which refers to the transaction as a "lease," the installments as "lease payments," and the parties as "lessor" and "lessee," provides that the user has the option to purchase the equipment for $1 at the end of the "lease term" even though the parties anticipate that it will have significantly more value at that time. Because any rational economic actor would exercise the option and become the owner, the transaction is the economic equivalent of a sale and the "lessor's" right to repossess the "leased property" in the event of default is in effect a security interest. The Code directs the courts to look through the parties' terminology and sweeps the security aspects of the transaction into Article 9.[53] This approach means that the "lessor" will have to follow Article 9's foreclosure rules after repossession and will have to perfect its security interest under

---

45. A sale, by definition, involves the passage of title. U.C.C. § 2-106(1). Even if the seller and buyer agree that the seller will retain title to the goods pending full payment (sometimes called a "conditional sale"), the seller's interest is limited to a reservation of a security interest. U.C.C. §§ 1-201(b) (35), 2-401(1). *See also* U.C.C. § 9-110 (providing that security interests arising under Articles 2 and 2A are subject to Article 9); *In re* Wild West World, L.L.C., 66 U.C.C. Rep. Serv. 2d 1033 (Bankr. D. Kan. 2008).

46. U.C.C. § 9-609(a).

47. U.C.C. § 9-610(a).

48. U.C.C. § 9-615(a). This requirement assumes that the secured party does not use strict foreclosure. Chapter 18 discusses the different methods for disposing of collateral after default.

49. U.C.C. § 9-615(d)(1).

50. U.C.C. § 2A-525(2).

51. U.C.C. § 2A-527.

52. See the extensive caselaw citations in W. Lawrence & J. Minan, The Law of Personal Property Leasing 2-15 to 2-21 (1993).

53. U.C.C. § 9-109(a)(1).

Article 9 (usually by a public filing)[54] to obtain priority against third parties with competing interests in the goods.[55]

Prior to the promulgation of Article 2A, inadequate legal standards played a significant role in blurring the boundaries between true leases and disguised security interests. The original definition of "security interest" included a sentence directed toward distinguishing leases and secured transactions[56] that proved woefully inadequate.[57] The revised test is extremely long and complex, but it does provide an effective standard based on functional considerations. Rather than continuing the original test's unworkable central standard relying on the parties' intent, the current test focuses on the economics of the transaction. The basic economic reality of a true lease is that the lessor must retain a meaningful residual interest, and this will not be the case if the transaction actually compensates the purported lessor for the residual interest as well as for the use of the goods during the lease term.

Whether a transaction denominated a lease creates a true lease governed by Article 2A or a security interest governed by Article 9 depends on the facts of the case.[58] However, a transaction creates a security interest as a matter of law if (1) the lessee does not have a right to terminate the lease before its stated expiration date, and (2) any one of several enumerated factors is present.[59] If the lessee has a right of early termination, a facts-and-circumstances test must be applied, and typically the lessor will be found to have retained a meaningful residual interest unless the right to terminate cannot be exercised until the lessor has been compensated for the full economic value of the goods.

Assuming no right of termination, a transaction creates a security interest as a matter of law if any of the enumerated factors is present. One of these factors is that the original term of the lease equals or exceeds the remaining economic life of the goods.[60] The economic reality of such a transaction is that the purported lessor has not retained

---

54. Article 9 provides that a lessor, concerned that a court might conclude that a transaction called a lease in fact creates a disguised security interest, may make a protective filing, using the terms "lessor" and "lessee" instead of "secured party" and "debtor." U.C.C. § 9-505(a). Such a filing, standing alone, is not an admission that the transaction is not a true lease. U.C.C. § 9-505(b). This provision also applies to certain consignment and consignment-like transactions, a related topic that is discussed in the next subsection.

55. With one optional provision for leased goods that become fixtures (U.C.C. § 2A-309), a true lessor need not make a public filing to protect its residual interest. U.C.C. § 2A-301.

56. U.C.C. § 1-201(37) (1962 Official Text).

57. For a critique of the inadequacies of the original definition, see W. Lawrence & J. Minan, The Law of Personal Property Leasing 2–15 to 2–21 (1993).

58. U.C.C. § 1-203(a). Subsection (c) provides that a transaction in the form of a lease does not create a security interest merely because certain factors may be present. For example, a full payout lease does not create a security interest as a matter of law, nor does a typical net lease. In a full payout lease, the lessor receives rent equaling or exceeding the full cost of its investment in the leased goods. In a net lease, the lessee assumes responsibilities normally associated with ownership, such as the responsibilities to pay for insurance, taxes, or maintenance.

59. U.C.C. § 1-203(b).

60. The remaining economic life of the goods must be determined based on the facts and circumstances that exist at the time the parties enter into the transaction. U.C.C. § 1-203(e).

a meaningful residual interest in the goods but rather has sold the goods on credit and retained a security interest in them. The practical effect is precisely the same if a lessee that cannot terminate the lease is bound to renew it to the end of the economic life of the goods, or is bound to become the owner of the goods. The lessee is contractually obligated to pay for the remaining economic life of the goods, leaving no meaningful residual interest in the lessor.

The remaining factors address the role of options. They cover the circumstances in which a lessee, upon compliance with the terms of the lease, has the option to become the owner of the goods or to renew the lease for the remaining economic life of the goods. If the lessee can exercise either option for no additional consideration or for only nominal consideration,[61] the transaction is not a true lease but is rather a security interest. The purported rental payments in such a transaction obviously compensate the lessor not only for the lessee's use of the goods during the lease term but also for the residual value that remains in the goods following the lease term. Despite the labels applied by the parties, the economic reality is that a lessor willing to allow a lessee to retain the goods for nominal or even no additional consideration has not retained a meaningful residual interest. Conversely, a lessor has retained the requisite interest for a true lease if the lessee must pay more than nominal additional consideration to exercise an option to purchase the goods or to renew the lease until the end of the economic life of the goods.

[2] Disguised Consignments

In some trades, a supplier commonly sends goods to a merchant on consignment, with the understanding that the merchant will make an effort to sell the goods. If successful, the merchant retains a percentage of the sales price and remits the remainder to the supplier. Until and unless the consigned goods are sold, title remains with the supplier/consignor and does not pass to the merchant/consignee. The merchant can return unsold goods to the supplier with no further obligation. The consignment approach—which has the legal characteristics of a bailment with an authority in the bailee to sell—serves to entice the merchant to attempt sales of merchandise that the merchant would not purchase outright. It also serves as a type of inventory financing because the capital of the consignor maintains the merchant's inventory.

At common law, a consignor could reacquire consigned goods free of the interests of creditors of the consignee even if the consignor did nothing to provide public notice of its interest in them. This approach created an ostensible-ownership problem in that

---

61. Additional consideration is deemed to be nominal "if it is less than the lessee's reasonably predictable cost of performing under the lease agreement if the option is not exercised." U.C.C. § 1-203(d). It is not nominal if, at the time the option to renew or become the owner is granted, the agreed rent or price is to be based on fair market values for rent or price. *Id.* The various components of the test (reasonably predictable cost of performing, fair market rent or price) are to be determined based on the facts and circumstances that exist at the time the transaction is entered into. U.C.C. § 1-203(e).

a dishonest consignee could hold itself out as the true owner of the consigned goods and thereby deceive a lender into advancing funds against their value.[62]

The key feature of a true consignment is that the risk of non-sale falls on the supplier/consignor rather than the merchant/consignee. By contrast, a merchant that buys goods from a supplier must pay for them whether or not they are successfully resold. Under Article 2, an agreement in a contract for sale reserving title in the seller until the buyer fully pays for delivered goods is reduced in effect to the creation of a security interest.[63] Thus, if the parties call their transaction a consignment but the risk of non-sale falls on the "consignee" (i.e., the consignee must pay for the goods even if it cannot sell them), the economic reality is that the transaction is a credit sale with a title-retention agreement and the "consignor's" interest will be treated as a security interest.

Consignments that function as security devices are within the scope of Article 9 in the same way as leases that function in that manner.[64] In such cases, a repossessing "consignor" must follow Article 9's foreclosure rules and will have to perfect its security interest (usually by a public filing) to obtain priority against third parties with competing interests in the goods.[65]

[3] True Consignments

Although Article 9 governs disguised consignments for the reasons discussed in the preceding subsection, the article also brings within its scope most commercially valuable true consignments.[66] Article 9 defines "consignment"[67] as a transaction in which goods are delivered to a merchant for the purpose of sale and the merchant "(i) deals in goods of that kind under a name other than that of the person making delivery; (ii) is not an auctioneer; and (iii) is not generally known by its creditors to be substantially engaged in selling the goods of others." Further limiting the definition are require-

---

62. Ostensible-ownership problems arise when goods in one party's possession are subject to a property interest of another. Third parties, believing from appearances that the party in possession has unencumbered title, may acquire an interest in the goods, thereby creating a priority contest. Sometimes, the outcome turns on whether the third party has the attributes of a bona fide purchaser for value. *See, e.g.,* U.C.C. § 2-403(1). Statutes requiring public filing alleviate ostensible-ownership problems by giving notice of interests that would otherwise be hidden. A consignment is a type of bailment, meaning a transaction in which goods are placed in the rightful possession of one who is not their owner. R. BROWN, THE LAW OF PERSONAL PROPERTY § 10.1 (W. Raushenbush ed., 3d ed. 1975). There are numerous types of bailments, and the rules governing the rights of third parties misled by the bailee's ostensible ownership vary with the context. As a rule, though, the common law of bailment has not generally provided protection for such parties. *See* § 2.02[C], *infra.*

63. U.C.C. § 2-401(1).

64. For a discussion of the attributes of a disguised lease transaction, see § 1.03[B][1], *supra.*

65. As with leases, in case of doubt, a consignor can make a protective filing using the terms "consignor" and "consignee" rather than "secured party" and "debtor," and the filing, standing alone, is not an admission that the transaction is not a true consignment. U.C.C. § 9-505(a), (b). Unlike the lease situation, however, and for reasons discussed in the next subsection, a filing under Article 9 is generally necessary to protect the interest of even a true consignor.

66. U.C.C. § 9-109(a)(4).

67. U.C.C. § 9-102(a)(20).

ments that, for a transaction to qualify as a consignment, each delivery must have an aggregate value of $1,000 or more and, without regard to value, the goods must not be consumer goods immediately before delivery to the merchant.

Article 9 defines a "consignor"[68] as the person that delivers the goods to the merchant, or the "consignee,"[69] and the consignor's retained interest in the goods is a security interest[70] in inventory deemed to be purchase-money in nature.[71] The consignor's interest is subject to the claims of creditors of the consignee,[72] but the consignor can protect that interest by using the methods available to any other Article 9 secured party.[73] These methods include filing a financing statement to defeat the consignee's creditors generally, and making certain to file and provide appropriate notice before the goods are delivered to the consignee to defeat a prior-perfected inventory financer with an after-acquired property clause.[74]

Although true consignments are within the scope of Article 9, they have features that are inconsistent with an ordinary Article 9 security interest—most notably the fact that, once the goods have been returned by the consignee due to non-sale, they belong to the consignor. Accordingly, the consignor need not go through a foreclosure.[75] By contrast and as discussed above, an Article 9 foreclosure is necessary for a security interest disguised as a consignment.

Consignment-like transactions are outside the scope of Article 9 in four situations: (1) consumer goods consigned to a merchant for sale, (2) a delivery to a merchant for sale that in the aggregate has a value of less than $1,000, (3) a delivery to an auctioneer, and (4) goods delivered to a merchant that is generally known by its creditors to be substantially engaged in selling the goods of others.[76] The common law of bailments rather than Article 9 governs each of these transactions, and, as a general proposition, that law insulates the goods from the claims of the bailee's creditors.[77] For example, suppose the owner of a horse trailer that is used for a consumer purpose places the trailer with a dealer for sale on consignment. The trailer is part of the dealer's inventory, but a security interest in all inventory granted by the dealer to a lender will not attach to it.

---

68. U.C.C. § 9-102(a)(21).

69. U.C.C. § 9-102(a)(19).

70. U.C.C. § 1-201(b)(35).

71. U.C.C. § 9-103(d). For a discussion of purchase-money security interests generally, see § 10.04[A], *infra*.

72. U.C.C. § 9-319(a).

73. U.C.C. § 9-319(b).

74. For discussion of purchase-money priorities in inventory, *see* § 10.04[B][2], *infra*.

75. U.C.C. § 9-601(g) (exempting consignments from Part 6 of Article 9).

76. *See In re* Downey Creations, LLC, 70 U.C.C. Rep. Serv. 2d 44 (S.D. Ind. 2009) (majority of consignee's creditors, measured numerically and not by the total value of claims, must know that consignee is substantially engaged in selling goods of others).

77. *See In re* Music City RV, LLC, 304 S.W.3d 806, 71 U.C.C. Rep. Serv. 2d 957 (Tenn. 2010) (rights of consignor of consumer goods governed by common law of bailments rather than sale-or-return provision of Section 2-326(2)). A person that is in doubt about whether a transaction is within an excluded category can make a precautionary filing under Section 9-505.

§ 1.04 Types of Collateral

Any type of personal property can secure an obligation, but different types of personal property pose distinct issues in the context of secured financing. The rules of Article 9 have to function properly for each type of collateral, and thus the classification of the collateral is frequently critical with respect to the application of a particular provision.

Many important distinctions in the application of Article 9 turn on whether the collateral is goods or non-goods. "Goods" refers generally to assets that are movable at the time a security interest attaches to them, and the various other types of collateral are excluded from the definition.[78] Essentially, goods are a form of personal property in which value is a function of physical characteristics.

Non-goods collateral falls into numerous types, with different rules applicable to each type. The rules reflect the treatment of the collateral in the marketplace and are, of necessity, consistent with the property regime that governs the type generally. For just one example, the rules for negotiable instruments used as collateral are consistent with Article 3 of the U.C.C., which creates a property regime that governs the holding and transfer of such instruments. There are many non-goods types of collateral, and it is difficult to make sweeping generalizations. Several of the non-goods types represent a right to the payment of money, and there are important distinctions between these types. These rights are often evidenced by a record, and there is a wide divergence on the value of the record for purposes of Article 9.

Classifying collateral has numerous consequences, one of the most important of which relates to the use of generic descriptions. For example, if a security agreement uses a generic description like "all debtor's equipment," the security interest will attach to all assets that are within the definition of that collateral type at the moment it first attaches to any asset.[79] If the security agreement contains an after-acquired property clause, the security interest will also attach to subsequently acquired assets that fall within the definition of equipment.[80] Assets that are equipment at the time of attachment continue to be subject to the security interest if their classification later changes (e.g., an item of equipment that the debtor takes home and begins using primarily for household purposes, thus converting it to consumer goods). Classification also drives issues related to perfection, priority, and foreclosure.

---

78. U.C.C. § 9-102(a)(44).

79. The security agreement may also provide for the security interest to attach to after-acquired assets that fall within the description. For discussion of attachment and the effect of after-acquired property clauses, see Chapter 2 and § 3.02, *infra*.

80. For discussion of after-acquired property clauses, see § 3.02, *infra*.

The following material describes some of the more important kinds of assets that fall within the Code's various classifications.[81] Most of the substantive discussion concerning the effect of classification appears in other chapters.

[A] Goods—§ 9-102(a)(44)

Article 9 establishes four basic classifications of goods: (1) consumer goods, (2) farm products, (3) inventory, and (4) equipment. The proper classification of goods can change over time, depending on changes in their use.[82] For example, goods held as inventory by a dealer might be sold and used as consumer goods in the buyer's home and then later used as equipment in the buyer's office.[83] The classifications are mutually exclusive, however, so that at any given point in time the goods can fit into only one of them.[84]

An important distinction separates mixed usage and a permanent change in use. The drafters recognized that sometimes a use (or intended use) of the goods will not be exclusive. In cases of mixed use, the primary use predominates for classification purposes. For example, goods used most of the time for personal reasons and only occasionally in the owner's business are continuously classified as consumer goods.[85] As indicated above, though, a permanent change in the pattern of usage throws the goods into another category. For example, a lawnmower bought on secured credit to mow a grassy area on the person's business premises would be equipment, but if the person subsequently brings the lawnmower home on a permanent basis and uses it to mow the lawn, it becomes consumer goods. The change in classification does not affect the attachment of the security interest, but if there is a default, the secured party will have to follow the special rules governing foreclosure on consumer goods.

The definition of goods includes "(i) fixtures, (ii) standing timber that is to be cut and removed under a conveyance or contract for sale, (iii) the unborn young of animals, (iv) crops grown, growing, or to be grown, even if the crops are produced on trees, vines, or bushes, and (v) manufactured homes."[86]

---

81. For discussion of other kinds of assets covered elsewhere in this chapter, see §§ 1.04[D] (investment property), 1.06[F][2] (commercial tort claims), 1.06[H] (deposit accounts), and 1.07 (letter-of-credit rights).

82. *In re* Elie, 11 B.R. 24, 31 U.C.C. Rep. Serv. 687 (Bankr. D. Mass. 1981) (primary factor is principal use to which goods are put). *See also* U.C.C. § 9-102, Comment 4a.

83. First Nat'l Bank of Thomasboro v. Lachenmyer, 146 Ill. App. 3d 1035, 497 N.E.2d 844, 2 U.C.C. Rep. Serv. 2d 703 (1986) (airplane originally purchased in pursuit of hobby was later used for business purposes).

84. North Ridge Farms, Inc. v. Trimble, 37 U.C.C. Rep. Serv. 1280 (Ky. Ct. App. 1983). *See also* U.C.C. § 9-102, Comment 4a.

85. Commercial Credit Equip. Corp. v. Carter, 83 Wash. 2d 136, 516 P.2d 767, 13 U.C.C. Rep. Serv. 1212 (1973) (occasional use of airplane in new employment did not affect its classification as consumer goods). *See also* U.C.C. § 9-102, Comment 4a.

86. U.C.C. § 9-102(a)(44).

The goods category also includes certain "embedded" computer programs. A computer program that is not within the definition of goods constitutes software, a subset of general intangibles.[87] For a security interest to attach to software, the security agreement must provide an adequate description of the software; and for priority purposes, a secured party will want to perfect its security interest in the software by describing it in a financing statement. The software category is irrelevant for both attachment and perfection purposes if a computer program is within the definition of goods. A computer program is goods if it is embedded in goods and if "(i) the program is associated with the goods in such a manner that it customarily is considered part of the goods, or (ii) by becoming the owner of the goods, a person acquires the right to use the program in connection with the goods."[88] For example, suppose Bank takes a security interest in Debtor's car and the description does not refer to any of the software used with the car. Bank's security interest attaches to Debtor's rights in the computer program that runs the anti-lock brakes because the program meets the statutory test.[89] As noted above, Bank's security interest in the program need not be separately described in the security agreement or separately perfected. By contrast, suppose Bank takes a security interest in Debtor's computer. The computer is clearly goods. The operating system that Debtor uses to run the computer is separately licensed, and thus Debtor did not acquire the right to use the program merely by becoming the owner of the computer. Whether the program is associated with the goods in such a manner that it customarily is considered part of the goods is an issue of fact. If the program is customarily considered part of the goods, Bank need only describe and perfect as to the computer; otherwise, it must also describe and perfect as to the software.

[1] Consumer Goods and Manufactured Homes— §9-102(a)(23), (24), (53), (54)

Goods are consumer goods if they are "used or bought for use primarily for personal, family, or household purposes."[90] Actual use for any of these purposes generally controls; however, goods intended at the time of purchase for a personal, family, or household purpose qualify initially as consumer goods even though never actually used for that purpose. If their predominant use when placed in service is for a non-consumer purpose, the classification will ordinarily change to another appropriate category, although some courts decline to change the category if doing so would

---

87. U.C.C. §9-102(a)(76).
88. U.C.C. §9-102(a)(44).
89. In fact, the computer program that runs the anti-lock brake system undoubtedly meets both parts of the test. This will always be the case with computer programs that function as ordinary parts of ordinary goods.
90. U.C.C. §9-102(a)(23). *In re* Elia, 18 B.R. 89, 33 U.C.C. Rep. Serv. 750 (Bankr. W.D. Pa. 1982) (hospital beds purchased for personal use); *In re* Nicolosi, 4 U.C.C. Rep. Serv. 111 (Bankr. S.D. Ohio 1966) (purchase of engagement ring as gift to fiancée does not mean it was not for purchaser's own "personal, family, or household purposes").

be disadvantageous to a secured party that relied in good faith on a statement by the debtor regarding the use to which the goods would be put.[91]

Article 9's definitional scheme creates some complexities based on whether the collateral is consumer goods or other assets held for a consumer purpose and whether the obligation secured by the collateral is a consumer obligation. The term "consumer transaction" is used for a transaction in which an individual incurs an obligation primarily for personal, family, or household purposes and holds the collateral primarily for personal, family, or household purposes.[92] A consumer transaction in most cases is also a "consumer-goods transaction"—a transaction in which an individual incurs an obligation primarily for personal, family, or household purposes and secures that obligation by granting a security interest in consumer goods.[93] The definitions of consumer transaction and consumer-goods transaction at first blush may seem identical, but the difference reflects the nature of the collateral. For example, consider a transaction in which an individual borrows money to pay her personal medical expenses. If she secures the obligation by granting a security interest in her personal automobile, the transaction is both a consumer transaction and a consumer-goods transaction. However, if she secures the obligation by granting a security interest in 1,000 shares of stock in a corporation—investment property rather than goods—that she has been holding to pay for her children's education, the transaction is a consumer transaction but not a consumer-goods transaction. In other words, consumer-goods transactions are a subset of the broader category of consumer transactions. By contrast, if an individual secures a business loan with consumer goods or with investment property held for a personal, family, or household purpose, the transaction is neither a consumer-goods transaction nor a consumer transaction. Similarly, a consumer loan secured by business assets is neither a consumer-goods transaction nor a consumer transaction.

Article 9 contains a number of protective rules that apply if the collateral is consumer goods, even if the transaction is not a consumer-goods transaction.[94] Other rules apply only if the transaction is a consumer transaction (which includes consumer-goods

---

91. *In re* Pettit, 18 B.R. 8, 33 U.C.C. Rep. Serv. 1762 (Bankr. E.D. Ark. 1981) (even though goods were actually used in debtor's business, seller/secured party held to have an automatically perfected purchase-money security interest in consumer goods when debtor unambiguously represented to seller/secured party that the purchase was for personal, family, or household purposes); *In re* Troupe, 59 U.C.C. Rep. Serv. 2d 23 (W.D. Okla. 2006) (statements of debtors at time of purchase that they would use tractor for consumer purposes, coupled with provision in security agreement specifying that it would be so used, held to protect seller/secured party even if tractor used predominantly for ranching-business purposes).

92. U.C.C. § 9-102(a)(23).

93. U.C.C. § 9-102(a)(24).

94. For example, Section 9-204(b)(1) limits the effectiveness of an after-acquired property clause to the extent that it would otherwise apply to consumer goods. *See* § 3.02[B], *infra*. Likewise, Section 9-625(c)(2) provides that a secured party that fails to comply with its obligation to dispose of consumer goods in a commercially reasonable manner following default is liable for minimum statutory damages even if the debtor does not suffer actual harm as a result of the secured party's conduct. *See* § 19.03, *infra*.

transactions),[95] and still other rules apply only if the transaction is a consumer-goods transaction.[96] In addition to these protective rules, many states and the federal government have enacted consumer protection laws that either preempt or supplement the Code's provisions.[97] For example, the Federal Trade Commission has adopted a rule that makes it a deceptive trade practice for a lender to take a nonpossessory, non-purchase-money security interest in many kinds of consumer goods.[98]

Article 9 also provides for a type of collateral called "manufactured homes."[99] Manufactured homes are usually consumer goods, although one might be used as an office at a construction site and qualify as equipment. The use of a manufactured home that is consumer goods as collateral for an Article 9 transaction is subject to the applicable rules governing consumer goods, consumer transactions, and consumer-goods transactions. The transaction might also constitute a "manufactured-home transaction," meaning either a transaction that creates a purchase-money security interest in a manufactured home that is not inventory or a transaction in which a manufactured home that is not inventory serves as the primary collateral.[100] The fact that goods are a manufactured home has no relevance for purposes of Article 9 unless the transaction is a manufactured-home transaction. Manufactured-home transactions are relevant only for a limited set of perfection and priority issues. For example, a financing statement perfecting a security interest created by a manufactured-home transaction can be made effective for 30 years,[101] reflecting the duration of many loans to consumers using manufactured homes as their residence. Also, there is a special priority rule for a manufactured home in a manufactured-home transaction that has become a fixture and as to which a security interest has been perfected under a state certificate-of-title law rather than under the normal rules for perfection as to fixtures.[102]

---

95. For example, as explained in Chapter 18, the "safe-harbor" rule pursuant to which a notice of disposition sent at least ten days before the disposition is deemed timely as a matter of law does not apply to consumer transactions. U.C.C. § 9-612(b).

96. For example, as explained in Chapter 19, a court in a case involving a consumer-goods transaction could conclude that a secured party that failed to satisfy its obligation to conduct a commercially reasonable disposition of the collateral following default would be barred from recovering a deficiency judgment. See U.C.C. § 9-626(b). Such an "absolute bar" rule would not apply to transactions other than consumer-goods transactions.

97. See U.C.C. § 9-201(b), (c) (Article 9 defers to other law protecting consumers).

98. 16 C.F.R. Pt. 444. Regulation AA is a parallel rule adopted by the Federal Reserve Board. 12 C.F.R. Pt. 227. See discussion in §§ 3.02[B], 7.01[B], infra.

99. U.C.C. § 9-102(a)(53). Comment 4b to Section 9-102 states that "the definition borrows from the federal Manufactured Housing Act, 42 U.S.C. § 5401 et seq., and is intended to have the same meaning."

100. U.C.C. § 9-102(a)(54).

101. U.C.C. § 9-515(b). Many states subject manufactured homes to their certificate-of-title laws, and perfection by filing is not effective. Methods of perfection are discussed generally in Chapter 4 and specifically in other chapters.

102. U.C.C. § 9-334(e)(4).

[2] Farm Products—§ 9-102(a)(34)

Farm products consist of goods, other than standing timber, with respect to which the debtor is engaged in a farming operation and which consist of

(A) crops grown, growing, or to be grown, including: (i) crops produced on trees, vines, and bushes; and (ii) aquatic goods produced in aquacultural operations;

(B) livestock, born or unborn, including aquatic goods produced in aquacultural operations;

(C) supplies used or produced in a farming operation; or

(D) products of crops or livestock in their unmanufactured states.[103]

The term "farming operation" means "raising, cultivating, propagating, fattening, grazing, or any other farming, livestock, or aquacultural operation."[104]

Goods that constitute crops, livestock, and supplies are readily determinable, but an issue can arise as to whether the debtor was engaged in a farming operation with respect to them.[105] Vegetables grown in a family garden by a farmer are unlikely to qualify, as are horses ridden for pleasure or used for teaching equestrian skills. Farming operations can, however, be undertaken by someone who has a separate career or livelihood.[106] Seed and fertilizer held in stock to produce a farm crop are examples of goods that qualify as supplies, as is gasoline held in an underground tank installed on a farm and used to run farm machinery.[107]

A potentially difficult line-drawing problem arises with crops and livestock because the farm-products category includes the products of crops or livestock in their unmanufactured states.[108] The courts must determine whether the goods have been subjected to a manufacturing operation or whether their processing falls short of manufacturing.[109] Once farm products are subjected to a manufacturing process, they typically become inventory.[110] To illustrate, grapes harvested from a vintner's land are farm products but bottled wine is inventory (unless bottled for the vintner's personal use, in which case

103. U.C.C. § 9-102(a)(34).

104. U.C.C. § 9-102(a)(35).

105. Morgan County Feeders, Inc. v. McCormick, 836 P.2d 1051, 18 U.C.C. Rep. Serv. 2d 632 (Colo. Ct. App. 1992) (stipulating that longhorn cattle used for recreational cattle drives were not farm products); In re Creel, 118 B.R. 372, 13 U.C.C. Rep. Serv. 2d 943 (Bankr. D. S.C. 1988) (commercial logging not considered farming operation). "Animals in a herd of livestock are covered whether the debtor acquires them by purchase or as a result of natural increase." U.C.C. § 9-102, Comment 4a.

106. In re Blease, 24 U.C.C. Rep. Serv. 450 (Bankr. D.N.J. 1978) (veterinarian who owned and operated two farms qualified).

107. The tank and the machinery would be equipment, and the tank would also be a fixture.

108. U.C.C. § 9-102(a)(34)(D).

109. In re K.L. Smith Enterprises, Ltd., 2 B.R. 280, 28 U.C.C. Rep. Serv. 534 (Bankr. D. Colo. 1980) (highly mechanized process of washing, candling, spraying with oil, and packing eggs for shipment did not constitute manufacturing process).

110. U.C.C. § 9-102, Comment 4a.

the bottled wine is consumer goods).[111] Obviously, this particular characterization can present close questions on which reasonable persons might differ—questions that will be of critical importance depending on how a security agreement describes the collateral. If goods are farm products and later become inventory, the description "farm products" in the security agreement and financing statement will be adequate to cause the security interest to attach and become perfected, and neither description needs to be amended to account for the new category;[112] if, on the other hand, the goods were inventory when the security interest attached, the description "farm products" will not be sufficient. An attorney advising a secured party in a borderline case should suggest that the description refer to both farm products and inventory. The same approach should be used for other assets that sit on the borderline between classifications.

Prior to 1998, Article 9 explicitly required that, for goods to qualify as farm products, they had to be "in the possession of a debtor engaged in raising, fattening, grazing, or other farming operations."[113] Once the goods left the possession of the farming debtor, they lost their characterization as farm products,[114] and their subsequent characterization depended on their subsequent use.[115] For example, cattle on a rancher's land are farm products, but the same cattle held for sale in a commission merchant's barn are inventory. Current Article 9 does not expressly require the goods to be in a farmer's possession but the phrase "with respect to which the debtor is engaged in a farming operation" leads to the same result.[116]

[3] Inventory—§ 9-102(a)(48)

Goods are inventory if they are held by a person for sale or lease or are to be furnished under a contract of service.[117] This part of the definition is the principal test of inventory, and it is implicit that these transactions occur within the ordinary course of

---

111. The 1972 text gave as examples of manufactured goods "ginned cotton, wool-clip, maple syrup, milk, and eggs." U.C.C. § 9-109(3). U.C.C. § 9-102, Comment 4a, provides the following explanation: "At one end of the spectrum, some processes are so closely connected with farming—such as pasteurizing milk or boiling sap to produce maple syrup or sugar—that they would not constitute manufacturing. On the other hand an extensive canning operation would be manufacturing."

112. The inventory is proceeds of the farm products. *See* § 2.03, *infra.*

113. U.C.C. § 9-109(3) (1972 Official Text). *In re* Charolais Breeding Ranches, Ltd., 20 U.C.C. Rep. Serv. 193 (Bankr. W.D. Wis. 1976) (operator of breeding ranch that dealt with cattle under programs to provide tax benefits to investors engaged in farming operations); Baker Production Credit Ass'n v. Long Creek Meat Co., 266 Or. 643, 513 P.2d 1129, 13 U.C.C. Rep. Serv. 531 (1973) (debtor who bought cattle, fed and fattened them, and sold them for slaughter was engaged in farming operations).

114. U.C.C. § 9-109, Comment 4 (1972 Official Text).

115. First Nat'l Bank of Elkhart Cnty. v. Smoker, 153 Ind. App. 71, 286 N.E.2d 203, 11 U.C.C. Rep. Serv. 10 (1972) (cattle became inventory upon transfer of possession from farmer to packer).

116. U.C.C. § 9-102, Comment 4a.

117. U.C.C. § 9-102(a)(48)(B), (C).

business.[118] Thus, if a company occasionally sells its used machinery when it needs to be replaced, such sales are insufficient to characterize the machinery as inventory.[119]

Goods actually leased by a lessor or furnished under a contract of service are also inventory. Thus, for example, a secured party that takes a security interest in "all inventory" of a merchant acquires an interest in goods subject to an existing lease (or more accurately, the merchant's residual interest in the leased goods as lessor) even though, at the time of attachment, the goods are not available to the merchant for immediate lease.

Raw materials, works in process, or materials used or consumed in a business are also inventory.[120] Thus, a stockpile of packaging material used by a company to ship its manufactured goods and the coal used to fire its generators qualify as inventory. These types of goods are inventory even though they are not held for sale, lease, or any other type of transfer. The concept is similar to supplies used or consumed in a farming operation, which are part of the definition of farm products. In a sense, farm products are what a layperson might think of as the farmer's inventory, but the Code's definitions are entirely discrete; if goods are within the definition of farm products, they are not inventory.[121]

[4] Equipment—§ 9-102(a)(33)

The category "equipment" is residual in nature, that is, goods are equipment if they are not consumer goods, farm products, or inventory.[122] This definition can lead to some interesting results. For example, standing timber to be cut and removed under a conveyance or contract of sale is goods under the Code,[123] is excluded from the definition of farm products,[124] and is highly unlikely to qualify as consumer goods. If it is held for sale or lease, it is inventory; otherwise, it is equipment.

The category includes assets used in a business, but it cannot overlap with the definition of inventory, which refers to materials used or consumed in a business.[125] The borderline is not entirely clear and the Comments provide the following guidance: "In general, goods used in a business are equipment if they are fixed assets or have, as identifiable units, a relatively long period of use, but are inventory, even though not held for sale or lease, if they are used up or consumed in a short period of time in

---

118. U.C.C. § 9-102, Comment 4a. Nichols Motorcycle Supply, Inc. v. Regency Kawasaki, Inc., 295 S.C. 138, 367 S.E.2d 438, 6 U.C.C. Rep. Serv. 2d 823 (Ct. App. 1988) (bulk transfer of goods is transfer not in ordinary course of business).

119. The machinery is equipment under Section 9-102(a)(33). *See* § 1.04[A][4], *infra. In re* Benton Trucking Serv., Inc., 21 B.R. 574, 34 U.C.C. Rep. Serv. 332 (Bankr. E.D. Mich. 1982).

120. U.C.C. § 9-102(a)(48)(A), (C), (D).

121. U.C.C. § 9-102(a)(48).

122. *In re* Estate of Silver, 2003 Mich. App. LEXIS 1389 (Mich. Ct. App., June 12, 2003) (paintings that were displayed in model homes and in various offices of the debtor's company were properly characterized as equipment rather than consumer goods).

123. U.C.C. § 9-102(a)(44).

124. U.C.C. § 9-102(a)(34).

125. *See* § 1.04[A][3], *supra.*

producing a product or providing a service."[126] As a rule of thumb, goods used up are inventory while goods used again are equipment.

The category must be considered in any borderline case involving goods. Suppose, for example, that an individual who is the sole proprietor of a business buys a pick-up truck to make deliveries and to use as a family vehicle. If the business use predominates, the truck is equipment because it does not come within the definition of consumer goods. If the family use predominates, it is within the consumer-goods category. If a court finds that the buyer's mixed business and family uses balance evenly, there is no primary use, and the truck is equipment under the residual definition because it does not come within the definition of consumer goods.

[B] Collateral Other than Goods

Perhaps the best place to start our discussion of collateral other than goods is with the definition of general intangibles. This type of collateral is residual in nature, that is, it applies only if the collateral does not fall within the definition of another type of collateral. In order to make this clear, the definition lists all the other types of collateral. Here is the relevant language from the definition:

> "General intangible" means any personal property ... other than accounts, chattel paper, commercial tort claims, deposit accounts, documents, goods, instruments, investment property, letter-of-credit rights, letters of credit, money, and oil, gas, or other minerals before extraction.

The discussion that follows is not comprehensive and focuses primarily on the various collateral types that constitute a right to the payment of money. The mechanics of collection by a secured party after default by a debtor are discussed elsewhere in this book.[127]

[1] Accounts—§ 9-102(a)(2), (46)

An "account" is a right to the payment of money, whether or not earned by performance, arising in one of a number of specific contexts. Accounts include rights to payment:

> (i) for property that has been or is to be sold, leased, licensed, assigned, or otherwise disposed of, (ii) for services rendered or to be rendered, (iii) for a policy of insurance issued or to be issued, (iv) for a secondary obligation incurred or to be incurred, (v) for energy provided or to be provided, (vi) for the use or hire of a vessel under a charter or other contract, (vii) arising out of the use of a credit or charge card or information contained on or for use with the card, or (viii) as winnings in a lottery or other game of chance operated or sponsored by a State, governmental unit of a State, or person licensed or

---

126. U.C.C. § 9-102, Comment 4a.
127. See § 18.03, infra.

authorized to operate the game by a State or governmental unit of a State. The term includes controllable accounts and health-care-insurance receivables.[128]

The following example illustrates the effect of the phrase "whether or not earned by performance." Suppose a painting contractor needing a loan is owed $5,000 for a completed job and has a contract to paint a building the next week for another $5,000. The right to payment for the first job has been earned by performance and the right to payment for the second job has not, but this is irrelevant for classification purposes. The right to payment for each job is an account. Of course, the contractor cannot collect the $5,000 for the second job without performing, and neither can a secured party to whom the account has been assigned as collateral.[129]

Most commercially valuable accounts arise from transactions evidenced by a record, but with the exception of controllable accounts, the record plays no part in the Article 9 scheme. For example, suppose Buyer purchases expensive goods from Seller on unsecured credit, and the agreement of the parties is evidenced by either a tangible or electronic record. A secured party lending money to Seller and taking a security interest in its right to collect from Buyer (the account) generally must perfect that security interest by filing a financing statement; it cannot perfect its security interest by taking possession or control of the record, nor does it need possession or control in order to collect from Buyer if Seller defaults on the secured obligation.

By contrast, a secured party can perfect a security interest in an instrument either by filing a financing statement or by taking possession of the writing[130] evidencing the instrument. Moreover, if the instrument is negotiable, the secured party will generally need possession in order to collect from a person obligated on the instrument. The rules governing the mechanics of collecting on a negotiable instrument are in Article 3. A secured party with a security interest in chattel paper can perfect its security interest either by filing a financing statement or by taking possession of the record evidencing the chattel paper if it is tangible or control of the record if it is electronic.[131] Unlike instruments, however, the secured party does not generally need possession or control

---

128. U.C.C. §9-102(a)(2). Prior to the 1998 Official Text, Article 9 classified many of these rights as general intangibles, but they were shifted to accounts primarily to facilitate securitizations. Sales of accounts are governed by Article 9, which provides clear rules protecting parties participating in the securitization; sales of general intangibles that are not also payment intangibles are governed by other law under which the rules are not so clear. *See, e.g., In re* Nittolo Land Dev. Ass'n, 58 U.C.C. Rep. Serv. 2d 313 (Bankr. S.D.N.Y. 2005) (right to payment under contract to sell real estate held to be an account under revised Article 9 even though it would have been a general intangible prior to the revision).

129. A discussion elsewhere in this chapter covers the mechanics of assigning accounts, including the vulnerability of the assignee to defenses such as might arise if the contractor does not perform under the second contract. *See* § 1.04[C], *infra.*

130. A record evidencing an instrument must be a writing, meaning that it must be tangible and cannot be electronic. *See* U.C.C. § 1-201(b)(43) (writing defined as an intentional reduction to tangible form) and the discussion of instruments in the next subsection.

131. U.C.C. §9-314A (perfection by possession and control).

of the record to collect from the person obligated on the chattel paper,[132] and the rules governing the mechanics of collection are in Article 9.[133]

Health-care-insurance receivable is a subset of account that is defined as "an interest in or claim under a policy of insurance which is a right to payment of a monetary obligation for health-care goods or services provided."[134] Article 9 excludes from its scope most assignments of rights under policies of insurance,[135] but it governs assignments under private health-care insurance policies to providers of health-care goods or services. For example, if a patient visits a doctor and assigns to the doctor the right to collect from the patient's private insurer, the doctor's right to collect is a health-care-insurance receivable. The inclusion of these rights to payment facilitates commerce by making it easier for doctors, hospitals, drugstores, and the like to sell or borrow against their rights to the proceeds of their patients' health-care-insurance policies. Lawyers dealing with health-care-insurance receivables need to be aware of certain special rules regarding collection from an insurer that apply to these types of accounts but not to ordinary accounts.[136]

A controllable account is "an account evidenced by a controllable electronic record that provides that the account debtor undertakes to pay the person that has control under Section 12-105 of the controllable electronic record."[137] For example, suppose Buyer purchases expensive goods from Seller on unsecured credit and the contract is evidenced by an electronic record which provides that Buyer will pay whomever is in control of the record. Seller has a right to the payment of money arising out of the sale of property, and thus the right to payment is an account, but the promise by Buyer to

---

132. Chattel paper is sometimes evidenced by two records, one evidencing an obligation to pay money and the other evidencing a security interest in or lease of specific goods. If the record evidencing the payment obligation is a negotiable instrument, the rules governing the mechanics of collection are in Article 3. U.C.C. § 9-102(a)(3) defines the term "account debtor" to include a person obligated on an account, chattel paper, or a general intangible, and the rules governing the mechanics of collecting from an account debtor are located in Article 9. See U.C.C. § 9-406(a)-(c). However, the definition of account debtor excludes a person obligated on a negotiable instrument that is part of chattel paper.

133. U.C.C. § 9-406(a)–(c).

134. U.C.C. § 9-102(a)(46).

135. U.C.C. § 9-109(d)(8). See § 1.06[G], infra.

136. The treatment of ordinary accounts differs somewhat from the treatment of health-care-insurance receivables. Section 9-404(e), for example, excludes health-care-insurance receivables from the general rules governing the right of account debtors to assert claims and defenses against assignees. The rationale is that other law governs the obligation of an insurer (the account debtor in this context). For similar reasons, Section 9-405(d) excludes health-care-insurance receivables from the general rules governing the effects of contract modifications against assignees, and Section 9-406(e) excludes health-care-insurance receivables from other aspects of the assignment rules, such as the obligation to pay an assignee after receiving notification. Health-care-insurance receivables are subject to Section 9-408(a), which invalidates an anti-assignment clause in a health-care-insurance policy to the extent that it prohibits assignment or makes assignment an event of default between the account debtor (insurer) and the debtor (insured), but the section specifies that the account debtor need not honor the assignment if the anti-assignment clause would be effective under other law. U.C.C. § 9-408(d). See also the discussion of the effects of U.C.C. § 9-408 in § 18.03, infra.

137. U.C.C. § 9-102(a)(27A).

pay the person in control of the electronic record evidencing the transaction creates issues that do not arise with ordinary accounts. Obtaining control of an electronic record evidencing an ordinary account is irrelevant for purposes of Article 9, but if Seller borrows money from Bank and grants Bank a security interest in its right to collect from Buyer (the controllable account), Bank will want to obtain control of the controllable electronic record evidencing the controllable account. Taking control is the best way for Bank to perfect its security interest,[138] and if Seller defaults on its secured obligation and Bank wishes to collect from Buyer, it will have to provide, upon demand, reasonable proof that it has control of the record.[139]

It is important with accounts to understand not only what is included within the definition but also what is excluded. The term does not include the following types of payment rights:

> (i) chattel paper, (ii) commercial tort claims, (iii) deposit accounts, (iv) investment property, (v) letter-of-credit rights or letters of credit, or (vi) rights to payment for money or funds advanced or sold, other than rights arising out of the use of a credit or charge card or information contained on or for use with the card, or (vii) rights to payment evidenced by an instrument.[140]

The most important of these exclusions are discussed in the ensuing subsections.

[2] Instruments—§9-102(a)(47), (65)

An Article 9 "instrument" is either a negotiable instrument, governed by Article 3, or "any other writing evidencing a right to be paid money which is of a type that is, in the ordinary course of business, transferred by delivery with any necessary indorsement or assignment."[141] The latter type of instrument is technically nonnegotiable, but the market has imbued it with some of the key attributes of negotiability, and such instruments are sometimes called "quasi-negotiable." Article 3 requires that a negotiable instrument be in a writing,[142] and Article 9 requires the same for nonnegotiable instruments, and the definition of "writing" requires an "intentional reduction to tangible form."[143] Accordingly, the record evidencing an instrument will always be tangible and never electronic.

---

138. A secured party can perfect a security interest in a controllable account by filing a financing statement or by taking control of the controllable electronic record evidencing the controllable account, but a secured party that has perfected by control will always have priority over a secured party that has perfected by filing. U.C.C. §§ 9-310(a), (b)(8); 9-314(a); 9-326A.

139. U.C.C. § 12-106(d)(1).

140. U.C.C. § 9-102(a)(2).

141. U.C.C. § 9-102(a)(47). The definition excludes investment property (e.g., bonds), letters of credit, or rights arising out of the use of credit or charge cards. If an instrument is part of chattel paper, it falls within that definition. U.C.C. § 9-102(a)(11). See § 1.04[B][3], *infra*.

142. U.C.C. §§ 3-104(a) (instrument is an unconditional promise or order to pay a fixed amount of money); 3-103(a)(8), (12) (order and promise must be written).

143. U.C.C. § 1-201(b)(43).

Whether a writing generally in the form of an instrument is negotiable is determined by whether it meets the criteria for negotiability established by Article 3,[144] and determining whether a writing is or is not negotiable can sometimes be difficult. The inclusion of nonnegotiable writings in the definition provides protection for a secured party that uses the term to describe its collateral in the security agreement but may have made a mistake as to a writing's negotiability. If it functions like an instrument, it's an instrument for purposes of Article 9.

The most common forms of negotiable instruments are drafts (most commonly checks), promissory notes, and certificates of deposit.[145] A draft involves a written order to pay money.[146] If you visualize a check,[147] the most common type of draft, the drawer (the person who signs the check) orders its bank (identified on the bottom left of the check) to pay money to the order of the person named on the payee line. A promissory note involves a promise to pay money[148] and is the most common form of instrument for purposes of Article 9. With a promissory note, the maker (the person who signs the note) promises to pay money to the order of the person named in the note. A certificate of deposit contains an acknowledgment by a bank that it has received a sum of money and a promise to repay it.[149]

The key attribute of an instrument is that the obligation to pay money that it evidences is merged into the writing. An obligation to pay money is inherently intangible in nature, but the merger makes it real, or reifies it. To illustrate, suppose Maker enters into a contract with Payee and signs a negotiable note promising to pay a certain sum of money to Payee or its order (i.e., to Payee or another person that Payee orders Maker to pay). If Payee wishes to transfer the right to collect from Maker to a third person, it must do so by physically delivering the note to that person. If Payee delivers the note to the person with its indorsement (signature), the transfer is referred to as a negotiation and the third person will be a holder.[150] If the third person not only takes possession of the note but also gives value for it, in good faith, and without notice that Maker has a contract defense to enforcement that would be good against Payee, the third person will be a holder in due course.[151] Holder-in-due-course status is highly desirable because a person with that status takes the instrument free from all adverse property claims,[152] including security interests[153] and most contract defenses.[154] If Bank makes a loan to Payee and takes a security interest in the note, taking possession of it

---

144. U.C.C. § 3-104.

145. For discussion of certificates of deposit, see § 1.06[H], *infra*.

146. U.C.C. § 3-104(e).

147. U.C.C. § 3-104(f).

148. U.C.C. § 3-104(e).

149. U.C.C. § 3-104(j).

150. U.C.C. §§ 3-201(a), (b) (negotiation); 1-201(b)(21) (holder). An instrument payable to bearer is negotiated by delivery alone. *Id.*

151. U.C.C. § 3-302.

152. U.C.C. § 3-306.

153. U.C.C. § 9-331(a).

154. U.C.C. § 3-305(b).

will prevent anyone else from becoming a holder in due course and thereby taking it free from the security interest. Moreover, if the secured party itself is a holder in due course, it can enforce the instrument free from most contract defenses that Maker might have against Payee. A more detailed description of the functioning of negotiable instruments in the context of Article 9, and a comparison with accounts and chattel paper, is provided elsewhere in this chapter.[155]

In the case of a nonnegotiable instrument, holder-in-due course status is unavailable, and neither Article 3 nor Article 9 provide rules governing the mechanics of collecting from the person obligated on the instrument. Those rules must be found in the common law. Even so, a secured party taking a security interest in such an instrument may find it advantageous to perfect by taking possession, rather than by filing a financing statement, because a secured party that leaves possession with the debtor runs the risk that the debtor will transfer the instrument free of the security interest under a rule protecting transferees other than holders in due course.[156]

Article 9 recognizes "promissory notes" as a subset of instruments.[157] A promissory note must qualify as an Article 9 instrument, must contain a promise to pay money rather than an order to someone else to pay money, and must not contain an acknowledgment by a bank that it has received funds for deposit. This has the effect of excluding drafts and certificates of deposit from the definition. The primary significance of the category is that Article 9 governs sales of promissory notes but does not govern sales of instruments that are not promissory notes,[158] and the special rules applicable to these sales can be more precisely stated by reference to promissory notes rather than all instruments.

[3] Chattel Paper—§ 9-102(a)(11), (31), (79)

The basic definition of chattel paper is as follows:

"Chattel paper" means:

(A) a right to payment of a monetary obligation secured by specific goods, if the right to payment and security agreement are evidenced by a record; or

(B) a right to payment of a monetary obligation owed by a lessee under a lease agreement with respect to specific goods and a monetary obligation owed by the lessee in connection with the transaction giving rise to the lease, if:

(i) the right to payment and lease agreement are evidenced by a record; and

(ii) the predominant purpose of the transaction giving rise to the lease was to give the lessee the right to possession and use of the goods.

---

155. See § 1.04[C], *infra*

156. U.C.C. § 9-330(d).

157. U.C.C. § 9-102(a)(65).

158. U.C.C. § 9-109(a)(3). Sales of promissory notes and certain other payment rights are discussed in § 1.05, *infra*.

The term does not include a right to payment arising out of a charter or other contract involving the use or hire of a vessel or a right to payment arising out of the use of a credit or charge card or information contained on or for use with the card.[159]

One common pattern involving chattel paper arises when a merchant sells goods on a secured basis, retaining a purchase-money security interest. The seller typically documents this transaction with one record,[160] usually called a "retail installment contract," which combines features of a promissory note and a security agreement.[161] The record evidences both the buyer's payment obligation and the merchant's security interest. Title to the goods passes to the buyer as part of the sale,[162] but the merchant retains an Article 9 security interest that it can foreclose if the buyer defaults. In effect, the merchant has traded the goods for a set of intangible rights—the right to enforce the buyer's payment obligation (through litigation, if necessary), and the right to use Article 9's mechanisms to foreclose on the goods if the buyer defaults.

The record signed by the buyer is chattel paper, but this term has no significance if the merchant does not make use of the chattel paper in a secondary financing arrangement. In other words, if a third party does not acquire an interest in the chattel paper, the merchant simply has a garden-variety security interest in the buyer's goods. If, however, the merchant uses the chattel paper as collateral for a loan from a bank,[163] the bank's collateral is the rights of the merchant evidenced by the chattel paper rather than the goods sold by the merchant. The easiest way to understand this relationship is to visualize a two-tier arrangement in which one security agreement (the merchant/buyer agreement) serves as collateral for another security agreement (the merchant/bank agreement). The collateral in the merchant/buyer transaction is consumer goods; the collateral in the merchant/bank transaction is chattel paper. If the merchant defaults, the bank will foreclose on the chattel paper. Foreclosure entitles the bank to enforce the rights that, absent default, the merchant could have enforced. The Code has a provision that allows the bank to in effect require the buyer to begin making the installment payments to it by preventing the buyer from obtaining a discharge of its obligation if

---

159. U.C.C. § 9-102(a)(11). Prior to the 2022 amendments, the term was defined as "a record or records that evidence both a monetary obligation" and a security interest in or lease of specific goods. The revised definition makes it clear that the collateral is the right to payment of a monetary obligation, not the record or records that evidence that right.

160. The buyer need not be a consumer, nor do the payment and security aspects of the transaction have to be in one record. A writing that is a promissory note and a record that is a security agreement will be taken together and treated as chattel paper. U.C.C. § 9-102(a)(11).

161. A writing that includes both a monetary obligation and a security interest can qualify as a negotiable instrument under Article 3 (although most retail installment contracts contain provisions that render them nonnegotiable). U.C.C. § 3-104(a)(3). Such a writing would not qualify as an instrument for Article 9 purposes, however. Section 9-102(a)(47) specifies that an instrument cannot be a writing that itself qualifies as a security agreement or lease.

162. U.C.C. § 2-106(1). Even if the record states that the seller is to retain title pending final payment, its interest is limited to a security interest. U.C.C. §§ 1-201(b)(35), 2-401(1).

163. Article 9 is also triggered if the merchant sells the chattel paper outright. U.C.C. § 9-109(a)(3). For discussion of Article 9's treatment of sales of chattel paper, see § 1.05, infra.

it pays the merchant.[164] That provision permits an assignee[165] of chattel paper to notify the account debtor[166] (the buyer) and thereby divert the payments from the merchant to itself. The bank is in the same position with regard to the buyer's goods as the merchant, however, and cannot foreclose on them unless the buyer defaults.[167]

A lease of goods in record form also creates chattel paper if it includes the payment obligation of the lessee, which is almost invariably the case.[168] If the lessor borrows money from a bank on the security of the lease, the lease is chattel paper.[169] If the lessor defaults, the bank can enforce the payment obligation created by the lease using the mechanism discussed in the preceding paragraph. If the lessee in turn defaults, the bank can recover the leased goods under the self-help provisions of Article 2A,[170] which governs the relationship between lessor and lessee. If the bank also has a security interest in the lessor's inventory, it can foreclose on the formerly leased assets using Article 9's normal foreclosure rules.[171]

---

164. U.C.C. § 9-406(a). This rule applies to "account debtors," meaning persons obligated on an account, chattel paper, or a general intangible. U.C.C. § 9-102(a)(3). If the record evidencing the payment obligation is a negotiable instrument, the rules governing the mechanics of collecting from the person obligated on the instrument are in Article 3 rather than Article 9. *Id. See also* U.C.C. § 9-607(a)(3), which establishes the right of a secured party to enforce the obligations of account debtors and other persons obligated on collateral.

165. U.C.C. § 9-406(a) (and related provisions in other sections) use the terms "assignor" and "assignee," but definitions enacted as part of the 2022 amendments make clear what has always been the case. "Assignor" refers to a debtor that grants a security interest in collateral to secure an obligation or sells certain payment rights in a transaction governed by Article 9, and "assignee" refers to a secured party with a security interest in collateral that secures an obligation or arises as a result of buying the payment rights. U.C.C. § 9-102(a)(7A) (assignee), (7B) (assignor). The merchant/bank security agreement described in the text operates as a conditional assignment to the bank of the merchant's rights in the chattel paper. It is conditional in that, unless otherwise agreed, the bank cannot enforce its rights as assignee unless the merchant defaults. If the merchant had made an outright sale of the chattel paper to the bank, the assignment would have been unconditional.

166. The term includes a person obligated on an account, chattel paper, or a general intangible. U.C.C. § 9-102(a)(3). It does not include a person obligated on a negotiable instrument even if the instrument is part of chattel paper. *Id.*

167. U.C.C. § 9-607(a)(3) establishes the right of a secured party to exercise the rights of the debtor with respect to any property that secures the obligations of the account debtor or other person obligated on the collateral.

168. *In re ICS Cybernetics, Inc.*, 123 B.R. 467, 17 U.C.C. Rep. Serv. 2d 609, *aff'd w.o. op.*, 123 B.R. 480 (N.D.N.Y. 1990), dealt with multiple writings. Because the master agreement provided for payment of "the monthly rent set forth in [the] equipment schedules" and did not specify the basic lease terms, the court held that the equipment schedules alone constituted chattel paper. Compare this case with *In re Funding Systems Asset Management Corp.*, 111 B.R. 500, 11 U.C.C. Rep. Serv. 2d 205 (Bankr. W.D. Pa. 1990) (chattel paper consisted of twelve equipment schedules, which contained monetary obligations, and master leases, which contained lease terms).

169. *In re Keneco Fin. Group, Inc.*, 131 B.R. 90, 16 U.C.C. Rep. Serv. 2d 219 (Bankr. N.D. Ill. 1991) (equipment leases). Charters of vessels are excluded because they constitute accounts. U.C.C. § 9-102(a)(2).

170. U.C.C. § 2A-525(2).

171. The term "inventory" includes goods that are actually leased as well as those held for sale or lease. U.C.C. § 9-102(a)(48). *See also* § 1.04[A][3], *supra*.

Note that transactions using chattel paper based on an underlying lease or an underlying security agreement are comparable because the record in both instances includes a payment obligation that is tied to specific goods.[172] The rights that the chattel paper represents with respect to the goods are the feature distinguishing chattel paper from other forms of personal property that include an obligation to pay money (i.e., instruments, accounts, and payment intangibles).[173] These goods-oriented rights pose unique issues that justify identifying chattel paper as a separate category for Article 9 purposes. Thus, even if the monetary obligation is evidenced by a separate writing that, standing alone, qualifies as an instrument, it is treated as part of the chattel paper.[174]

Note also that chattel paper requires a security interest in specific goods, so a record evidencing a monetary obligation and a security interest in all the debtor's inventory would not be chattel paper. Even if a record evidences a monetary obligation and a security interest in a specific item of equipment coupled with other collateral, such as all the debtor's inventory, the right to payment would not be chattel paper. If it were to be characterized as chattel paper, "it would be possible to convert virtually any monetary obligation evidenced by records and secured by any collateral into chattel paper merely by including as collateral a specific item of goods."[175] Some additional collateral may be included, but the specific goods must be the primary collateral; otherwise, the purpose of the special rules governing priorities in chattel paper but not in other types of collateral would be frustrated.[176]

Prior to the 2022 amendments, chattel paper was further broken down into "tangible chattel paper"[177] and "electronic chattel paper."[178] The latter term, introduced in 1998, adapted Article 9 to the practice, mostly among lessors, of evidencing rights by records in electronic form. The main distinction between the forms of chattel paper was that perfection by possession was available for tangible chattel paper, while the electronic counterpart of possession—control—was available for electronic chattel paper.[179] This bifurcation proved unsatisfactory for a number of reasons—sometimes chattel paper consists of more than one record and the records can be in different forms (some written and some electronic), and there can be conversions of electronic records to written

---

172. Note that the problems that can arise in determining whether an agreement is a true lease or a security interest in the form of a disguised lease (*see* § 1.03[B][1], *supra*) are not important in this context because the definition of chattel paper includes both leases and security agreements.

173. Berkowitz v. Chavo Int'l, Inc., 74 N.Y.2d 144, 544 N.Y.S.2d 569, 542 N.E.2d 1086, 9 U.C.C. Rep. Serv. 2d 4 (1989) (written purchase agreement was not chattel paper because it did not create a security interest in the goods sold under it); *In re* Padgett, 49 B.R. 212, 41 U.C.C. Rep. Serv. 1020 (Bankr. W.D. Ky. 1985) (monetary obligation alone not sufficient to create chattel paper).

174. U.C.C. § 9-102(a)(11).

175. U.C.C. § 9-102, Comment 5(b).

176. *Id.*

177. U.C.C. § 9-102(a)(79) (1998 Official Text).

178. U.C.C. § 9-102(a)(31) (1998 Official Text).

179. U.C.C. § 9-313(a) (possession of tangible chattel paper); §§ 9-314(a), 9-105 (control of electronic chattel paper). Security interests in both forms of chattel paper may also be perfected by filing. U.C.C. § 9-312(a).

records and vice-versa. The 2022 amendments eliminated the separate terms "tangible chattel paper" and "electronic chattel paper"—but not the concepts themselves—by creating a perfection rule called "possession and control." Section 9-314A(a) provides that:

> A secured party may perfect a security interest in chattel paper by taking possession of each authoritative tangible copy of the record evidencing the chattel paper and obtaining control of each authoritative electronic copy of the electronic record evidencing the chattel paper.

Hybrid transactions in which a lease of goods is combined with other property or services is common, and under the definition of chattel paper a right to payment of a monetary arising from a lease of specific goods is not chattel paper unless the predominant purpose of the transaction is to provide the lessee the right to possession and use of the goods. The following example from the Official Comments illustrates the point:

> Customer and Cableco enter into a transaction, evidenced by one or more records, pursuant to which, in exchange for a payment of $200 per month, Cableco will provide Customer with specified television programming and a device needed to access the programming (a "lease" of the device). If the components of the transaction were priced separately, the price for the programming would be substantially more than the price for possession and use of the device. Because the goods aspect of this transaction does not predominate, under paragraph (11)(B)(ii) Customer's monetary obligation does not constitute chattel paper.[180]

[4] Controllable Electronic Records—§12-102(a)(1)

Until the promulgation of the 2022 amendments to the U.C.C., digital assets such as virtual currency were classified under Article 9 as general intangibles, but the rules for general intangibles were not suitable for this type of asset. For example, the only way to perfect a security interest in a general intangible was (and except for controllable payment intangibles remains) the filing of a financing statement, but no prudent secured party will leave control of virtual currency in the hands of its debtor. The secured party will want to take control of the virtual currency in order to prevent the debtor from spending it, and doing so should be the preferred method of perfection.

The 2022 amendments introduced a new Article 12 governing the holding and transfer of digital assets, although that term is not used. Instead, the assets are called "controllable electronic records." This builds on existing Code definitions and concepts. "Record" means "information that is inscribed on a tangible medium or that is stored in an electronic or other medium and is retrievable in perceivable form,"[181] and "electronic" means "relating to technology having electrical, digital, magnetic,

---

180. U.C.C. §9-102, Comment 5(b).
181. U.C.C. §1-201(b)(31).

wireless, optical, electromagnetic, or similar capabilities."[182] "Control" as a means of perfection in the electronic world is also a familiar concept—it was first introduced into the U.C.C. in 1998 as a method of perfecting a security interest in chattel paper evidenced by an electronic record.[183] Putting the terms together, a controllable electronic record is "a record stored in an electronic medium that can be subjected to control under Section 12-105."[184] Controllable electronic records are often referred to as CERs. They are a subset of general intangibles for purposes of Article 9;[185] thus, a security agreement describing the collateral as "all general intangibles" will cover all controllable electronic records.

Laws other than Article 12 have rules for several types of assets that must or might exist in electronic form, and it is important that they be excluded from Article 12 in order to avoid confusion. As will be discussed below, Article 12 contains a broad take-free rule that insulates certain purchasers of CERs from adverse claims, and it is critical that assets such as electronic chattel paper,[186] for which Article 9 provides less expansive take-free rules that are relied on heavily by actors in the marketplace, not be treated as a CER. Thus, the definition of CER excludes:

- a deposit account;
- an electronic copy of a record evidencing chattel paper;
- an electronic document of title;
- electronic money;[187]
- investment property; and
- a transferable record.[188]

A key feature of Article 12 is the take-free rule of Section 12-104, which imbues CERs with the same level of negotiability as negotiable instruments under Article 3. Just as Article 3 provides that a "holder in due course" takes free from adverse prop-

---

182. U.C.C. § 1-201(b)(16A).

183. *See, e.g.,* U.C.C. §§ 9-314(a), 9-105. See also the discussion of chattel paper in § 1.04[B][3], *supra.*

184. U.C.C. § 12-102(a)(1).

185. General intangibles are discussed in § 1.04[B][7], *infra.*

186. This wording conforms to a revision of the definition of chattel paper in Article 9. *See* U.C.C. § 9-102(a)(11). The term "electronic chattel paper" is no longer used.

187. This is a new term used in Article 9 for what is sometimes referred to as a central bank digital currency, or CBDC. If a domestic or foreign government issues its own CBDC, it will be classified as electronic money under Article 9, not a CER under Article 12. Virtual currencies (e.g., Bitcoin) are excluded from the definition of money in Article 1 and thus are not electronic money under Article 9. They qualify as CERs under Article 12. Some states enacting the 2022 amendments have excluded any reference to electronic money out of a misplaced concern that its inclusion would encourage the federal government to issue a CBDC. Even in those states, however, virtual currencies such as Bitcoin are excluded from Article 1's definition of money and qualify as CERs under Article 12.

188. U.C.C. § 12-102(a)(3) defines "transferable record" as a record created under the Uniform Electronic Transactions Act § 16(a) or the federal Digital Signatures in Global and National Commerce Act (E-Sign), 15 U.S.C. § 7021(a)(1).

erty claims to a negotiable instrument,[189] so Article 12 provides that a "qualifying purchaser" takes free from adverse property claims to a CER.[190] Under Section 12-102(a)(2), a qualifying purchaser is a purchaser "of a controllable electronic record or an interest in a controllable electronic record that obtains control of the controllable electronic record for value, in good faith, and without notice of a claim of a property right in the controllable electronic record."

The reach of Article 12's take-free rule is illustrated by the following example from Comment 7 to Section 12-104:

> **Example 3:** Hacker, a thief, "steals" and obtains control of a controllable electronic record. Hacker then sells the controllable electronic record to Buyer, who obtains control and otherwise meets the requirements for a qualifying purchaser (by obtaining control and purchasing for value, in good faith, and without notice of a claim of a property right).
>
> As a general matter, law other than Article 12 would determine whether any particular transaction creates a property interest in a controllable electronic record. Section 12-104(c). However, even if under other applicable law Hacker has no rights in, and no right to transfer, the "stolen" controllable electronic record, Section 12-104(e) enables Buyer, a qualifying purchaser, to take the controllable electronic record free of claims of a property right—including that of the rightful owner.

Some CERs have inherent value in and of themselves. As noted in Paragraph 1 of the Prefatory Note to Article 12:

> [p]eople have begun to assign economic value to some electronic records that bear no relationship to extrinsic rights and interests. For example, without any law or legally enforceable agreement, people around the world have agreed to treat virtual currencies such as bitcoin (or, more precisely "transaction outputs" generated by the Bitcoin protocol) as a medium of exchange and store of value.

Other CERs do not have inherent value but rather function as evidence of the rights of parties to a transaction or rights of a person in property other than the CER. In language commonly used to describe the phenomenon, the rights and property evidenced by the CER are "tethered" to it. With two exceptions discussed in the next section, Article 12 addresses only the CER and not the tethered rights. As stated in Section 12-104(f), "[e]xcept as provided in … law other than this article, a qualifying purchaser takes a right to payment, right to performance, or other interest in property evidenced

---

189. U.C.C. § 3-306.

190. U.C.C. § 12-104(e). The analogy between Articles 3 and 12 is further strengthened by the definition of value. The Article 3 definition (U.C.C. § 3-303(a)) is narrower than the Article 1 definition (U.C.C. § 1-204), and Article 12 adopts the Article 3 definition (U.C.C. § 12-102(a)(4)).

by the controllable electronic record subject to a claim of a property right in the right to payment, right to performance, or other interest in property."[191]

Differentiating between a CER and rights tethered to it is critical. The following discussion from Paragraph 4(a) of the Prefatory Note is instructive. It begins with a transaction that occurs in the paper world:

> Suppose, for example, that S and B enter into a written contract for the sale of 100 air purifiers. The contract provides that at a specified time in the future, S is to deliver the goods and B is to pay for them. B may sell (assign) to P the right to receive delivery of the goods from S. P has acquired a valuable asset, i.e., the right to receive delivery.

> In contrast, if B sells to P only the paper (record) on which the contract is written, P might or might not acquire the right to delivery of the goods, depending on whether applicable law treats the sale of the paper as an assignment of the right to delivery (as can be the case with a negotiable document of title under UCC Article 7). P would become the owner of the paper in any event, but the paper itself may be of little value.

Now transition the transaction to the electronic world and posit that the record is a CER and P is a qualifying purchaser. The Prefatory Note continues:

> If the contract for the sale of air purifiers were electronic rather than written, the same analysis would apply. The right evidenced by the electronic record (i.e., B's right to receive delivery from S) would be the valuable asset, not the record itself.

> Suppose that the contract of sale between B and S is evidenced by a controllable electronic record that B sells to P. Under Section 12-104(d), P would acquire all rights *in the controllable electronic record* that the transferor (B) had or had power to transfer. If P obtains control of the controllable electronic record for value, in good faith, and without notice of any claim of a property right in the controllable electronic record, P will become a qualifying purchaser and, as such, would acquire its rights *in the controllable electronic record* free of any claim of a property right under Section 12-104.

> But the controllable electronic record itself may or may not be a valuable asset. In this example, unlike bitcoin, the record would have value to P only if by virtue of acquiring rights in the controllable electronic record, P would also acquire the right to receive delivery of the goods from S.

The point is critical and bears both repeating and embellishing. A qualifying purchaser of a CER takes the CER free from adverse claims, but if the value of the CER is that it evidences contract or property rights, whether the purchaser acquires those rights, and if so whether they are acquired free from adverse claims, is left to other

---

191. U.C.C. § 12-104(f) does not apply to controllable accounts and controllable payment intangibles.

law. Using a simple example, two parties might agree that a token represents property rights (e.g., in real estate or goods), but whether a purchaser of the token acquires those property rights and, if so, whether they are acquired free from adverse claims, is not addressed by Article 12. All we know for sure is that the qualifying purchaser takes the token itself free from adverse claims.[192]

There is an exception to the above analysis for controllable accounts and controllable payment intangibles.[193] These rights are explicitly tethered to the CER that evidences them, and a transferee of the CER acquires the controllable account or controllable payment intangible evidenced by the CER. A qualifying purchaser of the CER takes the CER and the tethered controllable account or controllable payment intangible free from adverse claims.

[5] Documents—§ 9-102(a)(30)

Article 9 defines "document" to mean either a document of title (a term defined in the general definitions of Article 1) or a receipt of the kind described in Section 7-201(2).[194] The Article 1 definition sets forth the essence of this form of property: "[A] record … that in the regular course of business or financing is treated as adequately evidencing that the person in possession or control of the record is entitled to receive, control, hold, and dispose of the record and the goods the record covers."[195] The record must purport "to be issued by or addressed to a bailee and to cover goods in the bailee's possession which are either identified or are fungible portions of an identified mass."[196] The most common documents are bills of lading issued by a carrier upon shipment of goods and warehouse receipts issued by a warehouse upon storage of goods.[197]

A document of title, whether or not it is negotiable, operates as a receipt for goods placed in the custody of a bailee[198] and also controls access to the goods. In other words, the bailee will not release the goods to anyone that cannot present a document in proper form. With a negotiable document, title to the covered goods is merged into

---

192. For further discussion on controllable electronic records generally, see § 6.04[C]. That section includes in note 145 a discussion of tethering in the context of tokenization.

193. Controllable accounts are discussed in § 1.04[B][1], *supra*, and controllable payment intangibles are discussed in § 1.04[B][7], *infra*.

194. U.C.C. § 9-102(a)(30). The reference to Section 7-201(2) (Section 7-201(b) in the 2003 Official Text) is to receipts in the nature of warehouse receipts issued under other statutes governing distilled spirits or agricultural commodities.

195. U.C.C. § 1-201(b)(16). The use of the term "record" in the definition signifies that documents may either be in tangible or electronic form. See various provisions of Article 7 that provide for electronic documents, and the use of the terms "tangible negotiable documents" and "electronic negotiable documents" in Article 9. U.C.C. §§ 9-313(a) (perfection by possession of tangible negotiable documents), 9-314(a) (perfection by control of electronic negotiable documents).

196. U.C.C. § 1-201(b)(16)(ii).

197. *Id. See also* U.C.C. §§ 1-201(b)(42) (warehouse receipt defined), (b)(6) (bill of lading defined).

198. "Bailee" means "a person that by a warehouse receipt, bill of lading, or other document of title acknowledges possession of goods and contracts to deliver them." U.C.C. § 7-102(a)(1). Article 7 provides substantive rules governing the use of warehouse receipts and bills of lading, including the obligation of the bailee to deliver the goods to the proper party.

the record just as an obligation to pay money is merged into an instrument. This means that title to the goods can be transferred to a third party by transferring possession or control the document to that party even though the goods remain in the custody of the bailee.[199] The bailee need not (and should not) release the goods unless the transferee is a "person entitled under the document."[200] Both negotiable and nonnegotiable documents play important roles in secured financing, and those roles are discussed later in this book.[201]

[6] Investment Property—§ 9-102(a)(49)

"Investment property" is a broad category of assets within one or more of the following subsets: securities (both certificated and uncertificated), security entitlements, securities accounts, commodity contracts, and commodity accounts.[202] Although "investment property" is an Article 9 term, it relies to a large extent on terminology and concepts developed in Article 8. As explained below, Article 8 deals with securities held directly by an investor and with financial assets, including securities, held indirectly through a securities intermediary (e.g., a broker). Investments in commodities are beyond the scope of the U.C.C., and Article 9 is self-contained with respect to security interests in such investments.

A security is an obligation of an issuer or a share or other interest in an issuer or its property that is or is of a type commonly dealt with in the securities markets, or that is a medium for investment that by its terms expressly provides that it is within

---

199. A transferee to whom a negotiable document is "duly negotiated" acquires title to both the document and the underlying goods. U.C.C. § 7-502(a)(1), (2). Section 7-501 defines due negotiation. At the core of the concept is a requirement that the transferee have the characteristics of a good-faith purchaser for value. A transferee of a nonnegotiable document acquires the title and rights that the transferor had or had actual authority to convey (as does a transferee of a negotiable document that does not take by due negotiation). U.C.C. § 7-504(a). In other words, the transferee derivatively acquires the transferor's title (with whatever defects may exist), but the document does not represent complete title.

200. A "person entitled under the document" means the holder of a negotiable document or the named consignee under a nonnegotiable document (or delivery order issued pursuant to a nonnegotiable document). U.C.C. § 7-102(a)(9). A person becomes a holder of a negotiable document when it is issued or negotiated to that person. The process for negotiation of tangible and electronic documents is governed by Section 7-501(a) (tangible) and (b) (electronic). A nonnegotiable document will inevitably name a consignee (without additional words indicating that the document runs to the order of the named person). That consignee is a person entitled under the document. If the named consignee wants another person to obtain possession, it can surrender the nonnegotiable document to the bailee in exchange for a new document running to the other person, or the named consignee can issue a delivery order (defined in Section 7-102(a)(5)) directing the bailee to release all or a portion of the goods to the other person. Once accepted by the bailee, a delivery order functions like an ordinary document in that the bailee's obligation to deliver the goods runs to the person named in the order. U.C.C. § 7-502(a)(4).

201. See §§ 6.02[B][1] (terminal warehousing), 6.02[B][2] (field warehousing), 6.02[C] (goods in transit), infra.

202. U.C.C. § 9-102(a)(49).

the scope of Article 8.[203] A certificated security is a security represented by a physical certificate.[204] The most common forms of certificated securities are stock and bond certificates.[205] The represented rights are commonly transferred by delivery of the certificate.[206] This analogous to the manner in which the right to payment evidenced by an instrument is transferred.[207]

An uncertificated security, sometimes called a book-entry security, is a security for which there is no certificate.[208] The security holder's interest is represented by a notation in books or records maintained by or on behalf of the issuer. Uncertificated securities are typically transferred by making appropriate changes in these records. For example, mutual funds do not ordinarily issue certificates to their shareholders but instead show shareholder interests as notations in their records.

The term "security" includes both certificated and uncertificated securities,[209] and it is primarily used when there is a direct relationship between the investor and the issuer. Most assets held indirectly through a broker are called "security entitlements,"[210] which are defined in terms of "financial assets." A financial asset may be a security, but the term also includes investment vehicles that are not securities but are either of a type commonly traded on financial markets or are a recognized medium for investment.[211] Article 8 contains a section that further differentiates between financial assets that are securities and those that are not.[212] A financial asset that is not a security and is held directly by the debtor is not investment property and is almost certainly a general intangible. A financial asset held by a broker is almost always a security entitlement, whether or not it qualifies as a security, and is therefore investment property.[213]

Assume, for example, that an investor owns 100 shares of ABC Corp. If the investor is in possession of a certificate showing this interest, the asset is a certificated security.

---

203. U.C.C. § 8-102(a)(15). An asset need not actually be dealt with in the securities markets as long as it is of a type that is traded. Thus, a stock certificate representing an ownership interest in a closely held corporation is a security even though the stock is not publicly traded.

204. U.C.C. § 8-102(a)(4).

205. *In re* H.J. Otten Co., Inc., 8 B.R. 781, 31 U.C.C. Rep. Serv. 702 (W.D.N.Y. 1981) (municipal bonds included); Traverse v. Liberty Bank & Trust Co., 5 U.C.C. Rep. Serv. 535 (Mass. Super. Ct. 1967) (convertible debentures included).

206. *See* U.C.C. §§ 8-104(a)(1) (describing how a person acquires an interest in a security), 8-302 (describing the rights acquired by a purchaser of a security), 8-301(a) (defining delivery in the context of certificated securities).

207. See discussion in § 1.04[B][2], *supra*.

208. U.C.C. § 8-102(a)(18).

209. U.C.C. § 8-102(a)(15)(i).

210. U.C.C. § 8-102(a)(17). The investor is called an "entitlement holder." U.C.C. § 8-102(a)(7).

211. U.C.C. § 8-102(a)(9). The term also includes any other asset that is held in a securities account and that the broker and customer have agreed will be treated as a financial asset.

212. U.C.C. § 8-103.

213. It is possible for a financial asset held through a broker to be treated as if it were held directly by the debtor. *See* U.C.C. § 8-501(d) (financial asset registered in the name of, payable to the order of, or specially indorsed to the debtor and not indorsed by the debtor to the broker or in blank). If such a financial asset is a security, it is investment property. If it is not a security, it is a general intangible.

If there is no certificate but the books of ABC Corp. reflect the investor's interest, the asset is an uncertificated security. If the investor indirectly holds 100 shares of ABC Corp. through a broker, the asset is a security entitlement. A securities account consists of all security entitlements held in a particular account by a securities intermediary.[214]

Now assume that the same investor directly owns a membership interest in a limited liability company. Unless the terms that define the interest specify that it is a security governed by Article 8, the interest is a financial asset but not a security.[215] It does not qualify as investment property and is instead a general intangible; moreover, since the principal right associated with the interest is not the payment of money, it is not a payment intangible (a subset of general intangibles). If, however, a broker holds the financial asset for the investor, it is a security entitlement and therefore qualifies as investment property.

The treatment of investments in commodity contracts is similar to that for security entitlements and securities accounts. A commodity account is an account maintained by a commodity intermediary (dealer) on behalf of an investor.[216] A commodity contract is a commodity futures contract or option that is traded on a commodities market.[217] Commodity contracts are functionally identical to security entitlements. A commodity account includes all the commodity contracts in an account maintained by a dealer and is functionally identical to a securities account.[218]

A security agreement that describes the collateral as "all investment property" will cover every asset within each category. The parties can also carve up the assets: The security agreement might, for example, cover "all securities," giving the secured party an interest in all certificated and uncertificated securities held directly by the debtor and all financial assets that are securities held through a broker. The secured party would not have a security interest in other financial assets held through a broker, nor would its interest attach to any commodity contract or commodity account. On the other hand, a security agreement that covers "all security entitlements" will reach each financial asset held through a broker but will not reach securities held directly by the debtor, nor will it reach commodity contracts or commodity accounts. A security agreement that describes the collateral as a particular securities account attaches to all security entitlements within the account, and a security agreement that describes the collateral as a particular commodity account attaches to all commodity contracts within the account.[219] Of course, the parties need not select a generic category. If the debtor holds a stock certificate representing an interest in a closely held corporation, the description in the agreement can be tailored to that asset. Likewise, if the parties

---

214. U.C.C. § 8-501(a). Attachment of a security interest to a securities account carries with it automatic attachment to each security entitlement within the account. U.C.C. § 9-203(h).

215. U.C.C. § 8-103(c). Partnership interests are treated similarly.

216. U.C.C. § 9-102(a)(14). The investor is called a "commodity customer." U.C.C. § 9-102(a)(16).

217. U.C.C. § 9-102(a)(15).

218. As is true with securities accounts, attachment of a security interest to a commodity account carries with it automatic attachment to each commodity contract within the account. U.C.C. § 9-203(i).

219. U.C.C. § 9-203(h), (i).

want to use a particular security entitlement without using all the assets in a particular account, they are free to do so.[220]

[7] General Intangibles (Other than Controllable Electronic Records) — § 9-102(a)(42), (61)

Article 9 defines "general intangibles" in residual terms, meaning any personal property that does not fall within one of the other types of property to which the article applies.[221] Just a few examples of personal property categorized by the courts as general intangibles are patent rights,[222] trademark rights,[223] rights to tax refunds,[224] rights to refunds for overpayments to an employee pension plan,[225] claims for breach of contract,[226] liquor licenses,[227] FCC licenses,[228] state water permits,[229] and refunds from security retainers.[230]

The value of a general intangible as collateral is easily understood. To illustrate, a patent represents a federally guaranteed right to exclusive exploitation of an invention for a defined term.[231] The patent holder can produce the invention and sell it or license its use by others. A secured party with a security interest in the patent can sell the patent, including the patent-holder's exploitation rights, at foreclosure in the event of default. Likewise, a secured party with a security interest in a government-issued license can sell the license at foreclosure in the event of default.[232] Often the license is the single most valuable asset owned by a business.

---

220. U.C.C. § 9-108(d) validates generic descriptions that use investment property or any of its subcategories, as well as specific descriptions of the underlying asset. Further, U.C.C. § 9-108(b) permits the description to identify the collateral by category or type, by quantity, by a computational or allocational formula or procedure, or by any other method that renders the identity of the collateral objectively determinable. In a consumer transaction, however, a description of a security entitlement, securities account, or commodity account only by one of the defined types is insufficient as a matter of law. U.C.C. § 9-108(d).

221. U.C.C. § 9-102(a)(42).

222. *In re* Emergency Beacon Corp., 23 U.C.C. Rep. Serv. 766 (S.D.N.Y. 1977).

223. *In re* Roman Cleanser Co., 43 B.R. 940, 39 U.C.C. Rep. Serv. 1770 (Bankr. E.D. Mich. 1984), *aff'd*, 802 F.2d 207, 2 U.C.C. Rep. Serv. 2d 269 (6th Cir. 1986).

224. *In re* Metric Metals Int'l, Inc., 20 B.R. 633, 33 U.C.C. Rep. Serv. 1495 (S.D.N.Y. 1981).

225. *In re* Long Chevrolet, Inc., 79 B.R. 759, 5 U.C.C. Rep. Serv. 2d 462 (N.D. Ill. 1987).

226. Merchants Nat'l Bank of Mobile v. Ching, 681 F.2d 1383, 34 U.C.C. Rep. Serv. 270 (11th Cir. 1982).

227. Queen of the North, Inc. v. LeGrue, 582 P.2d 144, 24 U.C.C. Rep. Serv. 1301 (Alaska 1978).

228. *In re* Ridgely Communications, Inc., 139 B.R. 374, 17 U.C.C. Rep. Serv. 2d 877 (Bankr. D. Md. 1992).

229. Lake Region Credit Union v. Crystal Pure Water, Inc., 502 N.W.2d 524, 21 U.C.C. Rep. Serv. 2d 774 (N.D. 1993).

230. *In re* E-Z Serve Convenience Stores, Inc., 299 B.R. 126, 51 U.C.C. Rep. Serv. 2d 858 (Bankr. M.D.N.C. 2003) (debtor's right to receive refund on unearned portion of retainer paid to a law firm constituted general intangible).

231. 35 U.S.C. § 154.

232. Statutes or regulations make some government licenses non-transferable. *See, e.g.*, Brown v. Baker, 688 P.2d 943, 39 U.C.C. Rep. Serv. 1105 (Alaska 1984) (state statute invalidated security interest

Although one would not ordinarily anticipate any difficulties in characterizing property as either goods or general intangibles, courts occasionally have faced the necessity of distinguishing the two. For example, in one case, a court appropriately held that blueprints, drawings, and technical data produced by a company's engineering staff constituted general intangibles rather than goods.[233] It reasoned that, even though reduced to tangible form, the value was in the concepts and ideas represented by the paper. Similarly, the court found that the written bids, proposals, and cost estimates that various departments of the company had preserved so that they could be drawn upon in preparing future bids were general intangibles.

The category of general intangibles has three discrete subsets—software, controllable electronic records, and payment intangibles—and payment intangibles has a subset called controllable payment intangibles. Software means "a computer program and any supporting information provided in connection with a transaction relating to the program."[234] A secured party can take a security interest in software as part of an integrated transaction in which it also takes a security interest in the goods for which the software is being acquired, in which case the security interest in the software qualifies for purchase-money status to the same extent as the security interest in the goods.[235] The term is also relevant to the definition of chattel paper.[236] Note that the term soft-

---

in limited-entry fishing permits); *In re* Chris-Don, Inc., 367 F. Supp. 2d 696, 57 U.C.C. Rep. Serv. 2d 496 (D.N.J. 2005) (state statute precluded licensee from using liquor license to secure loan). Other licenses are transferable, although typically the issuing governmental agency must approve of the transferee. This requirement simply means that the foreclosing secured party must locate a qualifying buyer. A similar problem arises with certain contract rights. For example, some franchise agreements are assignable if the franchisor approves of the transferee, while others are by their terms non-assignable. Article 9 includes provisions that makes any legal rule or contract term ineffective to the extent that it either impairs the creation, attachment, or perfection of a security interest in a general intangible or causes any of those events to constitute a default. U.C.C. § 9-408(a), (c). However, to the extent that such limitations are generally effective under law other than Article 9, the affected governmental agency or franchisor need not recognize the security interest or the rights of a foreclosure-sale transferee. U.C.C. § 9-408(d). Put another way, a debtor can grant a valid security interest in an otherwise non-transferable license without suffering any penalties, but that does not mean that it will have value in the event of default. A secured party with an interest in a franchise agreement can do no more than ask the franchisor to waive the anti-assignment clause. Perhaps the most important effect of these provisions is that they may provide a basis for increasing the value of secured claims in bankruptcy. See discussion in § 16.02[C], *infra*.

233. United States v. Antenna Systems, Inc., 251 F. Supp. 1013, 3 U.C.C. Rep. Serv. 258 (D.N.H. 1966).

234. U.C.C. § 9-102(a)(76). The discussion, in note 232, *supra*, of Section 9-408(a) and (d), which overrides contractual restrictions that would be enforceable under other law, is relevant to a security interest in a licensee's right to use software. A transfer restriction in a license agreement is ineffective to the extent it impairs the creation, attachment, or perfection of a security interest or causes any of those events to constitute a default by the licensee, but the security interest may not be enforced unless the account debtor (licensor) waives its rights under the term prohibiting transfer.

235. U.C.C. § 9-103(b).

236. *See* § 1.04[B][3], *supra*.

ware does not include embedded computer programs that are part of goods under the definition of that term.[237]

A payment intangible is "a general intangible under which the account debtor's principal obligation is a monetary obligation."[238] Sales of payment intangibles are within the scope of Article 9,[239] but sales of general intangibles that are not payment intangibles are not within its scope. Thus, the payment intangible subset of general intangibles is similar to the promissory note subset of instruments.[240]

An example of a payment intangible is a transferable record. In the discussion of instruments in this subsection, it was noted that an instrument must be evidenced by a writing and cannot be in electronic form. This led the drafters of the Uniform Electronic Transactions Act (U.E.T.A.), which has been adopted in almost all states, to create an electronic substitute for negotiable promissory notes. A transferable record is an electronic record that would be a promissory note under Article 3 if it was in writing[241] and that the issuer has expressly agreed is an electronic record.[242] A person in control of a transferable record under a test established by U.E.T.A.[243] is a holder as that term is defined in the U.C.C., and a person to whom control is transferred for value, in good faith, and without notice of defenses is a holder in due course.[244] Transferable records are, in effect, electronic promissory notes, but they cannot be classified as instruments under Article 9 because they are not in writing. They are, therefore, payment intangibles. Even though a secured party with a security interest in a transferable record will need to take control of the record in order to collect from

---

237. Section 9-102(a)(44) defines goods. *See also* § 1.04[A], *supra.*

238. U.C.C. § 9-102(a)(61). The discussion of accounts provides an example of a payment intangible (payment rights that are a fractional share of a package of loans not represented by instruments). *See* § 1.04, *supra. See also In re* Wiersma, 324 B.R. 92, 106–07 (Bankr. 9th Cir. 2005) (discussing why the definition of payment intangibles includes assignment of rights under settlement agreement); *cf. In re* Cohen, 305 B.R. 886, 53 U.C.C. Rep. Serv. 2d 148 (Bankr. 9th Cir. 2004) (security interest in potential settlement proceeds of tort claim prior to judgment or settlement did not create a payment intangible because alleged tortfeasors' liability had not been established, and thus they were not obligated to pay debtors anything). Also, a right to payment arising out of the use of a credit card is an account, but other rights to payment are payment intangibles. Thus, the right of a credit-card system to collect for a charge that its customer made purchasing goods or services from a merchant is an account, but the merchant's right to collect the charged amount from the credit-card system does not arise out of the use of the card and is a payment intangible. U.C.C. § 9-102, Comment 5a.

239. U.C.C. § 9-109(a)(3).

240. For discussion of promissory notes and other instruments, see § 1.04[B][2], *supra.*

241. U.E.T.A. § 16(a)(1). Transferable records can also be created under the federal Electronic Signatures in Global and National Commerce Act, 15 U.S.C. § 7021(a)(1). The federal act is commonly referred to as E-Sign.

242. U.E.T.A. § 16(a)(2).

243. U.E.T.A. § 16(b), (c). The control test created by the U.E.T.A. was adopted as the original test for control of electronic chattel in the 1998 Official Text of Article 9. That test was amended in 2010, and a new test for control was developed as part of the 2022 amendments. Both the original test for control as amended and the test introduced in 2022 are available to perfect a security interest in chattel paper.

244. U.E.T.A. § 16(d).

the issuer, doing so will not perfect its security interest. That must be accomplished by the filing of a financing statement.

A controllable payment intangible is a "payment intangible evidenced by a controllable electronic record that provides that the account debtor undertakes to pay the person that has control under Section 12-105 of the controllable electronic record." The term was introduced in the 2022 amendments, and the characteristics of a controllable payment intangible are similar to the characteristics of a controllable account.[245] Unlike an ordinary payment intangible, perfection can be accomplished by taking control of the controllable electronic record evidencing the payment right, and a secured party that perfects by control has priority over a secured party that perfects by any other method, such as by the filing of a financing statement.[246] Controllable electronic records, a term that equates roughly with digital assets, require extensive explanation and are covered in a separate subsection.[247]

[C] A Comparison of Accounts, Instruments, and Chattel Paper

Assume that a farm-implement dealer sells a tractor to a farmer. The farmer might be willing to pay cash for the tractor but may prefer to buy on credit, and the dealer may feel compelled to provide credit to close the deal. The dealer will then receive one of the forms of personal property typically created in a noncash sale—an account, an instrument (most likely in the form of a negotiable promissory note), or chattel paper. The account might be an ordinary account, or it might be a controllable account. Distinctions among these forms of property can be explained by comparing them in the context of this simple hypothetical.

If the dealer sells the tractor to the farmer on an open account (i.e., unsecured credit), the dealer acquires an Article 2 contract right to payment.[248] If the buyer breaches, the dealer does not have a right to repossess the tractor.[249] The dealer must instead sue the farmer for breach.[250] If the suit is successful and the farmer does not pay the judgment, the dealer may then have the sheriff execute on the judgment by seizing available assets of the farmer, selling them, and remitting the proceeds to satisfy the judgment in whole or in part. In the suit for breach, however, the farmer can assert any applicable defenses, such as breach of a warranty of quality with respect to the tractor.

---

245. See discussion in § 1.04[B][1], *supra*.

246. U.C.C. §§ 9-310(a), (b)(8); 9-314(a); 9-326A.

247. *See* § 1.04[B][4], *supra*.

248. U.C.C. § 2-301.

249. The sale passes title to the buyer (U.C.C. §§ 2-106(1), 2-401), and the dealer receives an enforceable promise in exchange. Section 2-702 provides a limited right to reclaim goods delivered pursuant to a credit transaction if the buyer is insolvent at the time of receipt.

250. The dealer's cause of action in this context is predicated on Section 2-607(1), which makes the buyer liable for the contract price once the tractor has been accepted. *See also* U.C.C. § 2-709(1)(a) (seller's action for the price of accepted goods).

If the dealer takes a negotiable promissory note for the farmer's payment obligation, the dealer will acquire Article 3 rights in the note, in addition to the Article 2 rights arising from the sale. The major significance of the additional Article 3 rights of a dealer/payee that retains the note are procedural in nature. The dealer may still have to sue to enforce the payment obligation, but Article 3 has provisions that make the case easier to prove on a negotiable instrument.[251] The farmer can still assert any available contract defenses.

If the dealer sells the tractor on secured credit and takes back chattel paper from the farmer, the dealer will acquire both Article 2 rights arising from the sales contract and Article 9 rights on the security agreement that is part of the chattel paper.[252] If the farmer defaults on the payment obligation, the dealer can repossess the tractor, hold a foreclosure sale, and use the sale proceeds to satisfy the outstanding indebtedness. The dealer thus can protect its interests without having to reduce its claim to judgment, although it can sue the farmer for a deficiency judgment if the proceeds of foreclosure do not satisfy the farmer's obligation. Once again, the farmer can assert any available defenses.

Selling the tractor on any of these noncash bases creates a problem for the dealer. The dealer must replenish its inventory of tractors, and if its supplier will not sell to the dealer on credit or deliver on consignment, the dealer must pay for replacement inventory on delivery. Payment for the tractor sold to the farmer, however, will be made over time. Confronted with this cash-flow problem, the dealer is likely to seek inventory financing and will probably secure the financing with its rights against the farmer. Thus, the dealer might borrow from a bank, granting the bank a security interest in the account, the promissory note, or the chattel paper, or it might sell the account, the promissory note, or the chattel paper to the bank. Article 9 governs both the sale of each of these assets and their use as collateral for an obligation.[253]

Further aspects of the three types of property can be illustrated by comparing their use in a loan transaction between the dealer and a bank. Note carefully, however, that the hypothetical now involves the dealer's offering as collateral the rights created in the dealer's favor by the sale to the farmer. In Article 9 terminology, the bank will be the secured party, the dealer will be the debtor, and the dealer's rights against the farmer will be the collateral. If the collateral consists of an account or chattel paper, the farmer will be the "account debtor," a term that means an obligor on an account, chattel paper, or a general intangible.[254] If the collateral consists of an instrument, Article 9 refers to the farmer as the person obligated on the instrument.

---

251. U.C.C. § 3-308.

252. If the chattel paper consists of two writings, a negotiable promissory note and a security agreement, the dealer will also have Article 3 rights, meaning that it can use the procedural advantages of Article 3 if it brings an action to enforce the payment obligation. However, the writings together comprise chattel paper. U.C.C. § 9-102(a)(11). Because the dealer sold the tractor to the farmer, the lease aspect of chattel paper is not applicable to this hypothetical.

253. U.C.C. § 9-109(a)(1), (3).

254. U.C.C. § 9-102(a)(3). The term does not include a person obligated to pay a negotiable instrument that is part of chattel paper. *Id.*

Assume the bank accepts the account as collateral and the dealer later defaults. The bank can then either require that the farmer make future payments directly to the bank[255] or it can sell the account at foreclosure. In either event, the money it receives will go to reduce the indebtedness of the dealer. Because the enforcement rights of the bank and any foreclosure-sale purchaser are predicated on the farmer's Article 2 obligation, they are subject to most contract defenses that the farmer could have asserted against the dealer had the account not been assigned (the merchandise risk). This risk can be avoided if the contract between the dealer and the farmer contains a waiver-of-defenses clause and if the bank has certain characteristics normally associated with a bona fide purchaser for value.[256] The bank and a foreclosure-sale purchaser also run the risk that the farmer might become insolvent (the credit risk). Lenders discount the value of accounts when lending against them based on the level of risk they assume.

The position of the bank significantly improves if the dealer acquired the farmer's payment obligation in the form of a negotiable promissory note. The bank then will have much less concern about the underlying transaction between the dealer and the farmer because of the enhanced rights that it obtains under Article 3. As with the account, if the dealer defaults, the bank can either apply the farmer's payments on the note to the dealer's debt or it can sell the note, in either event using the money it receives to reduce the dealer's debt. The enhanced position of the bank or the foreclosure-sale purchaser becomes relevant only if the farmer stops paying on the note. Unlike the dealer, the bank did not deal with the farmer. Provided the bank qualifies under Article 3 as a holder in due course, a particular type of bona fide purchaser for value, the bank and any foreclosure-sale purchaser will take free of most contract defenses of the farmer.[257] In effect, a holder in due course gets the benefit of a waiver of defenses without the inclusion of such a waiver in the instrument. The elimination of the risk that the farmer may have an effective defense, combined with the procedural advantages discussed previously, render a payment obligation in the form of a negotiable instrument more marketable than payment obligations in other forms.

---

255. See § 1.04[B][1], *supra,* for a discussion of the mechanics by which the bank will assert its collection rights.

256. U.C.C. §§ 9-404(a), 9-403. In effect, the waiver-of-defenses clause permits the bank to acquire rights that are indistinguishable from those of a holder in due course of a negotiable instrument, discussed in this subsection. The characteristics required of the bank are set forth in U.C.C. § 9-403(b). In consumer purchases of goods, a Federal Trade Commission rule makes it an unfair or deceptive act for certain sellers to take a contract that does not contain a notice preserving the consumer's defenses against assignees. The FTC rule applies whether the consumer buyer's payment obligation takes the form of an account, an instrument, or chattel paper. Trade Regulation Rule Concerning Preservation of Consumer Claims and Defenses, 16 C.F.R. § 433. U.C.C. §§ 9-403(d) and 9-404(d) provide that, in a consumer transaction, a record that *should* contain the required FTC notice will be treated as if it *did* contain the notice.

257. U.C.C. §§ 3-302(a)(2), 3-305(b).

If the underlying transaction created chattel paper, the bank will again have a form of property that represents the farmer's Article 2 payment obligation.[258] Furthermore, with the inclusion of the security interest in the tractor, if both the dealer and the farmer default on their payment obligations, the bank as assignee or a foreclosure-sale purchaser from the bank will be able to enforce the dealer's right to foreclose on the tractor. Whether the bank is subject to the farmer's contract defenses turns on whether the contract between the dealer and the farmer contains either an effective waiver-of-defenses clause or an obligation in the form of a negotiable promissory note.[259] If so, and if the bank has the requisite characteristics under either Article 9 (waiver-of defenses clause) or Article 3 (negotiable promissory note), it will take free of most contract defenses.

As this hypothetical demonstrates, the greatest bundle of property rights in a credit sale is created when the seller takes chattel paper that contains an effective waiver-of-defenses clause or a negotiable promissory note. Legal rights alone, however, do not drive all business transactions. Transaction costs are higher with notes and chattel paper, and these costs may outweigh the enhanced rights provided, particularly with relatively small amounts of debt involved. Alternative methods of risk assessment may also lessen the need for additional rights, and the rights themselves may not be particularly valuable in some transactions. For example, the right to foreclose on the underlying collateral when chattel paper is involved may not be viable if the property is difficult to resell or if an entity like a bank is not well-suited to undertake its sale. Subsequent parts of this book develop practical aspects of structuring a transaction with respect to accounts, notes, or chattel paper.[260]

§ 1.05 Sales of Accounts, Chattel Paper, Payment Intangibles, and Promissory Notes — § 9-109(a)(3)

Many Article 9 transactions are loan transactions, and the security interest is a device that serves the function of providing collateral in the event of default. An ostensible-ownership problem arises if the secured party lacks possession of the collateral, but the public filing of a financing statement resolves that problem. The filing protects the secured party from most adverse claims to its collateral.

---

258. If the chattel paper is a package that includes both a negotiable instrument and a security agreement, the bank's rights and duties are governed by Articles 3 and 9 to the extent they are consistent. In case of a conflict, Article 9 governs. U.C.C. § 3-102(b).

259. If the chattel paper consists of two writings (a negotiable instrument and a security agreement), the package of writings would still be chattel paper, but the bank would have the benefit of the Article 3 rules associated with negotiable instruments, including both the procedural advantages and the rights of a holder in due course.

260. *See, e.g.,* § 3.04, *infra.*

In real estate recording systems, any person with an interest in land, including mortgagees and buyers, must record that interest to gain protection against adverse claimants. A buyer, for example, will record a deed so that the seller cannot fraudulently reconvey an interest in the property to a third party whose claim might defeat the buyer's interest. Buyers of most goods need not record their interests because the mere fact of possession is sufficient to put third parties on notice. Public recording is necessary, however, for certain types of goods. Title certificates evidence ownership of motor vehicles, and buyers of aircraft must register with the Federal Aviation Administration to gain protection from adverse claimants.[261]

Recall that an account is an intangible asset, meaning that there is no record that must be transferred to assign the right to payment represented by the account.[262] If the owner of an account wants to realize upon it before payment is due from the account debtor, it can either conditionally assign the account as collateral for a loan or sell it via an unconditional assignment. In either case, the underlying mechanism for transfer of the right to payment is assignment.

Assignment of accounts is important in the context of merchants that sell some of their inventory on an installment plan.[263] Because of the need to replenish inventory and the desire to free the capital represented by the account, many merchants seek to finance against the value of their accounts. Various dynamics of the marketplace, explained later,[264] tend to dictate whether the merchant can borrow against the accounts or must sell them outright. The driving force in both circumstances, however, is the need of the merchant to finance the acquisition of additional inventory.

In a loan transaction, an Article 9 security agreement effectuates the assignment, and the secured party (assignee) must file a financing statement to protect its security interest in the event the owner fraudulently assigns the account a second time. The intangible nature of the collateral facilitates fraudulent reassignment, and the filing puts third parties on notice of the secured party's interest and establishes priority should a third party take an assignment anyway. The same problems can arise with the sale of an account by an unconditional assignment. The drafters of the original article wanted a mechanism that would encourage the buyer of an account to make a public filing to warn third parties that might either buy or lend against the same account. Their resolution was to expand the scope of Article 9 to cover "any sale of accounts or chattel paper."[265] Revised Article 9 adds sales of payment intangibles (a subset of general intangibles) and promissory notes (a subset of instruments) to its scope.[266]

The fact that Article 9 governs sales of accounts and chattel paper encourages buyers of these assets to give public notice by filing financing statements or, in the case

---

261. 49 U.S.C. § 1403.

262. See § 1.04[C][1], [D], *supra*.

263. See § 1.04[D], *supra*.

264. See § 3.04, *infra*.

265. U.C.C. § 9-102(1)(b) (1962 Official Text).

266. U.C.C. § 9-109(a)(3).

of chattel paper, by taking possession or control. The mechanism employed by the drafters to achieve their goal is awkward and confusing. The Code defines a "security interest" to include the interest of a buyer of accounts or chattel paper (or, in revised Article 9, also payment intangibles or promissory notes),[267] "secured party" to include a buyer of such assets,[268] and "debtor" to include a seller of such assets.[269] Because a buyer of accounts or chattel paper is a secured party with a security interest, it needs to file a financing statement to protect that interest. Under the normal Code priority rule governing contests among secured parties,[270] a buyer of accounts that fails to file will lose to a subsequent buyer or secured lender that does file.[271]

This mechanism accomplished the drafters' goal, but calling a buyer's interest a security interest when there is no loan (and therefore the security interest does not function as a security device) inevitably has consequences. For example, the sales agreement between the buyer and seller is a "security agreement"[272] and to be enforceable must meet the formalities required of any security agreement.[273] Also, because the security interest does not operate as a security device, the Code's foreclosure procedures do not apply to covered sales.[274] For example, if a lender acquires a security interest in accounts to secure a loan, following default it must adhere to Article 9's provisions governing foreclosure. Most importantly, it is subject to a standard of commercial reasonableness in either collecting the accounts[275] or selling (reassigning) them at a foreclosure sale.[276] If the collection or foreclosure brings a surplus, it belongs to the debtor, and if proper procedures have been followed, the obligor is liable for any remaining deficiency.[277] By contrast, if a buyer of accounts acquires a security interest that does not secure an obligation, these procedures make no sense. The buyer bought the entire interest and can keep whatever it collects on the accounts or generates by their resale. Because there will typically be neither a surplus nor a deficiency,[278] it should not matter whether the buyer's collection or resale efforts are commercially reasonable.

At least one court applying former law was thoroughly fooled by Article 9's terminology. It concluded that, because an account buyer's interest was limited to a security interest, Article 9 precluded the seller from transferring outright ownership of the

---

267. U.C.C. §1-201(b)(35).
268. U.C.C. §9-102(a)(73)(D).
269. U.C.C. §9-102(a)(28)(B).
270. U.C.C. §9-322(a)(1).
271. For discussion of priorities among secured parties, see Chapter 10, *infra*.
272. U.C.C. §9-102(a)(74).
273. U.C.C. §9-203.
274. U.C.C. §9-601(g).
275. U.C.C. §9-607(c).
276. U.C.C. §9-610(b).
277. U.C.C. §9-615(d).
278. The parties sometimes agree that the seller of accounts or chattel paper will make up any deficiency if collections do not bring a projected amount and/or the seller will be liable for any surplus if they exceed a projected amount. These consensual risk-allocation mechanisms are enforceable. U.C.C. §9-607(c)(2).

account. Accordingly, it held that the account was still owned by the seller and was part of the seller's bankruptcy estate.[279] Of course, the decision was wrong,[280] but using "security interest" to describe a buyer's interest invites confusion. Revised Article 9 overruled the decision by providing that "[a] debtor that has sold an account, chattel paper, payment intangible, or promissory note does not retain a legal or equitable interest in the collateral sold."[281]

Prior to revised Article 9, many payment rights were general intangibles and sales of all general intangibles, even those representing primarily the right to collect money, were outside the scope of the article. The drafters of the revision made a decision to support the securitization industry by bringing many of these collection rights into the definition of accounts. This approach made their sale subject to Article 9 and had the desirable effect of imposing on buyers the need to file financing statements giving public notice of their interests. In a typical securitization transaction, a company that needs immediate funds creates a special-purpose vehicle (SPV), often a business trust, and then sells a package of collection rights to the SPV.[282] The company raises capital through the sale to investors of shares in the SPV, sometimes called "asset-backed securities." Investors need certainty that the SPV's interest in the collection rights is protected against adverse claimants, primarily a trustee in the event the company seeks protection in bankruptcy. For collection rights that qualify as accounts or chattel paper, this means giving public notice through perfection.

A loan participation transaction, like a securitization transaction, involves the sale of collection rights. To illustrate, suppose a bank with a portfolio of loans (the lead bank) wishes to sell fractional shares in the collection rights that comprise the portfolio to other banks (participating banks). The lead bank's collection rights might or might not be instruments; in either event, under pre-revision law their sale was outside the scope of Article 9. Major banks involved in loan participation transactions wanted the simplicity and predictability offered by Article 9 but feared that, because of the volume

279. Octagon Gas Sys., Inc. v. Rimmer, 995 F.2d 948, 20 U.C.C. Rep. Serv. 2d 1330 (10th Cir. 1993).

280. P.E.B. Commentary No. 14 (June 10, 1994) disapproved of *Octagon Gas* and cited with approval *Major's Furniture Mart v. Castle Credit Corp.*, 602 F.2d 538, 26 U.C.C. Rep. Serv. 1319 (3d Cir. 1979). The Permanent Editorial Board (P.E.B.) is a joint committee of the Uniform Law Commission and the American Law Institute that oversees the development of the Uniform Commercial Code. One of the responsibilities of the P.E.B. is to provide commentaries that clarify issues that have troubled the courts.

281. U.C.C. §9-318(a). The drafters should have said no more because subsection (b), which was intended to reinforce the rule of subsection (a), is subject to being misconstrued. The subsection provides that "[f]or purposes of determining the rights of creditors of, and purchasers for value of an account or chattel paper from, a debtor that has sold an account or chattel paper, while the buyer's security interest is unperfected, the debtor is deemed to have rights and title to the account or chattel paper identical to those the debtor sold." The deeming rule only means that, while the debtor does not have the right to reassign the assets, it has the power to do so. Courts should not construe the subsection to mean that, as between the debtor and the buyer, the debtor retains any interest that might become part of its bankruptcy estate.

282. The company can also structure the transaction as a secured loan from the SPV with the receivables serving as collateral.

of transactions, a requirement that a buying bank be required to do anything to perfect its interest would be impractical. Revised Article 9 addresses the banks' concerns through a package of provisions. Although expanded as described above, the definition of account excludes rights to payment for money or funds advanced or sold (other than rights arising out of the use of a credit or charge card).[283] The drafters created two new asset types—promissory notes[284] (a subset of instruments) and payment intangibles[285] (a subset of general intangibles)—and they expanded the scope of Article 9 to govern the sale of promissory notes and payment intangibles.[286] Finally, the interest of a buyer of a promissory note or payment intangible is automatically perfected, meaning the buyer need not take any steps to notify the public of its interest.[287]

§ 1.06 Exclusions from Article 9— § 9-109(c), (d)

Some types of transactions fit the definition of a security interest and would otherwise clearly be within the scope of Article 9 except that the drafters chose to exclude them. The discussion below summarizes the policies that support the exclusions.

[A] Federal Statutes

Based on the principle of federal preemption, Article 9 does not apply to a security interest that is subject to a federal statute to the extent that the statute governs the rights of the parties.[288] A number of federal statutes govern aspects of security interests in a

---

283. U.C.C. § 9-102(a)(3). Instruments are also (and have always been) excluded from the definition of account, without regard to whether they represent a right to collect money or funds advanced or sold. *Id.*

284. U.C.C. § 9-102(a)(65). A promissory note is an instrument that evidences a promise to pay a monetary obligation and is neither an order to pay (if negotiable, such an instrument would be a draft for purposes of Article 3 as provided in Section 3-104(e)) nor a bank's acknowledgement of receipt for deposit of money or funds (if negotiable, such an instrument would be a certificate of deposit for purposes of Article 3 as provided in Section 3-104(j)). If negotiable, a promissory note would be a note for purposes of Article 3 as provided in Section 3-104(e).

285. U.C.C. § 9-102(a)(61). A payment intangible is a general intangible under which the principal obligation of the account debtor is the payment of money. The term "account debtor" refers to an obligor on an account, chattel paper (unless it is represented by multiple records, one of which is an instrument), or a general intangible. U.C.C. § 9-102(a)(3).

286. U.C.C. § 9-109(a)(3). Article 9 does not govern the sale of general intangibles that are not payment intangibles and promissory notes that are not instruments.

287. U.C.C. § 9-309(3) (payment intangible), (4) (promissory note). Buyers of loan participations should be wary. Some courts have held that participation arrangements characterized as "sales" by the parties are in fact disguised security transactions. *See, e.g., In re* Coronet Capital Co., 142 B.R. 78 (Bankr. S.D.N.Y. 1992) (discussing factors indicative of disguised security transaction). Automatic perfection applies to outright sales of payment intangibles and promissory notes but not to their use as collateral for loans.

288. U.C.C. § 9-109(c)(1).

variety of kinds of personal property.[289] None of these statutes, however, is comprehensive in its regulation of secured financing. Because the exclusion applies only "to the extent" of federal preemption, Article 9 applies to any aspect of a transaction not covered by the statute.[290] For example, the Federal Aviation Act of 1958 establishes a federal recording system for interests, including security interests, in aircraft, but most courts have determined that priority issues are to be decided under Article 9 because the Aviation Act does not address them.[291]

Some of the most complex issues of federal preemption occur in the area of intellectual property. For example, copyrights are general intangibles under Article 9, but assignments of such rights are the subject of federal law, and the perfection of a security interest in a registered copyright requires recording the security agreement with the U.S. Copyright Office.[292] A lawyer must carefully consider the relevant statutes and cases in determining the extent to which Article 9 is preempted.

[B] Landlord and Statutory Liens

Article 9 does not apply to a landlord's lien or to a lien created by statute or common-law rule for the provider of services or materials[293] unless the lien qualifies as an agricultural lien (discussed below). These exclusions simply reiterate the intention

---

289. *See, e.g.,* 17 U.S.C. § 205 (copyrights); 46 U.S.C. §§ 911–961 (ship mortgages); 49 U.S.C. § 1403 (aircraft); 49 U.S.C. § 11304 (railroad rolling stock).

290. Despite the clear intent of the drafters, not every court under former law understood that preemption is only partial. *See, e.g., In re* Peregrine Entertainment, Ltd., 116 B.R. 194, 11 U.C.C. Rep. Serv. 2d 1025 (C.D. Cal. 1990) (copyrights). Revised Article 9 makes clear that it defers to federal law only when, and to the limited extent that, it must. U.C.C. § 9-109(c)(1) and § 9-109, Comment 8.

291. *Cf.* Carolina Aircraft Corp. v. Commerce Trust Co., 289 So. 2d 37, 14 U.C.C. Rep. Serv. 505 (Fla. Dist. Ct. App. 1974) (repairman's lien priority); Suburban Trust & Sav. Bank v. Campbell, 250 N.E.2d 118, 6 U.C.C. Rep. Serv. 964 (Ohio Ct. App. 1969) (buyer of aircraft in ordinary course of business prevails). In 2004, the United States ratified the "Cape Town Convention" (the Convention on International Interests in Mobile Equipment, as modified by the Protocol to the Convention on International Interests in Mobile Equipment on Matters Specific to Aircraft Equipment), thereby recognizing an international registry established by the convention and located in Ireland as an additional place for the filing of interests in certain airframes, helicopters, and aircraft engines. *See* Cape Town Treaty Implementation Act of 2001, Pub. L. 108-297, Aug. 9, 2004, 118 Stat. 109.

292. *In re* Peregrine Entertainment, Ltd., 116 B.R. 194 (C.D. Cal. 1990); *In re* AEG Acquisition Corp., 127 B.R. 34 (Bankr. C.D. Cal. 1991), *aff'd,* 161 B.R. 50 (Bankr. 9th Cir. 1993). Recordation with the Copyright Office is not required for an unregistered copyright; rather, perfection requires the filing of an Article 9 financing statement. *In re* Auxiliary Power Co., 303 F.3d 1120 (9th Cir. 2002). Perfection is also accomplished by filing a financing statement if the collateral is a trademark (Trimarchi v. Together Dev. Corp., 255 B.R. 606 (D. Mass. 2000)) or a patent (*In re* Cybernetic Servs., Inc., 252 F.3d 1039 (9th Cir. 2001)).

293. U.C.C. § 9-109(d)(1) (landlord's liens), (d)(2) (liens for providers of services or materials). *See* Universal C.I.T. Credit Corp. v. Congressional Motors, Inc., 228 A.2d 463, 4 U.C.C. Rep. Serv. 152 (Md. 1967) (common-law landlord's lien excluded); *In re* Tacoma Aviation Ctr., Inc., 23 B.R. 326, 35 U.C.C. Rep. Serv. 298 (Bankr. W.D. Wash. 1982) (statutory mechanic's lien excluded).

generally to limit the scope of Article 9 to consensual security interests.[294] This means that a security agreement is not necessary for the creation of such a lien and that the lienor need not follow Article 9's rules for giving public notice or for foreclosing on assets subject to the lien.

Even though Article 9 generally does not apply to liens that arise by operation of law, Section 9-333 governs the priority of certain of these lien interests as against a security interest in the property subject to the lien.[295] The section generally grants priority to a lienor that, in the ordinary course of business, furnishes services or materials with respect to goods.[296] For example, an auto-body repair shop might have a statutory lien covering body restoration work performed on an automobile that was in a collision. Section 9-333 applies only to possessory liens, meaning liens whose existence depends on the goods' being in the lienholder's possession. The section does not apply to a priority contest between a secured party and the holder of a nonpossessory lien that arises by operation of law. The section also does not apply to a priority contest between a secured party and a person holding a landlord's lien,[297] even if the landlord is in possession of the goods, because a landlord, by definition, provides land rather than services or materials.

The decision of the court in *Leger Mill Co. v. Kleen-Leen, Inc.*,[298] provides an example of the proper application of the exception with respect to liens for services or materials. The court held that the predecessor to Section 9-333[299] did not provide a pig feeder with priority over a prior-perfected Article 9 security interest in the pigs because the feeder did not have possession of them at the time it attempted to enforce its lien. The court did not conclude by negative implication, however, that the secured party prevailed. Rather, it concluded that the nonpossessory lien fell within the Article 9 exclusion and therefore the priority determination was outside the scope of the article.[300]

Article 9 does govern a type of nonconsensual lien called an "agricultural lien."[301] An agricultural lien is, by definition, a nonpossessory lien, and it must arise under a statute other than Article 9 and not under the common law. Agricultural liens are limited to assets within the Article 9 definition of farm products, and the farm products subject to the lien must secure payment to a person that in the ordinary course of business fur-

---

294. U.C.C. § 9-109(a)(1). Article 9 does apply to security interests arising under other articles of the U.C.C. that are not consensual in nature. U.C.C. § 9-109(a)(5), (6). Article 1 defines "security interest," and the definition does not contain a requirement that the interest arise consensually. U.C.C. § 1-201(b)(35). *See generally* § 1.07, *infra*.

295. U.C.C. § 9-109(d)(2).

296. For discussion of this priority, see § 13.01, *infra*.

297. This is true unless the landlord's lien is an agricultural lien, in which case Article 9 applies to all issues other than creation of the lien.

298. 563 P.2d 132, 21 U.C.C. Rep. Serv. 896 (Okla. 1977).

299. U.C.C. § 9-310 (1972 Official Text).

300. The court ultimately found priority for the secured party, but it reached that result by shaping a common-law rule. The court might alternatively have granted priority to the secured party under Article 9's "default" priority provision found in U.C.C. § 9-201. *See* § 12.01, *infra*.

301. U.C.C. § 9-109(a)(5). *See* § 13.02, *infra*.

nishes goods or services, or a person that leases real property, to assist with a debtor's farming operation. An example of an agricultural lien would be the pig feeder's lien in the case described in the preceding paragraph. Revised Article 9 would not cover the creation of the pig-feeder's lien, which would arise as a result of the statute without the need for a security agreement. Article 9 would, however, apply to the priority of the lien; to obtain priority, the pig feeder would have to file a financing statement.[302] In other words, agricultural liens arise outside Article 9 but, once in existence, are swept into the article for other purposes as if they were consensual security interests.

[C] Real Estate Interests

Article 9 generally does not apply to the creation or transfer of real estate interests, including liens on real estate and leases or the rents due thereunder.[303] This exclusion reiterates the general scope provision that Article 9 applies to transactions creating security interests in personal property or fixtures.[304] Real estate law governs mortgages; both real estate law and Article 9 govern fixtures.[305]

Article 9 explicitly applies to a security interest in a promissory note secured by a mortgage on real estate. The relevant provision states as follows: "The application of this article to a security interest in a secured obligation is not affected by the fact that the obligation is itself secured by a transaction or interest to which this article does not apply."[306] In other words, even though the creation of a mortgage on real estate is beyond its scope, Article 9 applies to a security interest in a mortgage-backed debt. If a credit buyer of land executes a promissory note that embodies the payment obligation and secures it with a mortgage, the entire transaction is beyond the scope of Article 9. If the mortgagee subsequently uses the note and mortgage to secure a loan or sells them, Article 9 governs that transaction.[307] The primary collateral is the promissory note, but the lender or buyer will also take an assignment of the mortgage, giving it

---

302. *See* U.C.C. §§ 9-308(a) (agricultural lien perfected when it becomes effective and proper step has been taken), 9-310(a) (proper step for perfecting agricultural lien is filing financing statement), 9-509(a)(2) (person holding agricultural lien entitled to file financing statement), 9-322 (agricultural lienor treated like secured party for priority purposes, except that statute creating agricultural lien can provide that it takes priority over all secured parties if it is perfected (§ 9-322(g)).

303. U.C.C. § 9-109(d)(11). *See* Wells Fargo Home Mortgage, Inc. v. McCarthy, 51 U.C.C. Rep. Serv. 2d 853 (Minn. Ct. App. 2003) (unpublished) (agreement purporting to grant security interest in parcel of land did not create Article 9 security interest); *In re* Moukalled, 59 U.C.C. Rep. Serv. 2d 301 (Mich. Ct. App. 2006) (even though titled "security agreement," document did not create Article 9 security interest in two parcels of real estate).

304. U.C.C. § 9-109(a)(1).

305. For discussion of the nature of fixtures and the relationship between real estate law and Article 9, see Chapter 15, *infra*.

306. U.C.C. § 9-109(b).

307. *See* U.C.C. § 9-109, Comment 7, Example 1. A promissory note is a subset of the larger class of instruments and may be either negotiable or nonnegotiable. See discussion in § 1.04[B][2], *supra*. A negotiable note is within the scope of Article 3.

foreclosure rights in the event both its borrower and the note's maker (the buyer of the land) default on their payment obligations.[308]

A related problem arises if a vendor sells land pursuant to an installment land contract, sometimes called a contract for deed. Instead of taking back a note and mortgage, the vendor retains title to the land until payment of the last installment. This transaction is entirely outside the scope of Article 9, but what if the vendor sells the right to the stream of payments or uses it as collateral for a loan? The secondary financing transaction is within the scope of Article 9,[309] and the collateral is an account.[310] Along with the assignment of the account, there will be an assignment of the vendor's interest in the land.

Article 9 addresses the secured party's relationship with the underlying land by providing that a security interest in a secured obligation automatically attaches to the interest that secures the obligation.[311] In other words, attachment of a security interest to a note secured by a mortgage automatically causes the security interest to attach to the mortgagee's interest in the mortgage; and attachment of a security interest to an installment-contract vendor's account automatically causes the security interest to attach to the vendor's interest in the underlying land.[312] Further, perfection of the security interest in the note or account perfects the security interest in the underlying land.[313] These rules bring the entire transaction within the scope of Article 9.

----

308. An assignment of the mortgage is not necessary; even without an assignment, the mortgage follows the note, and thus the person entitled to enforce the note can enforce the mortgage. U.C.C. § 9-607(a)(3). *See also* Report of the Permanent Editorial Board for the Uniform Commercial Code, Application of the Uniform Commercial Code to Selected Issues Relating to Mortgage Notes (Nov. 14, 2011). An assignment is useful for establishing chain of title to the real estate in the event of foreclosure, and a recorded assignment protects the mortgagee from a collusive release by the assignor.

309. Not all courts have so held. *See, e.g.*, *In re* Shuster, 784 F.2d 883, 42 U.C.C. Rep. Serv. 1433 (8th Cir. 1986) (third party tracing title to land would not check U.C.C. filings). The *Shuster* decision is wrong. The vendor's title-retention scheme is a security device, rendering the underlying transaction a secured obligation within the meaning of U.C.C. § 9-109(b).

310. U.C.C. § 9-102(a)(2). *See In re* Tops Appliance City, Inc., 372 F.3d 510, 54 U.C.C. Rep. Serv. 2d 68 (3d Cir. 2004) (secured party's interest in right to payment arising from a contract to sell leasehold interest qualified as account for purposes of Article 9).

311. U.C.C. § 9-203(g). Article 9 uses a similar approach with what it calls a "supporting obligation," meaning a letter-of-credit right or other secondary obligation (such as a guaranty) that supports payment or performance under an account, chattel paper, document, general intangible, instrument, or investment property. U.C.C. § 9-102(a)(78). A security interest in a supported obligation automatically attaches to the supporting obligation, and perfection of the security interest in the supported obligation also perfects the security interest in the supporting obligation. U.C.C. §§ 9-203(f) (attachment), 9-308(d) (perfection). If, for example, a secured party has a perfected security interest in a negotiable promissory note (an instrument) that is supported by a standby letter of credit, it automatically has a perfected security interest in the underlying letter-of-credit rights.

312. Section 9-607(a)(1) provides that after default by the obligor (and earlier if so agreed), the secured party may notify the account debtor (vendee in an installment land contract) or person obligated on an instrument (e.g., maker of a note secured by a mortgage) to make payment to or for the benefit of the secured party. If that person defaults, the secured party may enforce the debtor's rights in the underlying mortgage or installment land contract. U.C.C. § 9-607(a)(3).

313. U.C.C. § 9-308(e).

The intent is to make recording in the real estate records unnecessary to defeat a lien creditor (including a bankruptcy trustee) or a subsequent assignee of the payment rights.[314] Nothing in Article 9, however, preempts the real estate recording acts to the extent that they protect a bona fide purchaser of an interest in the land. For example, if the developer in one of the prior examples colludes with a buyer to place a fraudulent deed of release in the real estate records and the secured party fails to record an assignment of the mortgage or the vendor's interest, a purchaser protected by the recording act will acquire its interest in the land free of the secured party's security interest.

[D] Wage Claim Assignments

Article 9 does not apply to a transfer of a claim for wages, salary, or other employee compensation.[315] It excludes these claims because their assignment presents "important social problems whose solution should be a matter of local regulation."[316] Many states have enacted laws that either prohibit or significantly limit wage assignments. The laws are designed to protect wage earners from financially overburdening themselves and their families.[317]

[E] Government Transfers

Former law excluded entirely a transfer by a government or governmental agency. For example, a governmental agency might have borrowed money and provided collateral in the form of a revenue stream based on its charges for water, electricity, or sewer service. Government transfers were excluded because other law generally applies.[318]

Revised Article 9 significantly narrows the exception. It applies to a government-created security interest unless preempted by a state statute that expressly governs the creation, perfection, priority, or enforcement of the interest.[319] In other words, govern-

---

314. Section 9-607(b) provides that if necessary to permit a secured party to enforce a mortgage nonjudicially, the secured party may record in the land records a copy of the security agreement along with a sworn affidavit in recordable form stating that there has been a default by the person whose obligation is secured by the mortgage and that the secured party is entitled to enforce the mortgage nonjudicially. For a detailed description of the rights of a secured party with respect to a mortgage following a default by its obligor, see American Law Institute (ALI) & the Uniform Law Commission (ULC), Report of the Permanent Editorial Board for the Uniform Commercial Code: Application of the Uniform Commercial Code to Selected Issues Relating to Mortgage Notes (Nov. 14, 2011).

315. U.C.C. § 9-109(d)(3). *See* Massachusetts Mutual Life Ins. Co. v. Central Penn Nat'l Bank, 372 F. Supp. 1027, 14 U.C.C. Rep. Serv. 212 (E.D. Pa. 1974), *aff'd mem.*, 510 F.2d 970 (3d Cir. 1975) (agent for insurance company held to be more like independent contractor than employee, so that renewal commissions were not employee compensation).

316. U.C.C. § 9-109, Comment 11.

317. *See In re* Gwynn, 82 B.R. 121, 5 U.C.C. Rep. Serv. 2d 1136 (Bankr. S.D. Cal. 1988) (California statutory prohibition against wage assignments absent permission of wage earner's spouse).

318. U.C.C. § 9-104, Comment 5 (1972 Official Text).

319. U.C.C. § 9-109(c)(2).

ment transfers are now within the scope of Article 9 except to the extent that another state statute expressly takes them out.[320]

Article 9 also creates a new category of transactions called "public-finance transactions."[321] A public-finance transaction is a secured transaction in which the secured obligation is represented by debt securities (e.g., bonds, indentures, certificates of participation) issued by a state or governmental unit of a state with an initial stated maturity of at least 20 years. The only importance of the category is that a financing statement perfecting a security interest in the collateral securing the debt securities in a public-finance transaction can be made effective for a period of 30 years.[322]

[F] Transfers Irrelevant to Commercial Finance

The objective of Article 9 has always been to facilitate commercial financing. The paradigmatic transactions involve a person using personal property or fixtures as collateral to secure a debt and a person selling accounts, chattel paper, payment intangibles, or promissory notes. The underlying assumption is that these transactions are motivated primarily by commercial financial considerations, although there is a recognition that the rules can sweep in some noncommercial transactions. Certain categories of transactions fit within the transactional models but have little or nothing to do with commercial financing, and Article 9 excludes these transactions.

[1] Specified Transfers of Rights to Payment

Several types of transfers of accounts, chattel paper, payment intangibles, or promissory notes are irrelevant to commercial financing interests and are excluded from Article 9.[323] These transfers are: (1) the sale of any of the listed assets as part of a sale of the business out of which the asset arose, (2) the assignment of any of the listed assets for the purpose of collection, (3) a transfer of any right to payment under a contract to an assignee that is also to render the performance due under the contract, and (4) a transfer of a single account, payment intangible, or promissory note to an assignee in whole or partial satisfaction of a preexisting debt.[324] These exclusions enable transferees like collection agencies and delegates to take assignments without having to comply with the Article 9 perfection provisions to protect their interests against other parties that deal with the assignor.

---

320. In enacting revised Article 9, many states retained the original, broader exception for all governmental transfers.

321. U.C.C. § 9-102(a)(67).

322. U.C.C. § 9-515(b).

323. U.C.C. § 9-109(d)(4)–(7).

324. *See* Bramble Transp., Inc. v. Sam Senter Sales, Inc., 294 A.2d 97, 10 U.C.C. Rep. Serv. 939 (Del. Super. Ct. 1971), *aff'd*, 294 A.2d 104, 10 U.C.C. Rep. Serv. 939 (Del. 1972) (transfer under collection-only exclusion requires transfer after accounts are in default).

[2] Judgment Rights and Tort Claims

Article 9 does not apply to "a right represented by a judgment."[325] Thus, if a party obtains a judgment and then assigns the right to collect on it as collateral to secure a loan, the assignee need not file a financing statement with respect to the assignment because the assignment is expressly exempt from the application of Article 9.[326] An assignee should be cautious, however. Except for claims arising in tort that are not commercial tort claims, for which there is a separate exclusion (discussed below), an assignment covering rights which might arise from litigation that has not yet commenced or has not yet reached the judgment stage will be within the scope of Article 9.[327]

The exclusion from Article 9 does not include "a judgment taken on a right to payment that was collateral."[328] A security interest, for example, might attach to an instrument or an account. If the obligation to pay that the collateral represents is reduced to judgment, an assignment of that judgment right is covered by Article 9.

With the exception of commercial tort claims, Article 9 does not apply to a transfer of all or part of a claim arising in tort.[329] This treatment stands in stark contrast to the assignment of contract claims as collateral, which are central to the Article 9 scheme. Once a claim is reduced to judgment without attachment of a security interest to the pre-judgment rights, whether the claim sounds in tort or contract or otherwise, the exclusion with respect to judgments applies. By contrast, the obligation that flows from the settlement of a tort claim is a payment intangible, and its assignment is within the scope of the article.

The exclusion for claims arising in tort does not apply to commercial tort claims,[330] meaning claims sounding in tort that arise out of the debtor's business or profession. If the debtor is an individual rather than an organization, the tort claim must not include a claim for death or personal injury. The security agreement may not describe commercial tort claims generically by type (i.e., "all commercial tort claims"),[331] which means that a security interest cannot attach to a commercial tort claim pursuant to an after-acquired property clause.[332]

---

325. U.C.C. § 9-109(d)(9).

326. Sun Bank, N.A. v. Parkland Design & Dev. Corp., 466 So. 2d 1089, 40 U.C.C. Rep. Serv. 636 (Fla. Dist. Ct. App. 1985).

327. Estate of Hill, 557 P.2d 1367, 20 U.C.C. Rep. Serv. 1319 (Or. Ct. App. 1976).

328. U.C.C. § 9-109(d)(9).

329. U.C.C. § 9-109(d)(12).

330. U.C.C. § 9-102(a)(12).

331. U.C.C. § 9-108(e)(1). Complete specificity is not a requirement. Comment 5 to Section 9-108 states that "a description such as 'all tort claims arising out of the explosion of debtor's factory' would suffice, even if the exact amount of the claim, the theory on which it may be based, and the identity of the tortfeasor(s) are not described. (Indeed, those facts may not be known at the time.)"

332. U.C.C. § 9-204(b)(2).

[3] Rights of Set-Off

Another exclusion from Article 9 covers any right of recoupment or set-off.[333] The exclusion exempts banks from having to obtain security agreements or to perfect their interests to preserve their set-off rights. Subject to certain limitations beyond the scope of this book, a bank that is not paid money that is due and owing to it by a depositor has a common-law right to set-off the money owed, which it accomplishes by reducing the depositor's account balance.

Two exceptions affect the exclusion. Article 9 governs, except in consumer transactions,[334] the use of deposit accounts as collateral. If the bank at which the account is maintained exercises a set-off right against a deposit account in which a secured party has a security interest, Article 9 governs the resolution of the priority issue that arises. The bank exercising set-off will have priority unless the secured party perfected its security interest by becoming the customer with respect to the account (i.e., by having its name shown as the customer on the records of the maintaining bank).[335] The other exception to the exclusion of rights of recoupment or set-off is that, if the person obligated (the account debtor) has a defense or claim that it could assert against an assignee under Article 9,[336] the defense or claim is available against the party exercising recoupment or set-off.

[G] Insurance Assignments

Subject to an exception for health-care-insurance receivables,[337] Article 9 does not govern the transfer of an interest in or the assignment of a claim under a policy of insurance.[338] It thus does not apply to a security assignment of the cash surrender value of a life insurance policy or the assignment of an insured's right to recover unearned premiums following cancellation.[339]

The exclusion does not encompass all transactions related to insurance. Article 9 covers an assignment of renewal commissions earned by an insurance agent.[340] The exclusion also specifically indicates that it does not extend to proceeds or to priorities in proceeds. The term "proceeds" includes "insurance payable by reason of the loss or nonconformity of, defects or infringement of rights in, or damage to, the collateral."[341]

---

333. U.C.C. § 9-109(d)(10).

334. For discussion of consumer transactions, see § 1.04[A][1], *supra*.

335. U.C.C. §§ 9-340(c) (priority rule), 9-104(a)(3) (perfection by becoming customer). The secured party can also perfect by obtaining a control agreement authenticated by itself, the debtor, and the maintaining bank; however, this will not provide it with priority in the event of set-off (although nothing prevents the maintaining bank from agreeing to subordinate its interest).

336. U.C.C. § 9-404 governs the effectiveness of an account debtor's claims and defenses as against an assignee. *See* § 1.04[D], *supra*.

337. For discussion of health-care-insurance receivables, see § 1.04[C][1], *supra*.

338. U.C.C. § 9-109(d)(8).

339. *In re* Duke Roofing Co., 47 B.R. 990, 40 U.C.C. Rep. Serv. 1431 (E.D. Mich. 1985).

340. The right to payment is an account. U.C.C. § 9-102(a)(2)(iii).

341. U.C.C. § 9-102(a)(64)(E).

The reasons given by the original drafters for the insurance exclusion were that "[s]uch transactions are often quite special, do not fit easily under a general commercial statute and are adequately covered by existing law."[342] The exclusion does not mean that insurance interests are not transferable, just as the other exclusions do not prohibit parties from entering into the excluded transactions.[343] Most states allow parties to assign insurance rights as long as the policy does not prohibit assignment.

[H] Deposit Accounts

Former law entirely excluded interests in deposit accounts,[344] although a secured party could trace proceeds of its collateral into such an account. Revised Article 9 limits the exclusion to consumer transactions.[345] This approach eliminates the confusing state laws governing common-law pledges and provides lenders with clear rules for creating and perfecting security interests in, and resolving priority disputes regarding, these assets. Security interests can be created in deposit accounts maintained at any bank, including a bank that is not the secured party,[346] and they are not invalid merely because the debtor has access to the funds in the account pending default.[347]

---

342. U.C.C. § 9-104, Comment 7 (1962 Official Text).

343. Other law governs whether parties can enter into an excluded transaction and, if so, its effect on third parties.

344. A deposit account is "a demand, time, savings, passbook, or similar account maintained with a bank." U.C.C. § 9-102(a)(29). The term does not include investment property or an account evidenced by an instrument. In other words, an account with deposited funds invested in money-market securities and an account represented by a certificate of deposit are, respectively, investment property and an instrument for purposes of Article 9. Lawyers must look beyond the labels used by banks in determining the appropriate category. For example, banks sometimes call accounts "money-market" but do not invest the deposited funds in money-market securities. Such an account is a deposit account, not investment property. Also, not every account represented by what a bank calls a "certificate of deposit" involves an instrument. For example, banks sometimes label accounts "book-entry certificates of deposit." When funds are deposited to a book-entry certificate, the depositor is given a receipt for the deposit, but not a writing that comes within the definition of instrument. The depositor's right to the funds qualifies as a deposit account.

345. U.C.C. § 9-109(d)(13). For discussion of consumer transactions, see § 1.04[D], *supra*.

346. If the secured party is the bank with which the deposit account is maintained, the fact that it takes a security interest in the account under Article 9 does not affect any set-off or recoupment rights that it may have under other law. U.C.C. § 9-340(b).

347. U.C.C. § 9-104(b). Although the debtor's access does not invalidate the security interest, it may create a choateness problem that would subordinate the interest to the federal government making a claim under the Tax Lien Act (26 U.S.C. § 6321 *et seq.*) or the federal claims priority statute (31 U.S.C. § 3713(a), usually referred to by its Revised Statute designation, R.S. § 3466). For discussion of choateness, see § 13.03, *infra*.

§ 1.07 Relationship between Article 9 and Other Articles

Although Article 9 is the primary source for determining the existence and effect of security interests, it is by no means the only source. It is just one article of the U.C.C., and it must be viewed in relation to the other articles.

Article 2 has a number of rules that intersect with Article 9. If a seller and buyer of goods agree that the seller will retain title pending full payment of the purchase price, Article 2 limits the effect of the term to the reservation of a security interest.[348] If a lender extends funds on the strength of goods being bought by an Article 9 debtor, Article 2 determines when the debtor has sufficient rights in the goods for a security interest to attach to them.[349] If a buyer in possession of goods rightfully rejects or justifiably revokes acceptance of them and the seller fails to refund the money the buyer has paid for them, Article 2 grants the buyer a security interest in the goods as collateral for any payments made on the price and for certain expenses.[350] Article 2 even contains priority rules protecting good faith purchasers for value that secured parties can use.[351]

Article 2A also contains provisions that intersect with Article 9. For example, a lessee in possession of goods that rightfully rejects or justifiably revokes acceptance of them has a security interest in them for any lease payments made and for certain expenses.[352] The article also contains provisions governing the priority rights of secured parties with interests in both the lessor's and lessee's interest in the goods.[353]

Security interests arising under Article 2 or 2A are subject to special Article 9 rules.[354] Specifically, the security interest is enforceable without a security agreement complying with Article 9's attachment rules,[355] filing is not required to perfect the security interest, Articles 2 and 2A govern the rights of the secured party after default,[356] and the security interest has priority over a conflicting security interest created by the debtor. With regard to priority, suppose Seller owns equipment subject to a perfected security

---

348. U.C.C. § 2-401(1).

349. The buyer acquires a special property interest in the goods with their identification to the contract for sale. U.C.C. § 2-501(1). For discussion of issues involving rights in the collateral, see § 2.02[C], *infra*.

350. U.C.C. § 2-711(3).

351. U.C.C. § 2-403(1). *See also* U.C.C. § 1-201(b)(30), (b)(29) (defining "purchaser" to include party with consensual lien). For an example of the operation of the priority rule, see *In re Samuels & Co.*, 510 F.2d 139, 16 U.C.C. Rep. Serv. 577 (5th Cir. 1975), *rev'd*, 526 F.2d 1238 (5th Cir. 1975) (secured party with security interest in debtor's inventory qualified as good faith purchaser for value under Section 2-403(1), thereby defeating reclamation rights of unpaid seller).

352. U.C.C. § 2A-508(5).

353. U.C.C. § 2A-307.

354. U.C.C. § 9-110.

355. The rules are set forth in U.C.C. § 9-203(b)(3).

356. *See* U.C.C. §§ 2-711(3) and 2-706; 2A-508(5) and 2A-527(5).

interest in favor of Bank and sells the equipment to Buyer, who justifiably rejects it. Buyer's Article 2 security interest is senior to Bank's Article 9 security interest.[357]

Article 4, which deals with bank deposits and collections, provides that a collecting bank (usually a depositary bank) that has given its customer access to funds represented by a deposited item such as a check before the item clears the payor bank has a security interest in the item and its proceeds.[358] The security interest is subject to Article 9, but a security agreement is not necessary to make it enforceable, filing is not necessary to perfect it, and it has priority over conflicting security interests.[359]

Under Article 5, the beneficiary of a letter of credit can assign its right to the proceeds[360] of the letter, either outright or as collateral for a loan.[361] That article differentiates between an assignment of a beneficiary's right to the proceeds of a letter of credit and a transfer of the beneficiary's right to draw or demand performance under the letter. Transactions in the latter category are analogous to novations which substitute a new beneficiary for the original beneficiary.[362] Because of this distinction, Article 5 provides that an issuer (or nominated person) need not recognize an assignment of the proceeds of the letter until it consents to the assignment. In other words, a secured party with a security interest in the proceeds cannot enforce the beneficiary's rights as against a nonconsenting issuer.[363] Article 9 calls the right of a beneficiary under a letter of credit to assign its right to the proceeds a "letter-of-credit right,"[364] meaning "a right to payment and performance under any letter, written or otherwise[;] but the term does not include the right of a beneficiary to demand payment or performance." This definition maintains the Article 5 distinction between the right to the proceeds of a letter of credit and the right of a beneficiary to demand payment or performance.

Article 7 contains rules that govern warehouse receipts and bills of lading, including, as of the most recent revision in 2003, electronic warehouse receipts and bills of lading. Article 9 deals extensively with security interests in such documents and the goods they represent.

Article 8 governs transfers of securities held directly by investors and certain financial assets held indirectly through financial intermediaries. Security interests in such assets are governed in part by Article 8 and in part by Article 9.

---

357. U.C.C. § 9-110, Comment 4.

358. U.C.C. § 4-210(a). Receipt of a final settlement for the item is a realization upon the security interest. U.C.C. § 4-210(c). The statutory grant of a security interest has ramifications for Article 3 as well as Article 9 because the collecting bank is deemed to have given value for holder-in-due-course purposes to the extent that it has a security interest. U.C.C. § 4-211.

359. U.C.C. § 4-210(c).

360. U.C.C. § 5-114(a) defines the term "proceeds of a letter of credit" to mean value given by the issuer or any nominated person under the letter.

361. U.C.C. § 5-114(b).

362. See U.C.C. § 5-112 and Comment 2.

363. U.C.C. § 5-114(c).

364. U.C.C. § 9-102(a)(51).

In sum, understanding secured-transactions law requires more than understanding Article 9. It requires that Article 9's rules be placed in the context of a unified code. Moreover, the Uniform Commercial Code itself must be placed in the context of the broader world of commercial law. It is, in effect, a "common-law code" because of the extent to which its provisions interface with and depend upon principles developed at common law (and in equity). Indeed, Article 1 specifically provides that, unless displaced by a particular Code provision, "the principles of law and equity, including the law merchant and the law relative to capacity to contract, principal and agent, estoppel, fraud, misrepresentation, duress, coercion, mistake, bankruptcy, and other validating or invalidating cause supplement its provisions."[365]

---

365. U.C.C. § 1-103(b).

Part II

Attachment of Security Interests

Chapter 2

Creation and Enforceability of Security Interests

Synopsis

§ 2.01 Overview:
The Concept of Attachment

A security agreement is a specialized type of contract entered into between a secured party and a debtor. The security agreement creates a security interest in personal property or fixtures that runs in favor of the secured party. The voluntary association of the parties that underlies any contract satisfies the requirement that an Article 9 security interest be consensual in nature.[1]

There are three requirements for the creation of an enforceable security interest: (1) there must be a security agreement, (2) value must be given by the secured party, and (3) the debtor must have rights or the power to transfer rights in the collateral.[2] Arti-

---

1. U.C.C. § 9-109(a)(1). *See* § 1.03[A], *supra. In re* Burival, 72 U.C.C. Rep. Serv. 2d 742 (Bankr. D. Neb. 2010) (landlord did not have a security interest in the corn crop grown on its land because it could not unilaterally create the interest).

2. U.C.C. § 9-203(b).

cle 9 additionally includes a statute-of-frauds provision, but it is part of the security-agreement requirement and not a separate element.[3] Upon satisfaction of each of these requirements, in whatever order, the security interest "attaches."[4]

The term "attachment" goes to the essence of contracts of this type. An Article 9 security interest cannot exist as an abstract or generalized concept. Rather, a security agreement creates a property interest with respect to specific collateral identified by the parties. The parties cannot create an Article 9 security interest in just any nondesignated property of the debtor that might be sufficient to satisfy the outstanding indebtedness.

Unless another provision of the Code yields a contrary result, the terms of a security agreement are effective between the parties to the agreement, against purchasers[5] of the collateral, and against creditors that assert a claim to the collateral.[6] Many exceptions qualify this general rule with respect to third parties, but only a few exceptions apply between the secured party and the debtor.[7] Their security agreement establishes the relationship between the secured party and the debtor, and it is subject to the general principle of freedom of contract.

The differentiation between the concepts of attachment and perfection is important to note at the outset. A security interest is enforceable against the debtor once it attaches,[8] meaning that the secured party can foreclose on the collateral in the event of default. Perfection is irrelevant in a dispute between the secured party and the debtor.[9] Perfection, which is best understood as a method for giving public notice of a security interest, becomes important only in the context of a dispute between the secured party and a third party asserting a claim to the collateral.[10]

---

3. U.C.C. § 9-203(b)(3).

4. U.C.C. § 9-203(a).

5. The term "purchaser" broadly includes any person that acquires an interest in the collateral through a voluntary transaction (e.g., buyer, lessee, licensee, etc.). U.C.C. § 1-201(b)(30), (29).

6. U.C.C. § 9-201(a).

7. Certain terms in their agreement might be unenforceable. *See, e.g.,* U.C.C. §§ 9-204(b), 9-602. Also, a secured party's failure to comply with the foreclosure procedures dictated in Article 9 might cause it to suffer a loss of rights. Chapter 19 discusses the consequences of creditor misbehavior.

8. U.C.C. § 9-203(a),(b).

9. As used in this context, "debtor" is limited to the person that signs the security agreement and does not include a person that becomes a debtor by transfer, such as a person that buys the collateral from the authenticating debtor. *See* U.C.C. § 9-102(a)(28) (defining debtor).

10. Chapter 4 provides an overview of the concept of perfection.

§ 2.02 Creation of an Enforceable
Security Interest—§ 9-203

An Article 9 security interest attaches only if the parties enter into a security agreement that satisfies a statute-of-frauds provision or falls within an exception; that is, the debtor must sign the agreement or there must be an exception that excuses the lack of a signature.[11] Even though attachment can occur in some cases without a signed record, such as when the secured party takes possession or control of the collateral, there must still be an oral security agreement. Attachment additionally requires that the secured party give value and that the debtor have rights or the power to transfer rights in the collateral. These requirements for attachment can occur in any order. With satisfaction of the last of the requirements, the security interest attaches and is enforceable.[12] The discussion below covers each of these requirements.

[A] Security Agreement—§ 9-203(b)(3)

Article 9 defines "security agreement" as an agreement that "creates or provides for a security interest."[13] An "agreement" means "the bargain of the parties in fact, as found in their language or inferred from other circumstances, including course of performance, course of dealing, or usage of trade as provided in Section 1-303."[14] The parties need only enter into a contractual relationship that falls within the scope of Article 9 to have a security agreement; they do not have to reference Article 9.[15] A record might describe particular goods yet evidence a transaction for their sale, lease, or bailment, or the record might be ambiguous with respect to the type of transaction involved. A record cannot qualify as a security agreement unless there is evidence from

---

11. U.C.C. § 9-203(b)(3). *In re* Seibold, 351 B.R. 741, 61 U.C.C. Rep. Serv. 2d 308 (Bankr. D. Ida. 2006) (no enforceable security interest in the absence of a signed security agreement).

12. U.C.C. § 9-203(a). Commercial Credit Group, Inc. v. Falcon Equip., LLC, of JAX, No. 3:09CV376-DSC, 2010 U.S. Dist. LEXIS 56544 (W.D.N.C. June 7, 2010) (security interest attached to debtor's heavy equipment and was enforceable upon completion of the three prerequisites). If the parties prefer, they can explicitly postpone the time for attachment. U.C.C. § 9-203(a).

13. U.C.C. § 9-102(a)(74).

14. U.C.C. § 1-201(b)(3).

15. The parties also do not have to intend for their transaction to be a security arrangement. The 1972 text was misleading on this point, providing that Article 9 applied "to any transaction (regardless of its form) which is intended to create a security interest." U.C.C. § 9-102(1)(a) (1972 Official Text). The parties must intend a contractual relationship, but they do not have to intend for it to create a security interest. For example, a transaction intended by the parties as a lease of goods nevertheless can be within the scope of Article 9 by operation of law. *See* U.C.C. § 1-203; § 1.03[B][1], *supra*. The 1998 revision resolved the problem by providing that it applies to "a transaction, regardless of its form, that creates a security interest." U.C.C. § 9-109(a)(1). An amendment to Section 9-109, Comment 2, approved in 2010, makes the point explicitly and indicates that this approach was the intent of the original drafters.

the language of the agreement or the surrounding circumstances that this is what the parties intended.[16]

Some courts have been too rigid in construing the agreement requirement. They inject into the Article 9 realm a degree of formalism generally associated with real estate conveyances by requiring that the parties use formal granting language (e.g., "I hereby grant to the secured party a security interest").[17] A security agreement is not a formal conveyancing document. Although reference to the prerequisites for attachment as the "formalities" for the creation of a security interest is common, the requirements are both simple in nature and easy to satisfy. Formalistic or magic words are not required.[18]

A comparison of the findings of the bankruptcy referee[19] and the decision of the appellate court in *In re Amex-Protein Development Corp.*[20] is illustrative. The parties intended to create a security interest, with recently purchased equipment to serve as the collateral for an obligation evidenced by a promissory note signed by the debtor (buyer of the equipment). The note contained the following language: "This note is secured by a Security Interest in subject personal property as per invoices."[21] The referee held that the note was insufficient to constitute a security agreement because the quoted language was passive and informative, not active or creative. The Ninth Circuit properly found the referee's construction to be too restrictive and held that the language was sufficient because it demonstrated that the parties had agreed to secure the obligation on the note.[22]

Occasionally, parties adopt a record that categorizes their transaction as something other than a secured transaction, and one of the parties later attempts to prove that the record in fact is a security agreement. For example, a record might indicate that one party delivered goods to another party as part of a credit sales transaction. After payment of the stipulated "price," the "seller" may argue that the goods actually were delivered to the "buyer" as security for a loan that has now been satisfied. In other words, the argument is that the seller in reality is an Article 9 debtor and the buyer is a secured party with a possessory security interest in the goods. Traditionally, courts

---

16. Allete, Inc. v. GEC Engineering, Inc., 726 N.W.2d 520, 61 U.C.C. Rep. Serv. 2d 906 (Minn. Ct. App. 2007) (filed standard financing statement standing alone does not create a security interest).

17. *In re* Modafferi, 45 B.R. 370, 40 U.C.C. Rep. Serv. 268 (Bankr. S.D.N.Y. 1985); Mitchell v. Shepherd Mall State Bank, 458 F.2d 700, 10 U.C.C. Rep. Serv. 737 (10th Cir. 1972).

18. *In re* Thompson, 315 B.R. 94, 54 U.C.C. Rep. Serv. 2d 1017 (Bankr. W.D. Mo. 2004) (language in installment sales agreement for cattle providing that, if any payment was ten days late, the personal property listed in the agreement became the property of the seller until the debt and incurred expenses were paid in full was sufficient to show intent to create security interest).

19. The presiding judicial officer in bankruptcy proceedings is now referred to as a "bankruptcy judge." Chapter 16 discusses the relevance of bankruptcy in detail.

20. 504 F.2d 1056, 15 U.C.C. Rep. Serv. 286 (9th Cir. 1974).

21. 504 F.2d at 1057, 15 U.C.C. Rep. Serv. at 287. *See also* Fantry v. Medical Capital Corp., 47 U.C.C. Rep. Serv. 2d 354 (Conn. Super. Ct. 2002) (recital in a security agreement to the effect that property had been attached and was to be secured held to create a security interest).

22. *See also* Simplot v. William C. Owens, MD, PA, 119 Ida. 243, 805 P.2d 449, 14 U.C.C. Rep. Serv. 2d 896 (1990) (note stating "SECURITY: 1956 GMC bus" sufficient when accompanied by debtor's indorsement and delivery of certificate of title to bus).

have allowed parties to introduce extrinsic evidence to the effect that a bill of sale absolute on its face was actually given as security, and the drafters did not intend for the Code to change this right.[23] Establishing that the transaction was in fact for security entitles the "seller" (debtor) to the return of the asset upon complete satisfaction of its obligation.

Article 9, on the other hand, rejects the principle of equitable mortgage, which allows a creditor to enforce a real estate security arrangement that does not comply with the requisite formalities by presenting clear and convincing evidence of intent to create a mortgage.[24] A lender that cannot satisfy the minimal formalities required by Section 9-203(b)(3)(A) (a signed record that describes the collateral) cannot use extrinsic evidence to establish its secured status.

[1] The Signature Requirement and Exceptions

Unless the secured party takes possession or control of the collateral, the debtor must sign the agreement. The signature requirement serves as a statute of frauds,[25] providing probative evidence that an alleged security interest rests on a real transaction between the parties. The party that must sign the agreement is the party against whom the security interest is to be enforced—the debtor.[26] A security agreement must satisfy the Article 9 statute of frauds (i.e., debtor signature or an exception) or no attachment occurs.[27]

The agreement must be in record form for the debtor to be able to sign it.[28] Prior to the 2022 amendments, the term "authenticate" was used instead of "sign,"[29] but it was defined to mean a physical or electronic signature and has been replaced by "sign" for the sake of clarity. "'Sign' means, with present intent to authenticate or adopt a record: (A) execute or adopt a tangible symbol; or (B) attach to or logically associate with the record an electronic symbol, sound, or process."[30]

---

23. U.C.C. § 9-203, Comment 3.

24. U.C.C. § 9-203, Comment 5 (1962 Official Text).

25. "[E]nforceability requires the debtor's security agreement and compliance with an evidentiary requirement in the nature of a Statute of Frauds." U.C.C. § 9-203, Comment 3. Tate v. Gallagher, 116 N.H. 165, 355 A.2d 417, 19 U.C.C. Rep. Serv. 281 (1976).

26. The term "debtor" refers to a person with an interest in the collateral. U.C.C. § 9-102(a)(28)(A). The term also includes a seller of accounts, chattel paper, payment intangibles, or promissory notes as well as a consignee. U.C.C. § 9-102(a)(28)(B), (C). If a debtor is an organization (e.g., a corporation, limited liability company, or general partnership), the signature must be made by a representative acting with actual or apparent authority. Extrinsic evidence of actual or apparent authority can bind an organization not identified in a security agreement signed by an agent. In re Mid-Atlantic Piping Prods. of Charlotte, Inc., 24 B.R. 314, 35 U.C.C. Rep. Serv. 618 (Bankr. W.D.N.C. 1982).

27. In re R. & L. Cartage & Sons, Inc., 118 B.R. 646, 13 U.C.C. Rep. Serv. 2d 543 (Bankr. N.D. Ind. 1990) (oral agreement with debtor not sufficient for enforceable security interest).

28. The term "record" means "information that is inscribed on a tangible medium or which is stored in an electronic or other medium and is retrievable in perceivable form." U.C.C. § 9-102(a)(70). The term encompasses both a traditional physical writing and information stored in electronic form.

29. U.C.C. § 9-102(a)(7) (1998 Official Text)

30. U.C.C. § 1-201(b)(37).

Consistent with the approach to the statute of frauds in Article 2,[31] Article 9 provides exceptions to the signature requirement. A security agreement is enforceable, even in the absence of a signed record, if the secured party has possession or control of the collateral pursuant to a security agreement.[32] The secured party's possession or control provides an alternative form of corroborative evidence to support its assertion that the parties entered into a security agreement.

[2] Description of the Collateral—§9-108

The signed security agreement required by Section 9-203(b)(3)(A) must provide a description of the collateral and, in the case of timber to be cut, a description of the land involved.[33] The description is the means to identify the property to which the security interest attaches. Identification of the affected property is necessary because a security interest cannot attach indiscriminately to a debtor's assets.[34] A description is not necessary if the secured party takes possession or control of the collateral pursuant to agreement because the possession or control provides the identification.[35]

The description in a security agreement delineates the assets of the debtor that are subject to the security interest.[36] If the debtor defaults and the secured party is undercollateralized (i.e., the value of the collateral is not sufficient to satisfy the balance of the outstanding indebtedness), the secured party might try to extend the reach of its security interest. The description requirement protects the debtor against such overreaching—the collateral consists only of the property encompassed within the description.[37]

---

31. U.C.C. §2-201(3).

32. U.C.C. §9-203(b)(3)(B), (D). See In re Miller, 320 B.R. 911, 56 U.C.C. Rep. Serv. 2d 499 (Bankr. E.D. Mo. 2005) (no security interest can attach based on a purely oral agreement if the debtor remains in possession of the purported collateral); In re Timothy Dean Restaurant & Bar, 59 U.C.C. Rep. Serv. 2d 485 (D.D.C. 2006) (lessor both created and perfected a security interest in a security deposit by taking possession of the money provided by the tenant); In re WL Homes, LLC, 452 B.R. 138, 74 U.C.C. Rep. Serv. 2d 599 (Bankr. D. Del. 2011) (bank that maintained a deposit account had the control over it required for the bank to have an enforceable security interest).

33. U.C.C. §9-203(b)(3)(A).

34. See §2.01, supra.

35. U.C.C. §9-203(b)(3)(B), (D). See In re Airwest Int'l, 70 B.R. 914, 3 U.C.C. Rep. Serv. 2d 1936 (Bankr. D. Haw. 1987) (sufficiency of description of two certificates of deposit in written security agreement was irrelevant because certificates had been pledged and were in the possession of secured party). See also In re Midland Transp. Co., 292 B.R. 181, 50 U.C.C. Rep. Serv. 2d 579 (Bankr. N.D. Iowa 2003) (security interest intended by parties did not attach to trucks because secured party did not take possession of the trucks and debtor did not sign a security agreement).

36. Personal Thrift Plan of Perry, Inc. v. Georgia Power Co., 242 Ga. 388, 249 S.E.2d 72, 25 U.C.C. Rep. Serv. 310 (1978) (descriptions in security agreement have the purpose of avoiding disputes over identity of the collateral); In re S.M. Acquisition Co., 296 B.R. 452, 51 U.C.C. Rep. Serv. 2d 867 (Bankr. N.D. Ill. 2003) (provision in security agreement consisting of the debtor's promise to keep collateral at designated locations did not alter the description that clearly showed the intent to create a security interest in debtor's assets located anywhere).

37. In re Levitz Ins. Agency, Inc., 152 B.R. 693, 19 U.C.C. Rep. Serv. 2d 1177 (Bankr. D. Mass. 1992) (description in security agreement as "customer list" did not extend to cover accounts). The court in In re Quisenberry, 295 B.R. 855, 51 U.C.C. Rep. Serv. 2d 548 (Bankr. N.D. Tex. 2003), held that a

Subject to certain exceptions discussed below, "a description of personal or real property is sufficient, whether or not it is specific, if it reasonably identifies what is described."[38] This standard is an explicit direction to analyze descriptions under a functional test. The objective is to be able to identify the property that comprises the collateral with a reasonable degree of certainty.

The court's opinion in *In re Drane*[39] provides valuable insight into the proper application of the standard. The secured party filed a proof of claim in a bankruptcy proceeding in which it claimed a perfected security interest in specified furniture. A part of the description of the collateral was as follows: "1–2 pc. Living room suite, wine."[40] The bankruptcy referee determined that the description was insufficient because the two-piece suite could consist of any of a variety of combinations of furniture commonly used in a living room, such as two chairs, a chair and a couch, or a chair and a couch that could be converted into a bed. The referee's position was essentially that a description must be sufficient on its face to identify the property subject to the security interest. The federal district court appropriately rejected this position and held that extrinsic evidence was admissible to aid in resolving the ambiguity in the description. The relevant evidence in *Drane* was that the debtor owned only one living-room suite and that it consisted of two pieces that were wine-colored. The description reasonably identified the collateral because of the extrinsic evidence.[41]

In re Drane by no means stands for the proposition that a nonspecific description always passes muster. The description likely would have failed if the debtor owned two separate living room suites consisting of two wine-colored pieces each, or if the debtor had owned a single wine-colored living-room suite consisting of three pieces. Evidence

---

bank did not have a security interest in a checking account that the debtor maintained with the bank because the description in the security agreement did not include the checking account. A section of the agreement that reserved the bank's right to exercise set-off against the account did not create a security interest because it was not part of the collateral description. The bank had a right of set-off by virtue of its deposit agreement with the debtor, irrespective of the security agreement. The court noted that a right to set-off is neither a security interest nor a lien.

38. U.C.C. § 9-108(a). A description reasonably identifies the collateral if it describes the collateral by specific listing, category, Code type, quantity, or computational or allocational formula or procedure. U.C.C. § 9-108(b). The parties can use any other method that makes identification of the collateral objectively determinable. *Id.* Section 9-108(d) includes a special rule for investment property. Because much of the terminology comes from Article 8 and is unfamiliar to many lenders, the special rule minimizes the damage from selection of the wrong term. With certain exceptions for consumer transactions discussed in the next paragraph of the text, a description of a security entitlement, securities account, or commodity account is sufficient if it uses those terms or the term "investment property," or if it describes the underlying financial asset or commodity contract. The special rule invites courts to accept extrinsic evidence to ascertain the intent of the parties even though their description uses a term that facially appears to be unambiguous. For discussion of investment property, see § 1.04[D], *supra*.

39. 202 F. Supp. 221, 1 U.C.C. Rep. Serv. 436 (W.D. Ky. 1962).

40. *In re* Drane, 202 F. Supp. at 221, 1 U.C.C. Rep. Serv. at 436.

41. *See also In re* Simplified Data Processing Sys., 55 B.R. 77, 42 U.C.C. Rep. Serv. 1441 (Bankr. E.D.N.Y. 1985) (description of collateral as "Prime 550" and "Prime 650" computer upheld because the debtor had only one Prime 550 and one Prime 650 system).

of the living room furniture owned by the debtor in either case would not have facilitated the identification of the two pieces of furniture intended to serve as collateral.[42]

A detailed description, though not required in most cases, often helps identify collateral with great precision and lessens problems that flow from ambiguities. But increased specificity may also lead to errors. Including a serial number, for example, enhances the specificity of the description[43] but creates a risk for misstatement of the number. The measure of acceptable error requires an assessment of the error in light of the total circumstances of the case. Transposing two digits in a long serial number is not likely to be fatal to the description,[44] whereas a number that does not correspond at all with the number on the collateral poses a much greater problem. A court nevertheless upheld a description with a seriously inconsistent serial number because the rest of the description of a tractor and its make and model corresponded to the only tractor that the debtor owned.[45] Other courts have not been as lenient.[46] Courts considering whether a description is legally sufficient should be mindful of the Official Comment that states "[t]his section rejects any requirement that a description is insufficient unless it is exact and detailed (the so-called 'serial number' test)."[47]

Increased specificity also increases the risk of debtor deceit. For example, enhanced specificity through an indication of the location of the collateral or features like its color can create identification issues if the debtor relocates or repaints it.[48] The secured party in *American Indian Agricultural Credit Consortium, Inc. v. Fort Pierre Livestock,*

---

42. *See* Raasch v. Tri-County Trust Co., 712 S.W.2d 5, 2 U.C.C. Rep. Serv. 2d 294 (Mo. Ct. App. 1986) (description of hogs only by breed is insufficient if debtor owns other hogs of the same breed); Pontchartrain State Bank v. Poulson, 684 F.2d 704, 34 U.C.C. Rep. Serv. 693 (10th Cir. 1982) ("various equipment totaling $158,600.00 located at Haskel County, Oklahoma" failed as description because it did not enable identification of the specific equipment covered).

43. *In re* Richman, 181 B.R. 260, 26 U.C.C. Rep. Serv. 2d 506 (Bankr. D. Md. 1995) (description as "all amounts on deposit in brokerage firm account no. 6282588026038 upheld"); Personal Thrift Plan of Perry, Inc. v. Georgia Power Co., 242 Ga. 388, 249 S.E.2d 72, 25 U.C.C. Rep. Serv. 310 (1978) (use of model and serial numbers to identify consumer appliances).

44. Dick Hatfield Chevrolet, Inc. v. Bob Watson Motors, Inc., 10 Kan. App. 2d 350, 699 P.2d 566, 40 U.C.C. Rep. Serv. 1876 (1985) (inadvertent addition of extra digit to the serial number of pickup truck held not to affect sufficiency of description).

45. Appleway Leasing, Inc. v. Wilkin, 39 Or. App. 43, 26 U.C.C. Rep. Serv. 209 (1979). *See also In re* Vintage Press, Inc., 552 F.2d 1145, 21 U.C.C. Rep. Serv. 1197 (5th Cir. 1977) (erroneous serial number of offset press not fatal because the rest of the description sufficiently identified collateral). *But see In re* Pickle Logging, Inc., 286 B.R. 181, 49 U.C.C. Rep. Serv. 2d 971 (Bankr. M.D. Ga. 2002) (description of collateral as a 648G skidder serial number DW648GX568154 when it was actually a 548G skidder serial number DW548GX568154 was inadequate because of the substantial difference between the two types of skidders and debtor's ownership of at least two units of each type).

46. *In re* Elridge, 10 B.R. 835, 36 U.C.C. Rep. Serv. 1422 (Bankr. E.D. Mich. 1981) (mistake in the last four digits of vehicle information number held fatal to description); *In re* Bolinger, 3 B.R. 186, 28 U.C.C. Rep. Serv. 1119 (Bankr. E.D. Mich. 1980) (correct serial number listed, but the Pontiac automobile was described as a Chevrolet).

47. U.C.C. § 9-108, Comment 1.

48. *In re* Freeman, 33 B.R. 234, 37 U.C.C. Rep. Serv. 268 (Bankr. C.D. Cal. 1983) (description of collateral as "all furniture and fixtures and inventory of debtor now or at any time located or installed" at a specified location held inadequate to cover inventory kept at a different location). *But see* Baldwin v. Castro Cnty. Feeders I, Ltd., 678 N.W.2d 796, 53 U.C.C. Rep. Serv. 2d 1 (S.D. 2004) (description of

Inc.,[49] was fortunate that the court upheld its description even though the collateral did not fit part of the description. The agreement described the cattle subject to the security interest as branded and tagged as follows: "-W on their right ribs, with an orange ear tag right ear." The court upheld the description with respect to the cattle with the "-W" brand alone, contending that the reference to the ear tag was unreliable surplusage because of the ease with which ear tags can be removed. All courts would not be this accommodating, which suggests the importance of devising descriptions that can withstand the tests of time, debtor manipulation, and judicial vagaries.

Although broad, generic descriptions might appear as potentially more vulnerable to attack on grounds of sufficiency, these descriptions often are the most precise. A description providing "all of the equipment and inventory" of the debtor has the virtues of being both inclusive and precise.[50] The description is certainly more efficient, and ultimately likely to be more accurate, than one that attempts to state each separate item of the debtor's equipment and inventory.

Broad descriptions pose a concern other than reasonable identification of the collateral. The broadest possible description would be "all personal property and fixtures" of the debtor. Although some courts upheld such "supergeneric" descriptions under former law,[51] other courts resisted.[52] The latter maintained an attitude that a single creditor should not be able to encumber all of the assets of a debtor and struck such broad descriptions as "dragnet clauses" that were unconscionable or in violation of public policy. Although the policy justifications are debatable, the drafters of the 1998 Official Text provided that a supergeneric description is not sufficient as a matter of law.[53] Nevertheless, a secured party can achieve virtually the same result by listing separately each of the types of personal property that Article 9 defines.[54] The result is not precisely the same because a description by type of collateral will not suffice for a

---

collateral as the livestock debtor delivered to secured party's feedlot in a stated community held to be sufficient even though it did not specify a particular lot or lots).

49. 379 N.W.2d 318, 42 U.C.C. Rep. Serv. 1443 (S.D. 1985).

50. With certain exceptions discussed below, Article 9 explicitly approves a description by types of collateral defined in the article (e.g., inventory, accounts). U.C.C. § 9-108(b)(3). The parties also can create their own generic "category" (e.g., machinery, cattle). U.C.C. § 9-108(b)(2). *See* Credit Alliance Corp. v. Trigg, 41 U.C.C. Rep. Serv. 208 (S.D. Miss. 1985) (description of collateral as "all … equipment" belonging to debtor sufficient to include a bulldozer used in debtor's business).

51. *In re* Legal Data Systems, Inc., 135 B.R. 199, 16 U.C.C. Rep. Serv. 2d 519 (Bankr. D. Mass. 1991) (all of debtor's "properties, assets, and rights of every kind and nature" sufficient); Federal Deposit Ins. Corp. v. Hill, 13 Mass. App. 514, 434 N.E.2d 1029, 33 U.C.C. Rep. Serv. 1510 (1982) (description as "all personal property" upheld).

52. *In re* Wolsky, 68 B.R. 526, 2 U.C.C. Rep. Serv. 2d 1689 (Bankr. D.N.D. 1986) ("all property of every kind and description in which the Debtor has or may acquire any interest" held insufficient).

53. U.C.C. § 9-108(c). In contrast, a financing statement must contain either a description of the collateral that complies with the requirements of Section 9-108 or an indication of the collateral that can be in the form of "all assets" or "all personal property." U.C.C. § 9-504(2). The distinction is appropriate because the function of a financing statement is to provide notice, not to identify the collateral subject to a security agreement. *See* § 5.03[A][4], *infra*.

54. *See In re* Lifestyle Home Furnishings, LLC, 68 U.C.C. Rep. Serv. 2d 825 (Bankr. D. Ida. 2010) (although the supergeneric description was insufficient, the reference to all inventory, equipment, accounts, and general intangibles qualified).

few categories. A description of "all commercial tort claims"[55] is insufficient as a matter of law;[56] likewise, in a consumer transaction, a generic description using the terms consumer goods, security entitlements, securities accounts, and commodity accounts is legally insufficient.[57]

The use of Article 9 types of collateral as a description might also raise issues of ambiguity. One concern is whether the parties intended to use the term consistent with its Article 9 meaning.[58] For example, the creditor of a manufacturing concern with a stockpile of its physical fitness products might describe the collateral as "all of the debtor's equipment," whereas Article 9 would characterize the finished products as inventory. The courts should seek to ascertain the intent of the parties.[59] The risk, however, is that a court will simply apply the Code classifications to terms of the description that correspond with the categories included in Article 9.[60] Secured parties for this reason often describe their collateral in multiple, overlapping categories, and when they intend for a term to have the meaning ascribed to it in the Code, it is best to state that in the security agreement. The parties sometimes create their own category of collateral, such as "all machinery,"[61] and when they do so it is important that they define the term unless its meaning is obvious (e.g., "all cattle").

[3] Multiple-Source Approach

A number of courts have been willing to consider multiple sources to locate the signature, the present intent necessary for the creation of a security interest, and the description of the collateral necessary for a signed security agreement. In *Amex-Protein*, for example, the requisite intent to contract and the signature were in the note, and

---

55. U.C.C. § 9-102(a)(13). For an explanation of commercial tort claims, see § 1.06[F][2], *supra*.

56. U.C.C. § 9-108(e)(1). Shirley Medical Clinic, P.C. v. U.S., 446 F. Supp. 2d 1028, 60 U.C.C. Rep. Serv. 2d 1033 (S.D. Iowa 2006) (the language "proceeds from any lawsuit due or pending" held to be insufficient). Comment 5 to Section 9-108 indicates that "a description such as 'all tort claims arising out of the explosion of debtor's factory' would suffice, even if the exact amount of the claim, the theory on which it may be based, and the identity of the tortfeasor(s) are not described."

57. U.C.C. § 9-108(e)(2). For discussion of consumer transactions, see § 1.04[A][1], *supra*. For discussion of descriptions of consumer goods in the context of after-acquired property clauses, see § 3.02, *infra*.

58. A prudent secured party needs to clarify in the security agreement whether a description by type corresponds to the relevant Article 9 definition.

59. Fifth Third Bank v. Comark, Inc., 794 N.E.2d 433, 51 U.C.C. Rep. Serv. 2d 533 (Ind. Ct. App. 2003) (security agreement incorrectly described collateral as inventory rather than equipment, but the court found the description to be adequate because the remainder of language in the description clearly showed the intent to include computer products bearing the name Comark).

60. K.L. Smith Enterprises v. United Bank, 2 B.R. 280, 28 U.C.C. Rep. Serv. 534 (Bankr. D. Colo. 1980) (description of inventory of debtor farmer's egg business held not to include eggs).

61. Description by category is acceptable. U.C.C. § 9-108(b)(2). Article 9 uses "type" to refer to a generic grouping defined in the text and "category" to refer to other generic groupings.

the collateral description was in the invoices.[62] In *In re Bollinger Corp.*,[63] a promissory note indicated that it was secured by a security agreement to be delivered by the debtor to the secured party, but the referenced agreement was never delivered.[64] The note by itself did not suffice as a security agreement because it did not show the requisite intent. A financing statement describing the collateral and signed by the debtor contemporaneously with the note likewise did not by itself show the requisite intent.[65] The court, however, read the note and the financing statement in conjunction with correspondence between the parties (subsequent to the execution of the note) in which they clarified whether the debtor could substitute or replace collateral in the ordinary course of its business. Although the court did not find the type of passive language referenced by the *Amex-Protein* court, it concluded that the correspondence did not make any sense if the parties had not intended their transaction to be secured. To summarize *Bollinger*, the signature was on both the note and the financing statement, the description was in the financing statement, and the present intent necessary to create a security interest was inferred based on the correspondence.[66]

The court applied the parol evidence rule incorrectly to defeat a secured party's claim in *In re Martin Grinding & Machine Works, Inc.*[67] The parties in the case apparently intended a loan to be secured by equipment, fixtures, inventory, and accounts. The security agreement inadvertently omitted inventory and accounts, but the descriptions in an SBA authorization, the debtor's corporate resolution authorizing the transaction, and the financing statement all included them. The description in the security agreement was unambiguous, which the court held precluded the introduction of extrinsic

---

62. *See also In re* Flager, Jr., 63 U.C.C. Rep. Serv. 2d 22 (Bankr. M.D. Ga. 2007) (debtor signed a bill of sale for the purchase of a truck, a note for the debt, and a title application for the described truck that listed the creditor as a lienholder). *But see In re* Jojo's 10 Restaurant, LLC, 455 B.R. 321, 74 U.C.C. Rep. Serv. 2d 441 (Bankr. D. Mass. 2011) (purchase agreement and related bill of sale identified the assets purchased, but neither of them created a security interest or stated which, if any, of the items were intended to serve as collateral).

63. 614 F.2d 924 (3d Cir. 1980).

64. Reference to a nonexistent record can be fatal. *See, e.g.,* Wilmot v. Central Oklahoma Gravel Corp., 620 P.2d 1350, 29 U.C.C. Rep. Serv. 1650 (Okla. Ct. App. 1980) (note stated that it was secured by a security agreement bearing the same date, but no such agreement existed).

65. A financing statement can be filed before a security interest attaches. U.C.C. § 9-502(d). Numerous decisions hold that a financing statement standing alone does not constitute a security agreement. *See, e.g.,* American Card Co. v. HMH Co., 196 A.2d 150, 1 U.C.C. Rep. Serv. 447 (R.I. 1963). *But see* Gibson Cnty. Farm Bureau Co-op Ass'n v. Greer, 643 N.E.2d 313, 25 U.C.C. Rep. Serv. 2d 954 (Ind. 1994) (extrinsic evidence admissible to show that debtor intended to grant a security interest to secured party whose only record was a signed financing statement). *See also* § 5.03[D], *infra.*

66. *See* Sears, Roebuck & Co. v. Conry, 321 Ill. App. 3d 997, 748 N.E.2d 1248, 46 U.C.C. Rep. Serv. 2d 859 (2001) (customer signed credit card receipts granting retailer a security interest in items purchased and incorporating by reference a security agreement included in the credit-card application). *Compare In re* Shirel, 251 B.R. 157, 42 U.C.C. Rep. Serv. 2d 604 (Bankr. W.D. Okla. 2000) (description of collateral in credit card agreement as all merchandise purchased using the card was too vague to satisfy description requirement; signed purchase receipt describing refrigerator did not contain cross-reference to security agreement).

67. 793 F.2d 592, 1 U.C.C. Rep. Serv. 2d 1329 (7th Cir. 1986).

evidence, but the court's analysis of the parol evidence rule is not convincing. The court did not discuss whether the parties intended the security agreement to be a complete integration of their agreement.[68] A record intended as merely a partial integration can be supplemented by evidence of consistent additional terms, although in the case of a security agreement any additional descriptive terms would have to be in record form to satisfy the statute-of-frauds requirement. Nothing in the security agreement was inconsistent with the addition of inventory and accounts as collateral categories. Moreover, the court failed to consider the fact that the parol evidence rule does not exclude evidence from contemporaneous records,[69] which must be read together to determine the intent of the parties.[70] The court's policy rationale—that third parties would be misled by the description in the security agreement—cannot withstand scrutiny. The description of the assets in the security agreement shows the intent of the secured party and debtor only and does not perform a notice function; notice to third parties is provided through a financing statement or other method of perfection.

[B] Value—§§ 9-203(b)(1), 1-204

A security interest does not attach until the secured party gives value.[71] One way that a secured party can give value is to provide consideration. The U.C.C. provides that "a person gives value for rights if the person acquires them ... in return for any consideration sufficient to support a simple contract."[72]

Value, however, is broader than consideration. The common-law theory of consideration manifested in the preexisting duty rule is too restrictive for many commercial transactions, and thus the definition of value rejects it, providing that a person gives value for rights if the person acquires them "as security for ... a preexisting claim."[73] Under this definition a secured party gives value by taking a security interest to collateralize an already existing, legally enforceable obligation.[74] For example, the court in

---

68. *See In re* Maddox, 92 B.R. 707, 9 U.C.C. Rep. Serv. 2d 333 (Bankr. W.D. Tex. 1988) (*Martin Grinding* analysis not applicable because the security agreement was not a completely integrated record).

69. *Cf.* U.C.C. § 2-202.

70. Dickason v. Marine Nat'l Bank of Naples, N.A., 898 So. 2d 1170, 57 U.C.C. Rep. Serv. 2d 127 (Fla. Dist. Ct. App. 2005) (provision in promissory note stating that note was secured by a financing statement on all business assets of the maker held to incorporate the collateral description included on the financing statement, including the after-acquired property clause).

71. U.C.C. § 9-203(b)(1).

72. U.C.C. § 1-204(4); Trinity Holdings, Inc. v. Firestone Bank, 24 U.C.C. Rep. Serv. 2d 1263 (W.D. Pa. 1994) (forbearance to commence collection on two delinquent loans).

73. U.C.C. § 1-204(2). The more restrictive meaning of value in Section 3-303(a) is adopted if the issue involves the right of an assignee to enforce an account debtor's agreement not to assert defenses. U.C.C. § 9-403(a). This puts the assignee on an equal footing with a holder in due course under Article 3.

74. Chicago Limousine Service, Inc. v. Hartigan Cadillac, Inc., 191 Ill. App. 3d 886, 548 N.E.2d 386, 10 U.C.C. Rep. Serv. 2d 1418 (1989) (preexisting indebtedness owed to lender by debtor constituted value with respect to subsequently-acquired limousines).

Hillman's Equipment, Inc. v. Central Realty, Inc.,[75] recognized that the debt incurred for the purchase price of restaurant equipment constituted value even though the parties did not enter into the security agreement with respect to the equipment until after the purchase. In *Ford Motor Credit Co. v. State Bank & Trust Co.*,[76] a finance company gave value even though it took a security interest in all of a car dealer's inventory only after the dealer failed to pay for the new cars that the finance company had financed.

The preexisting-claim aspect of value is particularly important with after-acquired property clauses.[77] For example, suppose a debtor signs a security agreement granting a secured party a security interest in all of the debtor's equipment, including after-acquired equipment, in exchange for a loan. The debtor later acquires a new item of equipment. The security interest cannot attach to that new item until all of the requirements for attachment are met. The single security agreement signed by the debtor satisfies the agreement requirement because it includes the after-acquired property clause that describes the collateral to include subsequently acquired items of equipment. The preexisting claim created through the loan advanced by the secured party satisfies the value requirement. The security interest attaches at the moment the debtor acquires rights in the new item.

The definition of value includes another alternative that is directly relevant to secured financing. It provides that "a person gives value for rights if the person acquires them … in return for a binding commitment to extend credit or for the extension of immediately available credit, whether or not drawn upon and whether or not a charge-back is provided for in the event of difficulties in collection."[78] A binding executory promise to extend credit provides value under this provision.[79] For example, a merchant and a bank might agree to a revolving line of credit which entitles the merchant on demand to draw up to a prescribed amount of money, and the merchant might sign a security agreement granting the bank a security interest in its inventory. Even though the merchant has not yet demanded any funds, the bank has given value and the security interest attaches as soon as the other requirements are met. Of course, the merchant will not have any repayment obligation until it draws against the line of credit, and the bank would not have any reason to foreclose on the inventory.[80] Nevertheless, attachment at the earliest possible moment is in the secured party's best interest.

---

75. 144 Ind. App. 18, 242 N.E.2d 522, 5 U.C.C. Rep. Serv. 1160 (1968), *rev'd on other grounds*, 253 Ind. 48, 246 N.E.2d 383 (1969).

76. 571 So. 2d 937, 13 U.C.C. Rep. Serv. 2d 548 (Miss. 1990).

77. For discussion of after-acquired property clauses, see § 3.02, *infra*.

78. U.C.C. § 1-204(1). Pittsburgh Tube Co. v. Tri-Bend, Inc., 185 Mich. App. 581, 463 N.W.2d 161, 14 U.C.C. Rep. Serv. 2d 230 (1990) (extension of credit by agreeing to receive payment over five years).

79. *In re* Air Vermont, Inc., 45 B.R. 817, 39 U.C.C. Rep. Serv. 1534 (D. Vt. 1984) (value given by binding commitment to extend credit even though money not transferred to debtor until six days later).

80. Although unlikely, the merchant could possibly breach its agreement with the bank before drawing against the credit line, in which case any obligation to pay damages to the bank would be secured by the inventory.

Article 9 requires that the secured party give value, but it does not require that the party providing the collateral receive the value. *In re Valle Feed of Farmington, Inc.*,[81] involved the use of the assets of a corporation as collateral to secure a loan from a bank to the corporation's sole shareholders. Value supported the security interest even though that value did not flow to the corporation.

[C] Rights or the Power to Transfer Rights in the Collateral—§ 9-203(b)(2)

The debtor must have rights or the power to transfer rights in the collateral before a security interest can attach.[82] This requirement is readily understandable because the debtor in an enforceable secured transaction must transfer a property interest to the secured party and, therefore, must itself have a transferable property interest or the power to transfer such an interest. The extent to which the debtor has transferable rights in the asset generally controls the interest that the secured party receives.[83] Stated another way, a security interest does not attach to the described asset itself; it attaches to the debtor's rights in the asset.

The common conceptualization of property rights as consisting of a bundle of sticks is helpful in understanding when a debtor has sufficient rights in an asset to grant an enforceable Article 9 security interest. Full ownership of an asset includes, *inter alia*, the rights to possess and use the asset and the right to transfer all or some of the owner's rights by, for example, sale, lease, or license. A person with transferable rights can grant an enforceable security interest in those rights. If the debtor has full ownership of the asset serving as collateral, the security interest attaches to the full panoply of property rights, and with a default the secured party can convey full ownership to a transferee through a foreclosure disposition, most often a sale.[84] At the opposite end of the scale of property interests, a thief with mere possession of goods does not have any transferable rights and thus cannot create an enforceable security interest in the goods.[85] Some cases fall between these two extremes: A debtor might

---

81. 80 B.R. 150, 5 U.C.C. Rep. Serv. 2d 1499 (Bankr. E.D. Mo. 1987). *Cf.* RESTATEMENT (SECOND) OF CONTRACTS § 71(4) (performance or return promise constituting consideration may be given to the promisor or to some other person).

82. U.C.C. § 9-203(b)(2).

83. Peoples Bank v. Bryan Bros. Cattle Co., 504 F.3d 549, 64 U.C.C. Rep. Serv. 2d 113 (5th Cir. 2007) (lower court improperly granted summary judgment in favor of secured parties because if the cattle pre-conditioning business operated as a partnership or LLC, the individual debtor did not have sufficient rights in the cattle to encumber them).

84. U.C.C. § 9-617(a) (disposition after default transfers all of debtor's rights in collateral).

85. *See, e.g.*, First Southern Ins. Co. v. Ocean State Bank, 562 So. 2d 798, 11 U.C.C. Rep. Serv. 2d 1255 (Fla. Ct. App. 1990). A thief of a negotiable instrument that qualifies as bearer paper is a holder and has the power to transfer an interest in the instrument free of the claim of the true owner to a secured party that qualifies as a holder in due course. U.C.C. § 3-306. The opportunity to receive good title despite a thief in the prior chain of title highlights a fundamental distinction between a transfer of negotiable property compared to property like goods, which are not negotiable.

have transferable rights that amount to something less than the full panoply of rights represented by full ownership.[86]

The foregoing analysis is nothing more than a particularized application of the doctrine of derivative title. The doctrine provides that a transferee's interest in property is derived from, and coextensive with, the interest of the transferor.[87] A debtor with limited rights in an asset generally lacks either the right or the power to transfer more than its own bundle of rights.[88] The limitations on the debtor's rights also constitute limitations on the interest taken by the secured party and on the interest that the secured party can transfer to a buyer through a post-default disposition. Remember that the "collateral" to which the security interest attaches is not the asset itself; it is the sum total of the debtor's transferable rights with respect to the asset.

The limits on a debtor's ability to create a security interest in goods that it acquired through a lease governed by Article 2A of the Code provide a good illustration.[89] A lessee does not acquire any of the residual interest[90] in the leased goods and therefore cannot create a security interest that effectively encumbers that interest.[91] The lessee does, however, acquire the right to the exclusive use and enjoyment of the goods for the duration of the lease term,[92] and those property rights can serve as the basis for a security interest.[93] If the debtor/lessee were to default, the secured party could not dislodge the lessor's residual interest in the goods but could proceed against the debtor's remaining

---

86. State Bank of Young Am. v. Vidmar Iron Works, Inc., 292 N.W.2d 244, 28 U.C.C. Rep. Serv. 1133 (Minn. 1980) (debtor's rights consisted of statutory lien for services provided on goods owned by third party).

87. The doctrine of derivative title underlies the common expression that an assignee "stands in the shoes" of the assignor. See U.C.C. § 9-404(a) for a statement of this doctrine in the context of Article 9. See Delacy Investments, Inc. v. Thurman, 693 N.W.2d 479, 56 U.C.C. Rep. Serv. 2d 84 (Minn. Ct. App. 2005) (assignee of accounts receivable subject to account debtor's right of set-off for past-due overhead fees that assignor owed under an independent-contractor agreement with the account debtor); Magill v. Schwartz, 197 Or. App. 334, 105 P.3d 867, 55 U.C.C. Rep. Serv. 2d 1002 (Or. Ct. App. 2005) (because a member of a limited liability company (LLC) does not have any interest in specific LLC property under Washington law, a debtor with an interest in the LLC did not have rights in the company's anticipated proceeds from settlement of litigation, and its lender's security interest did not attach to those proceeds).

88. *National City Bank, N.W. v. Columbian Mutual Life Insurance Co.*, 282 F.3d 407, 47 U.C.C. Rep. Serv. 2d 361 (6th Cir. 2002), is illustrative. An insurance company advanced substantial amounts of unearned commissions to an agent and retained a right to recoup payments for policies that were not finalized or that lapsed. The court held that the secured party's perfected security interest in the agent's accounts receivable was subject to the recoupment provision because it was part of the underlying contract that gave rise to the accounts.

89. Article 2A includes provisions on the transferability of leasehold interests in goods. See U.C.C. § 2A-303. For assistance in working through the thicket posed by this section, see W. LAWRENCE & J. MINAN, THE LAW OF PERSONAL PROPERTY LEASING 8-4 to 8-13 (1993).

90. *See* U.C.C. § 2A-103(1(q) (defining a lessor's residual interest).

91. *In re* Holiday Airlines Corp., 647 F.2d 977, 31 U.C.C. Rep. Serv. 1172 (9th Cir. 1981).

92. *See* U.C.C. § 2A-103(1)(j) (defining lease).

93. A term in a lease agreement is ineffective to the extent that it invalidates an assignment or transfer of an interest of either the lessor or the lessee under the lease, including a transfer that creates an enforceable security interest, and it is also ineffective to the extent that it provides that an

leasehold interest.[94] The secured party could convey through a foreclosure disposition the right to the exclusive use and enjoyment of the goods for the remainder of the lease term, subject to continued rental payments under the terms of the lease contract.[95]

A secured party that takes a security interest in a joint tenant's interest in an asset similarly cannot thereby dislodge the interest of the other joint tenant. The secured party at foreclosure can convey only the rights to which its security interest attached, and the buyer at foreclosure becomes a tenant-in-common with the non-debtor co-owner.[96]

A buyer of goods often grants a security interest in the goods purchased to either the seller in a credit sale or to a lender that provides the financing used to acquire the goods.[97] Article 2 provides that the buyer acquires an insurable interest and a special property interest when the goods become "identified" to the contract. Identification is an Article 2 concept that essentially signifies the earliest point in time at which the actual goods that the seller will deliver to the buyer are designated.[98] For example, if a seller with a contract to deliver 100 units of a specific model of television has 1,000 of the units in its warehouse, identification occurs at the moment the seller designates the units to be delivered. By contrast, if a buyer agrees to buy a specific car from a dealer, the car is identified when the contract becomes enforceable. The buyer's special property interest provides sufficient rights for attachment to occur.[99]

The significance of attachment upon identification is easily overstated. Because identification creates an insurable interest, a secured party might reach insurance proceeds if the buyer's interest was insured and the goods were lost or damaged.[100] The secured party could not defeat the seller, however, if the buyer were to repudiate the contract before taking delivery of the goods. The breach would entitle the seller to cancel the

---

assignment or transfer constitutes an event of default. U.C.C. § 9-407(a). This provision preserves for a secured party the value of a lessee's interest in leased goods.

94. *See* U.C.C. § 2A-103(1)(m) (defining leasehold interest to include the interest of the lessor or lessee under a lease). *See also* Franklin Bank v. Tindall, 66 U.C.C. Rep. Sev. 2d 133 (E.D. Mich. 2008) (security interest attached to the lessee/debtor's remaining interest in the boat).

95. United States v. PS Hotel Corp., 404 F. Supp. 1188, 18 U.C.C. Rep. Serv. 770 (E.D. Mo. 1975), *aff'd*, 527 F.2d 500, 18 U.C.C. Rep. Serv. 775 (8th Cir. 1975). The transferee at the post-default disposition is not personally obligated to pay rent, but a failure to pay gives the lessor the right to cancel the lease and repossess the goods. U.C.C. § 2A-523(1). Other events of default under the lease agreement can also give the lessor the right to cancel and repossess.

96. The foreclosure transaction creates a tenancy in common because the unity of title is severed. The disposition buyer as a tenant in common can sue for partition, which would cause the asset to be sold and the proceeds to be distributed according to the interests of the co-tenants.

97. These transactions typically create purchase-money security interests. U.C.C. § 9-103. For a discussion of purchase-money security interests, see § 7.01, *infra*.

98. U.C.C. §§ 2-401(1), 2-501(1).

99. Kendrick v. Headwaters Prod. Credit Ass'n, 523 A.2d 395, 3 U.C.C. Rep. Serv. 2d 1551 (Pa. Super. Ct. 1987). *Compare In re* Diversified Traffic Serv., Inc., 72 U.C.C. Rep. Serv. 2d 531 (Bankr. S.D. Ga. 2010) (debtor acquired rights in contracts to provide services when each contract was signed).

100. The insurance would have to be payable to the buyer or to the secured party. U.C.C. § 9-102(a) (64)(D). For a discussion of proceeds, see § 2.03, *infra*.

contract, thereby ending the debtor's rights in the goods.[101] The secured party's rights in the goods would also end because they are coextensive with the rights of the debtor.[102]

A secured party's rights expand if additional parties with rights in the collateral consent to the encumbrance of their rights. For example, if both a lessee and a lessor consent to a security interest, the secured party's interest attaches cumulatively to the full ownership interest. The effect of consent by all joint tenants to a security interest is identical. Consent to use a person's property rights as collateral, however, does not in itself make that person liable for the underlying indebtedness. The value given by a secured party can run to an obligor even though another person provides part or all of the collateral.[103]

A person that does not consent to a security interest may nevertheless be estopped to deny its effectiveness by a common-law rule or statute. The effect of estoppel is equivalent to consent in that the estopped person cannot contest the secured party's claim that the security interest attached to the person's rights in the collateral. The premise for the estoppel is the actions of the estopped person in clothing the debtor with indicia of ownership.[104] The analysis is comparable to the reasoning that underlies the doctrine of voidable title.[105] Estoppel provides a debtor with the power, but not the right, to grant a secured interest that has the effect of encumbering the estopped person's property rights.[106]

Many of the estoppel cases arise in the context of a bailment, meaning a transaction in which an owner of goods (a bailor) places them in the rightful possession of another person (a bailee).[107] The bailor clothes the bailee with the appearance of ownership through the transfer of possession. The question arises whether the grant

---

101. U.C.C. § 2-703(2)(f).

102. These limitations generally should not be a problem for purchase-money secured parties. If the seller retains a security interest in the goods sold, the seller will simply retain title to those goods following the breach by the buyer/debtor. If the purchase-money secured party is a lender that loans the money for the buyer/debtor to obtain the goods, the lender should protect itself by loaning the money in a form that will go directly to the seller of the goods. A seller that is paid lacks the grounds to retain title to the goods.

103. *In re* Terminal Moving & Storage Co., 631 F.2d 547, 28 U.C.C. Rep. Serv. 1146, *rev'd on rehearing en banc,* 631 F.2d 547, 29 U.C.C. Rep. Serv. 679 (8th Cir. 1980).

104. First Nat'l Bank v. Kisaare, 22 Okla. 545, 98 P. 433 (1908).

105. The doctrine of voidable title, itself predicated on estoppel principles, can be directly relevant. A person with voidable title has power to transfer full title to a good-faith purchaser for value. U.C.C. § 2-403(1). The term "purchaser" includes, *inter alia,* a secured party. U.C.C. § 1-201(b)(30), (29). Thus, a person with voidable title has the power to grant a security interest that attaches to the true owner's rights to a secured party that gives value and lacks notice of the true owner's interest. Section 2-403(1) not only gives a person with voidable title the power to grant an enforceable security interest but also functions as a priority rule in favor of the secured party. *See, e.g., In re* Samuels & Co., 526 F.2d 1238, 18 U.C.C. Rep. Serv. 545 (5th Cir. 1976) (secured financer of cattle buyer prevailed as good-faith purchaser for value over cash seller of cattle's reclamation rights when buyer's checks to seller bounced).

106. U.C.C. § 9-203(b)(2) (debtor must have rights or power to transfer rights in collateral).

107. R. BROWN, THE LAW OF PERSONAL PROPERTY § 10.1 (W. Raushenbush ed., 3d ed. 1975). Unlike a sale, title to the goods does not pass in a bailment, and the doctrine of voidable title is thus inapt.

of a security interest by the bailee causes the security interest to attach by estoppel to the bailor's rights.

In the simplest type of bailment, a bailor turns goods over to a bailee for storage or carriage but does not give the bailee permission to use the goods. This type of bailee lacks the power under common law to alienate the bailor's rights, even to a good-faith purchaser for value.[108] A security agreement signed by the bailee will not cause a security interest to attach to the bailor's rights because the bailee cannot alienate the rights of the bailor. Numerous cases hold that such a bailee lacks sufficient rights to grant a security interest in the bailed goods.[109]

At the other extreme is a "consignment," a type of bailment in which a consignor delivers goods to a consignee and authorizes the consignee to sell them. For example, suppose a manufacturer of goods consigns them to a merchant in the business of selling such goods with the understanding that the merchant can return any unsold goods. Because a third party would naturally believe that the goods are part of the consignee's inventory and could be misled more easily than a third party dealing with a bailee for storage or carriage, the case for estoppel is especially strong. Indeed, Article 9 explicitly governs most commercially valuable consignments and provides that the consigned goods are subject to the claims of the consignee's creditors.[110] The consignee accordingly has the power to cause a security interest to attach to the consignor's rights in the goods.

A consignment of goods to a merchant for the purpose of sale also qualifies as an "entrustment," an aspect of the transaction governed by Article 2.[111] In an entrustment, a person delivers (or acquiesces in the delivery of) goods to a merchant that deals in goods of the kind, which gives the merchant the power to convey the entruster's rights in the goods to a buyer in ordinary course of business.[112] A variation of the classic example is a watch owner that delivers a watch to a jeweler for repair and the jeweler negligently or fraudulently places the watch in its inventory and sells it to an ordinary-course buyer. The sale transfers the owner's title to the buyer. Because the entrustment provision protects only buyers in ordinary course of business, a secured party to which the jeweler grants a security interest cannot use it. The jeweler also lacks the power under the common-law rules governing bailments to grant an enforceable security interest in the watch. Without a cause of action under either Article 2 or the common law, a secured party has only one remaining possibility. If the bailor that entrusted the goods into the possession of the bailee used language or engaged in conduct that led the secured party to believe that the bailee had the power to transfer

---

108. E. GODDARD, THE LAW OF BAILMENTS AND CARRIERS § 29 (2d ed. 1908); Smith v. Clews, 114 N.Y. 190, 21 N.E. 160 (1889).

109. *See, e.g.,* Evergreen Marine Corp. v. Six Consignments of Frozen Scallops, 4 F.3d 90, 21 U.C.C. Rep. Serv. 2d 502 (1st Cir. 1993).

110. For discussion of consignments governed by Article 9, see § 1.03[B][2], *supra.*

111. *See* U.C.C. § 2-403(3), (2).

112. For discussion of buyers in ordinary course of business, see § 11.03[A][1], *infra.*

full ownership, general estoppel principles might cause the security interest to attach to the bailor's interest.[113]

Kinetics Technology International Corp. v. Fourth National Bank[114] provides an example of general estoppel in a bailment context. The plaintiff delivered certain goods that it owned to a manufacturer so that the manufacturer could add components to the goods to create finished products for delivery back to the plaintiff. The court invoked estoppel principles to subject the plaintiff's ownership interest in the goods still in the manufacturer's hands to a security interest that the manufacturer granted to the defendant. The court's rationale was that the plaintiff was a type of lender that loaned goods rather than money to enable the manufacturer to produce the finished product. If the plaintiff had loaned money to enable the manufacturer to acquire the goods, it could have taken a security interest in the goods and filed a financing statement to protect its interest. The financing statement would have warned the defendant of the plaintiff's interest. Even though it supplied goods rather than money to acquire them, the plaintiff should have taken and perfected a security interest in the goods. Courts in similar circumstances reach the same result by holding that the goods in question were actually sold to the manufacturer and that the attempt to retain title amounted to nothing more than a security interest.[115] The manufacturer as the owner of the goods would clearly have sufficient rights to grant a security interest in them, and the secured party/supplier should file a financing statement to assure itself of priority over third-party claims.[116]

In *Fifth Third Bank v. Comark, Inc.*,[117] the bank entered into a security agreement with Vertica, Inc., for assets owned by Vertica, LLC, a separate but related entity. The bank argued that Vertica, LLC, should be estopped from asserting that Vertica, Inc., did not have rights in the collateral, but the court disagreed. The bank could not prove (a) that Vertica, LLC, had consented to Vertica, Inc.'s encumbering its assets, (b) that Vertica, Inc., had ever been in possession of the assets, (c) that Vertica, Inc., had allowed Vertica, LLC, to appear as the owner of the collateral, or (d) that Vertica, Inc., had notice of the secured transaction.[118]

---

113. U.C.C. § 1-103(b) (unless displaced, principles of law and equity supplement the Code). *Cf.* Tumber v. Automation Design & Mfg. Corp., 130 N.J. Super. 5, 324 A.2d 602 (1974) (a person that does not qualify as a buyer in ordinary course of business may nevertheless prevail under estoppel principles).

114. 705 F.2d 396, 36 U.C.C. Rep. Serv. 292 (10th Cir. 1983). *See also In re* Pubs, Inc., 618 F.2d 432, 28 U.C.C. Rep. Serv. 297 (7th Cir. 1980) (closely held corporation estopped when two key officers used its assets as collateral for a personal loan).

115. *See* U.C.C. §§ 2-106(1) (sale is passing of title from seller to buyer for a price), 2-403(1) (contract term providing for title to remain in seller until buyer pays for goods reduced in effect to retention by seller of a security interest).

116. *See, e.g.,* Morton Booth Co. v. Tiara Furniture, Inc., 564 P.2d 210 (Okla. 1977).

117. 794 N.E.2d 433, 51 U.C.C. Rep. Serv. 2d 533 (Ind. Ct. App. 2003).

118. The bank's due diligence should have included the execution of entity resolutions by Vertica, LLC, that would have made its consent clear.

§ 2.03 Proceeds

Debtors sometimes dispose of collateral in their possession or control. The secured party might authorize the disposition, as commonly occurs when the secured party expects the debtor to sell financed inventory to acquire the money to repay the loan, or it might be without the awareness of the secured party and in violation of a prohibition in the security agreement.[119] Either way, the secured party will likely want to pursue the proceeds that the debtor receives from its disposition of the collateral. The discussion below explains the concept and the classifications of proceeds and describes how a security interest attaches to proceeds. Discussion elsewhere in the text covers perfection and priority of a security interest in proceeds.[120]

[A] Defined — § 9-102(a)(64)

The term "proceeds" means:

(A) whatever is acquired upon the sale, lease, license, exchange, or other disposition of collateral;

(B) whatever is collected on, or distributed on account of, collateral;

(C) rights arising out of collateral;

(D) to the extent of the value of collateral, claims arising out of the loss, nonconformity, or interference with the use of, defects or infringement of rights in, or damage to the collateral; and

(E) to the extent of the value of collateral and to the extent payable to the debtor or the secured party, insurance payable by reason of the loss or nonconformity of, defects or infringement of rights in, or damage to, the collateral.[121]

Virtually anything that replaces the economic value of collateral constitutes proceeds.

Proceeds can take almost any form. Courts have characterized as proceeds such items as cash,[122] checks,[123] promissory notes,[124] payments of principal and interest on promissory notes,[125] used cars accepted as trade-ins on sales of automobile inventory,[126]

---

119. Under Section 9-401(b), an agreement between the debtor and secured party prohibiting transfer or making the transfer a default does not prevent the transfer from being effective.

120. *See* §§ 8.02 (perfection),10.05 (priority), *infra.*

121. U.C.C. § 9-102(a)(64).

122. Bank of Kansas v. Hutchinson Health Servs., Inc., 12 Kan. App. 2d 87, 735 P.2d 256, 3 U.C.C. Rep. Serv. 2d 1537 (1987).

123. Farms Associates, Inc. v. South Side Bank, 93 Ill. App. 3d 766, 417 N.E.2d 818, 30 U.C.C. Rep. Serv. 1729 (1981).

124. *In re* Guil-Park Farms, Inc. v. South Side Bank, 90 B.R. 180, 7 U.C.C. Rep. Serv. 2d 1675 (Bankr. W.D.N.C. 1988).

125. *In re* Charter First Mortgage, Inc., 56 B.R. 838, 2 U.C.C. Rep. Serv. 2d 1409 (Bankr. D. Or. 1985).

126. Chrysler Credit Corp. v. Knebel Chevrolet-Buick, Inc., 976 F.2d 1012, 20 U.C.C. Rep. Serv. 2d 645 (7th Cir. 1992).

shares of stock received in the sale of partnership assets,[127] and a new certificate of deposit resulting from rolling over two other certificates.[128] By contrast, calves are not proceeds of the cattle that give birth to them because they do not in any sense replace those cattle.[129]

Under original Article 9, a majority of courts applied a misguided "passage-of-title" theory and held that casualty-insurance payments arising out of damage to insured collateral did not qualify as proceeds because of the absence of a disposition of the original collateral.[130] The passage-of-title theory was predicated on the then-current definition of proceeds as assets acquired upon the "sale, exchange, collection or other disposition" of collateral. The terms "sale," "exchange," and "collection" refer to transactions with the surrender of title or the satisfaction of payment rights.[131] The 1972 Official Text expressly overruled the insurance cases but did not amend the language that gave rise to the passage-of-title theory.[132] The 1998 revision continued the 1972 approach for insurance payments and extends it to insurance payments for lost economic value of the collateral as well as physical damage.[133] It also amended the definition of proceeds to include "whatever is acquired upon the sale, *lease, license,* exchange, or other disposition of collateral."[134] Lease and license transactions do not involve passage of title.[135]

---

127. *In re* Guaranteed Muffler Supply Co., Inc., 1 B.R. 324, 27 U.C.C. Rep. Serv. 1217 (Bankr. N.D. Ga. 1979).

128. *In re* Airwest Int'l, 70 B.R. 914, 3 U.C.C. Rep. Serv. 2d 1936 (Bankr. D. Haw. 1987).

129. Citizens Sav. Bank, Hawkeye, Iowa v. Miller, 515 N.W.2d 7, 24 U.C.C. Rep. Serv. 2d 1032 (Iowa 1994). *See also* PNC Bank v. Marty's Mobile Homes, Inc., 45 U.C.C. Rep. Serv. 2d 659 (Del. Ct. Ch. 2001) (sales tax receipts not proceeds from the sale of mobile home because they were never intended to be part of seller's assets and were regularly forwarded to state agency in the normal course of business); Western Farm Serv., Inc. v. Olsen, 114 Wash. App. 508, 59 P.3d 93, 49 U.C.C. Rep. Serv. 2d 936 (2002) (cash received as a separate allowance to reimburse grower/debtor for expenses incurred in delivering potatoes to a processing site was not a proceed because it did not result from the sale, exchange, lease, license or other disposition of the potato crop).

130. *See, e.g.,* Universal C.I.T. Credit Corp. v. Prudential Inv. Corp., 222 A.2d 571, 3 U.C.C. Rep. Serv. 696 (R.I. 1966).

131. U.C.C. § 9-306(1) (1962 Official text). The passage-of-title theory was inconsistent with Article 9's basic approach, which is that the location of title to collateral is immaterial. *See* U.C.C. § 9-202 (1962 and 2003 Official Texts). *See also* R. Wilson Freyermuth, *Rethinking Proceeds: The History, Misinterpretation and Revision of U.C.C. Section 9-306,* 69 Tulane L. Rev. 645 (1995).

132. U.C.C. §§ 9-306(1) (defining proceeds), 9-104(g) (1972 Official Text) (narrowing the exclusion from Article 9 so that transfers of insurance interests that constitute proceeds are within its scope).

133. U.C.C. § 9-102(a)(64)(E). *In re* Wiersma, 283 B.R. 294, 49 U.C.C. Rep. Serv. 2d 309 (Bankr. D. Idaho 2002) (settlement payments by insurance company represented compensation to debtors for the loss of and damage to secured party's collateral); Price v. Nationwide Mut. Ins. Co. of Des Moines, 62 U.C.C. Rep. Serv. 2d 276 (Kan. Ct. App. 2007) (unpublished) (settlement to cover the theft of collateral constituted proceeds).

134. U.C.C. § 9-102(a)(64)(A) (emphasis added).

135. Some courts applying the passage-of-title theory held that lease payments did not constitute proceeds. *See, e.g., In re* Cleary Bros. Constr. Co., 9 B.R. 40, 30 U.C.C. Rep. Serv. 1444 (Bankr. S.D. Fla. 1980). Such decisions defied economic reality. Leased property depreciates in value as it ages and the lessee uses it, and the rental payments, which reflect that depreciation, are direct economic substitutes for the collateral's lost value. Prior to the promulgation of the 1998 revision, the drafters amended

The 1998 revision also continued a rule first adopted in a conforming amendment to Article 9 that was part of the 1994 revision of Article 8: proceeds includes "whatever is distributed on account of" collateral.[136] The drafters adopted the rule for the express purpose of overruling the decision in *In re Hastie*,[137] a case in which the court relied on the passage-of-title theory to hold that cash dividends paid on account of stock were not proceeds because the debtor did not give up title to the stock to obtain them.

Although the 1998 revision extended the definition of proceeds to cover any rights arising out of collateral or claims predicated on a loss of the economic value of collateral,[138] it did not deal directly with "nonexistent collateral." Suppose, for example, that a secured party acquires a security interest in a debtor's crops. The parties anticipate at the time that the debtor will plant crops annually, but subsequently the debtor enrolls in a federal program that pays a subsidy to farmers that permit their land to lie fallow. The subsidy is a direct economic substitute for a crop that never existed and therefore ought to qualify as proceeds, but most courts facing this issue have held otherwise.[139] The textual treatment of proceeds in Article 9 reflects a value-based approach to proceeds that honors the *ex ante* expectations of the parties. Courts considering nonexistent collateral cases should carefully consider the implications of this approach.[140]

After not receiving payment, the landlord in *U.S. Bank Trust National Association v. Venice MD LLC*[141] wrongfully took possession of the debtor's inn and operated it using assets subject to the bank's security interest. The bank argued that the landlord's conduct constituted an unauthorized disposition of its collateral and sought to recover the gross revenues generated during the landlord's operation as proceeds of that disposition. Because most of the collateral remained intact after the landlord relinquished possession, the landlord did not dispose of it and thus did not create proceeds. Al-

---

the Comments to disapprove of these holdings. U.C.C. §9-306, Comment 6 (authorized by P.E.B. Commentary No. 9, June 25, 1992).

136. U.C.C. §9-102(a)(64)(B).

137. 2 F.3d 1042, 21 U.C.C. Rep. Serv. 2d 212 (10th Cir. 1993).

138. U.C.C. §9-102(a)(64)(C), (D). A claim might consist of a debtor's right to recover against its seller or lessor for a breach of warranty, a claim against an economic competitor for infringement of an intellectual property right, or even a tort claim, such as a right to payment for the negligent destruction of collateral. The extension of the definition corresponds with a narrowing of the exclusion from Article 9 for claims arising in tort. In addition to a proceeds interest, a secured party can also take an original security interest in a commercial tort claim. See §1.06[F][2], *supra*.

139. *See, e.g., In re* Schmaling, 783 F.2d 680, 42 U.C.C. Rep. Serv. 1074 (7th Cir. 1986) (federal Payment-in-Kind (PIK) program). *Contra* Sweetwater Production Credit Ass'n v. O'Briant, 764 S.W.2d 230, 7 U.C.C. Rep. Serv. 2d 1247 (Tex. 1988).

140. Another example of "nonexistent collateral" arises in the context of business-interruption insurance. A secured creditor might claim that a debtor's insurance claim is a proceed of accounts or general intangibles that would have existed but for the interruption of the business. Cases dealing with this issue include *CPC Acquisitions, Inc. v. Helm*, 64 U.C.C. Rep. Serv. 2d 669 (N.D. Ill. 2007) (settlement with insurance company for negligent procurement of insurance constituted proceeds to the extent that it compensated for damaged collateral, but not for recovery related to business-interruption losses from the fire), and *MNC Commercial Corp. v. Rouse*, No. 91-0615-CV-W-2, 1992 U.S. Dist. LEXIS 22166 (W.D. Mo. Dec. 15, 1992) (business-interruption insurance qualifies as proceeds).

141. 53 U.C.C. Rep. Serv. 2d 394 (4th Cir. 2004) (unpublished).

though the landlord did dispose of food and beverage inventory during its operation of the inn, the court held that the gross revenues could not be traced to these dispositions. Unlike the direct sale of inventory from a grocery store, the gross proceeds from the restaurant and bar operation also reflected preparation, atmosphere, and service.

Article 9 distinguishes between cash proceeds and noncash proceeds for some purposes of perfection and priority. Cash proceeds[142] include assets like money, checks, and deposit accounts. The definition is open-ended to cover an asset that is a cash equivalent, like a money-market account that is a financial asset in a securities account.[143] All other proceeds are noncash proceeds.[144] For example, suppose a secured party has a security interest in a debtor's inventory. If the debtor sells the inventory for cash or a check, the proceeds are cash proceeds. If the debtor takes a used item in trade or sells the inventory on account, the proceeds are noncash proceeds.[145] If the debtor takes a check for the inventory and later deposits it to a bank account, the bank's obligation to repay the deposited funds is proceeds of proceeds (and therefore qualifies as proceeds),[146] and, because it is a deposit account, it is cash proceeds. If money is later withdrawn from the account, the money is cash proceeds, and if the money is used to buy a piano, the piano is noncash proceeds.

[B] Attachment—§§ 9-203(f); 9-315(a)(2), (b)

Attachment applies automatically to most proceeds. The section on attachment provides that a security interest in collateral attaches automatically to proceeds as soon as they come into existence even if the security agreement is silent on the matter.[147] A corresponding provision limits attachment to proceeds that are identifiable.[148] Identification means that the secured party can trace the proceeds back to the disposition of the collateral.[149] A secured party can look to two separate sources of assets to secure the indebtedness. It might consider the proceeds because, as long as they are identifiable, the security interest attaches automatically.[150] Alternatively, the secured party might continue to assert its security interest in the original collateral that was subject to the

---

142. U.C.C. § 9-102(a)(9).

143. U.C.C. § 9-102, Comment 13(e).

144. U.C.C. § 9-102(a)(58).

145. The buyer's payment obligation could be an account. U.C.C. § 9-102(a)(2). An account is noncash proceeds, while a deposit account is cash proceeds.

146. U.C.C. § 9-102(a)(12)(A).

147. U.C.C. § 9-203(f).

148. U.C.C. § 9-315(a)(2). If goods, including goods that are proceeds, are commingled in such a way that their separate identity is lost, a security interest ceases to attach to them and instead attaches to the product or mass into which they have been subsumed. U.C.C. §§ 9-315(b)(1), 9-336. For discussion of commingled goods, see § 15.06, *infra*.

149. *See, e.g.,* Universal C.I.T. v. Farmers Bank, 358 F. Supp. 317, 13 U.C.C. Rep. Serv. 109 (E.D. Mo. 1973); *In re* Superior Used Cars, Inc., 258 B.R. 680, 44 U.C.C. Rep. Serv. 2d 293 (Bankr. W.D. Mich. 2001) (secured party could not meet its burden of tracing cash proceeds).

150. U.C.C. § 9-315(a)(2).

disposition.[151] A secured party that consents to disposition of the collateral free from its security interest can only pursue the identifiable proceeds from the disposition.[152] If the disposition occurs without such consent, in addition to its interest in the identifiable proceeds, the secured party's interest continues in the collateral, unless a provision of Article 9 or Section 2-403 provides to the contrary.[153]

What is the impact on identification of the deposit of cash proceeds into a deposit account? Depositing proceeds into a deposit account that contains only proceeds permits easy identification[154] but is not mandatory for a security interest in the deposited proceeds to remain valid.[155] Commingling funds in a deposit account, by contrast, raises serious identification problems. Because former law did not specifically provide for the identification of commingled cash proceeds, courts turned to equitable tracing concepts developed in the law of trusts.[156] The 1998 revision adopted this approach.[157] The applicable equitable tracing rule is the "lowest intermediate balance" rule, an approach based on the following assumptions: (1) as a debtor spends funds from a deposit account, it spends the proceeds of a security interest last,[158] and (2) a later deposit of non-proceeds funds does not increase the amount that constitutes identifiable proceeds unless the debtor intends that the later deposit restore, or partially restore, the proceeds balance.[159] For example, suppose a secured party has a security interest in a debtor's inventory and permits the debtor to deposit cash proceeds into its general checking account. On Day 1, the debtor has a balance of $10,000 in the account, none of which represents proceeds. On Day 2, the debtor deposits $5,000 in cash proceeds, resulting in an overall balance of $15,000 and a proceeds balance of $5,000. The next

---

151. U.C.C. § 9-315(a).

152. U.C.C. § 9-315(a).

153. U.C.C. § 9-315(a). Dry Canyon Farms, Inc. v. United States Nat'l Bank of Oregon, 84 Or. App. 686, 735 P.2d 620, 4 U.C.C. Rep. Serv. 2d 277 (1987) (security interest continues in proceeds, whether or not secured party authorizes disposition). For discussion of a secured party's continuing interest in the collateral following a disposition by a debtor, see §§ 11.01 and 11.02, *infra*.

154. *In re* Delco Oil, Inc., 365 B.R. 246, 62 U.C.C. Rep. Serv. 2d 257 (Bankr. M.D. Fla. 2007) (deposits of cash proceeds into an unauthorized bank account traced through bank records).

155. A security interest is not invalid or fraudulent merely because the debtor has the right or the ability to use, commingle, or dispose of all or part of the collateral. U.C.C. § 9-205(a)(1). "Collateral" includes proceeds. U.C.C. § 9-102(a)(12)(A). *See* § 3.01, *infra*.

156. Bank of Kansas v. Hutchinson Health Serv., Inc., 12 Kan. App. 2d 87, 735 P.2d 256, 3 U.C.C. Rep. Serv. 2d 1537 (1987). The tracing concept is not limited to deposits into a debtor's deposit account. Fricke v. Valley Prod. Credit Ass'n, 778 S.W.2d 829, 10 U.C.C. Rep. Serv. 2d 1454 (Mo. Ct. App. 1989) (secured party traced deposit of cash proceeds into the business account of debtor's business partner); Farns Assoc., Inc. v. South Side Bank, 93 Ill. App. 3d 766, 417 N.E.2d 818 (1981) (secured party traced proceeds by showing that bank received checks representing the proceeds directly from the account debtor and then cashed the checks).

157. U.C.C. § 9-315(b)(2).

158. *Ex parte* Alabama Mobile Homes, Inc., 468 So. 2d 156, 40 U.C.C. Rep. Serv. 1898 (Ala. 1985).

159. The deposit of new proceeds is distinguishable. In *Central Production Credit Association v. Hans*, 189 Ill. App. 3d 889, 545 N.E.2d 1063, 11 U.C.C. Rep. Serv. 2d 696 (1989), identifiable proceeds that had been deposited in a deposit account were withdrawn to purchase investments. After the sale of those investments, the proceeds were deposited into the same account. Because the second deposit also constituted identifiable proceeds, it increased the balance of proceeds in the account.

day, the debtor withdraws and spends $4,000.[160] This withdrawal reduces the overall balance to $11,000, but applying the first assumption leaves the proceeds balance at $5,000. On Day 3, the debtor withdraws an additional $7,000 and buys an item of equipment. The overall balance is $4,000, all of which is proceeds. In addition, the secured party has an interest in the equipment to the extent of $1,000 (the amount of proceeds used for the purchase). On Day 4, the debtor deposits $15,000, none of which is proceeds. The overall balance is $19,000, but applying the second assumption leaves the proceeds balance at $4,000. In other words, the proceeds balance is the lowest balance between the time proceeds are first withdrawn and the time the account balance later rises as a result of non-proceeds deposits—i.e., the lowest intermediate balance. If the debtor deposits $6,000 in new proceeds on Day 5, the overall balance will rise to $25,000 and the proceeds balance will rise to $10,000.

Former law provided that a security interest continued in identifiable proceeds "received by the debtor."[161] The 1998 revision eliminated the phrase, thereby making it clear that a security interest attaches to proceeds even if they are received by a person other than the debtor. The Comments state that "[t]his Article contains no requirement that property be 'received' by the debtor for the property to qualify as proceeds. It is necessary only that the property be traceable, directly or indirectly, to the original collateral."[162]

---

160. U.C.C. § 9-332(b) provides that a transferee of funds from a deposit account, even a transferee that does not give value, takes the funds free of even a perfected security interest in the account unless the transferee acts in collusion with the debtor to violate the rights of the secured party. *In re Cumberland Molded Products, LLC*, 69 U.C.C. Rep. Serv. 2d 371 (Bankr. M.D. Tenn. 2009) (bank lost its security interest in funds from a deposit account that it controlled by honoring a check drawn by the debtor on the account). U.C.C. § 9-332(a) provides a similar rule for transferees of money. U.C.C. § 9-332, Comment 3, explains the rule as follows:

> Broad protection for transferees helps to ensure that security interests in deposit accounts do not impair the free flow of funds. It also minimizes the likelihood that a secured party will enjoy a claim to whatever the transferee purchases with the funds. Rules concerning recovery of payments traditionally have placed a high value on finality. The opportunity to upset a completed transaction, or even to place a completed transaction in jeopardy by bringing suit against the transferee of funds, should be severely limited. Although the giving of value usually is a prerequisite for receiving the ability to take free from third-party claims, where payments are concerned the law is even more protective.

See Keybank Nat'l Ass'n v. Ruiz Food Products, Inc., 59 U.C.C. Rep. Serv. 2d 870 (D. Ida. 2005) (Section 9-332 protects innocent transferee of funds wrongfully paid by the debtor from a perfected security interest in the funds as identifiable proceeds from the sale of debtor's inventory).

161. U.C.C. § 9-306(2) (1972 Official Text).

162. U.C.C. § 9-102, Comment 13(d). *See* Case Corp. v. Gehrke, 208 Ariz. 140, 91 P.3d 362, 55 U.C.C. Rep. Serv. 2d 1 (Ariz. Ct. App.2004) (because security interest extended to proceeds and security agreement required debtor to transfer proceeds from sale of inventory to secured party within seven days, secured party had a viable claim for conversion against debtor because the proceeds could be identified even though they had been commingled with other funds in the debtor's general operating account).

§ 2.04 Attachment to Underlying Obligations—§ 9-203(f), (g)

Article 9 has special attachment rules that apply to (1) obligations that support payment or performance of collateral and (2) property, including real estate, that secures a right to payment or performance that is within the scope of Article 9. Section 9-203(f) provides that attachment of a security interest to collateral causes the security interest to attach also to any "supporting obligation" for the collateral. A supporting obligation is a letter-of-credit right or other type of secondary obligation, such as a guaranty, that supports payment or performance of a supported obligation that itself is within the scope of Article 9.[163] A supported obligation might be an account, chattel paper, a document, a general intangible, an instrument, or investment property. A security interest that attaches to a supported obligation automatically attaches to any supporting obligation.[164] For example, suppose that a secured party has a security interest in a negotiable promissory note (an instrument) that is supported by a standby letter of credit. The security interest automatically attaches to the letter-of-credit right even though the security agreement does not refer to the right.[165]

Section 9-203(g) contains a similar attachment rule for property that secures a right to payment or performance. For example, suppose a secured party lends money and takes a security interest in a note that is secured by a mortgage on real estate. Even though the initial acquisition of the mortgage by the payee of the note was outside the scope of Article 9, the secondary financing transaction that uses the note and mortgage as collateral is within its scope. The security interest automatically attaches to the mortgage when it attaches to the note.[166] This area presents complex issues that overlap with aspects of real-estate law. The discussion of the Article 9 scope provisions provides more detail.[167]

---

163. U.C.C. § 9-102(a)(78).

164. U.C.C. § 9-203(f). Moreover, perfection of the security interest in the supported obligation also perfects the security interest in the supporting obligation. U.C.C. § 9-308(d). This perfection applies even though a security interest in a letter-of-credit right that is not a supporting obligation must be perfected by control. U.C.C. §§ 9-312(b)(2), 9-107.

165. U.C.C. § 9-102(a)(51) defines "letter-of-credit right." See § 1.07, supra.

166. U.C.C. § 9-308(e). Perfection of the interest in the note automatically perfects the interest in the mortgage. Although the drafters' intent in adopting these provisions was to preempt real estate law, a legislative note appended to Section 9-308 suggests that each state legislature should provide further clarification by enacting an amendment to the state's real-estate recording act expressly providing that perfection under Article 9 is sufficient for all purposes.

167. See § 1.06[C], supra. See also Report of the Permanent Editorial Board of the Uniform Commercial Code, Application of the Uniform Commercial Code to Selected Issues Relating to Mortgage Notes (Nov. 14, 2011).

Chapter 3

Ongoing Financing Relationships

Synopsis

§ 3.01 Facilitating Clauses Generally

The parties to some financing arrangements do not view their initial security agreement as a static, one-shot transaction. They anticipate at least the potential for a dynamic, ongoing financing relationship with additional funds to be advanced by the secured party, after-acquired property of the debtor to serve as collateral, or both.

The parties to such transactions would incur considerable burdens if they had to formalize all subsequent additions to their agreement. The transaction costs associated with a requirement that they enter into a new security agreement each time the secured party advances additional funds, or each time the debtor acquires additional collateral, would be significant. Requiring new agreements would also slow the processing of some transactions, as well as increase the chances of overlooking a necessary formality. The parties would be better served if they could incorporate their long-term intent into their initial security agreement.

Consider the following hypothetical: D is the owner of a retail furniture outlet. SP provides D with financing for the acquisition of inventory and takes as collateral a security interest in all of D's inventory. The parties anticipate that D will repay SP with the proceeds derived from inventory sales and envision a long-term financing arrangement under which SP will finance D's acquisitions of inventory for many years to come. They want each future extension of credit to be secured by D's entire stock of inventory, and, accordingly, they want SP's security interest to attach to new inventory as D acquires it.

Article 9 includes provisions that facilitate such transactions. It enables parties to include terms in their security agreement that will implement their intentions with respect to the continuing nature of their financing arrangement. The use of an after-acquired property clause or a future-advances clause, or both, enables parties to craft their transaction with efficiency.

Although both an after-acquired property clause and a future-advances clause refer to events that transpire in the future, they cover distinct concepts and should not be confused. An after-acquired property clause concerns future assets that will serve as collateral for an obligation. It reflects the parties' understanding that the security interest will attach to property within the security agreement's description of the collateral that the debtor acquires subsequent to the effective date of the agreement. For example, if a security agreement provides for after-acquired inventory, the secured party acquires a security interest not only in the debtor's existing inventory but also in additional inventory as the debtor acquires rights in it. A future-advances clause, on the other hand, concerns the money or other value advanced by the secured party. If a security agreement includes a future-advances clause, the debtor's interest in the collateral will be encumbered to the extent of the initial advance of value and all subsequent advances of value.

Article 9 thus validates "floating liens"—that is, liens that expand the pool of collateral with the acquisition of new assets and that expand the debtor's secured obligation with the advance of new value.[1] This approach historically created considerable judicial hostility.[2] The drafters of the initial U.C.C. concluded that the hostility was premised "on a feeling, often inarticulate in the opinions, that a commercial borrower should not be allowed to encumber all his assets present and future, and that for the protection not only of the borrower but of his other creditors a cushion of free assets should be preserved."[3] Judicial resistance reached its zenith with the U.S. Supreme Court opinion in *Benedict v. Ratner*.[4] The Court struck down as a fraudulent conveyance an assignment of present and future accounts receivable. It reasoned that the debtor's unfettered dominion and control over the collateral and its proceeds created such an ostensible ownership problem that the entire transaction was void as a matter of law.

The effect of rulings like *Benedict* was to impose expensive formalities on the ongoing financing of accounts and inventory. For example, "it was thought necessary for the debtor to make daily remittances to the lender of all collections received, even though the amount remitted is immediately returned to the debtor in order to keep the loan

---

1. Article 9 security interests also "float" in the sense that they attach automatically to proceeds. *See* § 2.03[B], *supra.*

2. *See generally* 1 G. GILMORE, SECURITY INTERESTS IN PERSONAL PROPERTY §§ 2.2–2.5, 11.6–11.7 (1965).

3. U.C.C. § 9-204, Comment 2 (1962 Official Text).

4. 268 U.S. 353, 45 S. Ct. 566, 69 L. Ed. 991 (1925).

at an agreed level."[5] Many states overcame the policing requirements that constituted the substance of the *Benedict* rule by enacting laws that countered its effect.[6] Section 9-205(a) repeals the *Benedict* rule:

> A security interest is not invalid or fraudulent against creditors solely because:
>
> > (1) the debtor has the right or ability to:
> >
> > > (A) use, commingle, or dispose of all or part of the collateral, including returned or repossessed goods;
> > >
> > > (B) collect, compromise, enforce, or otherwise deal with collateral;
> > >
> > > (C) accept the return of collateral or make repossessions; or
> > >
> > > (D) use, commingle, or dispose of proceeds; or
> >
> > (2) the secured party fails to require the debtor to account for proceeds or replace collateral.[7]

A lender with a nonpossessory security interest[8] might, as a practical matter, feel a need to police the activities of its debtor with respect to collateral and its proceeds. Business rather than legal considerations, however, determine the extent of policing measures implemented.[9]

§ 3.02 After-Acquired Property— § 9-204(a), (b)

[A] General Applicability

Article 9 explicitly validates the use of terms providing for a security interest in after-acquired property.[10] The terms are common with regard to many types of commercial loans, but they are most important with "revolving" forms of collateral like inventory and accounts. These forms of collateral by their nature will dissipate over time. Inventory will be sold to buyers in ordinary course of business that will take it free from the security interest,[11] and the obligations that constitute accounts will be satisfied with payment of the accounts.

A secured party that continues to loan money against inventory or accounts must have its interest attach to additional inventory or accounts as the debtor acquires them,

---

5. U.C.C. § 9-205, Comment 1 (1962 Official Text).

6. U.C.C. § 9-205, Comment 1. New York law, rather than federal law of bankruptcy, was the basis for *Benedict v. Ratner.*

7. U.C.C. § 9-205(a).

8. Section 9-205(b) clarifies that nothing in the section relaxes the requirements for possession if attachment, perfection, or enforcement depends on a secured party's possession. For discussion of possession, see Chapter 6, *infra.*

9. U.C.C. § 9-205, Comment 2.

10. U.C.C. § 9-204(a).

11. U.C.C. § 9-320(a), discussed at § 11.03[A][1], *infra.*

or its collateral will ultimately disappear as the debtor sells its existing inventory or collects its existing accounts. An after-acquired property clause extends the scope of the security interest to cover the additional property as the debtor acquires it.[12] Without this clause, a secured party would have to enter into a new security agreement with respect to each of the debtor's new acquisitions of inventory or accounts. In the absence of both an after-acquired property clause and a new security agreement, the secured party would not have a security interest in the new acquisitions.[13]

An after-acquired property clause is part of the description of the collateral in the security agreement. Rather than being limited to existing collateral of the specified type (e.g., inventory, accounts, equipment), the description includes any property of the type that the debtor subsequently acquires.[14] This arrangement creates a floating lien on a shifting pool of collateral.[15]

How does a security interest attach to after-acquired property? When the parties initially enter into their security agreement, the debtor does not have rights in the property yet to be acquired. Indeed, the property might not yet even exist. The security interest cannot attach at that time because of the debtor's lack of rights in the anticipated property.[16] Attachment occurs immediately, however, when the debtor acquires rights in the collateral.[17] The security agreement with the after-acquired property clause provides in advance the necessary agreement, description of the collateral, and signature of the debtor,[18] and the value initially given by the secured party supports extension of the security interest to the newly acquired assets.[19]

---

12. The case of *In re Travelers Petroleum, Inc.*, 86 B.R. 246, 6 U.C.C. Rep. Serv. 2d 911 (Bankr. W.D. Okla. 1987), shows how an after-acquired property clause also can later bring some of the debtor's existing property within the scope of the security agreement. Trucks that the debtor used as equipment later became inventory subject to the after-acquired property clause when leased.

13. New assets might qualify as proceeds, but tracing requirements make identification problematic. *See* § 2.03[B], *supra*.

14. Parker Roofing Co. v. Pacific First Fed. Sav. Bank, 59 Wash. App. 151, 796 P.2d 732, 13 U.C.C. Rep. Serv. 2d 501 (1990) ("general intangibles ... now or hereafter owned"); *In re* Penn Housing Corp., 367 F. Supp. 661, 13 U.C.C. Rep. Serv. 947 (W.D. Pa. 1973) ("inventory present and after-acquired" and "all present and future accounts receivable submitted, including new accounts receivable whenever acquired"); South Cnty. Sand & Gravel Co., Inc. v. Bituminous Pavers Co., 256 A.2d 514, 6 U.C.C. Rep. Serv. 901 (R.I. 1969) (all of debtor's accounts receivable "now existing and hereafter arising").

15. U.C.C. § 9-204, Comment 2.

16. *See* U.C.C. § 9-203(b)(2); § 2.02[C], *supra*. Valley Nat'l Bank of Arizona v. Flagstaff Dairy, 116 Ariz. 513, 570 P.2d 200, 22 U.C.C. Rep. Serv. 787 (Ariz. Ct. App. 1977) (security interest cannot attach in after-acquired property until debtor acquires rights in it).

17. Babson Credit Plan, Inc. v. Cordele Prod. Credit Ass'n, 146 Ga. App. 266, 246 S.E.2d 354, 24 U.C.C. Rep. Serv. 437 (1978). With respect to accounts, the interest in after-acquired property attaches with the creation of the accounts. Shaw Mudge & Co. v. Sher-Mart Mfg. Co., Inc., 132 N.J. Super. 517, 334 A.2d 357, 16 U.C.C. Rep. Serv. 847 (Super. Ct. App. Div. 1975).

18. "This section follows Section 9-203, the section requiring a written security agreement, and its purpose is to make clear that confirmatory agreements are not necessary where the basic agreement has the clauses mentioned." U.C.C. § 9-204, Comment 5 (1972 Official Text).

19. "[A] person gives 'value' for rights if the person acquires them ... as security for ... a preexisting claim." U.C.C. § 1-204(2). *See also* Barry v. Bank of New Hampshire, N.A., 113 N.H. 158, 304 A.2d

A question litigated several times is whether a security agreement covering all of a particular type of collateral extends to after-acquired collateral of the same type in the absence of an explicit clause in the agreement. For example, suppose a security agreement describes the collateral as "inventory" or "all inventory." Do these descriptions mean "existing inventory" or "existing and future" inventory? A judicial finding that the term is ambiguous allows the use of extrinsic evidence to explain the parties' intent. If a bank lends against a revolving type of asset like inventory or accounts, it can introduce evidence of a course of performance, course of dealing, or usage of trade to support its argument for an expansive interpretation.[20] Suppose, however, an individual sells a business enterprise to another party on credit and retains a security interest in "all inventory." Because the secured party is not providing ongoing financing, convincing extrinsic evidence supporting an expansive interpretation is less likely.[21] The most plausible meaning is that the parties intended the security interest to attach only to the inventory delivered to the buyer as part of the sale of the business.

Although the courts generally have been permissive with ordinary-course financers of inventory and accounts,[22] some decisions are to the contrary.[23] The secured party's argument for implicit coverage of after-acquired assets is much weaker for non-revolving types of collateral such as equipment.[24] The ease of avoiding litigation of the issue should provide ample motivation to include an after-acquired property clause in any security agreement that contemplates the inclusion of such assets.[25]

879, 12 U.C.C. Rep. Serv. 732 (1973); *In re* King-Porter Co., Inc., 446 F.2d 722, 9 U.C.C. Rep. Serv. 339 (5th Cir. 1971).

20. U.C.C. § 1-303(a)((c). *Cf.* U.C.C. § 2-202 and Comment 1(c) (extrinsic evidence based on course of performance, course of dealing, or usage of trade admissible for purposes of interpretation without a showing of ambiguity).

21. *See* Stoumbos v. Kilimnik, 988 F.2d 949, 20 U.C.C. Rep. Serv. 2d 333 (9th Cir. 1993).

22. *In re* Shenandoah Warehouse Co., 202 B.R. 871, 32 U.C.C. Rep. Serv. 2d 573 (Bankr. W.D. Va. 1996). *See also* Peoples Bank v. Bryan Bros. Cattle Co., 504 F.3d 549, 64 U.C.C. Rep. Serv. 2d 113 (5th Cir. 2007) (security interests taken in the inventory of a business automatically cover after-acquired property unless the interest is limited specifically to only certain items).

23. Wollenberg v. Phoenix Leasing Inc., 182 Ariz. 4, 893 P.2d 4, 24 U.C.C. Rep. Serv. 2d 770 (Ct. App. 1994) (accounts); *In re* Balcain Equip. Co., Inc., 80 B.R. 461, 5 U.C.C. Rep. Serv. 2d 766 (Bankr. C.D. Ill. 1987) (inventory).

24. *See, e.g.*, Dowell v. D.R. Kincaid Chair Co., 125 N.C. App. 557, 481 S.E.2d 670, 31 U.C.C. Rep. Serv. 2d 987 (1997) (court refused to imply after-acquired property clause for security agreement covering equipment); Yatooma v. Barker, 73 U.C.C. Rep. Serv. 2d 176 (Mich. Ct. App. Dec. 28, 2010) (because the relevant assets were not by their nature in constant fluctuation, the security agreement did not reach after-acquired property).

25. U.C.C. § 9-204, Comment 7, indicates states that "[t]he references to after-acquired property clauses and future advance clauses in this section are limited to security agreements. There is no need to refer to after-acquired property or future advances or other obligations secured in a financing statement."

[B] Exceptions

Article 9 limits the reach of after-acquired property clauses in the context of consumer goods.[26] The limitation precludes the attachment of a security interest in consumer goods, other than an accession, given as additional collateral unless the debtor acquires rights in the goods within ten days after the secured party gives value.[27] For example, suppose that a secured party makes a loan and takes a security interest in a consumer's computer pursuant to a security agreement that includes an after-acquired property clause covering all computers and computer peripherals. The security interest will not attach to a new printer that the debtor acquires two weeks later unless the secured party extends additional value.[28] Note that the limitation applies to all consumer goods without regard to whether the transaction is a consumer-goods transaction, and thus the result would be the same in the case of a business obligation incurred by the sole proprietor of a business and secured by the proprietor's consumer goods.

A secured party needs to be careful with respect to after-acquired property clauses covering consumer goods, and perhaps the best advice is to avoid using the clause at all. If in the previous illustration the debtor defaults and the secured party forecloses on the computer and the printer, it could incur conversion liability for its actions with respect to the printer.[29]

A secured party must also address compliance with applicable state and federal consumer protection laws.[30] For example, a Federal Trade Commission rule makes it an unfair trade practice for a lender or a retail installment seller to take from a consumer a nonpossessory security interest in household goods other than a purchase-money

---

26. If the transaction is a consumer transaction, a description using "consumer goods" is insufficient as a matter of law. U.C.C. § 9-108(b)(3), (e)(2). Thus, in a consumer transaction, a security agreement covering "all present or after-acquired consumer goods" would not attach to any collateral, including consumer goods owned by the debtor at the time of attachment and those acquired within ten days after value is given. Article 9 leaves open the possibility that a description using a category not defined in the Code might suffice. Even though such a description is not *per se* insufficient under the Code, other law might invalidate it and, even if valid, the ten-day rule would limit the reach of its after-acquired aspect. For discussion of consumer transactions, see § 1.04[A][1], *supra.*

Similarly, a description using the generic types "security entitlement," "securities account," or "commodity account" is ineffective. U.C.C. § 9-108(b)(3), (e)(2). Article 9 does not include any explicit limitations on descriptions using categorical groupings it does not define. U.C.C. § 9-108(b)(2). For discussion of investment property generally, see § 1.04[B][6], *supra.* Article 9 also contains limitations that preclude the use of "all commercial tort claims" to describe existing or after-acquired collateral of that type. U.C.C. §§ 9-108(e)(1), 9-204(b)(2). Epicentre Strategic Corp.-Mich. v. Perrysburg Exempted Village School Dist., 60 U.C.C. Rep. Serv. 2d 166 (N.D. Ohio 2005) (unreported). For discussion of commercial tort claims generally, see § 1.06[F][2], *supra.*

27. U.C.C. § 9-204(b)(1).

28. *In re* Harris, 23 U.C.C. Rep. Serv. 220 (Bankr. N.D. Ga. 1977) (clause giving secured party security interest in replacement household consumer goods was ineffective to give security interest in such goods acquired more than ten days after the loan).

29. For a discussion of conversion liability, see § 19.01, *infra.*

30. Article 9 explicitly subordinates its rules to such laws. U.C.C. § 9-201(b).

security interest.[31] The Federal Reserve Board adopted a parallel rule that applies the same constraint on financial institutions.[32] The rules define "household goods" to include clothing, furniture, appliances, one radio and one television set, linens, china, crockery, kitchenware, and personal effects (including wedding rings).

The federal Truth-in-Lending Act and Regulation Z include another limitation that requires clear identification of the property affected by a security interest.[33] The Federal Reserve Board interprets the statute and regulation to mean that a creditor cannot claim a security interest in all after-acquired property of the debtor in transactions to which the act applies.[34] A number of court opinions concur with the interpretation.[35]

The limitation on the effectiveness of after-acquired property clauses does not apply to consumer goods that qualify as accessions. An accession is an item of personalty that retains its separate identity even though attached to another item of personalty, meaning that it can be removed and sold separately.[36] If a secured party takes a security interest in a debtor's personal car, a clause in the security agreement extending the security interest to after-acquired accessions is fully enforceable. The secured party's interest thus attaches to assets like replacement tires and batteries upon their acquisition and installation.

§ 3.03 Future Advances —
§ 9-204(c)

Article 9 validates the use of clauses that encumber the collateral as security for advances or other value made in the future, whether such advances are obligatory or discretionary.[37] A future-advances clause eliminates the need for the parties to enter into another security agreement every time the secured party advances more money to the debtor. The debtor agrees through the clause to grant a security interest in the

---

31. 16 C.F.R. § 444.2(a)(4).

32. 12 C.F.R. § 227.13(d) (Regulation AA). The Federal Reserve Board must promulgate deceptive trade practice rules that are substantially similar to designated rules prescribed by the FTC. This approach ensures that the limitations imposed by the FTC will also govern banks, savings and loans, and federal credit unions.

33. 15 U.S.C. § 1638(a)(9); 12 C.F.R. §§ 226.8(b)(5), 226.18(m).

34. Public Loan Co. v. Hyde, 47 N.Y.2d 182, 390 N.E.2d 1162, 4117 N.Y.S.2d 238, 26 U.C.C. Rep. Serv. 781 (N.Y. 1979).

35. *In re* McCausland, 63 B.R. 665, 1 U.C.C. Rep. Serv. 2d 1372 (Bankr. E.D. Pa. 1986); Smith v. No. 2 Galesburg Crown Fin. Corp., 615 F.2d 407, 28 U.C.C. Rep. Serv.212, 53 A.L.R. Fed. 406 (7th Cir. 1980).

36. For discussion of accessions generally, see § 15.05, *infra*.

37. U.C.C. § 9-204(c). Article 9 uses the phrase "pursuant to commitment" to refer to advances or other value that a secured party must extend under the terms of the security agreement or another agreement. U.C.C. § 9-102(a)(69). In certain circumstances, obligatory advances enhance a secured party's priority rights. *See* §§ 11.03[A][3], 12.02[C], and 12.03[C], *infra*. An advance can be pursuant to commitment even though an event of default or other event not within control of the secured party occurred that permits the secured party's release from its obligation. U.C.C. § 9-102(a)(68).

described collateral to the extent of any subsequent advances as well as the initial advance.[38]

A future-advances clause is an efficient means to extend a secured party's status with each new advance because it precludes the need for a new security agreement at the time of the advance. A secured party that advances additional money under a security agreement that lacks the clause will be unsecured with respect to the new advance unless it obtains a new security agreement to cover the advance.[39] In the absence of either a future-advances clause or a new security agreement, the debtor has not agreed to allow a security interest to attach to the collateral to cover the advance. A new security agreement provides the necessary debtor consent at the time of the advance; a future-advances clause provides it at the time of the original agreement.

Issues sometimes arise concerning the scope of a future-advances clause. The parties might include a clause with broad language yet nevertheless intend a narrower scope. For example, the security agreement in In re Eshleman[40] had a clause providing that the debtor's automobile "shall secure Debtor's obligations to pay the note of the Debtor of even date herewith ... [and] all other liabilities of Debtor to Lender, now existing or hereinafter incurred...."[41] A year and a half later, the secured party loaned the debtor additional money and obtained a new security agreement covering inventory, equipment, and accounts. The secured party forgot to perfect its security interest under the second agreement, leaving it subordinated to a bankruptcy trustee with respect to the collateral described in that agreement.[42] The bankruptcy referee refused to allow the secured party's claim that the automobile served as security for the second loan through the future-advances clause. The referee reasoned that the second loan "was so unrelated to the earlier loan transaction ... as to negate the inference that the debtor consented to its inclusion."[43] The Eshleman court concluded that the parties never intended a security interest in consumer goods to cover funds advanced under a separate security agreement for collateral of a commercial nature.

---

38. Farmers Nat'l Bank v. Shirey, 126 Idaho 63, 878 P.2d 762, 25 U.C.C. Rep. Serv. 2d 566 (1994) (security agreement provided that security interest "is to secure payment and performance of the liabilities and obligations of Debtor to Secured Party of every kind and description ... due or to become due, now existing or hereafter arising"); In re Branch, 368 B.R. 80, 62 U.C.C. Rep. Serv. 2d 585 (Bankr. D. Colo. 2006) (complete payment of the first loan did not preclude the secured party from foreclosing on the collateral also encumbered through an after-acquired property clause on a second loan in default).

39. Idaho Bank & Trust Co. v. Cargill, Inc., 105 Idaho 83, 665 P.2d 1093, 36 U.C.C. Rep. Serv. 691 (Ct. App. 1983) (in the absence of future-advances clause, such advances are not within the scope of the security agreement); Thorp Fin. Corp. of Wisconsin v. Ken Hodgins & Sons, 73 Mich. App. 428, 251 N.W.2d 614, 21 U.C.C. Rep. Serv. 881 (1977) (must enter into a new security agreement with the debtor to become secured with respect to a subsequent additional advance).

40. 10 U.C.C. Rep. Serv. 750 (E.D. Pa. 1972).

41. Id. at 751.

42. Perfection was necessary because second security agreement covered new collateral not covered in the original description. A future advance does not in itself require a new act of perfection.

43. Eshleman, 10 U.C.C. Rep. Serv. at 753.

Traditional judicial hostility continued to assert itself in construing future-advances clauses. Courts derisively labeled broad clauses as "dragnet clauses" and routinely refused to enforce them. Remnants of that judicial attitude, in the guise of the "same-class rule," survived the adoption of Article 9. A clause describing future advances in general terms is enforceable under this rule only if the later advances are of the same class as the initial obligation;[44] otherwise, the advance is not considered to be related to the financing contemplated by the parties when they entered into the security agreement.[45] The decision in *In re Eshleman* discussed above reflects the same-class rule.

The drafters of the 1998 Official Text sought to rein in judicial hostility to dragnet clauses. The Comments state a single criterion for assessing the scope of a future-advances clause and explicitly reject the use of other tests:

> Determining the obligations secured by collateral is solely a matter of construing the parties' agreement under applicable law. This Article rejects the holdings of cases decided under former Article 9 that applied other tests, such as whether a future advance or other subsequently incurred obligation was of the same or a similar type of class as earlier advances and obligations secured by the collateral.[46]

The court in *Pride Hyundai, Inc. v. Chrysler Financial Company, L.L.C.*,[47] predicted that the Massachusetts Supreme Judicial Court would follow the direction of the comment if faced with the issue and applied the test set forth in the Official Comments. The debtor argued that it had not intended to secure certain debts arising out of an existing retail financing agreement when it signed a security agreement containing a future-advances clause. The court, however, concluded that the language used in the clause was clear and unambiguous in securing without exception all future and past obligations.

Notwithstanding the position stated in the Official Comments, some courts may continue to apply the same-class rule, and secured parties thus should draft their future-advances clauses with care. A broad general clause is simply an invitation for a court to strike the clause with respect to future unrelated financing. The clause should express an intent to include unrelated financing to increase its chances of being upheld. The future-advances clause upheld in *In re Dorsey Electric Co.*[48] is illustrative. It included "all other indebtedness of every kind and nature, direct and indirect ...

---

44. *In re* Smith & West Constr., Inc., 28 B.R. 682, 36 U.C.C. Rep. Serv. 989 (Bankr. D. Or. 1983) (all loans were of a commercial nature related to debtor's construction business).

45. *In re* Blair, 26 B.R. 228, 36 U.C.C. Rep. Serv. 985 (Bankr. W.D. Tenn. 1982) (two personal loans on vehicles were sufficiently related, but business loan was not).

46. U.C.C. § 9-204, Comment 5.

47. 369 F.3d 603, 53 U.C.C. Rep. Serv. 2d 423 (1st Cir. 2004). *See also In re* Nagata, 60 U.C.C. Rep. Serv. 2d 255 (Bankr. D. Haw. 2006) (used the revised Comment as definitive in upholding provision in security agreement that extended the interest to any additional loans that the lender extended to the borrower, including a credit card loan); *In re* Renshaw, 447 B.R. 453, 74 U.C.C. Rep. Serv. 2d 24 (Bankr. W.D. Pa. 2011) (court cites Comment in concluding that Pennsylvania legislature reversed "relatedness rule").

48. 344 F. Supp. 1171 (E.D. Ark. 1972).

whether or not the same shall be similar or dissimilar or related or unrelated to the primary indebtedness."[49] A clause that shows an intent to include unrelated financing is a good response to the same-class rule because the rule precludes inferring the consent of the debtor if an advance does not relate to the same class of collateral as the initial obligation.[50]

§ 3.04 Financing Inventory and Accounts

Some of the most sophisticated financing transactions involve inventory, accounts, and their proceeds. Because these assets are expected to turn over on a regular basis,[51] they are the most likely candidates for financing transactions that use after-acquired property and future-advances clauses. The parties can creatively tailor these transactions to meet their specific needs with respect to an ongoing financing relationship.

Three financing patterns have become common: (1) factoring of accounts, (2) general financing of inventory, accounts or both, and (3) floor planning of inventory. The discussion below develops some of the parameters of these common financing patterns.

[A] Factoring of Accounts

Factoring of accounts is the purchase of accounts from their owner by a financing agency (typically called a factor). It does not involve a secured loan from the financing agency; rather, the owner sells the accounts. The customers on the accounts (the account debtors)[52] typically receive notice that their accounts have been sold and that they are to make payments to the factor when payments are due.[53] The factor typically

---

49. *Id.* at 1175.

50. Pellegrini v. Nat'l Bank of Washington, 28 U.C.C. Rep. Serv. 209 (D.C. Super. Ct. 1980).

51. Inventory will be sold to buyers in ordinary course of business, and such buyers take inventory free of even a perfected security interest. *See* § 11.03[A][1], *infra*. The obligation to pay money that is at the core of an account is satisfied as the account is paid.

52. An "account debtor" is a person obligated on an account, chattel paper, or a general intangible. A person obligated on a negotiable instrument is not an account debtor even if the instrument is part of chattel paper. U.C.C. § 9-102(a)(3). If the person obligated is an account debtor, Section 9-406(a)–(c) sets forth the mechanics of collection. Article 3 covers the collection from an obligor on a negotiable instrument.

53. Although notification of the account debtor is typical, the parties can structure the transaction so that the merchant continues to collect the accounts as an agent for the factor. If the merchant fails to remit the collections, the factor cannot recover from the account debtor for payments made to the merchant. An account debtor receives credit for payments made to the assignor prior to receiving notice that the account has been assigned and that payments are to be made to the assignee. The notice must be signed by either the assignor (the owner) or assignee (the factor). U.C.C. § 9-406(a).

purchases the accounts without recourse, meaning that the factor cannot recover from the owner that sold the account if an account debtor does not make timely payment.[54]

Even though factoring of accounts does not involve a secured loan, the transaction nevertheless falls within the scope of Article 9. For reasons already discussed, Article 9 applies to sales of accounts.[55] The agreement between the parties is a security agreement, and a factor's interest is called a security interest even though the accounts do not serve as security for an obligation.[56] A factor, accordingly, must be certain to observe Article 9 formalities. The factor must reduce the agreement with the owner to a record that describes the accounts and that the owner signs.[57] In addition, a factor needs to perfect its security interest by filing a financing statement in the appropriate office.

Factoring is a service that enables a merchant to contract to have another party conduct the activities related to extending credit to the merchant's customers and assume the risk that accompanies credit-related activities. A typical factor investigates the creditworthiness of customers, establishes available credit lines for those customers, does the bookkeeping with respect to accounts, sends the billing statements, undertakes collection of the accounts, and assumes the risk of any credit losses. The factor purchases each account at the time the merchant provides its customers with goods or services. Factoring allows the merchant to eliminate a credit department in its business and use the savings to pay the factor.

In exchange for assuming these duties and risks for the merchant, the factor receives compensation according to the terms of the factoring agreement. The parties negotiate the amount typically based on a percentage of the value of the accounts purchased, such as between 1 and 2 percent.[58] Whether the amount is higher or lower depends on factors such as the number of accounts handled, the average value of each account, the projected volume, and the expected losses.

The factoring business is highly specialized and requires careful assessment of all relevant criteria. Keeping compensation low creates a competitive advantage that attracts business, but miscalculations can have disastrous consequences for a factor.

---

54. A factor is subject to "all terms of the agreement between the account debtor and the assignor and any defense or claim in recoupment arising from the transaction that gave rise to the contract" unless the account debtor entered into an enforceable agreement not to assert defenses or claims. U.C.C. § 9-404(a)(1). *See* Systran Fin. Servs. Corp. v. Giant Cement Holding, Inc., 252 F. Supp. 2d 500, 50 U.C.C. Rep. Serv. 2d 305 (N.D. Ohio 2003) (factor bound by arbitration clause in agreement between debtor and account debtor). Hence, many factoring agreements provide for a right of recourse when the account debtor fails to pay because of a defect in the goods or services or if the account debtor does not have a satisfactory credit rating.

55. Although the discussion in this section involves only accounts, Article 9 also governs sales of chattel paper, payment intangibles, and promissory notes. U.C.C. § 9-109(a)(3). For discussion of the rationale for the inclusion of sales of these payment rights and for some aspects of the mechanics of such transactions, see § 1.05, *supra*.

56. U.C.C. § 1-201(b)(35).

57. U.C.C. § 9-203(b)(3)(A).

58. Obviously, amounts negotiated vary with economic conditions. The figures used in the discussion are illustrative only.

Economies of scale and modern credit information networks that use computers enable factors to provide efficient and effective service.

Some merchants cannot wait until the accounts become due to receive the payment from the factor. These merchants can negotiate an advance from the financing agency against some or all of the sales price of the accounts. These advances are relatively expensive, such as 3 percent or more over the prime rate.

[B] Financing against Inventory and Accounts

Rather than sell its accounts to a factor, a merchant that needs money immediately might use its accounts as collateral for a loan. If the merchant uses the accounts as collateral, it commonly collects them and remits the proceeds to the lender to reduce the outstanding indebtedness—i.e., account debtors do not receive notice to pay the lender directly unless the merchant defaults.[59] The merchant also typically bears the entire risk of nonpayment. The merchant must repay its loan to the secured party, and nonpayment by an account debtor will not discharge any part of the merchant's indebtedness.

A merchant alternatively might seek to use its inventory as collateral. Lenders do not generally consider inventory to be a particularly desirable form of collateral, however, because of certain practical difficulties. With "big-ticket" items, lenders often insist that debtors remit a percentage of the proceeds of each sale to reduce the outstanding indebtedness, but desperate debtors can sell "out of trust," diverting proceeds for use in their day-to-day operations. Other problems accompany a foreclosure. If a merchant defaults because it could not sell its inventory, a secured lender will not likely fare any better. Problems such as obsolescence and erroneous judgment concerning consumer tastes can leave the lender greatly under-collateralized notwithstanding the high costs associated with the acquisition of the inventory. Even if the inventory has good value, the secured lender faces the necessity of making a forced sale of a large volume of merchandise. The value of the inventory often diminishes considerably following default.

Because of these problems and risks, many secured lenders pursue conservative strategies when lending against inventory. Lenders usually will not advance more than a small percentage of the value of the dealer's inventory. In other words, lenders typically require very high loan-to-value ratios. For example, a lender may be willing to advance only 25 to 40 percent of the inventory's value. A 40 percent loan-to-value ratio means that for every dollar of inventory acquired by the dealer, the lender is willing to advance only forty cents.

Because the amounts available for financing against inventory are so low, most parties seek alternatives. One approach is a warehousing arrangement that reduces the

---

59. The parties can agree in their security agreement to instruct the account debtors to pay the secured party prior to default. Payments received by the secured party reduce the outstanding indebtedness. *See* U.C.C. § 9-607(a) (secured party may notify account debtors to remit payments directly to the secured party pursuant to either its agreement with the debtor or, in any event, on default).

risks associated with inventory financing.[60] Another approach is to floor plan inventory that consists of big-ticket items.[61] Inventory financing also is often used in conjunction with accounts financing or factoring.[62] Accounts are generally more attractive than inventory as collateral. The merchant creates accounts when it sells or leases its inventory to willing buyers or lessees, eliminating concerns about the merchant's ability to sell or lease the goods and the realistic value of the goods. A lender usually can better assess the value of a merchant's accounts than predict the value of its inventory in a forced-sale context. The lender generally can proceed more easily in the event of default against a merchant's accounts than against the bulk of its inventory. The marketplace reflects these advantages. A secured lender might be willing to advance as much as 85 percent of the face value of quality accounts.

Accounts financing provides a merchant with great flexibility. It can borrow more money against new accounts as they are created. It can use the proceeds of accounts that it collects to repay the borrowed funds. Many agreements provide a merchant with an assured line of credit that it can draw upon as needed. The percentage of collateralization agreed upon in the security agreement establishes the limit to the credit. The costs of this financing can be fairly high, such as 6 or 7 percent over the prime rate. The advantage, however, is that the merchant has to pay that amount only on the outstanding balance. The merchant can reduce its capital costs by keeping its balance low. It has the credit line, however, to take advantage of business opportunities that require liquidity.

Accounts financing poses significant risks of fraud. A merchant that encounters severe cash-flow difficulties may succumb to the temptation to use an accounts-financing arrangement as a means to obtain additional money. Because the merchant can borrow based on the volume of accounts generated in its business, it might falsify some accounts in the hope that it can borrow and repay the additional funds without the secured lender's learning of its dishonest activity. Falsification of accounts is tempting because they are so easy to fabricate.

Commercial finance companies that lend against accounts employ mechanisms to detect fraud in order to minimize losses. They often seek verifications from the identified customers of the merchant to ascertain whether they really ordered and received the stated goods or services. They often insist that payments to the merchant be remitted to the lender without a change in form. One example of this practice is a "lock-box" arrangement in which account debtors receive instructions to send checks payable to the merchant to a particular post office box that the lender controls. The security agreement authorizes the lender to collect the checks, thereby reducing the indebtedness. Secured lenders also make unannounced inspections of a merchant's

---

60. For discussion of warehousing arrangements, see § 6.02[B], *infra.*

61. For discussion of floor planning, see § 3.04[C], *infra.*

62. Indeed, a security interest in inventory attaches automatically to the accounts that are proceeds of that inventory. For discussion of proceeds generally, see § 2.03, *supra.* For discussion of priorities in accounts that are proceeds of inventory, see § 10.05, *infra.*

books and records, using personnel with special training to detect signs of fraudulent accounts. Lenders should carefully supervise their personnel to minimize the risk of collusion between inspectors and merchants.

Because controls against the risk of fraud impose higher costs on accounts financers, accounts financing is economically feasible only if a merchant has a high volume of accounts. Depending on the nature of the business and the types of accounts created, lenders commonly require a volume of between $500,000 and $1 million in outstanding accounts at any given time. Merchants with smaller volumes that need advances against accounts must factor their accounts and draw some of the payment price as an advance. The choice between accounts financing and factoring of accounts thus often is not made by the merchant but rather by the market forces that impose restrictions based on the volume of business. Factoring can be a good source of immediate liquidity, but it does not provide the flexibility available with accounts financing.

[C] Floor-Planning Inventory

Parties commonly use one of the most attractive forms of inventory financing when a dealer's inventory consists of big-ticket items, such as automobiles, construction equipment, or manufactured homes. Suppliers of such goods generally do not deliver them on consignment or even extend much credit to their dealers. They generally insist that dealers pay at least most of the price at the time of delivery. Because most dealers do not have that kind of liquidity, they need to finance the acquisition of their inventories. Floor planning is the predominant method.

Floor planning consists of a two-part transaction. In the first part, the lender provides the funds to pay all or most of the dealer's costs in acquiring big-ticket items and takes back a purchase-money security interest that attaches to each item.[63] The purchase-money status of the lender enables it to prevail with respect to the goods it finances against any prior secured party with an interest in the dealer's inventory. For example, the dealer might have secured an operating loan from another lender with a blanket lien on all its assets, including inventory.[64]

The second part of floor planning concerns the dealer's retail transactions. Most buyers of big-ticket items cannot afford to pay cash and thus must finance their purchases. The dealer could sell to a buyer on an unsecured basis, thereby generating an account. Given the amounts involved, however, a secured sale that involves the creation of chattel paper is much more likely. In the retail market, chattel paper generally consists of a single record, sometimes called a "retail installment sales contract," that combines the payment obligation and a security interest.[65] The buyer can also create chattel paper

---

63. For discussion of purchase-money security interests, see § 10.04, *infra*.
64. For a discussion of priority in this context, see § 10.04 [B][2], *infra*.
65. Chattel paper is also generated if the dealer leases the goods. U.C.C. § 9-102(a)(11).

by issuing a promissory note to the dealer for the unpaid purchase price, together with a security agreement granting the dealer a security interest in the item purchased.[66]

The availability of a security interest is valuable for big-ticket items like automobiles because the value of the item and the existence of established markets for used goods of the type mean that the secured party can readily convert the item into cash if repossession becomes necessary. Of course, a dealer too strapped for cash to purchase its inventory without outside financing is not going to be in a position to carry the paper of its customers who will be paying on the chattel paper over a period of several years. The solution is to sell the chattel paper to the secured lender.[67]

The retail side can be the most attractive aspect of floor planning to the lender. The finance charge included in the chattel paper often is quite high, which enables the buyer of the chattel paper to realize a good return. The secured lender often finances the dealer's acquisition of inventory at a relatively attractive rate of interest as the means to assure itself of acquiring the dealer's chattel paper with its high interest rate. The security agreement may link these two transactions with a requirement that the dealer sell all of its chattel paper to the secured lender.

---

66. For discussion of chattel paper, see § 1.04[B][3], *supra*.

67. Sales of chattel paper, like sales of accounts, payment intangibles, and promissory notes, are within the scope of Article 9. *See generally* § 1.05, *supra*. For discussion of the similar practice of factoring accounts, see § 3.04[A], *supra*. The parties to a sale of chattel paper often agree that the dealer will buy the paper back if the account debtor (or the obligor, if the chattel paper includes a negotiable instrument) defaults, thereby shifting to the dealer the costs associated with foreclosing on the underlying big-ticket item.

Part III

Perfection of Security Interests

Synopsis

The creation of a security interest in one or more items of a debtor's property creates a problem sometimes identified as the "ostensible-ownership" problem.[1] When the debtor grants a security interest to a secured party, this typically does not happen in a public event obvious to third parties or widely reported in news outlets. Third parties who are engaging in negotiations or transactions with the debtor may have no idea that the debtor has granted a security interest in some or all of its assets. These third parties could thus agree to buy, or take a security interest in, some or all of those assets—even though they presumably would not do so if they knew of the secured party's prior interest. This can result in a priority dispute where multiple persons claim competing interests in the same property. An array of potential claimants is possible—including, *inter alia*, a purchaser (other than a secured party), another secured party, or a lien creditor (e.g., a trustee in bankruptcy). Part IV, *infra*, addresses the priority rules that govern the resolution of these competing claims. The concern in Part III is to focus on the options for how a secured party can perfect its security interest to enhance the likelihood that it will prevail in a subsequent priority dispute with one or more competing claimants.

Satisfying one of the designated options the Code identifies in Article 9, Part 3 perfects a security interest. Attachment of a security interest establishes the relationship between the secured party and the debtor and gives the secured party a special property interest in the collateral.[2] Perfection is relevant only to the secured party's position vis-à-vis third-party claims to the collateral. Perfection generally has no bearing on the relationship between the debtor and the secured party; where there are no competing third-party interests, an unperfected secured party has the right to enforce its security interest in the event of default.[3] By perfecting the security interest, a secured party

---

1. For an overview of ostensible ownership problems, see § 1.03[B][2], *supra*.

2. Farmers' State Bank of Palestine v. Yealick, 69 Ill. App. 3d 353, 387 N.E.2d 399, 26 U.C.C. Rep. Serv. 509 (1979) (even an unperfected security interest is enforceable against the debtor); Melancon v. Countrywide Bank, 73 U.C.C. Rep. Serv. 2d 739 (E.D. La. 2011) (unperfected security interest valid between the secured party and the debtor).

3. Doyle v. Northrop Corp., 455 F. Supp. 1318, 25 U.C.C. Rep. Serv. 932 (D.N.J. 1978) (determining the sufficiency of financing statement to perfect security interest is unnecessary in an action between debtor and secured party because perfection only affects priority among competing claimants and is

reduces the risk that a third-party claimant can successfully assert a superior claim to the collateral.

Although Article 9 recognizes a variety of methods of perfection, the general principle underlying the concept is simple. Perfection generally requires the secured party to take specific steps deemed sufficient to publicize its interest to other parties that might obtain an interest in the same property—in other words, to address (if not cure) the ostensible-ownership problem. Perfection thus typically entails the steps that a secured party must take to provide adequate public notice of the existence of its security interest.[4] Although perfection does not guarantee priority against all potential competing claimants, it substantially improves the secured party's chances of achieving priority.

---

irrelevant to validity of security interest). The statement in the text assumes that the obligor has not filed for bankruptcy. If the obligor files for bankruptcy, the Bankruptcy Code permits the bankruptcy trustee to invalidate an unperfected security interest. *See* § 16.04[B][1], *infra*.

4. Perfection sometimes occurs automatically without providing notice to third parties. *See* § 4.01[C], *infra*.

Chapter 4

Perfection in General

Synopsis

§ 4.01 The Alternative Methods of Perfection—§ 9-310

Article 9 identifies eight different methods by which secured parties may perfect a security interest. Section 9-310 describes the various alternatives, with applicable cross-references to other sections. The availability of any given method of perfection depends on the kind of personal property used for the collateral. More than one method of perfection is often available, with different methods of perfection usually providing different levels of protection against third-party claimants (although every method provides protection against lien creditors, including a trustee in bankruptcy). The method chosen by the secured party frequently reflects an assessment of the practicality of alternative methods and the risks associated with the available methods. For example, if the collateral is manufacturing equipment in the hands of a debtor, it is impractical for the secured party to perfect by taking possession of the equipment because the debtor needs to use the equipment in manufacturing its products; however, perfection by the filing of a financing statement in the Article 9 filing records may be ideal.

[A] Filing a Financing Statement

Article 9's default perfection rule requires the filing of a financing statement to perfect all security interests and agricultural liens.[5] All other methods of perfection are exceptions to this general rule.[6]

A financing statement is a simple form filed in the appropriate public-filing office to enable interested parties to obtain information indicating the possibility of a security interest in personal property of the debtor. It is analogous to the public filing of a mortgage or deed of trust to show to potential buyers or mortgagees of real property that a mortgage interest already exists in that real property. The filing systems for personal property and for real property are distinct, however, and a financing statement is considerably simpler than a real estate filing. Chapter 5 provides extensive coverage of perfection by filing a financing statement.

[B] Possession

A secured party generally may perfect a security interest in goods or in any other tangible asset by taking possession of the collateral.[7] With respect to tangible money, other than tangible money that is cash proceeds of other collateral, perfection by possession is the only method available.[8] Filing is available with respect to other tangible assets, but possession maximizes the secured party's protection from third-party claimants. Chapter 6, *infra*, discusses perfection by possession.

[C] Automatic Perfection

In a few circumstances, a security interest becomes automatically perfected when it attaches even if the secured party takes no other steps to publicize its interest.[9] Chapter 7, *infra*, explores the policy justifications and implications of exempting the applicable transactions from the normal public-notice requirements.

[D] Temporary Perfection

Article 9 allows automatic perfection of a limited duration in certain circumstances.[10] Temporary perfection is possible with instruments, certificated securities, negotiable documents, and goods in the possession of a bailee other than one that issued a

---

5. U.C.C. § 9-310(a).

6. U.C.C. § 9-310(b) (listing exceptions), and Comment 2 to that section.

7. U.C.C. §§ 9-310(b)(6), 9-313.

8. U.C.C. § 9-312(b)(3). A security interest in identifiable cash proceeds of the original collateral is perfected as long as the secured party properly perfected its security interest in the original collateral. U.C.C. § 9-315(c), (d)(2).

9. U.C.C. §§ 9-310(b)(2), 9-309.

10. U.C.C. § 9-310(b)(5), (9).

negotiable document for them.[11] Temporary perfection is also generally available with respect to certain kinds of proceeds of collateral.[12] Chapter 8, *infra*, explains the details of temporary perfection.

[E] Perfection under Federal Law

Federal law includes some requirements concerning methods of perfecting a security interest in certain types of collateral.[13] For example, the Federal Aviation Act requires a security interest in an airplane to be perfected by filing with the Federal Aviation Administration.[14] Bowing to principles of federal preemption, Article 9 recognizes that filing a financing statement is not required and cannot even be effective to perfect a security interest if a federal statute or treaty provides for the use of a national or international registration system, a national or international certificate of title, or otherwise requires a different method of perfection than compliance with Article 9.[15]

[F] State Certificate-of-Title Statute

All states have enacted certificate-of-title statutes that cover motor vehicles and that may cover similar goods, such as trailers, boats, manufactured homes, and tractors. In addition to establishing a presumption of ownership of the designated goods in favor of the person shown as title-holder on a certificate issued by the state, these statutes also provide for a person holding a lien on those goods to have information about the existence of a security interest in the goods noted on the face of the certificate (if written) or stored in an electronic record associated with the certificate (if the state maintains certificates in electronic form). Generally, providing that information on or in a record associated with the certificate of title is the best method of giving notice to third parties, and thus Article 9 provides that compliance with the certificate-of-title act is the exclusive method of perfecting a security interest in the designated classes of goods,[16] except when they are held for sale or lease by a person in the business of selling

---

11. U.C.C. § 9-312(e), (f), (g).

12. U.C.C. § 9-315(c), (d). With the satisfaction of certain conditions, temporary perfection in proceeds extends automatically beyond the applicable period, thereby constituting a form of extended automatic perfection.

13. For discussion of federal preemption, see § 1.06[A], *supra*.

14. 49 U.S.C. § 1403; *In re* AvCentral, Inc., 289 B.R. 170, 49 U.C.C. Rep. Serv. 2d 1336 (Bankr. D. Kan. 2003).

15. U.C.C. §§ 9-310(b)(3), 9-311(a)(1).

16. *See, e.g., In re* Morgan, 291 B.R. 795, 50 U.C.C. Rep. Serv. 2d 596 (Bankr. E.D. Tenn. 2003) (exclusive method in Tennessee to perfect a security interest in automobiles not part of inventory is through notation of the interest on certificate of title in compliance with the state's motor vehicle title and registration laws, and secured party cannot supplement these laws with principles based on equitable doctrine of subrogation); *In re* Charley's Automotive, Inc., 50 U.C.C. Rep. Serv. 2d 927 (M.D. Ga. 2003) (secured creditor possession of certificates of title signed by seller of the vehicles insufficient for perfection because security interest was not noted on the certificates).

goods of that kind.[17] To achieve consistency with these state statutes, Article 9 provides that, with the exception noted in the previous sentence, the filing of a financing statement is neither necessary nor effective to perfect a security interest in collateral within the scope of a state certificate-of-title statute.[18] Chapter 9, *infra*, details the nuances posed by these statutes.[19]

[G] Control

The primary method to perfect a security interest in deposit accounts, controllable accounts, controllable electronic records, controllable payment intangibles, letter-of-credit rights, investment property, and electronic chattel paper is control.[20] Control is the exclusive method to perfect a security interest in deposit accounts,[21] letter-of-credit rights,[22] and electronic money;[23] it is optional for perfection of an interest in investment property and electronic chattel paper.[24] Control takes different forms depending on the type of asset. Chapter 6, *infra*, covers the specifics on perfection by control.

[H] Delivery

Article 9 permits a security interest in a certificated security in registered form to be perfected by delivery of the security certificate to the secured party even though the indorsement necessary for the secured party to take control is missing.[25] Delivery is nothing more than possession of the security certificate, but the term conforms Article 9 with the terminology of Article 8.[26]

---

17. U.C.C. §9-311(d). The exception, for example, permits a secured party to perfect a security interest in the inventory of a car dealer by filing a financing statement.

18. U.C.C. §§9-310(b)(3); 9-311(a)(2), (3). *But see* Carcorp, Inc. v. Bombardier Cap., Inc., 272 B.R. 365, 47 U.C.C. Rep. Serv. 2d 374 (Bankr. S.D. Fla. 2002) (motor vehicles that are part of a debtor dealer's inventory must be perfected by filing a financing statement rather than through the certificate-of-title statute.).

19. *See* §9.06, *infra*.

20. U.C.C. §§9-314(a), 9-106.

21. U.C.C. §§9-312(b)(1), 9-104.

22. U.C.C. §§9-312(b)(2), 9-107.

23. Electronic money is a new term introduced by the 2022 amendments and refers to money issued by a government in electronic form, as opposed to the traditional, tangible form. U.C.C. §9-102(a)(31A). Electronic money is sometimes referred to as a central bank digital currency, or CBDC. Virtual currencies like Bitcoin that are not issued by a government are not electronic money.

24. U.C.C. §§9-314(a), 9-105.

25. U.C.C. §9-313(a).

26. U.C.C. §8-301(a)(1) (delivery requires possession of the security certificate).

§ 4.02 When Perfection Occurs— § 9-308(a)

A security interest becomes perfected at the moment of attachment *and* satisfaction of the applicable steps for perfection.[27] In other words, the secured party must satisfy all of the steps for both attachment and perfection before perfection occurs.[28] The Code does not recognize the perfection of an interest that does not exist.[29] It allows for completion of the steps in any order; if the applicable steps required for perfection are completed prior to attachment, perfection is delayed until the security interest attaches.[30] Perfection occurs at the point in time of satisfaction of all the requirements for both attachment and perfection.

Because of practical aspects of achieving priority that we address later,[31] a prospective secured party sometimes wants to complete the applicable steps for perfection before the security interest attaches. For example, when the parties are about to reach a final agreement, a lender might insist that the prospective debtor authorize the filing of a financing statement that the lender then files in the appropriate office. The debtor might not sign the written security agreement or the secured party might not give value, each of which is a requirement for attachment to occur, until after filing of the financing statement. The order of completion of each requirement does not matter,[32] but fulfillment of all of the requirements for both attachment and perfection is required for a perfected security interest.

The opportunity to file a financing statement prior to attachment is also significant in the context of an after-acquired property clause. A security interest in property acquired by the debtor after initial attachment cannot attach until the debtor obtains rights in the after-acquired property.[33] The secured party, nevertheless, can file a financing statement with respect to the original collateral, and, if the description in the financing statement is sufficient to describe the after-acquired collateral, the financing

---

27. U.C.C. § 9-308(a). In the case of automatic perfection, the only requirement is attachment. *Id.*; U.C.C. § 9-309.

28. In *In re* Browning, 66 B.R. 79, 2 U.C.C. Rep. Serv. 2d 724 (S.D. Ill. 1986), a financing statement filed in 1983 described the collateral as the debtor's crops to be grown during 1983 through 1987. Perfection did not occur immediately for the later crops, because perfection requires attachment, and attachment requires that the debtor have rights in the collateral. *See also In re* Lanzatella, 254 B.R. 84, 42 U.C.C. Rep. Serv. 2d 1156 (Bankr. W.D.N.Y. 2000) (creditor complied with the perfection requirements but did not have a written agreement that created a security interest).

29. Bradley v. K&E Inv., Inc., 847 S.W.2d 915, 22 U.C.C. Rep. Serv. 2d 915 (Mo. Ct. App. 1993) (lender that failed to enter an agreement that met requirements for a security agreement could not have perfected security interest in cars of debtor).

30. U.C.C. § 9-308(a).

31. *See* §§ 5.04, 10.01, *infra.*

32. NBD-Sandusky Bank v. Ritter, 437 Mich. 354, 471 N.W.2d 340, 15 U.C.C. Rep. Serv. 2d 260 (1991) (order of applicable steps is not determinative for perfection).

33. *See* §§ 2.02[C], 3.02[A], *supra.*

statement filed with respect to the original collateral will also be sufficient to perfect the security interest in after-acquired collateral of the same type.[34] The secured party then will have perfected status in the after-acquired collateral as soon as the debtor obtains rights in that collateral.[35]

§ 4.03 Continuity of Perfection— § 9-308(c)

A secured party can use more than one method of perfection and remain continuously perfected through the process of tacking. With the use of different but nevertheless appropriate methods of perfection, the security interest is deemed to be continuously perfected from the date of the original perfection, *provided* that the interest does not become unperfected during any interim period.[36] Tacking cannot bridge a gap during which the interest was unperfected, meaning that the subsequent perfection would date only from the time of completion of the steps necessary to achieve perfection taken after the gap. Allowing a gap to occur endangers the secured party's interest because the rules of priority generally follow the principle of first-in-time, first-in-right. A secured party thus wants to establish rights based on the earliest point in time.

A simple example illustrates the application of the continuity-of-perfection provision. Assume that a secured party takes a security interest in the debtor's stamp collection on March 1 and perfects the interest by taking possession of the collection. On August 31, the parties agree that the secured party will return the collection to the debtor so that the debtor can remount several of the stamps. The secured party decides to perfect the interest further by filing a financing statement, which it accomplishes on September 1. Filing the financing statement before relinquishment of possession of the collection makes the security interest continuously perfected through tacking from March 1.[37] Return of the collection to the debtor prior to the filing, however,

---

34. A previously filed financing statement, however, is insufficient to perfect an interest in after-acquired property if the parties do not have a security agreement. J.I. Case Credit Corp. v. Foos, 11 Kan. App. 2d 185, 717 P.2d 1064, 1 U.C.C. Rep. Serv. 2d 250 (1986).

35. Bank of the West v. Commercial Credit Fin. Servs, Inc., 852 F.2d 1162, 6 U.C.C. Rep. Serv. 2d 602 (9th Cir. 1988) (bank acquired perfected security interest in debtor's after-acquired inventory).

36. U.C.C. § 9-308(c). *See* Mims v. First Citizens Bank, 913 So. 2d 1098, 56 U.C.C. Rep. Serv. 2d 383 (Ala. Ct. App. 2005) (even though assignor's financing statement lapsed and assignee filed its statement after lapse had occurred, assignee had continuous perfection, initially under the assignor's filing and subsequently through the assignee's possession of the collateral on the date of assignment and prior to lapse).

37. The reverse sequence of perfecting methods provided continuous perfection in *First Interstate Bank of Arizona, N.A. v. Interfund Corp.*, 924 F.2d 588, 14 U.C.C. Rep. Serv. 2d 247 (5th Cir. 1991). A security interest in a horse farm's chattel paper perfected originally by filing and subsequently by possession was deemed to be continuously perfected.

leaves an intervening period of unperfection. The perfected status then dates only from September 1, the date of filing.[38] The secured party will be vulnerable to any competing interest that arose between March 1 and September 1, a result that could have been avoided by maintaining continuity of perfection.

---

38. *See In re* Stewart, 74 B.R. 350, 4 U.C.C. Rep. Serv. 2d 271 (Bankr. M.D. Ga. 1987) (secured party became unperfected upon releasing possession of diamond ring back to debtor because the execution of a document to the effect that debtor held ring in trust for secured party was not an adequate method of subsequent perfection).

Chapter 5

Perfection by Filing

Synopsis

§ 5.01 General Method— § 9-310(a)

By filing a form that includes a limited amount of required information in a designated public office, a secured party publicly announces the possibility that it holds a security interest to any third parties concerned enough to search the public files. The filing of a financing statement for purposes of perfecting a security interest is somewhat analogous to the public recording of a mortgage to indicate an encumbrance on real estate.[1] Third parties considering a transaction with the debtor concerning personal property in which a security interest can be perfected by filing should first examine the filing records for a financing statement evidencing someone else's possible interest in that property.

The default method for perfecting an Article 9 security interest is to file a financing statement.[2] Alternative methods of perfection are available in numerous situations, but these alternatives are exceptions to the general rule.[3] Article 9, Part 5, covers the filing process. This chapter explains and analyzes its provisions.

§ 5.02 What Constitutes Filing— § 9-516

As explained below, Article 9 envisions the possibility of a variety of filings in the public records, including initial financing statements, various amendments (including continuation and termination statements), and information statements. The generic term "record" refers to any of these filings.[4] If the objective of a filing is the initial perfection of a security interest, the required record is an "initial financing statement."

---

1. The analogy is not perfect. A mortgagee records the mortgage document itself, and thus a prospective mortgage lender practically cannot "pre-record" a mortgage before the mortgage is actually executed. By contrast, as discussed in §§ 5.04 and 10.01, *infra*, a secured party contemplating a secured transaction in personal property can "pre-file" a financing statement in advance, even before the parties actually execute the security agreement and the security interest attaches.

2. U.C.C. § 9-310(a). The same section requires filing to perfect an agricultural lien. *Id.*

3. U.C.C. § 9-310(b). *See generally* Chapter 4, *supra*.

4. "Record" means "information that is inscribed on a tangible medium or which is stored in an electronic or other medium and is retrievable in perceivable form." U.C.C. § 9-102(a)(70).

The term "financing statement" means the sum of the filed records, including the initial financing statement and any subsequent filings that relate to it.

Filing can occur in either of two ways: (1) "communication of a record to a filing office and tender of the filing fee" or (2) "acceptance of the record by the filing office."[5] Filing does not require completion of the ministerial task of "indexing" the record, that is, properly entering the information in the record into the files maintained by the office for access by searchers.[6] Because secured parties cannot complete this task—which is the responsibility of the filing office—secured parties are not responsible for errors made by filing officers in indexing a record.[7]

The first method of filing requires the communication of a record to the filing office and tender of the filing fee. "Communicate" in the case of the transmission of a record to a filing office is limited to the means of transmission prescribed by filing-office rule.[8] This approach maximizes the opportunities for filing officers to authorize the use of technology in the transmission of records.

A record properly communicated to an office does not become a filed record if the filing office rejects it for certain statutorily defined reasons.[9] The responsibilities of the filing office with regard to acceptance and rejection of a record are purely ministerial; Section 9-520(a) provides that "[a] filing office shall refuse to accept a record for a reason set forth in Section 9-516(b) and may refuse to accept a record for filing *only* for a reason set forth in Section 9-516(b)."[10] Although the discussion below covers the specifics in detail,[11] Section 9-516(b) lists as reasons to reject an initial financing statement the following: communication by a method that is not authorized, failure to tender the filing fee, omission of a required description of the real property to which the initial financing statement relates,[12] a failure to provide a name and mailing address for the debtor and the secured party of record,[13] and the omission of certain required information for a debtor that is an organization.[14]

---

5. U.C.C. § 9-516(a).

6. U.C.C. § 9-517 ("The failure of the filing office to index a record correctly does not affect the effectiveness of the filed record.").

7. *In re* Masters, 273 B.R. 773, 47 U.C.C. Rep. Serv. 2d 398 (Bankr. E.D. Ark. 2002) (secured party was properly perfected and did not bear the risk that the filing officer would erroneously terminate the financing statement without authorization of the secured party); Chattanooga Agricultural Ass'n v. Sapp, 54 U.C.C. Rep. Serv. 2d 114 (Tenn. Ct. App. 2004) (secured party that complied with filing requirements perfected even though financing statement and attached exhibit detailing collateral were never indexed into the records).

8. U.C.C. § 9-102(a)(18)(C).

9. U.C.C. § 9-516(b).

10. U.C.C. § 520(a) (emphasis supplied).

11. *See* § 5.02, *infra.*

12. A description of real estate is necessary only for a financing statement that serves as a fixture filing or that covers as-extracted collateral or standing timber. *See* U.C.C. § 9-502(b).

13. A secured party of record is "a person whose name is provided as the name of the secured party or a representative of the secured party in an initial financing statement that has been filed." U.C.C. § 9-511(a).

14. See also § 5.03[A], *infra,* on the required content for initial financing statements.

Under Section 9-520(a), the list in Section 9-516(b) serves not only to establish the exclusive grounds for which a filing officer *may* reject a record communicated for filing; it provides that the filing officer *must* reject a record for those reasons. Nevertheless, if a filing officer fails in this duty and accepts a record that the officer should have rejected, filing of the record occurs.[15] If the filing officer neither accepts nor rejects a communicated record but the filing fee is tendered, filing is deemed to have occurred.

Because "filing" occurs before the filing officer performs the ministerial act of indexing the filing in the name of the debtor, a gap can exist between the time of perfection and the time a searcher can reasonably learn of the fact of perfection. Anyone conducting a search during this interim may be misled by the failure of the search to show a recent filing that is nevertheless effective. Contributing further to a searcher's concern is the fact that filings sometimes become backlogged, even though the filing office is required to complete the indexing within two business days after filing occurs.[16]

As between a searcher and a secured party that communicates a financing statement for filing, the latter might appear to be in the better position to initiate action that might alleviate the misleading appearances attributable to filing delays and errors; that is, the filing party could initiate a search for its own financing statement to determine whether the filing office handled it properly. Imposition of a search obligation on the filing party would, however, shift a significant risk to that party because the timing of effective filing can be crucial in deciding the outcome of a priority dispute.[17] The drafters chose not to impose this obligation on filers.[18]

Because parties that conduct searches bear much of the risk of these latent problems in the filing system, those parties should be aware of how to protect their interests as much as possible. For example, they should be aware of the extent of the backlog in filings in jurisdictions in which they conduct searches. A prospective purchaser (e.g., a buyer or a secured party) can then, before consummating a transaction with the debtor, insist upon protecting itself until that backlog clears. For example, a secured lender could insist on waiting for the backlog to clear after making its filing before giving value.

Article 9 addresses the backlog problem through two approaches. First, it requires the filing office to respond to a search request no later than two business days after receiving it,[19] and the information provided to the searcher must be current based on a date no earlier than three business days before receipt of the request.[20] Because filing offices sometimes cannot comply with such time requirements, the drafters included

---

15. U.C.C. § 9-516(a).

16. U.C.C. § 9-519(h).

17. Recognizing the critical role of time of filing, Article 9 requires filing officers to mark the time of filing on each financing statement. U.C.C. §§ 9-519(a)(2), 9-523. It does not include a specific requirement on how to determine the time of filing. This determination is to be made by rules adopted by each filing office. U.C.C. § 9-519, Comment 4.

18. U.C.C. §§ 9-519(a), 9-517.

19. U.C.C. § 9-523(e).

20. U.C.C. § 9-523(c)(1). Section 9-526 imposes requirements on the appropriate official or agency to adopt and publish rules consistent with Article 9. Delays beyond the prescribed time limits are

another provision aimed at surmounting the backlog problem. A filing office or the appropriate official must offer to sell or license to the public, on a nonexclusive basis, copies of all records filed with it.[21] It must provide the copies in bulk in every medium available to the filing office and make them available at least weekly. This provision facilitates access to the records by private companies that maintain parallel filing systems. If the official filing office fails to meet its mandate to file financing statements in the time prescribed, searchers can choose to rely on such privately maintained systems.

A searcher is additionally vulnerable to an effective financing statement that the filing officer accepted but which the search cannot reveal because the filing officer lost it prior to indexing it or misindexed it.[22] Under Section 9-517, the failure of the filing office to index a record correctly does not affect the filed record's effectiveness, even if the error makes it difficult or impossible for later searchers to find the record.[23]

§ 5.03 What to File

[A] Requirements—§§ 9-502, 9-516(b)

Section 9-502 sets forth the information that a filed financing statement *must* contain for it to be sufficient to perfect a security interest. To be effective, an initial financing statement must include:

- the name of the debtor;
- the name of the secured party or a representative of the secured party;
- an indication of the collateral covered; and
- a real property description, but only if the collateral is as-extracted collateral or timber to be cut, or if the financing statement constitutes a fixture filing.[24]

---

excusable for circumstances beyond the control of the filing office, provided that it exercises reasonable diligence under the circumstances. U.C.C. §9-524.

21. U.C.C. §9-523(f).

22. Some courts have held filing officers liable for losses to searchers caused by their errors. *See, e.g.*, Hudleasco, Inc. v. State, 90 Misc. 2d 1057, 396 N.Y.S.2d 1002, 22 U.C.C. Rep. Serv. 545 (Ct. Cl. 1977) (error by filing officer in certifying absence of prior financing statement). The claims lie in negligence, however, and governmental immunity may be available under state tort law. After the Kansas Supreme Court in *Borg-Warner Acceptance Corp. v. Secretary of State*, 240 Kan. 598, 731 P.2d 301, 2 U.C.C. Rep. Serv. 2d 1725 (1987), upheld negligence liability of the secretary of state for several certifications that failed to disclose a prior filing, the Kansas legislature amended Article 9 to grant immunity to filing officers in conducting searches. A common response in jurisdictions in which filing officers remain potentially subject to claims for loss is for the officers to reduce their risk by offering very little assistance to searchers.

In addition to filing officers, abstract companies hired to conduct a search have been sued for negligence. *See, e.g.*, Chemical Bank v. Title Servs., Inc., 708 F. Supp. 245, 9 U.C.C. Rep. Serv. 2d 402 (D. Minn. 1989) (title abstractor found not negligent for failing to conduct search under various misspellings of debtor's name).

23. *See, e.g., In re* Feed Store, LLC, 95 U.C.C. Rep. Serv. 2d 339 (Bankr. N.D. W. Va. 2018).

24. U.C.C. §9-502(a), (b).

An initial financing statement that does not contain this minimal information is not sufficient and thus is not effective to perfect a security interest[25] even if the filing officer accepts it.[26]

Section 9-516(b) lists the following additional information that must be included in an initial financing statement:[27]

- a mailing address for the debtor;
- a mailing address for the secured party; and
- an indication whether the debtor is an individual or an organization.

This additional information is required because a filing officer may,[28] and in fact must,[29] reject a financing statement that does not include it. At the same time, this additional information is not necessary for the financing statement to be legally sufficient to perfect a security interest in the indicated collateral; only the Section 9-502(a) required information is necessary for the financing statement to be effective. If the filing officer accepts an initial financing statement that satisfies Section 9-502(a) but that should have been rejected because it lacks some of the additional Section 9-516(b) information, the financing statement is still effective,[30] meaning that the security interest is perfected.[31] In summary, even if the filing officer is required to reject an initial financing statement for the omission of any of the information listed in Section 9-516(b), the filed financing statement is nevertheless legally sufficient to perfect a security interest if the filing officer accepts it anyway and it contains the information required by Section 9-502.

If a filing officer rejects a record, the officer must communicate the reason for the rejection to the person that communicated the record.[32] If a filing officer rejects a record for a reason not specified in the statute, filing is deemed to have occurred

---

25. U.C.C. § 9-502(a), (b).

26. U.C.C. § 9-520(c). Section 9-516(b) provides a list of reasons why a filing officer must reject (i.e., refuse to accept for filing) a record. If the record omits the debtor's name or the secured party's name, or omits the land description for a real-property-related filing, the filing officer must reject it. U.C.C. § 9-520(a) ("A filing office shall refuse to accept a record for filing for a reason set forth in Section 9-516(b) ..."); U.C.C. § 9-516(b)(3)(A) (name of the debtor); (b)(4) (name of the secured party); (b)(3)(D) (real property descriptions). Oddly, Section 9-516(b) does not list omission of an indication of the collateral as a ground for rejection; however, a financing statement can only be effective to perfect a security interest in the indicated collateral, and thus a filed financing statement cannot be legally sufficient without an indication of at least some collateral.

27. For discussion of requirements for other records presented for filing and the filing office's responsibilities regarding such records, see § 5.06, *infra*.

28. U.C.C. § 9-516(b).

29. U.C.C. § 9-520(a).

30. U.C.C. § 9-520(c) ("A filed financing statement satisfying Section 9-502(a) and (b) is effective, even if the filing office is required to refuse to accept it for filing under subsection (a).").

31. U.C.C. § 9-310(a) ("[A] financing statement must be filed to perfect all security interests and agricultural liens.").

32. U.C.C. § 9-520(b) (communication of the reason for rejection must be according to filing-office rules, but in no event more than two days after the filing office receives the record).

anyway—and that deemed filing is effective "except as against a purchaser of the collateral which gives value in reasonable reliance upon the absence of the record from the files."[33] The rationale for this exception is that rejections for invalid reasons should be rare (given the severe restrictions on the filing office's discretion), and the gap in the record caused by an invalid rejection should be short-lived because the filing officer must communicate the reason for the rejection promptly to the secured party, which can then take steps to resolve the problem and get its record filed. Because the rejected filing is ineffective only as to purchasers for value—persons that typically rely on the filing system—a secured party whose initial financing statement is wrongly rejected will still be perfected as against a lien creditor, including a trustee in bankruptcy.

The simplicity of the financing statement stands in sharp contrast to the typical security agreement. Terms in a security agreement that are significant to the parties—such as the extent of indebtedness, the terms for payment, events of default, and covenants regarding the use of the collateral—have no place in a financing statement. Article 9 includes a statutory form which, if completed properly, will be sufficient to qualify as an initial financing statement.[34]

[1] Debtor Names—§ 9-503(a)–(c)

The names of the parties play significant roles in the filing system. The filing officer places financing statements into the public files according to the name of the debtor.[35] This is logical because a searcher will want to ascertain whether a particular person[36] previously granted a security interest in that collateral that would undermine the searcher's anticipated transaction. The basis of this search is that person's name. If the debtor's name as it appears on the financing statement or as it is indexed is incorrect, a search under the debtor's correct name may not reveal the financing statement. Although later discussion will address the effect of mistakes in the debtor's name,[37] it is important to note at the outset that Article 9 has very little tolerance for such mistakes. *Any* mistake in the debtor's name renders the filing presumptively insufficient, with the presumption rebutted only if a search of the files under the correct name, using the

---

33. U.C.C. § 9-516(d).

34. U.C.C. § 9-521(a) (initial financing statement form). The section does not mandate the use of the form; rather, it provides that a filing office that accepts written initial financing statements must accept an initial financing statement in that form. U.C.C. § 9-521(b) provides an all-purpose amendment form.

Prior to 2010, the statutory form contained a box for taxpayer identification or social security numbers. Its inclusion was not mandatory but rather for convenience—the information, if provided, can help searchers distinguish among persons with similar names. The 2010 amendments deleted the box because privacy concerns had caused filing offices in most states to request omission of the information.

35. Article 9 requires that filings be indexed in the name of the debtor. U.C.C. § 9-519(c).

36. "Person" includes an individual or organization. U.C.C. § 1-201(b)(27). "Organization" includes, *inter alia*, corporations, partnerships, associations, and governmental entities.

37. *See* § 5.03[C], *infra*. The section also discusses the effect of post-filing name changes.

filing office's standard logic, would have revealed the mistaken filing.[38] This requirement protects a searcher that exercises due diligence and places pressure on a filer to
provide the debtor's name with precision.

[a] Registered Organizations

Special rules apply if the debtor is a "registered organization." A registered organization is "an organization formed or organized solely under the law of a single State
or the United States[39] by the filing of a public organic record with, the issuance of a
public organic record by, or the enactment of legislation by the State or the United
States."[40] The kinds of organizations covered by the definition are those created by
a public filing, the classic examples being a state-created corporation formed by the
public filing of articles of incorporation and a limited liability company formed by
the public filing of a certificate of formation. Limited partnerships are also registered
organizations. General partnerships, which are formed by contract rather than the
filing of a public record, are not registered organizations. Their status does not change
if the general partnership files a public record for the purpose of becoming a limited
liability partnership.[41]

Article 9 adopted the concept of the registered organization in 1998, and the adoption constituted a significant improvement over prior law. The primary advantage
relates to choice-of-law rules: the law of the debtor's location governs perfection,[42]
and a state-created registered organization is deemed to be located in the state whose
law governs its formation.[43] This designation provides a level of certainty unavailable
under prior law (and even under current Article 9 for organizations that are not registered organizations).[44] A side benefit is the ease of determining the name to use on
a financing statement. The secured party makes this determination by looking to the
"public organic record," which is the document that created the organization (e.g., the
articles of incorporation for a corporation or the certificate of formation for an LLC).[45]
The secured party must use "the name that is stated to be the registered organization's
name on the public organic record most recently filed with or issued or enacted by the

---

38. U.C.C. § 9-506(b), (c).

39. A foreign corporation is not a registered organization, nor is a domestic corporation that has
articles filed in more than one state. Such "double domestications" are rare.

40. U.C.C. § 9-102(a)(71).

41. The filing provides partners with a liability shield but does not relate to the creation of the partnership. *See* Permanent Editorial Board Commentary No. 17, Limited Liability Partnerships under the
Choice of Law Rules of Article 9 (June 29, 2012).

42. U.C.C. § 9-301(1).

43. U.C.C. § 9-307(e).

44. For example, if an organization that is not a registered organization has more than one place of
business, the Code deems the organization to be located at its chief executive office. U.C.C. § 9-307(b)
(3). The determination of which office qualifies as the chief executive office may be difficult if the
organization is large and management is decentralized.

45. U.C.C. § 9-102(a)(68). To qualify as a public organic record, a formation document must be
available to the public for inspection.

registered organization's jurisdiction or organization which purports to state, amend, or restate the registered organization's name."[46]

A state or federal organization might be formed not by the filing of a public organic record but rather by government issuance of a formation document (e.g., a charter for a state bank) or by legislation without the necessity of a formation document. Both types of entities are registered organizations, and the name to be used is the name on the government-issued formation document or in the legislation,[47] each of which constitutes a public organic record.[48] The Code also includes as a registered organization a particular kind of common-law business trust formed by contract rather than by the filing of a formation document. After noting that a common-law trust is ordinarily not a registered organization,[49] the Comments explain the inclusion as follows:

> In some states, however, the trustee of a common-law trust that has a commercial or business purpose is required by statute to file a record in a public office following the trust's formation. See, e.g., Mass. Gen. Laws Ch. 182, § 2; Fla. Stat. Ann. § 609.02. A business trust that is required to file its organic record in a public office is a "registered organization" ... if the filed record is available to the public for inspection.[50]

[b] Decedents' Estates

When an individual dies, it may become necessary for a personal representative to administer the property in the decedent's estate. A financing statement covering such property sufficiently provides the debtor's name only if it contains the "name of the decedent" and also, in a separate part of the financing statement, "indicates that the collateral is being administered by a personal representative."[51] The Code also provides a safe harbor rule for identifying the decedent's name: "the name of the decedent indicated on the order appointing the personal representative of the decedent issued by the court having jurisdiction over the collateral is sufficient as the 'name of the decedent.'"[52]

---

46. U.C.C. § 9-503(a)(1).

47. U.C.C. § 9-102(a)(71).

48. U.C.C. § 9-102(a)(68).

49. Some states have statutes governing the creation of a type of business trust that is formed by the filing with the state of a formation document, and these trusts are (and have always been) within the basic definition of registered organization.

50. U.C.C. § 9-102, Comment 11. The term "organic record" in the statute refers to the document that creates the trust by contract (e.g., the trust indenture). When the organic record is filed as required by statute, it becomes the trust's public organic record and provides the name to be used on a financing statement. U.C.C. §§ 9-102(a)(68) (defining public organic record), 9-503(a)(1) (name to be used on financing statement).

51. U.C.C. § 9-503(a)(2).

52. U.C.C. § 9-503(f). As discussed below, the ordinary individual-name rules rely heavily on the debtor's name as it appears on an unexpired driver's license, which would not be appropriate in the context of a decedent.

[c] Trusts That Are Not Registered Organizations

A common-law trust is not a juridical entity capable of owning property. Property held in a common-law trust is not owned by the trust; it is owned by the trustee, acting in the capacity as trustee for the benefit of the beneficiaries identified in the trust documents. While the trustee would typically have authority to grant a security interest in the trust property, a financing statement that identified the trustee as the debtor could create potential uncertainty for searchers. For example, suppose Abigail Jones is the trustee of a trust that owns stocks. If a secured party files a financing statement under the name "Abigail Jones" and identifying stock, it may not be clear to a searcher whether the financing statement covers stock owned by Abigail Jones in her personal capacity as an individual or whether it covers stock owned by her as a trustee. Resolving this potential confusion requires the financing statement to indicate in some manner that the indicated collateral is held in trust.

Section 9-503(a)(3) provides that the financing statement must use the name for the trust provided in the trust's organic record[53]—i.e., the record that created the trust[54]—and must indicate in a separate part of the financing statement that the property is held in a trust.[55] The standard financing statement form contains a single box to check if the collateral is held in a trust. If the trust's organic record does not provide a name for the trust, the secured party must use the name of the settlor or testator[56] as identified in the trust's organic record.[57] Furthermore, in the case of an inter vivos trust, there must, in a separate part of the financing statement, be sufficient information to distinguish the trust at issue from other trusts having more than one of the same settlors.[58]

[d] Organizations That Are Not Registered Organizations

The general rule for organizations that are not registered organizations is that, if the debtor has a name, the financing statement must provide the organizational name of the debtor.[59] Thus, if the partnership agreement of a general partnership specifies a name for the partnership, the financing statement must use that name.[60] If the organization does not have a name, as is true of some informal partnerships and unincor-

---

53. U.C.C. § 9-503(a)(3)(A)(i).

54. In a common-law trust, the trust agreement typically is not filed in any public record. To obtain the name, a prudent secured party would obtain the trust agreement from the trustee and would typically ask the trustee to certify that the trust agreement has not been amended and remains in effect.

55. U.C.C. § 9-503(a)(3)(B)(i).

56. U.C.C. § 9-503(a)(3)(A)(ii).

57. U.C.C. § 9-503(h)(2). If the settlor is a registered organization, the name to be used is the name on the settlor's public organic record. U.C.C. § 9-503(h)(1).

58. U.C.C. § 9-503(a)(3)(B)(ii).

59. U.C.C. § 9-503(a)(4)(A).

60. See, e.g., In re Webb, 520 B.R. 748, 85 U.C.C. Rep. Serv. 2d 1 (Bankr. E.D. Ark. 2014) (financing statement filed in name of joint venture sufficient even though it did not include the individual names of each joint venturer).

porated associations, the financing statement must provide the names of the partners, members, associates, or other persons comprising the debtor.[61]

Rejecting an alternative approach previously followed in some jurisdictions, Article 9 explicitly states that a financing statement that includes only a trade name does not sufficiently name the debtor.[62] A financing statement that contains an organization's name is not rendered ineffective merely because it omits the organization's trade name or (where the organization has a name) the names of partners, members, associates, or the like.[63] In documenting a loan to an individual who operates a sole proprietorship, the secured party should state the individual name of the debtor rather than the trade name under which the debtor conducts the business.[64] If desired, the secured party may add the trade name to the financing statement as an additional name.[65] The reason for this approach in the case of a sole proprietorship is that the proprietorship is not a juridical entity (i.e., it cannot own property in its trade name[66]). More broadly, trade names are too uncertain and can lack enough common recognition among both secured parties and persons searching the records to form the basis for a filing system.

[e] Individuals

Prior to 2010, the rules governing how to determine the name of an individual debtor were unclear. Article 9 always required that a financing statement had to contain the "individual name," but people often use names somewhat flexibly. Some may use first names, some may use middle names, some may use nicknames. Some may use different names in different settings. What if an individual's name as shown on a birth certificate or social security card differs from the name shown on their driver's license, passport, checking account, or other documents? While the instructions on the

---

61. U.C.C. §9-503(a)(4)(B). A lender could resolve any uncertainty simply by insisting that the organization amend its partnership agreement to adopt a name as a condition of making the loan.

62. U.C.C. §9-503(c). *See In re* Silver Dollar, LLC, 65 U.C.C. Rep. Serv. 2d 516 (Bankr. E.D. Tenn. 2008) (filing under assumed name "Silver Dollar Stores, LLC" rather than legal name "Silver Dollar, LLC" erroneous even though assumed name registered with state; summary judgment denied because of factual dispute over whether a search of the records under the correct name would reveal the filed financing statement); Dickason v. Marine Nat'l Bank of Naples, N.A., 898 So. 2d 1170, 57 U.C.C. Rep. Serv. 2d 127 (Fla. Dist. Ct. App. 2005) (financing statement in trade name "Patio Plus/Inside Out" instead of the corporate name "The Sawgrass Group, Inc." ineffective).

63. U.C.C. §9-503(b). *See In re* Wisniewski, 265 B.R. 897, 46 U.C.C. Rep. Serv. 2d 1192 (Bankr. N.D. Ohio 2001) (a reference to an incorrect trade name of the debtor did not make the financing statement seriously misleading because the financing statement correctly listed the debtor's name). A financing statement is also not ineffective merely because it fails to indicate the representative capacity of the secured party or a representative of the secured party. U.C.C. §9-503(d).

64. *In re* Stanton, 254 B.R. 357, 42 U.C.C. Rep. Serv. 2d 1190 (Bankr. E.D. Tex. 2000) (filing in trade name "Elkhart Pharmacy" was ineffective when the debtor Stanton operated it as a sole proprietorship).

65. Cross-filing under trade names can be useful because it might enable a later searcher who does not know the rules (and searches under the trade name rather than the legal name) to stumble across the filing, thus preventing a later dispute.

66. This is true also of an organization that does business under a trade name. The trade name is fictitious, and it is the organization, a juridical entity, that has rights in the collateral.

safe-harbor financing statement form in Section 9-521(a) call for the debtor's "exact full legal name"—and, as applied to individuals, provides blocks for the last name, first name, middle name, and suffix—the instructions do not constitute a legal standard.

The lack of clarity led to a few cases holding that the name provided on a financing statement was insufficient.[67] In one notable case, *In re Miller*,[68] the debtor's driver's license and social security cards identified the debtor as "Bennie A. Miller," and he used that name on his bank account, tax returns, and in executing the security agreement at issue in the case. However, the name on his birth certificate was "Ben," and the court ultimately held that his correct legal name was thus "Ben Miller." Because a search of the files under the correct name "Ben Miller" did not reveal the secured party's financing statement (filed under the name "Bennie A. Miller"), the court held that the security interest was unperfected.

The lack of clarity had other costs for searchers as well. Without certainty as to an individual's legal name, a prudent searcher would need to search under every possible permutation of a debtor's name, including common nicknames. Lender concerns were heightened by the ill-considered opinion in *Peoples Bank v. Bryan Brothers Cattle Co.*,[69] in which the court held that a financing statement that identified the debtor by his nickname, Louie, rather than his legal first name, Brooks, was sufficient to perfect the bank's security interest. The court did not even mention that under Section 9-506, any mistake in the debtor's name renders a financing statement seriously misleading unless a search of the files using the correct name and conducted using the filing office's standard search logic would reveal the financing statement.[70]

Lenders wanting the same sort of certainty for individual-debtor filings that exists for registered-organization filings began to promote nonuniform legislation to accomplish their goal. Texas was first, amending its version of Section 9-503(a)(4) to provide that the name of an individual debtor on a financing statement is sufficient if it is the name shown on the individual's driver's license or state-issued identification card. To ensure that rules would be as uniform as possible, the drafters amended Article 9 in

---

67. *See, e.g., In re* Borden, 63 U.C.C. Rep. Serv. 2d 801 (D. Neb. 2007) (financing statement using nickname "Mike Borden" insufficient when individual debtor's name was "Michael Ray Borden," and searches under the names "Michael Borden" and "Michael R. Borden" failed to disclose financing statement); *In re* Kinderknecht, 308 B.R. 71, 53 U.C.C. Rep. Serv. 2d 167 (Bankr. 10th Cir. 2004) (reversing Kansas bankruptcy court decision holding that financing statement using debtor's nickname is not seriously misleading when a search under the debtor's legal name using the filing office's standard search logic would not produce the filed financing statement); Pankratz Implement Co. v. Citizens Nat'l Bank, 55 U.C.C. Rep. Serv. 2d 245 (Kan. Ct. App. 2004), *aff'd*, 59 U.C.C. Rep. Serv. 2d 53 (Kan. 2006) (lower court erred in failing to find seriously misleading a financing statement that spelled the debtor's name as "House, Roger" rather than "House, Rodger" because a search using the standard search logic would not produce the filed financing statement); *In re* Fuell, 64 U.C.C. Rep. Serv. 2d 722 (Bankr. D. Idaho 2007) (financing statement indicating debtor's last name as "Fuel" rather than "Fuell" held insufficient). Most of the cases involve the use of a nickname or an obvious misspelling.

68. 2012 Bankr. LEXIS 70 (Bankr. C.D. Ill. Jan. 6, 2012).

69. 504 F.3d 549, 64 U.C.C. Rep. Serv. 2d 113 (5th Cir. 2007).

70. U.C.C. § 9-506(b), (c).

2010. The ultimate result was not a single uniform rule but rather two uniform alternatives for the states to choose from.

[i] Alternative A: The Only-If Approach

Under the first alternative, a financing statement sufficiently shows the name of "an individual to whom this State has issued a [driver's license] that has not expired, only if it provides the name of the individual which is indicated on the [driver's license]."[71] Subject to a limited exception for residents of foreign countries,[72] an individual debtor's location is the individual's principal residence,[73] and the law of the jurisdiction where the individual is located generally governs perfection of a security interest in assets of the individual.[74] Thus, if an individual's state of principal residence is Alabama and Alabama adopts Alternative A, the name of an individual on a financing statement will be sufficient only if coincides precisely with the name as it appears on the individual's unexpired Alabama driver's license. If an individual does not have an unexpired driver's license from the state of principal residence, a filing will be sufficient only if it indicates the individual name of the debtor (the pre-2010 requirement) or the individual's surname and first personal name. This latter option operates as a safe-harbor—but it is only safe if the individual does not have an unexpired driver's license. It might be helpful to think of the approach as a two-tier system, with the top tier being the name on the driver's license and the bottom tier being the individual's name but with a surname/first-personal-name safe harbor. Lenders generally prefer Alternative A because it provides them with additional certainty not only in filing but in searching. As we shall see, however, it does not provide them with absolute certainty.[75]

[ii] Alternative B: The Safe-Harbor Approach

The safe-harbor alternative is much easier to describe and apply, and it avoids the complexities associated with Alternative A. The safe-harbor approach does not reduce the burden on searchers because the name of the individual (the pre-2010 requirement) continues to suffice to perfect a security interest. This alternative has two safe harbors. The first is the same as the safe harbor on the second tier of Alternative A—the

---

71. U.C.C. § 9-504(a)(4) [Alternative A]. In the unlikely event that an individual holds two unexpired driver's licenses from the state of principal residency, the later-issued license controls. U.C.C. § 9-504(g) (rule applies under both only–if and safe-harbor approaches). A legislative note appended to amended Section 9-504 advises that if "a single agency issues driver's licenses and non-driver identification cards as an alternative to a driver's license, such that at any given time an individual may hold either a driver's license or an identification card but not both," the term "driver's license" should be replaced with appropriate terminology reflecting both types of identification.

72. Under Section 9-307(c), an individual located in a foreign country under the normal debtor-location rule of Section 9-307(b) is deemed located in Washington, D.C., if the foreign country location does not have a filing system that meets the statutory test.

73. U.C.C. § 9-307(b).

74. U.C.C. § 9-301(1).

75. For a discussion of some of the problems that may arise in a state that adopts Alternative A, see § 5.03[C], *infra*.

surname and first personal name of the individual. The second safe harbor is the name indicated on an unexpired driver's license issued by the state of the debtor's location.

Under either alternative, the court's decision in *In re Miller*[76] would have come out the other way, as the secured party's financing statement identified the debtor using the exact name shown on the unexpired driver's license.

[2] Authorization—§§ 9-509, 9-510

Article 9 originally required a signature of the debtor on the financing statement. Two related considerations justified this requirement. First, the mandate of the signature meant that the debtor had to cooperate before an effective filing could occur. This prevented a secured party from overstating, deliberately or inadvertently, the scope of the encumbered assets.[77] Second, the signature requirement served a verification function. Because the debtor had to participate at least to the extent of signing the financing statement, an effective financing statement reflected voluntary dealings between the parties with respect to the described collateral.

Article 9 eventually eliminated the requirement of the debtor's signature on an initial financing statement to facilitate electronic filing.[78] Today, alternative methods now satisfy the control and verification objectives. Section 9-509 provides that the debtor[79] must authorize the filing of an initial financing statement or an amendment that adds either collateral or a debtor.[80] By authenticating a security agreement, the debtor authorizes the filing of an initial financing statement that covers collateral described in the security agreement, as well as an amendment that describes proceeds of that collateral.[81] If the financing statement or an amendment indicates that it covers collateral not described in the security agreement or if an amendment adds a debtor, it must be authorized by the debtor in a signed record.[82] Any person that files an unauthorized record is liable for a statutory penalty of $500 and any additional actual damages that result.[83] Furthermore, a filing is effective only to the extent that it is authorized.[84] Thus,

76. 2012 Bankr. LEXIS 70 (Bankr. C.D. Ill. Jan. 6, 2012).

77. The potential of a tort action for slander of title also operates to control overreaching.

78. U.C.C. § 9-502, Comment 2.

79. The term "debtor" means any person with an interest in collateral other than a person with a security interest or lien, and includes transferees of collateral and new debtors. U.C.C. § 9-102(a)(28). In some instances, a secured party will want to file in the name of a transferee or new debtor, and it has statutory authority to do so. U.C.C. § 9-509(c), (b).

80. U.C.C. § 9-509(a).

81. U.C.C. § 9-509(b). The signature may be either manual or electronic. U.C.C. § 1-201(b)(37). *See* Hancock Bank of La. v. Advocate Fin., LLC, 73 U.C.C. Rep. Serv. 2d 425 (M.D. La. 2011) (signing of security agreement authorized secured party to file second financing statement after first one lapsed); *In re* Aliquippa Machine Co., Inc., 59 U.C.C. Rep. Serv. 2d 773 (Bankr. W.D. Pa. 2006) (same).

82. U.C.C. § 9-509(a). Only the secured party need authorize the filing of an amendment that releases collateral. U.C.C. § 9-509(c).

83. U.C.C. § 9-625(e)(3) (penalty); U.C.C. § 9-625(b) (actual damages).

84. U.C.C. § 9-510(a). *See, e.g.,* AEG Liquidation Trust v. Toobro NY LLC, 32 Misc. 3d 1202(A), 932 N.Y.S.2d 759, 74 U.C.C. Rep. Serv. 2d 675 (N.Y. Sup. Ct. 2011) (unauthorized termination statement ineffective to terminate financing statement).

if the debtor authorizes a filing to cover the debtor's inventory but the secured party files covering both the debtor's inventory and equipment, the filing is effective only as to inventory.[85]

[3] Addresses

A financing statement must contain the addresses of the parties[86]—although, as discussed above,[87] a filed financing statement can be legally sufficient to perfect a security interest even if it lacks one or both addresses.[88] The inclusion of the mailing address of the debtor can aid a searcher in determining the identity of the debtor because a searcher should know the debtor's address as well as its name. This information can help a searcher in distinguishing between individual debtors who have the same name and in overcoming the misleading effect of filings that are legally sufficient but contain errors in the debtor's name.

The drafters assumed that searchers would contact the secured party to obtain relevant information concerning any transaction between the secured party and the named debtor. In fact, very few secured parties will reveal confidential information to searchers without permission from the debtor. A secured party's address is thus significant primarily as the place to which others may send notifications. If a person required to send a notification to a secured party sends it to the address provided on a financing statement, the sender satisfies its notification requirement.[89] The secured party will also be deemed to have received a notification delivered to that address.[90] Of course, a searcher will not want to rely exclusively on explanations provided by the debtor, and the Code provides a mechanism by which the debtor can confirm information regarding its transaction with the secured party of record.[91] A prudent searcher will require the debtor to obtain information through the use of this mechanism.

---

85. U.C.C. § 9-510, Comment 2. In this situation, the debtor could demand that the secured party file an amendment deleting "equipment."

86. U.C.C. § 9-516(b)(4) (secured party), (b)(5)(a) (debtor).

87. *See* § 5.03[A], *supra*.

88. *Cf.* U.C.C. § 9-502(a) (contents required for sufficient financing statement). *See In re* Hergert, 275 B.R. 58, 47 U.C.C. Rep. Serv. 2d 1 (Bankr. D. Ida. 2002) (errors in the address of the filed financing statement did not adversely affect the sufficiency of the financing statement as the address serves to indicate where required notifications can be sent to the secured party rather than to identify the secured party). *See also In re* Bonds Distrib. Co., Inc., 48 U.C.C. Rep. Serv. 2d 1212 (4th Cir. 2002) (unpublished) (substantial compliance was found despite the omission of the address of the secured party based on the policies underlying the new revision of Article 9 even though the revision was not yet in effect); *In re* Grabowski, 277 B.R. 388, 47 U.C.C. Rep. Serv. 2d 1220 (Bankr. S.D. Ill. 2002) (use of the debtor's separate business address sufficient to perfect a security interest in the debtor's farm equipment).

89. U.C.C. § 9-516, Comment 5. *See also* U.C.C. § 9-102(a)(75) (defining "send").

90. U.C.C. § 9-516, Comment 5. *See also* U.C.C. § 1-202(d) (defining "notifies").

91. U.C.C. §§ 9-210, 9-102(a)(4). For discussion of this mechanism, see § 5.03[B][2], *infra*.

[4] Indication of Collateral

A financing statement is sufficient to perfect a security interest only if it "indicates the collateral covered by the financing statement."[92] Although "indication" is broader than description, a financing statement sufficiently indicates the collateral if it provides a description of the collateral effective under Section 9-108.[93]

The basic test for a description of personal or real property is that, whether or not specific, it must reasonably identify the collateral.[94] The drafters of original Article 9, where the test originated, clearly intended a more liberal, functional approach to descriptions than the fanatical "serial-number" test that often characterized earlier chattel-mortgage cases.[95] The Comments stress this functional approach to description sufficiency: "The test of sufficiency of a description under this section ... is that the description do the job assigned to it: make possible the identification of the collateral described."[96] A greater degree of precision may be necessary in a security agreement than in a financing statement because the security agreement establishes the intent of the parties regarding the assets to be subject to the security interest.[97] As in other contractual contexts, ambiguities are often resolved against the drafter.[98] A financing statement, in contrast, serves merely to notify interested third parties that the secured party

---

92. U.C.C. § 9-502(a)(3); First Nat'l Bank of Lewisville v. Bank of Bradley, 80 Ark. App. 368, 96 S.W.3d 773, 49 U.C.C. Rep. Serv. 2d 959 (2003) (description of "[a]ll equipment and machinery, including power driven machinery and equipment" in the first secured party's financing statement was sufficient to cover the 113 specific pieces of equipment listed in the second secured party's filing); *In re* Systems Eng'g & Energy Mgmt. Assocs., Inc., 284 B.R. 226, 49 U.C.C. Rep. Serv. 2d 608 (Bankr. E.D. Va. 2002) (description of debtor's accounts, equipment, and other collateral did not include litigation recoveries); *In re* Waldick Aero-Space Devices, Inc., 49 B.R 192, 42 U.C.C. Rep. Serv. 723 (Bankr. D.N.J. 1985) (security interest was unperfected because financing statement referred to collateral "[p]er the attached Schedule 'A' to be made part hereof," but no schedule was attached to the financing statement).

93. U.C.C. § 9-504(1).

94. *See* U.C.C. § 9-108; § 2.02[A][2], *supra*.

95. U.C.C. § 9-108, Comment 2. *See* Maxus Leasing Grp., Inc. v. Kobelco America, Inc., 63 U.C.C. Rep. Serv. 2d 140 (N.D.N.Y. 2007) (description of crane upheld despite one-digit error in serial number); McGehee v. Exchange Bank & Trust Co., 561 S.W.2d 926, 23 U.C.C. Rep. Serv. 816 (Tex. Civ. Ct. App. 1978) (description upheld despite errors of one digit in model year, engine number, and license number of boat); *In re* Delta Molded Products, Inc., 416 F. Supp. 938, 20 U.C.C. Rep. Serv. 795 (N.D. Ala. 1976) (upholding description that stated model number, type of machine, factory modifications, and list of attached auxiliary equipment despite inclusion of incorrect serial number).

96. U.C.C. § 9-108, Comment 2. *See* Planned Furniture Promotions, Inc. v. Benjamin S. Youngblood, Inc., 57 U.C.C. Rep. Serv. 2d 678 (M.D. Ga. 2005) (although financing statement described collateral as the assets of "Old Salem Furniture" and did not mention assets held under two other company names subsequently used by debtors, the court pointed to the inclusion of the address where the collateral was located as being sufficient to enable a prudent searcher to identify the described property).

97. World Wide Tracers, Inc. v. Metropolitan Protection, Inc., 384 N.W.2d 442, 42 U.C.C. Rep. Serv. 1573 (Minn. 1986).

98. Shelby Cnty. State Bank v. Van Diest Supply Co., 303 F.3d 832, 48 U.C.C. Rep. Serv. 2d 790 (7th Cir. 2002) (court construed security-agreement description of "all inventory, including but not limited to ... materials sold to Debtor by [Creditor]" against the secured party that drafted it).

might have a security interest in assets of the debtor that fall within the description, thereby alerting the searcher to investigate further before transacting with the debtor.[99]

Descriptions in security agreements and indications in financing statements must be sufficient to fulfill their respective functions.[100] For example, if a security agreement describes the collateral as "inventory and accounts" but the financing statement indicates only "accounts," perfection does not extend to the security interest in inventory[101] because a searcher would have notice only of a potential security interest in accounts.[102] Conversely, had the security agreement covered only "accounts" and the financing statement indicated "inventory and accounts," the security interest would probably be

---

99. U.C.C. § 9-504, Comment 2. *See* § 5.03[B], *infra. See, e.g., In re* I80 Equipment, LLC, 938 F.3d 866, 100 U.C.C. Rep. Serv. 2d 37 (7th Cir. 2019) (financing statement that described collateral as "all collateral described in a First Amended and Restated Security Agreement dated March 9, 2015 between Debtor and Secured Party" was sufficient to perfect security interest because the collateral was objectively determinable by reference to the security agreement). The decision places an unreasonable burden on searchers and has been severely criticized. *See, e.g.,* Bruce A. Markell, *The Road to Perdition:* I80 Equipment, Woodbridge *and* Liddle *Pave the Way*, 39 Bankr. Law Letter No. 11 (Nov. 2019). *See also* Kubota Tractor Corp. v. Citizens & S. Nat'l Bank, 198 Ga. App. 830, 403 S.E.2d 218, 14 U.C.C. Rep. Serv. 2d 1247 (1991).

100. *In re* Lynch, 313 B.R. 798, 54 U.C.C. Rep. Serv. 2d 849 (Bankr. W.D. Wis. 2004) (financing statement describing collateral as "general business security agreement now owned or hereafter acquired" described the financial transaction under which the bank claimed its security interest, but it did not indicate any of the collateral described in the referenced security agreement).

Disputes sometimes arise in cases where the financing statement covers a type of collateral but also includes a reference to a specific address even though the debtor operates (and collateral is located) at multiple locations. For example, a financing statement that described the collateral as "all furniture located at 813 State Street" would not be sufficient to perfect a security interest in furniture located at a different location as it would not reasonably alert a searcher that a security agreement might cover furniture at other locations. *See, e.g., In re* Freeman, 33 B.R. 234 (Bankr. C.D. Cal. 1983). By contrast, a financing statement that described the collateral as "[a]ll accounts receivable, inventory, equipment, and all business assets located at 1803 W. Main Street" was held sufficient to perfect a security interest in equipment and inventory located at other locations. The court reasoned that a fair reading of the financing statement was that the language "located at 1803 W. Main Street" referred only to "business assets" and that a security interest might exist in any inventory or equipment at other locations. *See, e.g., In re* 8760 Service Group, LLC, 586 B.R. 44 (Bankr. W.D. Mo. 2018).

101. *In re* Katz, 563 F.2d 766, 22 U.C.C. Rep. Serv. 1282 (5th Cir. 1977). *See also In re* American Home Furnishings Corp., 48 B.R. 905, 4 U.C.C. Rep. Serv. 631 (Bankr. W.D. Wash. 1985) (inclusion in security agreement of intangibles held broad enough to cover tax refund, but omission from financing statement left the interest unperfected).

102. *In re* Marta Coop., Inc., 344 N.Y.S.2d 676, 12 U.C.C. Rep. Serv. 955 (Cnty. Ct. 1973).

limited to accounts.[103] The security agreement, of course, is the contract that creates the security interest.[104]

A statement in a security agreement that "all assets" of the debtor are covered is not sufficient as a description under Section 9-108(c),[105] but Section 9-504(2) provides that "all of the debtor's assets" is sufficient as an indication of collateral on a financing statement and thus suffices to perfect a security interest in any asset for which filing is a viable method of perfection.[106] Section 9-504(2) was a response to some court decisions under prior law that had been unwilling to uphold broad descriptions in financing statements.[107] The notice function that financing statements are intended to serve discredits these holdings.[108] The primary advantage of an all-assets filing is that it is sufficient to cover any identifiable proceeds of collateral that are of a type capable of being perfected by filing but outside the rules of Section 9-315(d) that permit perfection of a security interest in proceeds to continue beyond the 20-day grace period of temporary perfection.[109] Because the description in the security agreement is unlikely to cover every type of collateral within the scope of Article 9, the security agreement will not itself authorize the secured party to make an all-assets filing, and thus the secured party will need to obtain explicit authorization in a record signed by the debtor.[110]

A financing statement need not indicate that it covers after-acquired property. An after-acquired property clause may be included in a security agreement to eliminate

---

103. The issue turns on whether the court will admit extrinsic evidence to supplement the description in the security agreement. See discussion in § 2.02[A][3], *supra*, of *In re* Martin Grinding & Machine Works, Inc., 793 F.2d 592, 1 U.C.C. Rep. Serv. 2d 1329 (7th Cir. 1986) (inclusion of inventory and accounts receivable in the financing statement description does not expand scope of security interest when those categories of property were inadvertently omitted from the security agreement's description of collateral). *See also* Landen v. Production Credit Ass'n of the Midlands, 737 P.2d 1325, 4 U.C.C. Rep. Serv. 2d 240 (Wyo. 1987) (narrower description of "cattle" in the security agreement controlled over the description in the financing statement of "livestock" to exclude a security interest in the debtor's horses).

104. *In re* Marta Coop., Inc., 344 N.Y.S.2d 676, 12 U.C.C. Rep. Serv. 955 (Cnty. Ct. 1973).

105. U.C.C. § 9-108(c).

106. U.C.C. § 9-504(2) ("A financing statement sufficiently indicates the collateral that it covers if the financing statement provides ... an indication that the financing statement covers all assets or all personal property."); *In re* Lull, 386 B.R. 261, 65 U.C.C. Rep. Serv. 2d 194 (Bankr. D. Hawaii 2008).

107. *See, e.g., In re* Boogie Enters., Inc., 866 F.2d 1172, 7 U.C.C. Rep. Serv. 2d 1662 (9th Cir. 1989) (description of "personal property" lacks required specificity); *In re* Grey, 29 B.R. 286, 36 U.C.C. Rep. Serv. 724 (Bankr. D. Kan. 1983) (description "all personal property" held insufficient to perfect an interest in grain).

108. *See* § 5.03[B], *infra*.

109. *See, e.g., In re* Scorpion Fitness Inc., 2020 WL 2529357 (Bankr. S.D.N.Y. Apr. 3, 2020) (secured party with blanket lien on debtor's assets, perfected by financing statement covering "all assets," had perfected security interest in insurance proceeds from the destruction of collateral even though secured party was not named as the loss payee on debtor's insurance policy). For discussion of the rules governing perfection of a security interest in proceeds, see § 8.02, *infra*.

110. Any indication of collateral in a filed financing statement that goes beyond the description in the security agreement and is not otherwise authorized by the debtor in a signed record opens the secured party to damages and penalties. *See* § 5.03[A][2], *supra*.

the necessity for the debtor and secured party to enter subsequent security agreements each time the debtor acquires additional property that fits the description of the collateral.[111] A financing statement, however, functions without regard to the time at which the debtor acquires the collateral. The financing statement may be filed before a security agreement has been entered into,[112] which means that it may be filed before the debtor has rights or the power to transfer rights in the initial collateral. The searcher must determine through inquiry the property to which a security interest has attached. Thus, a filed financing statement covering "debtor's equipment" is sufficient to perfect a security interest both in equipment the debtor owns at the time of the filing and a security interest that attaches to equipment acquired by the debtor thereafter. Though the Comments make this explicit[113] and nearly all decisions so recognize,[114] an occasional court decision has refused to recognize perfection as to after-acquired property because the financing statement did not mention after-acquired property.[115]

If the collateral is as-extracted collateral or timber to be cut, or if it is fixtures and the filing is to be a fixture filing, a financing statement must also include a description of the affected real property.[116] In these situations, the financing statement must also indicate that it is to be filed in the real property records and, if the debtor does not have an interest of record in the real property, provide the name of at least one record owner, thereby permitting the filing to be properly indexed into the real estate recording system.[117] A security interest in these types of collateral may also be perfected from the date of the recording of a real property mortgage, if the mortgage both indicates the assets covered and satisfies the requirements for a financing statement.[118]

[B] Notice Filing

[1] The Function of Notice

The filing of an effective financing statement does not indicate as much as an uninitiated searcher is likely to assume. For example, a recorded mortgage usually contains the entire mortgage document, and by the time it is recorded, the mortgagor will already have executed the mortgage (thus creating the mortgage lien on the real property). By contrast, an Article 9 financing statement does not even show that the

---

111. U.C.C. § 9-204(a). U.C.C. § 9-204, Comment 7 ("The references to after-acquired property clauses and future advance clauses in this section are limited to security agreements.").

112. U.C.C. § 9-502(d). *See* § 5.04, *infra*.

113. U.C.C. § 9-204, Comment 7 ("There is no need to refer to after-acquired property or future advances or other obligations secured in a financing statement.").

114. *In re* Brace, 163 B.R. 274, 22 U.C.C. Rep. Serv. 2d 1184 (Bankr. W.D. Pa. 1994); American Nat'l Bank & Trust Co. of Sapula v. Nat'l Cash Register Co., 473 P.2d 234, 7 U.C.C. Rep. Serv. 1097 (Okla. 1970).

115. *In re* Young, 42 B.R. 939, 39 U.C.C. Rep. Serv. 1041 (Bankr. E.D. Pa. 1984).

116. U.C.C. §§ 9-516(b)(3)(D), 9-502(b).

117. U.C.C. § 9-502(b).

118. U.C.C. § 9-502(c).

parties have entered into a security agreement. Article 9 specifically provides that "[a] financing statement may be filed before a security agreement is made or a security interest otherwise attaches."[119] For reasons explained in a later chapter,[120] prudent secured parties in large transactions commonly insist upon "pre-filing," that is, filing a completed financing statement before making a commitment to give the value necessary for the creation of a security interest. At most, therefore, a filed financing statement indicates only that the indicated secured party *might* have a security interest affecting the indicated collateral. The function that the filing system serves is strikingly modest; it serves in effect as a bulletin board.

The function of this system of "notice filing" is described in the Comments to Section 9-502:

> What is required to be filed is not, as under pre-UCC chattel mortgage and conditional sales acts, the security agreement itself, but only a simple record providing a limited amount of information (financing statement). The financing statement may be filed before the security interest attaches or thereafter.... The notice itself indicates merely that a person may have a security interest in the collateral indicated. Further inquiry from the parties concerned will be necessary to disclose the complete state of affairs.[121]

Once placed on notice of the possible existence of a security interest, the searcher can protect itself through further inquiry.[122]

[2] Requests for Information—§§ 9-210; 9-625(f), (g)

A searcher should not unquestioningly accept a debtor's explanation of the nature and extent of a secured party's interest. A searcher that contacts the secured party for information directly, however, is likely to be rebuffed.[123] Accordingly, the prudent searcher asks the debtor to employ a Code mechanism that enables the debtor to verify its position vis-à-vis the secured party. The debtor may submit a signed record requesting a list of the collateral,[124] a statement of account (i.e., a confirmation of the aggregate

---

119. U.C.C. § 9-502(d). For discussion of the desirability of pursuing this option, see §§ 5.04 and 10.01, *infra*.

120. *See* § 10.01, *infra*.

121. U.C.C. § 9-502, Comment 2.

122. *In re* Wak Ltd., Inc., 147 B.R. 607, 19 U.C.C. Rep. Serv. 2d 915 (Bankr. S.D. Fla. 1992) (description directed reader to specific lease). The requirement that the financing statement include at least a statement indicating the types of collateral is designed to spare every prospective creditor from the need to make further inquiry of every party who has filed a financing statement against the debtor. *In re* Kirk Kabinets, Inc., 15 U.C.C. Rep. Serv. 746 (Bankr. M.D. Ga. 1974).

123. Secured lenders, particularly banks, are often subject to confidentiality requirements. Comment 3 to Section 9-210, reflecting this fact, states that "the secured party should not be under a duty to disclose any details of the debtor's financing affairs to any casual inquirer or competitor who may inquire."

124. U.C.C. § 9-210(a)(3) (request to approve or correct a list stating collateral and reasonably identifying the transaction or relationship that is the subject of the request).

balance of the debt),[125] or an "accounting (i.e., a confirmation of the aggregate balance of the debt and each component of that debt, such as principal, interest, late charges, attorney fees, or other sums for which the obligor is liable)."[126] A secured party must respond to the request within 14 days after its receipt.[127] A secured party that fails to comply with this duty is liable to the debtor for $500 and for any actual damages caused by its failure.[128] As against a party misled by its failure to respond to a request for a list of collateral, the secured party may claim an interest only as shown in the debtor's list.[129] Although the use of these mechanisms appears to protect a searcher by providing information directly from the secured party, an understanding of the Article 9 priority rules will caution the searcher against transacting with the debtor with respect to collateral described in an effective filed financing statement even if the secured party disclaims any current interest in the described collateral.[130]

[C] Effect of Errors and Changes

[1] Errors—§§ 9-506(a), 9-518

[a] Information Required for Sufficiency

Even when parties prepare the simplest of records, errors occur. Article 9 provides a standard for resolving the effect of errors that appear on filed financing statements: "A financing statement substantially satisfying the requirements of this part is effective, even if it has minor errors or omissions, unless the errors or omissions make the financing statement seriously misleading."[131] The objective is clear from the accompanying Comments: "[The provision] is in line with the policy of this Article to simplify formal requisites and filing requirements [and] ... is designed to discourage the fanatical and impossibly refined reading of statutory requirements in which courts occasionally have indulged themselves."[132] Bear in mind that if the issue is the sufficiency of a filed financing statement to perfect a security interest, the court may consider only the items listed in Section 9-502.[133]

---

125. U.C.C. § 9-210(a)(4) (request to approve or correct a statement of the aggregate unpaid balance as of a specified date and reasonably identifying the transaction or relationship that is the subject of the request).

126. U.C.C. § 9-210(a)(2) (request must reasonably identify the transaction or relationship that is the subject of the request). An accounting is a record signed by the secured party that indicates the aggregate unpaid secured obligations (as of a date not more than 35 days before or after the date of the record) and identifies the components of the obligation in reasonable detail. U.C.C. § 9-102(a)(4).

127. U.C.C. § 9-210(b). A secured party who is a consignor or a buyer of accounts, chattel paper, payment intangibles, or promissory notes need not respond. *Id.*

128. U.C.C. § 9-625(f).

129. U.C.C. § 9-625(g).

130. *See* § 10.02, *infra.*

131. U.C.C. § 9-506(a).

132. U.C.C. § 9-506, Comment 2.

133. *See* § 5.03[A], *supra.*

The effect of errors essentially is a matter of degree. The purpose of a filed financing statement is to provide notice that informs interested parties that a particular person might have granted a security interest in particular property. If the filing, despite some error, is reasonably sufficient to place searchers on notice, the error should not affect the filing's effectiveness.[134] The savings provision that permits effectiveness for financing statements that contain minor errors places a greater degree of responsibility on searchers. While even minor errors might tend to mislead, searchers have grounds to complain only if they have been seriously misled. For example, the Comments suggest that searchers will rarely be seriously misled by an error in the secured party's name.[135]

Some mistakes in the identification of the collateral will be seriously misleading and defeat the effectiveness of the financing statement to perfect the security interest.[136] For example, if Bank has a security interest in all of Debtor's present and after-acquired equipment, but the filed financing statement identifies the collateral as "Debtor's inventory," the error is seriously misleading. Any secured party reviewing Bank's financing statement will reasonably conclude that it would not indicate the possibility of a security interest in Debtor's equipment.

By contrast, other mistakes will not affect the ability of the financing statement to warn subsequent parties that a prior security interest may exist. For example, consider the situation in *In re Murray*,[137] where an individual debtor granted a security interest in his shares in a cooperative apartment association and his accompanying proprietary lease on his cooperative apartment. The financing statement correctly identified the debtor, the secured party, and the street address for the apartment; however, the collateral description also identified the cooperative association as "235-21 79 St Tenants Corp" instead of its correct name "35-21 79 St Tenants Corp." The court held that the error in the misidentification of the cooperative association was not seriously mislead-

---

134. The financing statement in *Fifth Third Bank v. Comark, Inc.*, 794 N.E.2d 433, 51 U.C.C. Rep. Serv. 2d 533 (Ind. Ct. App. 2003), incorrectly described the collateral as inventory rather than equipment. The appellate court nevertheless affirmed the trial court decision that the description was adequate because additional language in the description referring to computer products bearing the name Comark was sufficient to place searchers on notice.

135. U.C.C. § 9-506, Comment 2. *See In re* Hergert, 275 B.R. 58, 47 U.C.C. Rep. Serv. 2d 1 (Bankr. D. Idaho 2002) (name of secured creditor that was incorrect at the time of the effective date of the new revision to Article 9 was not seriously misleading). However, where a security agreement grants a security interest to secure debts owed to both the secured party and an affiliate of the secured party, but the financing statement only identifies the secured party and not the affiliate, the affiliate's security interest is not perfected. *See, e.g., In re* Jarvis, 100 U.C.C. Rep. Serv. 2d 1260 (Bankr. W.D.N.C. 2020); *In re* Borges, 75 U.C.C. Rep. Serv. 2d 538 (Bankr. D.N.M. 2011).

136. A description in a financing statement is subject to the same statutory standard for sufficiency—whether it reasonably identifies the collateral—as a description in a security agreement. U.C.C. §9-504(1) ("A financing statement sufficiently indicates the collateral that it covers if the financing statement provides ... a description of the collateral pursuant to Section 9-108...."). *See* the discussion of security-agreement descriptions in §2.02[A][2], *supra*. A description (other than an indication that the financing statement covers "all assets") that fails to reasonably identify the collateral renders the description in the financing statement seriously misleading and thus insufficient to perfect the security interest.

137. 624 B.R. 532, 103 U.C.C. Rep. Serv. 2d 752 (Bankr. E.D.N.Y. 2020).

ing and would not have prevented a searcher from discovering the financing statement (which was filed under the debtor's correct name) or from appreciating that it covered the shares and the proprietary lease (further investigation to confirm the name of the association at that street address would have revealed the association's correct name).

Likewise, consider the financing statement in *In re Sterling United*,[138] which described the covered collateral as "all assets of the Debtor including, but not limited to, any and all equipment, fixtures, inventory ... located at or relating to the operation of the premises at 100 River Rock Drive, Suite 304, Buffalo, NY... ." By the time of the debtor's bankruptcy filing several years later, the debtor no longer operated at that location. The debtor's bankruptcy trustee argued that the secured party was unperfected because a reasonable searcher would conclude that the secured party's interest was limited to collateral located at that specific location (and not other locations). The court disagreed, concluding that the language specifying the location modified the phrase "including, but not limited to" and not the broader phrase "all assets of the debtor." The court held that the financing statement covered "all of the debtor's assets" and "clearly informs a prospective creditor that the list of affected collateral was non-exhaustive."[139] Further, even if a searcher found the language ambiguous, a prudent searcher would have inquired further. Thus, the financing statement was sufficient to perfect the secured party's interest.

The Code has much less tolerance for error if the information at issue is the debtor's name. Although the standard remains the same—whether the error is seriously misleading—there is a statutory presumption that *any* error is seriously misleading.[140] The presumption is rebutted only if a search of the filing records using the debtor's correct name using the standard search logic of the filing office would nevertheless disclose the erroneous financing statement to the searcher.[141] This rule properly allocates to the filer the risk of a mistake in the debtor's name. However, the rule promotes differences among jurisdictions in the near-term because the standard search logic can vary among filing offices with computerized systems. For example, many offices use search logic based on standards adopted by the International Association of Commercial Administrators (IACA). That search logic ignores what are sometimes called "noise words," such as the designations of the type of entity at the end of an organization's name (e.g., "Inc." or "LLC"). It also ignores middle initials in individual names. Thus, in a jurisdiction using that search logic, a search under the correct name "Bryant Corporation, Inc." would

---

138. 88 U.C.C. Rep. Serv. 2d 340 (W.D.N.Y. 2015).

139. *Id.*

140. U.C.C. § 9-506(b); Matter of Keast Enters., Inc., 101 U.C.C. Rep. Serv. 2d 157 (Bankr. S.D. Iowa 2020).

141. U.C.C. § 9-506(c). With regard to mistakes as to entity names, see, for example, *In re* Tyringham Holdings, Inc., 354 B.R. 363, 61 U.C.C. Rep. Serv. 2d 339 (Bankr. E.D. Va. 2006) (secured party left out "Inc." and search under the correct name using Virginia Secretary of State's standard search logic did not disclose the filing); *In re* C.W. Mining Co., 69 U.C.C. Rep. Serv. 2d 830 (Bankr. D. Utah 2009) (financing statement that identified debtor as "CW Mining Company" instead of correct name "C.W. Mining Company" ineffective). For cases involving individual debtor names, see § 5.03[A][1], *supra.*

reveal both a financing statement that had been filed under "Bryant Corporation, Inc." as well as one that had been filed under "Bryant Corporation." Likewise, a search under the correct name "April C. Smith" would reveal both a financing statement filed using the name "April C. Smith" and one filed using the name "April Smith." By contrast, if the jurisdiction's standard search logic returns only exact matches, then a search under the correct name "April C. Smith" would not reveal a financing statement that had been filed under the name "April Smith" (i.e., the error would be seriously misleading and prevent the financing statement from being effective to perfect the secured party's interest). Given the consequences of being wrong—being unperfected and at risk of losing priority—the prudent filer must take care to get the name exactly right. Even the most seemingly trivial errors in the preparation of a financing statement, such as the inclusion of an inadvertent space while typing the debtor's name, may render the filed financing statement ineffective if the secured party does not catch the error and the filing office's search logic is too rigid to overcome the error.[142]

Note that the term "financing statement" includes "any filed record relating to the initial financing statement," and the first record filed is referred to as the initial financing statement.[143] Through this mechanism, the seriously-misleading standard is made applicable to both the initial financing statements and all amendments.

[i] "Standard Search Logic"

As the foregoing discussion demonstrates, whether an error in the debtor's name is seriously misleading may depend on the state's "standard search logic." The Code does not define "standard search logic," but its meaning has become clearer thanks to litigation that culminated in the Florida Supreme Court's decision in *1944 Beach Boulevard, LLC v. Live Oak Banking Co.*[144] The debtor in that case was 1944 Beach Boulevard, LLC, which granted a security interest in most of its business assets to secure two loans. The secured party filed a financing statement identifying the debtor as "1944 Beach Blvd., LLC." After the debtor filed a bankruptcy petition, it argued that the financing statement did not contain the debtor's legal name and thus failed to perfect the security interest—in turn, permitting the debtor to invalidate the security interest under the Bankruptcy Code's "strong-arm" avoiding power.[145] Florida's filing office used search logic that, when the searcher enters the debtor's name, returns the 20 "closest" matches, then the next 20 closest, and so on—essentially, allowing the searcher to navigate through the entire index of filed financing statements. The secured party thus argued that the error was not seriously misleading under Section 9-506(c)'s safe harbor

---

142. *See, e.g.*, United States SEC v. ISC, Inc., 93 U.C.C. Rep. Serv. 2d 729 (W.D. Wis. 2017) (secured party's financing statement identified debtor as "ISC, Inc ." rather than "ISC, Inc."; the inadvertent space rendered financing statement seriously misleading given Wisconsin's search logic); *In re* PTM Technologies, Inc., 452 B.R. 165 (Bankr. M.D.N.C. 2011) (financing statement that identified debtor as "PTM Tecnologies, Inc." was ineffective to perfect security interest).

143. U.C.C. § 9-102(a)(39).

144. 346 So. 3d 587, 108 U.C.C. Rep. Serv. 2d 747 (Fla. 2022).

145. For further discussion of the strong-arm avoidance power, see § 16.04[B], *infra*.

because a search under the correct name would have eventually returned the secured party's filing. Ultimately, the Eleventh Circuit certified to the Florida Supreme Court whether the secured party's erroneous filing fell within the protection of the Section 9-506(c) safe harbor. The Florida Supreme Court held that it did not:

> [A]lthough the Registry offers an option for searching its records, that option is not a "standard search logic." Instead of returning a finite list of hits when a search is conducted, the Registry returns a list of twenty names starting with the name that most closely matches the name entered. That list of names is but a point from which the user can navigate forward and backward through all of the names indexed in the Registry. In other words, a "search" of the Registry returns an index of all of the financing statements in the Registry. The Registry's current search option also produces inconsistent results depending upon the date a search is conducted. This is true because as financing statements are filed, amended, and removed, the position of a financing statement on the Registry's index changes, which means that a financing statement included in a list of twenty today might not be on the same list tomorrow.
>
> ... [A] search procedure that returns as hits, for any search string, all financing statements in the filing office's database cannot rationally be treated as a "standard search logic."[146]

The court held that because the Florida filing office did not use a standard search logic, the safe harbor of Section 9-506(c) was unavailable to save the secured party's erroneous filing. Without the safe harbor, Section 9-506 provides zero tolerance for a financing statement that does not contain the debtor's correct legal name.[147] Thus, because the secured party's filing did not contain the debtor's correct legal name, the secured party's interest in the collateral was unperfected.

The decision was harsh for the secured party—especially since users cannot dictate the filing office's search mechanism—but it nevertheless makes good sense. A searcher should not have the burden of having to review every single financing statement in the filing system before it can safely conclude that there are no financing statements on file covering the particular debtor and the collateral. A standard search logic must "narrow down" the entire index, using the search logic to eliminate filed financing statements that reflect a name sufficiently inconsistent with the debtor's correct legal name. The burden on the secured party to get it right here was minimal—all it had to do was spell the full word "Boulevard" rather than abbreviating it.[148]

---

146. *1944 Beach Blvd.*, 346 So. 3d at 592.

147. U.C.C. § 9-506(b).

148. Note that if the filing office did have a standard search logic—and that search logic treated "Boulevard" and "Blvd." as equivalents—then a search under the correct name would have produced the secured party's financing statement, and thus the secured party would have been perfected under the safe-harbor. The IACA search logic discussed in the text does not anticipate such an abbreviation (i.e., it does not treat "St." as the equivalent of "Street"), but nothing would preclude a filing office from adopting standard search logic that did.

It is one thing for the filing office to establish a standard search logic. It is another thing to communicate successfully to searchers how to use it (and to courts how to apply it). Two Georgia decisions demonstrate the potential pitfalls. In the case of *In re Wynn*,[149] the secured party filed a financing statement identifying the debtor as "Jerry W. Wynn," even though the debtor's unexpired driver's license identified the debtor as "Wilson Jerry Wynn." The secured party argued that because a certified search under the name "Wilson Wynn" would have produced the filing under the name "Jerry W. Wynn,"[150] its error was not seriously misleading. The court held that Georgia's published search logic (established by the Georgia Superior Court Clerks' Cooperative Authority) did not contemplate a certified-search but instead an exact-name search mechanism whereby a search under the name "Wilson Wynn" would not have disclosed the secured party's filing under "Jerry W. Wynn." Thus, the secured party's failure to use the correct legal name rendered its security interest unperfected.

Likewise, consider the situation in *In re Bryant*,[151] where a secured party took a security interest in property owned by Darren Eugene Bryant (the name shown on the debtor's unexpired Georgia driver's license) but filed its financing statement under the name "Darren E. Bryant." Georgia's published search logic provided that "[w]hen searching for an individual, [the Debtor's] last name and first name are required, [the Debtor's] middle name is optional."[152] One reading this statement might think it means that the search logic will simply ignore middle names, that is, that a search under "Darren Eugene Bryant" would return any financing statement that had the first name "Darren" and the last name "Bryant."[153] Notwithstanding the description, however, the actual search logic did not work that way; a search under "Darren Eugene Bryant" did not return the secured party's filing under "Darren E. Bryant."[154] Thus, the court held that the secured party's financing statement was seriously misleading as to the debtor's name. The *Wynn* and *Bryant* cases demonstrate that no prudent secured party should ever plan for the safe harbor to save them; instead, the secured party should take great pains to get the name exactly right and make the safe harbor irrelevant.

[b] *Other Required Information*

If an error in a financing statement relates to information other than that required by Section 9-502 (i.e., information not necessary for a filed financing statement to be sufficient to perfect a security interest), the "seriously misleading" standard does

149. 627 B.R. 192, 104 U.C.C. Rep. Serv. 2d 705 (Bankr. M.D. Ga. 2021).

150. A certified search is one in which the searcher asks the filing officer (for a fee) to provide a certified copy of all filings in the name of a particular debtor. U.C.C. §9-523(c), (d). As explained in *Wynn*, the certified search went further than the exact-name search identified as the filing office's standard search logic and thus returned more results than an exact name search would have disclosed.

151. 630 B.R. 671, 105 U.C.C. Rep. Serv. 2d 1 (Bankr. M.D. Ga. 2021).

152. *Bryant*, 630 B.R. 671, 676 (Bankr. M.D. Ga. 2021).

153. In fact, this is the way that the IACA's model search logic would work.

154. By contrast, a search under "Darren Bryant" would have returned the secured party's financing statement. Of course, "Darren Bryant" was not the debtor's legal name as shown on the debtor's unexpired driver's license, which is the basis for the safe-harbor rule.

not apply. In this situation, the issue is not whether the secured party is perfected—it is perfected as long as the financing statement contains the Section 9-502 information—but whether the secured party can claim that perfected status as against a specific searcher who was misled by the error.[155] Section 9-338 contains rules that in effect estop a secured party from taking advantage of even a sufficient financing statement if a subsequent purchaser of the collateral (e.g., a buyer or a secured party) gives value in reasonable reliance on the erroneous information.[156] For example, suppose the debtor has a common name, such as Jane Smith, and the secured party's financing statement is otherwise correct but contains an address that is not her address. Later, Barbara agrees to buy the collateral from Jane; Barbara searches the records, and the search reveals the financing statement, but Barbara concludes—based on the incorrect address—that the financing statement relates to a different Jane Smith and thus does not actually cover the collateral. Even though the mistake did not affect the secured party's perfected status, the secured party will nonetheless be unable to assert that status if Barbara gave value and bought the collateral in reasonable reliance on the belief that the financing statement referred to a different Jane Smith. This approach properly balances the equities. As against a lien creditor, including a trustee in bankruptcy, the error in the address is irrelevant; such creditors do not customarily rely on the records in transacting with the debtor. By contrast, searchers that give value in reasonable reliance on the appearance created by the erroneous record gain appropriate protection.

[c] Information Statements

Article 9 provides a nonjudicial method for a debtor to complain in a filed record about a financing statement that contains errors or was wrongfully filed.[157] The debtor may file a record that indicates that it is an "information statement" and that states the basis for the debtor's belief that there is an error or a wrongful filing. The statement must also indicate any way to amend the financing statement to eliminate the error. A filed information statement is part of the financing statement[158] but does not negate its effectiveness.[159] In other words, an information statement provides searchers with additional information but has no legal effect.

Prior to 2010, only debtors could file information statements. Today, a secured party may do so where that is necessary. For example, a secured party may have transposed digits on a termination statement, leading the filing office to associate the termination statement with another secured party's financing statement. Of course, such a termination statement would not terminate the other secured party's financing statement

---

155. U.C.C. § 9-520(c) (cross-referencing § 9-338).
156. U.C.C. § 9-338. A buyer like Barbara must also receive delivery of assets capable of being possessed.
157. U.C.C. § 9-518(a), (b). Prior to 2010, the Code called this record a "correction statement," but this was misleading in that the statement had no legal effect and thus did not "correct" the problem that it addresses.
158. U.C.C. § 9-102(a)(39).
159. U.C.C. § 9-518(e).

because it is unauthorized, but searchers (who would not be aware of this) are likely to be misled. Today, a secured party of record may file an information statement indicating that it believes that a record associated with its financing statement is unauthorized.[160] Because only the secured party of record may file an information statement, the secured party that filed the unauthorized record will, if it discovers the mistake, need to advise the secured party of record to file an information statement to give searchers appropriate notice.[161]

[2] Changes—§§ 9-507, 9-508

[a] Changes Related to the Debtor's Name

Even if a financing statement does not contain any errors, changes might occur after filing that can mislead subsequent searchers. The general rule under Article 9 is that such post-filing changes do not render a properly completed filed financing statement ineffective.[162] There is an exception, however, for events related to the debtor's name that render a financing statement seriously misleading:

If the name that a filed financing statement provides for the debtor becomes seriously misleading under Section 9-506:

(1) the financing statement is effective to perfect a security interest in collateral acquired by the debtor before, or within four months after, the financing statement becomes seriously misleading; and

(2) the financing statement is not effective to perfect a security interest in collateral acquired by the debtor more than four months after the filed financing statement becomes seriously misleading, unless an amendment to the financing statement which renders the financing statement not seriously misleading is filed within four months after that event.[163]

An event that renders the name on a financing statement seriously misleading has a limited impact on the effectiveness of a properly prepared financing statement.[164] The original filing continues to perfect the security interest with respect to the collateral

---

160. U.C.C. § 9-518(c), (d).

161. If the person who filed the erroneous statement in this example failed to warn the secured party of record, and the secured party of record was later injured because a searcher was misled, the person who filed the erroneous statement would likely be exposed to a claim for damages.

162. U.C.C. § 9-507(b). *See In re* Hergert, 275 B.R. 58, 47 U.C.C. Rep. Serv. 2d 1 (Bankr. D. Ida. 2002) (change in secured party's name after an effective filed financing statement did not render the original filing ineffective under Section 9-504). For the consequences of filing a financing statement that contains incorrect information at the time filed, see U.C.C. § 9-338 and § 5.03[C][1], *supra*.

163. U.C.C. § 9-507(c). Prior to the 2010, this provision referred to "changes" in the debtor's name, but under the new rules regarding the use of a driver's license as a source for an individual debtor's name, a financing statement might become seriously misleading without a name change.

164. A change in the trade name but not the legal name of a debtor will not bring Section 9-507(c) into play. *In re* Miraglia, 11 B.R. 77, 31 U.C.C. Rep. Serv. 1196 (Bankr. W.D.N.Y. 1991) (debtor's change of trade name from "Louie's Deli" to "Pizza Pit" held irrelevant because financing statement was in name of individual proprietor).

to which it attached prior to the event. This means that a secured party with a security interest in a discrete item of collateral (and not an interest in after-acquired collateral) need not worry about an event related to the debtor's name that occurs after it files a sufficient initial financing statement.[165] Even with an after-acquired property clause, the original filing remains effective as to any collateral acquired by the debtor within four months after an event related to the debtor's name that renders the financing statement seriously misleading—even if the secured party never files an amendment indicating the new legally sufficient name.[166] Thus, the secured party needs to file an amendment to the financing statement only to perfect its security interest in after-acquired collateral acquired by the debtor more than four months after the event,[167] and then only if the event rendered the original financing statement seriously misleading.[168] An amendment will be sufficient if it either provides the debtor's new legally sufficient name or comes close enough that the financing statement is no longer seriously misleading. The four-month period allows the secured party to check on the debtor's name on a periodic basis without having to monitor the debtor constantly.

For example, assume that the debtor is an individual running a sole proprietorship who grants a bank a security interest in all present and after-acquired inventory. Assume also that with regard to individual debtor names, the jurisdiction has adopted Alternative A to Section 9-503(c)(4), meaning that as long as the debtor has an unexpired driver's license issued by the state of the debtor's residence, the only legally sufficient name for a financing statement is the name as it appears on the driver's license.[169] The name on the debtor's driver's license is Bennie Miller, and the secured party properly files in that name even though the name on the debtor's birth certificate is Ben J. Miller.[170] On May 1, the debtor's driver's license expires, and he fails to renew it. The names sufficient to perfect a security interest under Alternative A now are the individual's name, with all the ambiguity this formulation created prior to 2010, and

---

165. *In re* Custom Coals Laurel, 258 B.R. 597, 44 U.C.C. Rep. Serv. 2d 1 (Bankr. W.D. Pa. 2001) (amendment to the financing statement is not required with respect to collateral acquired prior to the name change).

166. Fleet Factors Corp. v. Bandolene Indus. Corp., 27 U.C.C. Rep. Serv. 2d 1105 (N.Y. 1995) (amended financing statement not required with respect to assets acquired by debtor six weeks after changing its name).

167. *In re* Motrobility Optical Sys., Inc., 279 B.R. 37, 48 U.C.C. Rep. Serv. 2d 727 (Bankr. D.N.H. 2002) (filing made six months after name change from "Lancast, Inc." to "Aura Networks, Inc." held ineffective with respect to collateral acquired more than four months after the name change); *In re* Cohuta Mills, Inc., 108 B.R. 815, 11 U.C.C. Rep. Serv. 2d 338 (N.D. Ga. 1989) (failure to file in name of new corporation within four months of its creation left secured party unperfected with respect to all collateral acquired after the grace period).

168. U.C.C. § 9-507(c). This standard is identical to the standard for determination of the effect of errors in the initial preparation of financing statements. First Agri Servs., Inc. v. Kahl, 385 N.W.2d 191, 42 U.C.C. Rep. Serv. 1583 (Wis. Ct. App. 1986) (financing statement listing debtor as "Gary and Dale Kahl" held seriously misleading when debtors began operating their farm as a partnership under the name "Kahl Farms" and filing officer had separate indexes for individual and organizational debtors).

169. For discussion of the alternatives provided for individual debtor names, see § 5.03[A][1], *supra*.

170. The facts of *In re* Miller, 2012 Bankr. LEXIS 70 (Bankr. C.D. Ill. Jan. 6, 2012), loosely provide the basis for this hypothetical.

the debtor's surname and first personal name. Even though the debtor's name has not legally changed, the expiration of the driver's license is an event that will render the financing statement seriously misleading if a search of the files using the filing office's standard search logic under either of the now-sufficient names (i.e., Ben J. Miller or Ben Miller) does not produce the financing statement filed under "Bennie Miller."

Assume further for purposes of this hypothetical that the financing statement has become seriously misleading and that the bank does not file an amendment using a legally sufficient name. On December 1, a finance company takes a competing security interest in the debtor's inventory and perfects by filing under a legally sufficient name. Despite its failure to file an appropriate amendment within the statutory four-month grace period, the bank will be perfected and thus have priority over the finance company[171] as to all inventory on hand at the time the driver's license expired (May 1) and all inventory acquired through the end of August (the end of the four-month period). As to all inventory acquired on or after September 1, the bank will be unperfected and thus subordinate to the finance company.[172] Although the prior example does not involve a change in the debtor's legal name, the same analysis would apply to such a change.

The practical implications behoove searchers to know any prior names the debtor may have used or that may have been legally sufficient for perfection purposes; otherwise, a search under the currently sufficient name may not reveal an effective financing statement. As indicated above, because many secured parties do not look to after-acquired property for security, post-filing events related to the debtor's name will not affect their interests. The secured parties that most commonly look to after-acquired property, and thus have the most at stake regarding the refiling requirement, are financers against inventory or accounts.

[b] Transferees and New Debtors

Rather than just a change in the debtor's name, a change might relate to the debtor's business structure. For example, an individual debtor that operates a sole proprietorship—and had granted a bank a security interest in its existing and after-acquired inventory—might incorporate and thereafter carry out its business activities in corporate form. Likewise, a corporate debtor that had granted a bank a similar security interest might dissolve after merging into another corporation.[173] In the first transaction, the individual debtor has essentially transferred the collateral to the new corporate entity; in the second, the original corporate debtor has essentially transferred the

---

171. For discussion of priority contests between secured parties, see Chapter 10, *infra*.

172. If the bank had filed an appropriate amendment after the expiration of the grace period but before December 1, it would have priority over the finance company as to all inventory, including the inventory acquired on or after September 1. There will have been a gap in the bank's perfection that the bank could have avoided if it had filed the amendment prior to September 1, but if no third party acquired an interest in the collateral during that gap, the bank will have suffered no harm. *See, e.g.,* Ratcliff v. Rancher's Legacy Meat Co., 2020 U.S. Dist. LEXIS 127276 (D. Minn. July 20, 2020).

173. U.C.C. § 9-508, Comment 2.

collateral to the acquiring corporation. When the existing collateral transfers from the debtor that granted the security interest to the new entity, does the bank's security interest in that collateral remain perfected by its filing in the name of the transferor?

The general rule on continuation of perfection in transferred collateral is that a filed financing statement remains effective with respect to any collateral that is disposed of and in which a security interest continues, "even if the secured party knows of or consents to the disposition."[174] This must be read in connection with Section 9-315(a)(1), which provides that a security interest continues in collateral notwithstanding its disposition "unless the secured party authorized the disposition free of the security interest."[175] Thus, in the first example above, as to inventory transferred by the proprietor to the corporation, the bank continues to have an enforceable, perfected security interest in that inventory unless the bank had authorized the transfer clear of its security interest. An exception applies if the transferee is located in a different jurisdiction from that of the transferor, but interjurisdictional issues are discussed elsewhere, and for current purposes, we will assume that everything occurs within a single jurisdiction.[176] Because the transferee (the new corporation) succeeded to the proprietor's rights with respect to the existing collateral, it becomes the debtor with respect to that collateral. Recall that the term "debtor" refers not to a person that owes payment or performance of the secured obligation but rather to a person with an interest in the collateral.[177] But since the filed financing statement remains generally effective, the bank need not amend that statement to reflect the name of the corporation—at least as far as the inventory existing on the date of the transfer.

Suppose the new corporation subsequently acquires new inventory. Will the bank's security interest attach to the new inventory? Obviously, if the corporation signs a new security agreement covering the corporation's inventory, the answer is yes. But if the bank was unaware of this change, no such new agreement will have been executed, and the new corporation never signed the original security agreement containing the after-acquired property clause. Thus, the bank's security interest will not attach to the new collateral unless the new corporation qualifies as a "new debtor" under Article 9.

The term "new debtor" means a person bound by the terms of the security agreement entered into by the original debtor.[178] The mere fact that a transferee acquires the collateral makes them a "debtor," but it does not make them a "new debtor," nor is

---

174. U.C.C. § 9-507(a).

175. U.C.C. § 9-315(a)(1). The provision is discussed in §§ 11.01 and 11.02, *infra*.

176. If the transferee is located in a different jurisdiction, the secured party will generally have a one-year grace period of temporary perfection following the transfer, but this temporary perfection will lapse unless the secured party files a financing statement in the transferee's name in the transferee's jurisdiction within that one-year period or otherwise perfects its security interest (such as by taking possession of the collateral) during that time. *See* U.C.C. § 9-316(a). The secured party has statutory authority to make such a filing. U.C.C. § 9-509(c). For further detail, see § 9.04, *infra*.

177. U.C.C. § 9-102(a)(28)(A).

178. U.C.C. § 9-102(a)(56). The "original debtor" is a person that, as the debtor, entered into the security agreement to which the "new debtor" becomes bound. U.C.C. § 9-102(a)(60).

the transferor an "original debtor." Only if the transferee is a "new debtor" within that term's definition does it become bound by all of the terms of the transferor's (original debtor's) security agreement, including (in our example) the after-acquired property clause. Section 9-203(d) determines whether a person is a "new debtor" and provides as follows:

> A person becomes bound as debtor by a security agreement entered into by another person if, by operation of law other than this article or by contract:
>
> (1) the security agreement becomes effective to create a security interest in the person's property; or
>
> (2) the person becomes generally obligated for the obligations of the other person, including the obligation secured under the security agreement, and acquires or succeeds to all or substantially all of the assets of the other person.

Law other than Article 9 thus determines whether a person becomes bound as a new debtor. The applicable sources of this law are the law of contracts and the law of business organizations.

Continuing with the sole proprietor example described above, suppose the individual who is the proprietor not only transferred all her business-related assets to the newly formed corporation but also arranged for the corporation to assume all of her business-related contractual obligations. As to the inventory on hand at the date of the transfer, the corporation becomes the debtor, and a filing in the name of the corporation is unnecessary to continue the bank's perfected status.[179] And because the corporation assumed the contractual obligations of the proprietor and succeeded to all or substantially all her assets, the corporation is also a "new debtor" as well. This means that the bank's after-acquired property clause is effective to cause a security interest to attach to the new inventory acquired by the corporation even if the corporation did not sign the security agreement containing the clause.

That resolves the attachment question, but now a separate perfection question arises: does the bank's original filing in the name of the individual proprietor perfect its security interest in the inventory acquired by the new debtor following its incorporation? As an initial proposition, a filed financing statement is effective against a new debtor to the same extent it would be effective against the original debtor, but there is an exception if, as will virtually always be the case, the difference between the name of the original debtor and the name of the new debtor is sufficient to render the filing seriously misleading to someone searching under the correct name of the new debtor.[180]

---

179. The security interest continues perfected by a filing naming the transferor as debtor, and the rules governing perfection as to new debtors are not applicable. U.C.C. §§ 9-507(a) (filed financing statement continues effective notwithstanding disposition by the debtor), 9-508(c) (rules governing perfection as to new debtor inapplicable to financing statement that remains effective under U.C.C. § 9-507(a)).

180. As with transferees, the discussion in the text assumes that the original debtor and the new debtor are located in the same jurisdiction. For discussion of inter-jurisdictional issues, see § 9.04, *infra*.

In that case, the filing is effective only as to (1) collateral of the new debtor, other than collateral transferred to it, in existence at the time the person becomes bound as new debtor (in this example, there is none[181]), and (2) collateral acquired by the new debtor during the four months after it becomes bound as a new debtor.[182] The filing in the name of the individual will not perfect the bank's security interest in inventory acquired by the new debtor more than four months after it becomes bound, unless the secured party files an initial financing statement in the name of the new debtor before the four-month period expires.[183]

Now suppose the person that granted the bank a security interest in existing and after-acquired inventory is Corporation A. Suppose further that Corporation A merges into Corporation B, which acquires all of Corporation A's existing inventory, and Corporation A is dissolved. If the law governing the merger makes Corporation B liable for Corporation A's debts, Corporation B will qualify as a new debtor. As to the assets of Corporation A acquired by Corporation B, the transfer rules (rather than the new-debtor rules) apply. Unlike the corporation that succeeded the sole proprietorship in the prior example, however, assume that Corporation B had its own stockpile of existing inventory at the time it became bound as new debtor. Because a new debtor is bound by all the terms of the original debtor's security agreement, the bank has a security interest in Corporation B's existing and after-acquired inventory.[184] The financing statement filed in the name of Corporation A is effective as to Corporation B's existing inventory and as to inventory acquired by it within four months after the merger. For inventory acquired by Corporation B more than four months after the merger, the bank needs to file an initial financing statement covering the inventory in Corporation B's name.[185]

---

181. The hypothetical assumes that the corporation was created to receive the transfer of inventory and to carry on the business, and thus it did not have, at the time it became bound by the security agreement, any assets that qualified as inventory other than the transferred assets. The new-debtor perfection rules thus apply only to the corporation's after-acquired inventory. Contrast this situation with the hypothetical involving merging corporations discussed next in the text.

182. U.C.C. § 9-508(b)(1).

183. U.C.C. § 9-508(b)(2). The secured party has statutory authority to make such a filing. U.C.C. § 9-509(b). As with name changes, a secured party that files its initial financing statement in the name of the new debtor after the four-month period expires will have a gap in its perfection but will still be perfected as to a third party whose interest arises after the belated filing.

184. U.C.C. § 9-203(e)(1). Section 9-326 governs priority contests between the original debtor's secured party and a secured party that has dealt directly with the new debtor. Even if it files an initial financing statement within four months after the new debtor becomes bound, the secured party of the original debtor will not obtain priority over a perfected security interest of the secured party of the new debtor in collateral of the new debtor in existence at the time it became bound or after-acquired collateral. It will have priority, however, with regard to transferred collateral even if the secured party of the new debtor now has a perfected security interest in that collateral as a result of an after-acquired property clause. U.C.C. § 9-326(a), (b).

185. The hypothetical assumes the filing in the name of Corporation A would seriously mislead a searcher using the correct name of Corporation B.

[D] May a Financing Statement Function as a Security Agreement?

With perfection by filing, a typical secured transaction involves at least two separate records: (1) a security agreement that meets the requirements of Section 9-203 for attachment, and (2) an initial financing statement that complies with Sections 9-502 and 9-516(b). A security agreement is often lengthy because it includes provisions that go far beyond the minimum requirements for attachment. An initial financing statement, in contrast, is generally a simple form that follows the model provided in Section 9-521(a). The use of the simple form is efficient. The limited, basic information required facilitates the practice of filing even before creation of the security interest. Filing fees based on the number of pages and whether the financing statement is in a standard form also create an incentive to keep filings simple.

The question sometimes arises whether a financing statement can serve both functions.[186] The court's decision in *Evans v. Everett*[187] is instructive in this regard. It stated that "[a] financing statement which does no more than meet the [statutory] requirements ... will *not* create a security interest in the debtor's property."[188] The court considered a basic financing statement to be insufficient because it does not create or provide for a security interest; that is, it does not contain language indicating an intent that there be a security interest. The financing statement before the court in *Evans*, however, contained more than the basic statutory requirements; it stated that it "*covers the following type of collateral: (all crops now growing or to be planted on 5 specified farms) same securing note for advanced money to produce crops for the year 1969.*"[189] The court held that this additional language was sufficient to show that the debtor

---

186. A copy of the security agreement was sufficient under prior law to constitute a valid financing statement if it was filed and included all of the information required for a valid financing statement. U.C.C. §9-402(1) (1972 Official Text). This provision created problems for filing officers because a typical security agreement is much more detailed than a financing statement and is formatted quite differently. As a result, if a secured party filed a security agreement as its financing statement, it created more work for the filing officer in indexing the filing correctly (and, correspondingly, increased the likelihood of a filing or indexing error). Article 9 no longer expressly authorizes the use of a security agreement as a financing statement, and many filing offices have adopted rules that discourage or prohibit secured parties from filing copies of security agreements.

187. 279 N.C. 352, 183 S.E.2d 109, 9 U.C.C. Rep. Serv. 769 (1971).

188. *Evans*, 279 N.C. at 358, 183 S.E.2d at 113, 9 U.C.C. Rep. Serv. at 774. For a similar result in a case involving a vehicle covered by a certificate of title, see *In re* Buttke, 76 U.C.C. Rep. Serv. 2d 875 (Bankr. D.S.D. 2012) (application for certificate of title and certificate itself did not contain language creating or providing for a security interest and thus did not constitute a security agreement).

189. *Evans*, 279 N.C. at 359, 183 S.E.2d at 114, 9 U.C.C. Rep. Serv. at 775. The debtor had also signed a promissory note that contained a statement that it "*is secured by* Uniform Commercial Code financing statement of North Carolina." *Id. See In re* Outboard Marine Corp., 300 B.R. 308, 52 U.C.C. Rep. Serv. 2d 488 (Bankr. N.D. Ill. 2003) (additional documents were invoices that included a reservation of a security interest by the seller as part of the terms and conditions of the sales of pieces of machinery; the court declined to grant summary judgment because, although the writings clearly showed the seller's intent to create security interest, a genuine issue remained as to whether the buyer had the same intention).

had granted a security interest to the plaintiff.[190] Thus, a financing statement can serve both functions, but only provided it satisfies the formal requirements for an enforceable security agreement—including a signature by the debtor. Because revised Article 9 does not require that a financing statement be signed, the requirement in Section 9-203(b)(3)(A) that the debtor sign the security agreement would have to be satisfied either by the debtor's signing the financing statement (though the form includes no place for the debtor's signature) or by the debtor's signing another record.[191]

§ 5.04 When to File—§ 9-502(d)

One caveat on the timing of filing is readily apparent: a secured party perfects to enhance its position vis-à-vis potential competing claimants. It is therefore in the secured party's interest to file sooner rather than later because, as a general proposition, the secured party will defeat most claimants whose conflicting interests arise after perfection but will be subordinate to most claimants whose conflicting interests arose earlier. This ranking of competing claimants is the concept of priorities, which subsequent chapters cover in detail. Nevertheless, the basic importance of perfecting promptly is easy to grasp. Delay in perfection leaves the secured party vulnerable to competing claimants.

Because a person cannot perfect a security interest that has not yet attached and therefore does not exist,[192] it is logical to assume that parties will first create a security interest and that the secured party will then perfect that interest by filing. The logic is not reliable in this case because Section 9-502(d) specifically authorizes pre-attachment filing: "A financing statement may be filed before a security agreement is made or a security interest otherwise attaches."[193] This provision allows a secured party to "pre-file," thereby "staking out" priority in the indicated collateral against possible compet-

---

190. The courts have been virtually unanimous in holding that a financing statement that does not create or provide for a security interest cannot qualify as a security agreement. *See, e.g., In re* Arctic Air, Inc., 202 B.R. 533, 31 U.C.C. Rep. Serv. 2d 233 (Bankr. D.R.I. 1996). Professor Grant Gilmore, a principal drafter of the original version of Article 9, disagreed, arguing that "nothing in § 9-203 requires that the 'security agreement' contain a granting clause." 1 G. GILMORE, SECURITY INTERESTS IN PERSONAL PROPERTY § 11.4, at 347 (1965). For a case that relies on Prof. Gilmore's analysis to conclude that a financing statement qualifies as a security agreement if extrinsic evidence shows that the parties so intended, see Gibson County Farm Bureau Co-op Ass'n v. Greer, 643 N.E.2d 313, 25 U.C.C. Rep. Serv. 2d 954 (Ind. 1994). *See also* § 2.02[A], *supra*.

191. *See, e.g., In re* Jojo's 10 Restaurant, LLC, 455 B.R. 321, 74 U.C.C. Rep. Serv. 2d 441 (Bankr. D. Mass. 2011) (no authenticated security agreement existed even though asset purchase agreement provided that buyer's obligation would be secured by a standard form security agreement that was never executed although filed financing statement described the collateral; asset-purchase agreement lacked granting language and the financing statement was not signed by debtor).

The use of multiple sources to satisfy the formal requirements for an enforceable security agreement is discussed in § 2.02[A][3], *supra*. Of course, if the necessary signature comes via the signing of another record, then the secured party is not really relying solely on the financing statement.

192. U.C.C. § 9-308(a). *See* § 4.03, *supra*.

193. U.C.C. § 9-502(d).

ing claimants while the secured party makes a decision whether to make a secured loan to the debtor.[194] Knowing about the priority advantage and the risks that it can help eliminate, lenders often require a prospective debtor to sign a record authorizing the filing of a financing statement[195] as a condition to continuing the negotiations that might lead to a secured transaction. If the transaction proceeds as anticipated, the secured party's priority date vis-à-vis other secured parties will be the date of its filing, not the date of attachment and perfection (which will occur simultaneously when the secured party has pre-filed).[196] If the debtor does not authorize the filing in a signed record but later, as part of the now-approved transaction, signs a security agreement that describes the same collateral as that covered by the unauthorized filing, the signing of the security agreement gives the secured party statutory authority to file an initial financing statement covering the collateral described in the agreement,[197] and that authority serves to ratify the previously unauthorized filing.[198] If the transaction is not consummated, the debtor is entitled to a termination statement that will end the effectiveness of the financing statement and its potential to perfect a subsequent transaction involving the same collateral.[199]

The pre-filing option illustrates another consequence to the disassociation of perfection and filing. After the full satisfaction of a secured obligation, a financing statement that had perfected the security interest will remain effective until it either lapses or is terminated. As long as it remains filed, the financing statement will still be effective to perfect a security interest created later (and not originally anticipated), provided that the description in the financing statement covers the collateral in the later transaction.[200] A third party contemplating a secured transaction with the debtor using the same collateral should insist on a termination statement[201] or require a subordination agreement[202] with the person that filed the financing statement.

---

194. U.C.C. § 9-322(a). For a more detailed discussion of Article 9's "first-to-file-or-perfect" rule for governing priority between conflicting security interests in the same collateral, see § 10.01, *infra*.

195. U.C.C. § 9-509(a)(1).

196. U.C.C. § 9-322(a)(1) (as between competing perfected security interests first to either file or perfect has priority). See discussion in § 10.01, *infra*.

197. U.C.C. § 9-509(a)(1).

198. U.C.C. § 9-509, Comment 3. *See, e.g., In re* Adoni Group, Inc., 530 B.R. 592, 86 U.C.C. Rep. Serv. 2d 540 (Bankr. S.D.N.Y. 2015) (relying on Comments as authority for holding that financing statement filed one day before debtor signed the security agreement became authorized the following day and was effective for perfection). The Comments are explicit that a secured party's priority date in the case of a ratification is the date of filing rather than the date of ratification. U.C.C. § 9-322, Comment 4. The rationale for the position taken in the Comment is that the notice value of the filing is independent of the time of ratification.

199. U.C.C. § 9-513(c), (d).

200. *In re* Payless Cashways, Inc., 273 B.R. 789, 47 U.C.C. Rep. Serv. 2d 366 (Bankr. W.D. Mo. 2002) (filing of a financing statement three years prior to the debtor's granting a security interest led to a perfected security interest).

201. For discussion of termination statements, see § 5.06[C], *infra*.

202. U.C.C. § 9-339. Article 9's priority rules are default rules, and the parties are free to alter them by agreement.

§ 5.05 Where to File

[A] In What State?

While Article 9 is generally "uniform" law, each state adopts Article 9 as state law, and each state maintains its own filing system. This means that in any secured transaction, the secured party must ascertain which state's law will govern whether the security interest is perfected—because this will determine in which state the secured party must file if it wishes to perfect its security interest by filing. A secured party that files in the wrong state has not perfected its security interest. Likewise, searchers must ascertain which state's law governs perfection, so that they know that they are searching in the correct set of filing records to permit them to ascertain whether a prior perfected security interest may exist in the intended property.

Because many secured transactions involve parties with locations or contacts in more than one state, identifying which state's law will govern perfection becomes critical. For the sake of clarity, Article 9, Part 3, Subpart 1, provides choice-of-law rules in Sections 9-301 through 9-307 that dictate in which state a secured party must file to perfect a security interest. These provisions are discussed in greater detail in Chapter 9.[203]

[B] In What Office?—§ 9-501

Once the secured party determines the appropriate state in which to file, the secured party must then identify the appropriate office within that state in which to file its financing statement. Interested parties are likely to search the files only in the office designated in Article 9 as the proper place for filing, and thus a filing in the wrong office cannot meet the notice function that the filing system serves.[204]

Because Article 9 is state law, its provisions designating the office in which to file refer to offices within the borders of the enacting state.[205] The vast bulk of filings under Article 9 are made centrally, at the state level, in what is often called the "central" filing office. When each state enacted Article 9, its legislature designated within its enactment of Section 9-501(a) which state official would operate the filing system and receive filed financing statements.[206] To perfect a security interest in most Article 9 collateral, the secured party must file in that central office.

---

203. *See* §§ 9.01, 9.02, *infra*.

204. *See* § 5.03[B], *supra*.

205. The Code makes the point clear: "if the local law of this State governs perfection of a security interest or agricultural lien." U.C.C. § 9-501(a).

206. U.C.C. § 9-501(a)(2). This explains the "empty brackets" that appear in the uniform version of Section 9-501(a)(2)—each state, in adopting Article 9 as state law, fills in that "blank" by identifying an agency to operate the central Article 9 filing system in that state. In some states (e.g., Missouri), the central Article 9 filing system is maintained by the Secretary of State. In other states, it is maintained by a different official (in Delaware, by the Division of Corporations; in Wisconsin, by the Department of Financial Institutions).

The only exception is for filings covering certain real-estate-related collateral, specifically, (1) timber to be cut, (2) as-extracted collateral,[207] and (3) fixture filings for goods that are or are to become fixtures.[208] These filings are made locally, in "the office designated for the filing or recording of a record of a mortgage on the related real property,"[209] that is, the office for recording interests in real estate. That office is most likely to be in the county in which the affected real property is located. Third parties that are considering buying land (or making a mortgage loan on it) would expect title to that land to include growing timber, minerals, or fixtures. Further, they would customarily search in the real property records to ascertain the possibility of conflicting interests in the land. Thus, Section 9-501(a)(1) requires that a secured party taking a security interest in these types of collateral must file in the real estate recording system to provide effective notice to third parties interested in the real estate.

§ 5.06 Lapse and Termination of Filing

[A] Lapse of Initial Financing Statement—§ 9-515(a)

The general rule under Article 9 is that a financing statement is effective for five years after filing.[210] Unless continued through the mechanisms discussed below, the effectiveness of the financing statement lapses at the end of this five-year period.[211]

When Article 9 was first enacted, many states required certain categories of Article 9 filings to be made at the local county, parish, or township level. The assumption was that the local availability of the files would facilitate searches. With the introduction and evolution of computerized systems capable of handling massive quantities of information, it was inevitable that efficiency concerns would drive the system to evolve toward centralized filing. Today, the only financing statements that are filed locally are those involving real-estate-related collateral as described in the text.

207. The term "as-extracted collateral" has two basic applications. First, the term applies to "oil, gas, or other minerals that are subject to a security interest that (i) is created by a debtor having an interest in the minerals before extraction; and (ii) attaches to the minerals as extracted." U.C.C. § 9-102(a)(6)(A). Second, the term refers to "accounts arising out of the sale at the wellhead or minehead of oil, gas, or other minerals in which the debtor had an interest before extraction." U.C.C. § 9-102(a)(6)(B).

208. For discussion of fixture filings, see § 15.02, *infra*.

209. U.C.C. § 9-501(a)(1).

210. U.C.C. § 9-515(a). A recorded mortgage can be effective as a fixture filing if satisfies the requirements for a financing statement (U.C.C. § 9-502(c)), and in such cases, the mortgage is effective until it "is released or satisfied of record or its effectiveness otherwise terminates as to the real property." U.C.C. § 9-515(g). The Code also permits a filing as to the assets of a transmitting utility to be made centrally even though the filing covers fixtures. U.C.C. § 9-501(b). The central filing serves as a fixture filing for fixtures located within that state. U.C.C. § 9-301, Comment 5b. The rationale is that the fixtures of a transmitting utility are typically located in numerous counties, rendering local filings impractical. A filing as to a transmitting utility is effective until a termination statement is filed. U.C.C. § 9-515(f). A special 30-year period of effectiveness is available for public-finance transactions and manufactured-home transactions, as these transactions involve obligations customarily repaid over longer terms (up to 30 years). U.C.C. § 9-515(b).

211. U.C.C. § 9-515(c). *See In re* Hurst, 308 B.R. 298, 53 U.C.C. Rep. Serv. 2d 342 (Bankr. S.D. Ohio 2004) (perfection lapsed when five years expired because secured party had not undertaken any measures to continue its perfected status).

Lapse provides a means to keep the filing system from being cluttered with financing statements unlikely to have further commercial relevance.[212] The five-year period runs from the date of filing of the financing statement, not the date of attachment of the security interest. Because the filing is effective for five years after filing, it lapses at the end of the anniversary date, not the day before. The filing office may destroy any written record immediately on lapse[213] but must maintain a record of the information destroyed for at least one year thereafter.[214]

[B] Continuation Statements—§ 9-515(c)–(e)

If the obligor repays the loan in less than five years, and the security interest is thus extinguished, the secured party may no longer care whether its financing statement lapses. But some credit arrangements remain in place for longer than five years, and secured parties in these transactions will want their interests to remain continuously perfected beyond the initial five-year period. The solution is to file a continuation statement. A timely continuation statement prevents a filed financing statement from lapsing.[215]

A continuation statement is a type of amendment that provides notice of the extension of the lapse date of the initial financing statement. It must identify the initial financing statement to which it relates by its file number[216] and indicate that it is filed as a continuation statement or to continue the effectiveness of the identified financ-

---

212. If financing statements never lapsed, someone searching the records today would theoretically have to search more than 60 years of financing statement records. But most of those records would relate to transactions that were paid off long ago and cover collateral that no longer exists. The Code's lapse feature permits searchers to limit their searches to filings appearing on the records during the most recent five years, thus reducing transaction costs.

213. U.C.C. § 9-522(b).

214. U.C.C. § 9-522(a). The record must be maintained for one year after the financing statement would have lapsed even if it is terminated earlier. Thus, information will always be available for at least six years after initial filing.

215. U.C.C. § 9-515(c). The courts have disagreed on the necessity of filing a continuation statement after a secured party commences litigation. *Compare* Hassell v. First Pa. Bank, N.A., 41 N.C. App. 296, 254 S.E.2d 768, 26 U.C.C. Rep. Serv. 1380 (1979) (secured party held to be unperfected despite having obtained judgment against debtor prior to expiration of five-year period), *with* Chrysler Credit Corp. v. United States, 1978 U.S. Dist. LEXIS 19263, 24 U.C.C. Rep. Serv. 794 (E.D. Va. Mar. 3, 1978) (filing of litigation tolled any obligation of plaintiff to file continuation statement because defendant was clearly aware of plaintiff's security interest). However, a prudent secured party should simply file a continuation statement in a timely manner rather than rely upon questionable case authority that a continuation statement is unnecessary.

216. The filing officer assigns a unique file number to each initial financing statement as it is filed. U.C.C. § 9-519(a). The file number must contain a digit that is "mathematically derived from or related to the other digits of the file number." *Id.* § 9-519(b)(1). Because amendments must contain the file number of the initial financing statement, this digit can assist the filing officer in determining whether the person filing the amendment made a single-digit or transpositional error in entering the file number on the amendment.

ing statement.[217] A filing fee also must be paid.[218] The filing office must index all filed records that relate to an initial financing statement, including continuation statements, in a way that associates the related records to the initial financing statement.[219]

A continuation statement may be filed at any time during the six months that precede lapse of the financing statement.[220] A timely filing with the correct information extends the effectiveness of the financing statement for an additional five years.[221] The additional five years begin not from the date of filing of the continuation statement but rather from the date the five-year period under the original filing ends.[222] A secured party that desires to extend the effectiveness of a financing statement even further may file additional continuation statements during the six-month periods that precede lapse *ad infinitum*.[223] A continuation statement requires authorization by the secured party of record but not by the debtor.[224]

Unless perfected through some means other than filing,[225] a security interest becomes unperfected prospectively upon lapse.[226] The security interest is also "deemed never to have been perfected as against a purchaser of the collateral for value."[227] Even

---

217. U.C.C. §9-102(a)(27). *See* Nat'l Bank of Fulton Cnty. v. Haupricht Bros., Inc., 55 Ohio App. 3d 249, 564 N.E.2d 101, 14 U.C.C. Rep. Serv. 2d 215 (1988) (nonconforming filings not effective as continuation statement). If a security interest is assigned, it makes sense to file a record of the assignment; otherwise, the assignor will continue as the secured party of record, and a continuation statement signed by the assignee will have to be accompanied by a separate statement of assignment signed by the secured party of record. The assignment of a security interest of record can be made in two ways: naming the assignee in the initial financing statement or making a subsequent amendatory filing. U.C.C. §9-514.

218. U.C.C. §9-525.

219. U.C.C. §9-519(c). This requirement ensures that the contents of the initial financing statement being continued will appear during the five-year search period.

220. U.C.C. §9-515(d). A filing office is required to reject a continuation statement not filed within this six-month period. U.C.C. §§9-520(a), 9-516(b)(7). A continuation statement accepted for filing outside this time frame is ineffective. U.C.C. §9-510(c); *In re* Quality Seafoods, Inc., 104 B.R. 560, 9 U.C.C. Rep. Serv. 2d 1156 (Bankr. D. Mass. 1989) (filing continuation statement five years and one day after filing of financing statement caused security interest to be unperfected because financing statement had lapsed before filing of continuation statement).

221. U.C.C. §9-515(e); Bank of Holden v. Bank of Warrensburg, 15 S.W.3d 758, 41 U.C.C. Rep. Serv. 2d 708 (Mo. Ct. App. 2000) (filing a continuation statement on January 30, 1997, with respect to a financing statement with effectiveness running from January 30, 1992, through January 30, 1997, was sufficient to prevent perfection in the collateral from lapsing).

222. U.C.C. §9-515(e). *See also In re* Davison, 29 B.R. 987, 36 U.C.C. Rep. Serv. 717 (Bankr. W.D. Mo. 1983).

223. U.C.C. §9-515(e). *See also* United States v. Branch Banking & Trust Co., 11 U.C.C. Rep. Serv. 2d 351 (E.D.N.C. 1990).

224. U.C.C. §9-509(d) provides that "[a] person may file an amendment other than an amendment that adds collateral covered by a financing statement or an amendment that adds a debtor to a financing statement only if" it is authorized by the secured party of record. For discussion of an exception for debtor-filed termination statements, see §5.06[C], *infra*.

225. *See* Chapter 4, *supra*.

226. U.C.C. §9-515(c). *See also* State Bank of Harland v. Arndt, 129 Wisc. 2d 411, 385 N.W.2d 219, 42 U.C.C. Rep. Serv. 1850 (Ct. App. 1986).

227. U.C.C. §9-515(c).

though a filing is effective and the security interest is thus perfected when the interest of a purchaser for value arises, this "retroactive invalidation" provision will cause the unperfected status that the secured party acquires upon lapse to relate back *ab initio* in the case of a later priority dispute with the purchaser.[228] In other words, a secured party that allows its filing to lapse will be treated, as against a purchaser for value, as if it had never filed at all.[229] Retroactive invalidation does not apply in favor of persons who are not purchasers, notably lien creditors (including a trustee in bankruptcy). The trustee will lose to a secured party perfected on the date of the debtor's bankruptcy filing (and whose interest is not otherwise avoidable under bankruptcy law)[230] even if lapse later occurs.

The array of competing claimants that fall within the scope of the retroactive-invalidation rule is broader than it initially appears. The term "purchaser" includes a buyer, secured party, and any other party that acquires an interest in property through a voluntary transfer.[231] For example, suppose SP-1 takes and perfects by filing a security interest in Debtor's equipment. A year later, SP-2 does likewise. If a priority dispute comes to trial before SP-1's financing statement lapses, SP-1 will have priority over SP-2. If SP-1 permits its filing to lapse, however, SP-2 will gain priority over SP-1. Even if SP-1 files a new financing statement after the initial one lapses, it cannot repair the gap in perfection caused by lapse. The new filing will only operate to perfect SP-1 prospectively for five years.[232]

---

228. *In re* Hilyard Drilling Co., Inc., 60 B.R. 500, 2 U.C.C. Rep. Serv. 2d 370 (Bankr. W.D. Ark. 1986) (upon lapse, prior-perfected secured party became junior to competing security interest that had been perfected during five-year period of effective filing of prior-perfected secured party).

229. Federal Fin. Co. v. Grady Cnty., Okla., 988 P.2d 908, 40 U.C.C. Rep. Serv. 2d 574 (Okla. Ct. Civ. App. 1999) (once creditor with priority allowed its financing statement to lapse, it lost its position of priority); Charles Ligeti Co., Inc. v. Ernie Goldberger & Co., 51 U.C.C. Rep. Serv. 2d 822 (Cal. Ct. App. 2003) (senior secured party that allowed perfection to lapse treated as unperfected at all times against perfected junior secured party even though junior secured party at all relevant times had actual knowledge of the senior's perfected status and the lapse of its financing statement).

230. *See, e.g.*, Ratcliff v. Rancher's Legacy Meat Co., 2020 U.S. Dist. LEXIS 127276 (D. Minn. July 20, 2020). For discussion of applicable bankruptcy law, see Chapter 16, *infra*.

231. "Purchaser" means "a person who takes by purchase." U.C.C. § 1-201(b)(30). The term "purchase" is, in turn, defined to include "taking by sale, discount, negotiation, mortgage, pledge, lien, issue or re-issue, gift or any other voluntary transaction creating an interest in property." U.C.C. § 1-201(b)(29).

232. The rationale for the retroactive invalidation rule is that it reduces the circumstances in which priorities will be resolved in a circular fashion. If the rule were otherwise—that is, if a secured party retained priority against all parties whose interests arose before lapse—the following scenario might occur: Bank lends money to Debtor and takes a security interest in Debtor's equipment, which it perfects by filing. Before Bank's financing statement lapses, Finance Company takes and by filing perfects a security interest in the same collateral. Bank then allows its financing statement to lapse and Debtor, while Finance Company is still perfected, files a petition in bankruptcy. As between Bank and Finance Company, Bank would have priority; as between Finance Company and the bankruptcy trustee exercising the rights of a lien creditor, Finance Company would have priority; as between Bank and the trustee, the trustee would have priority. Around we go! Under the retroactive invalidation rule, Finance Company has priority over both Bank and the trustee, and the trustee has priority over Bank.

[C] Termination Statements and Releases of Collateral — §§ 9-513, 9-509

A debtor will encounter significant difficulty obtaining secured financing against any property indicated as collateral on a filed financing statement that has not lapsed.[233] For this reason, a debtor that pays off the debt and does not have an ongoing financing relationship with its secured party will want to terminate the effectiveness of the secured party's filed financing statement without waiting for that statement to lapse.

The solution for such a debtor is a termination statement.[234] A termination statement is an amendment to a financing statement that identifies the initial financing statement to which it refers by its file number and either indicates that it is a termination statement or that the identified financing statement is no longer effective.[235] As with continuation statements and all other records that relate to an initial financing statement, the filing office must index a termination statement in a way that associates it with the initial financing statement.[236]

A debtor may make a signed demand on the secured party to provide the debtor with a termination statement if "there is no obligation secured by the collateral covered by the financing statement and no commitment to make an advance, incur an obligation or otherwise give value."[237] A debtor may also demand a termination statement with respect to the filing of an initial financing statement that the debtor did not authorize.[238] Subject to an exception for consumer goods discussed below, the secured party must then cause the secured party of record[239] either to communicate a termina-

---

A full analysis of priority issues must await later chapters. See §§ 10.01 (secured party versus secured party) and 12.02 (secured party versus lien creditor), infra.

233. For a complete explanation of why a prudent lender would be unwilling to make a secured loan to the debtor while the unlapsed financing statement of another creditor remains on file, see § 10.02, infra. For a case in which a subsequent creditor did not concern itself with a prior-filed financing statement on a debt that had been paid in full but found itself ultimately in a subordinate position, see Provident Finance Co. v. Beneficial Finance Co., 36 N.C. App. 401, 245 S.E.2d 510, 24 U.C.C. Rep. Serv. 1332 (1978).

234. U.C.C. § 9-513(d) ("[U]pon the filing of a termination statement with the filing office, the financing statement to which the termination statement relates ceases to be effective.").

235. U.C.C. § 9-102(a)(80).

236. U.C.C. § 9-519(c).

237. U.C.C. § 9-513(c)(1).

238. U.C.C. § 9-513(c)(4). Article 9 also includes other grounds for which a debtor may make a signed demand on a secured party for a termination statement: the financing statement covers accounts or chattel paper on which the person obligated has been discharged (U.C.C. § 9-513(c)(2)), and the financing statement covers goods that were on consignment but are not in the debtor's possession (U.C.C. § 9-513(c)(3)).

239. A termination statement (and any amendment other than an amendment that adds a debtor or adds collateral) must be authorized by the secured party of record. U.C.C. § 9-509(d)(1). If the secured party of record assigns its rights to a third party, the third party will be the secured party, but unless an amendment providing the name of the assignee is communicated to the filing office, the assignor will remain the secured party of record. Amendments to the Comments in 2010 make the

tion statement to the filing office and pay the statutory fee or to deliver a termination statement to the debtor, which may then communicate it to the office and pay the fee.[240] A filed termination statement ends the effectiveness of a financing statement earlier than would occur through lapse.[241] If a termination statement is not communicated for filing or delivered within 20 days after a proper demand,[242] the secured party incurs the same liability as that imposed for filing an unauthorized initial financing statement or amendment: a civil penalty of $500[243] and liability for any losses incurred by the debtor as a result of the secured party's failure to comply.[244]

Although a secured party does not ordinarily have a duty to provide a termination statement absent a demand from the debtor,[245] an exception applies if the financing statement covers consumer goods. The secured party then must cause the secured party of record to file a termination statement within one month after the outstanding secured obligation is extinguished, even without a demand from the debtor.[246] The secured party of record does not have the option of delivering the termination statement to the debtor.[247] If the secured party receives a signed demand from the debtor, it must cause the secured party of record to file a termination statement within 20 days thereafter.[248]

If the secured party of record fails to file (in the case of consumer goods) or communicate for filing or deliver (in other cases) a required termination statement, a termination statement may be filed without the secured party's authorization.[249] The filed termination statement is effective, however, "only if the debtor authorizes the filing and the termination statement indicates that the debtor authorized it to be filed."[250]

---

obvious but helpful point that authorization by the secured party of record need not be evidenced by a signed record. U.C.C. § 9-509, Comment 6.

240. U.C.C. § 9-525.

241. J.I. Case Credit Corp. v. Foos, 11 Kan. App. 2d 185, 717 P.2d 1064, 1 U.C.C. Rep. 2d 250 (1986) (filing of termination statement under erroneous belief that debtor had paid in full was nevertheless effective to terminate perfection).

242. U.C.C. § 9-513(c).

243. U.C.C. § 9-625(e)(4). See Household Fin. Corp. of Atlanta v. Raven, 136 Ga. App. 424, 221 S.E.2d 488, 18 U.C.C. Rep. Serv. 540 (1975).

244. U.C.C. § 9-625(b). For example, the secured party's failure to file a timely termination statement could cause the debtor to be unable to borrow money from another secured party on favorable terms. The debtor's foreseeable consequential damages in such a case could include the additional cost of obtaining substitute financing on less favorable terms (such as a higher interest rate).

245. Full payment of all outstanding indebtedness does not terminate the effectiveness of a filed financing statement. In re Bishop, 52 B.R. 470, 41 U.C.C. Rep. Serv. 1491 (Bankr. N.D. Ala. 1985). Absent the required demand from the debtor, a secured party is not under a duty to prepare or file a termination statement. Texas Kenworth Corp. v. First Nat'l Bank of Bethany, 564 P.2d 222, 21 U.C.C. Rep. Serv. 1512 (Okla. 1977).

246. U.C.C. § 9-513(a).

247. Id.

248. U.C.C. § 9-513(b).

249. U.C.C. § 9-509(d)(2).

250. Id. If the debtor requests a termination statement under circumstances in which the debtor is not entitled to one under Section 9-513, the debtor's self-filed termination statement would not be

Because a termination statement filed by a party with the authorization to file it terminates the effectiveness of the financing statement, a secured party should take care to ensure before filing the termination statement that the secured obligation has indeed been satisfied. If the secured party inadvertently or incorrectly terminates the financing statement, it cannot file a subsequent amendment "undoing" the termination and reinstating the previously terminated statement. The secured party that makes this error could file a new financing statement that would be sufficient to re-perfect the security interest, but if there was any gap in the secured party's perfection—even just a gap of a few minutes—the secured party could end up losing priority to another secured party that had previously held only a junior security interest in the collateral.[251]

In certain circumstances, a secured party may choose to release some or all of the collateral described in its financing statement (such as where the debtor wishes to sell an item of collateral free and clear and the secured party has agreed). A release is a type of amendment to the financing statement. As with other amendments, including termination and continuation statements, a release must identify the initial financing statement by file number[252] and must be filed in a manner that relates it to the initial financing statement.[253] An amendment that adds collateral or adds a debtor must be authorized by the debtor in a signed record,[254] but an amendment that operates as a release of collateral or a debtor need only be authorized by the secured party of record.[255] The caselaw demonstrates that secured parties intending to make a partial release of collateral should be careful not to inadvertently create a termination statement instead. For example, in one case, a bank erroneously checked a box on the form which indicated that its filing was a "termination statement" rather than a "partial release of collateral."[256] The description portion of the form showed that the bank intended to release only two specific items of collateral, whereas its security interest

authorized by Section 9-509(d). Such a self-filed termination statement would thus not be effective (U.C.C. §9-510(a)) and not operate to terminate the financing statement (U.C.C. §9-513(d)). *See also* AEG Liquidation Trust v. Toobro N.Y. LLC, 32 Misc. 3d 1202(A), 932 N.Y.S.2d 759 (Table) (Sup. Ct. 2011).

251. *See, e.g., In re* Wheeler, 580 B.R. 719, 94 U.C.C. Rep. Serv. 2d 528 (Bankr. W.D. Ky. 2017); *In re* Hickory Printing Group, Inc., 479 B.R. 388, 78 U.C.C. Rep. Serv. 2d 314 (Bankr. W.D.N.C. 2012); Official Committee of Unsecured Creditors of Motors Liquidation Co. v. JP Morgan Chase Bank, N.A., 103 A.3d 1010, 84 U.C.C. Rep. Serv. 2d 1046 (Del. 2014) (termination statement authorized by secured party terminated effectiveness of financing statement, without regard to whether secured party subjectively so intended). See also §5.06[B], *supra*, for a discussion of the effect of lapse of a financing statement's effectiveness on the rights of a purchaser of the collateral for value whose interest arose prior to lapse (the "retroactive invalidation" rule).

252. U.C.C. §9-512(a)(1).
253. U.C.C. §519(c).
254. U.C.C. §9-509(a)(1).
255. U.C.C. §9-509(d)(1).
256. *In re* Kitchin Equip. Co. of Va., Inc., 960 F.2d 1242, 17 U.C.C. Rep. Serv. 2d 322 (4th Cir. 1992). *See also In re* Silvernail Mirror & Glass, Inc., 142 B.R. 987, 18 U.C.C. Rep. Serv. 2d 322 (Bankr. M.D. Fla. 1992); *In re* Pacific Trencher & Equip., Inc., 735 F.2d 362, 38 U.C.C. Rep. Serv. 1121 (9th Cir. 1984).

was in nearly all of the debtor's assets. The court held that, by checking the box, the bank had created an effective termination statement and was thus unperfected as to all of the collateral, not just the two intended items. While harsh, the court was correct, as to hold otherwise would potentially mislead subsequent searchers who would conclude that the financing statement was terminated and thus would ignore it as irrelevant.

Chapter 6

Perfection by Possession and Control

Synopsis

§ 6.01 Possession Generally

[A] History

Understanding the Code's approach to perfection by possession starts with understanding the problems surrounding 19th-century secured financing. Common-law judges in the first half of that century refused to enforce "chattel mortgages," under which the debtor retained possession of the collateral. The perceived problem was ostensible ownership—that is, that the arrangement could mislead third parties into believing that the debtor had unfettered ownership of the collateral. The concern was that other creditors might make ill-advised loans because the debtor's apparent ownership of the collateral would lead them to miscalculate the debtor's net worth. Courts thus routinely voided nonpossessory security arrangements, classifying them as fraudulent conveyances.[1] Because the arrangements were void *ab initio*, creditors could not foreclose even if no third party was misled.

An ostensible-ownership problem did not exist if a debtor surrendered possession of collateral to a creditor.[2] This arrangement, called a "pledge" at common law,[3] provided sufficient notice to third parties to overcome judicial concerns about fraud.[4] The pledge, however, failed to meet the needs of the marketplace because it was entirely impractical for a borrower to surrender possession of assets that the borrower needed to use in the ordinary course of its business affairs.

In response, state legislatures began to enact chattel-mortgage recording acts that permitted nonpossessory security interests—conditioned on creditors' placing notices describing their interests in the public records. The legislatures saw filing as a satisfactory substitute for possession, but the courts remained hostile. They required the description of the collateral in the filing to be very specific, and any mistake, such as transposing digits within a serial number, could lead to judicial invalidation of the arrangement as fraudulent. Of course, a failure to file at all led to the same result.

The Code's approach to filing and possession is radically at odds with this history. Filing is the default method of perfection,[5] with possession being one of several sub-

---

1. *See, e.g.*, Clow v. Woods, 5 Sergeant & Rawle 275, 9 Am. Dec. 346 (Pa. 1819). This line of cases can be traced to *Twyne's Case*, 76 Eng. Rep. 809, 3 Coke 80 (Star Ch. 1601).

2. Although courts routinely enforced common-law pledges, the pledge did not entirely resolve the ostensible-ownership problem. The debtor could still mislead third parties about the nature of a creditor's interest in pledged assets (e.g., the debtor could advise a prospective third-party lender that the creditor in possession of a pledged asset was merely a bailee of that asset).

3. *See* RESTATEMENT OF SECURITY § 1 (1941) (a pledge constitutes a bailment to secure an obligation). The origins of the pledge are traceable to all of the ancient nations. A. DOBIE, HANDBOOK ON THE LAW OF BAILMENTS AND CARRIERS § 70, at 173–74 (1914).

4. For an extensive array of citations to pre-Code authorities on the law of the pledge, see R. HILLMAN, J. MCDONNELL & S. NICKLES, COMMON LAW AND EQUITY UNDER THE UNIFORM COMMERCIAL CODE § 23.01 (1985).

5. U.C.C. § 9-310(a) (filing mandatory absent provision to the contrary).

stitutes.[6] The Code facilitates filing by dramatically reducing the formal requirements for an effective financing statement. Serial-number specificity is no longer necessary; the only requirement is an indication of the collateral sufficient to place a searcher on notice.[7] The Code also specifies that a security interest is not fraudulent merely because the debtor retains control of the collateral.[8]

The provisions authorizing (or, in the case of tangible money, mandating)[9] possession as a method of perfection are the modern counterpart of the pledge. Although the term "pledge" is still a common reference, the designation of the arrangement as a "possessory Article 9 security interest" is more precise.

[B] Possession under Article 9—§ 9-313

Section 9-313 provides that possession is an appropriate method of perfection for goods, instruments, negotiable tangible documents, or tangible money.[10] In addition, a secured party can perfect a security interest in a certificated security by taking delivery of the certificate as provided in Section 8-301.[11]

Perfection by possession is unavailable for the purely intangible types of collateral, such as accounts and general intangibles.[12] With some exceptions (mostly minor

---

6. U.C.C. § 9-310(b)(6) (possession available if permitted by Section 9-313).

7. *See* § 5.03[A][4], *supra.*

8. U.C.C. § 9-205(a)(1)(A). *See* § 3.01, *supra.*

9. U.C.C. § 9-312(b)(3). Section 1-201(b)(24) defines money as a "medium of exchange that is currently authorized or adopted by a domestic or foreign government." As used in Article 9, money is either "electronic money" (money in electronic form), U.C.C. § 9-102(a)(31), or tangible money (money in tangible form), U.C.C. § 9-102(a)(79A). The term does not include a deposit account or money in electronic form that cannot be subjected to control under Section 9-105A. U.C.C. § 9-102(a)(54A). The court in *State of Minnesota v. 14,000 Dollars*, 345 N.W.2d 277, 38 U.C.C. Rep. Serv. 1007 (Minn. Ct. App. 1984), held that a security interest cannot attach to money, but the decision is clearly wrong given that Section 9-313 explicitly recognizes that a security interest in money can exist. *In Goldberg & Connolly v. New York Community Bancorp, Inc.*, 565 F.3d 66, 68 U.C.C. Rep. Serv. 2d 804 (2d Cir. 2009), a bank's security interest was in the funds recovered from a judgment, and it did not take an assignment of the judgment itself. The bank's interest thus was in money, and it failed to perfect that interest by taking possession of the funds recovered.

10. *In re* Liddle, 613 B.R. 186, 101 U.C.C. Rep. Serv. 2d 499 (S.D.N.Y. 2020).

11. Delivery is nothing more than possession, but the term is used to conform with the usage of Article 8, which governs investment securities. *See* U.C.C. § 8-301(a)(1). Certificated securities are a subset of investment property. For discussion of perfection of security interests in certificated securities, see generally § 6.04, *infra.*

12. *In re* Coldwave Systems, LLC, 368 B.R. 91 (Bankr. D. Mass. 2007) (security interest in patent not capable of being perfected by possession); *In re* Kanoff, 408 B.R. 53, 69 U.C.C. Rep. Serv. 2d 405 (Bankr. M.D. Pa. 2009) (liquor license is general intangible, and security interest in license could not be perfected by possession). For discussion of the concept of intangibles, see § 1.04[B][7], *supra.* The 2022 Code revisions have introduced two new forms of collateral called *controllable accounts* and *controllable payment intangibles.* If an account or payment intangible is evidenced by a controllable electronic record as to which the account debtor has undertaken to pay the person that has control of the controllable electronic record, the account or payment intangible is *controllable.* A secured party can perfect its security interest in a controllable account or a controllable payment intangible by

except for controllable electronic records, controllable accounts, and controllable payment intangibles as discussed in more detail later in this chapter), security interests in intangible assets can be perfected only by filing a financing statement.[13] For collateral other than goods, perfection by possession generally requires the existence of a writing[14] that is the physical embodiment of underlying rights in such a form that the holder of those rights may transfer them by transfer of the writing itself.[15] The right to payment created by an account does not satisfy this requirement.[16] There are tangible writings that indicate the existence of an account (e.g., ledger entries, invoices, written contracts), but the legal and business communities do not recognize these writings as the physical embodiment of the right to be paid. They have evidentiary value, but even without acquiring possession of any of them, an assignee of the account may enforce the right to be paid.

In contrast, instruments[17] and negotiable tangible documents are the exclusive representation of the rights indicated. The person entitled to enforce payment of an obligation represented by an instrument thus normally transfers that right by delivery of the writing to the transferee.[18] Likewise, the owner of goods covered by a negotiable tangible document normally transfers title to those goods by delivery of the document.[19] Possession serves as a reliable means of perfection only if it provides notice comparable to what filing provides.[20] If a debtor seeks to induce subsequent parties to enter into a transaction with respect to pledged property, those parties should appreciate the need to inquire as to why the debtor does not have possession of the property.

---

obtaining control of the controllable electronic record evidencing the account or payment intangible. Perfection by control as to these forms of collateral is discussed in § 6.04[C], *infra*.

13. Automatic perfection is occasionally available. *See* § 7.02, *infra*.

14. The term "writing" means a record that is printed, typewritten, or otherwise intentionally reduced to tangible form. U.C.C. § 1-201(b)(43). A writing necessarily must be in tangible form and must exist at the time it is signed. *Id.*, Comment 43.

15. Chattel paper is something of an anomaly. A right to payment that is chattel paper and is evidenced by a tangible record is transferred by assignment and not by transfer of the record, but perfection can be accomplished by taking possession of the record (and, if the chattel paper is also evidenced by an electronic record, by taking control of the electronic record). For discussion of perfection by possession of a tangible copy of the record evidencing chattel paper, see § 6.05, *infra*.

16. *In re* Sanelco, 7 U.C.C. Rep. Serv. 65 (Bankr. M.D. Fla. 1969) (account not capable of being possessed); First Bethany Bank & Trust, N.A. v. Arvest United Bank, 50 U.C.C. Rep. Serv. 2d 1209 (Okla. 2003) (security interest in account may not be perfected by possession).

17. For a nonnegotiable writing to fall within the definition of "instrument," the market must treat the writing as a tangible embodiment of a right to be paid. Such instruments sometimes are referred to as "quasi-negotiable." U.C.C. § 9-102(a)(47). *See* § 1.04[B][2], *supra*.

18. U.C.C. §§ 3-203(a) (transfer requires delivery), 1-201(b)(15) (delivery requires voluntary transfer of possession), 3-203(b) (transfer vests in the transferee any enforcement rights of the transferor).

19. U.C.C. § 7-502(a)(2). For discussion of the use of negotiable documents in commercial financing transactions, see §§ 6.02[B][1] and 6.02[C], *infra*.

20. The court in *Hutchison v. C.I.T. Corp.*, 726 F.2d 300, 37 U.C.C. Rep. Serv. 1760 (6th Cir. 1984), stressed that for the purpose of notice to third parties, possession must be unequivocal, absolute, and notorious. A night watchman on the property where collateral was located indicated that he would keep an eye on it for the secured party. The court appropriately concluded that the arrangement was insufficient to provide notice to third parties and thus did not constitute perfection.

Adequate notice through possession is thus possible only with goods and with property recognized as the single physical embodiment of the represented rights.

Failure to take possession of the physical embodiment of the collateral cost a bank
perfection of its security interest, worth more than $5 million, in *In re Funding Systems
Asset Management Corp.*[21] The collateral consisted of chattel paper made up of a note
and leases of underlying equipment. The leases had been prepared in duplicate originals
(original ink signatures without any designation of one as the original). The secured
party took possession of one set of originals but left another set in the possession of
the debtor. The court properly noted that a subsequent lender would not have received
adequate notice if the debtor had decided to offer the duplicate originals as collateral.[22]

§ 6.02 Possessory Security Arrangements in Specific Types of Personal Property

Article 9 permits possession as a method of perfection for security interests in a
wide array of collateral, but practical considerations narrow considerably the circumstances in which possession is a useful form of perfection. For example, a manufacturer that delivers its equipment to a creditor cannot produce its products. The same
problem exists for a consumer that needs to make home use of collateral consisting of
appliances or furniture. Any collateral that a debtor must use is ill-suited to a possessory security interest.

Another practical problem applies to collateral of great bulk. A bank cannot store
a debtor's stockpiled inventory of finished goods in the lobby or the vault. Although
the parties could arrange for more appropriate facilities, the transaction costs associated with transport and storage are significant and perhaps prohibitive. In addition, a
secured party in possession of collateral incurs an obligation to "use reasonable care in
the custody and preservation" of the collateral.[23]

Secured lenders have responded to these practical problems in two distinct ways.
One approach is to confine possessory-secured lending to transactions in which the
lender can easily manage receipt and custody of the collateral. The other approach is
to use documents to facilitate possessory security interests in goods. The discussion
below explains the basic patterns of the two approaches.

---

21. 11 U.C.C. Rep. Serv. 2d 205 (Bankr. W.D. Pa. 1990).

22. The secured party could have solved this problem by having the chattel paper indicate on its
face that it had been assigned to a named assignee, that is, the bank. See § 11.03[C], *infra.*

23. U.C.C. § 9-207(a); First Nat'l Bank of Thomasboro v. Lachenmyer, 131 Ill. App. 3d 914, 476
N.E.2d 755, 41 U.C.C. Rep. Serv. 234 (1985) (debtor allowed to set off damages to property in bank's
possession). The duty of reasonable care applies to possessory security interests and to collateral repossessed following default. For a discussion of the duty of reasonable care in the context of default,
see Chapter 17, *infra.*

[A] Pledges of Valuables, Instruments, and Chattel Paper

As noted above, secured lenders realistically can take delivery and maintain a possessory security interest in a relatively narrow range of goods. For lenders like banks, these goods typically include valuables, like jewelry or collectibles (e.g., coins, stamps, baseball cards), that the bank can store in its vault. Pawnbrokers have more expanded facilities for dealing with goods, but they also generally limit their transactions to items that are not bulky. Some of the items against which a pawnbroker extends loans become the inventory of the pawnbroker's shop.

Most possessory secured financing involves the use of promissory notes or chattel paper evidenced by a writing or writings[24] as the collateral. Financing institutions can easily take a pledge of paper like a promissory note or tangible chattel paper that represents an obligation to pay money. Although a secured party may perfect its interest in this type of collateral by filing,[25] taking possession of the note or the tangible chattel paper[26] deprives the debtor of the power to transfer rights in the collateral to a subsequent transferee that are superior to those of the secured party[27] and thus enhances the priority of the secured party against more categories of potential competing claimants. The secured party's possession also facilitates its collection or disposition of the collateral in the event of default.[28] A secured party that takes possession of an instrument or a tangible copy of a record evidencing chattel paper incurs an obligation to take "necessary steps to preserve rights against prior parties unless otherwise agreed."[29] The rights and responsibilities with respect to these types of paper are well within the expertise of

---

24. The Code uses "writing" to refer to a record in tangible form. U.C.C. § 1-201(b)(43). Instruments must be evidenced by a writing; chattel paper may be evidenced by a writing or writings, an electronic record or records, or any combination thereof.

25. U.C.C. § 9-312(a). Filing is sufficient to obtain priority over a lien creditor, including a trustee in bankruptcy. U.C.C. § 9-201(a).

26. Under the 2022 Amendments, the Code no longer uses the defined terms "tangible chattel paper" and "electronic chattel paper," and perfection as to chattel paper is accomplished by possession and control. However, the term "tangible chattel paper" is descriptive of the concept under discussion in the text. For more information on the effect of the 2022 Amendments and perfection as to chattel paper, see § 6.05, *infra.*

27. Article 9 contains a series of rules that protect good-faith purchasers for value that acquire possession of negotiable and quasi-negotiable collateral that is subject to a perfected security interest. To qualify, a purchaser must satisfy slightly different requirements depending upon the circumstances. *See* § 11.03[C] and [D], *infra.*

28. For example, only a "person entitled to enforce" a negotiable instrument can collect it. U.C.C. § 3-301. That status typically requires physical possession of the instrument. *See id.* (persons entitled to enforce a negotiable instrument include a holder and a transferee in possession with the rights of a holder). The definition of holder in U.C.C. § 1-201(b)(21) requires possession.

29. U.C.C. § 9-207(a). For example, a person that indorses a negotiable instrument may be discharged from liability by lack of timely notice of dishonor. U.C.C. § 3-503(a). Courts generally have found secured parties liable for failure to make a favorable conversion of pledged debentures into common stock. Traverse v. Liberty Bank & Trust Co., 5 U.C.C. Rep. Serv. 535 (Mass. Super. Ct. 1967). Although secured parties are responsible for the physical care of pledged stock, they have, almost without exception, not been held liable for failing to sell the stock in a declining market. Layne v. Bank

most financial institutions, however, and do not constitute barriers to the effective use of possession as a method of perfection.

Negotiable tangible documents are another form of collateral that is ideal for a possessory security interest. The document controls access and title to specified goods in the hands of a third-party bailee, thereby facilitating a possessory security interest without the secured party's having to deal with the covered goods directly. Possession is preferable to filing[30] as a method of perfection of an interest in a negotiable document because it eliminates the risk that the debtor may "duly negotiate" the document to a person that would thereby take free of the security interest.[31] It also facilitates the secured party's disposition of the goods in the event of default. The discussion below in the contexts of terminal warehousing and goods in transit delineates the role of the pledge of negotiable tangible documents in possessory secured financing.[32]

A secured party cannot perfect a security interest in an asset subject to a state certificate-of-title law by taking possession of the certificate.[33] A state issues a certificate of title as a fraud-prevention mechanism, and while the certificate represents the best evidence of title to the covered goods, title is not merged into it. Thus, it does not qualify as a document under Article 9.[34]

The preceding discussion of this section and the discussion that follows focus on possession of paper assets. Chattel paper can also exist in electronic form, as can negotiable documents.[35] As explained later in this chapter, any of the advantages achieved by possession of paper can also be achieved by obtaining control of the electronic equivalent of the paper.[36]

One, Ky., N.A., 395 F.3d 271, 55 U.C.C. Rep. Serv. 2d 704 (6th Cir. 2005); Beal Bank, SSB v. Sarich, 147 Wash. App. 1030, 67 U.C.C. Rep. Serv. 2d 281 (Wash. Ct. App. 2008).

30. Section 9-312(a) permits perfection of a security interest in a negotiable document by filing. As with instruments and chattel paper, filing is sufficient to obtain priority over a lien creditor, including a bankruptcy trustee. U.C.C. § 9-201(a).

31. U.C.C. § 9-331(a). A holder to whom a negotiable document is duly negotiated is the Article 7 equivalent of a bona-fide purchaser for value. U.C.C. § 7-501(b)(3).

32. See §§ 6.02[B][1], 6.02[C], infra.

33. In re Global Envtl. Serv. Group, LLC, 59 U.C.C. Rep. Serv. 2d 655 (Bankr. D. Haw. 2006); In re Davis, 269 B.R. 914, 46 U.C.C. Rep. Serv. 2d 879 (Bankr. M.D. Ala. 2001). See also In re Hadley, 541 B.R. 829 (Bankr. N.D. Ohio 2015) (attorney's taking possession of vehicle title certificate was not sufficient to constitute possession of vehicle for purposes of common-law retaining lien).

34. Nationwide Mut. Ins. Co. v. Hayes, 276 N.C. 620, 174 S.E.2d 511, 7 U.C.C. Rep. Serv. 1105 (1970).

35. See § 1.04[B][3], supra. Both the Uniform Electronic Transactions Act and the federal Electronic Signatures in Global and National Commerce Act (E-Sign) provide for the use of "transferable records," meaning electronic records that are the equivalent of electronic negotiable instruments. U.E.T.A. § 16, 15 U.S.C. § 7021(a)(1). Because a transferable record is not an instrument for purposes of Article 9, it qualifies as a general intangible and perfection must be by filing a financing statement. Transferable records are discussed further in § 1.04[B][7], supra.

36. See §§ 6.04[B] (electronic negotiable documents), 6.05 (chattel paper, whether evidenced in tangible or electronic records), infra.

[B] Goods in Storage or Manufacture

Manufacturers often store finished goods and raw materials used in a manufacturing process. This storage often involves a considerable capital investment by the manufacturer. Consequently, many manufacturers would like to use these goods as collateral to facilitate the financing of their operations. A prospective secured lender may balk at relying upon perfection by filing because it does not provide the same level of protection against debtor dishonesty as perfection by possession. The financing community has developed mechanisms by which a secured party can attain protection comparable to possession without having to take delivery of the goods.

[1] Terminal Warehousing—§ 9-312(c)

Terminal warehousing is used to store goods. The name derives from the fact that many such warehouses are located at railroad terminals to facilitate shipment of the stored goods. The warehouse company is responsible for the care and custody of the goods placed in its charge.[37] It usually issues a negotiable document to a party that deposits goods for storage. One might think of this document as a form of "goods paper" because it can be presented to the issuing bailee to recover goods, whereas an instrument is "money paper" in that it can be presented to the person obligated on the instrument to recover money.[38] The Comments stress that Article 9, like Article 7, "takes the position that, as long as a negotiable document covering goods is outstanding, title to the goods is, so to say, locked up in the document."[39] Accordingly, a security interest in goods covered by a negotiable document may be perfected by perfecting a security interest in the document."

To illustrate, a farmer that harvests wheat might transport it to a local grain elevator for its proper drying and storage. The elevator operator gives the farmer a negotiable document for the quantity of the grade of wheat the farmer delivered. The farmer then can sell the wheat by delivering the document to the buyer. In fact, the document might pass through the hands of several buyers until, ultimately, a buyer like a cereal manufacturer takes delivery of the wheat. The elevator will not deliver the wheat to anyone without surrender of the document to the elevator operator.[40] Until this surrender occurs, the document facilitates the marketing of the wheat without its removal from the elevator.

A negotiable document can also facilitate secured financing. While goods are in the possession of a bailee that has issued a negotiable document for them, a security

---

37. U.C.C. § 7-204.

38. As noted previously, instruments must be in writing, but negotiable documents can be either tangible or electronic.

39. U.C.C. § 9-312, Comment 7. *See* U.C.C. § 7-502(a) (holder to which negotiable document of title is duly negotiated receives title to the document, title to the goods, and the obligation of the issuer to hold or deliver the goods).

40. The issuer of the negotiable document must deliver the goods to the holder of the document. U.C.C. §§ 7-403(a), 7-102(a)(9).

interest in the goods is perfected by perfecting a security interest in the document.[41] The motivating interest of the creditor is the goods, of course, because they are the source of the collateral's value. For goods covered by a negotiable document, however, a prudent secured party will deal with the goods only through the document. The practical merger of title to the goods into the document facilitates secured lending because the lender can confidently control access to the goods by taking a security interest in (and possession of) the document if it is in written form. The same result can be accomplished by taking control of a negotiable document in electronic form.

The pledge of a negotiable tangible document perfects the lender's security interest.[42] The lender controls access to the goods because the warehouse will not release them without surrender of the document. If the obligor pays the outstanding indebtedness, the lender will return the document to the debtor so that the debtor can either sell it or acquire possession of the goods for use in its own operations. If the obligor defaults, the secured party can sell the document in satisfaction of the outstanding indebtedness.[43]

Most goods will have an existence both prior to and after being warehoused. During these prior and subsequent periods, the goods obviously are not in the possession of a person that issued a negotiable document for them. Accordingly, buyers or lenders that wish to deal with the goods during these periods cannot deal with them through a document but rather must deal with the goods themselves. Assume that goods are in the debtor's possession during Year 1, in the possession of a warehouse that issues a negotiable document for them during Year 2, and back in the debtor's possession during Year 3. Any security interest taken and perfected in the goods during Years 1 and 3 must be in the goods themselves. A secured party that takes a security interest in the goods during Year 1 and perfects by filing a financing statement describing the goods need not re-perfect as to the document to protect its security interest during Year 2.[44]

A secured party that takes a security interest during Year 2, however, should deal with the goods through the negotiable document. In other words, the security agreement should describe the document for attachment purposes, and the security interest should be perfected by filing a financing statement describing the document or, preferably, by taking possession of the document. What is the consequence to a lender that takes a security interest in the goods rather than the document during Year 2 and perfects by filing a financing statement covering the goods? The Code subordinates such a lender's interest to that of another secured party, *either earlier or later in time,* that takes and perfects a security interest in the document.[45] This result is an exception

---

41. U.C.C. § 9-312(c)(1).

42. U.C.C. § 9-313(a). *See* § 6.02[A], *supra.*

43. After default, the secured party can proceed against either the documents or the goods covered thereby. U.C.C. § 9-601(a)(2).

44. Article 7 is consistent. Absent specified entrustment or acquiescence, "[a] document of title confers no right in goods against a person that before issuance of the document had a legal interest or a perfected security interest in the goods." U.C.C. § 7-503(1).

45. U.C.C. § 9-312(c)(2).

to the general rule that rank orders perfected security interests on the principle of first-to-file-or-perfect.[46] The lender would, however, have a perfected security interest in the goods that would defeat any subsequent secured party that dealt with the goods rather than the document. It would also defeat lien creditors, including a bankruptcy trustee.

Continuing with the example, when Year 2 ends, the secured party will have to surrender the document to facilitate the debtor's reacquisition of the goods.[47] With surrender of the document to the bailee in exchange for possession of the goods, the document ceases to exist. If the secured party has, in addition to taking and perfecting through possession its security interest in the document, previously filed a financing statement describing the goods, it will continue its perfected status without interruption. If it filed a financing statement covering the document but not the goods, the goods are a proceed of the document and the secured party's interest will remain continuously perfected.[48] Relying on its proceeds interest is dangerous, however, because the secured party will have to identify the proceeds if it wishes to foreclose on them. Identification is difficult under any circumstances, and particularly so with fungible goods.[49] If the secured party perfected its security interest in the document by possession and did not file as to the goods, the goods still qualify as proceeds (if identifiable), but the secured party's interest in them becomes unperfected 20 days after their receipt by the debtor unless the secured party files a financing statement describing them.[50] Accordingly, the best practical advice to a secured party acquiring a security interest during the period when goods are subject to a negotiable document is not only to take a possessory security interest in the document but also to file a financing statement describing both the document and the goods.[51]

[2] Field Warehousing—§ 9-312(d)

A field warehouse is not for storage but rather is a device to facilitate secured financing of a debtor engaged in the sale of goods at retail or wholesale. It provides a possessory security interest by placing the goods in the actual possession and control of the secured party's agent, who acts as a warehouseman on the premises of the debtor. Field warehousing sharply reduces the transaction costs associated with a possessory security interest in bulky goods because the warehouse is created around the goods

---

46. For a discussion of the general rule of priority, see § 10.01, *infra*.

47. A security interest in a negotiable document that is perfected by possession remains perfected for 20 days without filing if the secured party makes the document available to the debtor for one of the purposes specified in Section 9-312(f). For discussion, see § 8.01[B], *infra*.

48. *See* § 8.01[B], *infra*.

49. Section 9-336 governs a secured party's interest and priority in commingled goods. *See* § 15.06, *infra*.

50. *See* §§ 8.02[A], 8.02[B][4], *infra*. The secured party could also remain perfected beyond the 20-day grace period by taking possession of the goods before the period expires.

51. The description of the document might seem superfluous, but it provides continuous perfection if the document is surrendered to the debtor and the debtor retains possession of it beyond the 20-day period of temporary perfection provided for by Section 9-312(f).

while they are located on the debtor's premises, thus eliminating any need to move them back and forth between the secured party and the debtor.

A field warehouse can be a very simple creation.[52] Assume that a debtor has a large stock of finished inventory, like Christmas ornaments, held for delivery to retail merchants for resale during the holiday season. A secured party would like to take possession of the inventory until the debtor needs it but does not want to pay transportation and storage costs. A field warehouse is an ideal solution. The key to the creation of the field warehouse is to exclude the debtor's access to the goods, both physically and legally. The warehouse can be created physically merely by enclosing the area around the finished goods with temporary walls of chicken wire, with access through a padlocked door. The debtor and secured party will enter a simple lease that transfers to the secured party control over the portion of the debtor's premises that comprises the warehouse.

The secured party is likely to be too busy to bother with operating the field warehouse itself and will appoint an agent to perform that task.[53] The agent generally will issue nonnegotiable warehouse receipts to the secured party for the goods that are located within the warehouse. These nonnegotiable documents, unlike the negotiable variety, do not embody title to the goods.[54] Like their negotiable counterparts, however, they serve as a receipt for goods delivered to the bailee and stored in the warehouse, and they establish a contractual relationship between the bailor and the warehouse agent.

Nonnegotiable warehouse receipts play a role in satisfying the notice requirement for perfection of a security interest in the underlying goods. Article 9 provides three perfection alternatives for a security interest in goods covered by a nonnegotiable document: (1) issuance of the document in the name of the secured party, (2) the bailee's receipt of notification of the secured party's interest, and (3) filing as to the goods.[55] Field warehousing typically uses the first alternative—the field warehouse agent issues warehouse receipts for the goods in the name of the secured party. This alternative makes the secured party the "person entitled under the document,"[56] giving it control over the disposition of the goods.[57]

---

52. For a description of a typical field warehouse, see *Scott v. Lawrence Warehouse Co.*, 227 Or. 78, 360 P.2d 610 (1961).

53. The agent, while frequently an employee of the debtor, must be made responsible to the secured party with respect to the warehoused goods and not to the debtor. U.C.C. § 9-313, Comment 3.

54. A transferee of a nonnegotiable document acquires only whatever title and rights the transferor has or has power to transfer, not necessarily complete title. U.C.C. § 7-504(a). Thus, secured parties do not take security interests in nonnegotiable documents (as opposed to the goods they represent), and the Article 9 perfection rules (discussed in this subsection) focus on the goods rather than the document.

55. U.C.C. § 9-312(d).

56. U.C.C. § 9-312, Comment 7. In the case of a nonnegotiable document, "person entitled under the document" means "the person to which delivery of the goods is to be made by the terms of, or pursuant to instructions in a record under" the document. U.C.C. § 7-102(a)(9).

57. U.C.C. § 7-403(a) (bailee must deliver the goods to a person entitled under the document).

If the debtor seeks to enter subsequent transactions concerning the goods with other parties, those parties are likely to inquire further when they discover that the debtor cannot open the lock on the field warehouse to gain access to the goods. After consulting with the only person that can gain access—the field-warehouse agent—an interested party will learn of the secured party's interest. Although not itself an act of perfection, the secured party may also give further notice of the security interest by placing signs outside the warehouse indicating that the goods contained within are subject to a security interest and providing the name and telephone number of the agent for purposes of any inquiries.

Secured lenders using a field warehouse should take the additional step of filing with respect to the goods. Then, in the event of a third-party challenge to any aspect of the field-warehousing arrangement—which, if successful, might defeat perfection by possession—the secured party can easily prove perfection by filing. The advantage of the field warehousing arrangement, however, is that it facilitates a secured financing agreement if the lender is unwilling to finance against goods that remain within the control and custody of the debtor.[58]

A field warehouse sometimes can be quite simple and not require much from the field-warehouse agent. For example, a large cask of whiskey might need to age for several years without being disturbed. Having the field-warehouse agent padlock the spigot denies the debtor access. Posting signs on the cask that indicate the goods have been pledged to the secured party and providing the name and address of the field-warehouse agent from whom further information can be obtained facilitates notice to interested parties. The agent need not be on the premises very often, but visits should be frequent enough to determine that the debtor has not removed posted signs and has not tampered with the padlocked access.

Parties can also establish more sophisticated field warehouses. Rather than locking up a completed seasonal inventory for several months, the parties might create a more fluid arrangement under which the debtor can receive some of the finished goods as they are sold and can store additional finished goods as they are manufactured. The field-warehouse agent will issue nonnegotiable documents in the name of the secured party for goods received into the warehouse, and the secured party can prepare delivery instructions to the agent concerning the release of collateral to the debtor.[59] The precise arrangements will depend on the terms negotiated between the secured party and the debtor. One possibility is instructions to the agent to release any goods requested by the debtor, but only if there remains within the warehouse finished goods whose value totals a particular amount relative to the outstanding debt (called in the

---

58. An article that focuses extensively on the control aspects of field warehousing and on the requirement of possession in this context is Skilton, *Field Warehousing as a Financing Device*, 1961 Wisc. L. Rev. 221 (Part I), 403 (Part II).

59. The debtor becomes the person entitled under the document to the extent of the secured party's written instructions. U.C.C. §7-102(a)(9). The bailee then must deliver the designated goods to the debtor. U.C.C. §7-403(a).

industry a "loan-to-collateral ratio").[60] The field-warehouse agent's compliance with such instructions will leave the lender with a perfected security interest in goods having a value considered sufficient to cover the outstanding indebtedness. If the obligor borrows more money against an established credit line or makes payments that reduce the extent of indebtedness, new delivery instructions from the secured party to the field-warehouse agent can change the amount of collateral the debtor must maintain within the warehouse.

Another possibility is to create two field warehouses—one for raw materials used in the debtor's manufacturing operations and the other for finished goods—and prepare delivery instructions that tie the two warehouses together. For example, the instructions to the field-warehouse agent might authorize the agent to release to the debtor ten units of raw materials for every three units of finished goods received. Extending field warehouses to the raw materials facilitates secured financing of those goods as well, allowing an enhanced borrowing position for the obligor.

Whitney National Bank of New Orleans v. Sandoz[61] demonstrates the consequences to a secured party that becomes too lax in establishing or monitoring a field warehouse. The bank took a security interest in the debtor canning company's inventory of canned goods and purportedly perfected by possession through a field-warehouse arrangement. Parts of the debtor's plants were leased to a warehouse company, which issued warehouse receipts for the goods. The debtor, however, retained possession of the leased spaces and had unfettered access to its inventory.[62] The appellate court found that the transaction was a sham and that the bankruptcy court had held properly that the warehouse receipts were invalid. The obvious lesson is that a field warehouse must exist in more than name only to provide perfection by possession. Its creation and operation must satisfy the notice function that underlies perfection of security interests.[63] Another lesson is that a proper filing as to the goods, while insufficient to protect against debtor defalcations, would have defeated the bankruptcy trustee.

---

60. Ribaudo v. Citizens Nat'l Bank of Orlando, 261 F.2d 929 (5th Cir. 1958) (warehousing company instructed by bank to retain in its custody warehoused merchandise worth 133 1/3% of $50,000 loan, or $66,666.67).

61. 362 F.2d 605 (1966).

62. One of the biggest business-fraud cases ever illustrates, in the extreme, the potential risk exposure that is associated with poorly-maintained field warehouses. Several banks in the United States and Britain extended loans for $150 million based on warehouse receipts for vegetable oils supposedly located in Bayonne, New Jersey. The contents actually located there were over a billion pounds short. *See* Proctor & Gamble Distrib. Co. v. Lawrence American Field Warehousing Corp., 16 N.Y.2d 344, 266 N.Y.S.2d 785, 213 N.E.2d 873, 21 A.L.R.3d 1320, 3 U.C.C. Rep. Serv. 157 (1965); N. MILLER, THE GREAT SALAD OIL SWINDLE (1965).

63. Article 9 stresses the importance of proper maintenance of a field warehouse. Although Section 9-205(a)(1)(A) allows the debtor to use and dispose of collateral without impairing the security interest's validity, Section 9-205(b) provides that the section "does not relax the requirements of possession if attachment, perfection, or enforcement of a security interest depends upon possession of the collateral by the secured party." *See* § 3.01, *supra*.

An alternative method of protecting a secured lender against a debtor's improper use of collateral has developed. Rather than creating a field warehouse and issuing warehouse receipts to the secured party, a bonded warehouse company may issue a certification in record form of the value of the collateral on the debtor's premises. The company also contracts to comply with the secured party's delivery instructions concerning the collateral and to assume liability for any losses that result from not fulfilling its duties. A three-way agreement among the debtor, the secured party, and the warehouse company authorizes policing and control by the warehouse company, and the secured party simply perfects by filing as to the goods. This approach to certified inventory control protects the secured party by passing the risk of debtor defalcation to the warehouse company.[64]

[C] Goods in Transit

Sometimes a person will wish to arrange financing secured by goods that are in transit. Assume a transaction in which an importer in the United States is purchasing several hundred tons of copper from Chile. The goods might take up to three weeks to arrive by ocean carrier at a U.S. port. The importer will then break down the shipment into domestic shipments that it will route to each of its pre-arranged buyers. An importer that must pay the seller shortly after shipment of the goods but that will not be paid on its resale transactions until delivery of the copper to domestic buyers might need financing to cover this interim period.

The importer can enter a transaction with a bank in this country under which the bank will issue a letter of credit to the exporter.[65] The bank will require that the importer execute a security agreement granting a security interest in the copper and in any documents covering the copper, and it will file a financing statement perfecting its security interest in the goods and documents. The letter of credit requires the bank to pay the Chilean seller's drafts, provided that the appropriate records accompany the drafts.[66] One of the required records will be a negotiable bill of lading, which will be issued by the carrier upon shipment of the goods.[67] After shipment, the seller will prepare a draft drawn on the bank demanding payment in the amount of the purchase

---

64. For descriptions of certified inventory-control arrangements, see McGuire, *The Impact of the UCC on Field Warehousing*, 6 U.C.C. L.J. 267, 280–82 (1974). The article further explains that warehouse companies also enter accounts-receivable programs in which they guarantee the validity of accounts and protect against debtor diversion of funds received on accounts.

65. A letter of credit is "a definite undertaking that satisfies the requirements of Section 5-104 by an issuer to a beneficiary at the request or for the account of an applicant or, in the case of a financial institution, to itself or for its own account, to honor a documentary presentation by payment or delivery of an item of value." U.C.C. § 5-102(a)(10).

66. A draft is a negotiable instrument that includes an order to pay money. U.C.C. § 3-104(e).

67. A bill of lading is "a document of title evidencing the receipt of goods for shipment issued by a person engaged in the business of directly or indirectly transporting or forwarding goods." U.C.C. § 1-201(b)(6). Provisions of Article 7 on documents cover bills of lading. For interstate shipments and exports, however, the Federal Bills of Lading Act governs bills of lading. 49 U.S.C. App. §§ 81–124 (1988).

price. It will then forward the draft and the negotiable bill of lading (together with other required records)[68] through banking channels to the bank. The bank will receive possession or control of the bill of lading when it pays the seller's draft.[69] Although the bank perfected its security interest with its financing statement, the bank's possession or control of the bill of lading enhances its position.[70]

This type of transaction can be desirable from the perspectives of all the parties. The Chilean seller need not relinquish ownership or control of the goods until it is paid, because it will not deliver the bill of lading to the bank until its draft is paid. The bank acquires control over the goods when it pays the draft. The importer can use the copper in transit as security to facilitate the transaction.

The bank, of course, will have to relinquish possession or control of the bill of lading for release of the goods by the ocean carrier. It will then have a perfected nonpossessory security interest in the importer's copper. The bank can further enhance its position by insisting that each sub-buyer of copper provide the importer with a letter of credit.[71] As the deliveries of copper to domestic shippers proceed, the transportation carriers will issue new negotiable bills of lading. These documents can be negotiated to the secured party, which will then forward them to the issuing banks with drafts ordering payment to itself. The secured-party bank will apply payments under the drafts to reduce the importer's indebtedness.

---

68. To assure itself that conforming goods have been shipped, the bank's letter of credit will probably require the seller to deliver certificates related to inspection of the goods. It will also require evidence of insurance and records demonstrating compliance with the laws of the exporting and importing countries.

69. The named consignee on the bill of lading, the exporter, will "negotiate" it to the bank by indorsing and delivering it. U.C.C. § 7-501(a)(1). Negotiation gives the bank the status of holder, making it the person entitled under the document. U.C.C. § 7-102(a)(9). The carrier will only release the goods to a person entitled to enforce the document. U.C.C. § 7-403(a).

70. *See* § 6.02[B][1], *supra.*

71. The bank's security agreement can cover the importer's rights to the proceeds of the letters of credit as additional collateral. The term "letter-of-credit rights" means the right to payment or performance under a letter of credit. U.C.C. § 9-102(a)(51). Except when the letter of credit represents a supporting obligation, a security interest in letter-of-credit rights must be perfected by control. U.C.C. §§ 9-312(b)(2), 9-107. Control requires that the issuer or its nominee consent to the security assignment. Without this consent, the secured party is not only unperfected but cannot require that the issuing bank honor the letter of credit. *See* § 1.07, *supra.* For discussion of supporting obligations, see § 1.06[C], *supra.*

§ 6.03 The Concept of Possession — § 9-313

[A] Possession by the Secured Party

Article 9 provides that "perfection occurs not earlier than the time the secured party takes possession and continues only while the secured party retains possession."[72] The first part of this sentence rejects the common-law theory of the "equitable pledge."[73] Under this theory, the taking of possession could relate back to the date of an original security agreement that included an agreement for future possession. Taking possession shortly before bankruptcy may create a voidable preference under federal bankruptcy law,[74] and to achieve consistency with this federal policy, the Code eliminates relation-back for possessory security interests.[75] Perfection by possession applies only during the time that the secured party takes and retains possession of the collateral.[76] Perfection either prior to or after the period of possession must be attained through tacking with other applicable methods of perfection.[77]

In *Transport Equipment Co. v. Guaranty State Bank*,[78] perfection by possession of the debtor's machinery occurred too late to protect the secured party against a second secured party perfected by filing. Although representatives of the first secured party arrived on the debtor's premises in the morning, they did not load the collateral onto their trucks until the afternoon. The court held that possession occurred only upon the loading, and thus the filing by the second secured party earlier in the afternoon afforded it priority. A purchase-money seller in *In re Automated Bookbinding Services*,

---

72. U.C.C. § 9-313(d).

73. *See* U.C.C. § 9-313, Comment 5. With respect to a security interest granted in exchange for new value in instruments, certificated securities, or negotiable documents, the Code provides for a 20-day period of temporary perfection without possession or filing. U.C.C. § 9-312(e). This period of automatic perfection can be seen as a limited relation-back rule. Short-term automatic perfection after the relinquishment of possession can also apply if the collateral consists of negotiable documents, goods in the possession of a bailee other than one that has issued a negotiable document, instruments, and certificated securities. U.C.C. § 9-312(f), (g). For discussion of temporary perfection, see § 8.01, *infra*.

74. 11 U.S.C. § 547. *See* § 16.04[E], *infra*.

75. *In re* Granite City Coop. Creamery Ass'n, Inc., 7 U.C.C. Rep. Serv. 1083 (Bankr. D. Vt. 1970). *See also In re* Clean Burn Fuels, LLC, 492 B.R. 445, 80 U.C.C. Rep. Serv. 2d 896 (Bankr. M.D.N.C. 2013) (mere intention or right to take possession of collateral by secured party is not alone sufficient to constitute possession for perfection purposes).

76. Except where the collateral is covered by a certificate-of-title statute, an otherwise unperfected secured party that takes possession of collateral following a default by the obligor thereby perfects its security interest. *In re* Osborn, 389 F. Supp. 1137, 16 U.C.C. Rep. Serv. 827 (N.D.N.Y. 1975); Walter E. Heller & Co. v. Salerno, 168 Conn. 152, 362 A.2d 904, 16 U.C.C. Rep. Serv. 840 (1975). Obtaining a default judgment against the defendant in a replevin action is not sufficient to perfect by possession because the right to take possession of the collateral is not the same as having actual possession. *In re* Walter Neilly & Co., Inc., 1 U.C.C. Rep. Serv. 364 (Bankr. W.D. Pa. 1961).

77. U.C.C. § 9-308(c). *See also* § 4.03, *supra*.

78. 518 F.2d 377, 17 U.C.C. Rep. Serv. 1 (10th Cir. 1975).

Inc.,[79] lost perfection when it shipped the goods by carrier under a nonnegotiable bill of lading showing the buyer as the consignee. Possession terminated because the seller lost control of the goods in transit.

[B] Possession by Agents and Bailees

A secured party may use an agent for purposes of possession.[80] In accordance with the principles of agency law, the agent acts on behalf of the principal, and thus possession by the agent serves as possession by the secured party.[81] The key is to exclude the debtor from both possession and control of the collateral.[82] The Comments succinctly state the necessary relationship as follows:

> The debtor cannot qualify as an agent for the secured party for purposes of the secured party's taking possession. And, under appropriate circumstances, a court may determine that a person in possession is so closely connected to or controlled by the debtor that the debtor has retained effective possession, even though the person may have agreed to take possession on behalf of the secured party. If so, the person's taking possession would not constitute the secured party's taking possession and would not be sufficient for perfection.[83]

Retention of possession or control by the debtor facilitates the possibility that the debtor might use its access to the collateral to deceive a subsequent party. Possession by the secured party or by an agent controlled by the secured party advances the notice function that lies at the core of the concept of perfection.

With collateral other than certificated securities and goods covered by a negotiable document, the secured party can also perfect by obtaining what is sometimes called "constructive possession."[84] Under former law, constructive possession commenced when a bailee (a person in possession of the collateral other than the debtor) received notification of the secured party's interest. Article 9 now restricts the receipt-of-notification method for obtaining constructive possession to bailees that have issued nonnegotiable documents covering the goods.[85] In other situations, constructive pos-

---

79. 471 F.2d 546, 11 U.C.C. Rep. Serv. 897 (4th Cir. 1972).

80. U.C.C. § 9-313, Comment 3. *See also In re* Bruce Farley Corp., 26 B.R. 164, 35 U.C.C. Rep. Serv. 1304 (Bankr. S.D. Cal. 1981).

81. RESTATEMENT (SECOND) OF AGENCY § 17, Comment a (1958) (delegated act done by representative has same legal effect as if done personally by the principal).

82. *In re* Maryville Sav. & Loan Corp., 27 B.R. 701, 35 U.C.C. Rep. Serv. 983 (Bankr. E.D. Tenn. 1983) (collateral that remained in debtor's possession was not constructively delivered for purposes of perfection by possession).

83. U.C.C. § 9-313, Comment 3. Prime Fin. Serv. LLC v. Vinton, 279 Mich. App. 245, 761 N.W.2d 694, 65 U.C.C. Rep. Serv. 2d 867 (Mich. Ct. App. 2008) (debtor's retention of possession of notes could not perfect the secured party's interest in the notes).

84. The term "constructive" is used in this discussion because it is a term commonly used elsewhere. However, a secured party that has "constructive" possession of collateral actually has possession through a bailee, just as it actually has possession through an agent.

85. U.C.C. §§ 9-312(d)(2); 9-313, Comment 7.

session requires that the bailee sign a record acknowledging that it holds, or as to future assets will hold, the collateral for the secured party's benefit.[86] This technique cannot be used if the bailee is a lessee of the collateral from a debtor that leased the goods in the ordinary course of its business.[87] The limitation represents a policy judgment that the lessee's possession of the goods in such circumstances is insufficient to provide adequate public notice of the secured party's interest.

A bailee is not under any legal obligation to sign an acknowledgment,[88] and unless the bailee otherwise agrees or law outside Article 9 otherwise provides, the fact that the bailee has chosen to do so does not subject the bailee to any duty to the secured party or to any third party.[89] Because of the risk that the bailee will refuse to sign an acknowledgment, a secured party should take the precautionary step of filing a financing statement to ensure perfected status.

Determining whether a third person is an agent or a bailee can occasionally be difficult. For example, in *In re Liddle*,[90] the secured party held a security interest in the proceeds of the debtor's sale of a cooperative apartment the debtor co-owned with his wife. The secured party had obtained a TRO to prevent the debtor from spending the funds. Pursuant to a stipulation modifying the TRO, the money was placed in an escrow account held by the debtor's lawyer. When the debtor later filed for bankruptcy, the secured party sought to prevent the debtor from using the money on the ground that it constituted the secured party's cash collateral. The secured party argued that its interest in the money was perfected under Section 9-313(a) by virtue of the lawyer's possession, because the lawyer was operating as an agent for both parties in handling the funds. Citing the Comments discussed above,[91] the court acknowledged that it was possible that a person could be a "dual" agent on behalf of two adverse parties—but held that the facts were insufficient to support a finding that the lawyer was also the secured party's agent for purposes of perfecting its interest in the money. The secured party also argued that its interest was perfected under Section 9-313(c) because the stipulation modifying the TRO was a record acknowledging that the lawyer held the funds for the secured party's benefit. The court disagreed, noting that although the stipulation could have sufficed for this purpose if worded appropriately, no language in the stipulation reflected that the lawyer had acknowledged that she would hold the funds for the secured party's benefit. The lesson of the case is obvious: if there is any ambiguity regarding the agency status of the person in possession, the secured party

---

86. U.C.C. § 9-313(c). S.E.C. v. Byers, 671 F. Supp. 2d 531, 71 U.C.C. Rep. Serv. 2d 364 (S.D. N.Y. 2009) (because secured party never took possession of mortgage and mortgage note, it did not have actual possession, and because party in possession did not authenticate a record acknowledging it held them for secured party, secured party did not have constructive possession).

87. U.C.C. § 2A-103(1)(u).

88. U.C.C. § 9-313(f).

89. U.C.C. § 9-313(g)(2). Section 9-313(g)(1) makes a signed acknowledgment effective to perfect a security interest even if it violates the debtor's rights.

90. 613 B.R. 186, 101 U.C.C. Rep. Serv. 2d 499 (S.D.N.Y. 2020).

91. *See* note 83, *supra*.

should obtain that person's signed acknowledgment to hold possession for the secured party's benefit.[92]

Because of concerns that the acknowledgment rule might interfere with mortgage warehouse lending, the Code provides a special rule for situations of delivery of collateral already in the possession of the secured party to a bailee. The secured party in that case is not deemed to have relinquished possession if it instructs the bailee, either before or contemporaneously with the delivery, to hold the collateral for the secured party's benefit or to redeliver it to the secured party.[93] For example, assume Mortgage Lender pledges its notes and mortgages as collateral for a series of short-term loans

---

92. *See also In re* American Pie, Inc., 361 B.R. 318, 61 U.C.C. Rep. Serv. 2d 1051 (Bankr. D. Mass. 2007) (secured party failed to prove perfection by possession through an agent because it did not provide a signed record from the attorney holding the collateral in escrow acknowledging that the attorney held the collateral for the benefit of the secured party).

Secured parties sometimes cite the case of *In re Rolain*, 823 F.2d 198, 4 U.C.C. Rep. Serv. 2d 5 (8th Cir. 1987), as support for the argument that possession by the debtor's lawyer can function as a dual agent for purposes of possession under Section 9-313(a). In *Rolain*, the collateral consisted of a promissory note issued to the debtor by a third party. The note contained confidential information which the debtor had agreed not to disclose, and by agreement of the secured party and debtor, the debtor's attorney held the note. When the debtor filed for bankruptcy, the trustee sought to avoid the security interest as unperfected. The court rejected the trustee's argument and concluded that the secured party was perfected.

Unfortunately, the *Rolain* court's opinion is unclear as to whether it was treating the attorney as an agent of the secured party or as a bailee. Under the provisions of Article 9 at that time, it did not matter, so the court ruled for the secured party without specifically deciding the issue. If the attorney was a bailee, he had received notification of the secured party's interest—which sufficed for constructive possession under Article 9 at the time. (As explained earlier in the text, today the bailee must acknowledge it holds the collateral for the benefit of the secured party and cannot have this status forced onto it by mere notification.) If the attorney was the secured party's agent, the court concluded that he was sufficiently independent of the debtor such that the lawyer's possession served to provide notice to third parties that the debtor no longer had unfettered control over the note. Section 9-313, Comment 3, appears to support this characterization of *Rolain* by stating that "[i]n a typical escrow arrangement, where the escrowee has possession of collateral as agent for both the secured party and the debtor, the debtor's relationship to the escrowee is not such as to constitute retention of possession by the debtor."

On the one hand, treating the debtor's lawyer as a dual agent for the secured party does not seem outrageous. After all, attorneys are capable of understanding situations involving divided loyalties and must act consistent with rules of professional conduct (indeed, both parties consented to the attorney's function as an escrow in *Rolain*, although the court was not clear on what sort of disclosure the attorney made). On the other hand, the agreement in *Rolain* appears to have been no more explicit than the agreement in *Liddle*—and the court in *Liddle* held that the placement of the funds in the lawyer's account "would not have placed other potential creditors on notice" that the secured party had an interest in the funds. *See also* Berkshire Bank v. Kelly, 109 U.C.C. Rep. Serv. 2d 1037 (Vt. 2022) (where ostensible security agreement covered a particular investment account "in the possession of, or subject to the control of, Lender," lender's security interest did not attach when account owner placed $208,000 from the account in escrow with account owner's attorney). Thus, rather than risk a fight over whether the debtor's attorney can suffice as the secured party's agent, the secured party should obtain the attorney's signed acknowledgment that the attorney serves as bailee for the secured party's benefit.

93. U.C.C. § 9-313(h). The secured party in *Rothrock v. Turner*, 72 U.C.C. Rep. Serv. 2d 103 (D. Me. 2010), did not qualify with respect to stock-certificate tenders to receive a cash payout as part of a merger involving the stock issuer. The instruction to the third party handling the payout was to transfer the merger proceeds to the debtor, not to the secured party.

from Bank. As each transaction closes, the note and mortgage are physically delivered to Bank, which is a mortgage warehouse lender. The loans provide operating capital to Mortgage Lender while it accumulates a sufficient pool of such assets to justify selling them as a package on the secondary mortgage market. A potential buyer may wish to inspect the documentation, and the common practice is for the warehouse lender (Bank) to forward a package of notes and mortgages under a cover letter advising the potential buyer of its security interest. The letter provides the notification that permits the mortgage warehouse lender to maintain its perfected status.

Although designed for mortgage warehouse lending, the notification-to-bailee rule also facilitates "repledges" of other kinds of collateral. An example may be found in Section 9-207(c)(3), which expressly authorizes a secured party to create a security interest in collateral in its possession. For example, suppose Finance Co. acquires a possessory security interest in Debtor's instruments. To obtain financing of its own, Finance Co. repledges the instruments to Bank as collateral for a loan. Finance Co. retains its perfected status vis-à-vis Debtor by instructing Bank to redeliver the collateral to Finance Co. upon repayment of Bank's loan to Finance Co.[94]

[C] Symbolic or Constructive Delivery

Possession is a concept that arises in numerous legal contexts and has varied meanings within those contexts. The popular saying that "possession is nine points in the law" reflects the fundamental significance that possession historically has enjoyed in our legal culture. In numerous contexts, possession has evolved to encompass symbolic or constructive delivery.[95] Although such delivery is appropriate in some contexts, it is not appropriate for the purpose of perfecting a security interest unless it provides sufficient notice to potential third parties.

The case of In re Bialk[96] is illustrative. The secured party sought to take a pledge of medals and coins that the debtor had placed in a bank safe-deposit box. The debtor gave his only keys to the box to the secured party, which argued that delivery of the keys constituted symbolic delivery of the contents sufficient to constitute perfection by possession. The bankruptcy court disagreed because the bank had not also been notified of the secured party's interest. The debtor could have gained access to the locked goods by advising the bank that the keys were lost. Consequently, delivery of the keys to the secured party did not provide the required level of notice to potential third parties.

---

94. A repledge will not excuse a secured party from its duty of reasonable care. U.C.C. § 9-207(a). See § 6.02, supra.

95. The differentiation between constructive delivery of an asset to a secured party and constructive possession by a secured party is important. The preceding subsection covers constructive possession.

96. 16 U.C.C. Rep. Serv. 519 (Bankr. W.D. Mich. 1974).

§ 6.04 Perfection by Control

The amendment of Article 9 to conform its provisions to the 1994 revision of Article 8 first introduced control as a method of perfection. At that time, control applied only to investment property that qualified as a financial asset under Article 8. The 1998 amendments to Article 9 extended perfection by control to deposit accounts, electronic chattel paper,[97] and letter-of-credit rights. Amendments to conform with the 2003 revision of Article 7 extended perfection by control to electronic documents. The 2022 amendments also permit perfection by control as to controllable accounts, controllable electronic records, controllable payment intangibles, and electronic money.

[A] Investment Property—§§ 9-314(a), 9-106

The Code's treatment of securities has evolved significantly over the past half-century. Prior to a revision of Article 8 and conforming amendments to Article 9 in 1977, the assumption was that physical certificates would be issued for investment securities. The owner of a certificated stock or bond could create a perfected security interest by entering into a security agreement and giving the secured party possession of the certificate. This type of asset was thus treated as form of indispensable paper, like an instrument.[98] Any interest that a debtor might have in an investment vehicle for which no certificate existed was as a general intangible.

The number of securities transactions increased so drastically during the 1960s that the industry looked for ways to reduce the amount of paperwork. One practice that developed was the issuance of certificates in "street name." Rather than issuing certificates to each individual investor, an issuing entity would issue only a few certificates in large amounts to stockbrokers. The certificates represented the ownership interests of each of a broker's customers.

Today, even a broker is unlikely to hold a certificate. Under the indirect holding system that developed in recent years, a more common approach is for a "jumbo certificate" to be held by a clearing corporation of which the broker is a member. Thus, the broker may own, for all its customers, 100,000 shares of a particular stock, and the books of the broker will reflect the ownership interests of each of the broker's customers. The certificate itself will be held by a clearing corporation and may represent many hundreds of thousands or millions of shares. The books of the clearing corporation will show that the broker owns 100,000 of these shares.

---

97. As discussed in § 6.05, *infra*, the 2022 amendments added Section 9-314A, which provides that a security interest in chattel paper (whether evidenced by a tangible or electronic record) may be perfected by "possession and control."

98. Indeed, what are now called certificated securities were defined as instruments for Article 9 purposes until the 1994 revision of Article 8 and the conforming changes to Article 9. *See* U.C.C. § 9-105(1)(i) (1972 Official Text).

Another practice is the issuance of uncertificated securities, sometimes referred to as "book entry" securities. The issuing entity does not issue a physical certificate; rather, the issuer or its agent records ownership and transfers through book or computer entries. A customer's interest in uncertificated securities held through a broker will be shown on the broker's records and confirmations of purchase. The government issues many securities in uncertificated form.

Perfection of a security interest in certificated securities held indirectly by a broker created problems under former law. Filing was ineffectual,[99] and for a pledge to work, a debtor would have to obtain a certificate from a broker (which, in turn, would typically have to obtain one from a clearing corporation). Perfecting an interest in uncertificated securities was also problematic. With such securities classified as general intangibles, the only means of perfection was to file a financing statement. The securities industry, however, was not in the practice of searching for financing statements because securities previously had all been certificated and filing had been excluded as a method of perfection. Although the use of uncertificated securities might have forced a change in industry practices, the imposition of a requirement for searching the U.C.C. filing systems would have undercut the objective of lessening transaction costs (which was a leading motivation for the introduction of uncertificated securities).

To accommodate the changes in the securities industry, Article 8 was revised in 1977. These changes proved unsatisfactory, and the article was revised again in 1994. The latter revision created, through conforming amendments to Article 9, "investment property" as an umbrella Article 9 category for most interests in investment vehicles.[100] Investment property consists of securities (whether held directly or indirectly and whether certificated or uncertificated), security entitlements, securities accounts, commodity contracts, and commodity accounts. Many of the key provisions governing non-commodity-related investment property were (and still are) in Article 8. Commodity-related assets have always been beyond the scope of Article 8, and provisions governing security interests in commodity contracts and commodity accounts are exclusively in Article 9. The 1998 amendments to Article 9 did some reorganizing of the relevant provisions but left the law essentially unchanged.

Control is the primary method to perfect a security interest in investment property.[101] A secured party has control if it has the power to control the disposition of the collateral. Filing is an alternative means of perfection.[102] Filing is unnecessary for a

---

99. Until the promulgation of revised Article 9, filing was unavailable as a method of perfection for security interests in instruments, the category to which certificated securities belonged until 1994. Permissive filing became available for certificated securities with the 1994 revision of Article 8 and conforming changes to Article 9.

100. For a detailed discussion of the definitions and basic structure for investment property, see § 1.04[B][6], *supra*.

101. U.C.C. §§ 9-314, 9-106.

102. U.C.C. § 9-312(a).

security interest created by a broker,[103] a securities intermediary,[104] or a commodity intermediary[105] because these security interests in investment property perfect automatically on attachment.[106] As will be shown below, however, filing is a decidedly inferior method of perfection.

As applied to a certificated security, uncertificated security, or security entitlement, control has the meaning specified in Article 8.[107] For a certificated security held directly by the debtor, control requires delivery of the certificate to the secured party.[108] If the certificate is in bearer form, the secured party need only gain possession.[109] If it is in registered form—meaning that it specifies the debtor as the person entitled under it[110]—the secured party must gain possession and must also either obtain the debtor's indorsement[111] or have the certificate registered with the issuer in the secured party's name.[112] The latter might occur, for example, if the debtor surrendered the certificate to the issuer and the issuer reissued it showing the secured party as the entitled person.

For uncertificated securities held directly by a debtor, control also occurs through delivery,[113] but delivery has an unusual meaning in this context. It means that the issuer has registered the secured party (or another person acting on the secured party's behalf) on its books as the owner of the security.[114] The secured party can also obtain control without delivery, but only if the issuer agrees to comply with the secured party's orders without the further consent of the debtor.[115]

A secured party can acquire control of security entitlements,[116] which the debtor by definition holds indirectly through a securities intermediary,[117] either by becoming the entitlement holder (meaning a change in the books of the broker to reflect ownership

103. A "broker" is a person defined as a broker or dealer under federal securities laws, including a bank acting in that capacity. U.C.C. §8-102(a)(3).
104. The term "securities intermediary" includes brokers and clearing corporations. U.C.C. §8-102(a)(14).
105. The term "commodity intermediary" includes persons registered under federal law as futures commission merchants and others who perform clearance or settlement services for certain boards of trade. U.C.C. §9-102(a)(17).
106. U.C.C. §9-309(10), (11).
107. U.C.C. §9-106(a).
108. U.C.C. §8-106(a), (b). Section 8-301(a) defines "delivery" as applied to certificated securities.
109. U.C.C. §§8-106(a), 8-301(a).
110. U.C.C. §8-102(a)(13)(i).
111. U.C.C. §§8-106(b)(1), 8-301(a). Section 8-304 governs indorsements.
112. U.C.C. §§8-106(b)(2), 8-301(a). If the secured party takes possession of the certificate but does not obtain control, it is nevertheless perfected by the delivery. U.C.C. §9-313(a). A security interest perfected by this method has priority over a security interest perfected by a method other than control (e.g., by filing). U.C.C. §9-328(5).
113. U.C.C. §8-106(c)(1).
114. U.C.C. §8-301(b).
115. U.C.C. §8-106(c)(2).
116. The definition of a "security entitlement" is in terms of financial assets, which may or may not be securities. U.C.C. §8-102(a)(17). See discussion in §1.04[B][6], supra.
117. U.C.C. §8-102(a)(14), (7).

by the secured party)[118] or by having the broker agree to comply with the secured party's orders without the further consent of the debtor.[119] With a commodity contract, control requires that the secured party, the debtor, and the commodity intermediary agree that any value on account of the contract will be distributed as the secured party directs without the further consent of the debtor.[120] A secured party that has control of all security entitlements or commodity contracts covered in a securities or commodities account also has control respectively of the applicable account.[121] Conversely, perfection as to a securities or commodity account carries with it perfection as to each security entitlement or commodity contract held in the account.[122]

Brokers often provide financing for their investors' purchases, taking security interests in the purchased financial assets.[123] A secured party that takes control of a financial asset held indirectly through a broker or other securities intermediary should obtain an agreement with the intermediary in which the intermediary agrees to subordinate any security interest it may have to the secured party's interest; otherwise, the intermediary will have priority over the secured party.[124]

As an alternative to control, Article 9 permits secured parties to perfect as to investment property by filing an ordinary Article 9 financing statement.[125] Filing is sufficient to obtain priority over lien creditors, including a bankruptcy trustee, but it exposes the secured party to significant risks. For example, a secured party that perfects by control takes priority over another secured party that perfects by filing, even if the filing predates control and the secured party with control knows of the other secured party's interest.[126] In addition, a person that acquires protected-purchaser status under Article 8 takes free of a security interest perfected by filing.[127] These rules derive from the realities of the securities market, where a requirement for investors to check the Article 9 filing system would be impractical.

---

118. U.C.C. § 8-106(d)(1).

119. U.C.C. § 8-106(d)(2).

120. U.C.C. § 9-106(b)(2).

121. U.C.C. § 9-106(c).

122. U.C.C. §§ 9-308(f) (security entitlements), 9-308(g) (commodity contracts).

123. An intermediary has control of all security entitlements or commodity contracts entrusted to it. *See* U.C.C. §§ 9-106(b)(1) (commodity intermediary), 8-106(e) (securities intermediary).

124. U.C.C. § 9-328(3), (4) (securities intermediary and commodity intermediary respectively).

125. *In re* Hawaiian Telcom Comms., Inc., 69 U.C.C. Rep. Serv. 2d 661 (Bankr. D. Haw. 2009).

126. U.C.C. § 9-328(1). If both secured parties perfect by filing, the normal first-to-file rule applies. U.C.C. § 9-328(7).

127. U.C.C. § 9-331(a), (b) (deferring to Article 8 for a description of protected purchasers). *See* U.C.C. § 8-303.

[B] Deposit Accounts, Electronic Documents, and Letter-of-Credit Rights—§§ 9-314(a), 9-104, 9-107

Control became a method of perfection of security interests in deposit accounts, electronic documents, and letter-of-credit rights once revised Article 9 extended the concept of control beyond investment property. Indeed, with certain limited exceptions, control is the exclusive method for deposit accounts[128] and letter-of-credit rights.[129] Filing is an alternative method of perfection for electronic documents.[130]

For a security interest in a deposit account, control is automatic (i.e., it occurs on attachment) if the secured party is the bank[131] that maintains the account.[132] If the debtor maintains the deposit account in a bank that is not the secured party, control requires either (i) that the secured party become the customer with respect to the deposit account[133] or (ii) that the secured party, the debtor, and the bank that maintains the deposit account agree that the maintaining bank will follow the secured party's orders without the further consent of the debtor.[134] A secured party that has satisfied one of the above requirements has control even if the debtor retains the right to direct disposition of the deposited funds.[135]

For example, suppose the secured party takes a security interest in a deposit account maintained at a bank that is not the secured party and enters into a control agreement with the debtor and the maintaining bank. This arrangement means that the maintaining bank must follow the secured party's orders.[136] The parties also agree, however,

---

128. U.C.C. § 9-312(b)(1).

129. U.C.C. § 9-312(b)(2).

130. U.C.C. § 9-312(a).

131. Section 9-102(a)(8) broadly defines "bank" to include, *inter alia*, savings and loan associations, credit unions, and trust companies.

132. U.C.C. § 9-104(a)(1). *In re* Versus Inv. Mgmt., LLC, 344 B.R. 536, 60 U.C.C. Rep. Serv. 2d 60 (Bankr. N.D. Ohio 2006) (bank that maintained a certificate of deposit not evidenced by an instrument had a perfected security interest through control and, pursuant to Section 9-310(c), that perfection extended to the assignee); Joseph Stephens & Co., Inc. v. Cikanek, 588 F. Supp. 2d 870, 67 U.C.C. Rep. Serv. 2d 384 (N.D. Ill. 2008) (bank automatically perfected through its maintenance of the deposit account).

133. U.C.C. § 9-104(a)(3). This method can also be used with a deposit account maintained with the secured party. Control by becoming the customer with respect to the account, whether maintained with the secured party or another bank, provides a secured party with priority over another secured party that has obtained control by another method. U.C.C. § 9-327. *See* § 10.03[A], *infra*. Also, a secured party that becomes the customer with respect to a deposit account maintained at a bank that is not the secured party has priority to the funds in the account in the event the maintaining bank exercises its common-law right of set-off. U.C.C. § 9-340(c). *See* § 11.03[E], *infra*.

134. U.C.C. § 9-104(a)(2). The agreement must be signed by each party. *Id. See In re* Hawaiian Telcom Communications, Inc., 69 U.C.C. Rep. Serv. 2d 661 (Bankr. D. Haw. 2009) (failure to provide evidence of an applicable agreement or whether the plaintiff was a customer of the banks with respect to the deposit accounts left a material issue of fact that precluded summary judgment).

135. U.C.C. § 9-104(b). Remember that a transferee of funds from a deposit account takes free of a security interest in the deposit account if the transferee receives the funds without acting in collusion with the debtor in violating the rights of the secured party. U.C.C. § 9-332(b).

136. A maintaining bank is not under a duty to enter into a control agreement. U.C.C. § 9-342.

that the maintaining bank must also follow the debtor's instructions until ordered to stop doing so by the secured party.[137] The secured party has a perfected security interest in whatever remains in the deposit account at the time it issues the stop order.[138] This flexibility permits a lending bank to take a security interest in a deposit account maintained with another bank,[139] leaves the debtor free to use the funds, and allows the lending bank to take priority over a trustee if the debtor subsequently files for bankruptcy protection. Article 8 contains a similar provision for uncertificated securities and security entitlements controlled through an agreement by which the issuer or securities intermediary agrees to comply with the secured party's orders.[140]

Control of letter-of-credit rights requires that the issuer or a nominated person consent to the security assignment of the proceeds of the letter.[141] This approach derives from the distinction in the letter-of-credit area between a right to the proceeds of the letter and a right to draw against the letter.[142]

Under Section 7-106(a), a secured party has control of an electronic document if "a system employed for evidencing the transfer of interests in the electronic document reliably establishes [the secured party] as the person to which the electronic document was issued or transferred."[143] The reliability standard is a high standard to meet, the key elements being the uniqueness, identifiability, and unalterability of the electronic record.[144]

---

137. Either the security agreement or the control agreement can establish the grounds (typically default by the obligor) for issuance of such an order by the secured party.

138. *In re* Cumberland Molded Prods., LLC, 69 U.C.C. Rep. Serv. 2d 371 (Bankr. M.D. Tenn. 2009) (bank in control of deposit account lost perfection when it honored a check issued by the debtor and turned the remainder of the funds over to the trustee).

139. The mechanism can also be used with an account maintained with the secured party, in which case it augments the bank's common-law right of set-off. For a discussion of set-off rights, see § 11.03[E], *infra*.

140. U.C.C. § 8-106(f).

141. U.C.C. § 9-107. Consent can be pursuant to Section 5-114(c) or any other applicable law or practice.

142. *See* § 1.07, *supra*.

143. U.C.C. §§ 9-314(a), 7-106(a). The rules governing perfection when a bailee has issued a nonnegotiable electronic document pose a subtle problem. Section 9-312(d) provides that perfection of a security interest in goods in the hands of a bailee that has issued a nonnegotiable document for them requires that the document be issued in the name of the secured party, that the bailee receive notification of the secured party's interest, or that the secured party ignore the document and file as to the goods. Unlike the situation with a negotiable document, neither filing with respect to a nonnegotiable document nor its possession is an appropriate means of perfection as to the goods because title to the goods is not reified in the document. Section 9-313(a), which governs perfection by possession, is appropriately limited to negotiable documents. Section 9-314(a), however, which governs perfection by control (the counterpart of possession in the electronic world), is not so limited. Because of this, a lawyer might be misled into thinking that obtaining control of an electronic nonnegotiable document accomplishes something worthwhile when, in fact, it does not protect a secured party's interest in the bailed goods. Accordingly, a secured party should not use control as a method of perfection for electronic nonnegotiable documents.

144. U.C.C. § 7-106, Comment 3. Section 7-106 provides safe harbor tests that, if satisfied, confirm the secured party's control of the electronic document of title. Subsection (b)'s safe harbor is available

[C] Controllable Accounts, Controllable Electronic Records, Controllable Payment Intangibles, and Electronic Money

In 2022, the new U.C.C. Article 12 introduced the concept of a "controllable electronic record" (CER), meaning a record stored in an electronic medium that can be subjected to control. Article 12 reflects an effort to adapt the U.C.C. to emerging technologies that affect electronic commerce, such as distributed ledger technology. Bitcoin and other virtual currencies are examples of CERs.[145] The drafters intended the term to be flexible enough to include other digital assets that may be created using yet-to-be-developed technologies. Article 12 seeks to reduce the commercial risks associated with transactions involving CERs by establishing legal rules governing the transfer of these records, both outright and for purposes of security. Our focus in this section is how a secured party that takes a security interest in a CER can perfect that interest.

Because many systems for transferring CERs are pseudonymous, the transferee of a CER may be unable to verify the real identity of the transferor or the source of the transferor's title. As a result, Article 12's rules make CERs "negotiable," that is, a qualifying purchaser of a CER—meaning a purchaser that has obtained control of the record for value, in good faith, and without notice of conflicting third-party claims[146]—will take

---

only where one authoritative copy of the document exists; subsection (c)'s safe harbor (added by the 2022 amendments) is available whether only one or multiple authoritative copies exist. U.C.C. § 7-106, Comment 4. Subsection (c)'s safe harbor generally tracks the new Article 12 test for control of controllable electronic records and the new Section 9-105 rules on control of chattel paper evidenced by electronic records. *Id.* Comment 6. The Article 12 test for control of controllable electronic records is discussed in § 6.04[C] *infra*; control of chattel paper is discussed in § 6.05 *infra*.

145. Another example of a CER is the "nonfungible token," or NFT. This is a unique digital identifier or "token" that is recorded on a blockchain and may contain references to some type of digital or tangible asset. Some innovators in the NFT market tout the potential of NFTs to "tokenize" ownership of digital or tangible assets (such as goods or land) and to streamline transactions by permitting the transfer of ownership of the underlying asset via transfer of the token.

One should take care to understand what "tokenization" does and does not accomplish. For example, suppose that Henning owns a racehorse that is subject to a security interest in favor of Bank, which holds a security interest (perfected by filing) in all of Henning's tangible goods and general intangibles. Henning later creates an NFT that purports to tokenize ownership of the horse, and then transfers the NFT to Gotberg (who pays value and lacks knowledge of the Bank's security interest in the horse and the token). It is tempting to say that if Gotberg is a "qualified purchaser" of the NFT (as discussed in the ensuing text and notes) and thus owns the NFT free of Bank's prior claim, she would also own the horse free and clear of Bank's security interest, but that is incorrect. Gotberg does own the NFT, but nothing in the Uniform Commercial Code—or other applicable law at this date—formally "tethers" ownership of tangible goods like the horse to the NFT. Even if the NFT purports to tokenize ownership of the horse, transfer of the NFT does not effect a transfer of ownership of the horse (i.e., the NFT does not actually "embody" ownership of the horse). Thus, even if ownership of the NFT gives Gotberg some legally enforceable rights vis-à-vis Henning, the horse itself remains subject to Bank's prior-perfected security interest.

146. U.C.C. § 12-102(a)(2). Chapter 12 gives the term "value" the same meaning that it has in U.C.C. Article 3, which means that the qualifying purchaser of a CER has rights equivalent to a holder in due course of a negotiable instrument. U.C.C. § 12-102(a)(4).

free of conflicting third-party claims. This means that while a secured party relying on a CER as collateral could perfect its security interest by filing,[147] reliance on filing alone is imprudent. A security interest in a CER that is perfected by control will have priority over a conflicting security interest perfected by any other method, including primarily filing.[148] Further, a qualifying purchaser of a CER would take its interest in the record free of the interest of a secured party perfected only by filing.[149] To assure its intended priority, the secured party must therefore perfect its security interest by obtaining control of the CER.

Section 9-107 provides that a secured party establishes control of a CER as provided in Section 12-105.[150] Under Section 12-105, a secured party has control of a CER if the CER, a record attached to or logically associated with the CER, or a system in which the CER is recorded meets the following criteria:

- It gives the secured party the power, which does not need to be exclusive, to avail itself of substantially all the benefit[151] from the CER, and the exclusive[152] power to prevent others from doing so;

- It gives the secured party the exclusive power to transfer control of the CER to another person or cause the transferee to obtain control of another CER; and

- It enables the secured party readily to identify itself in any way (including by name, identifying number, cryptographic key, office, or account number) as having the powers described above.[153]

While a power over a CER generally can be exclusive even if the power is shared with another person,[154] a secured party's power over such a record cannot be exclusive

---

147. U.C.C. § 9-312(a).

148. U.C.C. § 9-326A. A security interest in a CER that is proceeds could be perfected automatically for a 20-day period under U.C.C. § 9-315(c), (d), and the security interest of the buyer of a controllable payment intangible evidenced by a CER is perfected automatically under U.C.C. § 9-309(3).

149. U.C.C. § 12-104(e). Article 12 makes clear that "[f]iling of a financing statement under Article 9 is no notice of a claim of a property right in a controllable electronic record" so as to deprive a purchaser of the record of its qualifying status. U.C.C. § 12-104(h).

150. U.C.C. § 9-107A.

151. The "benefit" of a CER refers to the rights afforded by the record and the uses to which the record may be put. For example, the benefit accorded by control of a bitcoin is that the person in control can hold or dispose of it. Likewise, the benefit accorded by control of a CER that evidences a controllable account or controllable payment intangible is the right to collect the account or payment intangible from the account debtor. U.C.C. § 12-105, Comment 3.

152. The secured party's power is exclusive even if the CER, a record attached to or logically associated with the CER, or a system in which the CER is recorded limits the use of the CER or has a protocol programmed to cause a change, including a transfer or loss of control or a modification of benefits afforded by the CER. U.C.C. § 12-105(b)(1).

153. U.C.C. § 12-105(a). If the secured party has the powers described in the first two bulleted points in the text, a presumption arises that the powers are exclusive. U.C.C. § 12-105(d).

154. U.C.C. § 12-105(b)(2). The sharing of power over a CER pursuant to a multi-signature agreement can provide enhanced security where there are multiple persons holding the rights inherent within the record. For example, suppose that A and B are the sole members in an LLC that owns 200 Bitcoin. A and B have an agreement under which the exercise of power over the Bitcoin requires action

where that power is shared with the debtor.[155] Control in this context requires that the debtor must be "divested sufficiently of its powers over the relevant CER so as to warrant treating the transferee as a secured party having a security interest perfected by control or as having the requisite control to be a qualifying purchaser."[156]

Under Section 12-104(e), the secured party can establish control through another person if that person has control of the CER and acknowledges that it has control on behalf of the secured party, or if that person obtains control of the CER after having acknowledged that it will obtain control on behalf of the secured party.[157] However, the secured party does not establish control under Section 12-104(e) by having the debtor acknowledge that it has control on behalf of the secured party.[158] This is a logical extension of the principle that the debtor cannot function as the secured party's agent for purposes of perfection by possession.[159]

The 2022 amendments also introduced, as recognized forms of collateral, controllable accounts[160] and controllable payment intangibles.[161] If an account or payment intangible is evidenced by a CER as to which the account debtor has undertaken to pay the person that has control of the CER, the account or payment intangible is controllable.[162] A qualifying purchaser of a controllable account or a controllable payment intangible will take free of conflicting property claims.[163] Thus, to assure its intended priority, a secured party must perfect its security interest in a controllable account or a controllable payment intangible by obtaining control—which the secured party can do if it obtains control of the CER evidencing the account or payment intangible.[164]

---

by both, that is, neither person acting alone has the power to effect a transfer of the Bitcoin. If A is later hacked, the multi-signature agreement would prevent the hacker from exercising unauthorized power over the record (and effecting a transfer of the Bitcoin). U.C.C. § 12-105, Comment 5.

155. U.C.C. § 12-105(c)(2)(B). *See* U.C.C. § 12-105, Comment 9 ("Subsection (c)(2)(B) disqualifies a transferee (which includes a secured party in a secured transactions) of an interest in a controllable electronic record ... from the benefit of a shared power under subsection (b)(2) when the transferor retains a blocking power (i.e., when the transferee cannot exercise the power unless the transferor also exercises the power).")

156. U.C.C. § 12-105, Comment 9.

157. U.C.C. § 12-105(e).

158. *Id.*

159. *See* § 6.03[B], *supra. See also* U.C.C. § 12-105, Comment 9.

160. U.C.C. § 9-102(a)(27A).

161. U.C.C. § 9-102(a)(27B).

162. U.C.C. Article 12, Prefatory Note 4b. One might think of the right to payment evidenced by the account or the payment intangible as having been "tethered" to the electronic record evidencing them. U.C.C. § 12-104, Comment 9.

163. U.C.C. § 12-104(e). In this regard, the 2022 amendments allow the qualified purchaser of controllable accounts or controllable payment intangibles the benefit of take-free protections somewhat analogous to those enjoyed by the holder in due course of a negotiable instrument. U.C.C. § 12-105, Comment 10.

164. U.C.C. §§ 9-107A(b), 12-104(b). *See also* U.C.C. § 9-107A(a) ("A secured party has control of a controllable electronic record as provided in Section 12-105.").

Finally, the 2022 Article 9 amendments also added "electronic money" as a form of collateral.[165] A security interest in electronic money as original collateral can be perfected only by control as specified in Section 9-105A.[166] Section 9-105A's requirements for establishing control generally track those contained in Section 12-105 for establishing control over a CER.[167]

§ 6.05 Perfection by Possession and Control (Chattel Paper)

[A] Perfection in Chattel Paper Prior to 2022

When Article 9 was first promulgated in 1962, chattel paper was defined as "a writing or writings which evidence both a monetary obligation and a security interest or lease in specific goods."[168] This definition reflected the reality at the time that all chattel paper was tangible in nature. A secured party that took a security interest in chattel paper could perfect by filing a financing statement,[169] but doing so was potentially risky. Given the "quasi-negotiable" nature of chattel paper, if the debtor later assigned and delivered possession of the chattel paper to a good-faith purchaser for value, the secured party was at risk of the purchaser's taking the paper free of the secured party's interest.[170] One way for the secured party to prevent such an assignment was by taking possession of the chattel paper.[171] Taking possession of chattel paper was thus not only a permitted method of perfection as to chattel paper,[172] it was the preferred method.

By the time of the comprehensive revisions of Article 9 in 1998, innovation in electronic contracting meant that some transactions that would have created tangible chattel paper were being documented purely in electronic form. Consistent with the media-neutral emphasis of the 1998 revisions, the drafters redefined chattel paper as "a record or records that evidence both a monetary obligation and a security interest in specific goods … [or] a lease of specific goods…."[173] Further, the drafters divided chattel paper as a collateral form into "tangible chattel paper"[174] and "electronic chattel

---

165. U.C.C. § 9-102(a)(31A).

166. U.C.C. §§ 9-312(b)(4) (filing ineffective), 9-314(a) (perfected by control as specified in Section 9-105A).

167. U.C.C. § 9-105A, Comment 1.

168. U.C.C. § 9-105(1)(b) (1962 text). The definition was misleading, however, in suggesting that the chattel paper was the writing(s) itself rather than the monetary obligation it evidenced. This error was corrected in the amended definition of the term introduced in the 2022 amendments.

169. U.C.C. § 9-304(1) (1962 text).

170. U.C.C. § 9-308 (1962 text).

171. As noted earlier in the chapter, the secured party could not establish perfection by possession by taking one set of duplicate originals and leaving the debtor in possession of another set. If the obligor had signed multiple originals, the secured party had to take possession of all of them.

172. U.C.C. § 9-305 (1962 text).

173. U.C.C., § 9-102(a)(11) (2000 text).

174. U.C.C. § 9-102(a)(79) (2000 text).

paper."[175] For both types, filing remained a permissive method of perfection,[176] but they retained a quasi-negotiable character. Thus, for tangible chattel paper, the preferred method of perfection remained taking possession of the paper (thus preventing its transfer and delivery to a good-faith purchaser for value).[177] For electronic chattel paper—of which there was nothing tangible to possess—the drafters provided the functional equivalent of possession by permitting the secured party to establish "control" over the electronic chattel paper under Section 9-105. This required the secured party to establish that "a system employed for evidencing the transfer of interests in the chattel paper reliably establishes the secured party as the person to which the chattel paper was assigned."[178] Compliance with this standard required that the electronic record evidencing the chattel paper was stored in such a way that there was a single "authoritative" copy that identified the secured party and that could not be amended or altered in any way without the secured party's consent. The 1998 text required specific standards for how the objective of the control system had to be achieved. In 2010, the drafters restructured Section 9-105 as a safe harbor so that the marketplace could develop new technologies that might satisfy the general reliability standard. The 2022 amendments, discussed below, generally retain this approach as an alternative, so as not to upset existing systems, but also provide a different test for distributed ledger technologies.

Evolving commercial practices have made the distinction between "tangible chattel paper" and "electronic chattel paper" somewhat elusive, if not ethereal. The Comments to Section 9-314A (introduced in the 2022 amendments) highlight the difficulty:

> Perfection of a security interest in chattel paper by taking possession of the collateral generally has been understood to mean taking possession of the wet-ink "original." Experience has shown that the concept of an original breaks down when one allows for the possibility of the same monetary obligation being evidenced by different media over time, such as where electronic records evidencing chattel paper are "papered out" (replaced with tangible records evidencing the same chattel paper) or tangible records are "converted" to electronic records.[179]

Further, technological evolution (e.g., the development of distributed ledger technology like blockchain) has challenged the notion that there can be but one "authoritative" copy of an electronic record. These stresses increasingly made clear the need for the drafters to revisit perfection as to chattel paper, and the 2022 amendments do so by introducing the concept of "possession and control" for this purpose.

---

175. U.C.C. § 9-102(a)(31) (2000 text).
176. U.C.C. § 9-312(a) (2000 text).
177. U.C.C. § 9-313(a) (2000 text).
178. U.C.C. § 9-105(a) (2010 text).
179. U.C.C. § 9-314A, Comment 1.

[B] Perfection in Chattel Paper under the 2022 Amendments

Filing remains a permissive method of perfection for a security interest in chattel paper,[180] but it also remains inadequate alone, due to chattel paper's quasi-negotiable character. In Section 9-314A, the 2022 Code amendments introduce the concept of "possession and control" as a means of perfection for a security interest in chattel paper. To perfect under Section 9-314A(a), the secured party must (i) take possession of each authoritative tangible copy of the record evidencing the chattel paper and (ii) obtain control of each authoritative electronic copy of the electronic record evidencing the chattel paper.[181] A security interest remains perfected under Section 9-314A(a) only while the secured party retains possession and control.[182] Possession and control are also conditions for the secured party to ensure its priority vis-à-vis subsequent purchasers of the chattel paper under Section 9-330.[183]

Whether an electronic or tangible copy of a record evidencing chattel paper is "authoritative" depends in the first instance on the facts and circumstances. As the Comments explain:

> The determination should turn on whether the copy provides reasonable notice to third parties that it is one that must be subject to control or possession for purposes of perfection and priority. To accommodate current practices and future technology, parties are allowed considerable flexibility in determining the method used to establish whether a particular copy is authoritative, provided that third parties are able to reasonably identify the authoritative copies that must be possessed or controlled to achieve perfection. For example, the parties could develop a system or protocol where each tangible or electronic copy is "watermarked" as authoritative or nonauthoritative or where the terms of the records themselves describe how to determine which copies are authoritative and which are not.[184]

Traditionally, taking possession of chattel paper that existed in tangible form meant taking possession of the wet-ink-signed "original" record. As noted earlier in this chapter, this can pose a problem if the obligor signs duplicate originals and the debtor retains one of the duplicates. To establish the "possession" component of possession and control, the secured party would either have to (i) take possession of each and

---

180. U.C.C. § 9-312(a).

181. U.C.C. § 9-314A(a). By combining the concepts of possession and control, the drafters obviated any need to maintain separate definitions of "tangible chattel paper" and "electronic chattel paper," so those definitions have now been deleted. U.C.C. § 9-102, Comment 5b.

182. U.C.C. § 9-314A(b). If a secured party perfected both by filing and by possession and control, and later relinquished possession and control to the debtor, the secured party would remain perfected by virtue of the filing but would be at risk of losing priority to a subsequent good-faith purchaser for value under Section 9-330.

183. U.C.C. §§ 9-330(a)–(c); 9-105, Comment 1.

184. U.C.C. § 9-314A, Comment 1.

every signed duplicate original or (ii) ensure that one was sufficiently labeled as the "original" (i.e., the "authoritative" record) and others were labeled as "copies" (i.e., "nonauthoritative").

Under Section 9-105(a), a secured party has control of an authoritative electronic copy of a record evidencing chattel paper if "a system employed for evidencing the assignment of interests in the chattel paper reliably establishes [the secured party] as the person to which the authoritative electronic copy was assigned."[185] Section 9-105(b) and (c) then provides two "safe harbor" tests that (if satisfied) establish control under subsection (a).

The subsection (b) safe harbor applies when there is a single authoritative copy of the record or records evidencing the chattel paper. It sets forth standards that are functionally identical to those contained in the pre-2022 safe harbor for perfection by control of a security interest in electronic chattel paper.[186]

The subsection (b) safe harbor cannot apply if the record evidencing the chattel paper is maintained on a blockchain or another distributed ledger; such technology depends on there being multiple authoritative copies of a record.[187] Thus, subsection (c) provides a safe harbor for such a record; this provision generally tracks Article 12's rules for establishing control of CERs.[188] This safe harbor requires the secured party to identify each electronic copy of the record as authoritative or nonauthoritative and to identify itself as the assignee of the authoritative copy.[189] Further, the secured party must have exclusive power to transfer control of the authoritative copy and to prevent others from adding or changing an identified assignee.[190] As noted above, perfection (and priority vis-à-vis subsequent purchasers) requires the secured party to obtain control of each and every authoritative electronic copy of the record evidencing the chattel paper.[191]

Consistent with the control rules relating to CERs, a secured party's power over the authoritative electronic copy cannot be exclusive where that power is shared with the

185. U.C.C. § 9-105(a). This subsection essentially restates the general rule by which a secured party established control of "electronic chattel paper" under the 2000 revisions.
186. U.C.C. § 9-105(b) ("A system satisfies subsection (a) if the record or records evidencing the chattel paper are created, stored, and assigned in a manner that: (1) a single authoritative copy of the record or records exists which is unique, identifiable, and, except as otherwise provided in paragraphs (4), (5), and (6), unalterable; (2) the authoritative copy identifies the purchaser as the assignee of the record or records; (3) the authoritative copy is communicated to and maintained by the purchaser or its designated custodian; (4) copies or amendments that add or change an identified assignee of the authoritative copy can be made only with the consent of the purchaser; (5) each copy of the authoritative copy and any copy of a copy is readily identifiable as a copy that is not the authoritative copy; and (6) any amendment of the authoritative copy is readily identifiable as authorized or unauthorized.").
187. U.C.C. § 9-105, Comment 4.
188. See § 6.04[C], supra.
189. U.C.C. § 9-105(c)(1), (2).
190. U.C.C. § 9-105(c)(3).
191. U.C.C. § 9-314A(a).

debtor.[192] Control in this context requires that the debtor be sufficiently divested of its powers over the record to warrant a conclusion that the secured party has perfected by control.[193]

Under Section 9-105(g), the secured party can establish control of an electronic copy of a record evidencing chattel paper through another person, if that person has control of the authoritative electronic copy and acknowledges that it has control on behalf of the secured party or if that person obtains control of the authoritative electronic copy after having acknowledged that it will obtain control on behalf of the secured party.[194] The secured party cannot establish control by having the debtor acknowledge that it has control on the secured party's behalf.[195]

---

192. U.C.C. § 9-105, Comment 5. *See* § 6.04[C], *supra*.

193. U.C.C. §§ 9-105, Comment 5; 12-105, Comment 9.

194. U.C.C. § 9-105(g). This likewise tracks the comparable rules for perfection by control as to controllable electronic records in Section 12-105(e) and discussed in § 6.04[C], *supra*.

195. U.C.C. § 9-105(g). Again, this is a logical extension of the principle that the debtor cannot function as the secured party's agent for purposes of perfection by possession.

Chapter 7

Automatic Perfection

Synopsis

In some transactions, a security interest is perfected as soon as it attaches. The secured party need not take any further action to perfect because perfection occurs automatically with attachment.[1] Parties dealing with types of personal property that are eligible for automatic perfection need to be aware that a perfected security interest might exist despite the secret nature of the encumbrance. This chapter discusses the policies that led the drafters to permit automatic perfection and some practical consequences of this decision.

---

1. U.C.C. § 9-309 (identifying security interests that perfect "when they attach").

§ 7.01 Purchase-Money Security Interests in Consumer Goods—§ 9-309(1)

[A] Application of the Provision

The most important automatic-perfection provision applies to purchase-money security interests in consumer goods.[2] This instance of automatic perfection is the only one that completely eliminates the general filing requirement when a secured party leaves goods subject to a security interest in a debtor's possession.[3] A seller of goods used for a personal, family, or household purpose is automatically perfected with respect to a security interest retained in the goods to secure the unpaid purchase price. Similarly, a lender that provides an enabling loan to facilitate a debtor's acquisition of consumer goods obtains an automatically perfected security interest in the goods after the borrower buys them from a seller.[4]

Suppose that a debtor in a purchase-money transaction represents to the secured party that the debtor will use the purchase-money collateral for personal, family, or household purposes. Relying on this representation, the secured party files no financing statement (relying on the automatic-perfection rule). But suppose further that the debtor's representations were false, and the debtor intended to (and did) use the goods for business purposes. Is the secured party's security interest nevertheless automatically perfected?[5] Some courts have upheld automatic perfection when the debtor has

---

2. U.C.C. § 9-309(1); *In re* Haus, 18 B.R. 413, 33 U.C.C. Rep. Serv. 694 (Bankr. D. S.C. 1982) (household appliances); Meskell v. Bertone, 55 U.C.C. Rep. Serv. 2d 179 (Mass. Super. Ct. 2004) (boat). Although perfection is automatic with respect to purchase-money security interests in consumer goods, secured parties that rely on automatic perfection incur a unique risk with respect to consumers that buy the goods from the debtor. *See* U.C.C. § 9-320(b). For discussion of this priority issue, see § 11.03[A][2], *infra*.

As discussed later in this chapter, the automatic-perfection rule of Section 9-309(1) does not apply if the collateral is goods covered by a certificate-of-title statute. *See* § 7.01[C], *infra*; *In re* Mattes, 642 B.R. 1 (Bankr. D. Neb. 2022) (automatic-perfection rule of Section 9-309(1) inapplicable to purchase-money security interest in titled vehicle).

3. Although automatic perfection may extend indefinitely with respect to goods that constitute proceeds, appropriate filing or possession with respect to the original collateral is a prerequisite. U.C.C. § 9-315(d)(1). *See* § 8.02, *infra*.

4. The fact that a debtor subsequently installs the goods into the debtor's home, such that the goods become fixtures, does not affect the secured party's ability to claim that its security interest is automatically perfected under Section 9-309(1). *See, e.g., In re* Dabbs, 625 B.R. 15, 103 U.C.C. Rep. Serv. 2d 1477 (Bankr. D.S.C. 2021) (purchase-money security interest in siding installed on home); *In re* Dalebout, 454 B.R. 158, 74 U.C.C. Rep. Serv. 2d 531 (Bankr. D. Kan. 2011) (purchase-money security interest in windows installed in home). As to goods that become fixtures, however, automatic perfection would be sufficient only to establish the secured party's priority vis-à-vis other Article 9 secured parties and lien creditors. As discussed in Chapter 15, *infra*, it would not be sufficient to establish priority vis-à-vis conflicting claimants whose rights arise under real property law, such as a buyer of the land or a mortgagee. *See* § 15.03, *infra*.

5. Article 9 does not address the issue, but it does have a provision that insulates a secured party from liability or a reduction in its right to a deficiency if it reasonably believes that a transaction is not a consumer or consumer-goods transaction. U.C.C. § 9-628(c). Because the interests of third parties

unequivocally indicated to the secured party that the goods will be used for a consumer purpose.[6] A bankruptcy court in Pennsylvania approved this result but added the qualification that the secured party not have had reason to believe that the debtor would actually use the goods differently.[7] That court denied automatic perfection to the seller of a lawn tractor because the seller should have known that the buyer intended to use the tractor for a business purpose after the buyer initially tried to obtain the tractor in the name of the buyer's business. The seller's designation of the loan application as "personal" and its insistence that the buyer use a personal charge card were irrelevant.

[B] Policy

A provision permitting automatic perfection enables the creation of a secret lien—a circumstance that Article 9 generally avoids. Although several policy considerations underlie this departure from the norm, the Comments are not very helpful in explaining them. One reason for treating these transactions differently is the undesirable consequences that would result from requiring perfection by filing. Consumer transactions are so common that filing might overburden the filing system, although this rationale is considerably less compelling given modern electronic information-storage capacity. A related consideration is that most consumer transactions involve goods having a relatively low value.[8] The transaction costs associated with preparing and filing financing statements would thus be proportionately higher than in most other types of transactions, and the consumer would invariably bear those costs. Thus, automatic perfection in this context might be justified as reducing the costs of purchase-money financing for consumers.

The nature of the collateral provides another justification for automatic perfection. Consumer goods tend to depreciate rapidly and are difficult to deal with following a default by the debtor. As a result, many lenders do not favor using consumer goods as

---

become involved when perfection is at stake, the provision sheds no real light on the appropriate resolution of the problem.

6. *In re* Palmer, 365 B.R. 816 (Bankr. S.D. Ohio 2007); *In re* Troupe, 340 B.R. 86, 59 U.C.C. Rep. Serv. 2d 23 (Bankr. W.D. Okla. 2006); *In re* Pettit, 18 B.R. 8, 33 U.C.C. Rep. Serv. 1762 (Bankr. E.D. Ark. 1981); Franklin Inv. Co. v. Homburg, 252 A.2d 95, 6 U.C.C. Rep. Serv. 60 (D.C. Ct. App. 1969).

The court in *Troupe* justified its decision by stating that the debtor is bound by representations in the security agreement regarding the intended use of the collateral, and thus that the collateral was properly classified as consumer goods at the time the purchase-money security interest attached, triggering the automatic-perfection rule. The court then noted that even if the debtor used the collateral for business purposes, that "subsequent" change in the nature of the debtor's use did not change the secured party's perfected status. In this way, the court effectively treated the debtor's use of the collateral inconsistent with the representations as the equivalent of a post-transaction change in use. While such a change indeed would not affect a filed financing statement's effectiveness (U.C.C. §9-507(b)), this logic is much less compelling when the secured party is relying entirely on automatic perfection and, as such, no financing statement appears on the record.

7. *In re* Fiscante, 141 B.R. 303, 19 U.C.C. Rep. Serv. 2d 1188 (Bankr. W.D. Pa. 1992).

8. Some states had adopted a nonuniform provision that eliminated the option of automatic perfection when the value of the goods exceeded a specified dollar threshold. Adoption of the 1998 revisions eliminated most of these provisions. *See* note 21, *infra.*

collateral. Merchants that sell goods to consumers under installment sales contracts, on the other hand, sometimes retain purchase-money security interests. In the event of a default, the merchant (because it deals in goods of that kind) is in a somewhat better position to repossess and sell the goods than would be a lender with a similar security interest. The prospect of repossession in the event of default provides leverage to motivate a consumer to fulfill the obligation to pay the purchase price. Moreover, sellers have an incentive to sell to consumers on credit, and taking a security interest somewhat reduces their risk (and therefore the consumer's cost of credit).

In the past, secured lenders in non-purchase-money transactions with consumers often sought to improve their positions by taking a security interest in most or all of a debtor's consumer goods. This approach significantly enhanced their leverage by positioning them to threaten defaulting debtors with the loss of all or many of their worldly possessions. However, because this practice was perceived as abusive, the Federal Trade Commission promulgated a rule making it an unfair practice under federal law for a lender or a retail installment seller[9] to receive a consumer obligation that "[c]onstitutes or contains a nonpossessory security interest in household goods other than a purchase-money security interest."[10] Purchase-money security interests and possessory security interests are the only security interests that this rule permits in assets that qualify as household goods under the rule.[11]

Lenders and buyers of used goods that deal with consumers regularly should be aware of the possibility that a debtor's consumer goods may be subject to an automatically perfected purchase-money security interest. These parties can protect themselves by requiring satisfactory documentation from the consumer showing that the seller of the goods has received payment and that funds used for that payment were not borrowed from a lender that has not been repaid.

A consumer buyer of goods from another consumer is not expected to have the same degree of sophistication. Reflecting this assessment, a special priority provision enables such a buyer to take free of the interest of a purchase-money secured party that is relying on automatic perfection.[12] A purchase-money secured party can avoid the risk posed by consumer buyers by taking the additional step of filing a financing statement with respect to the goods.[13]

---

9. The rule defines a retail installment seller as "[a] person who sells goods or services to consumers on a deferred payment basis or pursuant to a lease-purchase arrangement within the jurisdiction of the Federal Trade Commission." 16 C.F.R. § 444.1(b).

10. FTC Rule on Credit Practices, Regulation AA, 16 C.F.R. § 444.2(a)(4) (1994).

11. A further reason for secured parties to avoid nonpossessory, non-purchase-money security interests in consumer goods is that such an interest can be invalidated in bankruptcy to the extent it impairs a bankrupt debtor's ability to claim an exemption in certain specified categories. 11 U.S.C. § 522(f)(1)(B). For discussion of "lien stripping" in bankruptcy, see § 16.01[C], *infra*.

12. U.C.C. § 9-320(b). For discussion of this provision, see § 11.03[A][2], *infra*.

13. U.C.C. § 9-320(b).

[C] Exceptions

The automatic-perfection provision with respect to consumer goods is subject to two exceptions. If the consumer goods become fixtures, the secured party must make a fixture filing to attain the priority that Article 9 allows with respect to most other realty interests, although automatic perfection will defeat lien creditors like a trustee in bankruptcy.[14] Chapter 15 provides further discussion of Article 9's priority rules for fixtures. Article 9 also precludes automatic perfection for goods subject to state certificate-of-title laws, as well as for goods subject to a federal statute, regulation, or treaty that preempts the general filing requirements of Article 9.[15] For example, if a motor vehicle is subject to a state certificate-of-title law, perfection may be accomplished only by compliance with that law, and a purchase-money security interest in the vehicle cannot be automatically perfected even if it is consumer goods.[16]

An occasional decision has created nonstatutory exceptions to automatic perfection for certain types of consumer goods. In *In re Sprague*,[17] the bankruptcy referee refused to characterize a mobile home as consumer goods even though the debtor purchased it for household purposes. The referee reasoned that the drafters did not intend for automatic perfection to apply to goods as large and expensive as mobile homes.[18] Similarly, the court in *Union National Bank of Pittsburgh v. Northwest Marine, Inc.*[19] held that a 33-foot motorboat purchased for family purposes for $8,000 was not consumer goods for purposes of automatic perfection. The court reasoned that the concept of consumer goods envisions a "using up" or "wasting away" of the asset to the extent that a second institution would not be inclined to loan money against it. It thus found

---

14. *In re* Weaver, 69 B.R. 554, 3 U.C.C. Rep. Serv. 2d 1231 (Bankr. W.D. Ky. 1987) (no automatic perfection for mobile home situated on permanent foundation); *In re* Hinson, 77 B.R. 34, 5 U.C.C. Rep. Serv. 2d 233 (Bankr. M.D.N.C. 1987) (fixture filing required for windows and gutters attached to house). *Cf. In re* Williams, 381 B.R. 742, 64 U.C.C. Rep. Serv. 2d 1034 (Bankr. W.D. Ark. 2008) (enabling lender with a purchase-money security interest in a guttering system installed to the debtor's dwelling held to be automatically perfected because the secured party and debtor explicitly agreed that the goods would remain as personal property rather than fixtures and the gutter system could be readily removed without material harm to the real estate).

15. U.C.C. §§ 9-309(1); 9-311(a)(1) (federal law), (a)(2) (state certificate-of-title law).

16. U.C.C. § 9-311(b). *See* United States v. One 1987 Cadillac DeVille, VIN 1G6CD5184H4348815, 774 F. Supp. 221, 16 U.C.C. Rep. Serv. 2d 1194 (D. Del. 1991) (automobile); *In re* Radny, 12 U.C.C. Rep. Serv. 583 (Bankr. W.D. Mich. 1973) (mobile home); *In re* Hicks, 491 F.3d 1136, 63 U.C.C. Rep. Serv. 2d 62 (10th Cir. 2007) (secured party with a purchase-money security interest in the debtor's vehicle was unperfected when the State of Kansas erroneously issued a certificate of title that failed to include a notation of the secured party's lien). *Compare In re* Lance, 59 U.C.C. Rep. Serv. 2d 632 (Bankr. W.D. Mo. 2006) (because Missouri law does not require snowmobiles to be covered by a certificate of title, a purchase-money security interest in a snowmobile used for consumer purposes became perfected upon attachment).

17. 4 U.C.C. Rep. Serv. 702 (Bankr. N.D.N.Y. 1966).

18. Note that in most states, manufactured homes are in fact subject to certificate-of-title statutes that would require a security interest to be perfected by having the secured party's lien noted on the certificate of title for the home. *See* § 15.03[G], *infra*. In those states, automatic perfection would not apply to a manufactured home, but not for the reason expressed by the referee in *Sprague*.

19. 27 U.C.C. Rep. Serv. 563 (Pa. Ct. Comm. Pl. 1979).

that the motorboat constituted goods of substantial magnitude compared to the "ordinary" concept of consumer goods and concluded that the secured lender that provided the enabling loan was not automatically perfected.[20] These decisions are wrong, as the drafters did not include any limiting criteria based on the size, value, or price of the consumer goods. Even if the results achieved by the courts are desirable, the standard articulated by them is far too vague for practical application.[21]

[D] The "Dual-Status" Rule and the "Transformation" Rule

Chapter 10 will explain how Section 9-103(f) generally adopts the "dual-status" rule, under which a security interest can be both a purchase-money security interest (to the extent that it secures the purchase-money obligation) and a non-purchase-money security interest (to the extent that it secures any other obligation).[22] Thus, a purchase-money security interest does not cease to be a purchase-money security interest merely because the purchase-money collateral also secures an unrelated obligation, because the debtor also has granted a security interest in other collateral to secure the purchase-money obligation or because the debtor has renewed, refinanced, consolidated, or restructured the purchase-money obligation.[23] In adopting the dual-status rule, the Code rejected judicial decisions that had adopted the "transformation" rule, under which courts had ruled that these transactions entirely transformed a purchase-money security interest into a non-purchase-money security interest.[24] If the Code's general approach also applies to purchase-money security interests in consumer goods, then the refinancing of the purchase-money obligation, for example, would not defeat the secured party's ability to rely on the automatic-perfection rule as a basis to claim perfection.

As Chapter 10 will explain, however, Section 9-103(f) explicitly applies only in non-consumer-goods transactions. In consumer-goods transactions, Section 9-103(h) leaves to courts whether to apply the transformation rule.[25] If a court applies the transformation rule, then the refinancing or consolidation of a purchase-money obligation would defeat the purchase-money status of a security interest securing that obligation—and if the secured party had been relying on the automatic-perfection rule, the security interest would become unperfected unless the secured party took another action sufficient to perfect (e.g., filing or possession).

---

20. Again, in some states, motorboats would be subject to certificate-of-title statutes, and in those states automatic perfection would not apply—but not for the reasons expressed in *Northwest Marine*.

21. Maine has narrowed the availability of automatic perfection for consumer goods by including a monetary limitation on the purchase price of the affected goods. Me. Rev. Stat. Ann. tit. 11, § 9-1309(1) ($10,000 or less). Colorado, Kansas, and Wisconsin eliminated prior monetary limitations when they enacted revised Article 9.

22. *See* § 10.04, *infra*.

23. U.C.C. § 9-103(f); *In re* Saxe, 491 B.R. 244, 80 U.C.C. Rep. Serv. 2d 245 (Bankr. W.D. Wis. 2013).

24. *See, e.g., In re* Matthews, 724 F.2d 798, 37 U.C.C. Rep. Serv. 1322 (9th Cir. 1984).

25. U.C.C. § 9-103(h).

Several court decisions involving consumer-goods transactions have simply adopted the dual-status rule in Section 9-103(h). For example, the court in *In re Madrid-Baskin*[26] stated that it saw "no reasoned legal basis to treat consumers and non-consumers differently" with respect to the applicability of the dual-status rule. Under this approach, a purchase-money secured party relying on automatic perfection as to consumer goods would not compromise its perfected status if it refinanced or restructured the purchase-money obligation. Likewise, several states have enacted nonuniform amendments to Section 9-103 that apply the dual-status rule to all transactions without regard to the nature of the collateral and have repealed Section 9-103(h).[27]

Nevertheless, there remain a few jurisdictions in which courts continue to apply the transformation rule in some circumstances, particularly in the context of bankruptcy decisions involving Bankruptcy Code § 1325(a) and its "hanging paragraph."[28] In those jurisdictions, a secured party that agreed to refinance or restructure the purchase-money obligation should appreciate the impact this action could have on its perfected status if the secured party was relying on the automatic-perfection rule.

§ 7.02 Certain Types of Assignments

Article 9 recognizes automatic perfection for assignments of specified types of assets. Among these are isolated assignments of accounts or payment intangibles, sales of payment intangibles and promissory notes, assignment of a health-care-insurance receivable to a provider of health-care goods or services, assignment of certain interests in investment property, an assignment for the benefit of all creditors, an assignment of a beneficial interest in a decedent's estate, and a sale by an individual of an account that constitutes lottery winnings. A security interest arising in these transactions is perfected automatically.

One must appreciate how automatic perfection in these limited circumstances interrelates with Section 9-109, Article 9's scope provision, which excludes certain transfers from the reach of Article 9 entirely.[29] Excluded transactions include a sale of accounts, chattel paper, payment intangibles, or promissory notes as part of a sale of

---

26. 619 B.R. 710, 102 U.C.C. Rep. Serv. 2d 1025 (Bankr. D. Colo. 2020).

27. *See, e.g.,* IDAHO CODE § 28-9-103; KAN. STAT. ANN. § 84-9-103; NEB. REV. STAT. § 9-103; N.D. CENT. CODE § 41-09-03; S.D. CODIF. LAWS § 57A-9-103.

28. *See, e.g., In re* Jett, 563 B.R. 206, 91 U.C.C. Rep. Serv. 2d 662 (Bankr. S.D. Miss. 2017); *In re* Mitchell, 379 B.R. 131, 64 U.C.C. Rep. Serv. 2d 483 (Bankr. M.D. Tenn. 2007). For further discussion of the dual-status and transformation rules in this particular context, see § 16.10[B] and [C], *infra*.

Courts in Missouri have adopted a hybrid approach. If the security agreement contains explicit provisions controlling how the secured party must apply payments on the debt toward the purchase-money and non-purchase-money components of the debt, then the dual-status rule will apply. By contrast, if the security agreement is not explicit, then the transformation rule will apply, and the entire transaction loses its purchase-money character. *See, e.g., In re* Weiser, 381 B.R. 263, 65 U.C.C. Rep. Serv. 2d 54 (Bankr. W.D. Mo. 2007).

29. U.C.C. § 9-109(d)(4)–(7). *See* § 1.06[F], *supra*.

the business out of which they arose;[30] the assignment of any such asset for the purpose of collection;[31] a transfer of any right to payment under a contract to an assignee that is also to render the performance due under the contract;[32] and a transfer of a single account, payment intangible, or promissory note to an assignee in whole or partial satisfaction of a preexisting debt.[33] Thus, suppose B assigns a specific account owing to B on account of a specific job done by B. If this assignment is governed by Article 9, the assignment is automatically perfected; by contrast, if the assignment was for the purpose of collection, Article 9 does not apply to the transaction and automatic perfection would not apply.

Article 9 also recognizes automatic perfection for security interests created under other articles of the Code, specifically security interests arising under Article 2 on sales or Article 2A on leases, and the security interest of a collecting bank under Article 4.[34] These security interests are unique to the transactions covered in those articles and thus are largely beyond the scope of this book.[35]

[A] Isolated Assignment of Account or Payment Intangible — § 9-309(2)

Automatic perfection applies to an assignment of accounts or of payment intangibles which, by itself or together with other assignments to the same assignee, does not transfer a significant part of the outstanding accounts of the assignor.[36] This exception saves "casual or isolated" assignments from potential invalidation by a lien creditor such as the bankruptcy trustee.[37] The original drafters included the exception in response to accounts-receivable statutes commonly enacted prior to the Code that encompassed "assignments which no one would think of filing."[38] The Comments caution, however, that a person that regularly takes assignments of accounts or payment intangibles should file[39] (except in the context of a sale of payment intangibles, in which case another automatic-perfection provision applies[40]). The Comments thus strongly suggest construing this automatic-perfection provision narrowly.

---

30. U.C.C. § 9-109(d)(4).
31. U.C.C. § 9-109(d)(5).
32. U.C.C. § 9-109(d)(6).
33. U.C.C. § 9-109(d)(7).
34. U.C.C. § 9-309(6), (7). *See also* U.C.C. § 9-110. Article 9 also provides for automatic perfection of a security interest of an issuer of a letter of credit (or that of a nominated person) arising under Article 5. U.C.C. § 9-309(8).
35. For a limited discussion, particularly of the Article 2 and 2A provisions, see § 1.07, *supra*.
36. U.C.C. § 9-309(2).
37. U.C.C. § 9-309, Comment 4.
38. *Id.*
39. *Id.*
40. U.C.C. § 9-309(3) (discussed in § 7.02[B], *infra*).

Courts have not taken a consistent approach in establishing or applying the criteria for this exception. Some courts apply the "casual-or-isolated" test suggested by the Comments.[41] Some have focused on the extent of business transacted between the assignor and assignee so that a one-shot transaction, even though for a considerable amount, qualifies for automatic perfection.[42] For other courts, the status of the assignee serves as the central feature of the casual-or-isolated test.[43] Under this view, automatic perfection is not available if the assignee regularly engages in commercial financing transactions, thereby precluding use of the exception by professional creditors.[44] Some courts applying the test have disqualified a transaction if it fails under either standard.[45]

Other courts have ignored the casual-or-isolated test in favor of a percentage test. Some of these courts evaluate whether the assignor has assigned a significant percentage of its accounts by reference to the number of outstanding accounts assigned,[46] while others refer to the dollar value of those accounts.[47] Courts focusing on the latter percentage have also been influenced by the amount involved.[48] Yet other courts have required that both a percentage test and the casual-or-isolated test be satisfied for

41. *Id.*

42. Architectural Woods, Inc. v. State of Wash., 88 Wash. 2d 406, 562 P.2d 248, 21 U.C.C. Rep. Serv. 1181 (1977) (assignment of $100,000, of an account for $144,953, held to be isolated). *See also In re* Fort Dodge Roofing Co., 50 B.R. 666, 41 U.C.C. Rep. Serv. 1839 (Bankr. N.D. Iowa 1985) (one-shot assignment).

43. Daly v. Shrimplin, 610 P.2d 397, 29 U.C.C. Rep. Serv. 237 (Wyo. 1980) (no automatic perfection because assignees each regularly took assignments of accounts from this assignor).

44. K.A.O.P. Co. v. Midway Nat'l Bank of St. Paul, 372 N.W.2d 774, 41 U.C.C. Rep. Serv. 1045 (Minn. Ct. App. 1985) (exception applicable only to assignee not regularly engaged in financing as a business).

45. M.D. Hodges Enters., Inc. v. First Ga. Bank, 243 Ga. 664, 256 S.E.2d 350, 26 U.C.C. Rep. Serv. 1333 (1979) (exception not available because, as part of its business, plaintiff bank regularly loaned money and accepted accounts as security).

46. *In re* Boughner, 8 U.C.C. Rep. Serv. 144 (Bankr. W.D. Mich. 1979) (no exception when assignor assigned all accounts due from his company, even though assignee was not a professional and did not regularly take assignments of accounts); *In re* Rankin, 102 B.R. 439, 9 U.C.C. Rep. Serv. 2d 301 (Bankr. W.D. Pa. 1989) (exception not applicable because entire account was assigned and it was debtor's only account of substance).

47. Fafinski v. Johnson, 104 U.C.C. Rep. Serv. 2d 1101 (Minn. Ct. App. 2021) (assignment by law firm of $3.3 million of accounts, constituting 87 percent of firm's total assets, did not qualify under Section 9-309(2) automatic-perfection rule); *In re* Crabtree Constr. Co., Inc., 87 B.R. 212, 6 U.C.C. Rep. Serv. 2d 1322 (Bankr. S.D. Fla. 1988) (transfer of 14 percent of debtor's overall accounts was not significant portion, even though transfer actually covered 25 percent of collectible accounts); *In re* Munro Builders, Inc., 20 U.C.C. Rep. Serv. 739 (Bankr. W.D. Mich. 1976) (40 percent of total accounts of bankrupt debtor was significant part).

48. Consolidated Film Indus. v. United States, 547 F.2d 533, 20 U.C.C. Rep. Serv. 1360 (10th Cir. 1977) (size of transaction did not suggest casual transaction that would ordinarily be exempt); Miller v. Wells Fargo Bank Int'l Corp., 406 F. Supp. 452, 18 U.C.C. Rep. Serv. 489 (S.D.N.Y. 1975) (no exemption for assignment of just under 20 percent of debtor's total outstanding accounts, particularly in view of $1,000,000 value of transaction).

automatic perfection to apply.[49] Given the uncertainty in the caselaw interpreting this automatic-perfection rule, no prudent assignee should ever rely on it.

[B] Sales of Payment Intangibles and Promissory Notes—§ 9-309(3), (4)

Article 9 provides for automatic perfection of the security interest acquired by the buyer of payment intangibles[50] or promissory notes.[51] Payment intangibles is a subset of general intangibles, and promissory notes is a subset of instruments. Article 9 introduced these provisions in the 1998 revision so that sales of such property would fall within its scope while sales of other general intangibles and instruments would remain outside its scope. The rationale for both the expansion in scope and the automatic-perfection rule is the protection of specialized financing arrangements like loan participations and securitizations, topics discussed elsewhere in this book.[52] Persons dealing with payment intangibles and promissory notes should be aware that automatic perfection applies only to the interest of a buyer. For a payment intangible or promissory note assigned as collateral for an obligation, automatic perfection is generally not available[53] (although it would apply to a casual or isolated assignment of a payment intangible[54]).

[C] Assignment of Health-Care-Insurance Receivables to a Provider—§ 9-309(5)

A health-care-insurance receivable is "an interest in or claim under a policy of insurance which is a right to payment of a monetary obligation for health-care goods or services provided."[55] The category is a subset of "account,"[56] and unless otherwise stated, rules applicable to accounts apply to health-care-insurance receivables.[57] Inclusion in the account category means that both sales of health-care insurance receivables

---

49. *In re* Tri-County Materials, Inc., 114 B.R. 160, 12 U.C.C. Rep Serv. 2d 869 (Bankr. C.D. Ill. 1990) (12 percent of outstanding accounts met percentage test, but formality and notice to account debtor meant it was not a casual transaction); H. & Val J. Rothschild, Inc. v. Northwestern Nat'l Bank of St. Paul, 309 Minn. 35, 242 N.W.2d 844, 19 U.C.C. Rep. Serv. 673 (1976) (assigned percentage exceeded one-third and bank engaged in business of interim financing, although it had not previously taken assignments of contract rights as security).

50. U.C.C. § 9-309(3); *In re* Oak Rock Fin., LLC, 527 B.R. 105, 86 U.C.C. Rep. Serv. 2d 137 (Bankr. E.D.N.Y. 2015) (security interest of buyer of participation interests in specific loans made by debtor held automatically perfected under § 9-309(3)).

51. U.C.C. § 9-309(4).

52. *See* § 1.05, *supra*.

53. *In re* Brooke Capital Corp., 588 Fed. Appx. 834, 85 U.C.C. Rep. Serv. 2d 349 (10th Cir. 2014).

54. U.C.C. § 9-309(2). *See* § 7.02[A], *supra*.

55. U.C.C. § 9-102(a)(46).

56. U.C.C. § 9-102(a)(2).

57. For discussion of some of the distinctions between health-care-insurance receivables and other accounts, see § 1.04[B][1], *supra*.

and assignments to secure an obligation are within the scope of Article 9.[58] An assignment of a health-care insurance receivable to the provider of the health-care goods or services is perfected automatically.[59] For example, suppose Patient assigns his rights under a private health-insurance policy to Doctor to pay for services rendered. Article 9 governs the transaction, and Doctor's security interest is automatically perfected. By contrast, if Doctor assigns all of her accounts, including health-care-insurance receivables, to Bank as collateral for a loan, Bank must file to perfect its security interest.

[D] Investment Property— § 9-309(9), (10), (11)

Article 9 provides special rules on security interests in investment property to provide certainty in the securities-settlement system. One set of rules applies to the rights of a seller that delivers, before receiving the agreed-upon payment, a certificated security or other financial asset represented by a writing of a kind that in the ordinary course of business is transferred by delivery (with any necessary indorsement or assignment) if both buyer and seller are in the business of dealing with such assets. This transaction often occurs when the seller's securities custodian delivers physical certificates to the buyer's securities custodian pursuant to an agreement that the buyer's custodian will remit payment. In accordance with the custom in the trade, the security is to be returned to the seller's custodian if payment is not forthcoming. Under the special rules, the seller has an attached security interest in the asset even without a signed security agreement,[60] and that interest becomes perfected automatically.[61] The rules promote efficiency in that they permit the delivery of high volumes of assets with minimal documentation.

Coordination of Article 9 with Article 8 also facilitates secured financing arrangements for securities firms. Lenders in some transactions require a transfer of securities maintained on a clearing corporation's books to the lender's account, resulting in perfection by control.[62] In other transactions, the lender allows the debtor to retain the positions in its own accounts under an agreement-to-deliver arrangement. The debtor's books reflect the security, and the debtor promises to transfer the security to the secured party's account upon demand. Perfection in these latter transactions occurs automatically if the debtor is a broker or securities intermediary.[63] Comparable automatic perfection applies for a security interest in a commodity contract or a commodity account created by a commodity intermediary.[64] The availability of auto-

---

58. U.C.C. § 9-109(a)(3).
59. U.C.C. § 9-309(5).
60. U.C.C. § 9-206(c), (d).
61. U.C.C. § 9-309(9).
62. For discussion of perfection of investment property by control, see § 6.04[A], *supra*.
63. U.C.C. § 9-309(10).
64. U.C.C. § 9-309(11).

matic perfection precludes the need for the parties to engage in their prior practice of indefinitely rolling over a new loan agreement every 20 days to qualify continually for temporary automatic perfection.[65]

[E] Assignment for the Benefit of All Creditors— § 9-309(12)

Another exception from the filing requirement for perfection applies to "an assignment for the benefit of all the creditors of the transferor and subsequent transfers by the assignee thereunder."[66] The Comments state that these assignments need not be filed because they "are not financing transactions, and the debtor ordinarily will not be engaging in further credit transactions."[67] This policy justification suggests that, rather than providing for automatic perfection of these assignments, the transactions should be excluded in their entirety from the scope of Article 9.[68]

[F] Assignment of a Beneficial Interest in a Decedent's Estate—§ 9-309(13)

Automatic perfection is available for "a security interest created by an assignment of a beneficial interest in a decedent's estate." Such an interest is a general intangible, and perhaps a payment intangible.[69] Article 9 governs the sale of payment intangibles but not the sale of other general intangibles.[70] Thus, a lender against a beneficial interest always gets the benefit of automatic perfection; a buyer of a beneficial interest gets the same benefit if the interest is a payment intangible, and Article 9, therefore, governs the transaction.

Prior law provided the same treatment for an assignment of a beneficial interest in a trust. As now revised, Article 9 eliminates automatic perfection in this context because of the more prevalent use of interests in trusts in commercial financing transactions.[71]

---

65. U.C.C. § 9-309, Comment 6. For discussion of temporary automatic perfection, see § 8.01, *infra*.
66. U.C.C. § 9-309(12).
67. U.C.C. § 9-309, Comment 8.
68. *See* U.C.C. § 9-109, Comment 6 (transfers of accounts excluded from Article 9 because, by their nature, they have nothing to do with commercial financing transactions).
69. U.C.C. § 9-102(a)(42), (61).
70. U.C.C. § 9-109(a)(3).
71. U.C.C. § 9-309, Comment 7.

[G] Sales of Lottery Winnings—
§ 9-309(14)

A right to payment of winnings in a lottery or other game of chance is an account,[72] and the interest of a buyer of such an account is automatically perfected.[73] The reason is that the payments are typically made over an extended period of time and, without this rule, the buyer would have to re-perfect within one year each time the seller changed its location.[74] Curiously, the same protection does not extend to a lender that takes an assignment of the right to payment, perhaps because the loan might be paid back over a shorter period of time.

72. U.C.C. § 9-102(a)(2).

73. U.C.C. § 9-309(14). A few states, including Alabama, Arizona, and Minnesota, have omitted this section in their enactment of Article 9, so automatic perfection as to the sale of the right to payment for lottery winnings would not apply in those jurisdictions.

74. U.C.C. § 9-316(a), (b). *See* § 9.04, *infra*.

Chapter 8

Temporary Perfection and Perfection of Proceeds

Synopsis

In addition to the normal methods of perfection, Article 9 includes some circumstances in which a secured party can either acquire or retain perfected status on a temporary basis. Although temporary perfection is a form of automatic perfection, it is distinguishable from the continuous automatic perfection discussed in Chapter 7. Temporary perfection under the rules discussed in this chapter is limited to a period of only 20 days.[1]

---

1. The one other context in which temporary perfection arises involves multi-state transactions where the law governing perfection changes because of the debtor's relocation or the transfer of the collateral to a debtor located in a different jurisdiction. Temporary perfection in this context is addressed in Chapter 9.

§ 8.01 Instruments, Certificated Securities, Documents, and Bailed Goods— § 9-312(e)–(h)

[A] Initial Perfection

Perfection with respect to a security interest in instruments, certificated securities, and negotiable documents is automatic for a period of 20 days after attachment if the secured party gives "new value."[2] Prior to expiration of the 20-day grace period, the secured party must comply with another appropriate method of perfection to remain continuously perfected thereafter without a gap.[3]

The new-value requirement means that the secured party is not perfected temporarily if it acquires its interest to secure an antecedent debt. New value means "(i) money, (ii) money's worth in property, services, or new credit, or (iii) release by a transferee of an interest in property previously transferred to the transferee." The definition excludes the substitution of one obligation for another obligation.[4]

Because perfection by filing is now available for security interests in these types of collateral,[5] temporary perfection is not really necessary, although it remains important in that it facilitates short-term transactions. For example, a bank might make a two-day loan to a mortgage lender secured by the lender's stockpile of promissory notes or make "day loans" to stockbrokers secured by certificated securities. Temporary perfection obviates the need for the bank either to file or take possession of the collateral.

Notwithstanding the convenience of the temporary perfection and permissive filing rules, there are inherent risks in relying on these types of perfection when the collateral is negotiable or quasi-negotiable.[6] Of course, any lender that agrees to a security interest based on collateral that the debtor claims to own always runs the risk that the property does not exist or that the debtor either does not own it or has already encumbered it. In the case of instruments, certificated securities, and negotiable documents, however, a significant risk persists even after the security interest attaches if the lender

---

2. U.C.C. § 9-312(e).

3. U.C.C. § 9-312(h).

4. U.C.C. § 9-102(a)(57). The requirement of new value eliminates temporary perfection for any collateral of these types to which a security interest attaches by virtue of an after-acquired property clause unless the secured party extends additional value to the debtor for this new collateral. *See In re* Reliance Equities, Inc., 966 F.2d 1338, 17 U.C.C. Rep. Serv. 2d 1316 (10th Cir. 1992) (automatic perfection with respect to each promissory note in issue because the secured party gave new value with respect to each note).

5. Perfection by filing of a security interest in instruments was not available until the 1998 revision.

6. The risk also applies in the case of a buyer of a promissory note that fails to obtain possession of the note. The buyer is deemed to be a secured party for purposes of Article 9, U.C.C. § 9-102(a)(73)(D), with automatic perfection of its security interest in the note. U.C.C. § 9-309(4).

relies on filing or temporary perfection.[7] Leaving this type of collateral in the debtor's dominion and control permits a wrongful transfer to a third party that might take priority over the secured party. A prudent secured party should consider the following priority rules:

- Nothing in Article 9 limits the rights of a holder in due course of a negotiable instrument, a holder to which a negotiable document has been duly negotiated, or a protected purchaser of a security. Furthermore, filing does not constitute notice to such persons.[8] This rule must be read in conjunction with provisions in Articles 3, 7, and 8 that permit certain holders and purchasers to take free of adverse claims.

- A purchaser of an instrument (whether negotiable or not) has priority over a secured party that perfects by a method other than possession if the purchaser gives value and takes possession in good faith and without knowledge that the purchase violates the secured party's rights.[9] If, however, a notation on the instrument states that it has been assigned to an identified assignee, any purchaser is deemed to have knowledge that the purchase violates the assignee's rights.[10] Accordingly, a secured party can insist that its debtor only take notes that contain a notation indicating that they have been assigned to the secured party, using the name of the secured party in the notation.[11] Bear in mind that "purchaser" means a person that acquires an interest in property as a result of a voluntary transaction;[12] thus, a secured party relying on filing or temporary perfection is at risk from both buyers and other secured parties.

The use of negotiable documents illustrates the advantage of permissive filing. A negotiable document represents title to goods. During the period of temporary perfection, the debtor might surrender the document and obtain the goods from a carrier or a warehouse. In fact, the very purpose of relying on temporary perfection might be to enable the debtor to acquire the goods for resale or other use. The advantage of filing is that it provides continuous perfection, whether the collateral is in the form of the document or the underlying goods. The filing will not be sufficient to overcome the

---

7. The risks are the same as those described in the text if perfection is accomplished by filing for a security interest in securities that are not certificated securities, controllable electronic records, controllable accounts, or controllable payment intangibles. Temporary perfection is not available for these types of assets except to the extent they constitute proceeds.

8. U.C.C. § 9-331. *In re* Kontaratos, 10 B.R. 956, 31 U.C.C. Rep. Serv. 1124 (Bankr. D. Me. 1981) (temporarily perfected security interest in shares of stock held subordinate to subsequent security interest of bank to which stock certificates were delivered as collateral). For further discussion of Section 9-331, see § 11.03[D], *infra*.

9. U.C.C. § 9-330(d).

10. U.C.C. § 9-330(f). For further discussion of Section 9-330 in the context of instruments, see § 11.03[C][2], *infra*.

11. The notation on a negotiable instrument would provide notice of a claim to the instrument and preclude the risk of a holder in due course. U.C.C. §§ 3-302(b), 3-306.

12. U.C.C. § 1-201(b)(30), (29).

loss of priority if the debtor, left in possession or control of the document, wrongfully transfers it to a person entitled to priority under Article 7.[13]

[B] Continuing Perfection for Collateral Made Available to Debtor

Article 9 also provides a temporary perfection period in certain cases of collateral made available to a debtor. If the collateral is a negotiable document or goods in the possession of a bailee that has not issued a negotiable document (including a bailee that has issued a nonnegotiable document), a perfected security interest remains perfected for 20 days without filing if the secured party makes available to the debtor either the goods or the document for the following limited purposes: "(1) ultimate sale or exchange; or (2) loading, unloading, storing, shipping, transshipping, manufacturing, processing, or otherwise dealing with them in a manner preliminary to their sale or exchange."[14] In addition, comparable continuing temporary perfection is available upon the delivery to the debtor of a certificated security or instrument for the purpose of "(1) ultimate sale or exchange; or (2) presentation, collection, enforcement, renewal, or registration of transfer."[15]

The foregoing rule on negotiable documents and goods in the possession of a bailee that has not issued such a document must be understood in the context of the following rules, which generally govern perfection in those categories of collateral:

- While goods are in the possession of a bailee that has issued a negotiable document, a security interest in the goods may be perfected by perfecting as to the document, and a security interest perfected in the document has priority over a security interest perfected in the goods by any other method during that time.[16]

- While goods are in the possession of a bailee that has issued a nonnegotiable document, a security interest must be perfected as to the goods, and not as to the document. Perfection results from giving the secured party control over access to the goods by issuance of a document in the name of the secured party, by the bailee's receipt of notification of the secured party's interest, or by filing as to the goods.[17]

---

13. U.C.C. §7-502. The only adequate protection against this risk is for the secured party to perfect by taking possession or control of the document, leaving the debtor unable to pass the possession or control that a subsequent transferee needs in order to attain priority. The risk of wrongful transfer explains why most secured lenders rely on possession or control of documents for perfection rather than on the filing of a financing statement. See U.C.C. §§9-331(a), 7-501, 7-502, 1-201(b)(20). The same analysis applies with respect to certificated securities and instruments.

14. U.C.C. §9-312(f).

15. U.C.C. §9-312(g). Subsections (f) and (g) deal only with perfection; they do not govern the priority of a security interest in goods after the surrender of possession or control of a document that governs them. U.C.C. §9-312, Comment 9.

16. U.C.C. §9-312(c). See §6.02[B][1], supra.

17. U.C.C. §9-312(d). See §6.02[B][2], supra.

- While goods are in the possession of a bailee that has not issued either a negotiable or nonnegotiable document, perfection may be accomplished by filing or
  by obtaining from the bailee a signed record acknowledging that it holds, or will
  hold, the collateral for the secured party's benefit.[18]

The temporary perfection period runs from the date the secured party makes the
document or goods available, or delivers the instrument or certificated security, to
the debtor. A secured party that wishes to remain perfected beyond the end of that
period must perfect by a different method prior to expiration of the 20-day temporary-
perfection period.[19]

For temporary perfection in these situations, new value is not a requirement, but the
return of the collateral must be to advance one of the stated purposes. This requirement
is not very limiting because it covers nearly all legitimate purposes for returning such
collateral. Caselaw recognizes the legitimacy of the return of a certificate of deposit for
its renewal by issuance of a new certificate,[20] the return of a negotiable bill of lading
to acquire the goods from a carrier and store them,[21] and the return of a promissory
note for purposes of collection.[22] Courts even recognize the return of the collateral for
purpose of sale as legitimate, based on the rationale that the parties may envision the
debtor's selling the collateral as a means to obtain the funds to pay the secured debt.

The secured party must balance the convenience associated with temporary perfection against the enhanced risk that accompanies debtor reacquisition of collateral
in the form of a negotiable document. The debtor then has the means to transfer the
collateral to a party that can achieve priority against even a perfected security interest.[23]
The prior subsection dealing with initial temporary perfection describes the risks in
more detail.[24]

---

18. U.C.C. § 9-313(c). *See* § 6.03[B], *supra*.

19. U.C.C. § 9-312(h). *See In re* Schwinn Cycling & Fitness, Inc., 313 B.R. 473, 54 U.C.C. Rep.
Serv. 2d 645 (D. Colo. 2004) (because the common carrier with the security interest did not file a
financing statement after releasing possession of the goods and the negotiable document to the debtor
for purpose of sale of the goods, the carrier did not have a continuously perfected security interest).

20. Wightman v. American Nat'l Bank of Riverton, 610 P.2d 1001, 29 U.C.C. Rep. Serv. 251 (Wyo.
1980).

21. Scallop Petroleum Co. v. Banque Trad-Credit Lyonnais S.A., 690 F. Supp. 184, 6 U.C.C. Rep.
Serv. 2d 1573 (S.D.N.Y. 1988).

22. McIlroy Bank v. First Nat'l Bank of Fayetteville, 252 Ark. 558, 480 S.W.2d 127, 10 U.C.C. Rep.
Serv. 1111 (1972).

23. *See* U.C.C. §§ 9-331 and 11.03[D], *infra*.

24. *See* § 8.01[A], *supra*.

§ 8.02 Proceeds—§ 9-315(c)–(e)

[A] The Grace Period of Temporary Perfection

Article 9 provides that a secured party's interest in collateral attaches automatically to identifiable proceeds of that collateral.[25] It also determines whether the secured party's interest in the proceeds is perfected.[26] "Proceeds" includes, *inter alia*, whatever the debtor receives on any kind of disposition of collateral.[27] Even if a disposition is unauthorized or constitutes a breach of the security agreement, the security interest continues automatically in the proceeds so long as they are identifiable.

Parties in some types of financing anticipate dispositions that will produce proceeds. A secured party engaged in inventory financing, for example, is virtually certain to authorize sale or lease of the inventory. An authorized disposition of the inventory will extinguish the security interest,[28] as will (in most circumstances) even an unauthorized disposition.[29] For continuing security, the secured party will look to proceeds, which are likely to be in the form of cash, checks, rights to payment resulting from the use of a credit or debit card, promissory notes, accounts, or chattel paper. Similarly, an accounts financier will claim the proceeds received from payments on accounts, which may be in the form of checks or rights to payment resulting from the use of credit or debit cards.

Although a security interest attaches automatically to identifiable proceeds, perfection is generally necessary to protect the secured party's interest against other claimants. If the secured party had perfected its security interest in the original collateral by any method, the secured party is automatically perfected as to the proceeds of the collateral.[30] This initial grant of perfection, however, is only temporary and lapses on the 21st day after attachment of the security interest to the proceeds unless one of the three conditions discussed below is satisfied.[31]

The secured party's goal is for its security interest in proceeds to be continuously perfected so that its priority will relate back to the date of its initial perfection as to the collateral that gave rise to the proceeds.[32] The Code grants temporary automatic per-

---

25. U.C.C. §§ 9-203(f), 9-315(a)(2). For a discussion of automatic attachment of security interests to identifiable proceeds, see § 2.03[B], *supra*.

26. U.C.C. § 9-315(c)-(e).

27. U.C.C. § 9-102(a)(64)(A). For discussion of the concept of proceeds, see § 2.03[A], *supra*.

28. U.C.C. § 9-315(a)(1). For discussion of these provisions, see §§ 11.01, 11.02, *infra*.

29. U.C.C. §§ 9-320(a) (buyer in ordinary course of business), 9-321(c) (lessee in ordinary course of business). For further discussion of these provisions, see § 11.03[A][1], *infra*.

30. U.C.C. § 9-315(c) ("A security interest in proceeds is a perfected security interest if the security interest in the original collateral was perfected.").

31. U.C.C. § 9-315(d).

32. Article 9 does not provide continuous perfection with respect to proceeds for a secured party unperfected in the original collateral. *In re* Beacon Light Marina Yacht Club, Inc., 125 B.R. 154, 14 U.C.C. Rep. Serv. 2d 1230 (Bankr. W.D. Va. 1990) (secured party, which did not perfect its interest in

fection for the duration of the 20-day grace period in every case. If the secured party satisfies one of the statutory conditions that does not require any further action by the secured party, perfection continues automatically beyond that period. Otherwise, the secured party will have to perfect its security interest *as to the proceeds* before the grace period expires, and if it does not, its interest in the proceeds becomes unperfected.[33]

[B] Continuous Perfection

Automatic temporary perfection in proceeds becomes continuous perfection if the secured party satisfies one of three conditions.[34] The discussion below covers these conditions.

[1] Identifiable Cash Proceeds

Perfection does not lapse at the end of the grace period if the proceeds are identifiable cash proceeds.[35] "Cash proceeds," defined to include only "money, checks, deposit accounts, or the like,"[36] are essentially cash or cash equivalents.[37] Cash proceeds most commonly arise when the debtor receives a form of full or partial payment for collateral in which the secured party has a perfected security interest.

Cash proceeds are easy to dissipate, and a secured party relying on such proceeds must be aware of the following risks:

- The secured party may lose its security interest in any proceeds that the debtor commingles with other funds because the commingling may prevent the secured party from being able to identify the proceeds. Article 9 permits a secured party to use equitable tracing principles, notably the lowest-intermediate-balance rule, to identify the extent of commingled proceeds.[38]

- A transferee of a check that qualifies as a holder in due course under Article 3 takes the check free of a perfected security interest.[39]

---

boat by complying with state certificate-of-title act, did not have perfected security interest in proceeds from sale of boat).

33. U.C.C. § 9-315(e)(2).

34. U.C.C. § 9-315(d).

35. U.C.C. § 9-315(d)(2); *In re* Luna Developments Group, LLC, 618 B.R. 595 (Bankr. S.D. Fla. 2020).

36. "[T]he like" almost certainly includes the right to payment for a credit-card system or bank based on a customer's use of a credit or debit card.

37. U.C.C. § 9-102(a)(9). *See* § 2.03[A], *supra*.

38. U.C.C. § 9-315(b)(2); HHH Farms, L.L.C. v. Fannin Bank, 648 S.W.3d 387 (Tex. Ct. App. 2022); *In re* Milton Abeles, LLC, 81 U.C.C. Rep. Serv. 2d 770 (Bankr. E.D.N.Y. 2013); RDLF Fin. Servs., LLC v. Esquire Capital Corp., 34 Misc. 3d 1235(A), 950 N.Y.S.2d 610 (Table) (Sup. Ct. 2012). For further discussion, see § 2.03[B], *supra*. Section 9-315(b)(1) provides that the identification of commingled goods that are proceeds is determined under Section 9-336.

39. U.C.C. § 9-331(a). For further discussion, see § 11.03[D], *infra*.

- A transferee of a check may take it free of a perfected security interest even if the transferee does not qualify as a holder in due course.[40] The transferee must give value and take possession of the check in good faith and without knowledge that the transfer violates the rights of the secured party.[41]

- A transferee of funds from a deposit account takes the funds free of a perfected security interest in the deposit account if the transferee receives the funds without acting in collusion with the debtor to violate the secured party's rights.[42] Similar rules apply to a transferee of money.[43]

Continuous perfection for identifiable cash proceeds most commonly applies to cash-proceed payments in full or partial satisfaction of accounts in which the secured party has a perfected security interest[44] and to cash proceeds received on the sale of inventory subject to a perfected security interest.[45] One bankruptcy opinion correctly concluded that perfection was continuous and automatic with respect to traceable cash proceeds from the sale of inventory in which the secured party had a perfected security interest, but not with respect to the proceeds of inventory in which the secured party did not have a perfected interest.[46] Another bankruptcy decision held that a filing for national registration with the FAA, which is required to perfect a security interest in an airplane,[47] led to continuous automatic perfection in the identifiable cash proceeds received from the debtor's sale of the airplane.[48]

The free alienability of cash proceeds suggests that great care is advisable in structuring transactions in which a secured party desires continuous automatic perfection. A secured lender might require the debtor to segregate all cash proceeds it receives and deposit them into a special deposit account (often called a "lockbox") to which the secured party can control access. The secured party then can make unannounced spot-checks to monitor the debtor's compliance.

The secured party in *In re Schwinn Cycling and Fitness, Inc.*[49] had temporary perfection under Section 9-312(f) in goods that it made available to the debtor for ultimate sale. The secured party did not take steps to re-perfect its interest in the goods that the

---

40. U.C.C. § 9-330(d).

41. *See* § 11.03[C][2], *infra*.

42. U.C.C. § 9-332(b); Amegy Bank Nat'l Ass'n, v. Deutsche Bank Corp., 917 F. Supp. 2d 1228 (M.D. Fla. 2013). For further discussion, see § 11.03[E], *infra*.

43. U.C.C. § 9-332(a) (transferee of tangible money), 9-332(c) (transferee of electronic money).

44. *In re* John Deskins Pic Pac, Inc., 59 B.R. 809, 1 U.C.C. Rep. Serv. 2d 1696 (Bankr. W.D. Va. 1986); Farns Assocs., Inc. v. South Side Bank, 93 Ill. App. 3d 766, 417 N.E.2d 818, 30 U.C.C. Rep. Serv. 1729 (1981).

45. Dixie Production Credit Ass'n v. Kent, 167 Ga. App. 714, 307 S.E.2d 277, 37 U.C.C. Rep. Serv. 595 (1983).

46. *In re* Critiques, Inc., 29 B.R. 941, 36 U.C.C. Rep. Serv. 1778 (Bankr. D. Kan. 1983).

47. The Federal Aviation Act of 1958 preempts Article 9 perfection rules. 49 U.S.C. § 1403. *See* § 1.06[A], *supra*.

48. *In re* Turner, 13 B.R. 15, 32 U.C.C. Rep. Serv. 1240 (Bankr. D. Neb. 1981).

49. 313 B.R. 473, 54 U.C.C. Rep. Serv. 2d 645 (D. Colo. 2004).

debtor sold within the 20-day temporary-perfection period. The secured party then claimed its interest in the proceeds of the sale. The bankruptcy court held that the secured party's failure to maintain continuous perfection of its security interest in the goods meant that its security interest in the proceeds was unperfected. On appeal, the district court held that the secured party should prevail if the proceeds were identifiable cash proceeds and remanded the case to the bankruptcy court for a determination of that issue. The court specifically referred to Comment 7 of Section 9-315, which provides that "if the security interest in the original collateral was perfected, a security interest in identifiable cash proceeds will remain perfected indefinitely, regardless of whether the security interest in the original collateral remains perfected."

[2] Same Filing Office: The Basic Rule

If the collateral is in the form of noncash proceeds, continuous perfection beyond the grace period sometimes applies, but only if the secured party perfected its security interest in the original collateral by filing and meets other conditions.[50] The conditions are that (i) the collateral must be of a type for which perfection by filing is permissible and (ii) the office in which a financing statement would be filed with respect to the proceeds must be the same office in which the secured party filed to perfect its security interest in the original collateral.[51] The prime example of this "same-office" rule is when a secured party perfected its security interest in inventory by filing and the debtor receives accounts or chattel paper from its disposition of the inventory. Because the secured party would have filed as to the accounts or chattel paper (had they been the original collateral) in the same office where it filed with respect to the inventory, the same-office rule applies, and perfection in the proceeds does not lapse at the end of the 20-day grace period. Perfection is predicated on the initial financing statement, and the secured party in this situation will become unperfected only if the financing statement lapses.[52]

This approach represents a compromise between the need to reduce transaction costs and the need for adequate notice to searchers. The basic idea is that in certain common financing transactions, a searcher should recognize that a particular type of described collateral will likely yield a particular type or types of undescribed proceeds, such as inventory sold to produce accounts or chattel paper. A searcher interested in buying or lending against a dealer's accounts or chattel paper should be aware that such assets typically arise with a credit sale or lease of inventory. Thus, a searcher that finds a financing statement covering the debtor's inventory is on notice that the secured party

---

50. U.C.C. § 9-315(d)(1).

51. For selection of the proper office for purposes of Article 9 filings, see U.C.C. § 9-501 (selection of the office within a given state) and U.C.C. §§ 9-301 through 9-307, 9-316 (selection of the state whose law governs perfection). *See also* § 5.05, *supra*; Chapter 9, *infra*.

52. Following the passage of the grace period of 20 days, a security interest in the proceeds perfected continuously will become unperfected if the effectiveness of the financing statement covering the original collateral lapses or is terminated. U.C.C. § 9-315(e).

identified in that financing statement may also claim a security interest in accounts and chattel paper received as proceeds of that inventory. This notice function explains why it is important that the filing for the original collateral appear in the same office in which a filing would be made for the proceeds. A searcher that looks in the proper office for accounts and does not find a financing statement describing inventory cannot draw the proper inference.

Because the same-office rule relies on the predictability of certain types of proceeds in common financing transactions, it tends to break down in less common situations. For example, suppose Secured Party files to perfect a security interest in Farmer's tractor, using a specific description (e.g., "Debtor's Deere S390 tractor"). Farmer later trades in the tractor for a new compressor. Secured Party's interest in the new compressor will remain perfected beyond the grace period under the same-office rule, meaning that it will have priority over a person that buys or lends against the new compressor even though the buyer or lender will not be on notice in any real sense (the buyer or lender is unlikely to have anticipated that Farmer may have acquired the compressor in exchange for the tractor). The same result would also apply if Farmer traded the original tractor to Neighbor for a valuable painting because filings for equipment and consumer goods are made in the same office. Such situations are, of course, relatively rare.[53]

A secured party can qualify for continuous perfection as to proceeds under the same-office rule only if the original collateral is perfected by a filed financing statement. If the original collateral is consumer goods in which the secured party holds a purchase-money security interest for which the secured party is relying on automatic perfection, the secured party cannot qualify for continuous perfection of a security interest in noncash proceeds under the same-office rule. Likewise, if the original collateral is deposit accounts as to which the secured party could perfect only by control, the secured party cannot qualify for continuous perfection of a security interest in noncash proceeds under the same-office rule.[54]

[3] Same Filing Office: The "Cash-Phase" Rule

Sometimes, a security interest in noncash proceeds arises in a series of transactions involving a "cash phase," that is, the debtor disposes of the original collateral in a transaction that produces cash proceeds and then uses the cash proceeds in another transaction to acquire noncash proceeds. In this second transaction, the debtor can use cash proceeds to purchase assets of any type, thus potentially undermining the predictability on which the same-office rule depends. The drafters, therefore, included another condition for the secured party's seeking continuous perfection as to noncash

---

53. *But see In re* Wiersma, 283 B.R. 294, 49 U.C.C. Rep. Serv. 2d 309 (Bankr. D. Ida. 2002), *aff'd*, 324 B.R. 92, 56 U.C.C. Rep. Serv. 2d 452 (Bankr. 9th Cir. 2005) (security interest in cows and milk was properly perfected in the office of the Secretary of State, which is the same office where a secured creditor would file to perfect an interest in an insurance settlement).

54. *See, e.g., In re* 3PL4PL, LLC, 619 B.R. 441 (Bankr. D. Colo. 2020). The same result occurs if the proceeds are goods subject to a certificate-of-title act.

proceeds acquired using cash proceeds. Perfection in the noncash proceeds lapses at the end of the grace period unless (i) the secured party has already filed a financing statement containing a description broad enough to cover the noncash proceeds or (ii) the secured party takes further action to perfect as to the noncash proceeds by any appropriate method before the grace period expires.

For example, suppose Secured Party has filed a financing statement covering all of Rancher's "cattle." Rancher later sells some of the cattle in exchange for a check, which Rancher deposits in a bank account. If Rancher later uses the proceeds in the account to purchase additional cattle, Secured Party's perfected status will not lapse at the end of the grace period—which makes sense, given that the description in the already filed financing statement ("cattle") is sufficient to cover the noncash proceeds. But if Rancher had used the proceeds in the deposit account to buy a tractor, the description in the existing filed financing statement would not be sufficient to cover the tractor. Thus, Secured Party's temporarily perfected security interest in the tractor as proceeds would lapse after 20 days, unless Secured Party amended the collateral description in its financing statement to cover the tractor or took possession of it before the grace period expired.[55]

The facts of *Citicorp (USA), Inc. v. Davidson Lumber Co.*[56] demonstrate the rules for perfection in noncash proceeds acquired with cash proceeds. Two banks had security interests in present and after-acquired general intangibles, and each had perfected by filing. The debtor later received a federal tax refund of approximately $1.3 million, which it used (without the knowledge of the banks) to purchase a certificate of deposit payable at a future date. The right to a tax refund is a general intangible, and the refund check was a cash proceed of that right. Transfer of the check in exchange for the certificate of deposit generated noncash proceeds from the cash proceeds.[57] The banks could have attained continuous perfection of their interests in the CD by taking the necessary steps for perfection of a security interest in the CD within the 20-day grace period.[58] The court properly rejected the policy argument of the banks that such a requirement was "preposterous" because it left them vulnerable to the actions of a debtor that secretly converted the collateral into a type of proceeds that necessitated action by them to attain continuous perfection. The court noted that this argument simply raises concerns regarding a secured party's need to implement adequate measures to police the actions of its debtor. It further noted that the banks could have protected

---

55. Similarly, a financing statement that describes the collateral as "accounts" is inadequate to perfect a security interest in inventory acquired with cash proceeds of the accounts. The result would be otherwise if the filed financing statement had also listed "inventory."

56. 718 F.2d 1030, 37 U.C.C. Rep. Serv. 324 (11th Cir. 1983).

57. The characterization of the certificate of deposit was one of the primary issues litigated. The appellate court properly held that the CD was noncash proceeds, thus precluding continuous perfection based on the filing with respect to the original collateral. The court followed prior decisions in holding that an instrument in the form of a certificate of deposit is more like a promissory note than a check.

58. *See* U.C.C. § 9-315(d)(3) and § 8.02[B][4], *infra*.

themselves with respect to the expected tax refund by using the federal Assignment of Claims Act.[59]

[4] Timely General Perfection

If neither the identifiable-cash-proceeds option nor the same-office option is available, perfection will lapse at the end of the grace period unless the secured party takes appropriate steps to perfect as to the proceeds. In other words, the secured party must take a step that would have been appropriate had the proceeds been the original collateral. This might involve, *inter alia*, the filing of a financing statement describing the proceeds, taking possession or control of them, or complying with a relevant certificate-of-title act or federal law. A secured party that allows the grace period to expire becomes unperfected. Even if the secured party later perfects its interest in the proceeds, the gap in perfection means that its priority cannot relate back to the date on which it perfected as to the original collateral.

An occasional case involves a secured party that succeeds in taking the timely action necessary to achieve continuous perfection in proceeds. In *In re Airwest International*,[60] a bank used possession to perfect its interest in two certificates of deposit and, when the bank "rolled over" the certificates at their maturity, to perfect its interest continuously in the resulting single new certificate. In *Wrightman v. American National Bank of Riverton*,[61] a bank, initially perfected by possession of an instrument in the form of a certificate of deposit, continued perfected by temporary perfection when it returned the certificate to its owner for the purpose of renewal by issuance of a new certificate.[62] The replacement certificate constituted proceeds of the first certificate, and the bank's interest in the proceeds continued perfected because the bank obtained possession of the new certificate before expiration of the grace period.[63]

Secured parties more often become unperfected with respect to proceeds because they fail to take timely steps to perfect their interests. An example is *Citicorp (USA), Inc. v. Davidson Lumber Co.*,[64] discussed in the preceding subsection. In *Security Savings Bank of Marshalltown, Iowa v. United States*,[65] the bank had a security interest in a Chevrolet truck which it had properly perfected by notation on a certificate of title. The bank agreed that the debtor could substitute a Ford truck for the Chevy; however, because the bank did not provide for notation of its security interest on a certificate of title covering the Ford within the grace period, it lost continuous perfection. Another case of lost continuous perfection in a vehicle as proceeds is *In re Charles E. Sutphin*,

---

59. 31 U.S.C. § 203 (1976), *amended by* 31 U.S.C. § 3727 (1983).
60. 70 B.R. 914, 3 U.C.C. Rep. Serv. 2d 1936 (Bankr. D. Haw. 1987).
61. 610 P.2d 1001, 29 U.C.C. Rep. Serv. 251 (Wyo. 1980).
62. *See* U.C.C. § 9-312(g).
63. *See* U.C.C. § 9-315(d)(3).
64. 718 F.2d 1030, 37 U.C.C. Rep. Serv. 324 (11th Cir. 1983).
65. 440 F. Supp. 444, 22 U.C.C. Rep. Serv. 1260 (S.D. Iowa 1977).

Inc.[66] The secured party properly perfected by filing with respect to farm vehicles that were part of the debtor's inventory. In exchange for two of the vehicles, the debtor received a tractor. The dealer did not add the tractor to its inventory but rather placed it in over-the-road service, making the tractor subject to a certificate-of-title requirement. Because the secured party failed to perfect under the certificate-of-title law within the grace period, its security interest in the tractor became unperfected.

---

66. 44 B.R. 533, 39 U.C.C. Rep. Serv. 1499 (Bankr. W.D. Va. 1984).

Chapter 9

Multistate Transactions

Synopsis

§ 9.01 The Code's Basic Choice-of-Law Provision

The Code's basic choice-of-law provision, which appears in Article 1 and is therefore generally applicable to all transactions within the scope of the other articles, permits the parties to select the state or nation whose laws will govern their rights and duties, but only if the transaction bears a "reasonable relation" to the selected state or nation.[1] If the parties fail to choose the governing law or their choice is unenforceable, the forum state's version of the Code applies if the transaction bears an "appropriate relation" to that state.[2]

Section 1-301(c) lists a number of Code provisions that mandate the applicable law and are not subject to either the reasonable-relation or the appropriate-relation test.[3] The Article 9 provisions are Sections 9-301 through 9-307, which designate the law governing perfection, the effect of perfection or nonperfection, and the priority of a security interest.[4] These sections implicate the rights of third persons that are not parties to the security agreement and that need a high degree of certainty as to the applicable law. For example, a potential lender or buyer considering a transaction with a particular person must be able to determine readily the filing office in which to search for a financing statement indexed in the name of that person. The Article 1 choice-of-law rules thus apply only to other issues concerning secured transactions, including attachment, validity, characterization, and enforcement.[5] This section of the chapter addresses the Code's basic choice-of-law rules, and the next section addresses the mandatory rules of Article 9.

---

1. U.C.C. § 1-301(a). Revised Article 1 initially adopted choice-of-law rules that relied more heavily on freedom of contract while retaining for consumers the benefit of certain non-waivable protections. U.C.C. § 1-301 (2003 Official Text). Because of significant but misguided opposition that prevented enactment, the sponsors withdrew the provision and reinstated the rules from original Article 1.

2. U.C.C. § 1-301(b).

3. If a mandatory choice-of-law rule applies, a contrary agreement is effective only to the extent permitted by the law that the rules indicate. *Id.*

4. In addition to referring to the law governing perfection and priority, the 1972 version of Article 9 referred to the law governing the effect of perfection or nonperfection. *See, e.g.,* U.C.C. § 9-103(1)(b) (1972 Official Text). A reference to the law governing priority was unnecessary because the law that governs the effect of perfection or nonperfection is the law that governs priority. Perhaps because the phrase "the effect of perfection or nonperfection" is somewhat murky, a reference to the law governing priority was added to Article 9 as a conforming amendment flowing from the 1994 revision of Article 8; however, perhaps out of concern that something might be lost, the reference to the law governing the effect of perfection or nonperfection was not deleted. U.C.C. § 9-103(6) (1994 Official Text). The drafters of the 1998 revision stayed with the 1994 formulation even though using both "the effect of perfection or nonperfection" and "priority" is redundant. For the sake of simplicity, this book generally refers to the law governing perfection and the law governing priority, and it omits any reference to the law governing the effect of perfection or nonperfection.

5. *See* Prefatory Comment, Part 3, Article 9.

[A] The Reasonable-Relation Test

The drafters of the original Code assumed that it would not be enacted in every state and were concerned that parties in a Code state might try to circumvent its rules by selecting the law of a non-Code state. They wanted to enhance the prospects that the Code's rules would be applied. The Code's choice-of-law provisions would only be consulted if the forum state (i.e., the state in which an action was brought) had enacted the Code, and thus the choice-of-law rules were heavily weighted toward selecting that jurisdiction. Another jurisdiction, which might be a non-Code jurisdiction, could be selected only if the transaction bore a reasonable relation to both that jurisdiction and to the forum jurisdiction. Although the Code recognized party autonomy, it was tightly conscribed.

The Comments[6] indicate that the reasonable-relation test is similar to the test laid down by the U.S. Supreme Court in *Seeman v. Philadelphia Warehouse Co.*[7] The lender in *Seeman* was a Pennsylvania corporation that regularly conducted business within the state, and the Court upheld a choice-of-law clause designating Pennsylvania law. The opinion validated party autonomy but with two important limitations: the chosen law must have a "natural and vital" connection with the transaction, and it must be selected in good faith and not for the purpose of disguising the transaction's true character.[8]

The courts routinely accede to the parties' choice if one of them is located in the selected state.[9] With neither party located in the chosen state, the nexus between the transaction and the state may nevertheless be sufficient to uphold the choice. For example, in *Key Bank of Maine v. Dunbar*,[10] the court upheld a choice-of-law clause selecting Maryland law because the collateral (a boat) was to be kept in that state. The courts do not require that the parties select the state that has the most significant contacts with the transaction, only that they select a state that has some legitimate contact with the transaction.[11]

Courts rarely invalidate choice-of-law agreements,[12] and when they do, the result is usually obvious. For example, in *WOCO v. Benjamin Franklin Corp.*,[13] the parties to a

---

6. U.C.C. § 1-301, Comment 1.

7. 274 U.S. 403 (1927).

8. *Id.*

9. *See, e.g., In re* Keene Corp., 188 B.R. 881, 28 U.C.C. Rep. Serv. 2d 651 (Bankr. S.D.N.Y. 1995) (selection of Illinois law upheld where debtor, a New York resident, granted secured party, an Illinois corporation, a security interest in book-entry Treasury securities).

10. 28 U.C.C. Rep. Serv. 2d 398 (E.D. Pa. 1995), *aff'd*, 91 F.3d 124 (3d Cir. 1996).

11. Comment 1 to Section 1-301 states that "[o]rdinarily the law chosen must be that of a jurisdiction where a significant enough portion of the making or performance of the contract is to occur."

12. Section 1-301(a) requires that the parties "agree" on the law of a particular state or nation, and "agreement" includes both the expressions of the parties and implications drawn from the surrounding facts. U.C.C. § 1-201(b)(3). While most choice-of-law agreements are memorialized in a record (and it is risky not to do so), a record is not required. *See, e.g.,* Neville Chem. Co. v. Union Carbide Corp., 422 F.2d 1205 (3d Cir. 1970) (court relies on fact that parties assumed Pennsylvania law would apply).

13. 20 U.C.C. Rep. Serv. 1015 (D.N.H. 1976), *aff'd on other grounds*, 562 F.2d 1339 (1st Cir. 1977).

lease agreement that was held to be a disguised security agreement selected California law, but the testimony failed to establish that either party was located or did business there, that the goods were kept there, or that the parties formed the contract there. The court properly applied the law of the forum state, New Hampshire, to resolve the dispute.

The universal success of Article 9 makes it unlikely that a party will designate the law of a state for the bad-faith purpose of avoiding its basic contractual obligations. This possibility is more significant in international transactions because not all countries have a well-developed secured transactions regime. Accordingly, more scrutiny of the law chosen by the parties is desirable in international transactions.[14] Sometimes, significant differences apply even among states. Virtually every state's version of Article 9 includes nonuniform provisions, and even uniform provisions have been subjected to varying judicial interpretations.

A court that determines that an agreed choice of law is effective ordinarily applies the law of the chosen jurisdiction routinely, but sometimes a party (usually the debtor) argues that doing so violates a fundamental public policy of the forum state. For example, suppose the forum state has an anti-deficiency rule in consumer transactions that penalizes secured parties that fail to follow the proper foreclosure procedures, but the parties designate another state's law that allows the secured party to overcome a negative presumption and recover a deficiency.[15] Courts faced with such arguments should ordinarily defer to the parties' choice and resist the temptation to apply local law.[16] However, the law governing conflicts of laws recognizes an exception to the application of another jurisdiction's law. The exception may be explained as follows:

> Under the fundamental policy doctrine, a court should not refrain from applying the designated law merely because this would lead to a result different than would be obtained under the local law of the State or country whose law would otherwise govern. Rather, the difference must be contrary to a public policy that is so substantial that it justifies overriding the concerns for certainty and predictability underlying modern commercial law as well as concerns for judicial economy generally.[17]

---

14. Revised Article 1's initial choice-of-law rules differentiated between domestic and international transactions. In a domestic transaction, the parties could choose the law of any state without regard to the relation of the transaction to the state but could not choose the law of another country. In international transactions, the parties were free to choose the law of any state or country. U.C.C. § 1-301(a) (defining domestic and international transaction), (c)(1) (rules governing domestic transactions), (c) (2) (rules governing international transactions) (2003 Official Text).

15. For discussion of the general rules regarding a secured party's ability to obtain a deficiency judgment following a commercially unreasonable disposition, see § 19.02, *infra*.

16. They have done so for the most part. *See, e.g.,* Interfirst Bank Clifton v. Fernandez, 853 F.2d 292, 6 U.C.C. Rep. Serv. 2d 1275 (5th Cir. 1988) (court refused to apply Louisiana anti-deficiency statute to protect Louisiana resident).

17. U.C.C. § 1-301, Comment 6 (2003 Official Text). The original version of Section 1-301 in revised Article 1, since withdrawn because of an inability to obtain enactment in the states, contained in subsection (f) a fundamental policy exception. The comment from which the quoted language is

The fundamental-policy exception is equally applicable if a court, in the absence of an effective party choice, selects the law of another jurisdiction to govern the transaction.

A court that applies the substantive law of another state will nevertheless apply the procedural law of the forum state. In *Nez v. Forney*,[18] for example, the parties selected the law of Texas. The court, however, applied New Mexico's statute of limitations because it was held to be procedural in nature.

Parties wishing to invoke rules from a jurisdiction that does not bear a reasonable relation to the transaction may in most instances simply draft them into their agreement. Unless the Code provides otherwise, the effect of its provisions may be varied by agreement.[19] The parties may not disclaim the obligations of good faith, diligence, reasonableness, and care but may determine the standards by which to measure those obligations if the standards are not manifestly unreasonable.[20]

[B] The Appropriate-Relation Test

Section 1-301(b) provides that if the parties fail to choose the governing law or make a choice that is unenforceable, the forum state's version of the Code "applies to transactions bearing an appropriate relation to this state." As noted above with regard to the reasonable-relation test, the drafters assumed the Code would not be enacted in every state and wanted it to apply to as many transactions as possible. One method for accomplishing this goal was to favor the law of the forum state if that state had enacted the Code. The following statement from the Comments, which uses an extreme example to illustrate a case in which the law of the forum state would not apply, suggests that the drafters intended "appropriate relation" to mean a minimum level of contact between the forum state and the transaction:[21]

> ... the mere fact that suit is brought in a state does not make it appropriate to apply the substantive law of that state. Cases where a relation to the enacting state is not "appropriate" include, for example, those where the parties clearly contracted on the basis of some other law, as where the law of the place of

---

excerpted explains the exception. *See, e.g.*, Patches Farms, Inc. v. Thompson Machinery Commerce Corp., 65 U.C.C. Rep. Serv. 2d 729 (N.D. Miss. 2008) (applying Mississippi statutes on privity, warranty disclaimers, and limitations of remedy notwithstanding effective choice of Tennessee law).

18. 109 N.M. 161, 783 P.2d 471, 10 U.C.C. Rep. Serv. 2d 289 (1989). *See also* Belleville Toyota, Inc. v. Toyota Motor Sales, U.S.A, Inc., 199 Ill. 2d 325, 264 Ill. Dec. 283, 770 N.E.2d 177, 47 U.C.C. Rep. Serv. 2d 1044 (2002) (applying Illinois statute of limitations notwithstanding effective choice of California law).

19. U.C.C. § 1-302(a).

20. U.C.C. § 1-302(b).

21. The Comments to the initial choice-of-law provision in revised Article 1, since withdrawn, reinforce this interpretation. "By using an 'appropriate relation' test, rather than, say, requiring that the forum be the location of the 'most significant' contact, [the Code's original choice-of-law rule] expressed a bias in favor of applying the forum's law." U.C.C. § 1-301, Comment 7 (2003 Official Text).

contracting and the law of the place of contemplated performance are the same and are contrary to the law under the Code.[22]

Although the original purpose of the appropriate-relation test was to weight the choice-of-law issue in favor of states that had adopted the Code, many courts have ignored the legislative history and applied the forum state's normal conflict-of-laws principles.[23] In most states, this has meant following the approach of Section 188(a) of the Restatement (Second) of Conflicts, which applies the law of the state that has the most significant relationship with the transaction and the parties.[24] Other courts have followed the text's mandate and applied the law of the forum state even though its connection to the transaction is more limited than that of another state.[25] For example, the court in *In re Roberts*[26] held that, absent an effective contractual choice of law, the forum state's version of the U.C.C. applies unless the transaction does not bear an appropriate relation to that state, in which case the approach adopted by the Restatement (Second) of Conflicts of Laws would apply.

Even if the parties have selected a state that satisfies the reasonable-relation test, the courts should apply the appropriate-relation test if one of the disputants is a third party that did not participate in the agreement process.[27] Of course, many issues involving the rights of third parties will turn on issues related to perfection and priority, in which case Section 1-301(c) defers to Article 9's mandatory choice-of-law rules.

---

22. U.C.C. § 1-301, Comment 2.

23. The initial choice-of-law provision in revised Article 1 took this approach. U.C.C. § 1-301(d) (2003 Official Text). *See, e.g.,* Butler v. Ford Motor Co., 724 F. Supp. 2d 575, 72 U.C.C. Rep. Serv. 2d 691 (D.S.C. 2010) (court in South Carolina applied that state's conflict-of-laws principles in determining that North Carolina law governed).

24. Section 188(b) of the Restatement (Second) of Conflicts identifies as points of contact the place of negotiation, the place of contracting, the place of performance, and the location of the subject matter of the contract, as well as the domicile, residence, nationality, place of incorporation, and place of business of the parties.

25. *See, e.g.,* Barclays Discount Bank Ltd. v. Levy, 743 F.2d 722, 39 U.C.C. Rep. Serv. 916 (9th Cir. 1984) (court applying California rather than Israeli law held that appropriate-relation test was intended to change common-law choice-of-law principles).

26. 110 U.C.C. Rep. Serv. 2d 597 (D. Colo. 2023).

27. *See, e.g.,* American Specialty Sys., Inc. v. Chicago Metallic Corp., 47 U.C.C. Rep. Serv. 2d 949 (N.D. Ill. 2002) (fundamental principles of contract law militate strongly against subjecting third parties to contracting parties' choice of law).

§ 9.02 The Article 9 Choice-of-Law Rules

Article 9 contains mandatory choice-of-law provisions governing the perfection and priority of a security interest. As noted in the preceding discussion, these rules are exceptions to Article 1's basic choice-of-law rules.[28] The reason for the exception is that issues related to perfection and priority invariably involve the rights of persons that are not parties to the security agreement and need a high degree of certainty as to the applicable law. Leaving the decision to the secured party and debtor under the reasonable-relation test or to the courts under the appropriate-relation test would not provide the necessary guidance.

[A] General Rule: Location of the Debtor — § 9-301(1)

Article 9's general rule on choice of law, which applies only to nonpossessory security interests (i.e., security interests in which the secured party does not take possession of the collateral), is that perfection and priority are governed by the local law of the jurisdiction of the debtor's location.[29] Subsequent sections of the chapter will discuss exceptions to the general rule, the most important of which are as follows:

- the local law of the jurisdiction where certain tangible collateral is located governs both perfection and priority if the secured party perfects by possession;[30]

- the local law of the jurisdiction where certain tangible collateral is located governs priority but not perfection if the secured party perfects by a method other than possession;[31] and there are special rules for perfection and priority as to certain types of collateral.[32]

Prior to the 1998 revision, for tangible collateral Article 9 designated the law of the jurisdiction where the collateral was located as the governing law. This approach frequently necessitated multiple filings because a financing statement had to be filed in each jurisdiction in which collateral was located to perfect a security interest in that collateral. Furthermore, because of the highly mobile nature of many goods, relocation of the collateral often required reperfection in another jurisdiction.[33] One of the

---

28. Section 1-105(2) (1998 Official Text) expressly subjected Section 1-105(1) to Sections 9-301 through 9-307 with respect to the law governing perfection and priority. The Official Text of revised Article 1 is comparable. U.C.C. § 1-301(g)(8) (2003 Official Text).

29. U.C.C. § 9-301(1). "Local law" means the version of Article 9, Part 5, in effect in the jurisdiction of the debtor's location.

30. See U.C.C. § 9-301(2), discussed in § 9.02[B], *infra*.

31. See U.C.C. § 9-301(3)(C), discussed in § 9.02[C], *infra*.

32. See U.C.C. §§ 9-302 through 9-306B, discussed in §§ 9.02[D] and 9.03, *infra*.

33. Reperfection in this context means taking steps in the other jurisdiction to maintain continuity of perfection.

1998 revision's greatest improvements is the reduction in the number of occasions requiring the filing of more than one financing statement at the outset of a transaction and a reduction in the circumstances that require reperfection.[34] The introduction in 1998 of the term "registered organization" further simplified the burden on filers and searchers.[35] Because a registered organization's location is deemed to be the jurisdiction whose laws govern its formation or organization,[36] its location does not change even if its chief executive office is moved to a new jurisdiction. Even if the debtor is not a registered organization and might change its location, the new rules are an improvement because a secured party can more easily detect a change in debtor location than a change in collateral location.

Determining the applicable law based on the debtor's location promotes additional efficiencies. A prospective secured lender that has filed its financing statement prior to the attachment of its security interest[37] does not have to worry that the debtor may have moved collateral to another jurisdiction between the time of filing and the time of attachment. Consider further a debtor that is a multinational corporation incorporated under the laws of New York and has offices and assets all over the world. The secured party needs to file and searchers need to search only in New York.

Article 9's rules establish the location of the debtor with a high level of precision.[38] An individual's location is the individual's principal residence.[39] An organization that is not a registered organization and that has only one place of business is located at that place; otherwise, its location is its chief executive office.[40] A registered organization formed or organized under the law of a state is located in that state.[41] For example, the location of a corporation is the state in which its articles of incorporation are filed, the location of a limited liability company is the state in which its certificate of organization is filed, and the location of a limited partnership is the state in which its certificate of limited partnership is filed. A registered organization's formation document is its "public organic record," a term introduced by the 2010 amendments.[42] Determining

---

34. U.C.C. §9-301, Comment 4. Debtors are far less likely to change their location than they are to change the location of their assets.

35. U.C.C. §9-102(a)(71). For discussion of registered organizations, see §5.03[A][1], *supra*.

36. U.C.C. §9-307(e). See the discussion, *infra*, and the discussion of registered organizations in connection with the appropriate name for a financing statement in §5.03[A][1], *supra*.

37. Pre-filing a financing statement is expressly permitted by U.C.C. §9-502(d). The rationale for doing so is discussed in §5.04, *supra*.

38. U.C.C. §9-307.

39. U.C.C. §9-307(b)(1).

40. U.C.C. §9-307(b)(2), (3). Section 9-307(a) defines "place of business" to mean "a place where a debtor conducts its affairs." U.C.C. §9-307(a). This broad definition encompasses organizations that do not engage in for-profit business activities. U.C.C. §9-307, Comment 2. Subsequent discussion in this section covers chief executive office.

41. U.C.C. §9-307(e). Events that affect the status of an organization, such as the dissolution of a corporation or the suspension or revocation of its charter, do not affect its location for purposes of Article 9. U.C.C. §9-307(g).

42. U.C.C. §9-102(a)(68). The term also includes a record issued by a state or the United States to form or organize an organization, legislation enacted by a state or the United States which forms or

the location of a registered organization formed or organized under the law of the United States is a bit more complicated. The location of the organization is (i) the state designated by federal law if the law designates a state,[43] (ii) the state designated by the organization if federal law authorizes it to designate a state,[44] or (iii) the District of Columbia if federal law neither designates a state nor authorizes the debtor to do so.

The designation of a single state for registered organizations represents a significant advantage over the rule applicable to other organizations which, as noted above, designates the debtor's chief executive office as its location if it has places of business in more than one state. Formation or organization of a corporation or limited liability company is ordinarily under the law of a single state,[45] and a prospective secured party can readily ascertain the corporation's location by inspecting its filed articles of incorporation (public organic record).[46] Comparable location information is not available for the chief executive office of a debtor that is not a registered organization. The Comments indicate that "[c]hief executive office means the place from which the debtor manages the main part of its business or other affairs."[47] This place, however, may be difficult to pinpoint in the case of an organization that operates in multiple jurisdictions and has a decentralized management structure. A prudent secured party will make a filing in each jurisdiction in which the debtor's chief executive office might plausibly be located.

Notwithstanding the simplicity of the debtor-location rules as compared with former law, tricky issues sometimes arise. For example, suppose a secured party makes a loan to a common-law trust, which is not a registered organization.[48] A trust is not a juridical entity capable of owning property and thus cannot be a debtor (i.e., a person

---

organizes an organization, and the organic record of a business trust if a state statute requires that the record be filed with the state. A record must be available to the public for inspection to qualify as a public organic record. For discussion of public organic record and registered organizations generally, see § 5.03[A][1], *supra*.

43. U.C.C. § 9-307(f)(1).

44. U.C.C. § 9-307(f)(2). If authorized by federal law, a registered organization may select its state of location by designating its main office, home office, or other comparable office. *Id*.

45. In rare cases, a corporation might have articles of incorporation on file in more than one state. Such a corporation is not a registered organization, and this leads to a tricky choice-of-law problem. The proper place to file would be the state in which the corporation's chief executive office is located, which might not be a state in which articles of incorporation are filed.

46. Reliance on a registered organization's public organic record provides a secured party with an additional benefit: it provides a reliable source for the debtor's name for purposes of a financing statement. For discussion of debtor names for purposes of a financing statement, see § 5.03[A][1], *supra*.

47. U.C.C. § 9-307, Comment 2.

48. A business trust is a registered organization if a state statute requires its organic record to be filed with the state. U.C.C. § 9-102(a)(71). The organic record becomes the trust's public organic record upon filing. U.C.C. § 9-102(a)(68). For discussion of common-law trusts that are registered organizations, including discussion of the distinction between such a trust's organic record and its public organic record, see § 5.03[A][1], *supra*.

with an interest in the collateral).[49] The debtor is the trustee acting in that capacity,[50] and a filing must be made in the trustee's location.[51]

Article 9 also provides rules for determining the location of non-U.S. debtors. The general debtor-location rules discussed above apply even if they designate a foreign country, if the designated country's laws require "information concerning the existence of a nonpossessory security interest to be made generally available in a filing, recording, or registration system as a condition or result of the security interest's obtaining priority over the rights of a lien creditor with respect to the collateral."[52] In other words, the law of the foreign country governs perfection, but only if that law provides a means for giving public notice of a security interest and obtaining priority over a person that is the equivalent of a lien creditor under Article 9. If a foreign country's law governs perfection, that law must be consulted to determine the type of record to file, its required contents, and the place of filing. Because the advantages of applying the normal debtor-location rules would be lost without a qualifying public-notice system, the debtor's location is the District of Columbia if the laws of the foreign country do not meet Article 9's statutory test.[53] For example, suppose a multinational corporation formed or organized under German law has places of business all over the world, but its chief executive office is in Riyadh, Saudi Arabia. Because it is an organization that is not a registered organization,[54] it is located in Saudi Arabia if that country has a qualifying public-notice system, in which case a filing must be made in that system. The filing must be made in the District of Columbia if Saudi Arabia does not have a qualifying system. In cases of doubt, a prudent secured party will file in the foreign system and in the District of Columbia.

[B] Possessory Security Interest Exception — § 9-301(2)

Possessory security interests (i.e., security interests as to which the secured party takes possession of the collateral) fall under a collateral-location rule rather than the debtor-location rule discussed above.[55] The efficiency of such an approach is obvious. Perhaps most importantly, the debtor-location rule makes it simple for a person

---

49. U.C.C. § 9-102(a)(28)(A).

50. The 2010 amendments make the point in a comment, and also make the point that the beneficiary of a trust is the debtor with respect to that person's beneficial interest but not with respect to the assets of the trust. U.C.C. § 9-307, Comment 2.

51. In the case of multiple trustees, a prudent secured party will make a filing in each jurisdiction in which a trustee is located. U.C.C. § 9-307, Comment 2.

52. U.C.C. § 9-307(c).

53. U.C.C. § 9-307(c). The same location is designated for the United States as a debtor. U.C.C. § 9-307(h).

54. It is not formed or organized under the law of a single state or the United States. *See* U.C.C. § 9-102(a)(71).

55. "While collateral is located in a jurisdiction, the local law of that jurisdiction governs perfection ... and the priority of a possessory security interest in that collateral." U.C.C. § 9-301(2).

contemplating a transaction to determine which system, among all state and foreign-country filing systems, it should search. This concern is not relevant if the secured party perfects by possession rather than by filing. The rules governing perfection by possession are the same everywhere, and because the secured party, its representative, or a bailee holding the collateral on the secured party's behalf is in possession, the secured party can prevent or control movement of the collateral to another jurisdiction. Moreover, because the rules governing perfection by possession are the same in every state, the secured party will be perfected under the law of the new state at the moment the goods are moved there, eliminating the possibility of difficult reperfection issues.[56] The law of the jurisdiction in which the collateral is located governs both perfection and priority of the possessory security interest.[57]

[C] Tangible Property Partial Exception for Priority—§ 9-301(3)(C)

The drafters of the 1998 revision recognized a problem in applying the general debtor-location rule for nonpossessory security interests to priority contests when the debtor and the collateral are located in different jurisdictions. The Comments use the following example to explain the problem:

> For example, assume a security interest in equipment located in Pennsylvania is perfected by filing in Illinois, where the debtor is located. If the law of the jurisdiction in which the debtor is located were to govern priority, then the priority of an execution lien on goods located in Pennsylvania would be governed by rules enacted by the Illinois legislature.[58]

The debtor-location rule of Section 9-301(1) applies generally to both perfection and priority, but there is an exception that addresses the problem described in the Comments. With respect to priority only, the law of the jurisdiction in which the collateral is located governs if the collateral consists of goods, instruments, negotiable tangible documents, or tangible money.[59] The exception applies to certain collateral that has a tangible form and is therefore capable of being located within a particular jurisdiction.[60] The law governing perfection remains the local law of the jurisdiction in which the debtor is located.[61] In other words, Article 9 bifurcates the designation of the governing law. Although this bifurcated approach adds an element of complexity,

---

56. *See* § 9-316(c); § 9.03, *infra.*

57. A collateral-location rule also applies in certain situations involving land-related collateral. *See* § 9.02[D][1], *infra.*

58. U.C.C. § 9-301, Comment 7.

59. U.C.C. § 9-301(3)(C).

60. The exception does not apply to all tangible collateral. For example, the rules governing both perfection and priority of a security interest in chattel paper, including chattel paper evidenced by a writing, are found in U.C.C. § 9-306A; goods covered by a certificate of title in U.C.C. § 9-303; and certificated securities in U.C.C. § 9-305.

61. U.C.C. § 9-301(1). *See* § 9.02[A], *supra.*

it preserves the benefit associated with a debtor-location perfection rule while avoiding the type of problem illustrated by the Comments.

The exception will not have any effect if the rules of the two jurisdictions regarding priority are the same, which will almost always be the case. The results will occasionally differ, however. The courts in the two states might interpret a uniform priority rule differently, or the laws of the states might differ on the time when a person becomes a lien creditor. The latter situation can be explained by the following example. Suppose that on February 1, Bank takes a security interest in the equipment of ABC, Inc., a Nevada corporation with equipment located in both Las Vegas and San Diego, and on the same day files an initial financing statement in Nevada. Unknown to Bank, Victim had obtained a tort judgment in a California court against ABC on January 15 and on the same day had filed a notice of judgment lien with California's Secretary of State.[62] On February 28, the sheriff executes on Victim's judgment by levying on equipment located at ABC's San Diego facility. Bank and Victim subsequently litigate the priority dispute.

Whether the forum court is located in Nevada or California (or any other state, for that matter), the forum state's version of Section 9-301(1) provides that Nevada law governs perfection and thus Bank is perfected without regard to the location of the collateral.[63] Under Nevada law, Victim would not have a lien and thus would not be a lien creditor[64] until levy occurred on February 28. If Nevada's priority rules governed, Bank's prior-perfected security interest would have priority over Victim's lien.[65] The forum state's version of Section 9-301(3)(C), however, provides that California law governs the priority dispute because the levied-upon collateral was located there. Because California allows a judgment lien on personal property to arise by public filing without an actual levy, Victim became a lien creditor on January 15 and prevails over Bank's later-perfected security interest.

The choice-of-law rules for nonpossessory security interests can be summarized as follows: (1) if the collateral is intangible, the law of the jurisdiction in which the debtor is located governs perfection and priority;[66] (2) if the collateral is tangible, the law of the jurisdiction in which the debtor is located governs perfection,[67] but the law of the jurisdiction in which the collateral is located governs priority.[68] In the case of a possessory security interest, the law of the jurisdiction in which the collateral is located governs perfection and priority.[69] This summary is subject to additional exceptions discussed below.

---

62. *See* Cal. Civ. Pro. Code §§ 697.510 to 697.530.
63. ABC is a registered organization located in Nevada. *See* U.C.C. § 9-307(e).
64. *See* U.C.C. § 9-102(a)(52)(A).
65. U.C.C. §§ 9-201, 9-317(a)(2) (converse reading).
66. U.C.C. § 9-301(1).
67. *Id.*
68. U.C.C. § 9-301(3)(c).
69. U.C.C. § 9-301(2).

[D] Additional Exceptions

[1] Chattel Paper—§ 9-306A

Perfection of chattel paper may be accomplished either by filing a financing statement, in which case the law governing perfection is the local law of the debtor's location,[70] or by possession and control under Section 9-314A.[71] If a security interest is perfected by possession and control, the local law of the chattel paper's jurisdiction governs perfection and priority. The following rules determine the chattel paper's jurisdiction:

(1) If the authoritative electronic copy of the record evidencing chattel paper, or a record attached to or logically associated with the electronic copy and readily available for review, expressly provides that a particular jurisdiction is the chattel paper's jurisdiction for purposes of this part, this article, or [the Uniform commercial Code], that jurisdiction is the chattel paper's jurisdiction.

(2) If paragraph (1) does not apply and the rules of the system in which the authoritative electronic copy is recorded are readily available for review and expressly provide that a particular jurisdiction is the chattel paper's jurisdiction for purposes of this part, this article, or [the Uniform commercial Code], that jurisdiction is the chattel paper's jurisdiction.

(3) If paragraphs (1) and (2) do not apply and the authoritative electronic copy, or a record attached to or logically associated with the electronic copy and readily available for review, expressly provides that the chattel paper is governed by the law of a particular jurisdiction, that jurisdiction is the chattel paper's jurisdiction.

(4) If paragraphs (1), (2), and (3) do not apply and the rules of the system in which the authoritative electronic copy is recorded are readily available for review and expressly provide that the chattel paper or the system is governed by the law of a particular jurisdiction, that jurisdiction is the chattel paper's jurisdiction.

(5) If paragraphs (1) through (4) do not apply, the chattel paper's jurisdiction is the jurisdiction in which the debtor is located.

These rules apply even the transaction does not bear any relation to the designated jurisdiction.[72]

---

70. U.C.C. § 9-306A(d).

71. U.C.C. § 9-314A provides that perfection may be accomplished "by taking possession of each authoritative tangible copy of the record evidencing the chattel paper and obtaining control of each authoritative electronic copy of the electronic record evidencing the chattel paper."

72. U.C.C. § 9-306A(a).

[2] Controllable Accounts, Controllable Electronic Records, and Controllable Payment Intangibles — § 9-306B

Section 9-306B(a) provides rules for determining the law that governs perfection and priority of a security interest in a controllable electronic record and a security interest in a controllable account or controllable payment intangible evidenced by the controllable electronic record if perfection is accomplished by control.[73] For these purposes, the governing law is that of the controllable electronic record's jurisdiction, which is established under Section 12-107(c) and (d). Subsection (c) creates what is in effect a waterfall:

(1) If the controllable electronic record, or a record attached to or logically associated with the controllable electronic record and readily available for review, expressly provides that a particular jurisdiction is the controllable electronic record's jurisdiction for purposes of this part, this article, or [the Uniform commercial Code], that jurisdiction is the controllable electronic record's jurisdiction.

(2) If paragraph (1) does not apply and the rules of the system in which the controllable electronic record is recorded are readily available for review and expressly provide that a particular jurisdiction is the controllable electronic record's jurisdiction for purposes of this part, this article, or [the Uniform commercial Code], that jurisdiction is the controllable electronic record's jurisdiction.

(3) If paragraphs (1) and (2) do not apply and the controllable electronic record, or a record attached to or logically associated with the controllable electronic record and readily available for review, expressly provides that the controllable electronic record is governed by the law of a particular jurisdiction, that jurisdiction is the controllable electronic record's jurisdiction.

(4) If paragraphs (1), (2), and (3) do not apply and the rules of the system in which the controllable electronic record is recorded are readily available for review and expressly provide that the controllable electronic record or the system is governed by the law of a particular jurisdiction, that jurisdiction is the controllable electronic record's jurisdiction.

(5) If paragraphs (1) through (4) do not apply, the controllable electronic record's jurisdiction is the District of Columbia.

Subsection (d) deals with the possibility that the District of Columbia might not have adopted the 2022 amendments and provides that in that case it will be presumed, for purposes of subsection (c)(5), that the District has adopted Article 12 as promulgated by the Code's sponsors without material modification.

Perfection of a security interest in a controllable electronic record and a security interest in a controllable account or controllable payment intangible evidenced by the

---

73. U.C.C. § 9-107A provides that perfection by control is accomplished by satisfying the test for control in U.C.C. § 12-105.

controllable electronic record may also be accomplished by the filing of a financing statement, although that is a decidedly inferior method of perfection.[74] In that case, the law governing perfection is the local law of the debtor's location. Controllable electronic records are general intangibles, and controllable accounts and controllable payment intangibles are subsets of accounts and payment intangibles, so this approach does not change pre-2022 law. The local law of the debtor's location also governs automatic perfection in the case of a sale of a controllable payment intangible.[75]

[3] Land-Related Collateral—§ 9-301(3), (4)

Article 9 includes special rules for collateral that has a close relationship to specific real estate. In the case of goods that are or are to become fixtures, if the secured party perfects by filing a fixture filing,[76] the law of the jurisdiction in which the goods are located governs perfection.[77] A collateral-location rule for perfection also applies if the collateral is timber to be cut.[78] Fixture filings and filings covering timber to be cut must be filed in the office in which a mortgage on the relevant real estate would be filed or recorded,[79] and that office is invariably in the state (and typically in the county) in which the real estate is located. Because fixtures and standing timber are goods, the law of the jurisdiction in which they are located also governs priority.[80]

In the case of as-extracted collateral, the law of the jurisdiction in which the wellhead or minehead is located governs perfection and priority.[81] As with fixture filings and filings covering timber to be cut, filings related to as-extracted collateral must be filed in the office in which a mortgage on the relevant real estate would be filed or recorded. As-extracted collateral generally consists of goods, as to which a collateral-location rule for priority-related issues is the norm. However, as-extracted collateral also includes "accounts arising out of the sale at the wellhead or minehead of oil, gas, or other minerals in which the debtor had an interest before extraction,"[82] and accounts are intangible. The law governing intangible collateral is ordinarily the law of the debtor's location, but states rich in this type of collateral, especially oil- and gas-producing states, often have nonuniform priority rules applicable to accounts arising out of sales at the point of extraction. Article 9 defers to those rules.

---

74. Under U.C.C. § 9-326A, a security interest perfected by control has priority over a security interest perfected by another method, even if control is accomplished after perfection by the other method occurs.

75. A security interest arising from the sale subject to Article 9 of a payment intangible is automatically perfected. U.C.C. § 9-309(3). For a discussion of the application of Article 9 to the sale of certain rights to payment, see § 1.05, *infra*.

76. For discussion of fixture filings, see § 15.02, *supra*.

77. U.C.C. § 9-301(3)(A).

78. U.C.C. § 9-301(3)(B).

79. U.C.C. § 9-501(a)(1).

80. U.C.C. § 9-301(3)(C). *See* § 5.02[C], *supra*.

81. U.C.C. § 9-301(4).

82. U.C.C. § 9-102(a)(6)(B).

[4] Agricultural Liens—§ 9-302

The law of the jurisdiction in which farm products are located governs perfection and priority of an agricultural lien on the farm products.[83] This rule can create a trap for an unwary secured party. For example, suppose Bank makes a loan to FarmCorp, a Kansas corporation in the business of farming, secured by all FarmCorp's crops. FarmCorp is a registered organization, and under the debtor-location rule, Kansas law governs perfection of Bank's security interest.[84] Bank files in that state after searching the Kansas records and finding no adverse interest. Unknown to Bank, FarmCorp leases cropland in Missouri from Landlord and is behind in its rent. Landlord has an agricultural lien for unpaid rent on FarmCorp's crops pursuant to a Missouri statute, and it perfected its lien by filing in Missouri before Bank filed in Kansas. Landlord's agricultural lien has priority over Bank's security interest.[85]

[5] Deposit Accounts—§ 9-304

Perfection and priority of a security interest in a deposit account are governed by the local law of the jurisdiction of the bank that maintains the account.[86] Article 9 provides a series of rules for determining a bank's jurisdiction.[87] The bank and its customer (the debtor) may by express agreement choose the law that will govern for purposes of the priority rules of Part 3 of Article 9, for purposes of all of Article 9, or for purposes of the entire U.C.C.,[88] even without any relationship between the chosen jurisdiction and either the parties or the transaction.[89] If the parties do not make a choice expressly referencing part or all of Article 9 or the U.C.C. but their agreement contains a general choice-of-law clause, the law of the chosen jurisdiction governs.[90] If the parties do not have an agreement on choice of law, the governing law is the law of the jurisdiction in which the bank office that maintains the deposit account is located if the parties' agreement expressly identifies that location; otherwise, it is the law of the location of the bank office identified in an account statement as the office serving the customer's account, or, if the account statement does not identify an office, the location of the bank's chief executive office.[91]

---

83. U.C.C. § 9-302. For discussion of agricultural liens, see § 13.02, *infra*.
84. U.C.C. § 9-301(1). *See* § 9.02[A], *supra*.
85. U.C.C. § 9-322(a)(1).
86. U.C.C. § 9-304(a).
87. U.C.C. § 9-304(b).
88. U.C.C. § 9-304(b)(1).
89. U.C.C. § 9-304, Comment 2. The parties can choose to apply the law of one jurisdiction to perfection and priority and the law of another jurisdiction for other purposes. *Id.*
90. U.C.C. § 9-304(b)(2).
91. U.C.C. § 9-304(b)(3)–(5).

[6] Investment Property—§ 9-305

Article 9 includes choice-of-law rules for perfection and priority of a security interest in investment property.[92] When perfection is based on control, the law of the jurisdiction in which the certificate is located governs in the case of a certificated security, the law of the issuer's jurisdiction as specified in Section 8-110(d) governs in the case of an uncertificated security, the law of the security intermediary's jurisdiction as specified in Section 8-110(e) governs in the case of a security entitlement or securities account, and the law of the commodity intermediary's jurisdiction as specified in Section 9-305(b) governs in the case of a commodity contract or commodity account. The 2022 amendments clarify that, with the exception of the rule stated above for certificated securities, the rules apply even if the transaction does not bear any relation to the designated jurisdiction.

Each of the cross-referenced rules is similar to the rules governing deposit accounts, and the reader can refer to the discussion in the preceding subsection for specifics. The selection of the choice-of-law rule in these cases reflects the principles used in Article 8 to determine other questions related to investment property.[93] If perfection is by filing, or automatic in certain cases involving a broker, securities intermediary, or commodity intermediary, the law of the debtor's location governs perfection but not priority.[94]

The United States is a party to the Hague Securities Convention, and the Comments contain the following cautionary note:

> The Hague Securities Convention generally preserves these rules for perfection by filing. However, if the debtor is located in a non-U.S. jurisdiction, or if the account agreement designates the law of a non-U.S. jurisdiction, then filing may be appropriate only in a different jurisdiction or altogether unavailable. See Convention articles 12(2)(b) and 4(1), respectively, and PEB Commentary No. 19, particularly footnote 25.

[7] Letter-of-Credit Rights—§ 9-306

A separate provision of Article 9 addresses the law governing perfection and priority with respect to a security interest in letter-of-credit rights.[95] The applicable law is the local law of the issuer's jurisdiction or the local law of a nominated person's jurisdiction, provided that the jurisdiction is a state. If the jurisdiction is not a state, the general Article 9 choice-of-law rule applies, meaning that perfection and priority are governed by the law of the debtor's location.[96] The objective is to prevent foreign law from controlling a transaction that, from the perspective of the debtor-beneficiary, its

---

92. U.C.C. § 9-305. For discussion of investment property generally, see § 1.04[B][6], *supra*.

93. U.C.C. § 9-305, Comment 2. *See* U.C.C. § 8-110. Article 9 contains the rules governing commodity intermediaries because commodities are outside the scope of Article 8, but the rules in the two articles are consistent. *Compare* U.C.C. § 9-305(b) *with* U.C.C. § 8-110(e).

94. For discussion of automatic perfection for investment property, see § 7.02[D], *supra*.

95. U.C.C. § 9-306.

96. U.C.C. § 9-306, Comment 2. *See* U.C.C. § 9-301(1).

creditors, and a domestic nominated person, is essentially domestic.[97] The determination of an issuer's or nominated person's jurisdiction is to be made in accordance with provisions in Article 5 on letters of credit.[98]

§ 9.03 Initial Perfection under a Certificate-of-Title Law — §§ 9-303, 9-311

Article 9 does not govern perfection of a security interest in goods subject to a certificate-of-title act in effect in any jurisdiction.[99] It provides instead that perfection must occur by compliance with the requirements of such an act (although, as subsequent discussion demonstrates, not necessarily the requirements of the act to which the goods are subject).[100] Filing a financing statement is neither necessary nor effective to perfect the security interest;[101] rather, "[c]ompliance with the requirements of [this or another jurisdiction's certificate-of-title act] for obtaining priority over the rights of a lien creditor is equivalent to the filing of a financing statement under this article."[102]

Certificates of title are issued by a state agency and provide information about the covered goods, including the name of the owner and any secured party with a security interest in the goods. Historically, certificates were in a physical form, but today many states have reduced paperwork by permitting or requiring the issuing agency to maintain an electronic record evidencing ownership and providing information about security interests.[103]

---

97. U.C.C. § 9-306, Comment 2.

98. U.C.C. § 9-306(b) (referencing U.C.C. § 5-116).

99. Section 9-311(a)(2) as enacted in a particular state contains a cross-reference to that state's certificate-of-title acts. Section 9-311(a)(3) refers generally to the certificate-of-title acts of other jurisdictions.

100. U.C.C. § 9-311(b). The requirement that perfection occur by compliance with the requirements of a certificate-of-title act does not apply to a security interest in inventory held for sale or lease by a person in the business of selling goods of the kind. See U.C.C. § 9-311(d), discussed *infra* this section. Also, perfection may be accomplished by possession in limited circumstances involving a change in the governing law. See U.C.C. § 9-313(b), discussed in § 9.04[C], *infra*.

101. U.C.C. § 9-311(b).

102. *Id.*

103. Electronic certificate-of-title systems generally maintain the information that would be included in a paper certificate in a centralized database and provide the owner of record with a receipt indicating that a certificate has been issued. Some states have adopted acts that create what are functionally electronic certificate-of-title systems but do not use the term "certificate-of-title." The definition of the term was amended in 2010 to include a "record maintained as an alternative to a certificate of title by the governmental unit that issues certificates of title if a statute permits the security interest in question to be indicated on the record as a condition or result of the security interest's obtaining priority over the rights of a lien creditor with respect to the collateral." U.C.C. § 9-102(a)(10); 9-102, Comment 11.

The rationale for the Code's approach is that every person should understand the imprudence of buying or lending against goods subject to a certificate-of-title act without first seeing the certificate (if physical) or obtaining the information stored in the record (if electronic). Accordingly, the best method of giving notice of a security interest is having it indicated on the face of a physical certificate or stored in the electronic record maintained by the state agency. While Article 9 defers to certificate-of-title acts for perfection, it governs the priority of a security interest in goods subject to such an act.

Every state has a certificate-of-title act for motor vehicles, although the definition of what constitutes a motor vehicle varies somewhat from state to state. Many states also have such acts for other types of goods, most commonly boats and manufactured homes. These acts have a great deal of variety, and many of them, especially those governing motor vehicles, were enacted before the widespread adoption of the Code and do not use the Code's terminology. For example, many acts refer to a security interest as a "lien" and a secured party as a "lienholder."

Perfection of a security interest in goods subject to the certificate-of-title act of any jurisdiction may not be accomplished under any of the normal Article 9 methods even if the general debtor-location rule of Section 9-301(1) designates a state that does not have a certificate-of-title act for the type of goods at issue.[104] For example, suppose Debtor, an individual whose principal residence is in State A, grants Bank a security interest in a boat regularly docked in State B. State A does not have a certificate-of-title act for boats; State B requires a certificate of title for any boat regularly docked in the state. If debtor regularly docked the boat in State A or in another state without a certificate-of-title act covering boats, Bank could perfect by filing an initial financing statement in State A. However, because the boat is subject to a certificate-of-title act, Bank must comply with the requirements of such an act to perfect its security interest.

The term "certificate of title" is defined somewhat redundantly to mean "a certificate of title with respect to which a statute provides for the security interest in question to be indicated on the certificate as a condition or result of the security interest's obtaining priority over the rights of a lien creditor with respect to the collateral."[105] The "condition or result" language recognizes that, in some states, perfection occurs upon delivery to the appropriate government agency of a valid application for a certificate of title and tender of the applicable fee,[106] whereas in other states, perfection occurs only upon the issuance of a certificate of title indicating the security interest.[107] The indication of the

---

104. U.C.C. § 9-311(a)(2) (designating state's certificate-of-title acts), (b) (security interest may be perfected "only by compliance" with provisions of a certificate-of-title act).

105. U.C.C. § 9-102(a)(10).

106. This is the approach taken in the Uniform Motor Vehicle Certificate of Title and Anti-Theft Act, which is in effect in a few states. The Uniform Certificate of Title Act, promulgated in 2002, takes the same approach but has not yet been enacted in any state.

107. *See, e.g.*, Johnson v. Branch Banking & Trust Co., 313 S.W.3d 557 (Ky. 2010) (under Kentucky law, perfection occurs upon issuance of certificate of title indicating security interest).

security interest on the certificate is a result of perfection under the first type of act; it is a condition of perfection under the second type of act.

Section 9-303, the choice-of-law provision for goods subject to a certificate-of-title act, can be confusing at first blush because it turns on the goods "becoming covered" by a certificate of title. The moment when goods subject to a security interest become covered by a certificate of title is not necessarily the moment when perfection of the security interest occurs, and goods may become covered by a certificate even though the state has not yet issued one. Under Section 9-303(b), goods become covered by a certificate of title "when a valid application for the certificate of title and the applicable fee are delivered to the appropriate authority." They cease to be covered when the certificate of title ceases to be effective under the law of the issuing jurisdiction or when the goods subsequently become covered by a certificate of title issued by another jurisdiction, whichever occurs earlier.[108] The problems that arise when goods covered by a certificate of title in one state become covered by a certificate of title in another state are discussed in the next section, which deals with changes in the governing law.[109]

The provisions of Section 9-303 are choice-of-law provisions only. They determine the state whose law governs perfection and priority of a security interest in goods subject to a certificate-of-title act, but they do not govern how or when the security interest becomes perfected. As noted above, in many states, perfection occurs upon delivery to the appropriate authority of a valid application and tender of the applicable fee; in those states, the goods become covered by a certificate of title, and the secured party becomes perfected simultaneously.[110] In states in which perfection occurs only upon issuance of a certificate of title indicating the security interest, the goods become covered by the certificate at the application stage, and perfection occurs at the issuance stage. Becoming covered simply means that perfection is governed by the law of the state under whose certificate the goods have become covered.

For example, suppose Debtor, a resident of State A, grants Bank a security interest in a car subject to State A's certificate-of-title act, which requires issuance of a certificate for all cars kept in the state. Until delivery of a valid application for a certificate of title to the appropriate authority in some state and tender of the applicable fee, the law of State A governs perfection under Section 9-301(1).[111] However, the moment a valid application is delivered to the appropriate authority in a state and the applicable fee is tendered, the car becomes covered by that state's certificate (even though no certificate has yet been issued), and that state's law governs perfection. As a practical matter, the application will be delivered to the issuing authority in State A because otherwise Debtor will be in violation of that state's requirement that a certificate of title be issued

108. U.C.C. § 9-303(b).
109. *See* § 9.04[C], *infra.*
110. This statement assumes that a "valid application" includes all the information and supporting documents required under state law for issuance of a certificate of title indicating a security interest.
111. *See* § 9.02, *supra.* Even though the law of State A governs perfection, Bank cannot perfect under any of the normal methods of perfection authorized by that state. U.C.C. § 9-311(a)(3), (b).

for all cars kept there, but that is not an Article 9 issue. A relationship between the state whose law governs perfection and the goods or the debtor is not a requirement for purposes of Article 9.[112] The fact that the car has become covered by a certificate of title does not mean that Bank's security interest is perfected; perfection depends on the provisions of the certificate-of-title act of the state whose law governs.

Article 9 includes an important exception to the rule that security interests in goods subject to a certificate-of-title act must be perfected by compliance with the requirements of that act. Section 9-311(d) provides that "[d]uring any period in which collateral [subject to a certificate of title statute] is inventory held for sale or lease by a person or leased by that person as lessor and that person is in the business of selling goods of that kind, [the certificate-of-title method of perfection] does not apply to a security interest in that collateral created by that person."[113] The reason for the exception is obvious. The titling process is complicated, time-consuming, and, if applied to a large volume of vehicles, expensive. Moreover, if perfection of a security interest in inventory held for sale or lease were governed by a certificate-of-title act, the secured party would no sooner apply for a certificate than its interest might be extinguished by a sale to a buyer in ordinary course of business. To avoid the paperwork and expense associated with such a procedure, the Code allows the secured party to perfect its security interest by filing an initial financing statement.

Perfection by filing is available only if the debtor is in the business of selling goods of the kind. If the debtor leases but does not sell the goods, as with a car rental company, perfection must be accomplished by the certificate-of-title method. If the debtor is in the business of selling goods of the kind, perfection as to its inventory of such goods—those held for sale and lease, and those subject to a lease—may be accomplished by filing.

---

112. Permitting perfection to occur in a state that has no contact with the parties or the goods is consistent with modern trucking practices. *See* U.C.C. § 9-303, Comment 2. An application delivered to an office in a state that does not issue certificates of title for out-of-state cars would not be a "valid" application, and Section 9-303 would not be triggered.

113. U.C.C. § 9-311(d). *See* Carcorp, Inc. v. Bombadier Capital, Inc., 272 B.R. 365, 47 U.C.C. Rep. Serv. 2d 374 (Bankr. S.D. Fla. 2002) (motor vehicles that are part of a debtor dealer's inventory must be perfected by filing a financing statement rather than under the certificate-of-title statute). *See also* First Nat'l Bank v. Automotive Fin. Corp., 661 N.W.2d 668 (Minn. Ct. App. 2003) (lender that perfected its security interest in a consumer's automobile under certificate-of-title act had priority over dealership's perfected-by-filing inventory financier when the consumer traded in its automobile on the purchase of a newer model; court did not cite Section 9-325(a), which would have awarded priority to lender even if inventory financier had filed its financing statement before lender perfected).

§ 9.04 Perfection Following Change in Governing Law—§ 9-316

Article 9's choice-of-law rules govern more than just the initial perfection of a security interest; they continue to apply throughout the life of a secured transaction. Complicated issues arise with changes in the governing law. For example, suppose Debtor, who operates a sole proprietorship, resides in State A, and Bank, which takes a security interest in all Debtor's existing and after-acquired inventory and equipment, properly perfects by filing in that state.[114] Debtor subsequently moves to State B. State B's law now governs perfection, and the question arises whether Bank's filing continues to be effective or whether it must reperfect in State B.

In the prior example, the determining factor in choosing the governing law was the debtor's location, but the same issue arises in other contexts. For example, the law of State A might govern perfection of a security interest in goods subject to a certificate-of-title act because the goods have become covered by a certificate of title in that state, but what is the effect on perfection if the goods cease to be covered by State A's certificate and become covered by a certificate in State B?[115] Similar issues arise from a transfer of collateral to a person that thereby becomes a debtor if the transferee is located in a jurisdiction other than the jurisdiction whose law governed perfection prior to the transfer. Yet another problem arises if a new debtor is located in a jurisdiction other than that of the original debtor.[116]

[A] Change of Location

[1] Nonpossessory Security Interests

Article 9's general choice-of-law rule for nonpossessory security interests provides that perfection is governed by the law of the jurisdiction in which the debtor is located.[117] If a debtor located in State A changes its location to State B, State B's law governs perfection immediately upon the change of location. However, a security interest in the debtor's assets perfected in State A does not become unperfected merely because the law of State B now governs.[118] State B's version of Section 9-316(a) will provide the secured party with a period of temporary automatic perfection. This "grace period" is intended to give the secured party sufficient time to learn of the change of location and to take the necessary steps to reperfect in State B.[119]

---

114. For discussion of the choice-of-law rules based on the debtor's location, see § 9.02[A], *supra*.

115. For discussion of the choice-of-law rules for goods subject to a certificate-of-title act, see § 9.03, *supra*.

116. For discussion of perfection in the context of transferees and new debtors generally, see § 5.03[C][2][b], *supra*.

117. U.C.C. § 9-301(1).

118. U.C.C. § 9-316, Comment 2.

119. *Id.*

Section 9-316(a) is complex and deals with more than just a debtor's change of location; it also deals with a transfer of collateral to a person that thereby becomes a debtor. The basic grace period is four months for a change of debtor location and one year for a transfer to a person that thereby becomes a debtor.[120] The provision states in full as follows:

> A security interest perfected pursuant to the law of the jurisdiction designated in Section 9-301(1) or Section 9-305(c)[121] remains perfected until the earliest of:
>
> (1) the time perfection would have ceased under the law of that jurisdiction;
>
> (2) the expiration of four months after a change of the debtor's location to another jurisdiction; or
>
> (3) the expiration of one year after a transfer of collateral to a person that thereby becomes a debtor and is located in another jurisdiction.

In a case involving a change of the debtor's location, only paragraphs (1) and (2) apply. In a case involving a transfer to a person that thereby becomes a debtor, only paragraphs (1) and (3) apply.

Recall the example at the beginning of this section: Debtor, who operates a sole proprietorship, resides in State A, and Bank, which takes a security interest in all Debtor's existing and after-acquired inventory and equipment, properly perfects by filing in State A.[122] Subsequently, Debtor moves to State B. No matter where the parties litigate, the forum court will look to its state's version of Sections 9-301(1) and 9-307(b)(1) and conclude that Debtor is located in State B and that its laws govern perfection.[123] Under State B's version of Section 9-316(a), Bank's security interest remains perfected until the earlier of the time perfection would have ceased in State A or the expiration of four months after the change of location to State B, which its own statute awkwardly designates as "another jurisdiction."

Suppose Debtor moves to State B on June 1, and Bank's State A financing statement will lapse on June 10. Bank's period of temporary automatic perfection is only ten days, and it cannot be increased by filing a continuation statement in State A because that state's law no longer governs perfection.[124] The grace period thus is not always four months in length. It may, in fact, be dramatically shorter.

---

120. This section of the book discusses a debtor's change of location. For discussion of a transfer to a person that thereby becomes a debtor, see § 9.04[B], *infra*.

121. Section 9-301(1) is the general choice-of-law rule for nonpossessory security interests. Section 9-305(c) is the choice-of-law rule for security interests in investment property perfected either by filing or automatically.

122. For discussion of the choice-of-law rules based on the debtor's location, see § 9.02[A], *supra*.

123. The court will look first to its state's version of U.C.C. § 1-301(c)(8) and determine that its state's version of Sections 9-301 through 9-307 are mandatory choice-of-law provisions. See discussion in § 9.01, *supra*.

124. Bank would have the full four-month grace period if it had filed a timely continuation in State A before the move, while that state's law still governed perfection. For discussion of the proper timing for filing a continuation statement, see § 5.06[B], *supra*.

In the example, suppose Debtor acquires new inventory or equipment after the move. Bank's security interest will not attach to the new collateral until Debtor acquires rights in it, and by that time State B's law will govern perfection. Bank's security interest in the after-acquired collateral was never perfected in State A because perfection cannot occur absent attachment,[125] and Section 9-316(a) is therefore irrelevant. The 1998 revision as originally drafted did not provide a grace period for this situation; Bank was unperfected as to the after-acquired collateral and remained unperfected until it perfected in State B. The 2010 amendments provide Bank with the same grace period for after-acquired collateral that it has for collateral on hand at the time of the move.[126]

If Bank reperfects in State B before its grace period expires, it will remain perfected thereafter without a gap in its perfected status. If it reperfects in State B by filing, its initial financing statement will be effective for five years, and that period can be extended by the filing of a continuation statement.[127] Failure to reperfect during the grace period leaves the security interest unperfected prospectively, and it is deemed never to have been perfected as against a purchaser of the collateral for value.[128] This "retroactive invalidation" rule operates in the same manner as the rule applicable to a financing statement that lapses.[129]

Although a person that becomes a purchaser of the collateral for value during the grace period gets the benefit of the retroactive invalidation rule if lapse occurs, it bears the risk that the secured party might reperfect after the purchaser searches the filings but before the grace period ends. Again, using our example, suppose Debtor, after moving to State B, applies for a loan from Finance Company, which makes the loan and takes a security interest in Debtor's inventory and equipment after searching State B's filing system 0and finding no financing statement covering the collateral. If Bank perfects in State B before the end of the grace period, it will have priority over Finance Company. Similarly, suppose Debtor sells a piece of equipment to Buyer, which searches in State B and finds nothing. If Bank reperfects during the grace period, it will have priority over Buyer.[130] The grace period represents a compromise between the interests of third parties and perfected secured parties, and it is not totally fair to either group. A filing is needed in State B because that is where third parties will naturally search.[131] However, Bank needs time to learn of the change of location and perfect in State B. Finance Company and Buyer can protect themselves by inquiring

---

125. U.C.C. § 9-308(a).
126. U.C.C. § 9-316(h).
127. U.C.C. § 9-316(b).
128. *Id.*
129. *See* § 5.06[A], *supra.*
130. Unless disclaimed, Buyer will have a cause of action against Debtor for breach of the Article 2 warranty of title. U.C.C. § 2-312.
131. Filing in State B will not be necessary if Bank takes possession of its collateral after the move, thereby perfecting its security interest in State B and providing notice to third parties. If the change of location constitutes a default under its security agreement with Debtor and as a result Bank repossessed its collateral, the repossession would also constitute perfection by possession.

about Debtor's location during the four months preceding their search (and hopefully obtaining a truthful answer).

[2] Possessory Security Interests

A grace period is not needed for security interests perfected by possession. The law governing perfection of a possessory security interest is the law of the jurisdiction in which the collateral is located,[132] and the secured party can prevent a change of location. If, for some reason, the collateral is moved to another jurisdiction while the secured party retains possession, the new jurisdiction's law will govern perfection, but the secured party will continue to be perfected by possession under that jurisdiction's version of Article 9.[133]

[B] Transferees and New Debtors

[1] Transferees

Suppose Bank has a security interest all of Manufacturer's equipment that is perfected by filing, and Manufacturer sells a piece of equipment to Buyer without Bank's having authorized the sale free of its security interest. The term "debtor" refers to a person with an interest in the collateral, and after the sale, Buyer is the debtor with regard to the purchased equipment.[134] The general rule on continuation of perfection is that a filed financing statement remains effective with respect to collateral disposed of and in which a security interest continues,[135] but an exception applies if Manufacturer and Buyer are located in different jurisdictions. Because Buyer is now the debtor, perfection is governed by the jurisdiction of its location.[136] That jurisdiction's version of Section 9-316(a) provides Bank with temporary automatic perfection, just as it would have provided Bank with that type of protection if Manufacturer had changed its location to the new jurisdiction.[137] Rather than a four-month grace period, however, Bank has one year to reperfect in the new jurisdiction (unless its filed financing statement would lapse sooner).

As in the case of a debtor's change of location, a continuation statement filed in the original jurisdiction after the transfer will be ineffective to continue perfection as to the transferred piece of equipment. Also as in the case of a debtor's relocation, if Bank does not reperfect in the new jurisdiction during the grace period, its security interest becomes unperfected prospectively and is deemed never to have been perfected as against a purchaser of the collateral for value. If the grace period lapses and Buyer

---

132. U.C.C. § 9-301(2). *See* § 9.02[B], *supra*.

133. U.C.C. § 9-316(c).

134. U.C.C. § 9-102(a)(28)(A).

135. U.C.C. § 9-507(a). *See* § 5.03[C][2][b], *supra*.

136. U.C.C. § 9-301(1).

137. For discussion of Section 9-316(a) in the context of a change of debtor location, see § 9.04[A][1], *supra*.

did not know of Bank's security interest when it gave value and took delivery of the equipment, it will have priority over Bank even though it was subordinate at the time of purchase.[138] Bank will also be unperfected for purposes of priority contests with other purchasers for value.

Bank may reperfect in the new jurisdiction by filing or by taking possession of the equipment. By acquiring collateral in which a security interest continues, Buyer is deemed to have authorized the filing of an initial financing statement covering the purchased equipment and, if necessary, an amendment covering identifiable proceeds.[139] Bank must be careful in filing against Buyer; its security interest is limited to the purchased equipment, and Bank is not statutorily authorized to use the kind of broad description that it no doubt used in its filing against Manufacturer.[140]

[2] New Debtors

The general rule governing perfection by filing against a new debtor is similar to the rule that applies if an event causes the name on a financing statement to become seriously misleading.[141] For example, suppose Corporation A grants Bank a security interest in existing and after-acquired inventory and that Bank perfects by filing. Corporation A subsequently merges into Corporation B, which qualifies as a new debtor.[142] Bank thus has a security interest in three distinct pools of inventory: (1) inventory that Corporation A transferred to Corporation B, (2) inventory held by Corporation B at the time it became a new debtor, and (3) inventory acquired by Corporation B after it became a new debtor. As to inventory in Pool 1, the transferee rules discussed in the preceding material apply. The inventory in Pools 2 and 3 are subject to the new-debtor perfection rules. If the two corporations are located in the same jurisdiction and the difference between their names causes Bank's financing statement to become seriously misleading, the financing statement is nevertheless effective to perfect Bank's security interest in the inventory held by Corporation B at the time it became a new debtor (i.e., the inventory in Pool 2) and inventory acquired by Corporation B within four months thereafter.[143] Bank must file an initial financing statement indicating Corporation B as a debtor to be perfected as to inventory acquired by it more than four months after it became a new debtor. By becoming a new debtor, Corporation B authorizes the filing of an initial financing statement covering the collateral described in Bank's security agreement with Corporation A and, if necessary, an amendment covering proceeds.[144]

---

138. U.C.C. § 9-317(b).

139. U.C.C. § 9-509(c).

140. Bank can also perfect in the new jurisdiction by possession. If the sale by Manufacturer constituted a default under the security agreement, Bank has a right to repossess the transferred equipment and would be perfected by the repossession.

141. *See* § 5.03[C][2][b], *supra*.

142. For discussion of the factors relevant to determining whether Corporation B qualifies as a new debtor, see § 5.03[C][2][b], *supra*.

143. U.C.C. § 9-508(b).

144. U.C.C. § 9-509(b).

Now suppose the corporations are located in different jurisdictions. As to the transferred inventory (Pool 1), Section 9-316(a), discussed in the preceding material, provides Bank with a four-month grace period[145] to reperfect in the new jurisdiction. As to the other two groups of inventory, however, the 1998 revision originally did not provide a grace period, meaning that Bank would be unperfected as to inventory held by Corporation B and after-acquired inventory until it files an initial financing statement in the jurisdiction in which Corporation B is located. The 2010 amendments contain a provision that gives a secured party the same four-month protection for new debtors located in a jurisdiction different from that of the original debtor that it has for new debtors located in the same jurisdiction.[146]

[C] Goods Subject to a Certificate-of-Title Act

As discussed previously,[147] in the case of goods subject to a certificate-of-title act, Section 9-301's choice-of-law rules govern perfection until the goods become covered by a certificate of title.[148] However, subject to an exception for goods that are inventory,[149] the secured party cannot perfect using any of the normal Article 9 methods; rather, the secured party must comply with the requirements of a certificate-of-title act,[150] although not necessarily the certificate-of-title act to which the goods are subject.[151] This situation inevitably requires that an application for a certificate of title be made to a governmental authority that issues certificates for goods of the kind involved in the transaction. With delivery of a valid application to such an authority and tender of the applicable fee,[152] the goods "become covered" by a certificate of title even though issuance of the actual certificate will not occur until later.[153] The moment the goods become covered by a jurisdiction's certificate of title, that jurisdiction's law governs perfection and priority.[154] In some jurisdictions, delivery of a valid application and tender of the fee constitutes perfection; in others, perfection occurs only with issuance of a

---

145. The grace period is shorter if the financing statement would have lapsed in the original jurisdiction before the grace period ends. U.C.C. §9-316(a).

146. U.C.C. §9-316(i).

147. See §9.03, supra.

148. For discussion of perfection under a certificate-of-title act generally, including discussion of what it means to become covered by a certificate of title, see §9.03, supra.

149. U.C.C. §9-311(d). See §9.03, supra. Also, perfection may be accomplished by possession in limited circumstances involving a change in the governing law. See U.C.C. §9-313(b), discussed infra this subsection.

150. U.C.C. §9-311(b).

151. U.C.C. §9-303(a). See §9.03, supra.

152. For convenience, subsequent references to an application for a certificate of title will assume tender of the applicable fee.

153. A certificate of title must, by definition, indicate the security interest as a condition or result of its obtaining priority over the rights of a lien creditor with respect to the collateral. U.C.C. §9-102(a)(10).

154. Unlike Section 9-301, discussed in §9.02, supra, Section 9-303 does not bifurcate the law governing perfection and the law governing priority.

certificate of title indicating the security interest. Analysis of the movement of goods from one title state to another title state, or from a non-title state to a title state, requires a clear understanding of the distinction between becoming covered and becoming perfected. As shown below, movement from a title state to a non-title state does not present a risk to a secured party.

Suppose Bank takes a security interest in Debtor's boat and delivers a valid application for a certificate of title to the appropriate authority in State A. State A's law now governs perfection and will continue to do so until the goods cease to be covered by the certificate.[155] This event will not happen until the earlier of the time the certificate ceases to be effective in State A or the time the boat becomes covered by a certificate in another jurisdiction.[156] Assuming the certificate remains effective in State A until Bank surrenders it or satisfaction of the secured obligation, Bank will remain perfected until a valid application for a certificate of title is made to the appropriate authority in another jurisdiction.[157] It does not matter whether Debtor moves to a state that does not have a certificate-of-title act for boats or moves to a state that has such an act but does not apply for a new certificate; without delivery of a valid application in another jurisdiction, State A's law governs and Bank is perfected.[158] Even if Debtor moves to a state with a certificate-of-title act for boats and wishes to comply with the act, it will have difficulty in delivering a *valid* application to the appropriate authority in that state without Bank's cooperation because certificate-of-title laws generally provide that an application must be accompanied by an existing certificate of title.

Suppose Debtor moves to State B and delivers an application for a certificate of title to the appropriate authority in that state. The application is accompanied by the State A certificate, which Bank is willing to surrender to facilitate the issuance of a new certificate. State B's law now governs, but if that law defers perfection until issuance of a certificate of title indicating Bank's security interest, the question whether Bank remains perfected in the interim arises. State B's version of Section 9-316 answers the question differently for lien creditors and purchasers of the boat for value. Subsection (d) provides that Bank remains perfected until its security interest would have become unperfected under the law of State A if the boat had not become covered by a certificate of title in State B, however long that might be. Subsection (e) creates an exception that applies only in the case of a purchaser for value. Under the exception, Bank's security interest will become unperfected as against a purchaser for value if its security interest

---

155. U.C.C. § 9-303(c).

156. U.C.C. § 9-303(b).

157. *See In re* Baker, 56 U.C.C. Rep. Serv. 2d 257 (W.D. Wis. 2005), *aff'd*, 430 F.3d 858 (7th Cir. 2005) (New Mexico law governed perfection as to goods covered by that state's certificate of title, even though debtor had moved to Wisconsin and more than three years had elapsed, because there had not been an application for a Wisconsin certificate).

158. This policy choice places an enormous burden on searchers in states that do not have certificate-of-title laws for assets like boats and mobile homes.

is not perfected in State B[159] before the earlier of the time the State A certificate would cease to be effective under the law of that state or the expiration of four months after the governing law shifts to State B. If Bank's security interest becomes unperfected, it will be deemed never to have been perfected against a purchaser for value. In other words, as long as Bank's State A certificate would be effective if that state's law continued to govern, Bank need not worry about a lien creditor, including a bankruptcy trustee.[160] However, if the four-month grace period expires and it has not perfected in State B, it is at risk of losing a priority contest with a buyer of or lender against the boat, even if the buyer or lender acquired its interest during the grace period.[161]

If each state's certificate-of-title act provided that perfection occurred upon delivery to the appropriate authority of a valid application for a certificate indicating a security interest, there would be no loss of perfection when a secured party perfected under the certificate-of-title act of one state facilitated the debtor's application for a certificate in another state. However, variations in existing acts can cause problems. For example, suppose State B's certificate-of-title act defers perfection until issuance of a certificate indicating Bank's security interest. If more than four months elapse between the time of the application and the time a new certificate is issued, or if the certificate when issued fails to indicate the security interest because of a mistake by the issuing authority, Bank is at risk from both subsequent and existing purchasers for value. It is not at risk, however, from lien creditors. The Comments stress that a security interest perfected under the certificate-of-title act of one state remains perfected even if the existing certificate is surrendered and the law of the state that issued it provides that a security interest becomes unperfected upon surrender of the certificate.[162]

The preceding discussion involves a shift in governing law from one title state to another title state. Assume now that State A does not have a certificate-of-title act governing boats, but State B does. Assume further that Bank's security interest is perfected in State A by filing a financing statement[163] before the boat becomes covered by

---

159. Perfection may be accomplished by becoming perfected under State B's certificate-of-title law or by taking possession of the boat. Although perfection by possession is generally unavailable for goods subject to a certificate-of-title act, a secured party faced with the risk from purchasers of the collateral for value created by Section 9-316 may perfect by taking possession of the goods. U.C.C. §§ 9-316(e), 9-313(b).

160. See In re Owen, 69 U.C.C. Rep. Serv. 2d 896 (Bankr. D. Idaho 2009) (bankruptcy trustee, ignoring Section 9-316(d), argued that security interest perfected by California certificate of title became unperfected upon application for Idaho certificate because under Idaho law perfection does not occur until issuance of certificate; court notes that perfection in Idaho occurred within four months but that this was irrelevant since trustee was lien creditor and secured party remained perfected under Idaho law without limitation).

161. For discussion of other "retroactive invalidation" rules applicable to purchasers for value, see §§ 5.06[A] (lapse of financing statement), supra, 9.04[A][1] (change in governing law caused by change of debtor's location), supra, and 9.04[C] (change in governing law caused by transfer to a person that thereby becomes a debtor), infra.

162. U.C.C. § 9-316, Comment 5, Example 8.

163. Perfection might also occur automatically because the secured party has a purchase-money security interest in a boat that qualifies as consumer goods.

a certificate of title in State B. Section 9-316(d) and (e) are every bit as operative in this situation as they are in a title-state-to-title-state situation. In other words, as long as the financing statement would be effective in State A if the boat had not become covered by a certificate of title in State B, Bank's security interest remains perfected under the law of State B as against a lien creditor and remains perfected for four months as against a purchaser for value.

In addition to the protection for purchasers for value provided by Section 9-316(e), Article 9 provides a special priority rule in Section 9-337 that protects certain buyers and secured parties that rely on a "clean" certificate of title.[164] The rule is an exception to the ordinary rule subordinating buyers to perfected security interests. To illustrate, suppose that during the time Bank's security interest in Debtor's boat remains perfected[165] against purchasers for value under State B's version of Section 9-316(e), State B issues a certificate of title that neither indicates Bank's security interest nor contains a statement that the boat might be subject to security interests not indicated on the certificate.[166] To qualify for priority, a buyer must give value and receive delivery of the boat after issuance of the clean certificate and without knowledge of the security interest and must not be in the business of selling goods of the kind.[167] A secured party must be without knowledge of Bank's security interest. Section 9-337 is only necessary if Bank reperfects in State B before the end of the grace period; if Bank fails to do so, Section 9-316(e)'s retroactive invalidation rule protects a buyer or secured party.

---

164. U.C.C. § 9-337(1).

165. The special priority rule of Section 9-337 applies without regard to the method of perfection used in the first state. Thus, it applies in both title-state-to-title-state and non-title-state-to-title state situations.

166. This situation will be rare if in a title-state-to-title-state situation in which the title issued by the first state is surrendered to the second state. The second state might inadvertently fail to indicate on its certificate a security interest known to it, or the debtor might through fraud induce the issuance of a clean certificate. The situation is more likely to occur if the first state is a non-title state and perfection there is accomplished by a method permitted by Article 9.

167. See Metzger v. Americredit Fin. Serv., Inc., 273 Ga. App. 453, 615 S.E.2d 120, 56 U.C.C. Rep. Serv. 2d 825 (2005) (buyer met all requirements after car originally titled in New York was re-titled in Georgia with a certificate that did not reflect the security interest due to a data-entry error).

Part IV

Priorities

Synopsis

[A] The Priority Concept
[B] Understanding Priorities

[A] The Priority Concept

Much of the discussion thus far has addressed the various mechanisms by which a secured party can attain and retain perfected status. Whether a secured party is perfected has significant consequences in the event of a competing third-party claim to the collateral but is irrelevant to the rights of the parties to the security agreement *inter se*. For example, if Debtor grants Bank a security interest in a car and then defaults, Bank can foreclose on the car even if it is unperfected. Perfection is relevant only when a third party asserts a claim to collateral that competes with a secured party's security interest.

A wide variety of third parties might assert a claim to the collateral of a secured party, including another secured party asserting a security interest in the same collateral; a person that buys, leases, or licenses the collateral from the debtor; and a creditor with a type of nonconsensual lien on the collateral, including a trustee in bankruptcy. Perfection generally enhances a secured party's position against these claimants, but, as the discussion in the next few chapters demonstrates, a secured party's position may not be unassailable even with perfection. Also, different methods of perfection may be available for a particular type of collateral and may provide different levels of protection.

A simple illustration demonstrates the importance of prevailing in a priority conflict. Assume Debtor borrows money from Bank and grants Bank a security interest in all its equipment, including after-acquired equipment. Later, without authorization, Debtor sells an item of equipment to Buyer. If Bank perfects its security interest before Buyer gives value and receives delivery of the item, Buyer takes it subject to Bank's security interest. This means that Bank can foreclose on the item if Debtor defaults on its obligation, just as it can foreclose on the items of equipment still owned by Debtor. By contrast, if Buyer gives value and takes delivery without knowledge of the security interest and before Bank perfects, Buyer takes the item free of Bank's security interest. If Debtor defaults, Bank's right to foreclose is limited to the items still owned by Debtor.[1]

As mentioned above, perfection does not always guarantee priority. To illustrate, let's change the prior example so that Bank takes and perfects a security interest in all Debtor's inventory, including after-acquired inventory, as collateral for its loan. Buyer later buys an item of inventory from Debtor in a normal, everyday type of transaction. Even though Bank is perfected, Buyer will be granted a special status—buyer in ordinary course of business—and will take the item free of Bank's security interest.[2]

Priority battles arise whenever two (or more) parties assert claims to the same asset. Many of these conflicts do not involve a secured party, such as competing claims between a buyer and a lessor of the same goods, or between a mortgagee and a trustee in bankruptcy competing for a parcel of real property. All of these conflicts are outside the scope of Article 9 and of this book. Article 9 governs priority conflicts between secured parties or between a secured party and a claimant whose rights in the secured party's collateral are grounded in another area of the law.

[B] Understanding Priorities

Understanding Article 9 priorities requires more than an appreciation of each individual rule. It also requires a recognition of the relationship among the various priority rules and how they operate together to cover entire categories of cases. Certain themes run through the priority provisions. The fundamental principle of prioritization is "first in time, first in right," under which the party that takes a specified action first prevails. There are numerous exceptions to this fundamental principle, and they also follow certain themes, particularly in cases of what are called "purchase-money security interests."[3] Understanding Article 9 priorities requires an understanding of the overall picture as well as each individual rule. Such an understanding inevitably requires an appreciation of the policies that underlie the provisions.

Article 9's priority rules, with good reason, are quite precise. Contracts generally affect only the contracting parties, and mechanisms are available for resolving ambiguities, but the broader contracts standards are not workable in the secured transactions priority context because the third parties whose rights are at stake are not parties to the security agreement. Article 9's precise priority rules delineate and protect the rights of both the secured party and the third-party claimants.

The starting point for priority issues is the residual rule governing the general validity of a security agreement, which makes it effective according to its terms "between the parties, against purchasers of the collateral, and against creditors."[4] This rule favors

---

1. The rights of a buyer in this situation are discussed in § 12.03[A], *infra*.

2. The rights of a buyer in ordinary course of business and the policy rationale for the special treatment given such a buyer are discussed in § 11.03[A], *infra*.

3. Purchase-money security interests are discussed generally in § 10.04[A], *infra*.

4. U.C.C. § 9-201. *See* § 12.01, *infra*.

secured parties in priority conflicts, and under it, a security interest prevails even if it is unperfected. The baseline established by the residual rule is subject to any exceptions that the Code otherwise provides, and the exceptions are numerous. The discussion of priorities in the next few chapters of this book is essentially a discussion of the exceptions to the residual rule.

The resolution of an Article 9 priority contest always involves at least the following basic steps. The first step is to determine the status of each of the competing claimants. One of them will be a secured party; the other could also be a secured party, or it could be a person asserting a different type of claim. The second step is to determine whether the secured party is perfected and, if so, when perfection occurred. In the case of a priority contest between secured parties, perfection will have to be analyzed for each of them. The third step is to apply the appropriate Article 9 priority rule to decide the outcome of the conflict. Other factors sometimes come into play as well. For example, there are special priority rules for purchase-money security interests, and if different methods of perfection are available, the method chosen by the secured party may affect its priority rights.

Chapter 10

Priority Contests: Between Secured Parties

Synopsis

§ 10.01 First to File or Perfect— § 9-322(a)

If a debtor grants a security interest in the same collateral to two or more secured parties, the secured parties have competing claims to the collateral. Section 9-322 generally governs priorities among conflicting security interests in the same collateral. Subsection (a) states the general rules of that section as follows:

> Except as otherwise provided in this section, priority among conflicting security interests and agricultural liens in the same collateral is determined according to the following rules:
>
> (1) Conflicting perfected security interests and agricultural liens rank according to priority in time of filing or perfection. Priority dates from the earlier of the time a filing covering the collateral is first made or the security interest or agricultural lien is first perfected, if there is no period thereafter when there is neither filing nor perfection.
>
> (2) A perfected security interest or agricultural lien has priority over a conflicting unperfected security interest or agricultural lien.
>
> (3) The first security interest or agricultural lien to attach or become effective has priority if conflicting security interests and agricultural liens are unperfected.

Paragraph (3) rests on the basic first-in-time, first-in-right principle but is rarely invoked because an unperfected secured party that faces a priority dispute with another unperfected secured party can simply perfect and attain priority under paragraph (2).[5] The rule of paragraph (2)—that a perfected secured party defeats an unperfected secured party—is straightforward and obvious. The most commonly applied priority rule is in paragraph (1), since most secured parties take care to perfect properly. Under paragraph (1), priority is awarded to the secured party that is the first to have filed a financing statement covering the collateral or to have perfected its security interest.[6] Understanding this rule requires understanding a concept that initially may not be intuitive: the fact that a person has filed a financing statement does not necessarily mean that the person has a perfected security interest as a result.

---

5. *See* U.C.C. § 9-322, Comment 4, Example 2; Engelsma v. Superior Prods. Mfg. Co., 298 Minn. 77, 212 N.W.2d 884, 13 U.C.C. Rep. Serv. 944 (1973).

6. Board of Cnty. Comm'rs, Cnty. of Adams v. Berkeley Village, 40 Colo. App. 431, 580 P.2d 1251, 24 U.C.C. Rep Serv. 975 (1978) (first secured party to perfect by filing had priority over both secured party that filed later and creditor that never filed); S. Lotman & Son, Inc. v. Southeastern Fin. Corp., 288 Ala. 547, 263 So. 2d 499, 11 U.C.C. Rep. Serv. 218 (1972) (B took security interest; A took competing security interest and filed; B filed later; A won as first to file and first to perfect); St. Paul Mercury Ins. Co. v. Merchants & Marine Bank, 882 So. 2d 766, 54 U.C.C. Rep. Serv. 2d 671 (Miss. 2004) (second secured party that filed a financing statement had priority over the first secured party that did not perfect, irrespective of whether the second secured party had knowledge of the first secured party's interest prior to extending its own loan).

Paragraph (1) does not simply recognize filing as the predominant method of perfecting a security interest; it grants a special priority advantage to filing that is not available through any alternative method of perfection.[7] Filing an initial financing statement does not result in perfection if attachment has not occurred. Perfection requires satisfaction of all the applicable steps required for both attachment and perfection.[8] Nevertheless, Article 9 explicitly permits a prospective secured party (if properly authorized) to "pre-file" by filing an initial financing statement prior to attachment.[9] A secured party that pre-files is not perfected at the moment of filing, but if attachment later occurs it will become perfected immediately as long as the collateral is of a type capable of perfection by filing. Moreover, the secured party who pre-files will have priority over another secured party that files or perfects after the pre-filing.[10] The pre-filer has, in effect, staked its claim to the collateral. Later-in-time secured parties should find the pre-filer's financing statement in the exercise of due diligence and take steps to protect themselves.

The significance of the priority advantage associated with filing becomes apparent when comparing the position of a secured party that files prior to attachment with what its position would have been had it taken possession of the collateral prior to attachment. Assume that SP-1 files a financing statement before it enters into a security agreement with a prospective debtor. SP-2 afterward takes and perfects a security interest in the same property described in SP-1's financing statement. SP-1 and the debtor subsequently complete the steps necessary for SP-1 to acquire a security interest. If the debtor later defaults on both loans, SP-1 will have priority in the collateral. Even though SP-2 perfected first, the pre-filing by SP-1 provides it with priority.[11]

In contrast, if SP-1 had taken possession of the collateral instead of pre-filing and SP-2 had perfected by filing before SP-1's security interest attached, SP-1 would not have priority. For priority based on possession, SP-1 would have had to perfect its security interest before SP-2 either filed or perfected its security interest.[12] Of course, debtors generally don't part with possessions before entering into a security agreement,

---

7. Priority in favor of the first secured party to file requires the filing to be made properly. Mountain Credit v. Michiana Lumber & Supply, Inc., 31 Colo. App. 112, 498 P.2d 967, 10 U.C.C. Rep. Serv. 1347 (1972) (defendant's financing statement was filed first but in wrong office). *See also* U.C.C. § 9-322, Comment 4.

8. U.C.C. § 9-308(a). *See* § 4.02, *supra*.

9. U.C.C. § 9-502(4). *See* § 5.04, *supra*.

10. *In re* McCorhill Pub., Inc., 86 B.R. 783, 8 U.C.C. Rep. Serv. 2d 203 (Bankr. S.D.N.Y. 1988). The priority also extends to after-acquired property within the scope of the secured party's interest. Wade Credit Corp. v. Borg-Warner Acceptance Corp., 83 Or. App. 479, 732 P.2d 76, 3 U.C.C. Rep. Serv. 2d 289 (1987).

11. Enterprises Now, Inc. v. Citizens & S. Dev. Corp., 135 Ga. App. 602, 218 S.E.2d 309, 17 U.C.C. Rep. Serv. 1114 (1975) (having filed first, appellee had priority over appellant even though appellant perfected first).

12. Bank of Okla., City Plaza v. Martin, 744 P.2d 218, 5 U.C.C. Rep Serv. 2d 222 (Okla. Ct. App. 1987) (first to record security interest in airplane with FAA); Barry v. Bank of N.H., N.A., 113 N.H. 158, 304 A.2d 879, 12 U.C.C. Rep. Serv. 732 (1973) (plaintiff perfected at the latest when it took possession of collateral).

and secured parties thus rarely if ever "pre-possess." Nevertheless, the point remains: the advantage of taking the step necessary for perfection before attachment occurs only gives an advantage under Article 9 to a secured party that files a financing statement.

The Comments provide the reason for giving special priority protection to filing, even filing before attachment: "The justification for determining priority by order of filing lies in the necessity of protecting the filing system—that is, of allowing the first secured party who has filed to make subsequent advances without each time having to check for subsequent filings as a condition of protection."[13] The availability of this special protection and the reasoning that supports it explain why lenders commonly insist on authorization from a prospective debtor to file an initial financing statement as a condition to finalization of a secured financing transaction.[14] The lender can pre-file and then search the filing system to make certain that there are no competing filings covering the anticipated collateral. It then can finalize its transaction with the debtor free of concerns that the debtor could be dealing with another lender that might obtain priority by perfecting a security interest before the first lender's security interest attaches.[15]

If a party that pre-files a financing statement later makes a loan but never enters into a security agreement with the debtor, should that party nevertheless prevail against a secured party that files later? Although the general rule awards priority to the secured party that filed first, it does not apply in this situation because it only governs priority battles between perfected secured parties. If the first party to file never enters into a security agreement, that party never becomes a secured party, and its filing is irrelevant for purposes of the priority rule.[16]

Even though a pre-filed financing statement doesn't perfect a security interest if attachment never occurs, it will remain effective for five years unless its effectiveness is ended by a termination statement.[17] For example, suppose Bank-1 and Manufacturer are contemplating a transaction in which Bank-1 will make a loan secured by all Manufacturer's equipment, including after-acquired equipment, and Bank-1 properly pre-files. Bank-1 decides not to make the loan. Bank-2 makes the loan and takes and

---

13. U.C.C. § 9-322, Comment 4. Enterprises Now, Inc. v. Citizens & S. Dev. Corp., 135 Ga. App. 602, 218 S.E. 2d 309, 17 U.C.C. Rep. Serv. 1114 (1975).

14. Pre-filing requires the prospective debtor's authorization in a signed record. U.C.C. § 9-509(a)(1).

15. Pre-filing protects a secured party from later-filing-or-perfecting secured parties but not from other claimants. For example, a person that buys the collateral before attachment need not worry about a pre-filed financing statement, even if the person knows of it. U.C.C. § 9-317(b) (knowledge of a security interest—not of a pre-filing—subordinates the buyer).

16. Although it reached the correct result, the Tenth Circuit could have been more accurate by recognizing these principles. Transport Equip. Co. v. Guaranty State Bank, 518 F.2d 377, 17 U.C.C. Rep. Serv. 1 (10th Cir. 1975). See also Wachovia Bank Nat. Ass'n v. EnCap Golf Holdings, LLC, 690 F. Supp. 2d 311, 72 U.C.C. Rep. Serv. 2d 352 (S.D.N.Y. 2010) (court construed the insurer's argument that the interests of the secured parties were unperfected as a red herring because a creditor without a security interest or a lien does not have any claim to specific property of the debtor).

17. U.C.C. § 9-513, discussed in § 5.06[A], supra. Termination statements are discussed generally in § 5.06[C], supra. The utility of a termination statement is also discussed in the next section in the context of future advances.

perfects by filing a security interest in all Manufacturer's equipment, including after-acquired equipment, but without insisting that Bank-1 terminate its filing. Four years after filing its financing statement, Bank-1 makes a loan to Manufacturer and takes a security interest in all Manufacturer's equipment, including after-acquired equipment. Bank-1 has priority over Bank-2 under the first-to-file-or-perfect rule. Bank-2 should have insisted on a termination statement.[18]

The general rule confers priority on a perfected secured party that was the first to file or perfect only if there is no period thereafter during which there is neither filing nor perfection.[19] In other words, to retain the advantage of being the first to file or perfect, the secured party's filing or perfection must be continuous.[20] In the example in the preceding paragraph, the result would have been different if Bank-1 had waited more than five years after pre-filing to take its security interest in Manufacturer's equipment. Even if it filed a new initial financing statement in connection with the transaction, there would have been a gap between the time the first financing statement lapsed and the time the second financing statement became effective. For purposes of the first-to-file-or-perfect rule, Bank-1 could not ignore the gap and use its pre-filing to establish priority.

The first-to-file-or-perfect rule is a pure-race rule—the first secured party to either file or perfect prevails without regard to knowledge.[21] For example, suppose SP-1 has an unperfected security interest in Debtor's equipment and Debtor applies to SP-2 for a loan secured by the same equipment. SP-2 can attain priority by filing or perfecting before SP-1 does either, even if SP-2 knows of SP-1's security interest.

In applying the first-to-file-or-perfect rule, bear in mind that the term "secured party" includes "a person to which accounts, chattel paper, payment intangibles, or promissory notes have been sold."[22] For example, if Debtor sells its accounts to Factor and then fraudulently resells them or uses them as collateral for a loan, Factor and the

---

18. If Bank-2 was comfortable with Bank-1's acquiring a security interest in Manufacturer's equipment as long as it had priority over Bank-1, it could have protected itself by entering into a subordination agreement with Bank-1 as an alternative to obtaining a filed termination statement. U.C.C. § 9-339. Article 9's priority rules are default rules and may be changed by agreement. The utility of a subordination agreement is discussed further in the next section in the context of future advances.

19. Stearns Mfg. Co., Inc. v. National Bank & Trust Co. of Cent. Pa., 12 U.C.C. Rep. Serv. 189 (Pa. Ct. Com. Pl. 1972) (defendant attained priority when plaintiff's previously filed financing statement lapsed).

20. See U.C.C. § 9-322, Comment 4, Example 2.

21. Knowledge that a prior party has taken an unperfected security interest is irrelevant in the priority determination. U.C.C. § 9-322, Comment 4. State of Alaska, Div. of Agric. v. Fowler, 611 P.2d 58, 29 U.C.C. Rep. Serv. 696 (Alaska 1980). Some priority provisions of Article 9 do refer to knowledge or notice, but not these general rules.

22. U.C.C. § 9-102(a)(73)(D). The definition implicitly applies only to buyers of payment rights in transactions within the scope of Article 9 because the Section 1-201(b)(35) definition of "security interest" includes the interest of a buyer of such payment rights only if the buyer acquires the rights in a transaction subject to Article 9. Section 9-109(d)(4)-(7) sets forth excluded transactions. See § 1.06[F][1], supra. See also § 12.03[A], infra, discussing buyers of payment rights that acquire their interests in transactions excluded from the scope of Article 9. The security interest of a buyer of pay-

competing buyer or lender are both secured parties with priority determined under the ordinary rules governing priority between secured parties.[23] An earlier discussion in this book explains the rationale for including sales of these types of payment rights within the scope of Article 9.[24]

§ 10.02 Future Advances—
§§ 9-323, 9-322

Article 9 includes a separate section that deals with future advances,[25] but the section does not include the general rule on competing security interests concerning future advances. The general rule of Section 9-322 discussed in the preceding section governs most cases concerning priority between secured parties with respect to future advances.[26] Priority under the first-to-file-or-perfect rule as to the initial advance gives the secured party priority against another secured party for all subsequent advances secured by its collateral.

Consider the following hypothetical. SP-1 loans Debtor $50,000, takes a security interest in Debtor's equipment, and files a financing statement, all on Day 1. SP-2 loans Debtor $75,000, takes a security interest in the same equipment, and files a financing statement, all on Day 20. SP-1 loans Debtor an additional $40,000 on Day 30. Under Section 9-322(a)(1), SP-1 clearly has priority with respect to its initial loan of $50,000. Does SP-1 also have priority with respect to its later $40,000 loan? The question cannot be answered without first characterizing SP-1's status with respect to the second loan, and the facts as presented are insufficient to establish that status. There are three possible scenarios. Under two of them, SP-1 is a secured creditor with respect to the second loan and prevails under the general rule. Under the third scenario, SP-1 is an unsecured creditor with respect to the second loan, and that loan is thus outside the scope of the provisions governing priority between secured parties.

In the first scenario, SP-1 made the second loan on Day 30 pursuant to a future-advances clause in the Day 1 security agreement between SP-1 and Debtor. The effect of the future-advances clause is to make SP-1 a secured party with respect to the second loan in the same collateral that secures the first loan. Because SP-1 filed a financ-

---

ment intangibles or promissory notes perfects automatically at the time the buyer's interest attaches. See § 7.02[B], *supra*.

23. Rentenbach Constructors, Inc. v. CM Partnership, 181 N.C. App. 268, 639 S.E.2d 16, 61 U.C.C. Rep. Serv. 2d 598 (N.C. Ct. App. 2007) (bank that perfected its security interest in accounts six months before a factor perfected its security interest in the same accounts had priority).

24. See § 1.05, *supra*.

25. U.C.C. § 9-323. For discussion of a secured party's priority in future advances against a lien creditor or a buyer or lessee of goods, see § 12.02[C] (lien creditors) and §§ 12.03[C] and 11.03[A][3] (buyers and lessees of goods), *infra*.

26. U.C.C. § 9-323, Comment 3.

ing statement that preceded filing or perfection by SP-2, SP-1 prevails over SP-2 with respect to both the first and second loans.[27]

In the second scenario, the Day 1 security agreement does not contain a future-advances clause, but SP-1 and Debtor enter a new security agreement in connection with the second loan on Day 30 that describes the same collateral as their original Day 1 security agreement. The second security agreement clearly gives SP-1 secured status with respect to the second loan. The issues are whether the security interest created by the Day 30 security agreement is perfected and whether SP-1 has priority over SP-2 with respect to the second loan. As to perfection, as long as the financing statement filed by SP-1 in connection with the original security agreement remains effective, it will perfect a later security interest in the same collateral.[28]

This priority issue proved to be controversial under original Article 9. The decision by a Rhode Island court in *Coin-O-Matic Service Co. v. Rhode Island Hospital Trust Co.*[29] epitomized a minority position that attracted considerable attention. The original parties in that case entered into a new security agreement with the advance of the subsequent loan because, at the time of their first loan, they had not contemplated additional advances by the secured party. The court held that the first-to-file-or-perfect rule did not apply if the original security agreement did not provide for future advances, and it concluded that the secured party did not have priority for the subsequent loan over a conflicting security interest perfected prior to the time of that loan.[30] Fortunately, most courts refused to follow the erroneous reasoning of the *Coin-O-Matic* case.[31] The drafters of the 1972 revisions to Article 9 rejected the decision and its progeny and, to emphasize their position, added language to the Comments that repudiated the decision.[32] A bankruptcy court in Rhode Island also later rejected the approach of *Coin-O-Matic* based on the changes stressed by the drafters.[33]

---

27. *In re* Leslie Brock & Sons, 147 B.R. 426, 21 U.C.C. Rep. Serv. 2d 154 (Bankr. S.D. Ohio 1992); *In re* Lombardo's Ravioli Kitchen, Inc., 70 U.C.C. Rep. Serv. 2d 418 (Bankr. D. Conn. 2009) (prior perfected secured party had priority in all subsequent advances on a line of credit, as well as the original loan, because the security agreement included a future-advances clause).

28. U.C.C. § 9-322(a)(1). First Nat'l Bank & Trust Co. of Vinita, Okla. v. Atlas Credit Corp., 417 F.2d 1081, 6 U.C.C. Rep. Serv. 1223 (10th Cir. 1969).

29. 3 U.C.C. Rep. Serv. 1112 (R.I. Super. Ct. 1966).

30. A few cases followed the same approach. ITT Indus. Credit Co. v. Union Bank & Trust Co., 615 S.W.2d 2, 30 U.C.C. Rep. Serv. 1701 (Ky. Ct. App. 1981) (future-advances clause required in security agreement to cover future advances). Some more recent decisions also suggested the need for a clause in the security agreement. *In re* Comprehensive Review Tech., Inc., 138 B.R. 195, 17 U.C.C. Rep. Serv. 2d 954 (Bankr. S.D. Ohio 1992).

31. *See, e.g.,* Provident Fin. Co. v. Beneficial Fin. Co., 36 N.C. App. 401, 245 S.E.2d 510, 24 U.C.C. Rep. Serv. 1332 (1978); *In re* Rivet, 299 F. Supp. 374, 6 U.C.C. Rep. Serv. 460 (E.D. Mich. 1969).

32. U.C.C. § 9-312, Comment 7 (1972 official text). The current version of Article 9 includes a comparable comment. U.C.C. § 9-323, Comment 3, Example 1.

33. *In re* Nason, 13 B.R. 984, 31 U.C.C. Rep. Serv. 1739 (Bankr. D.R.I. 1981). For consistent cases, see UNI Imports, Inc. v. Aparacor, Inc., 978 F.2d 984, 18 U.C.C. Rep. Serv. 2d 933 (7th Cir. 1992); State Bank of Sleepy Eye v. Krueger, 405 N.W.2d 491, 3 U.C.C. Rep. Serv. 2d 1145 (Minn. Ct. App. 1987).

Thus, if the Day 30 security agreement covers the same collateral that the Day 1 filed financing statement describes, SP-1 has priority for its second loan.[34] Although the subsequent loan is not a future advance but rather a new loan made contemporaneously with the new security agreement, SP-1 still prevails on the strength of the language and policy of the first-to-file-or-perfect rule. Earlier discussion of that rule[35] demonstrated that if SP-1 had pre-filed a financing statement and later entered into a security agreement with Debtor after SP-2 perfected its security interest, SP-1 would have attained priority as the first to file or perfect.[36] Conceptually, the relationship between SP-1's filed financing statement and its second security agreement with Debtor is no different merely because SP-1 also entered into an initial security agreement with Debtor contemporaneous with its filing.

The third possible scenario is that SP-1 made the $40,000 loan on Day 30 without the benefit of a future-advances clause in its Day 1 security agreement and without a entering into a subsequent security agreement with the debtor covering the same collateral. SP-1 then would be an unsecured creditor with respect to the second loan. SP-1 could not show that Debtor consented to attachment for the second loan, and thus the collateral described in the Day 1 security agreement would not also secure the Day 30 loan. The first-to-file-or-perfect rule would not apply because, beyond SP-1's initial loan, SP-2 would be the only secured party. A lender in SP-1's position, therefore, must either include a future-advances clause in its initial security agreement or remember to enter into another agreement to secure a subsequent loan.

The first-to-file-or-perfect rule has enormous practical consequences on secured financing. The reality is that a subordinate creditor does not have any certain safety.[37] If a debtor owes only $10,000 to a prior-perfected secured party and the value of the collateral exceeds $100,000, another lender might think it was safe to lend several thousand dollars against the remaining equity in the collateral. Subsequent advances from the first secured party, however, could encumber the remaining available equity. The second lender is not safe even if the original security agreement does not include a future-advances clause or, if the first secured party perfected by filing, even if the outstanding debt to the first secured party has been paid in full. All that must happen to undercut the second lender's position is for the first lender to make a subsequent advance and to enter into a new security agreement while the financing statement remains effective.

A prospective lender that wishes to make a loan to a debtor but wants to avoid these risks should follow one of three courses. If the debt to the first lender has been fully paid, the second lender should insist on the filing of a termination statement to end

---

34. Allis-Chalmers Credit Corp. v. Cheney Inv., Inc., 227 Kan. 4, 605 P.2d 525, 28 U.C.C. Rep. Serv. 574 (1980).

35. *See* § 10.01, *supra.*

36. U.C.C. § 9-322(a)(1). First Nat'l Bank & Trust Co. of Vinita, Okla. v. Atlas Credit Corp., 417 F.2d 1081, 6 U.C.C. Rep. Serv. 1223 (10th Cir. 1969).

37. *In re* Martin Grinding & Machine Works, Inc., 793 F.2d 592, 1 U.C.C. Rep. Serv. 2d 1329 (7th Cir. 1986) (not safe to loan against property described in prior financing statement).

any basis for further perfection based on the first lender's filing.[38] If the debtor still owes money to the first lender, the second lender could increase the amount of its loan, pay off the first lender, and require either an assignment of the first lender's rights[39] or a termination statement.[40] The third option is to negotiate with the first lender[41] for an agreement[42] in which the first lender agrees to subordinate itself with respect to any further loans that it might advance to the debtor.[43] Although such an agreement is not generally in the interest of the first lender, it might be attainable if the first lender would like to see a new infusion of capital into the debtor's operation or if the first lender is certain that it will not advance any more money to the debtor.[44]

The timing of an advance generally is not relevant to a priority conflict between secured parties: "[I]t is abundantly clear that the time when an advance is made plays no role in determining priorities among conflicting security interests except when a financing statement was not filed and the advance is the giving of value as the last step for attachment and perfection."[45] A special rule in Section 9-323(a), however,

---

38. Provident Fin. Co. v. Beneficial Fin. Co., 36 N.C. App. 401, 245 S.E.2d 510, 24 U.C.C. Rep. Serv. 1332 (1978) (defendant could have protected itself by insisting that a termination statement be filed but failed to do so). *See* § 5.06[C], *supra.*

39. *See* U.C.C. § 9-310(c) (assignee of perfected security interest need not file in its name to continue perfected status).

40. *In re* Bishop, 52 B.R. 470, 41 U.C.C. Rep. Serv. 1491 (Bankr. N.D. Ala. 1985) (bank received correspondence noting its payment of a prior-perfected finance company, but termination statement was not filed; court held that an enforceable subordination agreement was entered into with respect to the noted inventory but that it did not extend to after-acquired units).

41. Subordination agreements are generally entered into between two or more creditors. A secondary creditor that was not a party to a subordination agreement between the primary secured party and the debtor has been held to be a beneficiary of that agreement. *In re* Thorner Mfg. Co., Inc., 4 U.C.C. Rep Serv. 595 (Bankr. E.D. Pa. 1967).

42. A secured party's priority can also be subordinated through estoppel. Hillman's Equip., Inc. v. Central Realty, Inc., 144 Ind. App. 18, 242 N.E.2d 522, 5 U.C.C. Rep. Serv. 1160 (1968), *rev'd on other grounds*, 246 N.E.2d 383 (1969) (junior secured party changed his position in reliance on senior secured party's statement, prior to sale of collateral, that he would get his equipment).

43. "This article does not preclude subordination by agreement by a person entitled to priority." U.C.C. § 9-339. *See also In re* Smith, 77 B.R. 624, 5 U.C.C. Rep. Serv. 2d 496 (Bankr. N.D. Ohio 1987) (bank agreed to subordinate its lien on proceeds up to $8,000 per year for seven years). *But see* H. & Val J. Rothschild, Inc. v. Northwestern Nat'l Bank of St. Paul, 309 Minn. 35, 242 N.W.2d 844, 19 U.C.C. Rep Serv. 673 (1976) (telephone conversation in which parties assumed mistakenly that plaintiff had a prior claim did not subordinate defendant's claim). The security interest of a person entitled to priority under Article 9's priority rules cannot be subordinated by agreement unless that person is a party to the subordination agreement. One's rights cannot otherwise be adversely affected by an agreement to which one is not a party. U.C.C. § 9-339, Comment 2. First Dakota Nat'l Bank v. Performance Engr. & Mfg., Inc., 676 N.W.2d 395, 53 U.C.C. Rep. Serv. 2d 677 (S.D. 2004).

44. Western Auto Supply Co. v. Bank of Imboden, 17 Ark. App. 4, 701 S.W.2d 394, 42 U.C.C. Rep. Serv. 1506 (1985) (prior-perfected secured party consented because it recognized its own interest in debtor's obtaining bank loan). A secured creditor should be careful in agreeing to subordination. *In re* Bar-Cross Farms & Ranches, Inc., 48 B.R. 976, 1 U.C.C. Rep. Serv. 2d 256 (Bankr. D. Colo. 1985) (waiver by secured party did not merely subordinate its interest to another claimant but terminated the interest).

45. U.C.C. § 9-323, Comment 3.

applies to priority based on the time an advance is made. The special rule identifies the circumstances in which the timing of an advance affects priority between secured parties: priority dates from the time an advance is made to the extent the security interest secures an advance (1) made while the interest is perfected automatically or by temporary perfection, and (2) not made pursuant to a commitment entered into before or while the security interest was perfected by a method other than automatic or temporary perfection. The emphasis on these forms of perfection should be obvious because a security interest perfected by one of these methods is a hidden lien, and a subsequent secured party should not take subject to an advance when it does not have notice of the initial loan.[46]

For example, suppose Secured Party has a security interest in a negotiable promissory note executed by Obligor and payable to the order of Debtor. Secured Party perfects its security interest in the instrument by possession, and the security agreement contains an optional future-advances clause. Secured Party later delivers the instrument to Debtor so that Debtor can present it to Obligor for payment, thereby invoking temporary perfection.[47] If Secured Party makes an advance during the period of temporary perfection, its priority against another secured party for the advance will date only from the time the advance is made. If the security agreement obligated the secured party to make the advance, however, priority for the advance would date from the time Secured Party initially took possession. The practical effect of these rules is that the special provision of Section 9-323 governs very few cases: "Thus, an advance has priority from the date it is made only in the rare case in which it is made without commitment and while the security interest is perfected only temporarily under Section 9-312."[48] The first-to-file-or-perfect rule of Section 9-322(a)(1) governs most cases between competing secured parties involving future advances.

§ 10.03 Exceptions for Non-Filing Collateral

The Comments to Article 9 draw a distinction between "non-filing collateral" and "filing collateral." They describe the distinction as follows:

> As used in these Comments, non-filing collateral is collateral of a type for which perfection may be achieved by a method other than filing (possession or control, mainly) and for which secured parties who so perfect generally do not expect or need to conduct a filing search. More specifically, non-filing collateral is chattel paper, deposit accounts, negotiable documents, instruments, investment property, and letter-of-credit rights. Other collateral—accounts, commercial tort claims, general intangibles, goods, nonnegotiable documents, and payment intangibles—is filing collateral.[49]

---

46. For the definition of "pursuant to commitment," see U.C.C. § 9-102(a)(69).
47. U.C.C. § 9-312(f) (20-day period).
48. U.C.C. § 9-323, Comment 3.
49. U.C.C. § 9-322, Comment 7.

Although the Comment was not amended as part of the 2022 amendments, non-filing collateral today would also include controllable electronic records, controllable accounts, and controllable payment intangibles.

The distinction is important because Article 9 provides special priority rules with respect to non-filing collateral that override the first-to-file-or-perfect rule of Section 9-322(a).[50] Depending on the specific types of property, these rules on non-filing collateral provide for priority based on the first to perfect by taking control or possession of the collateral.

[A] Deposit Accounts—§ 9-327

A secured party must perfect a security interest in a deposit account by control.[51] The filing of a financing statement cannot be effective to perfect a security interest in a deposit account, even if the financing statement properly describes that account. A secured party may have a perfected security interest in certain funds inside that deposit account if they are identifiable cash proceeds of other collateral, but this interest is subordinate to the interest of another secured party with an interest in the entire deposit account perfected by control.[52]

A bank that maintains a deposit account in which it has a security interest automatically has control of the deposit account.[53] Other secured parties can acquire control of a deposit account by entering into a control agreement with the debtor and the maintaining bank, or by agreeing with the debtor to become the customer with respect to the account in the records of the maintaining bank.[54] If the bank maintaining a deposit account is a secured party with respect to it, the bank's interest takes priority over a conflicting security interest in the deposit account[55] unless the other secured party obtains control by becoming the customer with respect to the deposit account.[56] This rule leaves banks free to extend credit to their customers without having to consult their records for the possibility of another security interest in the deposit account.[57] A secured party that wishes to avoid this priority and that does not become the customer with respect to the account can prevail only by obtaining a subordination agreement from the maintaining bank.[58]

---

50. U.C.C. §§ 9-322(f)(1), 9-327 to 9-331.

51. U.C.C. § 9-312(a)(1). A secured party remains perfected by control only while it retains control. U.C.C. § 9-314(b); *In re* Cumberland Molded Prods., LLC, 69 U.C.C. Rep. Serv. 2d 371 (Bankr. M.D. Tenn. 2009) (bank in control of deposit account lost perfection when it honored a check issued by the debtor and turned the remainder of the funds over to the trustee). For a discussion of perfection by control in a deposit account, see U.C.C. §§ 9-312(b)(1), 9-314, and 9-104, and § 6.04[B], *supra*.

52. U.C.C. § 9-327(a).

53. U.C.C. § 9-104(a)(1).

54. U.C.C. § 9-104(a)(2), (3).

55. U.C.C. § 9-327(3).

56. U.C.C. § 9-327(4).

57. U.C.C. § 9-327, Comment 4.

58. U.C.C. §§ 9-327(4), 9-104(a)(3).

[B] Investment Property—§ 9-328

Article 9 allows a secured party to perfect a security interest in investment property by filing a financing statement[59]—but a prudent secured party will perfect as to investment property by control. A secured party that perfects a security interest in investment property by control has priority over a competing interest perfected by any other means.[60] This rule reflects unique aspects of the securities markets. It provides a clear mandate that a secured party that wants the greatest level of protection available must obtain control. The availability of filing as an alternative method of perfection for investment property does not alter the established practice of entering into securities transactions without first searching the U.C.C. files.[61] A secured party can attain control and proceed unaffected by any prior filings. Filing provides a secured party with protection only against lien creditors (including bankruptcy trustees) and other secured parties that fail to establish control.

A variety of rules determine priority of conflicting security interests in investment property perfected by control. A securities intermediary that holds a security interest in a security entitlement or in a securities account maintained with the intermediary has the primary advantage. Its priority extends over a conflicting security interest held by another secured party.[62] A rule of temporal priority applies to other cases involving conflicting security interests perfected by control.[63] In other words, the first secured party to obtain control has priority. The occurrence of such dual interests perfected by control is likely to be rare.[64]

A security interest perfected by delivery of a certificated security in registered form rather than by taking control of the certificate has priority over a conflicting security interest perfected by any method other than control.[65] Delivery falls short of control because control of a certificated security in registered form requires either the indorsement of the person in whose name the certificate is issued or registration of the certificate in the name of the secured party.[66] A secured party that takes possession of a certificated security registered in the debtor's name without obtaining the debtor's indorsement thus has priority over a prior secured party that perfected by filing.

---

59. U.C.C. § 9-312(a).

60. U.C.C. § 9-328(1). For discussion of perfection by control in investment paper, see U.C.C. §§ 9-314 and 9-106, and § 6.04[A], *supra*.

61. For discussion of practices in the securities markets, see § 6.04[A], *supra*.

62. U.C.C. § 9-328(3). Comparable priority is available for a commodity intermediary. U.C.C. § 9-328(4).

63. U.C.C. § 9-328(2).

64. U.C.C. § 9-328, Comment 5.

65. U.C.C. § 9-328(5). The fact that delivery is a half-step short of control justifies the rule. For discussion of delivery, see § 4.02[H], *supra*.

66. U.C.C. § 8-106(b). A secured party obtains control of a certificated security in bearer form merely by taking delivery. U.C.C. § 8-106(a).

[C] Letter-of-Credit Rights—§ 9-329

A secured party with control of a letter-of-credit right has priority over a conflicting security interest held by a secured party that does not have control.[67] The only alternative methods to perfect an interest in a letter-of-credit right are automatic perfection in a supporting obligation[68] or temporary perfection if the letter-of-credit right is a proceed of the secured party's original collateral.[69] This allocation of priority is consistent with international practice and promotes finality of payment made to recognized assignees of letter-of-credit proceeds.[70] Multiple secured parties with control rank according to the time of obtaining control.[71]

[D] Controllable Electronic Records, Controllable Accounts, and Controllable Payment Intangibles—§ 9-326A

Section 9-326A provides that "[a] security interest in a controllable account, controllable electronic record, or controllable payment intangible held by a secured party having control of the account, electronic record, or payment intangible has priority over a conflicting security interest held by a secured party that does not have control."

[E] Chattel Paper, Instruments, Negotiable Documents, Securities, Controllable Electronic Records, Controllable Accounts, and Controllable Payment Intangibles—§§ 9-330, 9-331

A purchaser might attain priority against even a prior-perfected secured party in chattel paper, instruments, negotiable documents, securities, controllable electronic records, controllable accounts, and controllable payment intangibles.[72] The term "purchaser" means a person that acquires a property interest in a voluntary transaction and thus includes a secured party.[73] A subsequent chapter explains the applicable provisions in detail.[74] Consistent with the approach taken for other non-filing collateral, priority that is an exception to the first-to-file-or-perfect rule is available under Section 9-330 for a purchaser of chattel paper and instruments, whether or not negotiable. Priority is available under Section 9-331 for a purchaser that qualifies as a holder in due course

---

67. U.C.C. § 9-329(1). For discussion of perfection by control for letter-of-credit rights, see U.C.C. §§ 9-312(b)(2), 9-314, and 9-107, and § 6.04[B], *supra*.

68. U.C.C. § 9-308(d).

69. U.C.C. § 9-315(c).

70. U.C.C. § 9-329, Comment 2.

71. U.C.C. § 9-329(2).

72. U.C.C. §§ 9-330, 9-331.

73. U.C.C. § 1-201(b)(30), (29).

74. *See* § 11.03[C], [D], *infra*.

of a negotiable instrument; a person to which a negotiable document has been duly negotiated; a protected purchaser of a security; or a qualifying purchaser of a controllable electronic record, controllable account, or controllable payment intangible to the extent of the purchaser's protection under Articles 3, 7, 8, and 12. To take advantage of either Section 9-330 or 9-331, a purchaser must obtain possession or control of the collateral and satisfy other requirements.

§ 10.04 Purchase-Money Security Interests

[A] Purchase-Money Security Interests Generally

Although Article 9 makes many distinctions based on the classification of the collateral involved in a transaction, the nature of the transaction itself can also be relevant.[75] One form of secured transaction does not involve the debtor's acquisition of the collateral; the debtor simply grants a security interest in assets in which the debtor already has an interest. For example, a consumer debtor might grant a security interest in a car she already owns or a business debtor might grant a security interest in its existing equipment.

Secured transactions also frequently play a significant role in the acquisition of goods. Many buyers cannot afford to pay the full purchase price at the time they enter into a sales contract, or they choose for a variety of reasons not to do so. One solution that facilitates these transactions is an unsecured installment sales contract. The seller allows the buyer to take immediate possession of the goods upon making a down payment and agreeing to pay the balance, plus interest and other charges, in installments. The seller, however, faces a risk that may make the transaction unpalatable. If the seller does not receive the promised installments, its options are generally limited to bringing an action for the unpaid balance.[76] A seller that has not reserved a security interest in the goods can only recover them *in specie* in limited circumstances.[77]

An alternative is for the seller and the buyer to enter into a secured installment sales contract, sometimes called a conditional sales contract. In this type of contract, the seller sells the goods on credit terms but retains an Article 9 security interest in them. The term "conditional sale" originated with a pre-Code security device pursuant to which a seller retained title to the goods until final payment of the purchase price. In a

---

75. For example, a purchase-money security interest, described in this section, can enable a creditor to acquire special rights in priority contests.

76. "Unless otherwise explicitly agreed title passes to the buyer at the time and place at which the seller completes his performance with reference to the physical delivery of the goods...." U.C.C. § 2-401(2). Although the seller in *Evans Products Co. v. Jorgensen*, 245 Ore. 362, 421 P.2d 978, 3 U.C.C. Rep. Serv. 1099 (1966), had intended to reserve title until paid for the veneer that it delivered to a plywood manufacturer, the delivery passed title.

77. The seller must ascertain that the buyer received the goods on credit while insolvent, and, even then, the seller generally must give notice of its intent to reclaim them within ten days of their receipt. *See* U.C.C. § 2-702.

contract for sale under the Code, title to the goods passes to the buyer notwithstanding a term reserving it to the seller until receipt of final payment. The reservation-of-title term is reduced in effect to the creation of an Article 9 security interest.[78]

In the case of a conditional sale, the seller's reserved security interest qualifies as a type of "purchase-money" security interest.[79] The Code provides that a security interest is purchase money in nature if the obligation was "incurred as all or part of the price of the collateral."[80] In effect, the seller has loaned the buyer the purchase price, and the collateral is the goods acquired with the loan.[81]

Many merchants do not have sufficient capital to finance the transactions with their buyers and lessees. These merchants must continually replenish their inventory, and, if their suppliers require payment on delivery, they cannot afford to wait for installment payments from their buyers and lessees. Their business depends on turning over inventory, not on earning the interest added to an installment-payment obligation. These credit-sale transactions can nevertheless go forward through the involvement of a bank or other lender. The debtor can borrow money from the lender to acquire the goods from the merchant and grant the lender a security interest in the acquired goods. The lender's security interest is a purchase-money security interest if the lender gives value to the debtor to enable the debtor to acquire rights in or the use of the collateral and the debtor in fact uses the value to acquire rights in or use of the collateral.[82] Loans of this nature are commonly referred to as "enabling loans" because the lender provides the financing that enables the debtor to acquire the collateral.[83]

A purchase-money lender must take care that the debtor actually uses the value provided to acquire rights in or the use of the collateral.[84] A lender will find itself unsecured if the debtor squanders the loan proceeds and never acquires the collateral described in the security agreement. Even if the debtor acquires the collateral so that a security interest attaches, it will not be purchase-money in nature if the lender cannot bear the burden of tracing its loan proceeds into the collateral. The lender can protect

---

78. U.C.C. § 2-401(1).

79. Burlington Nat'l Bank v. Strauss, 50 Wis. 2d 270, 184 N.W.2d 122, 8 U.C.C. Rep. Serv. 944 (1971) (defendant retained purchase-money security interest in cattle sold to debtor under conditional sales contract taken by defendant to secure sales price).

80. U.C.C. § 9-103(a)(2) (part of definition of "purchase-money obligation").

81. A merchant selling inventory can also enter into a consignment arrangement with a supplier under which the supplier delivers the goods but reserves title. The reservation of title is effective because the merchant can return the goods it cannot sell. The interest of a consignor (the supplier), like the interest of a secured credit seller, is a purchase-money security interest. U.C.C. § 9-103(d). For discussion of consignments generally, see § 1.03[B][3], *supra*.

82. U.C.C. § 9-103(a)(2).

83. Chrysler Credit Corp. v. B.J.M., Jr., Inc., 834 F. Supp. 813, 22 U.C.C. Rep. Serv. 2d 379 (E.D. Pa. 1993), *aff'd* 30 F.3d 1485 (3d Cir. 1994) (lender's financing was intended to permit dealer to acquire its inventory); Nauman v. First Nat'l Bank of Allen Park, 50 Mich. App. 41, 212 N.W.2d 760, 13 U.C.C. Rep. Serv. 1191 (1973) (bank made advances to customers to enable them to acquire rights in trailers).

84. *See* Mays v. Brighton Bank, 832 S.W.2d 347, 18 U.C.C. Rep. Serv. 2d 621 (Tenn. Ct. App. 1992) (question of fact as to whether loan given by bank was used to purchase trailer).

itself by making payment directly to the seller of the collateral or by issuing a check naming the seller and the debtor as joint payees.

Former law did not include an explicit limitation on the types of assets that could serve as purchase-money collateral. By contrast, the 1998 revision explicitly limited purchase-money collateral to goods and, in limited situations, software.[85] To qualify as purchase-money collateral, software must be acquired in an integrated transaction in which goods are also acquired, and the software must be acquired for the principal purpose of being used with the goods. If the test is met, a security interest in the software is purchase-money in nature to the same extent that the security interest in the goods is purchase-money in nature.[86]

A problem that has arisen with a 2005 amendment to the Bankruptcy Code is whether "negative equity" constitutes a purchase-money obligation. To illustrate negative equity, suppose Debtor buys a new car for $25,000 and, as part of the transaction, Dealer agrees to take her used car in trade and gives her a credit of $8,000 for it. Unfortunately, Debtor owes $13,000 on the used car, meaning that she is $5,000 "underwater." To make the transaction work, Bank lends Debtor $30,000—enough to pay for the new car and also to pay off her existing loan—and takes as collateral a security interest in the new car. The $5,000 by which the debtor was underwater on her used car is called negative equity. The federal circuit courts of appeal have split on the question of whether negative equity constitutes a purchase-money obligation. A discussion elsewhere this book covers the issue.[87]

[1] Adoption of the "Dual-Status" Rule

Purchase-money secured parties operating under former law sometimes ran into difficulties when they refinanced the original obligation. Refinancing can take many forms. For example, a financially troubled debtor might ask to restructure a purchase-money loan to reduce the monthly payments. If the secured party canceled the old agreement and substituted a new agreement reflecting new payment terms, some courts held there had been a new loan and that its proceeds were used to pay off the old loan—and thus that the refinanced loan did not enable the debtor to acquire the

---

85. U.C.C. §9-103(a)(1). Thus, suppose Bank extends a loan to Investor to enable Investor to buy all of the assets of ABC Corp. Investor uses the loan to acquire all of the assets of ABC Corp. and signs a security agreement sufficient to create a security interest in all of the assets purchased by Investor from ABC Corp. To the extent that the assets purchased by Investor are goods, the security interest in those assets is a purchase-money security interest. To the extent that the assets purchased by Investor are intangible personal property such as accounts or general intangibles, however, the security interest in those assets is not a purchase-money security interest (even though the loan may have enabled Investor to acquire those intangible assets).

86. U.C.C. §9-103(c). *See also* U.C.C. §9-324(f) (providing purchase-money priority in the software to the same extent such priority is provided for the associated goods).

87. *See* §16.10, *infra*.

collateral.[88] The secured party did not lose its security interest or its perfected status, but its security interest was no longer purchase-money in nature.[89]

A related problem occurred if the security interest in acquired goods secured more than their purchase price. For example, a seller with a purchase-money security interest in one item might sell a second item to the debtor, also on a purchase-money basis. Following the consolidation of the two loans into a single loan for which both items served as collateral,[90] some courts applied a "transformation rule" and held that the seller's combined security interest was not purchase-money as applied to either item. The rationale was that the security interest, as applied to each item, was not retained solely to secure all or part of its price.[91] Problems also arose when a purchase-money lender made a later advance to the debtor for a purpose other than the acquisition of collateral and combined the obligations (potentially making it unclear whether the combined obligation, or some portion of it, was purchase-money in nature).

Some courts under former law rejected the transformation rule and held that a secured party's interest was purchase-money in nature if it could prove the extent to which the outstanding balance at any given point in time retained its purchase-money character. The 1998 revision adopted this approach, called the "dual-status" approach, for transactions that are not consumer transactions.[92] Article 9 rejects the transformation rule by providing that a purchase-money security interest does not lose its status as such even if "(1) the purchase-money collateral also secures an obligation that is not a purchase-money obligation; (2) collateral that is not purchase-money collateral also secures the purchase money obligation; or (3) the purchase-money obligation has been renewed, refinanced, consolidated, or restructured."[93] It also adopts the dual-status rule by providing as follows:

A security interest in goods is a purchase-money security interest:

   (1) *to the extent* that the goods are purchase-money collateral[94] with respect to
       that security interest;

---

88. *See In re* Matthews, 724 F.2d 798, 37 U.C.C. Rep. Serv. 1332 (9th Cir. 1984). *But see In re* Billings, 838 F.2d 405, 5 U.C.C. Rep. Serv. 1259 (10th Cir. 1988) (refinancing did not amount to new loan).

89. As a result, such a secured party may have lost priority that it otherwise would have held as a purchase-money secured party. *See* §§ 10.04[B], 12.02[B], 12.03[B], *infra*.

90. This approach is called "cross-collateralization."

91. *See In re* Manuel, 507 F.2d 990, 16 U.C.C. Rep. Serv. 493 (5th Cir. 1975).

92. The appropriate approach in consumer transactions is left to the courts, and adoption of the dual-status rule for other transactions does not create an inference that the transformation rule should be adopted by the courts for consumer transactions. U.C.C. § 9-103(h). Consumers prefer the transformation rule because, in bankruptcy, a nonpossessory, non-purchase-money security interest can be invalidated to the extent the interest impairs a debtor's ability to claim an exemption in certain specified categories. 11 U.S.C. § 522(f)(1)(B). For discussion of "lien stripping" in bankruptcy, see § 16.07[B], *infra*.

93. U.C.C. § 9-103(f).

94. "Purchase-money collateral" means the goods or software that secure a purchase-money obligation. U.C.C. § 9-103(a)(1).

(2) if the security interest is in inventory that is or was purchase-money collateral, also *to the extent* that the security interest secures a purchase-money obligation[95] incurred with respect to other inventory in which the secured party holds or held a purchase-money security interest; and

(3) also *to the extent* that the security interest secures a purchase-money obligation incurred with respect to software in which the secured party holds or held a purchase-money security interest.[96]

The "to the extent" language makes it clear that a transaction can be part purchase-money and part non-purchase-money in nature. The burden of establishing the extent to which a security interest is purchase-money in nature is on the party claiming that status,[97] and, to aid the secured party in sustaining its burden, there is guidance as to how payments are to be allocated to the purchase-money and non-purchase-money components of the obligation. The parties can allocate payments in accordance with any reasonable method that they agree to,[98] and the secured party will want a term in its security agreement providing that payments will be allocated first to any unsecured obligations, next to any non-purchase-money secured obligations, and finally to any purchase-money secured obligations.[99] If the parties do not agree, any intent manifested by the obligor at or before the time payment is made controls the allocation.[100] Failing agreement or obligor manifestation, a default rule provides for allocation of payments first to any unsecured obligations, next to any purchase-money secured obligations, and finally to any non-purchase-money secured obligations.[101]

Section 9-103(b)(2), which adopts the dual-status rule for transactions involving inventory,[102] overrules a case that had sent shock waves through the secured lending industry.[103] The case held that a purchase-money inventory financer that relied on an after-acquired property clause to cover multiple transactions lost its purchase-money

---

95. "Purchase-money obligation" means a seller's retention of collateral to secure all or part of the purchase price or a lender's retention of collateral to secure an enabling loan. U.C.C. § 9-103(a)(2). Comment 3 to that section states that the "price" or "value given to enable" includes "obligations for expenses incurred in connection with acquiring rights in the collateral, sales taxes, duties, finance charges, interest, freight charges, costs of storage in transit, demurrage, administrative charges, expenses of collection and enforcement, attorney's fees, and other similar obligations."

96. U.C.C. § 9-103(b) (emphasis supplied).

97. U.C.C. § 9-103(g).

98. U.C.C. § 9-103(e)(1).

99. *See, e.g.,* In re Cersey, 321 B.R. 352, 56 U.C.C. Rep. Serv. 2d 772 (Bankr. M.D. Ga. 2004) (the contracts provided the following allocation for each payment: "all sales taxes, all finance charges, all insurance charges, all delinquency charges, all court costs, all dishonored payment fees, all delivery charges, all set-up or installation fees, and then to the purchase price of each item in order of earlier items paid for first, and in the case of multiple items purchased on the same day, in order of lesser value items paid for first").

100. U.C.C. § 9-103(e)(2).

101. U.C.C. § 9-103(e)(3).

102. U.C.C. § 9-103(b)(2).

103. Southtrust Bank of Alabama v. Borg-Warner Acceptance Corp., 760 F.2d 1240, 40 U.C.C. Rep. Serv. 1601 (11th Cir. 1985).

status entirely. The 1998 revision's solution might be called a "dual-status-plus" rule. To illustrate its application, suppose Manufacturer retains a purchase-money security interest in an item that will be inventory in the hands of Retailer as collateral for the item's price, and that the security agreement also grants Manufacturer a security interest to secure the price of any other items that Manufacturer might later sell to Retailer. Manufacturer later sells another item to Retailer on a purchase-money basis, and Retailer resells the second item to a buyer in ordinary course of business that takes it free from the security interest under the buyer-in-ordinary-course rule.[104] Under the 1998 revision, Manufacturer's security interest in the first item is still entirely purchase-money in nature even though it now secures the price of both items. Without this special provision, the dual-status approach would apply, and Manufacturer's security interest would only be partially purchase-money in nature.

[B] Application to Secured Party versus Secured Party Priorities

The first-to-file-or-perfect rule and the rules on priorities with respect to future advances could place a debtor in a difficult position. The debtor's secured lender might be unwilling to advance additional capital that the debtor needs to acquire more property of the type covered in a filed financing statement while other suppliers and lenders could refuse to extend credit because they would be vulnerable to any later advances that the secured lender might make. The first-to-file-or-perfect rule and the priority rules governing future advances thus could enable a secured lender to eliminate competing sources of financing and to exert excessive control over the direction of the debtor's business.

Article 9's provisions that favor purchase-money secured parties temper this position of excessive control. A purchase-money secured party under these provisions can finance the debtor's acquisition of additional goods despite a prior-filed financing statement covering goods of that type and attain priority with respect to the additional goods.[105] Even if the initial secured party's perfected security interest extends to the new goods under an after-acquired property clause, the interest of the initial secured party will be subordinate with respect to the new goods.

The prior secured party should have few complaints about the priority granted to later purchase-money secured parties. Because of the secondary source of financing, the debtor acquires additional assets without the prior secured party's having to finance

---

104. For discussion of the rights of a buyer in ordinary course, see § 11.03[A][1], *infra*.

105. A purchase-money security interest can attach only to an interest in goods and related software. U.C.C. § 9-103; First Bethany Bank & Trust, N.A. v. Arvest United Bank, 50 U.C.C. Rep. Serv. 2d 1209 (Okla. 2003) (cannot take a purchase-money security interest in accounts). *See* § 10.03[A], *infra*. A purchase-money security interest in software is possible only if the debtor acquires the interest for the purpose of using the software in goods subject to a purchase-money security interest. U.C.C. § 9-103(c). A perfected purchase-money security interest in software has the same priority as the purchase-money security interest in the related goods. U.C.C. § 9-324(f).

the new acquisition. Furthermore, the prior secured party relied on the additional collateral in making its original decision to extend financing only to a limited extent. The exceptions in favor of purchase-money secured parties are crucial to allow debtors to obtain alternative financing once they permit the filing of a financing statement.

[1] Collateral Other than Inventory—§ 9-324(a)

The general rule on purchase-money priority favors purchase-money secured parties that have interests in goods other than inventory or livestock.

[A] perfected purchase-money security interest in goods other than inventory or livestock has priority over a conflicting security interest in the same goods ... if the purchase-money security interest is perfected when the debtor receives possession of the collateral or within 20 days thereafter.[106]

The only requirement imposed on the purchase-money secured party is that it perfect in a timely manner, that is, within the 20-day grace period that begins to run when the debtor receives possession of the collateral.[107] The secured party can perfect by filing or by any other available method.[108] The purchase-money security interest is perfected automatically upon attachment if the collateral is consumer goods.[109] If the collateral is not consumer goods, however, the purchase-money secured party typically must file a financing statement before the expiration of the grace period.[110] Perfection by possession is possible, but both options are unlikely given the nature of the typical purchase-money secured transaction.

The grace period facilitates the completion of commercial transactions. A supplier can sell goods, retain a security interest in them, and conveniently allow the debtor to take possession without having to interrupt this sequence by first filing a financing statement. The supplier can conclude its deal with the debtor, confident that it can achieve

---

106. U.C.C. § 9-324(a). The grace period is comparable to the 20 days allowed for a purchase-money secured party to file or take possession of the collateral to achieve priority over an intervening lien creditor. See U.C.C. § 9-317(e) and § 12.02[B], infra.

107. State Bank & Trust Co. of Beeville v. First Nat'l Bank of Beeville, 635 S.W.2d 807, 33 U.C.C. Rep. Serv. 1775 (Tex. Ct. App. 1982) (purchase-money secured party filed one day later to qualify under exception); In re Wild West World, L.L.C., 66 U.C.C. Rep. Serv. 2d 1033 (Bankr. D. Kan. 2008) (failure to perfect within the grace period precluded use of the exception for priority); In re McAlmont, 385 B.R. 191, 65 U.C.C. Rep. Serv. 2d 562 (Bankr. S.D. Ohio 2008) (20-day period is a grace period to perfect to achieve non-temporal priority, not a deadline to prevent achieving priority under the general temporal rule against subsequent parties).

108. There are similar 20-day grace periods for obtaining purchase-money priority over buyers and lien creditors, but to take advantage of them the secured party must perfect by filing. Those grace periods and the requirement and the rationale for the filing requirement are discussed in §§ 12.02[B] (lien creditors) and 12.03[B] (buyers), infra.

109. U.C.C. § 9-309(1). The purchase-money secured party nevertheless may choose to file in order to ensure that it does not lose its priority as against a later consumer that buys the collateral without knowledge of the security interest. See § 11.03[A][2], infra.

110. U.C.C. § 9-324(a); Custer v. American Honda Fin. Corp., 50 U.C.C. Rep. Serv. 2d 608 (Bankr. N.D. Iowa 2003) (because purchase-money secured party failed to perfect its interest within the 20-day grace period, trustee in bankruptcy acquired superior rights in the vehicle).

priority if it completes the steps for perfection within the allotted grace period. The rationale that underlies pre-filing of financing statements does not apply in this context.

The grace period begins from the time the debtor receives possession of the collateral.[111] Prior to the 1998 revision, the provision generated some controversy in cases where a debtor acquired possession of goods through a sale on approval or through a lease with an option to buy. For example, suppose Debtor leases equipment from Supplier and, 30 days after receiving possession, exercises an option to purchase the equipment. Supplier then extends credit to finance payment of the option price, retains a security interest in the equipment, and immediately files a financing statement. Shortly thereafter, Bank challenges Supplier for priority based on Bank's prior-perfected security interest in the equipment under an after-acquired property clause. Bank asserts that Supplier does not qualify for purchase-money priority because it filed more than 20 days after Debtor acquired possession. Supplier counters that it filed its financing statement within 20 days after the equipment became "collateral," that is, when Debtor and Supplier entered into a security agreement.

The Comments now address the issue directly, indicating that "the 20-day period in subsection (a) does not commence until the goods become 'collateral' (defined in Section 9-102), i.e., until they are subject to a security interest."[112] Most courts already construed the language of Article 9 to support Supplier's position.[113] Even if a financing statement had been filed earlier, it would not have constituted perfection because a security interest did not attach until Debtor entered into the security agreement.[114]

Article 9 also includes a provision that governs priority between conflicting purchase-money security interests. A purchase-money security interest under which a seller secures the price of the collateral has priority over a purchase-money security interest acquired through an enabling loan.[115] The general "first-to-file-or-perfect" rule governs priority between multiple purchase-money security interests that secure enabling loans.[116]

---

111. *In re Ivy*, 37 B.R. 285, 38 U.C.C. Rep. Serv. 651 (Bankr. E.D. Ky. 1983) (filing financing statement within grace period [then ten days] after debtor received delivery of equipment was adequate even though security agreement was signed more than ten days before filing).

112. U.C.C. § 9-324, Comment 3.

113. *In re Hooks*, 40 B.R. 715, 39 U.C.C. Rep. Serv. 332 (Bankr. M.D. Ga. 1984) (shipment for inspection); Rainier Nat'l Bank v. Inland Mach. Co., 29 Wash. App. 725, 631 P.2d 389, 32 U.C.C. Rep. Serv. 287 (1981) (lease with option to buy).

114. "Collateral" means "the property subject to a security interest or agricultural lien." U.C.C. § 9-102(a)(12). The analysis in the text applies only to transactions in which a true lease has been created rather than a security interest disguised as a lease. For discussion of the requirements for a true lease, see § 1.03[B][1], *supra*.

115. U.C.C. § 9-324(g)(1). This priority allocation reflects the rule adopted in the RESTATEMENT (THIRD) OF PROPERTY (Mortgages) § 7.2(c) (1997). U.C.C. § 9-324, Comment 13. This allocation favors the purchase-money seller, who arguably may not be as well-suited as a purchase-money enabling lender to spread financial losses.

116. U.C.C. § 9-324(g)(2); Lashua v. La Duke, 707 N.Y.S.2d 542, 41 U.C.C. Rep. Serv. 2d 930 (App. Div. 2000) (although purchase-money secured party failed to perfect within the grace period, it nevertheless prevailed as the first party to perfect).

Purchase-money security interests are clearly fair as applied to a prior-perfected secured party but can create a problem for other secured parties. For example, suppose SP-1 takes a purchase-money security interest on June 1 but does not file until June 18. In the interim, on June 10, SP-2 makes a loan and takes a security interest in the purchase-money collateral. The rule requires that SP-1 prevail, but this places a substantial inquiry burden on SP-2 (who should have made sure that the collateral had been in the debtor's possession for more than 20 days prior to the June 10 loan).

[2] Inventory—§ 9-324(b), (c)

The exception favoring purchase-money secured parties is more complicated if the collateral is inventory.[117] The text of Article 9 provides:

> [A] perfected purchase-money security interest in inventory has priority over a conflicting security interest in the same inventory ... if:
>
> (1) the purchase-money security interest is perfected when the debtor receives possession of the inventory;
>
> (2) the purchase-money secured party sends a signed notification to the holder of the conflicting security interest;
>
> (3) the holder of the conflicting security interest receives the notification within five years before the debtor receives possession of the inventory; and
>
> (4) the notification states that the person sending the notification has or expects to acquire a purchase-money security interest in inventory of the debtor and describes the inventory.[118]

Although these provisions may at first appear quite daunting, they essentially require the purchase-money secured party to do only two things: (a) perfect its security interest at or before the time the debtor receives possession of the inventory (there is no grace period) and (b) ensure receipt of its notification (prior to the debtor's receiving possession of the inventory) by the holder of a conflicting security interest that filed a financing statement before the purchase-money secured party filed.

The specific requirements of this exception are best understood in the context of the underlying policy concerns. Consider a typical ongoing inventory-financing arrangement in which the secured party makes advances up to a specified percentage against invoices for new inventory acquired by the debtor. In this arrangement, lenders rely on invoices to determine their advances of additional funds. If a purchase-money secured

---

117. Article 9 also provides for the priority of purchase-money security interests in livestock that are farm products that is comparable to the purchase-money priority provided for inventory, the main difference being that the purchase-money secured party in the livestock must renew its notice to prior-perfected secured parties on a six-month rather than a five-year basis. U.C.C. § 9-324(d), (e).

118. U.C.C. § 9-324(b). "Subsections (b)(2) through (4) apply only if the holder of the conflicting security interest had filed a financing statement covering the same types of inventory: (1) if the purchase-money security interest is perfected by filing, before the date of the filing; or (2) if the purchase-money security interest is temporarily perfected without filing or possession under Section 9-312(f), before the beginning of the 20-day period thereunder." U.C.C. § 9-324(c).

party finances the debtor's acquisition of inventory covered by a particular invoice, a dishonest debtor can easily deceive the inventory financer by presenting that same invoice with a request for an additional advance. The purchase-money secured party, therefore, must protect the inventory financer by providing a signed notification[119] that it has acquired or intends to acquire[120] a purchase-money security interest in specific items or types of inventory.[121] The notice protects the original financer by alerting it to guard against the debtor's use of an invoice that covers any of the inventory described in the notification.[122]

The notification process would be burdensome to a purchase-money secured party that contemplates a series of transactions with the debtor if it had to provide notification prior to each transaction. A manufacturer, for example, might decide to finance all of a retailer's subsequent acquisition of its products. The manufacturer can simply notify the prior inventory financer that it expects to acquire a purchase-money security interest in these items of inventory[123] and that notification is valid for five years from the date the inventory financer receives it.[124] The inventory financer should implement a business procedure by which it can protect itself for the next five years in light of the information contained in the notification.

Because the notification can describe inventory in which the sender merely expects to acquire a purchase-money security interest,[125] a debtor might acquire some inventory that fits the description but, in fact, is not financed by the sender of the notifi-

---

119. Elhard v. Prairie Distrib., Inc., 366 N.W.2d 465, 40 U.C.C. Rep. Serv. 1968 (N.D. 1985) (oral notification invalid); Bank of Lincoln Cnty. v. G.E. Comm. Distrib. Fin. Corp., 73 U.C.C. Rep. Serv. 2d 93 (E.D. Tenn. 2010) (failure to send a signed notification precluded priority for the bank as a purchase-money secured party).

120. In re Daniels, 35 B.R. 247, 37 U.C.C. Rep. Serv. 967 (Bankr. W.D. Okla. 1983) (notification upheld against an attack that it should fail because it did not state explicitly that creditor planned to take a purchase-money security interest); In re Leading Edge Pork, LLC, 72 U.C.C. Rep. Serv. 2d 866 (Bankr. C.D. Ill. 2010) (e-mail that did not identify the debtor or indicate that the sender had or expected to have a purchase-money security interest in wiener pigs did not qualify as a signed notification).

121. U.C.C. § 9-324(b)(2), (4); Guaranty State Bank & Trust Co. v. Van Diest Supply Co., 55 P.3d 357, 48 U.C.C. Rep. Serv. 2d 1197 (Kan. Ct. App. 2002) (held that a notice that does not specifically indicate that a purchase-money security interest is retained or considered is not sufficient because it could mislead the secured party receiving the notice to believe that it retains its priority under the first-to-file rule).

122. The Comments explain the reason why a comparable notification requirement does not apply to purchase-money security interests for collateral other than inventory: "Inasmuch as an arrangement for periodic advances against incoming goods is unusual outside the inventory field, subsection (a) does not contain a notification requirement." U.C.C. § 9-324, Comment 4.

123. U.C.C. § 9-324(b)(4).

124. U.C.C. § 9-324(b)(3). The five-year duration of the notification corresponds to the period before a filed financing statement lapses. A purchase-money secured party engaged in ongoing financing of a debtor should provide new notification to all relevant parties when it files a continuation statement.

125. Fedders Fin. Corp. v. Chiarelli Bros., 289 A.2d 169, 10 U.C.C. Rep. Serv. 880 (Pa. Super. Ct. 1972) (written notification that described variety of types of appliances was valid even though the purchase-money secured party took an interest only in the air conditioners).

cation.[126] The inventory financer with an after-acquired property clause has the only interest in those items.[127]

The special priority rules are available to enable any purchase-money secured party to take priority over a prior-perfected secured party.[128] If a purchase-money secured party fails to comply with the procedures required to invoke them, however, it will be subordinate to a prior-perfected secured party that can use an after-acquired property clause to reach the collateral provided by the purchase-money secured party.[129] Because a grace period does not apply for filing on inventory, subsequent secured parties not do incur a risk.

§ 10.05 Proceeds

A secured party might take its interest in one type of collateral (such as inventory), and another secured party might acquire a security interest from the same debtor in a different type of collateral (such as accounts). What happens when some of the inventory is sold on unsecured credit and accounts are created? The accounts are proceeds of the inventory, and a priority dispute might arise between the two secured parties. Before turning to the priority rules, however, the first step is to characterize the interests of the competing claimants in the accounts. Because the inventory-based secured party can claim the accounts only as proceeds, the provisions relevant to attachment and perfection of security interests in proceeds need to be analyzed.

A security interest attaches automatically to identifiable proceeds received on the disposition of collateral.[130] The inventory financer's security interest thus attaches to accounts created from the sale of the inventory subject to its security interest if it can identify them, meaning trace them back to the inventory.[131] If the inventory financer perfects its interest in the inventory by filing a financing statement, perfection in the

---

126. For example, suppose Retailer sells tractors and finances its inventory through a line of credit from Bank. Retailer also sells John Deere tractors, but Retailer finances its acquisition of Deere tractors through purchase-money financing extended by John Deere Acceptance Corp. (JDAC). Now suppose that Retailer sells a new IH tractor to Customer, taking the Customer's used John Deere tractor as a trade-in. Only Bank, and not JDAC, would have a security interest in the trade-in.

127. Inventory financers rarely fail to include such a clause. See § 3.02[A], *supra*.

128. The term "secured party" in this context includes a consignor, U.C.C. § 9-102(a)(73)(C), and the interest of a consignor is deemed to be a purchase-money security interest in inventory. U.C.C. § 9-103(d). For discussion of consignments, see § 1.03[B][2], [3], *supra*.

129. U.C.C. § 9-322(a). Zink v. Vanmiddlesworth, 300 B.R. 394, 51 U.C.C. Rep. Serv. 2d 892 (N.D.N.Y. 2003) (because purchase-money secured party did not perfect its security interest before debtor received possession of the cattle, and did not notify a prior-perfected secured party with an interest in all of the current and after-acquired debtor's livestock, purchase-money secured party did not attain priority with respect to the cattle that it sold to debtor).

130. U.C.C. §§ 9-203(f), 9-315(a)(2). For discussion of attachment of security interests in proceeds generally, see § 2.03[B], *supra*.

131. It would not have a security interest in accounts arising from other sources, such as services provided by the debtor to third parties.

accounts as proceeds automatically extends beyond the grace period of temporary perfection because the office where the secured party filed is the same office in which a secured party would file with respect to accounts.[132] Assuming the accounts financer filed a financing statement perfecting its security interest in the debtor's accounts and the inventory financer did likewise as to the debtor's inventory, thus also giving it perfected status as to accounts that are identifiable proceeds of the inventory, we have a priority contest between two perfected secured parties. As we shall see below, this particular priority contest will be resolved under the basic first-to-file-or-perfect rule that governs perfected security interests in the same collateral and that was discussed previously in this chapter.[133]

There are, however, different rules governing priority contests in different contexts, such as transactions in which there are proceeds of purchase-money security interests[134] or proceeds of non-filing collateral.[135] The material below explores the various rules and their application.

[A] Non-Purchase-Money Security Interests

The Article 9 rules on priority with respect to proceeds of a security interest that is not purchase-money in nature include a general rule and special rules. The general rule is the first-to-file-or-perfect rule of Section 9-322(a)(1) that governs priority of competing perfected security interests and is based on temporal priority. The special rules are set out in other subsections of Section 9-322 and apply to situations in which application of the general rule would lead to an inappropriate result. The special rules apply only to non-filing collateral, and they encompass both a rule based on non-temporal priority and one based on special temporal priority. Recall that non-filing collateral is a type of collateral in which a secured party that perfects by possession or control does not expect or need to search the filing system.

[1] General Rule (First to File or Perfect)—
§ 9-322(b)(1)

The general rule for priority in proceeds makes the time of filing or perfection for proceeds the same as the time of filing or perfection as to the original collateral. It thus applies the first-to-file-or-perfect rule that governs conflicting perfected security interests in the same collateral.[136] The general rule applies when none of the special rules discussed in the subsequent subsections are applicable.

---

132. U.C.C. §§ 9-315(c), (d)(1); 9-501(a)(2). For discussion of perfection of security interests in proceeds, see § 8.02, *supra*.

133. *See* § 10.01, *supra*.

134. Purchase-money security interests are discussed in § 10.04, *supra*.

135. Non-filing collateral is discussed in § 10.03, *supra*.

136. "For the purposes of subsection (a)(1), the time of filing or perfection as to a security interest in collateral is also the time of filing or perfection as to a security interest in proceeds." U.C.C. § 9-322(b)(1). *See also In re* Topsy's Shoppes, Inc., of Kan., 118 B.R. 797, 12 U.C.C. Rep. Serv. 2d 1161

The previous subsection gave an example of the application of the general rule, with one secured party asserting a perfected-by-filing security interest in accounts that were proceeds of inventory and another secured party asserting a perfected-by-filing security interest in accounts as original collateral. The situation did not involve a purchase-money security interest or non-filing collateral, the situations to which the special rules apply, so priority went to the first secured party to either file a financing statement or perfect its security interest.

[2] Special Rules

As noted above, the special rules cover situations in which application of the general rule would lead to an inappropriate result.[137] The special rules apply only to certain types of non-filing collateral. Perfection by filing is available for each type of non-filing collateral except deposit accounts, but a purchaser that satisfies certain conditions takes the collateral free of an earlier filed financing statement.[138] The types of non-filing collateral are chattel paper, deposit accounts, negotiable documents, instruments, investment property, letter-of-credit rights, controllable electronic records, controllable accounts, and controllable payment intangibles.[139]

[a] Special Rule on Non-Temporal Priority— § 9-322(c)(2)

As noted in the preceding subsection, Article 9 includes a number of provisions that enable a secured party with a security interest in non-filing collateral to attain non-temporal priority, that is, priority over a prior-perfected conflicting security interest in the same collateral.[140] This priority is attainable only through perfection by possession or by control, as well as satisfaction of other requirements. It is an exception to the temporal priority rule (first-to-file-or-perfect rule) that generally governs conflicting perfected security interests.[141]

(Bankr. D. Kan. 1990) (secured party failed to establish priority in proceeds arising from sales of intangibles when it conceded that another secured party had prior perfection in the same intangibles); *In re* Montagne, 409 B.R. 685, 69 U.C.C. Rep. Serv. 2d 617 (Bankr. D. Vt. 2009) (agricultural lender prevailed on cash proceeds from a sale of livestock because it perfected prior to the other secured party).

137. U.C.C. § 9-322(c)–(e), and Comment 7.

138. U.C.C. §§ 9-328 (investment property), 9-329 (letter-of-credit right), 9-330 (chattel paper and instruments), and 9-331 (negotiable instruments, negotiable documents, securities, controllable electronic records, controllable accounts, and controllable payment intangibles). For discussion of these provisions, see § 10.03, *supra.*

139. The special rule of Section 9-322(c) applies to each type of non-filing collateral by cross-referencing the provisions under which a secured party may qualify for priority over a conflicting security interest applicable to each type. The special rule of Section 9-322(d) lists the types individually and omits controllable electronic records, controllable accounts, and controllable payment intangibles. It is likely that the omission was inadvertent.

140. The special rule of Section 9-322(c) applies to each type of non-filing collateral because it cross-references each of these provisions.

141. U.C.C. § 9-322(f)(1).

If a secured party with a security interest in non-filing collateral has taken the steps necessary for non-temporal priority,[142] Section 9-322(c)(2) extends that priority to the proceeds of the non-filing collateral if the security interest in the proceeds is perfected and the proceeds are either cash proceeds or are the same type of property as the original collateral. For example, assume that by filing, SP-1 perfects a security interest in all of Debtor's instruments, including after-acquired instruments. SP-2 later perfects a security interest in a promissory note owned by Debtor by taking possession of the note, acquiring priority in the note under Section 9-330(d) or Section 9-331(a). Debtor subsequently receives an installment payment on the note in the form of cash and also receives a check for the balance of the note. The temporal rule of Section 9-322(a)(1) would give priority in the proceeds to SP-1. Section 9-322(c)(2) applies, however, and gives priority to SP-2. The cash and the check are both cash proceeds, and the check is also the same type of collateral as the promissory note, that is, an instrument.[143]

The special rule of non-temporal priority in Section 9-322(c)(2) also governs proceeds of proceeds. Perfection under the special rule applies only if *all* of the intervening proceeds are cash proceeds, proceeds of the same type of property as the original collateral, or an account relating to the collateral.[144] If *any* of the intervening proceeds do not comply, the general first-to-file-or-perfect rules of Sections 9-322(a) and (b) govern priority in the proceeds.

[b] Special Rule on Temporal Priority— §9-322(d), (e)

Even if a secured party perfects a security interest in non-filing collateral by possession or control and attains priority over another secured party, it will not have priority

---

142. An actual conflicting security interest in the original non-filing collateral is not necessary. U.C.C. §9-322(c).

143. If a secured party perfects in the original non-filing collateral by taking control, the additional step of filing can be beneficial in certain situations. For example, assume SP-1 perfects a security interest in all of the investment property of Debtor by filing. Afterward, SP-2 perfects in a certificated security of Debtor by taking control. Debtor subsequently receives a stock dividend on the certificated security controlled by SP-2, in the form of a new certificated security. Even though the proceed is the same type of property as the collateral, if SP-2 does not take delivery or control, or file with respect to the proceeds before the expiration of its 20-day period of temporary perfection, SP-2 will be unperfected as to the proceeds pursuant to Section 9-315(e)(2), and SP-1 will have priority under Section 9-322(a)(2). In contrast, if SP-2 had filed as to investment property in addition to perfecting in the original certificated security by taking control, SP-2 would be continuously perfected in the certificate constituting proceeds pursuant to Section 9-315(d)(1) and would attain priority in the proceeds under Section 9-322(c)(2). The extent of benefit achievable through the additional step of filing with respect to original non-filing collateral, however, is limited. For example, if the proceeds received by Debtor took the form of a promissory note covering dividends, the filing by SP-2 in investment property would lead to continuous perfection in the note. SP-2 nevertheless could not prevail under Section 9-322(c)(2), however, because the note is neither cash proceeds nor proceeds of the same type as the original collateral (i.e., an instrument as opposed to investment property). SP-1 thus would have priority in the proceeds under Sections 9-322(a) and (b).

144. U.C.C. §9-322(c)(2)(C).

under Section 9-322(c)(2) in proceeds that constitute filing collateral.[145] The normal first-to-file-or-perfect rule of Section 9-322(a) does not apply; rather, subsections (d) and (e) provide a different temporal rule based on first-to-file to determine priority. This rule is consistent with normal expectations concerning proceeds that are filing collateral.[146]

For example, assume that SP-1 perfects its security interest in Debtor's deposit account by control. SP-2 thereafter files with respect to Debtor's inventory. Debtor subsequently uses funds acquired from the deposit account to purchase additional inventory, and SP-1 promptly files with respect to the inventory, thereby extending its perfected status beyond the 20-day grace period of automatic perfection for proceeds. SP-1 claims the inventory as proceeds, and SP-2 claims it as original collateral by virtue of its after-acquired property clause. SP-2 will have priority under Section 9-322(d) as the first party to file. This result, although based on the first filing, is an exception to the first-to-file-or-perfect rule of Section 9-322(a). If that subsection applied, SP-1 would prevail as the first party to perfect without any subsequent period during which it was unperfected.

[B] Purchase-Money Security Interests — §9-324(a), (b)

An earlier discussion in this chapter explains how Article 9 enables a purchase-money secured party to attain priority over an earlier-perfected competing secured party in the same collateral.[147] The steps needed to obtain this beneficial treatment vary depending on whether the purchase-money collateral is inventory or livestock, on the one hand, or another type of goods, on the other hand.[148] The same Article 9 provisions that establish purchase-money priority for the original collateral state the circumstances in which purchase-money priority passes through to the identifiable proceeds of that collateral.

If the collateral for a purchase-money security interest is goods other than inventory or livestock, the same priority rule applies to identifiable proceeds as applies to the original collateral.[149] Thus, if a secured party obtains purchase-money priority in an item of its debtor's equipment over a previously perfected security interest in the

---

145. Filing collateral is any collateral that is not non-filing collateral. Filing collateral could not qualify under subsection (c) as either cash proceeds or proceeds of the same type that constitute the secured party's non-filing collateral.

146. U.C.C. §9-322, Comment 9, Example 12. Oddly, Section 9-322(d) lists the types of non-filing collateral individually and omits the types introduced in the 2022 amendments—controllable electronic records, controllable accounts, and controllable payment intangibles. It is likely that the omission was inadvertent.

147. *See* §10.04[B], *supra*.

148. U.C.C. §9-324(a) (goods other than inventory and livestock), (b) (inventory), (d) (livestock).

149. Section 9-324(a) accomplishes this result through the language "a perfected security interest in its identifiable proceeds also has priority."

after-acquired equipment of the debtor and the debtor sells the equipment on unsecured credit, the purchase-money security interest will have priority over the account (the proceeds) generated by the sale. The Code does not revert back to the first-to-file-or-perfect rule in this situation. Even though the requirements for obtaining purchase-money priority in livestock are largely the same as the requirements when the purchase-money collateral is inventory, the rule governing priority in proceeds is the same as the rule for non-inventory. A secured party with purchase-money priority in livestock also has priority in all identifiable proceeds of the livestock and in all of its identifiable products in their unmanufactured state.[150]

The purchase-money priority rules work differently for the proceeds of purchase-money collateral that is inventory. A secured party with purchase-money priority in inventory also has purchase money priority in "identifiable cash proceeds of the inventory to the extent the identifiable cash proceeds are received on or before the delivery of the inventory to a buyer."[151] Thus, if a merchant sells inventory for cash or takes a check or credit card, a secured party with purchase-money priority in the inventory will also have priority in the cash, check, or right to payment from the credit card system. With exceptions discussed below, the secured party would not have priority in noncash proceeds like promissory notes, chattel paper, or accounts.[152] For example, suppose Bank has a purchase-money security interest in a merchant's inventory and has purchase-money priority over prior perfected security interest that covers all inventory, including after-acquired inventory, of the merchant. If the merchant sells some inventory on unsecured credit, generating accounts, and some for cash or a cash equivalent, the purchase-money secured party will have priority as to the cash and cash equivalents but will not have priority as to the accounts under the first-to-file-or-perfect rule.

A perfected purchase-money security interest does not automatically provide the secured party with priority for proceeds in the form of chattel paper and instruments, but the secured party can obtain priority in these types of proceeds by qualifying as a purchaser entitled to priority under Section 9-330.[153] That section requires the purchaser to give new value, which is not likely the case if the chattel paper is proceeds. However, Section 9-330(e) treats the holder of a purchase-money security interest in inventory as having given new value for chattel-paper proceeds, thereby enabling the secured party, if it meets the other requirements of Section 9-330, to take the chattel

---

150. U.C.C. § 9-324(d).

151. U.C.C. § 9-324(b). This provision recognizes an exception to the purchase-money priority for cash proceeds. If the cash proceeds are in the form of a deposit account, a secured party with a security interest in the deposit account perfected by control will have priority over a secured party with purchase-money priority in the deposit account. U.C.C. § 9-327(a).

152. Mbank Alamo N.A. v. Raytheon Co., 886 F.2d 1449, 10 U.C.C. Rep. Serv. 2d 35 (5th Cir. 1989) (prior-perfected accounts financer prevailed as to proceeds that were accounts against secured party with purchase-money priority as to inventory that was original collateral).

153. U.C.C. § 9-324(b). For discussion of the rights of purchasers of chattel paper subject to a prior-perfected security interest, see § 11.03[C], infra.

paper free of other claims, including a claim based on a prior-perfected security interest in the chattel paper.[154]

The limitations on the extent to which the priority of a purchase-money security interest in inventory extends to proceeds might at first glance seem questionable. After all, inventory consists of goods held for sale or lease, and these transactions often produce accounts or chattel paper. Pursuant to the limitations, a secured party with a purchase-money security interest entitled to priority in inventory loses priority in these types of proceeds to earlier secured parties with ongoing perfected financing arrangements in either inventory or in accounts or chattel paper as original collateral, although the availability of priority under Section 9-330 ameliorates the situation somewhat in the case of chattel paper.

The limitations purposely favor financing on the basis of accounts and chattel paper as original collateral. These types of financing are a critical aspect of commercial finance. The dangers associated with financing inventory—compared with the accounts or chattel paper that its sale or lease generates—are obvious and leave many lenders reluctant to lend against inventory.[155] Inventory financing for many lenders is only one facet of an ongoing arrangement that looks predominantly to the accounts or chattel paper proceeds generated by the sale or lease of the inventory. Because accounts and chattel-paper financing plays such a fundamental role in commercial finance, the drafters elected to protect the claims of these financers even against subsequent purchase-money secured parties that claim the accounts as proceeds of their collateral.

The position of the purchase-money secured party in inventory actually is not as precarious as it might first appear. The independent financing made available through an accounts or chattel-paper financer provides the debtor with funds it can use to pay the inventory lender.[156] The purchase-money priority in the inventory will serve the inventory lender well in the event the debtor defaults because it can take possession of the inventory that has not been sold or leased free of the claims of other parties.

---

154. Under Section 9-330(c), a secured party entitled to priority as a purchaser of chattel paper under Section 9-330 is also entitled to priority in the proceeds of the chattel paper "to the extent that: (1) section 9-322 provides for priority in the proceeds; or (2) the proceeds consist of the specific goods covered by the chattel paper or cash proceeds of the specific goods, even if the purchaser's security interest in the proceeds is unperfected." Section 9-322's rules regarding priority in proceeds are discussed in § 10.05[A][2][a], *supra.*

155. *See* § 3.04[B], *supra.*

156. "In some situations, the party financing the inventory on a purchase-money basis makes contractual arrangements that the proceeds of receivables financing by another be devoted to paying off the inventory security interest." U.C.C. § 9-324, Comment 8.

Chapter 11

Priority Contests: Purchasers versus Perfected Secured Parties

Synopsis

§ 11.01 General Rule on Disposition— § 9-315(a)

A secured party with a perfected security interest may face a challenge from a person that purchases the collateral from the debtor. As used in the Code, the term "purchaser" means any person that acquires an interest in property through a voluntary transaction and includes, *inter alia*, secured parties, buyers, and lessees.[1] This chapter deals primarily with purchasers that are not secured parties, but the superpriority rules for chattel paper and instruments are available to all purchasers, including secured parties.[2]

A purchaser of an asset subject to a security interest often asserts that it purchased the asset free of that interest. The secured party, to the contrary, may contend that the transfer was subject to its security interest, meaning the secured party can foreclose on the asset notwithstanding the transfer[3] following a default under the security agreement.[4] This chapter explains the provisions that govern disputes between purchasers and secured parties that have perfected their security interests. A subsequent discussion covers priorities between purchasers and unperfected secured parties.[5]

Article 9 includes a rule that, subject to exceptions, grants priority to the secured party if the debtor disposes of the collateral. Section 9-315(a)(1) provides that "a security interest or agricultural lien continues in collateral notwithstanding sale, lease, license, exchange, or other disposition thereof unless the secured party authorized the disposition free of the security interest or agricultural lien."[6] This rule defeats any argument that mere disposition of the collateral by itself terminates a security interest in the collateral; to the contrary, the starting premise is that the security interest remains enforceable despite the disposition.[7] The rule provides three exceptions: (1) cases in which the secured party authorizes the disposition free of the security

---

1. U.C.C. § 1-201(b)(30), (29). The term even includes a donee, but the Article 9 provisions that provide protection for purchasers are limited to purchasers for value.

2. *See* § 11.03, *infra*. Chapter 10, *supra*, covers the rights of secured parties generally.

3. Alternatively, if the purchaser refuses to return the collateral to the secured party, the purchaser may be liable in conversion for its fair market value. *See* U.C.C. 9-315, Comment 2; AAA Auto Sales & Rental, Inc. v. Security Fed. Sav. & Loan Ass'n, 114 N.M. 761, 845 P.2d 855, 19 U.C.C. Rep. Serv. 2d 923 (Ct. App. 1992). The mere fact of purchase does not make the purchaser personally liable for the secured obligation.

4. Most security agreements make disposition of the collateral by the debtor without the consent of the secured party an event of default. *See* § 17.01, *infra*.

5. *See* § 12.03, *infra*.

6. The first part of this rule simply reflects a specific application of the more general provision in Section 9-201(a) that "a security agreement is effective according to its terms ... against purchasers of the collateral...." Both provisions are merely the starting point of analysis, as a number of exceptions might apply in a particular case.

7. The continuation of the security interest had extensive reach in *Marine Midland Bank, N.A. v. Smith Boys, Inc.*, 129 Misc. 2d 37, 492 N.Y.S.2d 355, 41 U.C.C. Rep. Serv. 1843 (1985). The debtor traded in two inboard motors that were subsequently sold three times. The ultimate purchaser took subject to the bank's security interest.

interest; (2) cases in which a specific rule of Article 9 grants priority to the purchaser; and (3) cases in which Section 2-403(2) on entrustment grants priority to a buyer in ordinary course of business.[8]

Section 9-315(a) recognizes the dual baseline interests of a secured party following a disposition of collateral. The security interest remains enforceable against the collateral, which means the purchaser's rights are subject to the security interest to the extent of the outstanding secured obligation. Further, the security interest also attaches automatically to any identifiable proceeds.[9] These dual interests give the secured party the option to pursue the proceeds, the collateral, or both, although only to the extent of satisfying the secured obligation.[10] Previous chapters covered the secured party's right to proceeds.[11] This chapter covers the secured party's rights in the collateral following its voluntary transfer to a purchaser.

Another provision of Article 9 that sometimes causes confusion preserves the alienability of the debtor's rights in the collateral. Notwithstanding an agreement between the debtor and the secured party that prohibits transfer or makes transfer an event of default, the debtor's legal and equitable rights in the collateral may be voluntarily or involuntarily transferred.[12] This provision appears at first glance to conflict with the rule preserving security interests in transferred collateral, but the two provisions actually are complementary and must be read together. The provision preserving alienability focuses on the *debtor's rights only.* Those rights are transferable notwithstanding an agreement to the contrary, but the transferee takes the rights subject to an enforceable security interest unless it can take advantage of an exception.

For example, suppose Manufacturer grants a security interest in its equipment to Secured Party and agrees that it will not sell any item of equipment without Secured Party's consent in record form. In breach of this agreement, Manufacturer sells and delivers to Buyer an item of equipment. The sale is effective to transfer Manufacturer's rights in the item to Buyer,[13] but Secured Party's interest encumbers those rights[14]

---

8. Section 2-403 does not cut off the rights of a secured party unless the secured party is an entruster.

9. U.C.C. §§ 9-203(f); 9-315(a)(2).

10. *See* U.C.C. 9-315, Comment 2.

11. *See* §§ 2.03, 8.02, 10.04, *supra.*

12. U.C.C. § 9-401(b). An example of an involuntary transfer is a lien creditor's levy on collateral. *See* § 12.02[A], *infra. See* Clapp v. Orix Credit Alliance, Inc., 192 Or. App. 320, 84 P.3d 833, 52 U.C.C. Rep. Serv. 2d 1016 (2004) (even though a provision in a sales contract/security agreement prohibited the assignment of the contract note without the written consent of the holder, it did not prevent the assignment to the plaintiff of the vendee's rights under the contract). Voluntary transfers are the focus of this chapter.

13. Because the transaction is a sale, Buyer acquires Manufacturer's title to the equipment. U.C.C. § 2-106(1) (sale consists of passage of title for a price). Buyer is now the debtor with respect to the purchased item. U.C.C. § 9-102(a)(28)(A).

14. In this situation, Buyer will have, absent an effective disclaimer, a cause of action against Manufacturer for breach of the Article 2 warranty of title. U.C.C. § 2-312.

unless Buyer can take advantage of an exception.[15] In addition, the sale is a breach of the security agreement, entitling Secured Party to exercise its remedies under Part 6 of Article 9 as supplemented by the agreement.[16]

§ 11.02 Authorized Disposition— § 9-315(a)(1)

A secured party that authorizes the debtor to dispose of all or part of its rights in the collateral free of the security interest obviously agrees to give up its security interest.[17] The secured party must rely solely on its right to proceeds and to any other collateral the debtor has retained. Similarly, if the secured party authorizes the debtor to lease or to license the collateral free of the security interest, the interest of the lessee or of the licensee is unencumbered, but the debtor's residual rights remain subject to the security interest. The authorization can be either express or implied.

[A] Express Authorization

Secured parties commonly authorize dispositions of collateral free of their security interests in the context of inventory financing. Most inventory consists of goods held for sale or lease,[18] and a secured lender that takes a security interest in such inventory and then prohibits its sale or lease is acting in a counter-productive fashion. Without such dispositions, the debtor could not generate the income necessary to pay the secured obligation. Consequently, secured parties generally authorize sales or leases of inventory and look to the proceeds to protect themselves.

Even in inventory financing, however, secured lenders are not likely to give a blanket authorization sufficient to support all dispositions. For example, inventory financers typically authorize only sales and leases made in the ordinary course of the debtor's business[19] because other sales and leases may include features that would be disadvantageous to the financer.[20] Even if a sale or lease is made in the ordinary course of

---

15. Production Credit Ass'n v. Columbus Mills, 22 U.C.C. Rep. Serv. 228 (Wis. Cir. Ct. 1977). *See also* Decatur Production Credit Ass'n v. Murphy, 119 Ill. App. 3d 277, 456 N.E.2d 267, 37 U.C.C. Rep. Serv. 1736 (1983) (transferee acquired only rights of debtor and was not free of security interest).

16. U.C.C. § 9-601.

17. U.C.C. § 9-315(a)(1). *In re* Jorenby, 393 B.R. 663, 66 U.C.C. Rep. Serv. 2d 774 (Bankr. W.D. Wis. 2008) (even though the security agreement did not preclude the debtor's disposition of the tractor collateral, the security interest continued in the tractor because the secured party had not authorized the sale free from its interest).

18. *See* § 1.04[A][3], *supra.*

19. Universal C.I.T. Credit Corp. v. Middlesboro Motor Sales, Inc., 424 S.W.2d 409, 4 U.C.C. Rep. Serv. 1126 (Ky. 1968) (sales of automobiles by dealer to owner's wife and employee were in ordinary course of business).

20. The court in *Crocker National Bank v. Ideco Division of Dresser Industries, Inc.*, 889 F.2d 1452, 10 U.C.C. Rep. Serv. 2d 573 (5th Cir. 1989), held that a transfer of goods back to the seller that supplied

business, the debtor's authorization to dispose of the collateral might be conditioned on a satisfactory credit check to determine that the buyer or lessee is creditworthy.[21]

Another limitation, commonly used with collateral other than inventory, is to authorize disposition free of the security interest in the security agreement but to condition that authorization on the consent of the secured party to any specific disposition.[22] This condition permits the secured party to assess the situation at or near the time of the proposed disposition,[23] and, if it authorizes the disposition, the secured party can insist on a method of payment that preserves its interest in the proceeds.[24] Thus, the requisite consent is often given on condition that the debtor remit the proceeds of the disposition (or a specified portion thereof) to the secured party, or that the purchaser wire the proceeds to the secured party or make its check jointly payable to the debtor and the secured party.

If the debtor subsequently fails to account for the proceeds as required by the secured party as a condition of its authorization, the secured party sometimes contends that its interest in the collateral continues against the purchaser, arguing that the debtor's failure to satisfy the condition renders the disposition unauthorized. A few courts have accepted this position.[25] The Ninth Circuit held, for example, that a secured party did

---

them was not a sale in the ordinary course of business. The transfer was to cancel the debt owed for their purchase, which would not leave any proceeds to protect the security interest.

The bad faith of the debtor precluded finding a sale in the ordinary course of business in *Central Finance Loan Corp. v. Bank of Illinois*, 149 Ill. App. 3d 724, 500 N.E.2d 1066, 3 U.C.C. Rep. Serv. 2d 1178 (1986). A car dealer used false pretenses to obtain a duplicate certificate of title for a sale of an automobile in its inventory.

21. Other provisions of Article 9 discussed later in this chapter enable some buyers or lessees in ordinary course of business to take free of a prior perfected security interest in inventory even though the disposition is unauthorized. *See* § 11.03[A][1], *infra*.

22. United States v. E. W. Savage & Son, Inc., 343 F. Supp. 123, 10 U.C.C. Rep. Serv. 1093 (D.S.D. 1972) (cattle sold without written consent as required in security agreement); Smith v. Paccar Fin. Corp., 64 U.C.C. Rep. Serv. 2d 685 (Minn. Ct. App. 2007) (failure to comply with a written-consent requirement with respect to a truck); *In re* Jersey Tractor Trailer Training Inc., 580 F.3d 147, 69 U.C.C. Rep. Serv. 2d 748 (3d Cir. 2009) (because security agreement provided that debtor would not settle any accounts for less than their full value without written permission of secured party, secured party did not authorize sale of the accounts for only 61.5 percent of the amounts due free of its security interest).

23. First Nat'l Bank & Trust Co. of Oklahoma City v. Atchison Cnty. Auction Co., Inc., 10 Kan. App. 2d 382, 699 P.2d 1032, 41 U.C.C. Rep. Serv. 219 (1985) (where secured party waived written consent requirement but still required prior oral consultation, sale of livestock without consultation was unauthorized).

24. A secured lender required the debtor to have buyers of hogs issue checks jointly to the lender and debtor, and it informed buyers of this requirement. Sales made without compliance were unauthorized, and the buyers were liable for conversion. Lafayette Prod. Credit Ass'n v. Wilson Foods Corp., 687 F. Supp. 1267, 6 U.C.C. Rep. Serv. 2d 1278 (N.D. Ind. 1987).

25. *See, e.g.*, Southwest Wash. Prod. Credit Ass'n v. Seattle-First Nat'l Bank, 92 Wash. 2d 30, 593 P.2d 167, 26 U.C.C. Rep. Serv. 1346 (1979); RFC Capital Corp. v. Earthlink, Inc., 55 U.C.C. Rep. Serv. 2d 617 (Ohio Ct. App. 2004) (buyer bears the risk that the conditions established by secured party will be satisfied, even if buyer lacks control to satisfy the conditions).

not release its security interest in cattle until it actually received the proceeds from the debtor's sales.[26]

These decisions are unfair when the purchaser does not know of the secured party's condition at the time it pays for the collateral. The authorized-disposition rule is essentially an estoppel rule. Having clothed the debtor with authority to dispose of the collateral free of the security interest, a disappointed secured party ought not be allowed to pursue the collateral into the hands of a good-faith purchaser without notice of the condition.[27] Once the purchaser pays the debtor, it cannot control what the debtor does with the proceeds.[28] Imposing a condition of debtor compliance thus makes the purchaser an insurer of acts that are beyond both its knowledge and its control.[29] Most courts have correctly recognized that the failure to remit the proceeds constitutes a breach by the debtor[30] but does not retroactively negate the authority to dispose of the collateral free of the security interest.[31] The result should be different, however, if the purchaser knows that authorization for the sale has been conditioned on debtor remittance of the proceeds.[32] The equities in that situation require that the purchaser take steps, such as issuance of a check naming the secured party as joint payee or a wire transfer of the funds to the secured party, that protect the secured party's interest.[33]

The secured party can provide express authorization in the security agreement or otherwise.[34] The security agreement itself can include a term expressly authorizing anticipated dispositions.[35] The secured party can also give express authorization

---

26. *In re* Ellsworth, 722 F.2d 1448, 37 U.C.C. Rep. Serv. 1376 (9th Cir. 1984).

27. Moffat Cnty. State Bank v. Producers Livestock Mktg. Ass'n, 598 F. Supp. 1562, 40 U.C.C. Rep. Serv. 314 (D. Colo. 1984).

28. *In re* Cullen, 71 B.R. 274, 3 U.C.C. Rep. Serv. 2d 815 (Bankr. W.D. Wis. 1987) (condition ineffective unless purchaser can control satisfaction of condition).

29. Production Credit Ass'n of Baraboo v. Pillsbury Co., 132 Wis. 2d 243, 392 N.W.2d 445, 1 U.C.C. Rep. Serv. 2d 1352 (Ct. App. 1986) (conditions on authorization to sell are effective only if satisfaction of condition is within buyer's control).

30. Moffat Cnty. State Bank v. Producers Livestock Mktg. Ass'n, 598 F. Supp. 1562, 40 U.C.C. Rep. Serv. 314 (D. Colo. 1984).

31. Parkersburg State Bank v. Swift Indep. Packing Co., 764 F.2d 512, 41 U.C.C. Rep. Serv. 248 (8th Cir. 1985) (sale had been authorized even though debtor subsequently failed to apply sale proceeds to secured debt).

32. Lafayette Prod. Credit Ass'n v. Wilson Foods Corp., 687 F. Supp. 1267, 6 U.C.C. Rep. Serv. 2d 1278 (N.D. Ind. 1987) (secured party notified buyers that checks should be issued jointly to lender and farmer).

33. The same principle applies when the buyer agrees to a condition imposed by the secured creditor that upon transfer of the collateral the buyer assumes the debtor's obligations. *In re* Hanson Restaurants, Inc., 155 B.R. 758, 21 U.C.C. Rep. Serv. 2d 810 (Bankr. D. Minn. 1993); *In re* Dawley, 44 B.R. 738, 40 U.C.C. Rep. Serv. 1893 (Bankr. W.D. Pa. 1984).

34. U.C.C. §9-315, Comment 2.

35. Attempts by litigants to stretch common clauses in security agreements to include an authorization to dispose of the collateral have been rebuffed by the courts. Northern Commercial Co. v. Cobb, 778 P.2d 205, 10 U.C.C. Rep. Serv. 2d 197 (Alaska 1989) (inclusion of right to proceeds). The *Cobb* case also holds that the absence of any restrictions on sale in the security agreement cannot be construed as implying an authorization to sell.

in another record[36] or even orally.[37] The authorization need not even be express—a secured party can engage in conduct from which authorization to sell free of its security interest may be fairly inferred. The ensuing subsection discusses implied waivers.

[B] Implied Authorization

Even though a secured party does not expressly authorize a disposition of collateral free of its security interest, its conduct might provide a basis for inferring consent. Arguably, a secured party that knowingly acquiesces in the debtor's disposition impliedly authorizes the disposition. Some courts accept this argument, holding that a secured party that is aware of a transfer by the debtor and does not object tacitly consents.[38] Other courts refuse to recognize mere acquiescence as a sufficient basis to find implicit authorization.[39]

Another argument that purchasers sometimes make is that a secured party that accepts the proceeds of a disposition thereby ratifies it (i.e., authorizes it after the fact). Mere acceptance of proceeds, however, should not suffice to establish ratification.[40] Article 9 explicitly provides that a security interest continues in identifiable proceeds and, absent authorization or a contrary rule, in the collateral as well. A secured party thus has a right to the proceeds. The Comments to Section 9-315 make clear that "[t]he secured party's right to proceeds ... does not in itself constitute an authorization of disposition."[41]

The purchaser makes a better case if the secured party has engaged in a pattern of accepting proceeds from unauthorized dispositions that is sufficient to establish a course of dealing or course of performance. A course of dealing[42] provides an appro-

---

36. *In re* Dawley, 44 B.R. 738, 40 U.C.C. Rep. Serv. 1893 (Bankr. W.D. Pa. 1984) (written consent of secured party for debtor to transfer its equity in collateral to another person); Ottumwa Prod. Credit Ass'n v. Keoco Auction Co., 347 N.W.2d 393, 38 U.C.C. Rep. Serv. 624 (Iowa 1984) (letter instructing debtor to liquidate its hog holdings).

37. Wright v. Vickaryous, 611 P.2d 20, 28 U.C.C. Rep. Serv. 1177 (Alaska 1980) (secured creditors consented to auction sales of cattle in conversations with owner). *See also* First Nat'l Bank of Bethany v. Waco-Pacific, Inc., 9 U.C.C. Rep. Serv. 1064 (Okla. Ct. App. 1971) (secured party's promise to release its interest in airplane to facilitate its sale was not subject to statute of frauds).

38. Vacura v. Haar's Equip., Inc., 364 N.W.2d 387, 40 U.C.C. Rep. Serv. 1493 (Minn. 1985). *See also* Cessna Fin. Corp. v. Skyways Enters., Inc., 580 S.W.2d 491, 26 U.C.C. Rep. Serv. 212 (Ky. 1979) (prior consent requirement waived by secured party's acquiescence in sales of other airplanes subject to same requirement).

39. *See, e.g.*, Oxford Prod. Credit Ass'n v. Dye, 368 So. 2d 241, 26 U.C.C. Rep. Serv. 217 (Miss. 1979).

40. J.I. Case Credit Corp. v. Crites, 851 F.2d 309, 6 U.C.C. Rep. Serv. 2d 551 (10th Cir. 1988). *See also* Brown v. Arkoma Coal Corp., 276 Ark. 322, 634 S.W.2d 390 (1982) (no waiver of security interest in trying to prevent distribution of proceeds from judicial sale after collateral was taken by lien creditor).

41. U.C.C. § 9-315, Comment 2.

42. A course of dealing means "a sequence of conduct concerning previous transactions between the parties to a particular transaction that is fairly to be regarded as establishing a common basis of understanding for interpreting their expressions and other conduct." U.C.C. § 1-303(b).

priate basis for supplementing or qualifying the terms of the agreement.[43] For example, a course of dealing might develop between a farmer and a bank that have entered annually into a secured transaction with respect to the farmer's livestock, with each year's security agreement including a prohibition against the farmer's sale of any of the collateral without the bank's prior approval.[44] If, in a sequence of annual transactions, the bank ignored the prior-approval requirement and acquiesced in the debtor's sales, a purchaser could argue that this pattern of conduct created a course of dealing that implicitly authorized the sale under the current security agreement.[45] A course of performance[46] is comparable to a course of dealing except that, rather than a sequence of repeated conduct within the context of prior transactions between the same two parties, the sequence of conduct is under the existing contract. For example, a bank's repeated acquiescence to livestock sales by a debtor with respect to a current security agreement could result in implicit authorization to make additional, similar sales under that agreement.[47]

Although similar in that each is based on a sequence of conduct, the Code makes a functional distinction between a course of dealing and a course of performance. To illustrate the distinction, suppose a security agreement contains an express term prohibiting disposition by the debtor without the prior consent of the secured party. Evidence of a sequence of conduct permitting dispositions without consent, constituting either a course of dealing or course of performance, clearly contradicts the express term. Under the hierarchy established by Article 1, express terms and terms derived from a course of dealing or course of performance are to be construed wherever reasonable as consistent with each other; however, when such construction is unreasonable, express terms control.[48] If this hierarchical provision is applied literally, a course of dealing could not displace an express term prohibiting disposition. Several courts have used this rationale to defeat course-of-dealing arguments advanced by purchasers.[49] By con-

---

43. U.C.C. § 1-303(d). A course of performance or usage of trade can serve the same purposes. *Id.*

44. The U.C.C.'s "farm-products rule," discussed in § 14.01, *infra*, continued security interests in farm products notwithstanding their purchase by a buyer in ordinary course of business. The bulk of the implied-authorization cases arose in the context of such purchases. The federal Food Security Act of 1985 now preempts the U.C.C. rule. *See* §§ 14.02, 14.03, *infra*.

45. *See, e.g.,* Producers Cotton Oil Co. v. Amstar Corp., 197 Cal. App. 3d 638, 242 Cal. Rptr. 914, 5 U.C.C. Rep. Serv. 2d 32 (1988).

46. A course of performance means "a sequence of conduct between the parties to a particular transaction that exists if: (1) the agreement of the parties with respect to the transaction involves repeated occasions for performance by a party; and (2) the other party, with knowledge of the nature of the performance and opportunity for objection to it, accepts the performance or acquiesces in it without objection." U.C.C. § 1-303(a).

47. Farmers State Bank v. Farmland Foods, Inc., 225 Neb. 1, 402 N.W.2d 277, 3 U.C.C. Rep. Serv. 2d 902 (1987), *overruling* Garden City Prod. Credit Ass'n v. Lannan, 186 Neb. 668, 186 N.W.2d 99, 8 U.C.C. Rep. Serv. 1163 (1971).

48. U.C.C. § 1-303(e). With a conflict between a course of dealing and a course of performance, the course of performance controls. *Id.*

49. First Bank v. Eastern Livestock Co., 886 F. Supp. 1328, 27 U.C.C. Rep. Serv. 2d 1045 (S.D. Miss. 1995); *In re* Envtl. Electronic Sys., Inc., 2 B.R. 583, 29 U.C.C. Rep. Serv. 271 (Bankr. N.D. Ga. 1980); Wabasso State Bank v. Caldwell Packing Co., 251 N.W.2d 321, 19 U.C.C. Rep. Serv. 315 (Minn. 1976).

trast, a course of performance might constitute a waiver or modification of the express term.[50] Thus, an argument based on a course of performance might succeed where an argument based on a course of dealing would fail.

§ 11.03 Priorities

The disposition of collateral following an authorization by the secured party for a disposition free of the security interest terminates the security interest in the collateral. The termination avoids a priority conflict between the formerly secured party and the purchaser or a transferee from the purchaser. The situation differs for dispositions not similarly authorized. The residual rule of Section 9-315(a)(1) continues the secured party's interest in the collateral notwithstanding its disposition.[51] The residual rule, however, is expressly subject to exceptions provided in other sections of Article 9 and in Section 2-403.[52] The ensuing material explains the priority rules that protect purchasers (other than secured parties) of different types of collateral from prior-perfected security interests. Chapter 12 covers the rights of such purchasers against unperfected security interests.[53]

[A] Goods

[1] Buyers and Lessees of Goods in Ordinary Course of Business—§§ 9-320(a), 9-321(c)

Article 9 provides that a buyer in ordinary course of business (other than one that buys farm products from a farmer) or a lessee in ordinary course of business takes collateral free of a security interest created by the buyer's immediate seller or the lessee's immediate lessor, even if the security interest is perfected and the buyer or lessee knows of its existence.[54] These rules seek to protect parties that buy or lease goods in good faith from the inventory of a dealer.[55] These rules are superfluous to the extent that the secured party authorizes disposition free of the security interest, which is common with inventory.[56]

---

50. U.C.C. § 1-303(f).

51. See § 11.01, *supra*.

52. U.C.C. § 9-315(a).

53. See § 12.03, *infra*.

54. U.C.C. §§ 9-320(a), 9-321(c). *See* First Nat'l Bank of El Campo, Texas v. Buss, 54 U.C.C. Rep. Serv. 2d 706 (Tex. Ct. App. 2004) (buyers of automobiles from a used-car dealer qualified as buyers in ordinary course and took free of security interest that bank perfected by filing as to the used-car inventory of the dealer/debtor, despite the fact that the secured party retained certificates of title for the automobiles).

55. See U.C.C. § 1-201(b)(9) (defining "buyer in ordinary course of business") and the discussion in § 11.03[A][1][a], *infra*.

56. See § 11.02, *supra*.

These exceptions reflect the policy of removing obstacles that would unduly impede the free flow of commerce in goods. Buyers and lessees in ordinary course of business rely on the integrity of the marketplace to pass to them good title (buyers) or enjoyment of the right to possession and use without interference (lessees), and this well-placed reliance reduces transaction costs. The exceptions relieve the buyer or lessee from the burdens of checking the filing system and negotiating releases from secured parties.

[a] Defining the Buyer or Lessee— §§ 1-201(b)(9), 2A-103(o)

A buyer must qualify as a "buyer in ordinary course of business" to take free of a perfected security interest. The definition of this term establishes criteria for the buyer, the seller, and the sales transaction.[57] A buyer in ordinary course of business essentially is (1) a bona-fide purchaser for value of goods, (2) acquired in the ordinary course from the perspective of the buyer, (3) from a seller that deals in such goods, and (4) in the type of transaction by which such dealers normally conduct sales.

A buyer must buy the goods from a person, other than a pawnbroker, that is in the business of selling goods of the kind being purchased.[58] This requirement effectively limits the status to buyers from the inventory of a merchant.[59] The primary issue with respect to this part of the definition prior to the 1998 revision was whether a buyer could qualify when the transaction fell outside the seller's most common business activity. For example, in *Hempstead Bank v. Andy's Car Rental System, Inc.*,[60] a car rental agency was generally in the business of leasing automobiles but periodically sold automobiles in its inventory to keep its fleet modern. The court characterized the sales as merely incidental to the leasing business and therefore held that these sales were not made by a person engaged in the business of selling automobiles.[61]

The court in *Tanbro Fabrics Corp. v. Deering Milliken, Inc.*,[62] held in favor of a buyer even though the transaction differed from the seller's most common business prac-

---

57. U.C.C. § 1-201(b)(9). The buyer bears the burden of establishing that it qualifies as a buyer in ordinary course. Integrity Bank Plus v. Talking Sales, Inc., 56 U.C.C. Rep. Serv. 2d 400 (D. Minn. 2005). The definitions of "lessee in ordinary course of business" and "licensee in ordinary course of business" conform, for the most part, with the definition of "buyer in ordinary course of business." U.C.C. §§ 2A-103(1)(o) (lessee), 9-321(a) (licensee).

58. U.C.C.§ 1-201(b)(9). Sindone v. Farber, 105 Misc. 2d 634, 432 N.Y.S.2d 778, 31 U.C.C. Rep. Serv. 329 (Sup. Ct. 1980) (goods sold were equipment, not inventory, as debtor did not hold them for purposes of sale). The courts have clarified that sales between dealers can qualify because they frequently sell to one another. Taft v. Jake Kaplan, Ltd., 28 U.C.C. Rep. Serv. 253 (Bankr. D.R.I. 1980); Weidinger Chevrolet, Inc. v. Universal CIT Credit Corp., 501 F.2d 459, 15 U.C.C. Rep. Serv. 197 (8th Cir. 1974).

59. A buyer of farm products from a farmer can qualify as a buyer in ordinary course of business, but such buyers do not get the benefit of the Article 9 priority rule, and, in any event, preemptive federal law determines their rights. See § 14.02, *infra*.

60. 35 A.D.2d 35, 312 N.Y.S.2d 317, 7 U.C.C. Rep. Serv. 932 (Sup. Ct. 1980).

61. *Accord* O'Neill v. Barnett Bank of Jacksonville, N.A., 360 So. 2d 150, 24 U.C.C. Rep. Serv. 779 (Fla. Dist. Ct. App. 1978) (occasional sale of used airplane by seller in business of airplane rental and service held insufficient to qualify).

62. 39 N.Y.2d 632, 385 N.Y.S.2d 260, 350 N.E.2d 590, 19 U.C.C. Rep. Serv. 385 (1976).

tice. Deering sold unfinished fabric to Mill Fabrics, which then finished the fabric and resold it in the course of its business. Mill Fabrics lacked storage capacity, so Deering retained possession of the fabric (even though Mill Fabrics had paid for it) until the buyer needed it. Deering also retained a security interest in the fabric for obligations owed to it by Mill Fabrics under an open account. Mill Fabric on occasion sold unfinished fabric to other fabric converters, and it ordered Deering to make delivery to these buyers. Tanbro was such a buyer. When Deering refused to make delivery, Tanbro sued for conversion. Tanbro argued that it was a buyer in ordinary course of business and therefore took free from the security interest that Deering had perfected by possession. The court held in Tanbro's favor.

The finding that the sale to Tanbro was an ordinary-course transaction was appropriate. Although Mill Fabrics more commonly sold finished fabric, its sales of unfinished fabric were consistent with an industry-wide norm and thus reasonably to be expected.[63] As part of the 1998 revision to Article 9, the drafters also amended the Article 1 definition of buyer in ordinary course of business to ratify this aspect of *Tanbro*. The revised definition provides that "[a] person buys in the ordinary course if the sale to the person comports with the usual or customary practices in the kind of business in which the seller is engaged or with the seller's own usual or customary practices."[64]

Another aspect of *Tanbro*—its grant of priority to a buyer over a security interest perfected by possession—caused a stir in the marketplace. Nothing in former law restricted the exception favoring these buyers to security interests perfected by a method other than possession. Nevertheless, possession is a common element in rules that protect bona-fide purchasers,[65] and the 1998 revisions reversed this aspect of *Tanbro*. Section 9-320(e) modifies the exception favoring buyers in ordinary course of business by providing that it does "not affect a security interest in goods in the possession of the secured party under Section 9-313," and the definition of buyer in ordinary course of business states that "[o]nly a buyer that takes possession of the goods or has a right to recover the goods from the seller under Article 2 may be a buyer in ordinary course of business."[66] The circumstances in which Article 2 provides a buyer with a right of possession are quite limited.[67]

---

63. *Accord* Sea Harvest, Inc. v. Rig & Crane Equip. Corp., 181 N.J. Super. 41, 436 A.2d 553, 32 U.C.C. Rep. Serv. 1005 (Ch. Div. 1981) (sales of equipment were substantial part of lessor's business).

64. U.C.C. § 1-201(b)(9). Fordyce Bank & Trust Co. v. Bean Timberland, Inc., 369 Ark. 90, 251 S.W.3d 267, 62 U.C.C. Rep. Serv. 2d 133 (Ark. 2007) (sales of wood comported with the buyer's and the trade's customary practice of not conducting a prior lien search, and finding a filed financing statement would merely have indicated the possible security interest but not a violation of that interest through the sales). The revision process did not make a comparable change in the article on leases to Section 2A-103(1)(a) (definition of "buyer in ordinary course of business") or Section 2A-103(1)(o) (definition of "lessee in ordinary course of business").

65. See discussion in § 12.03, *infra*.

66. U.C.C. § 1-201(b)(9). The revision process did not make a comparable change in Article 2A on leases.

67. *See* U.C.C. §§ 2-502 (pre-paying buyer entitled to possession of consumer goods if seller repudiates or fails to deliver; buyer entitled to possession of any goods if seller becomes insolvent with-

A person must have the requisite bona fides to qualify as a buyer in ordinary course of business. The buyer must act in good faith, must not have knowledge that the sale violates the rights of another person (including the rights of a secured party), must buy in the ordinary course, and must give value for the goods. The buyer may give cash, may exchange property for the goods, may buy on secured or unsecured credit, and may buy under a preexisting contract of sale. The buyer may not, however, buy in bulk and cannot take the goods in total or partial satisfaction of a preexisting money debt.

The requirement that the buyer not know that the sale violates the rights of another person might appear to conflict with the part of Section 9-320(a) that allows a buyer in ordinary course of business to take free of a perfected security interest even though the buyer knows of its existence. The provisions actually do not conflict. A buyer that knows that a security interest exists qualifies for protection; a buyer that knows that the sale violates the terms of the security agreement does not qualify.[68] The Official Comments reconcile the two provisions as follows:

> The buyer in ordinary course of business is defined as one who buys goods "in good faith, without knowledge that the sale violates the rights of another person and in the ordinary course." Subsection (a) provides that such a buyer takes free of a security interest, even though perfected, and even though the buyer knows the security interest exists. Reading the definition together with the rule of law results in the buyer's taking free if the buyer merely knows that a security interest covers the goods but taking subject if the buyer knows, in addition, that the sale violates a term in an agreement with the secured party.[69]

Suppose, for example, that Bank has a perfected security interest in Dealer's inventory of consumer electronics. The security agreement requires Dealer to obtain a check made jointly payable to it and to Bank on any cash sale in excess of $2,000. Suppose further that two buyers purchase big-screen TVs on the same day, each paying with a $2,500 check made payable only to Dealer. Both buyers know of Bank's security interest, but only Buyer 1 knows of the joint-check requirement. If Dealer defaults, Bank can enforce its security interest against Buyer 1, who does not qualify as a buyer in

---

in ten days after receipt of first installment on the price); 2-716(1) (specific performance); 2-716(3) (buyer's right of replevin). *In re Dorsey Trailer Co., Inc.*, 68 U.C.C. Rep. Serv. 2d 335 (Bankr. M.D. Ala. 2009) (due to a scarcity of certain raw materials needed to manufacture the type of trailers in the contract, the trailers in the seller's possession were unique, and the buyer had the right to recover them through specific performance).

68. *Quinn v. Scheu*, 675 P.2d 1078, 38 U.C.C. Rep. Serv. 367 (Or. Ct. App. 1984) (buyer that paid seller after notification that payment was to be made directly to secured party bought in knowing violation); *DaimlerChrysler Serv. N. Am., LLC v. Labate Chrysler, Jeep, Dodge, Inc.*, 61 U.C.C. Rep. Serv. 2d 217 (N.D. Ohio 2006) (debtor dealership that purchased two automobiles from itself in direct contravention of a preclusion in the security agreement covering the dealership's inventory knew that the sales violated the rights of the secured lender).

69. U.C.C. § 9-320, Comment 3. *Indianapolis Car Exchange, Inc. v. Alderson*, 910 N.E.2d 802, 69 U.C.C. Rep. Serv. 2d 980 (Ind. Ct. App. 2009) (although buyer had an indication of a lender's interest in the vehicle, she did not know that her purchase of the vehicle would violate the lender agreement).

ordinary course of business. Buyer 2 qualifies, assuming satisfaction with all other elements, and takes free of Bank's security interest.

The requirement that the buyer buy in ordinary course means that the sale itself must be conducted in a manner consistent with the way that most sellers conduct such sales. For example, a sale of a new watch by a jeweler from its store would comply, whereas a sale of the same watch by the jeweler at a garage sale would not qualify. Note that the definition of "buyer in ordinary course of business" requires the seller to be in the business of selling goods of the kind sold, but it does not require the buyer to be in business or the transaction itself to relate to a buyer's business. The definition thus can be satisfied by a consumer who, by definition, buys for personal, family, or household purpose.[70]

[b] Created by Its Seller or Lessor

A buyer or lessee in ordinary course of business takes free of a perfected security interest only if the buyer's immediate seller or the lessee's immediate lessor created the security interest.[71] Put another way, only a person that acquires an interest in goods directly from the debtor that granted the security interest can take advantage of the special priority rules protecting ordinary-course buyers and lessees.

For example, assume Bank has a perfected security interest in Retailer's inventory of computers. If Corporation buys a computer from Retailer for use in its business operations, Corporation will almost certainly take the computer free of Bank's security interest. The sale of the computer was probably authorized free of the security interest by Bank. Even if not, Corporation probably qualifies as a buyer in ordinary course of business, and Retailer, its immediate seller, created the security interest. For purposes of comparison, assume now that Bank provides an enabling loan for Partnership to acquire a computer for use in its accounting business, and Bank takes and perfects a security interest in the computer. Partnership, in violation of the terms of the security agreement, sells the computer to Dealer, who specializes in used computers. Because Partnership is not in the business of selling computers, Dealer is not a buyer in ordinary course of business and thus takes the computer subject to Bank's perfected security interest.[72] If Dealer later resells the computer to Buyer, Buyer may qualify as a buyer in ordinary course of business, but it cannot take free of Bank's security interest under Section 9-320(a) because Buyer's immediate seller (Dealer) did not create the security interest. Buyer is lumped together with buyers not in ordinary course of

---

70. *See* U.C.C. § 9-102(a)(24)(A).

71. U.C.C. §§ 9-320(a), 9-321(c). *Compare* Bombardier Capital, Inc. v. Hensley, 69 U.C.C. Rep. Serv. 2d 1357 (Ky. Ct. App. 2006) (buyer in ordinary course of a mobile home from the inventory of a dealer financed by plaintiff took free of the security interest granted by their seller) *with* Walden v. Mercedes Benz Credit Corp., 57 U.C.C. Rep. Serv. 2d 182 (Pa. Ct. Com. Pl. 2005) (original purchaser of an automobile gave a security interest in the car and later sold it to another dealer, but buyer in ordinary course of the car from the dealer did not take free of the security interest because the interest had not been created by the dealer).

72. U.C.C. § 9-315(a)(1).

business for priority purposes and thus takes the computer subject to Bank's perfected security interest.[73]

What explains the differing treatment of Corporation, an ordinary-course buyer that takes free of a perfected security interest, and Buyer, an ordinary-course buyer that takes subject to the perfected security interest? The perspectives of the two buyers cannot provide the rationale. Both buyers made good-faith purchases of similar goods from a merchant, and neither expected to receive anything other than clear title.[74] As the explanation below develops, the doctrine of apparent authority provides the answer.[75] The doctrine focuses on the actions of the secured party and on the business status of the debtor, not on the qualifications of the buyer. If this result seems unfair, recall that it is not the only situation in which a buyer in ordinary course of business takes goods subject to the interest of another person. A good-faith purchaser for value from a thief cannot take goods free from the interest of their rightful owner, so if a thief steals goods and sells them to a good-faith dealer in that type of goods, the dealer will take them subject to the owner's interest. If the dealer subsequently sells the goods to a buyer in ordinary course of business, the buyer will also take them subject to the owner's interest.[76] Buyers in ordinary course of business receive enormous, but not blanket, protection.

As covered previously,[77] inventory financers almost invariably give their debtors authority to sell collateral in ordinary-course transactions, although they sometimes impose conditions that limit the debtor's authority. Buyers and lessees in such transactions do not need a special priority rule to take free of the financer's interest if all the conditions imposed by the secured party are satisfied because the debtor has actual authority to conduct the sale free of the security interest. However, suppose a debtor sells inventory on credit in violation of a requirement that the secured party first determine the creditworthiness of the prospective buyer and approve the sale. Even though the sale is unauthorized, the secured party will, and should, lose to a buyer in ordinary course of business.[78] The rationale for this result is that the secured party clothed the debtor with the appearance of authority to make the sale.

The Article 9 approach to ordinary-course buyers is similar to the Article 2 entrustment rule. Under that rule, a person that delivers goods to, or allows them to be retained by, a merchant that deals in goods of the kind gives the merchant the power (as distinct from the right) to transfer the entruster's rights to a buyer in ordinary course of business.[79] This result differs from the common law of bailments, which generally protects

---

73. *See* § 12.03, *infra*.

74. Both buyers are beneficiaries of the Article 2 warranty of title. U.C.C. § 2-312. A warranty against interference protects a similarly situated lessee. U.C.C. § 2A-211(1).

75. *See generally* William H. Lawrence, *The "Created by His Seller" Limitation of Section 9-307(1) of the UCC: A Provision in Need of an Articulated Policy*, 60 IND. L.J. 73, 80(83 (1984).

76. *Cf.* U.C.C. § 2-403(1).

77. *See* § 11.02, *supra*.

78. U.C.C. § 9-320(a).

79. U.C.C. § 2-403(3), (2).

ownership interests from claims by purchasers from a bailee. The premise for the rule is that the entruster clothes the merchant with apparent authority to sell inventory in ordinary-course transactions, just as the similar rule of Article 9 applies because the secured party clothes the merchant with similar apparent authority. By permitting a debtor to be in possession of goods when the debtor is in the business of selling goods of the kind, a secured party vests the debtor with apparent authority. A secured party's nonpossessory security interest in a debtor's inventory is an entrustment to the only entity—a merchant with respect to such goods—that can sell the goods to a buyer that can qualify as a buyer in ordinary course of business.[80]

The basis for apparent authority is missing if the secured lender entrusts the debtor with possession of goods other than inventory. A secured party's acquiescence in its debtor's possession of non-inventory collateral does not create appearances to third parties that the debtor's primary purpose for holding the goods is to sell them. Consequently, Section 9-320(a) does not provide protection for purchasers that buy these goods from the debtor.

The limitation in Sections 9-320(a) and 9-321(c) to persons that buy or lease directly from the person that created the security interest reflects the reality that a secured party only rarely would be responsible for clothing anyone other than its debtor with apparent authority to sell or lease collateral. However, a secured party occasionally delivers (or more likely acquiesces in the delivery of) its collateral to a remote party that deals in goods of that kind. In that case, the secured party comes within the Article 2 entrustment rule, which is expressly cross-referenced in Article 9,[81] and the merchant thus has the power to transfer all rights of the secured party to a buyer in ordinary course of business.[82] The situation is sometimes referred to as remote entrustment. Suppose, for example, that a financially distressed debtor convinces a secured party to permit the collateral to be placed with a dealer for sale on commission. A buyer in ordinary course of business from the dealer takes free of the rights of both the debtor and the secured party, as both are entrusters.[83]

---

80. Qualification for buyer-in-ordinary-course-of-business status requires, for both Article 2 and Article 9, that the buyer purchase from a person in the business of selling goods of that kind. U.C.C. § 1-201(b)(9).

81. U.C.C. § 9-315(a)(1). See § 2-403(2), (3).

82. Article 2A does not have a parallel rule for lessees in the ordinary course of business. Nevertheless, if goods are entrusted by a secured party to a merchant who deals in goods of that kind and subsequently leased to an ordinary-course lessee, the lessee should take free of the security interest on estoppel grounds.

83. By contrast, consider the situation in *Conseco Finance Servicing Corp. v. Lee*, 54 U.C.C. Rep. Serv. 2d 96 (Tex. Ct. App. 2004). The original buyer of a motor home from a dealer granted a security interest in the motor home which the dealer then assigned to Conseco. A few years later, the motor home ended up back in the hands of the same dealer, for reasons not clearly explained by the court (perhaps because the original buyer did not wish to continue making the payments and turned the motor home back over to the dealer, believing the dealer to be Conseco's agent). The dealer resold it to the Lees, who were not aware of Conseco's security interest. Conseco sought to repossess the motor home. The Lees were not entitled to protection under the buyer-in-ordinary-course rule because the security interest was created by the original buyer, not by the dealer. Further, the Lees were not entitled

Once a buyer takes free of a security interest, subsequent transferees acquire the buyer's right and also take free of the security interest (the "shelter" principle). For example, the plaintiffs in *Indianapolis Car Exchange, Inc. v. Alderson*[84] purchased a vehicle from a seller that bought it from a debtor/dealer that had given a security interest in the vehicle as part of its inventory. The defendant secured party argued that the plaintiffs could not take the vehicle free of the security interest because the interest had not been created by their seller. The plaintiffs' seller (the debtor/dealer), however, had taken the vehicle free of that interest because it was a buyer in ordinary course of business that qualified under Section 9-320(a).[85]

[2] Consumer Buyers of Consumer Goods— § 9-320(b)

Article 9 includes a provision that allows certain consumer buyers to take consumer goods free of automatically perfected purchase-money security interests. Automatic perfection of purchase-money security interests in consumer goods[86] is a practical necessity given the enormous volume of such transactions and it saves consumers the cost of filing, but it creates hidden liens. Strong policies support enforcement of such liens against nonreliance creditors (e.g., bankruptcy trustees). Enforcement against commercial buyers (e.g., second-hand stores) and other secured lenders is a closer case, but the drafters made the policy decision to subordinate such buyers and lenders on the grounds that they ought to be aware generally of such risks when they deal with used consumer goods and they can ask appropriate questions of their seller or borrower. Enforcement against consumer buyers (i.e., persons who buy consumer goods from another consumer for their own personal, family, or household purposes) goes too far. Accordingly, consumer buyers who give value take free of an automatically perfected security interest unless they know of it.[87]

The priority available through this provision has a narrow range. It applies only if the secured party relies upon automatic perfection and the buyer intends to use the goods for personal, family, or household purposes. The section thus governs only consumer-to-consumer sales[88] and is, for that reason, sometimes referred to as the "garage-sale" rule. The secured party can avoid the impact of the rule by filing a financ-

---

to protection under the entrustment rule, because there was no evidence that Conseco had entrusted the motor home to the dealer.

84. 910 N.E.2d 802, 69 U.C.C. Rep. Serv. 2d 802 (Ind. Ct. App. 2009).

85. U.C.C. § 2-403(1). *See also* Gary Aircraft Corp. v. General Dynamics Corp., 681 F.2d 365 (5th Cir. 1982) (sale to a buyer in ordinary course extinguished the lien, which did not resurrect on the subsequent sale).

86. *See* § 7.01, *supra.*

87. U.C.C. § 9-320(b).

88. Security Pac. Nat'l Bank v. Goodman, 24 Cal. App. 3d 131, 100 Cal. Rptr. 763, 10 U.C.C. Rep. Serv. 529 (1972); Meskell v. Bertone, 55 U.C.C. Rep. Serv. 2d 179 (Mass. Super. Ct. 2004) (even though a professional agent negotiated the sale of a boat, agreement between buyer and seller qualified as a sale between two consumers, and buyer took free of the security interest of the bank that did not file a financing statement).

ing statement covering the goods prior to the purchase. Although the belief that an average consumer will check the filing system before buying used goods from another consumer is far-fetched, as a practical matter, filing is all the secured party can do to stake its claim and thereby ameliorate the problem of ostensible ownership.

[3] Future Advances—§ 9-323(d)–(g)

Article 9 includes provisions that govern priority between a security interest covering future advances and a buyer or lessee not in ordinary course of business.[89] Even a buyer or lessee that takes subject to a security interest will generally take free of the security interest to the extent that it covers future advances made after the earlier of (1) the time the secured party acquired knowledge of the sale or lease or (2) forty-five days after the sale or lease.[90] Notwithstanding these limitations, the secured party has priority for the advance if it was made pursuant to a commitment[91] entered into without knowledge of the purchase and before the expiration of the 45-day period.[92] The commitment can be made either before or after the sale or lease, as long it is made without knowledge and the 45-day period has not expired. The "45-days-or-less" rule for gaining priority stands in contrast to the "45-days-or-more" rule that applies in priority disputes between a lien creditor and a secured party that makes future advances after the lien creditor's lien arose.[93]

A buyer or lessee in ordinary course of business takes free of any security interest created by the immediate seller or lessor and thus does not need protection against future advances.[94] Likewise, a buyer or lessee that takes delivery of the goods for value and without knowledge of an unperfected security interest takes free of that security interest[95] and, accordingly, free from future advances. Thus, the rules regarding future advances only apply if the buyer or lessee takes the goods subject to the security interest.

Obviously, a secured party that knows that its debtor has entered into an unauthorized transaction should not expect to be able to further encumber the collateral in the hands of the buyer or lessee by continuing to advance money to the debtor, unless it has made a commitment to do so.[96] Even in the absence of such knowledge, the secured party's interest will be cut off with respect to any advances made more than 45 days

---

89. U.C.C. §§ 9-323(d), (e) (buyer), 9-323(f), (g) (lessee).

90. U.C.C. §§ 9-323(d) (buyer), 9-323(f) (lessee).

91. *See* U.C.C. § 9-102(a)(68).

92. U.C.C. §§ 9-323(e) (buyer), 9-323(g) (lessee).

93. U.C.C. § 9-323(b). *See* § 12.02[C], *infra*.

94. *See* § 11.03[A][1], *supra*.

95. U.C.C. § 9-323(d)–(g). *See* § 12.03, *infra*. The provision applies equally to a buyer or lessee in ordinary course of business whose seller or lessor did not create the security interest.

96. The transfer by the debtor might constitute a default that would excuse the secured party from making further advances. Sometimes, however, the secured party's better interest is to keep the debtor afloat by making an advance anyway, and an advance in this context is still made pursuant to commitment. U.C.C. § 9-102(a)(69).

after the purchase.[97] Secured lenders thus have a grace period during which to extend advances, and they can investigate to make certain the debtor has not wrongfully disposed of the collateral if they want greater security when making a particular advance.

Buyers and lessees are on notice of perfected security interests and, as a practical matter, should contact the secured party and disclose the intended transaction before completing the sale or lease. This advice serves two functions: (1) it cuts off the secured party's right to make advances that will have priority against the buyer or lessee (absent a commitment, which can be inquired about), and (2) the buyer or lessee can determine whether the secured party intends to treat the sale or lease as a default under the security agreement. If the secured party intends to treat the sale or lease as a default, the buyer or lessee can take steps to avoid negative consequences. For example, the buyer or lessee might negotiate a waiver of the security interest by agreeing to pay all or part of the outstanding balance owed to the secured party. If the secured party will not agree to a waiver, the buyer or lessee should (if possible) avoid or cancel the transaction.[98]

The following hypothetical demonstrates the application of the future-advances provision. Assume a secured party took a perfected security interest in the debtor's business assets on June 1. On September 1, when the outstanding balance of the debt was $1 million, the debtor wrongfully sold the collateral to a buyer that took it subject to the security interest. On October 1, the secured party loaned the debtor an additional $500,000 pursuant to a future-advances clause in the security agreement, increasing the outstanding balance to $1.5 million. If the secured party knew of the purchase at the time of the October 1 advance, the security interest would only secure repayment of $1 million—not the $500,000 advance—unless the secured party made the advance pursuant to a commitment entered into without knowledge of the sale. By contrast, if the secured party did not know of the purchase at the time of the October 1 advance, the security interest would secure repayment of the entire $1.5 million balance. Likewise, assume that the wrongful sale of the collateral occurred on August 1 (two months prior to the future advance). In this case, the purchaser would take the collateral subject to the security interest, but that interest would only secure repayment of $1 million, not the additional $500,000 future advance, unless the secured party made that advance pursuant to a commitment entered into before September 15 and without knowledge of the sale.

---

97. The court in *Spector United Employees Credit Union v. Smith*, 263 S.E.2d 319, 28 U.C.C. Rep. Serv. 310 (N.C. Ct. App. 1980), held that a refinancing of the original secured debt, as distinct from a future advance, was not within the scope of Section 9-307(3), which was the predecessor of current Section 9-323(d). It denied summary judgment and remanded to determine the extent to which a subsequent loan that was extended to the debtor well beyond 45 days after the sale of the collateral was a refinancing of the original debt.

98. In a sales transaction, the buyer's right to cancel would be predicated on a breach of the warranty of title. U.C.C. § 2-312. In a lease transaction, the lessee's right to cancel would be based on a breach of the warranty against interference. U.C.C. § 2A-211(1).

[B] Licensees of General Intangibles in Ordinary Course of Business—§ 9-321(a), (b)

With regard to general intangibles, Article 9 provides that "[a] licensee in ordinary course of business takes its rights under the license free of a security interest in the general intangible created by its licensor, even if the security interest is perfected and the licensee knows of its existence."[99] The article also provides a definition for "licensee in ordinary course of business" that essentially parallels the definitions of ordinary-course buyers and lessees. The definition eliminates, for obvious reasons, any reference to possession.[100] Curiously, it omits the requirement that present value be given.

A license is a contract that authorizes the use of an asset without an accompanying transfer of ownership. Consider software as an example.[101] A security interest granted by the owner of software covers the owner's right to license authorized persons to use the software and the owner's right to prohibit unauthorized persons from doing so. If, however, a licensee acquires its rights from the owner in the ordinary course of business, the secured party cannot interfere with the licensee's right to continue using the software in a manner consistent with the license. As in the case of a lessor's residual interest in goods, a secured party can enforce its rights against the owner's interest in the licensed software.

[C] Chattel Paper and Instruments—§ 9-330

As was noted at the outset of this chapter,[102] the term "purchaser" is defined as a person that acquires a property interest in a voluntary transaction and thus includes buyers, lessees, licensees, and secured parties. Most secured-party-versus-secured-party priority contests were discussed in the preceding chapter, and the discussion up to this point in this chapter has involved only purchasers that are not secured parties. The superpriority rules for chattel paper and instruments discussed in this subsection are available to all purchasers, including secured parties.

[1] Chattel Paper

Article 9 includes two situations in which a purchaser of chattel paper can achieve priority over a perfected security interest in the same property. In one situation, the secured party takes a security interest in inventory and claims a security interest in chattel paper merely as proceeds of that inventory.[103] In the other situation, the secured party takes a security interest in both inventory and chattel paper, and the chattel paper

---

99. U.C.C. § 9-321(b).
100. *Id.*
101. "Software," defined in U.C.C. § 9-102(a)(75), is within the definition of general intangibles in Section 9-102(a)(42). Users of software generally acquire their rights by license rather than sale.
102. See the text of § 11.01 and note 1, *supra.*
103. U.C.C. § 9-330(a).

is an important part of the pool of collateral.[104] In each situation, obtaining priority requires the purchaser to give new value and to take possession of each authoritative tangible copy of the record evidencing the chattel paper and control of each authoritative electronic copy of the record in the ordinary course of the purchaser's business.[105]

A secured party can assure itself of priority in each of the described situations by perfecting its security interest through possession and control rather than by filing, as this will deprive purchasers of the opportunity to obtain possession and control themselves. Also in each situation, a secured party that perfects by filing will still be assured of priority if each authoritative copy of the record evidencing the chattel paper indicates that it has been assigned to an identified assignee other than the purchaser. The identified assignee typically is the secured party itself.

If a secured party claims chattel paper merely as proceeds of inventory,[106] a purchaser can prevail even if it knows that the sale violates the rights of the secured party.[107] The only way for the secured party to prevail in this context, absent perfecting by possession and control or a failure of the purchaser to satisfy one of the requirements for priority described above, is for each authoritative copy of the record evidencing the chattel paper to indicate that it has been assigned to an identified assignee other than the purchaser.[108]

If a secured party has more than a "mere proceeds" interest in chattel paper, a purchaser can achieve priority only if it lacks knowledge that the purchase violates the rights of the secured party. The lack-of-knowledge requirement does not create a duty for purchasers to check the filing system prior to making their purchase; indeed, the Official Comments make the point that a purchaser that performs a search and finds a financing statement would not thereby acquire the requisite knowledge unless it saw a statement in the financing statement indicating that any purchase would violate the secured party's rights.[109] If the secured party leaves each authoritative copy of the record evidencing the chattel paper in the possession or control of the debtor—as is common in the furniture field, where the debtor typically collects installment payments directly from account debtors—the secured party can protect itself by making sure that each authoritative copy indicates that the chattel paper has been assigned to an identified assignee other than the purchaser. In this context, the effect of the indication is to give a purchaser knowledge of the existence of the security interest.[110]

---

104. U.C.C. § 9-330(b).

105. The "ordinary course" requirement in this provision of Article 9 is individualized to the specific purchaser, as distinct from the "buyer in ordinary course of business" requirement. Blazer Fin. Serv., Inc. v. Harbor Fed. Sav. & Loan Ass'n, 623 So. 2d 580, 23 U.C.C. Rep. Serv. 2d 1241 (Fla. Dist. Ct. App. 1993) (bulk purchase of installment sales contracts was transaction in ordinary course of purchaser's business).

106. For discussion of attachment of a security interest to proceeds, see § 2.03[B], *supra*.

107. U.C.C. § 9-330(a).

108. U.C.C. § 9-330(a)(2).

109. U.C.C. § 9-330, Comment 6.

110. U.C.C. §§ 9-330(f).

As noted above, in each of the described situations, a purchaser desiring priority must give new value for the chattel paper. The pre-1998 text did not define "new value,"[111] but the courts refused to recognize a set-off against a preexisting debt owed to the purchaser by the debtor.[112] Policy grounds justified this refusal. Although a purchaser can sever a secured party's security interest in chattel paper, the new value provided by the purchaser is proceeds of the chattel paper and thus provides some protection for the secured party. The transaction in which the purchaser simply sets off a prior debt does not generate any proceeds that might benefit the secured party. The 1998 revision provided a definition of "new value" that advances the underlying policy. Specifically, "new value" means "(i) money, (ii) money's worth in property, services, or new credit, or (iii) release by a transferee of an interest in property previously transferred to the transferee. The term does not include an obligation substituted for another obligation."[113]

If a security agreement covers inventory alone, the secured party obviously is interested in any resulting chattel paper "merely as proceeds" of its collateral. This conclusion does not change merely because the security agreement also explicitly covers chattel paper. A court can still determine that the secured party's primary interest is in the inventory and that the agreement covers chattel paper to avoid the impact of Section 9-330(a).[114] This determination is appropriate if the inventory consists of big-ticket items being financed under a floor-plan arrangement.[115] In a typical floor plan, the secured party advances money to enable the debtor to purchase specific items of inventory and expects to be repaid with the sale or lease of each item. If the security interest at issue is a general floating lien, however, the typical secured party relies on a shifting pool of collateral that consists of the inventory and receivables (i.e., accounts, chattel paper, and instruments). Indeed, debtors commonly borrow up to a pre-set percentage of the cost of the inventory and a different percentage of the face amount of the receivables. With a general floating lien, the secured party's interest in chattel paper would not ordinarily be a "mere proceeds" interest.[116]

[2] Instruments

Article 9 also deals with the rights of purchasers of both negotiable and nonnegotiable instruments. Except as provided in section 9-331(a) dealing with the rights of a

---

111. U.C.C. §9-108 (1972 Official Text) provided that certain persons that took after-acquired collateral for pre-existing claims gave new value. The 1998 revision omitted this provision as "unnecessary, counterintuitive, and ineffective for its original purpose of sheltering after-acquired collateral from attack as a voidable preference in bankruptcy." U.C.C. §9-102, Comment 21.

112. General Elec. Capital Corp. v. Deere Credit Serv., Inc., 799 F. Supp. 832, 19 U.C.C. Rep. Serv. 2d 933 (S.D. Ohio 1992); In re Dr. C. Huff Co., Inc., 44 B.R. 129, 40 U.C.C. Rep. Serv. 284 (Bankr. W.D. Ky. 1984).

113. U.C.C. §9-102(a)(57).

114. Int'l Harvester Credit Corp. v. Assocs. Fin. Serv. Co., Inc., 133 Ga. App. 488, 211 S.E.2d 430, 16 U.C.C. Rep. Serv. 396 (1974).

115. For discussion of floor planning, see §3.04[C], supra.

116. See P.E.B. Commentary No. 8 (Dec. 10, 1991).

holder in due course of a negotiable instrument under Article 3,[117] a purchaser takes free of a security interest perfected by a method other than possession only if the purchaser gives value and takes possession of the instrument in good faith and without knowledge that the purchase violates the rights of the secured party.[118] A purchaser that fits these requirements does not need to qualify as a holder in due course to take free of a security interest in a negotiable instrument.

For example, suppose Buyer signs and delivers to Seller a negotiable promissory note payable to the order of Seller, who subsequently grants Bank a security interest in the note as collateral for a loan. Bank leaves possession of the note in Seller's hands and perfects by filing. Seller then sells the note to Purchaser or borrows from Purchaser and grants it a security interest in the note. Seller delivers possession of the note to Purchaser but does not indorse it. Purchaser gives value for the note in good faith and without knowledge of Bank's security interest. The delivery to Purchaser is a transfer under Article 3 but not a negotiation, and thus Purchaser is neither a holder nor a holder in due course.[119] Nevertheless, under Article 3 Purchaser acquires Seller's rights and is entitled to enforce the note against Buyer subject to any defenses Buyer might have against Seller.[120] Purchaser has priority over Bank's security interest under section 9-330(d) unless the note indicated that it had been assigned to an identified assignee. The indication would be deemed to have given Purchaser knowledge of Bank's security interest.[121] If Seller had indorsed the note and delivered it to Purchaser, Purchaser would have qualified as a holder in due course under Article 3 and would have had priority over Bank's security interest under section 9-331(a), discussed in the next subsection.

In the prior example, if the note qualified as an instrument under Article 9 but was nonnegotiable, the same analysis would apply with respect to the priority of Purchaser over Bank's security interest. However, none of the Article 3 analysis would apply, and Purchaser's right to collect from Buyer would be derived from the common law. While Purchaser could defeat Bank under Section 9-330(d), it could not qualify as a holder in due course — a purely Article 3 concept — and therefore could not take advantage of Section 9-331(a).

Prior to 1998, Article 9 followed the approach taken with respect to chattel paper by distinguishing between secured parties that claimed instruments merely as proceeds and other secured parties. The 1998 revision eliminated this distinction for instruments. It also eliminated the new value requirement, meaning that a purchaser can take free of a security interest even though it acquires the instrument in total or partial

---

117. *See* § 11.03[D], *infra.* A purchaser that so qualifies need not comply with the tests set forth in Section 9-330(d).

118. U.C.C. § 9-330(d).

119. A negotiable instrument payable to the order of a named person must be indorsed by that person for a subsequent transferee to acquire holder or holder-in-due-course status. U.C.C. §§ 1-201(b)(21), 3-201(b). A transfer occurs when an instrument is delivered by a person other than its issuer for the purpose of giving to the recipient the right to enforce the instrument. U.C.C. § 3-202(a).

120. U.C.C. § 3-301.

121. U.C.C. § 9-330(f).

satisfaction of a pre-existing debt. Interestingly, the revision did not adopt a definition of value consistent with the Article 3 requirement to qualify as a holder in due course. This omission means that a purchaser that acquires an instrument in exchange for an executory promise qualifies for protection.[122]

[D] Negotiable Instruments, Negotiable Documents, Securities, Controllable Electronic Records, Controllable Accounts, and Controllable Payment Intangibles—§ 9-331

While the provisions of Article 9 discussed in the preceding subsection provide protection for purchasers of instruments, another provision covers only purchasers that qualify for the highest status with respect to fully negotiable personal property.[123] The provision states that nothing in Article 9 limits the rights of a holder in due course of a negotiable instrument under Article 3,[124] a holder to whom a negotiable document of title has been duly negotiated under Article 7,[125] a protected purchaser of a security,[126] or a qualifying purchaser of a controllable electronic record, controllable account, or controllable payment intangible.[127] Moreover, filing under Article 9 does not constitute notice of the security interest to such holders or purchasers.[128]

The holders and purchasers referred to are types of bona-fide purchasers for value that are given priority over adverse claims of ownership under Articles 3 (negotiable instruments), 7 (negotiable documents), 8 (securities), and 12 (controllable electronic records). The provision of Article 9 under discussion provides an interface with those other articles and defers to the results that would follow under those articles.[129] The 1972 text provided that such holders and purchasers took priority over even a perfected security interest,[130] but that statement was overly broad. The 1998 revision appropriately clarified that such holders and purchasers take priority only to the extent provided in the other articles.[131] For example, a holder to whom a negotiable document

---

122. U.C.C. § 1-204(4). By contrast, a person claiming priority as a holder in due course of a negotiable instrument under Section 9-331(a) will not qualify for that status if it acquires the instrument in exchange for an executory promise. U.C.C. § 3-303(a)(1). *See also* U.C.C. § 9-403(a) (assignee must give value as defined in Article 3 to take free of account debtor's defenses under enforceable waiver-of-defenses term).

123. U.C.C. § 9-331.

124. U.C.C. §§ 3-302, 3-305, 3-306.

125. U.C.C. §§ 7-501, 7-502.

126. U.C.C. § 8-303. Even though uncertificated securities are not represented by indispensable paper, they are fully negotiable in that Article 8 provides protection for good-faith purchasers that give value, lack notice of adverse claims, and take control. For discussion of control, see § 6.04, *supra*.

127. U.C.C. § 12-104

128. U.C.C. § 9-331(c).

129. U.C.C. § 9-331(a).

130. U.C.C. § 9-309 (1972 Official Text).

131. U.C.C. § 9-331(a).

has been duly negotiated takes it subject to any security interest in the covered goods that attached and was perfected before issuance of the document.[132] Nothing in Article 9 changes this result.

This provision shows the risk inherent in leaving negotiable collateral in the possession or under the control of the debtor. The security agreement may flatly prohibit any transfer of the property by the debtor absent the secured party's authorization. By retaining possession or control, however, the debtor is nevertheless empowered to transfer the collateral free from the security interest.[133] Filing and temporary methods of perfection, and the automatic perfection provided to a buyer of a promissory note,[134] are extremely convenient ways to transact business, but they carry the risk associated with wrongful transfers to protected parties.

[E] Funds in Deposit Accounts; Tangible and Electronic Money — §§ 9-332, 9-340

Section 9-332(b) provides protection to transferees of funds from deposit accounts and applies without regard to the perfected status of a secured party with a security interest in either the entire account or the specific funds as proceeds. Transfers from deposit accounts normally occur by check, by funds transfer, or by an electronic debit of the account and a corresponding credit of another account.

The priority rule is that the transferee of the funds takes them free of the security interest, even if perfected by any available method, unless the transferee acts in collusion with the debtor in violating the rights of the secured party.[135] The transferee need not give value for the funds, and it does not matter whether the transferee acted with notice, or even knowledge, that the transfer violated the secured party's rights. Rather, the standard is whether the transferee acted in "collusion" with the debtor, a term borrowed from Article 8.[136] The Comments state the policy rationale for the rule as follows:

> Broad protection for transferees helps to ensure that security interests in deposit accounts do not impair the free flow of funds. It also minimizes the likelihood that a secured party will enjoy a claim to whatever the transferee

---

132. U.C.C. § 7-503(1). *See* § 6.02[B][1], *supra*.

133. Louisiana St. School Lunch Emp. Retirement Sys. v. Legel Braswell Gov't Sec. Corp., 699 F.2d 512, 35 U.C.C. Rep. Serv. 737 (11th Cir. 1983) (priority to bona-fide purchaser of securities); Bowles v. City Nat'l Bank & Trust Co. of Oklahoma City, 537 P.2d 1219, 16 U.C.C. Rep. Serv. 1396 (Okla. Ct. App. 1975) (priority to possessor of negotiable instrument that qualified as holder in due course).

134. *See* § 7.02[B], *supra*.

135. *In re* Cumberland Molded Prods., LLC, 69 U.C.C. Rep. Serv. 2d 371 (Bankr. M.D. Tenn. 2009) (rather than asserting its right to set-off and freezing the account that it controlled when debtor filed for bankruptcy, bank sent a check for the balance in the account to trustee and thereby lost its interest to trustee). U.C.C. § 9-330(a) provides a similar rule protecting the transferee when a customer withdraws money (currency) subject to a security interest from a deposit account and transfers it.

136. *Cf.* U.C.C. § 9-331, Comment 4 (bad actors). *See also* U.C.C. §§ 8-115, 8-503(e).

purchases with the funds. Rules concerning recovery of payments traditionally have placed a high value on finality. The opportunity to upset a completed transaction, or even to place a completed transaction in jeopardy by bringing suit against the transferee of funds, should be severely limited.[137]

Section 9-332(b) applies to a transfer of funds from a deposit account, not to a transfer of the deposit account itself. Other rules govern competing claims to a deposit account that arise when a debtor grants a security interest in the account to two or more secured parties.[138]

Section 9-340 states a related rule that deals with the priority of a bank that maintains a deposit account subject to another person's security interest and exercises set-off (or a right of recoupment) against funds in the account. The bank's set-off rights generally take priority over the rights of the secured party, even if the secured party perfected its interest in the account by means of a control agreement.[139] However, if the secured party perfected its security interest by becoming the customer with respect to the deposit account, its interest has priority over the bank's exercise of its set-off or recoupment rights.[140] Interestingly, although the bank cannot obtain priority by means of an involuntary transfer of the funds to itself, it can take advantage of the rule of Section 9-332(b) that protects voluntary transferees. Thus, if the debtor gives it a check drawn on the account, the bank will take the funds represented by the check free of a security interest in the account perfected in any manner unless it acts in collusion with the debtor to violate the rights of the secured party.

Prior to the 2022 amendments, money was defined in Article 1 as "a medium of exchange currently authorized or adopted by a domestic or foreign government."[141] It was assumed that money was tangible, and this assumption found expression in rules like pre-2022 Section 9-312(b)(3), which provided that a security interest in money could only be perfected by possession. Then, in September 2021, El Salvador adopted Bitcoin as legal tender, and there was concern that this made Bitcoin money for purposes of the U.C.C. The 2022 amendments make clear that non-government-issued virtual currencies like Bitcoin are not money by adding the following sentence to the definition of money: "The term does not include an electronic record that is a medium of exchange recorded and transferable in a system that existed and operated for the medium of exchange before the medium of exchange was authorized or adopted by the government."[142] The system in which rights in Bitcoin are recorded and by which they are transferred existed and operated before El Salvador adopted Bitcoin as legal tender. Accordingly, Bitcoin and similar virtual currencies are controllable electronic records under Articles 12 and 9.

---

137. U.C.C. § 9-332, Comment 3.
138. *See* § 10.03[A], *supra*.
139. U.C.C. §§ 9-340(b), 9-104(a)(2).
140. U.C.C. §§ 9-340(c), 9-104(a)(3).
141. U.C.C. § 1-201(b)(24) (1998 Official Text).
142. U.C.C. § 1-201(b)(24).

A few countries have issued their own virtual currencies, sometimes referred to as central bank digital currencies, or CBDCs. For example, the Marshall Islands issues and treats as legal tender a virtual currency called the SOV,[143] and the U.S. Federal Reserve Board has studied the advantages and disadvantages of issuing a digital currency.[144] A CBDC would qualify as money under the Article 1 definition, and rules were needed in Article 9 for taking a security interest in a CBDC. The 2022 amendments use "electronic money"[145] for CBDCs and "tangible money" for traditional, physical currency, and a new Section 9-312(a)(4) provides that a security interest in electronic money may be perfected only by control.[146]

Section 9-332 provides the same rules for transferees of money that it provides for transferees of funds from deposit accounts. A transferee of tangible money takes it free of a security interest if the transferee receives possession of the money without acting in collusion with the debtor in violating the rights of the secured party,[147] and a transferee of electronic money takes it free of a security interest if the transferee obtains control of the money without acting in collusion with the debtor in violating the rights of the secured party.[148]

Unfortunately, some have misconstrued the intent behind the reference to electronic money and have wrongly concluded that its enactment might lead to the adoption of a CBDC by the United States. In a few states adopting the 2022 amendments, the definition of money has been amended to exclude CBDCs, and the term "electronic money" has been deleted from Article 9. These nonuniform amendments do not change the fact that Bitcoin and other non-government-issued virtual currencies are controllable electronic records under Article 12, but it prevents the taking of an effective security interest in any CBDCs that might be issued by a country.

---

143. Marshall Islands Sovereign Currency Act of 2018 (Feb. 26, 2018). The Atlantic Council maintains a helpful online digital currency tracker: https://www.atlanticcouncil.org/cbdctracker/. As of January 2024, the tracker indicates that CBDCs have been launched in 11 countries and that there are pilot projects underway in 21 countries.

144. Bd. of Governors of Fed. Res. Sys., *Money and Payments: The U.S. Dollar in the Age of Digital Transformation* (Jan. 2022), https://www.federalreserve.gov/publications/files/money-and-payments-20220120.pdf.

145. U.C.C. § 9-102(a)(31A) (electronic money), (79A) (tangible money).

146. U.C.C. § 9-105A establishes a control test for electronic money based on the test for controllable electronic records in Article 12.

147. U.C.C. § 9-332(a).

148. U.C.C. § 9-332(c).

Chapter 12

Priority Contests:
Purchasers and Lien Creditors
versus Unperfected Secured Parties

Synopsis

§ 12.01 Article 9's Residual Priority Rule— § 9-201(a)

Article 9 has a residual rule that makes a security interest—even if unperfected—effective against the debtor, purchasers from the debtor, and creditors of the debtor.[1] This rule is subject to numerous exceptions that subordinate unperfected security interests to the rights of competing claimants, and this chapter examines those exceptions. In the absence of an exception, however, the residual rule is the rule of decision.[2]

---

1. U.C.C. § 9-201(a). The previous chapter discussed Section 9-315(a), which is also a residual rule but is more specific than Section 9-201(a) and is specific to purchasers. *See* § 11.01, *supra*.

2. Richard McCluhan Assocs., Inc. v. Shari Candies, Inc., 57 U.C.C. Rep. Serv. 2d 988 (Minn. Ct. App. 2005) (unpublished) (perfected secured party in debtor's assets was effective against a general creditor that continued to provide services on account despite debtor's financial distress; equitable principles could not alter the priority because secured creditor did not have any role in inducing the extension of further services).

§ 12.02 Lien Creditors

[A] General Rule—§ 9-317(a)(2)

Working in conjunction with Section 9-201(a), Section 9-317(a)(2) establishes priority between a secured party and a lien creditor.[3] "Lien creditor" is a misleading term[4] because Article 9 also refers to parties with liens that do not fall within the term's definition. A security interest is a lien, for example, but it is consensual in nature; therefore, secured parties are not "lien creditors." A creditor may also have a lien that arises by operation of a common-law or statutory rule,[5] but such creditors again are not "lien creditors." The common element among parties that qualify as lien creditors under the Article 9 definition is that their liens arise as the result of a judicial or quasi-judicial proceeding. It is important to note that lien creditors are not purchasers because they do not acquire their interest in the property subject to the lien in a voluntary transaction.[6]

The most important lien creditor, the trustee in bankruptcy, is the subject of extensive coverage in Chapter 16.[7] Next in order of importance is an initially unsecured creditor that acquires lien-creditor status through levy or a similar process. Suppose, for example, Seller sells hard drives to Debtor, a computer manufacturer, on unsecured credit. Because this transaction is a sale, Article 2 applies and Debtor acquires title to the drives when they are delivered to it.[8] By selling on unsecured credit, Seller chose to convey title without retaining a property interest in the drives, in effect trading the drives for a legally enforceable promise to pay the contract price. If Debtor fails to pay the price as it becomes due, Seller cannot repossess the drives.[9] Instead, Seller must file suit against Debtor claiming breach of contract. After recovering a judgment, Seller can use the state's debt-collection procedures, called the "execution" process.

Missouri's execution process, used here for illustrative purposes, is typical. If Debtor persists in not paying after the court's judgment in favor of Seller, Seller can apply to the court clerk for a writ of execution,[10] which is an order directing the sheriff to levy

---

3. U.C.C. § 9-102(a)(52). The term "lien creditor" means "(A) a creditor that has acquired a lien on the property involved by attachment, levy, or the like; (B) an assignee for benefit of creditors from the time of the assignment; (C) a trustee in bankruptcy from the date of the filing of the petition; or (D) a receiver in equity from the time of appointment."

4. One scholar labeled the term "gibberish." David Mellinkoff, *The Language of the Uniform Commercial Code*, 77 YALE L.J. 185 (1967).

5. *See* Chapter 13, *infra*.

6. *See* U.C.C. § 1-201(b)(30), (29).

7. *See* § 16.04[B], *infra*.

8. *See* U.C.C. §§ 2-106(1) ("sale" means passing title from seller to buyer for a price); 2-401(2) (unless otherwise agreed, title passes to buyer on physical delivery of goods).

9. Section 2-702 creates a limited exception to this rule. Seller can reclaim the drives *in specie* if Debtor was insolvent on the delivery date and Seller demands their return within ten days thereafter (or a longer reasonable time if Debtor misrepresented its solvency in writing during the three months preceding delivery).

10. Mo. R. CIV. P. 76.01.

on Debtor's assets. The sheriff, in essence, acts as Seller's agent for purposes of satisfying the judgment. "Levy" means to take into legal custody and, in the case of tangible goods capable of being moved, requires physical seizure by the sheriff.[11] Note that a writ of execution allows levy on *any* of the debtor's nonexempt assets.[12] The sheriff might levy on the drives, but Seller has no authority to direct the sheriff to levy on them or on any other particular asset, including real estate. The act of levy confers on the sheriff a power of sale,[13] and any proceeds derived from the execution sale will (after paying the sheriff's expenses) go to Seller for application to the judgment. The act of levy also creates a lien on the seized property in favor of Seller and converts Seller from a judgment creditor (still a general creditor) into a lien creditor.[14]

A lien on assets acquired by levy or the like gives the lien creditor priority over persons that acquire property interests in those assets subsequent to their seizure by the sheriff, but, under the residual priority rule of Section 9-201(a), it does not give priority over existing property interests. The U.C.C. contains an exception to this rule, providing that an *unperfected* security interest is subordinate to the rights of a subsequent lien creditor.[15] The practical effect of granting priority to the lien creditor is that the sheriff's execution sale extinguishes an unperfected security interest in the collateral.[16] Had the security interest been perfected prior to the sheriff's levy, the secured party would have priority, and its security interest would remain enforceable against the collateral in the hands of the execution-sale purchaser.[17]

---

11. Mo. R. Civ. P. 76.06. Different procedures are prescribed for levy on other types of assets. If an asset is in the custody or under the control of a third person, levy requires that the person be served with a writ of garnishment. Mo. R. Civ. P. 90.01 *et seq.*

12. A judgment debtor can claim certain assets as exempt, meaning that they can be placed beyond the reach of an executing creditor. *See generally* Mo. Rev. Stat. § 513.430 (list of exemptions); Mo. R. Civ. P. 76.075 (procedure for claiming exemptions). Each state has its own list of exempt property.

13. Mo. R. Civ. P. 76.18 (sets forth the procedures to be employed at an execution sale).

14. Mo. R. Civ. P. 76.07. In limited circumstances, levy may proceed from an attachment rather than an execution. Mo. R. Civ. P. 85.0 *et seq.* Attachment, an ancillary process used in conjunction with a creditor's suit for a money judgment, permits levy prior to judgment. Assets subjected to an attachment levy are held *in custodia legis* pending the outcome of the litigation. If the creditor recovers a money judgment, the assets are sold at an execution sale. For purposes of Article 9, the creditor becomes a lien creditor at the moment of levy.

15. U.C.C. § 9-317(a)(2)(A). *See* Citibank, N.A. v. Prime Motor Inns Ltd. P'ship, 98 N.Y.2d 743, 750 N.Y.S.2d 818, 780 N.E.2d 503, 49 U.C.C. Rep. Serv. 2d 934 (2002) (because bank levied on a $500,000 lawsuit settlement by initiating a turnover proceeding shortly before secured creditor filed its financing statement, bank had priority); In re Lortz, 344 B.R. 579, 60 U.C.C. Rep. Serv. 2d 90 (Bankr. C.D. Ill. (2006) (although initially perfected in debtor's automobile, secured party's mistaken release of the lien on the vehicle's certificate of title and return of the certificate to debtor left secured party unperfected and subordinate to trustee in bankruptcy exercising its powers as a lien creditor).

16. It is axiomatic that junior interests are eliminated by foreclosure sales, including execution sales and Article 9 foreclosure sales. *See* § 18.02[E], *infra.* Any excess funds from the execution sale are proceeds to which the junior interests attach automatically. *See* § 2.03[B], *supra.*

17. *See also* Myers v. Christensen, 278 Neb. 989, 776 N.W.2d 201, 70 U.C.C. Rep. Serv. 2d 577 (Neb. 2009) (judgment creditor that sought to levy on the judgment debtor's deposit accounts through a writ of garnishment did not take priority over the bank with a prior security interest in the deposit accounts perfected through control).

In certain cases, Article 9 gives a secured party priority even though it did not have a perfected security interest at the time a competing claimant became a lien creditor.[18] A secured party will prevail if, before the claimant becomes a lien creditor, the secured party satisfies one of the conditions of Section 9-203(b)(3) and also files a financing statement covering the collateral. For example, a secured party that has the debtor sign a security agreement describing the collateral[19] and files a financing statement in anticipation of an expected secured loan will have priority over a lien creditor even if attachment and perfection do not occur until the secured party later extends value to the debtor and that occurs after the lien creditor's interest arises.[20] The secured party would lose, however, if it merely filed the financing statement before the lien creditor's interest arose, and thus the rule is not the same as the first-to-file-or-perfect rule applicable to priority contests between secured parties.[21] The Comments indicate that the purpose of this provision is to treat the initial advance of value by the secured party the same as any subsequent advance.[22]

[B] Purchase-Money Security Interests— § 9-317(e)

An exception allows a secured party to prevail even though it perfects after a lien creditor's rights arise in the goods that serve as the secured party's collateral. Section 9-317(e) provides as follows:

> [I]f a person files a financing statement with respect to a purchase-money security interest before or within 20 days after the debtor receives delivery of the collateral, the security interest takes priority over the rights of a buyer, lessee, or lien creditor which arise between the time the security interest attaches and the time of filing.[23]

---

18. U.C.C. § 9-317(a)(2)(B).

19. U.C.C. § 9-203(b)(3)(A).

20. U.C.C. §§ 9-308(a), 9-203(b)(1).

21. See § 10.01, *supra*.

22. U.C.C. § 9-317, Comment 4. The stated rationale for the rule is not convincing. In most instances in which a debtor signs a security agreement and funds are not immediately disbursed by the secured party, the rule is unnecessary because value has been given in the form of a binding commitment to extend credit or the extension of immediately available credit (Section 1-204(1)) or in the form of consideration sufficient to support a simple contract (Section 1-201(4)). The secured party thus has priority over a lien creditor for the initial advance, and its priority for future advances is determined under Section 9-323(b). Without the rule, if value is not given, a secured party is subordinate to a lien creditor for the initial advance and all subsequent advances. The rule is helpful to a secured party that has agreed to extend a line of credit but, because of rights reserved to it in the agreement, has difficulty proving that it has made a binding commitment or given consideration. As against a lien creditor, the secured party is in the same position as if it had given value, that is, it has priority for the initial advance, and its priority for future advances is determined under Section 9-323(b). For discussion of a secured party's rights in future advances as against a lien creditor, see § 12.02[C], *infra*.

23. This provision is subject to Sections 9-320 and 9-321. U.C.C. § 9-317(e).

This provision applies only in favor of a purchase-money secured party.[24] Its primary rationale is to facilitate secured sales[25] by allowing buyers to take delivery without sellers' first having to file financing statements.[26] If a lien creditor's interest arises shortly after delivery, a diligent secured party should not be subordinated to the lien creditor, and this policy is facilitated by giving the secured party a 20-day grace period after delivery to a buyer during which the secured party can perfect and attain priority.[27] The provision does not prejudice lien creditors unduly because a lien creditor does not rely on the absence of a filed financing statement when it acquires its lien.[28]

Note that the grace period begins to run when the debtor receives delivery of the goods, which may or may not coincide with the time of attachment. For example, suppose Buyer purchases an item of equipment from Seller and grants Seller a purchase-money security interest that attaches on June 1. Seller delivers the goods to Buyer on June 10, Lien Creditor's interest in the goods arises on June 15, and Seller perfects on June 25. Seller's security interest has priority over Lien Creditor's rights because Seller perfected within 20 days after Buyer received delivery. It is irrelevant that perfection occurred more than 20 days after attachment.

The purchase-money exception applicable to lien creditors is comparable to the non-inventory purchase-money exception to the "first-to-file-or-perfect" priority rule that governs conflicting security interests in the same collateral.[29] The latter exception protects a purchase-money secured party that perfects during the 20-day grace period from (i) a prior-perfected secured party with an after-acquired property clause pro-

---

24. *See* § 10.04[C], *supra.* Purchase-money security interests exist only with respect to goods and associated software. *See* § 10.04[A], *supra.*

25. Although adopted primarily to protect sellers, the rule applies to all purchase-money secured parties.

26. *In re* Moore, 7 U.C.C. Rep. Serv. 578 (Bankr. C.D. Me. 1969) (provisions concerned only with allowing retroactive priority during the applicable grace period); *In re* Estergaard, 59 U.C.C. Rep. Serv. 2d 660 (Bankr. D. Colo. 2006) (because Section 9-317(e) applies to financing statements, and because the Colorado certificate of title act—unlike the acts in some other states—does not permit perfection by notation on the certificate of title to relate back to the creation of the lien, secured party was not perfected when debtor filed for bankruptcy between the time of purchase of the car and filing of certificate of title noting the security interest).

27. Secured sellers do not ordinarily file financing statements before goods have been delivered. Thus, the Code selects the buyer's receipt of possession as the triggering date for the grace period even though attachment of the security interest may have occurred earlier. *See, e.g.,* U.C.C. §§ 2-501(1) (buyer obtains rights in goods—a "special property interest"—upon their identification to a contract for sale); 1-204(4) (value includes any consideration sufficient to support a simple contract). A filing before the end of the grace period defeats any lien creditor whose rights arise between the time of attachment and the time of filing.

28. Compliance with a certificate-of-title statute "for obtaining priority over the rights of a lien creditor is equivalent to the filing of a financing statement under this article." U.C.C. § 9-311(b). As a result, a party that takes a purchase-money security interest in an automobile and properly perfects by compliance with the certificate-of-title statute will attain relation-back priority under Section 9-317(e). Some state certificate-of-title laws expand the grace period by giving secured parties 25 or even 30 days following attachment in which to perfect and still obtain relation-back priority.

29. *See* U.C.C. § 9-324(a); § 10.04[A], *supra.*

viding it with a security interest in the same collateral and (ii) a secured party whose interest attaches during the grace period and becomes perfected before the purchase-money secured party perfects. Note that a secured party must perfect by filing to obtain purchase-money priority if its competitor is a lien creditor[30] (or a buyer[31]) but can perfect in any manner, including possession, if its competitor is a secured party.[32] The limitation of perfection to filing in the case of a lien creditor (or buyer) is because the debtor will not have possession of the collateral and obtaining it would be difficult.

[C] Future Advances—§ 9-323(b)

Although this chapter deals generally with the rights of unperfected secured parties, it bears noting, briefly, that Article 9 also contains a provision that governs priority between a perfected security interest that extends to future advances pursuant to the terms of the security agreement and the rights of a lien creditor.[33] Under this provision, the lien creditor takes subject to the security interest only to the extent that it secures advances made (1) before the lien creditor's interest arises, (2) within 45 days after the lien creditor's interest arises, even if the secured party knows of that interest at the time it makes the advance, (3) more than 45 days after the lien creditor's interest arises, if made without knowledge of that interest, or (4) pursuant to a commitment entered into at any time as long as the commitment was made without knowledge of the lien creditor's interest.[34] The drafters included the absolute protection that is afforded the secured party for the initial 45-day period to protect security interests against liens arising under the Federal Tax Lien Act of 1966. The material discussing tax liens provides a more complete description of the provision.[35]

§ 12.03 Purchasers Other than Secured Parties

[A] General Rules—§ 9-317(b)–(d), (f)–(i)

Section 9-317(b) states that, except as provided in the exception dealing with purchase-money security interests,[36] "a buyer, other than a secured party, of tangible chattel paper, documents, goods, instruments, or a certificated security takes free of a security interest or agricultural lien if the buyer gives value and receives delivery of the collateral without knowledge of the security interest or agricultural lien and before

---

30. U.C.C. § 9-317(e).

31. U.C.C. § 9-317(e) applies equally to buyers other than buyers in ordinary course of business and lien creditors.

32. U.C.C. § 9-324(a).

33. For discussion of future-advances clauses, see § 3.03, *supra*.

34. U.C.C. § 9-323(b).

35. See § 13.03, *supra*.

36. See U.C.C. § 9-317(e); § 12.02[B], *supra*.

it is perfected." Although the provision seems somewhat unwieldy, its requirements correlate with other Article 9 priority provisions.[37]

To prevail under Section 9-317(b), a buyer must both give value and receive delivery[38] without knowledge of a security interest and before it is perfected.[39] A buyer that qualifies is a type of bona-fide purchaser for value—albeit one that does not meet all of the requirements of other sections for priority over perfected security interests. A buyer without knowledge receives protection from secured parties that fail to give notice in the Code's filing system because they are presumed to rely on the system.[40]

Section 9-317(d) includes a comparable provision that applies to buyers of all types of collateral not capable of being delivered.[41] It simply eliminates the requirement that the buyer take delivery to obtain priority because these types of property are intangible. Otherwise, the requirements for buyer priority are identical to the requirements in

---

37. In many circumstances, buyers take priority over conflicting interests by virtue of other provisions of Article 9. For example, a person that qualifies as a buyer in ordinary course of business takes free of a security interest in goods created by its seller, even if that interest is perfected and the buyer knows of it. U.C.C. § 9-320(a). A buyer of consumer goods from another consumer who gives value and buys the goods without knowledge of a purchase-money security interest in those goods perfected only by automatic perfection takes free of that security interest. U.C.C. § 9-320(b). Certain purchasers, a term which includes buyers of chattel paper and instruments, take free of conflicting perfected security interests under Section 9-330. A holder in due course of a negotiable instrument, a person to which a negotiable document has been duly negotiated, a protected purchaser of a security, and a qualifying purchaser of a controllable electronic record, controllable account, or controllable payment intangible takes free of a perfected security interest under Section 9-331.

38. Because a buyer under Section 9-317(b) must take delivery of the collateral, the section applies only when delivery is possible. Accordingly, the section covers only goods and other forms of tangible property. Section 9-317(c) provides a similar rule for lessees of goods that receive delivery. Section 9-317(d) deals with buyers of intangibles (i.e., collateral incapable of being delivered).

39. Chase Manhattan Bank, N.A. v. J & L General Contractors, Inc., 832 S.W.2d 204, 18 U.C.C. Rep. Serv. 2d 1286 (Tex. Ct. App. 1992) (purchaser was buyer not in ordinary course that gave value and received delivery of goods with no knowledge of creditor's security interest); Case Credit Corp. v. Barry Equip. Co., Inc., 2005 Mass. Super. LEXIS 61 (Mass. Super. Ct. Feb 7, 2005) (court rejected buyer's argument that the security interest itself became ineffectual when the perfection by the financing statement lapsed; material issue of fact presented as to whether buyer had knowledge of the security interest at the time that it received possession of the collateral).

40. The only method of perfection contemplated by this section is filing a financing statement. If the secured party perfected by possession or control, the buyer could not take delivery and therefore could not prevail. Further, the Code has separate rules protecting consumer buyers of consumer goods from purchase-money secured parties that rely on automatic perfection (U.C.C. § 9-320(b)) and protecting buyers in an interstate context that rely on clean certificates of title from secured parties that perfect as to goods covered by certificates of title (U.C.C. § 9-337(1)).

41. U.C.C. § 9-317(d) applies to "a buyer, other than a secured party, of collateral other than electronic money, goods, instruments, tangible documents, or a certificated security."

Section 9-317(b): the buyer cannot be a secured party[42] and must give value without knowledge of the security interest and before its perfection.[43]

Section 9-317 also deals with the rights of lessees of goods and licensees of general intangibles (other than lessees and licensees in ordinary course of business).[44] The rights of the lessees and the licensees are similar to the rights of buyers. A lessee of goods takes free of a security interest or agricultural lien[45] if the lessee gives value and takes delivery before perfection and without knowledge of the interest or lien.[46] A licensee of a general intangible cannot take possession and thus need only give value before perfection of the security interest and without knowledge of the security interest.[47] This provision is of particular importance because most software is a general intangible that is licensed rather than sold.[48]

The 2022 amendments added provisions under which buyers of certain types of assets that are, or in the case of chattel paper might be, in electronic form may take free of unperfected security interests. Each provision follows the pattern established by the provisions for buyers, lessees, and licensees described above in this subsection but adapts the pattern to the attributes of the collateral.

- Under subsection (f), a buyer of chattel paper takes free of an unperfected security interest if, without knowledge of the security interest and before it is perfected, the buyer gives value and: (i) receives delivery of each authoritative tangible copy of the record evidencing the chattel paper; and (ii) if each authoritative electronic copy of the record evidencing the chattel paper can be perfected by control, obtaining that control.

- Under subsection (g), a buyer of an electronic document takes free of a security interest if, without knowledge of the security interest and before it is perfected, the buyer gives value and, if each authoritative electronic copy of the document can be subjected to control under Section 7-106, obtains that control.

---

42. In the case of accounts, electronic chattel paper, and general intangibles that qualify as payment intangibles, the buyer will be a secured party unless the transaction of purchase is excluded from the scope of Article 9.

43. Gerardo A. Angulo-Mestas v. Editorial Televisa Intern., S.A., 747 F. Supp. 2d 255, 72 U.C.C. Rep. Serv. 2d 795 (D.P.R. 2010) (secured party with an unperfected interest in debtor's accounts held subordinate to assignee of the accounts that took them for value and without any knowledge of the secured party's interest).

44. As might be expected, a lessee or licensee in ordinary course of business takes free of a perfected security interest created by the lessor or licensor even if the lessee or licensee knows of its existence. U.C.C. §§ 9-321(c) (lessee), 9-321(b) (licensee). *See also* §§ 9-321(a) (defining "licensee in ordinary course of business"), 2A-103(1)(o) (defining "lessee in ordinary course of business"). *See also* § 11.03, *supra.*

45. Agricultural liens are effective only as to farm products (U.C.C. § 9-102(a)(5)), making lessees unlikely.

46. U.C.C. § 9-317(c).

47. U.C.C. § 9-317(d).

48. U.C.C. § 9-102(a)(42). *See also* U.C.C. § 9-102(a)(76) (defining software).

- Under subsection (h), a buyer of a controllable electronic record takes free of a security interest if, without knowledge of the security interest and before it is perfected, the buyer gives value and obtains control of the controllable electronic record.

- Under subsection (i), a buyer, other than a secured party, of a controllable account or a controllable payment intangible takes free of a security interest if, without knowledge of the security interest and before it is perfected, the buyer gives value and obtains control of the controllable account or controllable payment intangible.

[B] Purchase-Money Security Interests — § 9-317(e)

The purchase-money exception to the general rule that protects against lien creditors also protects secured parties that perfect during the 20 days following the debtor's receipt of the collateral from competing buyers and lessees whose rights arise between the time the security interest attaches and the time of perfection.[49] For example, suppose Seller sells a computer for business use to Buyer on credit and retains a purchase-money security interest in it. If Buyer resells the computer to Purchaser, who gives value and takes delivery without knowledge of the security interest and before Seller files a financing statement, Purchaser will nevertheless take subject to Seller's interest if Seller perfects by filing during the grace period. Unlike lien creditors, buyers and lessees generally rely on the filing system, and to avoid the harsh effects of the relation-back rule, they should ask their vendors appropriate questions and hopefully receive truthful answers.

Additional details about the application of the purchase-money exception may be found in the discussion of the exception's application to lien creditors.[50]

[C] Future Advances — § 9-323(d)–(g)

As is the case with lien creditors,[51] Article 9 includes provisions that govern priority between a perfected security interest that extends to future advances pursuant to the terms of the security agreement and the interests of buyers and lessees. A buyer or lessee of goods takes free of the security interest to the extent the secured party makes advances either with knowledge of the purchase or more than 45 days after it occurs, unless the advance is made pursuant to a commitment entered into without knowledge of the purchase and before the expiration of the 45-day period.[52] A buyer in ordinary course of business that takes free of a security interest under Section 9-320 and a lessee

---

49. U.C.C. § 9-317(e); *see* § 14.02[B], *supra*.
50. *See* § 12.02[B], *supra*.
51. *See* § 12.02[C], *supra*.
52. U.C.C. § 9-323(d), (e) (buyers); 9-323(f), (g) (lessees).

in ordinary course of business that takes free under Section 9-321 are not subject to future advances. This book covers in greater detail elsewhere a secured party's right to priority in future advances as against a buyer or lessee.[53]

§ 12.04 Claimants Not Expressly Governed by Article 9

Article 9 has rules that explicitly govern priority contests between a secured party and a purchaser (whether a secured party or otherwise), a lien creditor, and certain persons with liens that arise by operation of law. This list by no means exhausts the types of persons that might claim a competing interest. If the adverse claimant does not fall within one of the articulated categories, the court must decide between resolving the contest under the Code's residual priority rule[54] or resolving it by application of rules derived from the common law or equity.[55] Application of the residual priority rule enables the secured party to prevail regardless of perfection. The outcome is less certain with the application of non-Code rules.

Prior to the 1998 revision,[56] the most common example of a priority contest not expressly governed by Article 9 involved a bank exercising set-off against deposited funds that were subject to a security interest as identifiable proceeds of other collateral. The following hypothetical remains relevant to the extent it explores the approaches a court might take in resolving this type of priority dispute.

Suppose Finance Company, which has a security interest in Debtor's inventory, permits Debtor to retain cash proceeds from the sale of inventory and to commingle those proceeds with other funds in its general operating account that is maintained at Bank. Suppose further that Debtor owes money to Bank and is in default on its obligation. Bank has a common-law right of "set-off"—a right to seize funds in the account and apply them to reduce the outstanding indebtedness to Bank. Which creditor has priority if Bank seizes funds in which Finance Company claims an interest as identifiable proceeds of its inventory collateral?[57]

---

53. See § 11.03[A][3], *supra*.

54. U.C.C. § 9-201(a). See § 12.01, *supra*.

55. See U.C.C. § 1-103(b) (unless preempted, common-law and equitable rules applicable).

56. Original Article 9 excluded rights of set-off entirely from its scope but in 1998 the exclusion was made subject to then-new U.C.C. § 9-340, discussed in § 11.03[F], *supra*, governing set-off against funds in deposit accounts. See U.C.C. § 9-109(d)(10)(A).

57. U.C.C. § 9-315(a)(2). *See generally* William H. Henning, *Article 9's Treatment of Commingled Cash Proceeds in Noninsolvency Cases*, 35 ARK. L. REV. 191 (Winter 1982). Set-off is only one method by which a depositary bank can gain control of deposited funds. An advantage of set-off is that it is a self-help remedy that can be implemented without the cooperation of the debtor (depositor). If the debtor will cooperate, the bank will be better off having the funds in the account paid to it voluntarily. When cash proceeds in a deposit account are paid to a transferee, the transferee takes free of any security interest in the proceeds unless the transfer is a fraudulent conveyance or is in some other respect a collusive attempt to defraud the secured party. U.C.C. § 9-332. Further, if the funds are paid by check,

Perhaps the best discussion of the issues was in *National Acceptance Co. of Virginia v. Virginia Capital Bank*,[58] in which a federal district court had to resolve a dispute under Virginia law. Because Virginia's courts had not ruled on the proper interpretation of the exclusion for rights of set-off, the district court gave alternative analyses. The party claiming a security interest in the deposited funds would prevail under a narrow interpretation through Article 9's residual rule. Resolution under a broad interpretation would turn on non-Code law. The court found that the non-Code law of Virginia follows the majority rule that a bank exercising set-off is subordinate to an adverse claimant if it knows or has reason to know of the claimant's interest.[59] Because the evidence indicated that the bank, at a minimum, had notice of the secured party's interest, the court concluded that the secured party would prevail under either a narrow or broad interpretation.

As noted above, this specific priority contest was resolved in the 1998 revision, which for the first time introduced rules governing deposit accounts. A security interest in a deposit account must be perfected by control.[60] In the case of a deposit account maintained at a bank that is not the secured party, control requires the secured party to obtain a control agreement with the maintaining bank or to become that bank's customer with respect to the account.[61] If the secured party perfects by a control agreement, it is vulnerable to the maintaining bank's exercise of set-off[62] unless the control agreement provides for subordination of the set-off right.[63] If the secured party becomes the customer with respect to the account, it has priority over the maintaining bank's right of set-off.[64]

A current example may be found in Missouri's statutes governing liens for service to and storage of vehicles, which permit the lienor to retain the lien after surrendering possession by filing a statement with the county recorder.[65] The statute is silent regarding priority, and after surrender of possession the lien is no longer a possessory lien under Section 9-333[66] so there is not an applicable Article 9 priority rule. In the event of a priority contest between a lienor without possession and a secured party with a security interest in the vehicle, the court would have to decide whether to confer priority on the secured party through application of the residual rule or to decide the case based on the non-Code law of the state.

---

the transferee may qualify as a holder in due course and thereby defeat the security interest. U.C.C. § 9-331. For discussion of the rights of holders in due course, see § 11.03[D], *supra*.

58. 498 F. Supp. 1078, 30 U.C.C. Rep. Serv. 1145 (E.D. Va. 1980).

59. The majority rule is sometimes referred to as the "legal" rule. Under the minority, or "equitable," rule, a third-party claimant has priority even if the bank exercising set-off lacks knowledge or notice.

60. U.C.C. §§ 9-312(b)(1), 9-314(a), 9-104. For discussion of control of deposit accounts, see § 6.04[B], *supra*.

61. U.C.C. § 9-104(2), (3).

62. U.C.C. § 9-340(a).

63. Parties can alter the Code's normal priority rules through a subordination agreement. U.C.C. § 9-339.

64. U.C.C. § 9-340(c).

65. Mo. Rev. Stat. §§ 430.020, 430.082.

66. Possessory liens are discussed in § 13.01, *infra*.

Chapter 13

Creditors with Liens Arising by Operation of Law

Synopsis

§ 13.01 Possessory Liens That Arise by Operation of Law—§ 9-333

Section 9-333 provides priority over even perfected security interests for liens that arise by operation of law in favor of certain persons that provide services or materials with respect to goods. It refers to such liens as "possessory liens," which is an apt description in that only liens whose effectiveness depends upon possession of the goods by the provider qualify for priority under the section.[1]

Article 9 does not apply to a possessory lien except to the extent Section 9-333 governs priorities between a possessory lienor and a secured party.[2] This means, *inter alia*, that (i) a security agreement is not necessary for the lien's existence and, (ii) in the event of foreclosure by the possessory lienor, the provisions of Part 6 of Article 9 do not apply. The classic example of a possessory lien is one that arises from repair work conducted on goods like a car.[3] Most states give the garage that does the repair work an artisan's lien on the car so long as the garage retains possession of the car.[4] In other words, the garage can sell the car at foreclosure if the owner fails to pay the repair bill. The lien has priority over a perfected security interest because the following elements

---

1. A nonpossessory lien on farm products may qualify as an agricultural lien. *See* § 13.02, *infra*.
2. U.C.C. § 9-109(d)(2).
3. Schleimer v. Arrowhead Garage, Inc., 260 N.Y.S.2d 271, 2 U.C.C. Rep. Serv. 753 (Civ. Ct. 1965).
4. The term "mechanic's lien" generally refers to liens arising by operation of law in favor of persons who provide services or materials to improve land. An architect, who is an artisan, might have the benefit of a mechanic's lien, while a mechanic who repairs a car might have the benefit of an artisan's lien. Go figure!

are present: (1) the services or materials were furnished in the ordinary course of the provider's business; (2) the effectiveness of the lien depends upon retention of possession by the provider; and (3) the lien arises by operation of a statutory or common-law rule.[5] The key point with regard to the last element is that the lien must not be consensual and must not result from a judicial or quasi-judicial proceeding. Thus, the provider must be neither an Article 9 secured party nor a "lien creditor" as defined by Article 9.

The rationale for the priority granted for possessory liens is akin to the rationale that undergirds the special priority granted purchase-money security interests.[6] If a car needs repair, for example, its value as collateral has been reduced. Because the services and materials supplied by the garage restore the car's value, priority for the garage in the car for the purpose of recovering its repair bill is only fair. The remaining value of the car—the value present before the repairs were done—is still available to the secured party.[7]

States provide liens for a wide array of interests. Some liens have roots in the common law; others arise by statute. In addition to artisan's liens, there are carrier's liens, logger's liens, innkeeper's liens, and even plastic fabricator's liens. The original drafters designed the Code's priority rule to favor "liens securing claims arising from work intended to enhance or preserve the value of the collateral."[8]

As indicated above, a lien must be possessory in nature to fall within the priority rule of Article 9. The rule does not benefit a person that never acquires possession of the goods[9] or one that voluntarily surrenders possession.[10] Reacquiring possession of the goods after they have been surrendered does not improve the position of the unprotected lienholder.[11] By contrast, involuntary relinquishment of possession, such as by a secured party's replevy of the property,[12] will not defeat a lienholder's priority.[13] One court properly held that a statutory lienholder that temporarily surrenders possession to a subcontractor for purposes of doing a portion of the repair work does

---

5. U.C.C. § 9-333.

6. For discussion of the policy underlying purchase-money secured-party priority, see § 10.04, *supra*.

7. A secured party must be careful or this value could be lost. With the sale of the car at the garage's foreclosure sale, the purchaser will take free of the secured party's interest. *See* § 18.02[E], *infra* (junior liens destroyed through foreclosure). Whether the secured party is entitled to share in any surplus (i.e., amount in excess of the repair bill) received at the sale turns on the state law governing the foreclosure. Because of these risks, the secured party may simply choose to pay the repair bill prior to foreclosure and add the amount to the balance of the secured obligation.

8. U.C.C. § 9-310, Comment 1 (1962 Official Text).

9. Circle 76 Fertilizer, Inc. v. Nelson, 365 N.W.2d 460, 41 U.C.C. Rep. Serv. 1079 (Neb. 1985) (supplier of fertilizer with statutory lien never had possession of debtor's crops).

10. Forrest Cate Ford, Inc. v. Fryar, 465 S.W.2d 882, 8 U.C.C. Rep. Serv. 239 (Tenn. Ct. App. 1970).

11. Balzer Mach. Co. v. Klineline Sand & Gravel Co., 271 Or. 596, 533 P.2d 321, 16 U.C.C. Rep. Serv. 1160 (1975).

12. For discussion of replevin, see § 18.01[B], *infra*.

13. Finch v. Miller, 271 Or. 271, 531 P.2d 892 (1975); *In re* Borden, 361 B.R. 489, 62 U.C.C. Rep. Serv. 2d 158 (Bankr. 8th Cir. 2007) (artisan did not lose its priority from its lien on farm equipment

not jeopardize its priority.[14] This result is consistent with the constructive possession doctrine available to secured parties with possessory security interests.[15]

A state statute may in some instances entitle a lienholder to file a notice of its lien and return the property to the debtor rather than retain possession.[16] Following this option precludes the lienholder from the benefit of Article 9's priority rule. The secured party, however, does not necessarily prevail. The statutory lien is then entirely beyond the scope of Article 9,[17] and the court must determine priority without reference to Section 9-333. A court could apply Article 9's residual priority rule—Section 9-201(a)—and award priority to the secured party, or it could resolve the priority dispute under law other than Article 9.[18]

A common-law possessory lien has priority over a perfected security interest.[19] The priority applies equally to statutory liens, with one exception—a possessory lien created by a statute that expressly subordinates the lien to an Article 9 security interest loses the priority that otherwise would be available.[20] In the absence of the requirement that the subordination be express, pre-Code caselaw might still have construed a statute that creates a possessory lien as subordinate to security interests. Subordination based on case law is not sufficient. Article 9 "provides a rule of interpretation that the possessory lien takes priority, even if the statute has been construed judicially to make the possessory lien subordinate."[21]

Most jurisdictions have enacted forfeiture statutes under which a governmental entity can seize property. Sometimes the seized property is subject to a perfected security interest. Although the government's interest appears to be analogous to a possessory lien, the claim of the governmental entity that seizes the goods does not fit within the parameters of the Code's priority rule because the government's claim to the goods

---

when debtor wrongfully took the equipment from artisan's business premises without the knowledge or consent of artisan).

14. Beverly Bank of Chicago v. Little, 527 So. 2d 706, 7 U.C.C. Rep. Serv. 2d 1272 (Ala. 1988).

15. See § 6.03[B], supra.

16. See, e.g., KAN. STAT. ANN. § 58-201.

17. U.C.C. § 9-109(d)(2). See § 1.06[B], supra; see also In re Laurel Hill Paper Co., 387 B.R. 677, 65 U.C.C. Rep. Serv. 2d 374 (Bankr. M.D.N.C. 2008) (priority contests between nonpossessory artisan liens of suppliers of goods and a secured party not governed by Article 9).

18. See § 12.04, supra; see also Church Bros. Body Serv., Inc. v. Merchants Nat'l Bank & Trust Co. of Indianapolis, 559 N.E.2d 328, 13 U.C.C. Rep. Serv. 2d 537 (Ind. Ct. App. 1990) (pre-Code law applied to resolve priority dispute between security interest and nonpossessory artisan's lien).

19. Charter One Auto Fin. v. Inkas Coffee Distrib. Realty, 57 U.C.C. Rep. Serv. 2d 672 (Conn. Super. Ct. 2005) (storage company's common-law possessory lien for storage fees on an automobile had priority over the prior interest of the secured party that had perfected by notation on the certificate of title).

20. See, e.g., WIS. STAT. § 779.41(1) (priority of garage's possessory lien over prior-in-time perfected security interest limited to specified dollar amount unless the work was done with the express consent of the secured party). See also Affiliated Bank v. Evans Tool & Mfg. Co., Inc., 229 Ill. App. 3d 464, 593 N.E.2d 145, 19 U.C.C. Rep. Serv. 2d 928 (1992); In re S.M. Acquisition Co., 296 B.R. 452, 51 U.C.C. Rep. Serv. 2d 867 (Bankr. N.D. Ill. 2003).

21. U.C.C. § 9-333, Comment 2.

does not qualify as a lien. Resolution of the dispute in these cases falls outside the scope of Article 9.[22]

§ 13.02 Agricultural Liens— §§ 9-317, 9-322(a)(1)

An "agricultural lien"[23] is a nonpossessory statutory lien[24] on farm products[25] that is not a security interest (i.e., does not arise by virtue of a security agreement) and that secures payment to a person that in ordinary course of business furnishes goods or services, or leases real property, to assist with a debtor's farming operation.[26] Examples include a landlord's lien for unpaid rent on crops raised on the demised premises, a commercial harvester's lien for services rendered on crops left in the farmer's possession, and a feeder's lien for services rendered on livestock that remain on a rancher's land. Like possessory liens, such liens arise by operation of law other than Article 9, but once created they are swept into Article 9 for perfection, priority, and enforcement purposes.[27] In other words, once an agricultural lien becomes effective under other law, it receives the same treatment as an Article 9 security interest.[28] "Effectiveness" of an agricultural lien is the equivalent of "attachment" of a security interest.[29]

Because agricultural liens are, by definition, nonpossessory, perfection results from filing a financing statement.[30] Many of the priority rules include specific provisions dealing with agricultural liens, inevitably affording them the same treatment as secu-

---

22. *Compare* State v. One 1976 Pontiac Firebird, 402 A.2d 254, 26 U.C.C. Rep. Serv. 1306 (N.J. Super. Ct. 1979) (state statute made seizure subject to prior security interest) *with* United States v. One 1969 Plymouth Fury Auto., 476 F.2d 960, 12 U.C.C. Rep. Serv. 1228 (5th Cir. 1973) (forfeiture to government held superior to security interest because statute did not provide for subordination).

23. U.C.C. § 9-109(a)(2). *See* § 1.06[A], *supra*.

24. Article 9 does not apply to nonpossessory liens on farm products that arise pursuant to a common-law rule.

25. U.C.C. § 9-102(a)(34). *See* § 1.04[A][2], *supra*.

26. U.C.C. § 9-102(a)(5).

27. The term "secured party" includes a person that holds an agricultural lien. U.C.C. § 9-102(73) (B). Note the difference in the scope of Article 9 coverage of agricultural liens (everything except their creation) and of the possessory liens that arise by operation of law discussed in the previous section (priority only).

28. Agricultural liens are the only common-law or statutory liens governed to this extent by Article 9. *In re* Nicolls, 384 B.R. 113, 65 U.C.C. Rep. Serv. 2d 685 (Bankr. W.D. Pa. 2008) (perfection of a hospital lien for reasonable and necessary charges for hospital care that attached to a judgment or settlement against a tortfeasor that caused the injuries requiring hospital care was not within the scope of Article 9).

29. *Compare* U.C.C. § 9-308(a) (security interest is perfected when it *attaches* and all applicable requirements of Section 9-310 are satisfied) *with* § 9-308(b) (agricultural lien is perfected when it becomes *effective* and all applicable requirements of Section 9-310 are satisfied).

30. U.C.C. § 9-310(a). *Cf. In re* Shulista, 451 B.R. 867, 74 U.C.C. Rep. Serv. 2d 370 (Bankr. N.D. Iowa 2011) (in deference to a provision in the statute creating the Iowa dairy-cattle supply lien, the court held that a filed financing statement covered only feed sold during the 31-day period prior to the filing).

rity interests.[31] For example, Section 9-317(a) provides that an unperfected security interest or agricultural lien is subordinate to the rights of a lien creditor,[32] and Section 9-317(b) allows a buyer that both gives value and takes delivery of goods, without knowledge of a security interest or agricultural lien and before it is perfected, to take free of the interest or lien.[33] Similarly, Section 9-322(a)(1) provides that "conflicting security interests and agricultural liens rank according to priority in time of filing or perfection." If, for example, a bank takes a security interest in a farmer's crops and files its financing statement on November 5, it will be subordinate to a commercial harvester with a statutorily created agricultural lien on the same crops that filed on November 1.

A trap for the unwary lurks in the perfection rules for agricultural liens. Article 9 generally designates the state of the debtor's location as the place to file a financing statement to perfect a security interest.[34] With an agricultural lien, however, the place to file is the state of the location of the farm products subject to the lien.[35] For example, suppose Farmer, who lives in Iowa, rents crop land in Missouri from Landlord, who acquires by statute a lien on Farmer's crops as security for unpaid rent. To perfect its agricultural lien, Landlord must file centrally in Missouri. If Bank takes a security interest in the crops, it will perfect by filing in Iowa. If either Landlord or Bank limits its search for conflicting interests to the office in which it files its own financing statement, it will not locate a financing statement filed by the other party.

§ 13.03 Federal Tax Liens

The Tax Lien Act of 1966 grants to the federal government a lien on all property belonging to a taxpayer that neglects or refuses to pay taxes following a demand for payment.[36] Once created, the lien relates back to the date of the assessment,[37] and its scope is exceptionally broad, attaching to all existing and after-acquired real and personal property in which the taxpayer has an interest.[38] The lien is a "secret lien," meaning that the Internal Revenue Service need not give any public notice for the lien

---

31. Section 9-322(g) provides an exception to the rule that agricultural liens receive the same treatment as Article 9 security interests for priority purposes. A perfected agricultural lien takes priority over a conflicting security interest if the statute creating the lien so provides.

32. *In re* Mendonca, 63 U.C.C. Rep. Serv. 2d 276 (Bankr. E.D. Cal. 2007) (because dairy-cattle supply lien was effective and perfected before the lien in favor of trustee in bankruptcy arose, lien holder prevailed).

33. Buyers of farm products may take priority over even perfected security interests under the federal Food Security Act. 7 U.S.C. § 1631. *See* Chapter 14, *infra*.

34. *See* § 9.02[A], *supra*.

35. U.C.C. § 9-302. *See* § 9.02[D][2], *supra*.

36. I.R.C. § 6321. An excellent analysis of these issues can be found in Michelle Cecil, *Bankruptcy: Tax Issues Affecting Insolvent and Bankrupt Debtors*, in BUSINESS ORGANIZATIONS WITH TAX PLANNING CH. 158 (Zolman Cavitch, ed. 1996).

37. I.R.C. § 6322.

38. Treas. Reg. § 301.6321-1.

to arise and be enforceable. It continues in effect until payment of the tax or expiration of a ten-year limitation period.[39]

Because the lien is secret, third parties unaware of it that acquire an interest in the taxpayer's property—including Article 9 secured parties—are potentially at risk. To reduce the risk, the tax laws encourage the government to file a public notice of its lien[40] by providing that the lien is invalid as against certain interests that arise before the filing. The protected parties are purchasers, judgment lien creditors, mechanic's lienors, and, most importantly for our purposes, holders of security interests.[41]

The Tax Lien Act defines "security interest" to include only an interest that has been perfected under state law.[42] Thus, while Article 9 covers both perfected and unperfected security interests, the holder of an unperfected Article 9 security interest does not have a "security interest" at all for tax-law purposes—and thus has no protection against even an unfiled tax lien. Only secured parties that have perfected prior to the government's filing can prevail in a priority contest with the IRS.

Even if a secured party has properly perfected before filing of a notice of the federal tax lien, it will not prevail over the government unless its security interest is *choate*.[43] A security interest is choate if the identity of the secured party, the property to which the interest attaches, and the amount of the debt can all be accurately established. For a secured party with a single loan and a security interest in a readily identifiable asset, choateness is not a problem. For example, if the secured party has a security interest in the debtor's car and has properly perfected by compliance with the requirements of a certificate-of-title act, a hidden federal tax lien on the car at the time of perfection is irrelevant. All that matters is that the secured party perfected its interest before the government filed its tax-lien notice. The secured party will have no difficulty proving the elements necessary to show choateness.

The choateness doctrine is most troublesome when a secured party attempts to enforce a lien on after-acquired property or on collateral securing future advances. In *Rice Investment Co. v. United States*,[44] for example, a secured party with a properly perfected security interest in the debtor's inventory, including after-acquired inventory, lost a priority battle with the government because it could not establish that the inven-

---

39. I.R.C. §§ 6322, 6502(a)(1).

40. In the case of personal property, the filing must be made in a single office located in the taxpayer's state of residence. I.R.C. § 6323(f)(1)(A)(ii), (2)(B). Unfortunately, for organizations this office may be in a state other than the debtor's state of location for purposes of Article 9, creating difficulties for searchers.

41. I.R.C. § 6323(a). Planned Furniture Promotions, Inc. v. Benjamin S. Youngblood, Inc., 57 U.C.C. Rep. Serv. 2d 678 (M.D. Ga. 2005) (perfected security interest had priority over a subsequently filed tax lien).

42. I.R.C. § 6323(h)(1). Quad City Bank & Trust Co. v. United States, 69 U.C.C. Rep. Serv. 2d 399 (S.D. Iowa 2009) (prior perfected security interest on payments owed under a consulting agreement had priority over a subsequently filed tax lien).

43. Choateness is a judicially created doctrine. The seminal case under the Tax Lien Act of 1966 is *United States v. McDermott*, 507 U.S. 447 (1993).

44. 625 F.2d 565 (5th Cir. 1980).

tory in dispute was in existence and owned by the debtor at the time the government filed its notice of tax lien. Similarly, in *Texas Oil & Gas Corp. v. United States*,[45] the court held that a secured party's perfected security interest was inchoate because its future-advances clause rendered the amount of the indebtedness uncertain as of the time the government filed its notice.

The first of two important exceptions to the choateness doctrine in the Tax Lien Act applies only to security agreements that contain future-advances clauses and allows a secured party to obtain priority for its advances over a filed federal tax lien if certain conditions are met.[46] The secured party need only be perfected before the filing of the tax-lien notice to obtain priority for amounts already advanced at that time. Three requirements apply to obtain priority for a subsequent advance: (1) the advance must be made before the 46th day following the tax-lien filing; (2) the collateral must be covered by the terms of a written[47] security agreement entered into before the tax-lien filing; and (3) the advance must be protected under state law against a creditor with a judgment lien arising out of an unsecured obligation. The period during which the secured party can obtain priority for future advances terminates early if the secured party acquires knowledge or actual notice of the tax-lien filing.

This provision can best be understood by contrasting it with the Article 9 provision dealing with priority for future advances as against a lien creditor.[48] Because the Article 9 provision was drafted with the Tax Lien Act in mind, it always requires satisfaction of the third requirement for priority over the government (that future advances made before the 46th day after tax-lien filing must be protected under state law from a judgment lien creditor). Specifically, Article 9 provides that a secured party has priority over a person that becomes a lien creditor while the security interest is perfected for (1) all advances made before the person becomes a lien creditor, (2) all advances made within 45 days following the date on which the person becomes a lien creditor, irrespective of the secured party's knowledge of the person's interest, (3) all advances made more than 45 days following the date on which the person becomes a lien creditor if the secured party lacks knowledge of the person's lien at the time of the advance, and (4) all advances made pursuant to a commitment entered into without knowledge of the person's lien.

A few examples will help illustrate the differences between the treatment of future advances under the U.C.C. and under the Tax Lien Act. Suppose SP has a perfected security interest in D's equipment, which is collateral for a $10,000 loan. The security agreement includes a future-advances clause. On May 1, the government files its

---

45. 466 F.2d 1040 (5th Cir. 1972).

46. I.R.C. § 6323(d).

47. Although the statute uses the term "written," it is subject to the Electronic Signatures in Global and National Commerce Act (E-Sign), 15 U.S.C. § 7001 *et seq.*, meaning that an equivalent electronic record satisfies its provisions.

48. U.C.C. § 9-323(b). *See* § 12.02[C], *supra*.

tax-lien notice. On May 31, SP, which has neither actual notice[49] nor knowledge of the government's filing, lends D an additional $10,000. SP will have priority over the government for both the original loan and the advance.[50] If SP had made the advance on June 30, more than 45 days after the tax-lien filing, the government would have had priority as to the advance (but not the original loan). The fact that SP was still without actual notice or knowledge when it made the advance on June 30 would be irrelevant. The period of protection for future advances never exceeds 45 days under the Tax Lien Act, and actual notice or knowledge shortens it. The only way for a secured party making a series of future advances to be perfectly safe is to check for tax-lien filings every 45 days.

Article 9 operates somewhat differently. Again, assume SP has a perfected security interest in D's equipment as security for a $10,000 loan and the security agreement has a future-advances clause. On May 1, L, an erstwhile unsecured creditor that obtained a judgment against D, has the sheriff levy on the equipment. On May 31, SP, which does not have knowledge[51] of the levy, makes an advance. SP will have priority over L for both the original loan and the advance. The result would be the same if SP had knowledge of the levy because Article 9 protects all advances made during the 45-day period without regard to knowledge. Even if the advance was made on June 30, SP would have priority if it still lacked knowledge of the levy. In short, the tax laws protect future advances for 45 days at most and perhaps for a shorter period; Article 9 protects such advances for at least 45 days and perhaps longer.[52]

The second statutory exception to the choateness doctrine applies to after-acquired property clauses.[53] The exception applies to "commercial transactions financing agreements,"[54] meaning agreements entered into by lenders to make loans to taxpayers

---

49. The Internal Revenue Code does not define the term, but actual notice obviously means less than actual knowledge and more than either constructive or inquiry notice. For example, suppose a secured party does not know that the government has a tax lien but learns from a reliable source that the government has padlocked the debtor's plant. This information ought to constitute actual notice, and a future advance made after acquiring such information will be subordinate to the tax lien. *Cf.* U.C.C. § 1-202(a) (defining notice).

50. Without I.R.C. § 6323(d), the secured party would have priority as to its original loan (it was perfected before the tax-lien notice was filed), but its security interest would be inchoate with respect to the advance.

51. Article 9 does not use the term "actual notice."

52. The discussion of this area would not be complete without a reference to U.C.C. § 9-323, which provides a "forty-five day or less" rule for future advances made after a buyer or lessee not in ordinary course of business purchases the collateral. U.C.C. §§ 9-323(d), (e) (buyer); 9-323(f), (g) (lessee). *See* § 11.03[A][3], *supra*; *see also* U.C.C. § 9-323(a) (provides for unlimited priority for future advances against another secured party); § 10.02, *supra*.

53. I.R.C. § 6323(c). This provision also applies to a limited class of obligatory future-advances clauses.

54. I.R.C. § 6323(c)(1)(A)(i). The provision also applies to real property construction or improvement financing agreements and to obligatory disbursement agreements. I.R.C. § 6323(c)(1)(A)(ii), (iii). Discussion of these agreements is beyond the scope of this book, but if your curiosity is uncontrollable, see GRANT S. NELSON, DALE A. WHITMAN, ANN M. BURKHART & R. WILSON FREYERMUTH, REAL ESTATE FINANCE LAW § 9.9 (6th ed. 2015).

secured by "commercial financing security."[55] Commercial financing security in turn means paper of a kind ordinarily arising in commercial transactions, accounts receivable, mortgages on real property, and inventory. If a secured party has a written security agreement with the taxpayer that covers commercial-financing security, including after-acquired assets, and its security interest is protected under state law from a judgment lien arising out of an unsecured obligation (meaning properly perfected before the government files its notice), it will have priority over the government as to commercial-financing security acquired by the taxpayer before the 46th day following tax-lien filing.[56] As with the future-advances exception discussed above, the period during which the secured party can obtain priority for after-acquired property terminates early if the secured party acquires knowledge or actual notice of the tax-lien filing.

As with the exception for future advances, the only sure way for a secured party to protect itself is by checking for tax-lien filings every 45 days. A filing discovered during a search (or that otherwise comes to the attention of the secured party) should induce the secured party to repossess its collateral immediately. Allowing the debtor to retain the collateral beyond the protected period (45 days or less) will later require the secured party to prove what collateral was in the debtor's hands when the period ended. Otherwise, the secured party will face the inchoateness problem described in connection with the *Rice Investment Co.* case.

---

55. I.R.C. §6323(c)(2)(A). The lender must make the loan in ordinary course of business, and the taxpayer must acquire the commercial financing security in ordinary course of business. This section of the Tax Lien Act also applies to certain agreements to purchase commercial financing security (other than inventory) from the taxpayer. This application is roughly analogous to, although somewhat broader than, Article 9's coverage of sales of certain intangibles.

56. Old Nat'l Bank v. RCH Elec. Sys., Inc., 56 U.C.C. Rep. Serv. 2d 468 (S.D. Ind. 2005) (by filing tax liens in November 1999 and March 2000, the United States had priority over the bank's claim to after-acquired accounts that arose between August and November 2000); American Inv. Fin. v. United States, 364 F. Supp.2d 1321, 57 U.C.C. Rep. Serv. 2d 94 (D. Utah 2005) (IRS liens had priority over lender's security interest in health-care-insurance receivables for services that were performed outside the 45-day safe harbor provision, even though the contracts that gave rise to the receivables pre-dated the tax liens).

Chapter 14

The Farm Products Rule

Synopsis

§ 14.01 The Article 9 Rule

Article 9 includes an exception to the priority rule that favors a buyer in ordinary course of business over a prior-perfected security interest created by the buyer's seller.[1] But this priority rule does not protect "a person buying farm products from a person engaged in farming operations."[2] Even though the debtor's farm products are analogous to a merchant's inventory, and even though a buyer of farm products may qualify as a buyer in ordinary course of business, the Code does not permit the buyer to prevail over a prior-perfected agricultural lender.

A number of arguments support the exception, which dates to the original version of Article 9. The buyer-in-ordinary-course rule protects buyers, and, in many instances, consumers, that purchase inventory from a seller, and these buyers are often unaware of the need to check for filed financing statements before proceeding with a purchase. Buyers of farm products, however, generally are merchants that ought to know of the need to check for filed financing statements. These buyers thus are in a better position to protect their interests than is the typical inventory buyer. Agricultural lenders are, furthermore, more vulnerable than inventory lenders because farmers often sell all of their farm products at one time.[3] Policing measures that can detect an inventory seller

---

1. For discussion of this priority rule, see § 11.03[A][1], *supra*.
2. U.C.C. § 9-320(1). Section 9-102(a)(35) defines "farming operation."
3. A bulk sale by a nonfarmer would be unlikely to qualify as an ordinary-course transaction. *See* U.C.C. § 1-201(b)(9).

beginning to sell "out of trust"[4] cannot aid a lender after a farmer wrongfully sells all of the crops or livestock. Although the lender's interest extends automatically to the proceeds of the sale,[5] that protection is meaningless if the farmer is dishonest or desperate and the buyer's check does not include the lender as a joint payee.[6]

The farm-products rule has also had its detractors. The general rule favoring buyers in ordinary course of business protects the free flow of commerce—a principle that arguably applies to agricultural commodities as well as to other kinds of goods. Moreover, federal laws that require prompt payment for certain commodities make searches of the filing system particularly impractical and costly.[7] The impact of the farm-products rule fell with undue harshness on smaller businesses that bought farm products, and they derisively called it the "double-jeopardy" rule.[8]

§ 14.02 The Federal Food Security Act

Congress included a section in the Food Security Act of 1985 (Act) captioned "Protection for Purchasers of Farm Products."[9] The congressional findings for the provision determined that the possibility of double payment by a buyer of farm products that did not discover the existence of a perfected security interest constituted a burden on and an obstruction to interstate commerce.[10] Congress therefore provided that unless one of two exceptions applies, buyers of farm products in the ordinary course of business are to be treated like other buyers in ordinary course of business,[11] that is, they take free

---

4. This term is used primarily in floor planning, a type of inventory financing discussed in § 3.04[C], *supra*. It refers to a failure to remit to the lender an agreed percentage of the purchase price of big-ticket inventory items.

5. *See* § 2.03, *supra*.

6. For discussion of the risks to a lender in regard to cash proceeds, see § 8.02[B][1], *supra*.

7. *See* Packers & Stockyard Act, 7 U.S.C. § 2286 (1994) (full payment before close of next business day following purchase and transfer of livestock).

8. The term refers to the fact that a buyer could pay a farmer for farm products and then have to pay a secured party a second time to avoid foreclosure.

9. 7 U.S.C. § 1631.

10. *Id.* § 1631(a).

11. The protection of the federal legislation also extends to "commission merchants" and "sales agents" that sell farm products in the ordinary course of business, thereby insulating such merchants and agents from conversion liability.

of perfected security interests created by their sellers even if they have knowledge of the interests.[12] The federal legislation preempts the Code's farm-products rule.[13]

The federal law provides two alternative mechanisms that preserve a secured party's interest in farm products following an unauthorized disposition by the debtor. One approach is for the secured party or the debtor to provide advance notice of the security interest directly to the buyer. The other approach is to use a central registry that a state can elect to create for purposes of providing notification to buyers that request information concerning farm products.[14] The discussion below describes the two mechanisms.

---

12. *Id.* § 1631(d). Under Article 9, a person that knows its purchase violates the rights of a secured party does not qualify as a buyer in ordinary course of business. U.C.C. § 1-201(b)(9). The federal law does not include a similar provision. However, consistent with Article 9, a buyer of farm products in ordinary course takes free of a security interest only when the security interest is created by the buyer's seller. The buyer in *Fin Ag, Inc. v. Hufnagle, Inc.*, 720 N.W.2d 579 (Minn. 2006), ran afoul of this limitation. The secured party filed an "effective financing statement" with the Minnesota central registry on its debtor's corn crop that protected it on purchases made directly from the debtor. The buyer claimed, however, that a third party sold some of the debtor's corn to it under the third party's name. The buyer lost to the secured party under this scenario because the security interest in the corn was not created by the buyer's seller. The court in *Fin-Ag, Inc. v. Cimpl's, Inc.*, 754 N.W.2d 1 (S.D. 2008), came to a different conclusion. It distinguished *Hufnagle* on the grounds that, rather than using unrelated third parties to sell the farm products of the debtor, the individual debtors used their doing-business-as name to sell the cattle themselves. It also disagreed with the *Hufnagle* court's approach to the "created-by-the-seller" analysis, pointing out caselaw in the context of the U.C.C. that does not strictly construe the language when the seller and the creator of the prior lien are closely related or the seller was instrumental in creating the encumbrance.

13. Lisco State Bank v. McCombs Ranches, Inc., 752 F. Supp. 329, 13 U.C.C. Rep. Serv. 2d 927 (D. Neb. 1990) (federal statute applies retroactively to previously perfected security interests); Farm Credit Servs. of Mid Am. v. Rudy, Inc., 1995 U.S. Dist. LEXIS 22178 (S.D. Ohio Mar. 8, 1995) (the Act does not create a federal cause of action).

14. First Bank v. Eastern Livestock Co., 837 F. Supp. 792, 23 U.C.C. Rep. Serv. 2d 933 (S.D. Miss. 1993) (because the Act provides two exclusive means by which a buyer of farm products in ordinary course can be subject to the perfected security interest, actual knowledge of the buyer through other means would be irrelevant).

On its public website, the National Agricultural Law Center maintains a series of helpful factsheets that buyers and secured parties can use to navigate compliance with each alternative. According to the 2022 factsheet, 33 states follow the advance-notice approach, and 16 states use the state central-registry approach. *See* Micah Brown, Nat'l Agric. L. Ctr, *Figuring the Federal Farm Products Rule: Complying with the Notice Requirements* (2022).

[A] Advance-Notice Approach

A buyer of farm products that receives, within one year prior to the sale,[15] a written[16] notice containing statutorily prescribed information from either the lender or the debtor advising of the security interest will take subject to it unless the buyer complies with payment instructions included in the notice.[17] The secured party generally requires payment with a jointly payable check to ensure its control over the sale proceeds.[18] This approach shifts onto secured parties the burden of identifying adverse interests, a burden the Article 9 filing system imposes on buyers. The secured party must locate potential buyers and provide them direct notice.

The advance notice to buyers must satisfy several requirements.[19] The notice must be organized by the type of farm product affected. It must include the names and addresses of the secured party and the debtor, the social security or taxpayer identification number of the debtor, a description of the farm products subject to the security interest, the amount of the farm products if applicable (e.g., if less than all of a particular category is claimed), the crop year, a reasonable description of the land on which the crops are grown (including the county or parish), and any payment obligations imposed on

---

15. Pioneer Hi-Bred Int'l, Inc. v. Keybank Nat'l Ass'n, 742 N.E.2d 967 (Ind. Ct. App. 2001) (buyer held to be subject to secured party's interest in seed corn because buyer received notice from secured party within one year of the sale); First Midwest Bank, N.A. v. IBP, Inc., 314 Ill. App.3d 255, 731 N.E.2d 839, 41 U.C.C. Rep. Serv. 2d 1278 (Ill. Ct. App. 2000) (majority upheld lower court's ruling that bank's direct notice of its security interest in hogs lapsed after one year).

16. Although the Act uses the term "written," it is subject to the Electronic Signatures in Global and National Commerce Act (E-Sign), 15 U.S.C. § 7001 *et seq.* Under E-Sign, a writing requirement imposed by the Food Security Act may be satisfied by an electronic record.

17. 7 U.S.C. § 1631(e)(1)(A). The perfected secured party in *Ag Services of America, Inc. v. DeBruce Grain, Inc.,* 28 Kan. App. 2d 582, 19 P.3d 188, 45 U.C.C. Rep. Serv. 2d 1193 (Kan. Ct. App. 2001), provided the necessary advance notice to the defendant, which had a contract to buy 30,000 bushels of the debtor's corn crop. After the debtor delivered less than a third of the bushels and repudiated the remainder of the sales contract, the defendant covered on the open market and deducted the amount of its damages from the purchase price for the delivered corn. The majority held that the buyer of farm products in ordinary course could not reduce the secured party's interest through its set-off rights, as the secured party was not liable for claims that the buyer had against the seller. The dissent would have treated the secured party as an account debtor following delivery of the corn and thus would have held that the secured party was subject to the buyer's off-set claim under Section 9-318(1)(a) of the Code.

18. Farm Credit Bank of St. Paul v. F&A Dairy, 165 Wis. 2d 360, 477 N.W.2d 357, 16 U.C.C. Rep. Serv. 2d 885 (Ct. App. 1991) (buyer liable in conversion for failing to comply with advance notice requiring monthly milk payments to be made directly to secured party); Agriliance, L.L.C. v. Runnells Grain Elevator, Inc., 272 F. Supp. 2d 800, 51 U.C.C. Serv. 2d 756 (S.D. Iowa 2003) (buyer failed to comply with notice to issue payment jointly to the secured party and the farmer/seller). *But see* Mercantile Bank of Springfield v. Joplin Regional Stockyards, Inc., 870 F. Supp. 278, 27 U.C.C. Rep. Serv. 2d 269 (W.D. Mo. 1994) (buyer that did not comply with payment instructions still prevailed based on secured party's acquiescence through course of conduct).

19. Lisco State Bank v. McCombs Ranches, Inc., 752 F. Supp. 329, 13 U.C.C. Rep. Serv. 2d 927 (D. Neb. 1990) (oral notification ineffective).

buyers as a condition for release of the security interest.[20] Any material change in the information requires a written amendment of the notice within three months.[21]

The Act permits the secured party to require the debtor to provide a list of prospective buyers for the debtor's farm products.[22] A prudent secured party accordingly will include covenants in the security agreement requiring the debtor to provide such a list and to sell only to buyers on the list. The monetary fine for selling to an unlisted buyer, unless the debtor notifies the secured party in writing at least seven days prior to the sale,[23] is the greater of $5,000 or 15 percent of the value of the farm products sold.[24] A debtor that does not inform the secured party prior to an off-the-list sale can still avoid liability by remitting the proceeds to the secured party within ten days following the unauthorized sale.[25] The off-list buyer takes the farm products free of the security interest even if the buyer knows of it.

[B] State Central-Registry Approach

The alternative approach permitted by the federal Act requires a state to create a central-filing registry that complies with standards articulated in the Act. A registry must require secured lenders seeking priority to file with the registry (to be maintained by the Secretary of State or its designee[26]) a notice designated in the Act as an "effective financing statement" and known to lenders as an "EFS."[27] An EFS must include all the information mandated under the advance-notice alternative[28] and also must be amended within three months following any material change in the information pro-

---

20. 7 U.S.C. § 1631(e)(1)(A)(ii). Although the Act does not cover the effect of missing information in a notice under the advance-notice system, the court in *First National Bank & Trust v. Miami County Cooperative Association*, 257 Kan. 989, 897 P.2d 144 (1995), held that the more probable congressional intent was to avoid making a notice ineffective if it contains minor omissions or errors that are not seriously misleading. It upheld the effectiveness of a secured party's notices to the buyer, even though the notices did not describe the real property or the crop year, because the notices substantially complied and did not mislead the buyer. *Cf.* Farm Credit Midsouth, PCA v. Farm Fresh Catfish Co., 371 F.3d 450 (8th Cir. 2004) (because strict compliance is required for the secured party's advance notice, the secured party failed the test by sending a notice that did not include the debtor's taxpayer identification number, the debtor's address, or the counties in which the catfish subject to the security interest were produced).

21. 7 U.S.C. § 1631(e)(1)(A)(iii).

22. *Id.* § 1631(h)(1).

23. *Id.* § 1631(h)(2)(A).

24. *Id.* § 1631(h)(3).

25. *Id.* § 1631(h)(2)(B).

26. *Id.* § 1631(d)(11).

27. If the state permits electronic filings under Article 9, an electronically reproduced copy of the EFS may be filed. *Id.* § 1631(c)(4)(A).

28. *Id.* § 1631(c)(4)(D).

vided.[29] A filed EFS provides constructive notice of the security interest to all potential farm-product buyers.[30]

A central registry has several master lists. One of the lists is organized according to types of farm products, arranged alphabetically by the debtors' names,[31] numerically by their social security and taxpayer identification numbers, geographically by county, and temporally by crop year. Another master list indicates all of the buyers of farm products registered with the system. That list must show the name and address of each registered buyer and the types of farm products that interest the buyer. The Secretary of State on a regular basis must send registered buyers written notification[32] of the information on file regarding the types of farm products for which they registered.[33] The Secretary of State must also provide oral confirmation of the existence of an EFS within 24 hours, followed by written confirmation, upon request by an unregistered buyer.[34]

Buyers that do not register or request information from the Secretary of State about an EFS prior to purchasing farm products subject to a security interest take the farm products subject to the security interest if the secured party filed an EFS.[35] If the secured party did not file an EFS, even an unregistered buyer in ordinary course prevails.[36] A registered buyer that receives notification from the Secretary of State about an EFS on

---

29. *Id.* § 1631(c)(4)(E).

30. Lisco State Bank v. McCombs Ranches, Inc., 752 F. Supp. 329, 13 U.C.C. Rep. Serv. 2d 927 (D. Neb. 1990) (perfected secured party failed to file effective financing statement to take advantage of Nebraska's implementation of central-filing system). Like an Article 9 financing statement, an EFS is effective for a period of five years. 7 U.S.C. § 1631(c)(4)(F).

31. *But see* Peoples Bank v. Bryan Bros. Cattle Co., 504 F.3d 549, 64 U.C.C. Rep. Serv. 2d 113 (5th Cir. 2007) (genuine issue of material fact as to whether debtor operated as a sole proprietorship, partnership, or LLC because a security interest could have attached only if the debtor was a sole proprietorship).

32. The Electronic Signatures in Global and National Commerce Act (E-Sign) allows federal and state regulatory agencies to determine permitted formats. 15 U.S.C. § 7004.

33. *See* Fin-Ag, Inc. v. Cimpl's, Inc., 754 N.W.2d 1 (S.D. 2008). A meat-packing business purchased cattle from "C & M Dairy," a business name used by two individuals to buy and sell cattle. A lender had a security interest in the names of the two individuals, and the monthly portion of the master list that the packing business received after registering with the Secretary of State's central filing system showed those individual names but not the assumed business name. The court held that C & M Dairy was the seller of the cattle, and the secured lender failed to protect its interest by not including the business name.

34. 7 U.S.C. § 1631(c)(2)(F).

35. *Id.* § 1631(e)(2). Ag Servs. of Am., Inc. v. United Grain, Inc., 75 F. Supp. 2d 1037 (D. Neb. 1999) (unregistered buyer in Kansas took subject to creditor's security interest in debtor's corn grown in Nebraska and properly noted on the master lists of the Nebraska central registry).

36. 7 U.S.C. § 1631(e)(2). Consol. Nutrition, L.C. v. IBP, Inc., 669 N.W.2d 126, 2003 S.D. 107, 51 U.C.C. Rep. Serv. 2d 329 (S.D. 2003) (registered buyer took free of the security interest in debtor's hogs because at the time of the sales the secured party had neither filed an effective financing statement nor sent a written notice to the buyer concerning the security interest); Battle Creek State Bank v. Preusker, 253 Neb. 502, 571 N.W.2d 294 (Neb. 1997) (although bank's failure to list milk on the effective financing statement resulted in the purchaser of the milk's taking free of the security interest, this protection did not extend to unsecured creditors to whom the proceeds from the milk sales were transferred because the creditors did not qualify as buyers of farm products in ordinary course).

file can take free of the security interest by obtaining a waiver or release of the interest through compliance with specified payment conditions.[37]

§ 14.03 A Critique

The Food Security Act has some deficiencies. The Act impedes the important goal of promoting uniformity in commercial law:[38] The alternative mechanisms undercut uniformity. Moreover, the application of each mechanism undermines uniformity. The states may determine what constitutes "receipt" of a notification under the advance-notification approach.[39] Under the central-registry approach, each state prescribes what constitutes "regular" distribution of written notices to buyers.[40]

Although adopted based on a finding that the Article 9 farm-products rule was a burden to interstate commerce, the Act's cumbersome mechanisms are poorly designed to overcome such burdens. The central-filing approach is a particular source of confusion. It does not replace or provide a substitute for the Article 9 filing system—a secured party must still file an Article 9 financing statement to obtain priority over other secured parties and lien creditors.[41] The registry is relevant only in determining protection of a security interest with respect to a buyer of farm products. The Act thus constitutes a trap for the unwary. By using the term "central filing system" and referring to the secured party's filing as an "effective financing statement," it creates the impression that it supplants Article 9's filing requirements.[42] Needless

---

37. 7 U.S.C. § 1631(e)(3)(B).

38. *See* U.C.C. § 1-103(a)(3).

39. 7 U.S.C. § 1631(c)(2)(e).

40. *Id.* § 1631(f).

41. The commission agent in *Food Services of America v. Royal Heights, Inc.*, 123 Wash. 2d 779, 871 P.2d 590, 23 U.C.C. Rep. Serv. 2d 949 (1994), claimed priority in the proceeds of its sale of the debtor's apple crop made free of the competing bank's prior-perfected security interest. The court denied priority to the commission agent because of its failure to comply with the Article 9 perfection requirements. The Act's protection extended to the commission agent as a seller but not as a competing secured party. *See also* Consol. Nutrition, L.C. v. IBP, Inc., 669 N.W.2d 126, 2003 S.D. 107, 51 U.C.C. Rep. Serv. 2d 329 (S.D. 2003) (application of proceeds to a pre-existing claim that buyer had with seller was governed by state law and not by the provision of the Act because buyer in this context was acting as a lender and receiving the goods in satisfaction of a pre-existing claim rather than buying them); Fin-Ag, Inc. v. Pipestone Livestock Auction Market, Inc., 754 N.W.2d 29, 66 U.C.C. Rep. Serv. 2d 43 (S.D. 2008) (no federal protection for sale proceeds used to meet a preexisting debt).

42. For example, the bankruptcy court in *In re Duffin*, 226 B.R. 436 (Bankr. D. Idaho June 30, 1999), erroneously held that the central registry provided a separate and single index for all claims of creditors of interests in farm products in Idaho so that filing had to be made in that registry in order to perfect a security interest in farm products. Therefore, even though the secured party had filed a U.C.C. financing statement describing the collateral as all of the debtor's crops, because the "effective financing statement" of the central registry described only the debtor's wheat crop, the court held in error that the secured party was not perfected in the debtor's potato crops and was subordinate to the trustee in bankruptcy. Other cases have held that compliance with the requirements for an Article 9 financing statement constitutes an effective financing statement for purposes of the Act. People's Bank v. Bryan Bros. Cattle Co., 504 F.3d 549, 64 U.C.C. Rep. Serv. 2d 113 (5th Cir. 2007); Bryan Bros. Cattle

confusion has resulted from its duplicating terms used in Article 9 but assigning them different meanings.[43]

The mechanisms established by the Act also pose workability concerns. The provisions imposing fines on debtors that sell to buyers that are not on a list submitted to a secured party pursuant to a covenant in a security agreement may not provide a sufficient deterrent for farmers facing financial ruin. Fines collected by the government rather than applied to the secured debt do not protect the secured lender. Moreover, the advance-notice approach creates an incentive for a secured lender to send notification to all potential buyers. Rather than limiting notification to the buyers listed by the debtor, the secured party has an incentive to notify any other potential buyer in a relevant geographic area as a hedge against an off-list sale by the debtor. The incentive to over-notify imposes transactional costs on both secured lenders and potential buyers, which may be blitzed with notifications. Because the Act does not stipulate a uniform format for notices, buyers must be prepared to assimilate information that will arrive in a variety of formats.

Co. v. Glenbrook Cattle Co., 2006 U.S. Dist. LEXIS 29926 (N.D. Miss. May 1, 2005) (courts examine filed financing statements to determine whether secured parties had effective financing statements); Fin-Ag, Inc. v. Pipestone Livestock Auction Market, Inc., 754 N.W.2d 29, 66 U.C.C. Rep. Serv. 2d 43 (S.D. 2008) (parties agreed that a filed U.C.C. financing statement qualified as an effective financing statement under the Act).

43. The language in the Act does not state the requirements that a buyer act in good faith and without knowledge that the sale to it violates the interests of third parties in order to qualify as a buyer of farm products in ordinary course. 7 U.S.C. § 1631(c)(1). *See* Lisco State Bank v. McCombs Ranches, Inc., 752 F. Supp. 329, 13 U.C.C. Rep. Serv. 2d 927 (D. Neb. 1990).

Chapter 15

Fixtures, Accessions, and Commingled Goods

Synopsis

§ 15.01 Fixtures Defined— § 9-102(a)(41)

The U.C.C. defines "fixtures" as goods that have become so related to a particular parcel of land that an interest in them arises under real property law.[1] Under real property law, a "fixture" is an item of personal property that is so affixed to land (or to a structure on land) that a purchaser of the land[2] would expect that title to the item would pass with a deed to the land. Yet this affixation does not inherently cause a fixture to lose its separate identity such that it becomes merged into the realty for all purposes. As a result, a creditor may obtain an Article 9 security interest in a fixture (either before or after its affixation),[3] and following default, a secured party may remove a fixture and sell it as goods at an Article 9 foreclosure sale.[4] In other words, a fixture has attributes associated with both realty and personalty.

Courts use a facts-and-circumstances test to determine whether a particular asset qualifies as a fixture, typically focusing on three elements: (1) the intent of the annexor,[5] (2) the degree of physical affixation to the realty, and (3) the degree of adaptation of the asset to the particular characteristics of the real estate.[6] The first factor—the intent of the annexor—is important in disputes between a secured party and the party that owned the land at the time of affixation, but courts may give this factor less significance in disputes between a secured party and a subsequent purchaser of the land. In deciding whether to buy or lend, a purchaser typically will have relied on the appearance that the fixture was part of the land, and the reasonable expectations of the purchaser outweigh the hidden intentions of the annexor. Accordingly, in most disputes involving whether goods constitute a fixture, the issue turns on the degree of affixation and adaptation. While goods that are plugged into the wall are in some sense "affixed" to the land, a court is not likely to characterize such goods as a fixture. If a couple of screws connect goods to the land to keep the goods from vibrating, the goods may or may not be a fixture. If the goods are so extensively attached to or embedded in the land that the goods cannot be removed without intensive labor, the goods are almost certainly a fixture.[7] Adaptation may have special significance, even if the physical con-

---

1. U.C.C. § 9-102(a)(41). Thus, while Article 9 establishes a complex system of perfection and priority for security interests in fixtures, it leaves the basic definition of "fixture" to non-Code law.

2. Under both the Code and real estate law, the term "purchase" includes any voluntary transaction that creates or transfers an interest in property. As a result, the term "purchaser" of the land would include both buyers and mortgagees. *See* U.C.C. § 1-201(b)(29), (30); DALE A. WHITMAN, ANN M. BURKHART, R. WILSON FREYERMUTH, & TROY A. RULE, THE LAW OF PROPERTY § 11.10 (4th ed. 2019).

3. To acquire a security interest in an item that is a fixture or might become a fixture, the secured party must satisfy the basic requirements for attachment in Section 9-203. *See* § 2.02, *supra*.

4. *See* § 15.04, *infra*.

5. The "annexor" is the person affixing the asset to the land.

6. *See, e.g., In re* MBA Poultry, L.L.C., 291 F.3d 528, 47 U.C.C. Rep. Serv. 2d 1488 (8th Cir. 2002) (stainless steel superstructure in bird-processing plant satisfied all three criteria).

7. *Compare* Lewiston Bottled Gas Co. v. Key Bank of Me., 601 A.2d 91, 17 U.C.C. Rep. Serv. 2d 282 (Me. 1992) (air conditioning units in motel building were fixtures) *with* Federal Land Bank of

nection between the goods and the land is slight, when the goods have been specially designed to fit into a particular area.[8] For example, drapes that are loosely attached but are specifically designed for a particular room may qualify as fixtures.[9]

Certain goods become so embedded in land that they lose their individual identity and become part of the land for all purposes.[10] Many houses, for example, are technically movable[11] in that they can be lifted from their foundations; nevertheless, courts typically characterize a house as pure real property and not as a fixture.[12] Likewise, real property law considers most ordinary building materials that have been incorporated into a structure—such as mortar, paint, or lumber—to be pure realty. Real estate law does not treat such materials as fixtures because they are unlikely to retain their physical integrity or their value if removed from the land.

Conceptually, some ordinary building materials might qualify as fixtures under non-Code law, but policy suggests that they should not be subject to an Article 9 security interest. For example, bricks used to build a house might have significant value if removed from the house, but no Article 9 secured party should be allowed to remove the bricks because doing so would destroy the economic value of the house. Although removing a fixture often requires the secured party to inflict some physical damage to the land and may decrease the land's fair market value, allowing a secured party to disassemble a structure piecemeal and thereby destroy its capacity to carry out its basic functions would be wasteful. Article 9 thus precludes parties from claiming a security interest in ordinary building materials that have been incorporated into an improvement regardless of their classification under real estate law.[13] The distinction is

---

Omaha v. Swanson, 438 N.W.2d 765, 9 U.C.C. Rep. Serv. 2d 1125 (1989) (grain bins, while attached to concrete, were nevertheless readily removable and were not fixtures).

8. *See, e.g., In re* Troutt, 70 U.C.C. Rep. Serv. 2d 424 (Bankr. S.D. Ill. 2009) (energy guard insulation blanket that conformed to an attic, was adapted to fit the roof support beams, and was stapled into place constituted a fixture as it had no utility for another attic); *In re* Sand & Sage Farm & Ranch, Inc., 266 B.R. 507, 45 U.C.C. Rep. Serv. 2d 911 (Bankr. D. Kan. 2001) (pivot irrigation system constituted fixture; need for system in semi-arid conditions of western Kansas demonstrated relation between goods and use of land).

9. *See, e.g.,* Sears, Roebuck & Co. v. Seven Palms Motor Inn, 530 S.W.2d 695 (Mo. 1975). The concept of adaptation is sometimes called "constructive annexation."

10. *See, e.g., In re* Ojeda, 2020 WL 5746801 (Bankr. M.D. Fla. 2020) (in-ground swimming pool was neither goods nor a fixture).

11. "Goods" are "all things that are movable when the security interest attaches" and specifically includes fixtures. U.C.C. §9-102(a)(44).

12. *See, e.g., In re* Menorah Congregation & Religious Ctr., 554 B.R. 675 (Bankr. S.D.N.Y. 2016) (under New York law, bungalows on land used in seasonal vacation business were realty, not personalty). Smaller structures such as sheds may qualify as goods.

13. U.C.C. §9-334(a). *See, e.g., In re* Adkins, 444 B.R. 374 (Bankr. N.D. Ohio 2011) (windows installed in a home constituted "ordinary building materials incorporated into an improvement on land," and creditor's claimed security interest in the windows did not continue following installation). For a wrongly decided case, *see In re* Dabbs, 625 B.R. 15 (Bankr. D.S.C. 2021) (siding installed on debtor's home was a fixture and not ordinary building materials incorporated into an improvement).

more theoretical than practical; ordinary building materials that are so incorporated will almost certainly be classified as pure realty under non-Code state law.[14]

§ 15.02 Fixture Filings— § 9-102(a)(40)

A secured party may take a security interest in a fixture, but a buyer of the land would expect to become the owner of the fixture and a mortgagee would expect the fixture to serve as collateral for a mortgage loan. Because of the potential conflict between a secured party with an interest in the fixture as personalty and one or more parties with an interest in the fixture as realty, the filing system should provide for notice of a fixture interest to appear in the chain of title to the land. Article 9 facilitates this notice through the concept of a "fixture filing." A fixture filing is a financing statement that covers goods that "are or are to become fixtures" and that satisfies both the general requirements for the sufficiency of a financing statement and the specific requirements for the sufficiency of a real-property-related financing statement.[15] To be sufficient as a fixture filing,[16] the statement must:

- indicate that it covers goods that are fixtures or are to become fixtures,[17]
- indicate that it is to be filed in the real property records,[18]

---

14. Statutes in each state allow the unpaid supplier of such materials to assert a statutory mechanic's lien against the real property into which the materials were incorporated, permitting the supplier to foreclose against the entire land. *See, e.g.,* Mill Creek Lumber & Supply Co. v. First United Bank & Trust Co., 278 P.3d 12 (Okla. Ct. Civ. App. 2012). The creation and enforcement of mechanic's liens varies from state to state and is thus beyond the scope of this book.

15. U.C.C. § 9-102(a)(40) ("'Fixture filing' means the filing of a financing statement covering goods that are or are to become fixtures and satisfying Section 9-502(a) and (b).").

16. Allied Mut. Ins. Co. v. Midplains Waste Mgmt., L.L.C., 612 N.W.2d 488, 42 U.C.C. Rep. Serv. 2d 296 (Neb. 2000) (financing statement ineffective as fixture filing because it did not include required information).

17. U.C.C. § 9-502(b)(1).

18. U.C.C. § 9-502(b)(3). Because most jurisdictions provide for local (e.g., county, district, parish, or town) recording of real property interests, the secured party will typically file a fixture filing in the recording office in the locality where the relevant land (i.e., the land to which the goods are or are to be affixed) is located. U.C.C. § 9-501(a)(1)(B). Article 9 contains special provisions allowing a security interest in the real-property-related assets of a transmitting utility to be perfected by a single, central filing that has the effect of a fixture filing and that remains effective until a termination statement is filed. Because many utilities have operations spanning large parts of a state, the normal fixture filing rules would require filings in multiple counties. *See* U.C.C. §§ 9-102(a)(81) (defining "transmitting utility"); 9-501(b) (central filing operates as a fixture filing); 9-515(f) (duration of filing). A secured party must take care in this context. A fixture filing must be made pursuant to the law of the jurisdiction where the land is located, U.C.C. § 9-301(1)(A). In the case of a transmitting utility, a central filing is required in each state in which the utility has fixtures to perfect as to the fixtures in each state. U.C.C. §§ 9-301, Comment 5b; 9-501, Comment 5.

- provide a description of the real property to which the collateral is related,[19] and

- if the debtor does not have an interest of record in the real property, provide the name of a record owner of the land.[20]

The Code dictates that fixture filings be made in the office for recording a mortgage on the underlying land.[21] In other words, to serve as a fixture filing, an ordinary financing statement must be adapted to serve the functions of the real property recording system.[22] The financing statement thus must have the name of at least one record owner of the land. Priority contests frequently turn on whether the secured party has made a timely fixture filing.

A secured party that takes a security interest in goods that it expects to become fixtures should make dual filings, that is, both a fixture filing and a financing statement sufficient to perfect a security interest in the goods in their non-affixed form. This "belt-and-suspenders" approach protects the secured party against the risk that the debtor never affixes the goods, that a court later holds that the goods did not qualify as fixtures, or that the debtor later removes the goods and sells them to a buyer in their non-affixed form.

§ 15.03 Priorities in Fixtures

[A] The Code's Residual Rule—§ 9-334(c)

Article 9's residual priority rule for fixtures is Section 9-334(c), which provides that "a security interest in fixtures is subordinate to the conflicting interest of an encumbrancer[23] or owner of the related real property other than the debtor." Thus, in contrast

---

19. U.C.C. § 9-502(b)(3). The description of the land is sufficient for purposes of a fixture filing if it would be sufficient to give constructive notice to subsequent purchasers of the land if used in a recorded mortgage.

20. U.C.C. § 9-502(b)(4). Often, the debtor that creates an Article 9 security interest in the fixture will also be the record owner of the land. Sometimes this will not be the case. For example, a party granting a security interest in fixtures may be a tenant in possession of the land under an unrecorded lease or may be buying the land under an unrecorded installment land contract.

21. U.C.C. § 9-501(a)(1)(B). If the fixture filing is in proper form and is presented for filing with the proper fees, the secured party is perfected even if the filing officer mistakenly files it in the chattel records. U.C.C. §§ 9-516(a), 9-517.

22. A recorded mortgage can serve as a fixture filing if the mortgage sufficiently describes the goods, if the goods are or are to become fixtures to the land described in the mortgage, and if the mortgage contains all the information required by Section 9-502 for a financing statement (other than an instruction directing that it be filed in the land records). U.C.C. § 9-502(c). If a mortgage serves as a valid fixture filing, it remains effective until the secured debt is released or satisfied of record. U.C.C. § 9-515(g).

23. An "encumbrance" is "a right, other than an ownership interest, in real property." U.C.C. § 9-102(a)(32). The term includes a mortgage or other lien on real property. Id. Notwithstanding the occasional incorrect decision to the contrary, for example, In re Laurel Hill Paper Co., 387 B.R. 677, 65 U.C.C. Rep. Serv. 2d 374 (Bankr. M.D.N.C. 2008), the term also includes judicial and statutory liens on real property, such as a mechanic's lien or a judgment lien. See, e.g., Yeadon Fabric Domes, Inc. v. Maine Sports Complex, LLC, 901 A.2d 200, 60 U.C.C. Rep. Serv. 2d (Me. 2006).

to the Code's general residual priority rule,[24] the residual rule for fixtures is that the secured party loses to conflicting real property interests. As discussed below, numerous exceptions limit the potential reach of this rule and permit a security interest in fixtures to take priority over a conflicting real estate interest in appropriate cases. If the fixture secured party cannot assert any of these exceptions, the competing real property claimant has priority.[25]

[B] The Purchase-Money Priority Exception— § 9-334(d)

Article 9 provides special priority status for certain parties holding purchase-money security interests. As discussed in Chapter 10, a secured party that takes a purchase-money security interest in non-inventory collateral (and perfects within 20 days after the debtor takes possession) takes priority over a secured party holding a prior-perfected security interest in that collateral by virtue of an after-acquired property clause.[26] Section 9-334(d) provides a comparable priority rule for purchase-money security interests in fixtures. Section 9-334(d) provides:

> Except as otherwise provided in subsection (h), a perfected security interest in fixtures has priority over a conflicting interest of an encumbrancer or owner of the real property if the debtor has an interest of record in or is in possession of the real property and: (1) the security interest is a purchase-money security interest; (2) the interest of the encumbrancer or owner arises before the goods become fixtures; and (3) the security interest is perfected by a fixture filing before the goods become fixtures or within 20 days thereafter.[27]

For example, suppose Bank holds a recorded mortgage on Grocer's land and building. On July 31, Secured Party sells Grocer a walk-in freezer on credit, taking back a purchase-money security interest in the freezer. On August 1, Grocer installs the freezer in its store, thereby rendering it a fixture and giving Bank an interest in it by virtue of its mortgage. On August 9, Secured Party makes a proper fixture filing covering the freezer. On these facts, Secured Party's security interest has priority over Bank's interest in the freezer under its mortgage. This result makes good policy sense, because granting purchase-money priority to Secured Party facilitates commerce by encouraging credit sales and does not harm Bank. At the time Bank took its mortgage, there

---

24. Under the Code's general residual priority rule, the secured party wins unless another provision dictates a contrary result. U.C.C. § 9-201(a). Where the goods have become fixtures but the priority contest is between two parties claiming Article 9 security interests in the goods (i.e., where there is no competing real property claimant), the Code's regular priority rules apply rather than Section 9-334. *See, e.g.,* Sturtz Machinery, Inc. v. Dove's Indus., Inc., 83 U.C.C. Rep. Serv. 2d 425 (N.D. Ohio 2014).

25. Yeadon Fabric Domes, Inc. v. Maine Sports Complex, LLC, 901 A.2d 200, 60 U.C.C. Rep. Serv. 2d (Me. 2006).

26. U.C.C. § 9-324(a).

27. U.C.C. § 9-334(d).

was no freezer affixed to the land; accordingly, Bank cannot reasonably have expected to take priority with respect to the freezer (or any other subsequently attached fixtures Grocer obtains using purchase-money credit).[28]

It may not be entirely logical to require any form of perfection—much less a fixture filing—to enable a purchase-money creditor like Secured Party to prevail over Bank in this example if Bank has made no future advances after affixation. Nevertheless, for purchase-money priority, Article 9 requires a fixture filing within the grace period.[29] As a policy matter, the requirement provides the secured party with an incentive to act promptly to place its interest on the land records, thus providing a more complete set of records for persons that might subsequently consider purchasing an interest in the affected real property.

Note carefully that Section 9-334(d) does not provide the fixture secured party with priority over real property interests that arise *after the goods become fixtures*. For example, suppose that on July 31, Secured Party sells Grocer a walk-in freezer on credit and takes back a purchase-money security interest. On August 1, Grocer installs the freezer in its store, thereby rendering it a fixture. On August 5, Grocer borrows $100,000 from Bank and grants Bank a mortgage on the land, which Bank records that same day. On August 9—within 20 days after the freezer became a fixture—Secured Party finally makes a proper fixture filing. On these facts, Secured Party cannot claim purchase-money priority in the freezer; Bank takes priority under the residual priority rule of Section 9-334(c). Viewed from the perspective of third parties searching the land records, this result is sensible. If Bank had performed a title search on August 5 before taking its mortgage, the search would not have revealed a fixture filing covering the freezer. As a result, a reasonable person in Bank's position would have concluded that the freezer (which was already affixed to the land) was unencumbered.[30]

Note also that the purchase-money priority exception applies only if the debtor has an interest of record in the land or is in possession of it. A secured party cannot rely on purchase-money priority if its security interest is created by someone other than an owner or lessee of the land. For example, suppose Secured Party sells a furnace on credit to Contractor. Contractor is doing remodeling work on Owner's building, which is subject to a previously recorded mortgage in favor of Bank. Even if Secured Party takes a purchase-money security interest and makes a fixture filing within 20 days after

---

28. Secured Party's removal of the freezer might cause physical damage to the land, and this risk threatens the Bank's security as mortgagee. Section 9-604(d) ameliorates this risk by requiring that Secured Party "promptly reimburse any encumbrancer or owner of the real property, other than the debtor, for the cost of repair of any physical injury caused by the removal."

29. If the purchase-money fixture secured party fails to make a fixture filing within the grace period and fails to qualify for any other exception, the competing real property claimant has priority under the general rule of Section 9-334(c). *See, e.g., In re* Pierce, 621 B.R. 434, 103 U.C.C. Rep. Serv. 2d 341 (Bankr. S.D. Ind. 2020).

30. A buyer or mortgagee may not actually rely on fixtures in a particular case, but Article 9 bases its priority rules on the assumption that a typical buyer or mortgagee will so rely.

the furnace becomes a fixture, Secured Party will not obtain priority over Bank because Contractor had neither a record interest in nor possession of the land.[31]

[C] The "First-to-File-or-Record" Exception— § 9-334(e)(1)

Under Section 9-334(e)(1)'s "first-to-file-or-record" exception, a person that takes a security interest in fixtures and perfects by making a fixture filing takes priority over the interest of an owner or encumbrancer of the real property whose interest is recorded after the fixture filing.[32] This exception applies to both purchase-money and non-purchase-money security interests, as demonstrated by the following examples:

- On August 1, Secured Party sells Grocer a walk-in freezer, taking a security interest to secure the purchase price. That same day, Secured Party makes a fixture filing properly covering the freezer. Grocer installs the freezer in its store on August 2, rendering it a fixture. On August 5, Grocer borrows $100,000 from Bank, which takes and records a mortgage on the land and store. Because Bank recorded its mortgage after Secured Party's fixture filing, Secured Party's security interest in the freezer will take priority over Bank's interest in the freezer as mortgagee.

- On August 1, Merchant borrows $100,000 from Bank and grants Bank a security interest in all its personal property, now-owned or after-acquired, including fixtures located on Merchant's business premises. On August 5, Bank makes a fixture filing. On August 10, Merchant sells the premises to Buyer, who records a deed later that day. Because Bank made its fixture filing before Buyer recorded its deed to the premises, Buyer takes the premises subject to Bank's security interest in the fixtures.

- On August 1, Merchant borrows $100,000 from Bank and grants Bank a security interest in all its personal property, now-owned or after-acquired, including fixtures located on Merchant's business premises. On August 5, Bank files a regular financing statement (but does not make a fixture filing). On August 10, Merchant sells the premises to Buyer, who is unaware of Bank's security interest and records a deed later that day. Because Bank did not make a fixture filing before Buyer recorded its deed to the premises, Buyer takes the premises free and clear of Bank's security interest in the fixtures.

A secured party that makes a fixture filing before the conflicting real property interest is recorded will not prevail if the holder of the conflicting interest is a successor to a person that would have had priority over the secured party. For example, suppose Bank holds a recorded mortgage on Grocer's land and building. On July 31, Secured Party

---

31. U.C.C. § 9-334(c). If Secured Party wants priority over Bank or Owner, it can obtain that party's consent to its security interest. U.C.C. § 9-334(f)(1).

32. U.C.C. § 9-334(e)(1).

sells Grocer a walk-in freezer on credit, taking back a purchase-money security interest in the freezer. On August 1, Grocer installs the freezer in its store, thereby rendering it a fixture. Secured Party fails to make a fixture filing, however, until October 1. On November 1, Bank conducts a proper foreclosure sale under Grocer's mortgage, and Buyer purchases the land at the sale. Buyer records a deed on November 2. In this case, although Secured Party made its fixture filing (October 1) before Buyer recorded its deed (November 2), this is irrelevant. At the time of the foreclosure sale, Bank had priority in the freezer under the Code's residual fixture priority rule, because Secured Party had failed to qualify for purchase-money priority by making a fixture filing within the 20-day grace period. Thus, Bank's foreclosure sale extinguished Secured Party's subordinate interest in the freezer, and Buyer takes the freezer free of Secured Party's interest.

[D] The Nonreliance-Creditor Exception— § 9-334(e)(3)

Article 9 requires a secured party claiming an interest in fixtures to make a fixture filing to obtain priority against persons that might be called "reliance creditors"—that is, persons that typically rely on the real property records in deciding whether to buy or lend against land. Creditors that acquire a lien on land and/or fixtures by virtue of a judgment or an execution process[33] are "nonreliance" creditors and are typically not protected by recording statutes.[34] The same is true of other secured parties with a security interest in the fixtures but with no interest in the land. They rely on the U.C.C. filing system but not on the real property recording system.[35]

Because these creditors typically do not rely upon the real property records, it would be pointless to require a secured party to make a fixture filing to obtain priority over them. Any method of perfecting a security interest under Article 9 should be sufficient for this purpose. This principle finds expression in Section 9-334(e)(3), which states that a party claiming a perfected security interest in fixtures has priority if "the conflicting interest is a lien on the real property obtained by legal or equitable proceedings

---

33. Creditors that acquire an interest in personalty by virtue of an execution process are called lien creditors in Article 9. See § 12.02, *supra*. The concept is the same here, except that a creditor that levies on the land (and, therefore, is deemed to have levied on the fixtures as part of the land) is not strictly an Article 9 lien creditor (as the lien is attaching to realty, not personalty). It is possible, however, for such a creditor to have the sheriff levy on just the fixture and remove it from the land, at which point the creditor becomes an Article 9 lien creditor.

34. *See* U.C.C. § 9-334, Comment 9. State real property law is not unanimous on this point. Although most state recording acts do not protect judgment creditors, some do give such creditors priority over unrecorded interests. See, e.g., COLO. REV. STAT. ANN. § 38-35-109(1) (unrecorded instrument is invalid as "against *any person with any kind of rights* in or to such real property who first records") (emphasis added).

35. The general rule of Section 9-334(c) subordinating security interests in fixtures only applies if the adverse interest is that of an owner or encumbrancer of the related real property.

after the security interest was perfected *by any method permitted by this article....*"[36] The following examples demonstrate the application of the nonreliance creditor exception:

- On July 31, Secured Party sells a walk-in freezer to Grocer on credit, retaining a purchase-money security interest. On August 1, Grocer installs the freezer in its store premises, rendering it a fixture. Secured Party does not make a fixture filing but does file an Article 9 financing statement on August 2 that is sufficient to perfect a security interest in Grocer's equipment. On October 1, Customer obtains a judgment against Grocer arising out of a slip-and-fall accident, and the judgment constitutes a lien against all of Grocer's real property. Although Customer obtains a lien against the freezer by virtue of the judgment, this lien is subordinate to Secured Party's perfected security interest in the freezer.

- On July 31, Secured Party sells Tycoon a walk-in freezer on credit for use in his home, retaining a purchase-money security interest. On August 1, the freezer is installed in Tycoon's home, rendering it a fixture. Secured Party does not file a fixture filing or a financing statement covering the freezer. On October 1, Victim obtains a judgment against Tycoon for injuries sustained in an automobile accident caused by Tycoon's negligence, and the judgment constitutes a lien against Tycoon's home. Although Creditor obtains a lien against the freezer by virtue of the judgment, this lien is subordinate to Secured Party's security interest, which was automatically perfected upon attachment.[37]

- Bank has a security interest in all of Grocer's equipment, including after-acquired equipment, which is perfected by filing. On July 1, Secured Party sells Grocer a walk-in freezer on credit, retaining a purchase-money security interest. Secured Party perfects by filing a financing statement in the U.C.C. system on July 10 but does not make a fixture filing. Secured Party has priority over Bank. The result would not change if Bank had made a fixture filing for equipment that constitutes fixtures.

The most feared nonreliance creditor is the trustee in bankruptcy. If a secured party fails to make a fixture filing and finds itself in a priority contest with the trustee, can it prevail if it has perfected using one of the Code's non-fixture methods? The drafters of the U.C.C. assumed that the answer was "yes," but the issue was open until 1984, when Congress amended the Bankruptcy Code to make clear that if a trustee claims an interest in fixtures, the trustee stands in the position of a lien creditor levying on personalty under state law, not in the position of a bona fide purchaser of real property.[38]

---

36. U.C.C. § 9-334(e)(3) (emphasis added).

37. U.C.C. § 9-309(1); *In re* Hudgins, 2016 WL 5173239, 90 U.C.C. Rep. Serv. 2d 747 (Bankr. W.D.N.C. 2016) (creditor holding automatically perfected PMSI in home furnace took priority over interest of Chapter 7 trustee following debtor's bankruptcy, despite lack of fixture filing).

38. *See* 11 U.S.C. § 544(a)(3). *See also* 11 U.S.C. § 547(e)(1) (trustee treated as lien creditor of personalty rather than bona-fide purchaser of real estate for preferential-transfer purposes).

[E] The Exception for "Readily Removable Collateral"—§ 9-334(e)(2)

Another exception to the residual priority rule involves security interests in fixtures that are readily removable and that are (1) "factory or office machines," (2) "equipment that is not primarily used or leased for use in the operation of the real property" to which the goods are affixed, or (3) "replacements of domestic appliances that are consumer goods."[39] A secured party may perfect a security interest in any of these goods by any method permitted by Article 9, including filing and automatic perfection. Under this exception, no fixture filing is necessary—ordinary perfection is sufficient even against reliance creditors. To qualify for protection under this section, the secured party must perfect the security interest before the goods are affixed to the land.

The rationale for this exception rests in the reasonable contextual expectations of commercial parties. For example, suppose Secured Party sells a photocopier to Debtor on credit, retaining a purchase-money security interest. Debtor installs the photocopier into a recessed area in one wall of Debtor's office building to save office space. Unaware of Debtor's plan, Secured Party merely files an ordinary financing statement covering the copier and does not make a fixture filing. Shortly thereafter, Debtor obtains a loan from Bank and grants Bank a mortgage on its office building. Given the photocopier's readily removable character, Bank likely would not expect it to be a fixture and thus would not likely rely on the presence of the photocopier in deciding whether to make the mortgage loan. Nevertheless, a court might later conclude that the combination of affixation by a wall plug and adaptation to a particular feature of the building[40] rendered the copier a fixture. By virtue of the "readily removable" exception, Secured Party in this example will have priority in the photocopier over Bank.

For domestic appliances that are consumer goods, the exception requires that the collateral be a replacement, not an original. This limitation serves to protect a lender (typically a construction lender) that may have relied on having a lien on the original appliances when it provided financing to the debtor. Such a lender should realize that appliances eventually break down. A provision requiring a purchase-money secured party to make a fixture filing to obtain priority for an interest in a replacement appliance would drive up the transaction costs for what are routine sales and thus would serve no useful notice function.[41]

---

39. U.C.C. § 9-334(e)(2).

40. Adaptation is discussed in § 15.01, *supra.*

41. U.C.C. § 9-334, Comment 8.

[F] Special Rules for Construction Mortgages— § 9-334(h)

Article 9 provides a special priority rule designed to protect a construction lender's interest in fixtures under a construction mortgage:[42]

> Except as otherwise provided [in Sections 9-334(e) and (f)], a security interest in fixtures is subordinate to a construction mortgage if a record of the mortgage is recorded before the goods become fixtures and the goods become fixtures before the completion of the construction. A mortgage has this priority to the same extent as a construction mortgage to the extent that it is given to refinance a construction mortgage.[43]

This provision effectively precludes the operation of the purchase-money priority exception against construction lenders. For example, suppose Debtor is building an office building financed by a construction loan from First Bank, which has recorded a construction mortgage. On August 1, Secured Party sells Debtor 50 sets of cabinets for wall-mounted installation in the offices, retaining a purchase-money security interest in the cabinets. On August 2, the cabinets are installed and become fixtures. On August 3, Secured Party makes a fixture filing describing the cabinets. Without Section 9-334(h), Secured Party would take priority over Bank under the purchase-money priority exception.[44] Under Section 9-334(h), however, Secured Party's security interest in the cabinets is subordinate to First Bank's mortgage.[45]

Why this preference for a construction lender? Recall that the purchase-money priority exception rests on the assumption that a mortgagee whose interest arose before goods became fixtures will not have relied on the goods in deciding whether to lend money. This assumption is not valid for a construction mortgagee, however, who typically knows of the construction plans from the outset and makes its decision to lend assuming that the fixtures will become part of the structure.[46] Consequently, a construction mortgagee is a reliance creditor from the outset. The priority accruing to a construction mortgagee passes to a permanent (or "take-out") lender to which the mortgage is assigned when construction is complete.

---

42. Under Article 9, "[a] mortgage is a construction mortgage to the extent that it secures an obligation incurred for the construction of an improvement on land, including the acquisition cost of the land, if a recorded record of the mortgage so indicates." U.C.C. § 9-334(h).

43. U.C.C. § 9-334(h).

44. *See* § 15.03[B], *supra.*

45. In this example, state law might also permit Secured Party to claim a mechanic's lien against the land if Debtor does not pay for the cabinets. The relative priority of a mechanic's lien and a construction mortgage is not governed by Article 9 and is beyond the scope of this book.

46. In many circumstances, a construction lender will have factored the cost of fixtures into the amount of its construction loan and thus expects to finance the fixtures. As a result, enabling the debtor to grant purchase-money priority in the fixtures to a competing secured party would allow the debtor to "double finance" the fixtures.

If a construction lender or permanent lender acquires an interest in fixtures placed on the land after construction is complete (typically through an after-acquired fixtures clause in a mortgage), the rationale for this provision no longer applies. The priority for construction mortgages thus applies only to goods that become fixtures before construction is completed. For example, if six months after construction is complete, Secured Party sells Debtor 50 units of cabinets, and the cabinets become fixtures upon installation, Secured Party can acquire priority over a properly recorded construction mortgage or permanent take-out mortgage by making a proper fixture filing during the 20-day grace period in Section 9-334(d).

There are two other situations that are less significant but nevertheless deserve brief mention. First, if a construction lender or permanent takeout lender consents in writing to a security interest or disclaims an interest in fixtures, or if it gives a debtor consent to remove fixtures, the secured party acquires priority over the mortgage with respect to those fixtures.[47] Second, if a construction mortgagee fails to record its mortgage before the goods become fixtures (not likely, but possible if the construction lender is careless), it subjects itself to the risk of losing priority under the "first-to-file-or-record" exception to the residual priority rule.[48]

[G] Exception for Manufactured Homes— § 9-335(e)(4)

Article 9 contains a special priority rule addressing the potential conflict between a person that finances a debtor's purchase of a "manufactured home"[49] and a person holding a lien on the land to which the home becomes attached. In most states, manufactured homes are covered by certificate-of-title statutes. In those states, a secured party must perfect its security interest in a manufactured home (assuming that the manufactured home is not inventory in the debtor's hands) by compliance with a certificate-of-title act. Under Section 9-334(e)(4), a security interest in a manufactured home that is created in a "manufactured home transaction"[50] takes priority over the interest of an owner or encumbrancer of the land to which the home is attached, provided the secured party properly perfects under a certificate-of-title act. For example, suppose Debtor purchases a manufactured home on credit from Seller and grants Seller a purchase-money security interest in the home. Seller properly perfects by having its security interest noted on the certificate of title covering the home. The home is then affixed to land that Debtor is purchasing from Vendor on an installment land contract. Seller's security interest has priority over the claim of Vendor under the installment

---

47. U.C.C. § 9-334(f). *See* § 15.03[H], *infra.*

48. *See* § 15.03[C], *supra.*

49. The definition of "manufactured home" in Section 9-102(a)(53) includes a typical mobile home or prefabricated home that is movable in one or more sections. *See* § 1.04[A][1], *supra.*

50. A "manufactured home transaction" is either a transaction that creates a purchase-money security interest in a manufactured home or a transaction in which a manufactured home is the primary collateral. U.C.C. § 9-102(a)(54).

land contract.[51] Prudent title examiners in certificate-of-title states should check the records of the state agency that issues certificates of title if there is a manufactured home on the land.

[H] Exception Based on Consent or Right of Removal—§ 9-334(f)

Two additional exceptions to the residual priority rule merit brief mention. The first exception is based on consent. If an encumbrancer or owner that would otherwise have priority over a secured party with respect to fixtures either consents to the security interest or disclaims an interest in the fixtures, the secured party acquires priority.[52] This is merely a particular application of the general rule that parties may enter subordination agreements altering the priorities created by the U.C.C.'s normal rules.[53]

The final exception arises primarily in the case of fixtures attached to leased land. Most jurisdictions have adopted what is sometimes called the "trade-fixture" doctrine. Under this doctrine, goods affixed to leased business premises generally are treated as personalty as between the lessor and the lessee. As a result, the lessee may remove the goods at the conclusion of the lease term unless the lease expressly provides to the contrary. Further, most jurisdictions have expanded this doctrine to include goods affixed by lessees of residential property. Article 9 incorporates this concept, giving a secured party with an interest in fixtures priority over the conflicting claim of an encumbrancer or owner of the land if "the debtor has a right to remove the goods as against the encumbrancer or owner," regardless of whether the secured party's interest in the fixtures is perfected.[54] The Code provides that the secured party's priority continues "for a reasonable time" if the debtor's right to remove the goods terminates.[55] This provision is important in those jurisdictions where a lessee's right to remove fixtures terminates upon expiration of the lease (or expiration of the period during which the lessee is a holdover tenant), as it affords the secured party priority for a reasonable time so that it can repossess the fixtures.[56]

---

51. Conseco Fin. Servicing Corp. v. Old Nat'l Bank, 754 N.E.2d 997, 45 U.C.C. Rep. Serv. 2d 652 (Ind. Ct. App. 2001).

52. U.C.C. § 9-334(f)(1). The consent or disclaimer must appear in a signed record.

53. U.C.C. § 9-339.

54. U.C.C. § 9-334(f)(2). The rationale does not apply to parties that buy the land from, or become mortgagees of, the lessor.

55. U.C.C. § 9-334(g).

56. If a debtor no longer has access to the premises, a secured party would be well-advised to use judicial repossession rather than attempting to repossess by self-help. See discussion in Chapter 17, infra.

§ 15.04 Secured Party's Right to Remove Fixtures after Default—§ 9-604(c), (d)

Section 9-604 sets forth a secured party's rights with respect to fixtures after default. Not surprisingly, a secured party may not repossess fixtures if it lacks priority against an owner or encumbrancer of the land.[57] If the secured party does not have this priority, it cannot repossess the fixtures at all. Thus, unless the subordinate secured party obtains the consent of all parties having priority, its security interest is worthless, and it must rely for protection on any rights it may have under the state's laws governing mechanic's liens.

Even if a secured party has first priority, Section 9-604(d) constrains the secured party's repossession and enforcement rights to protect owners and encumbrancers from unjustified harm due to the removal of fixtures. In some circumstances, removal of a fixture will cause physical injury to the underlying land. Section 9-604(d) provides that a secured party repossessing fixtures must "promptly reimburse any encumbrancer or owner of the real property, other than the debtor, for the cost of repair of any physical injury caused by the removal."[58] While the repossessing secured party must compensate for physical injury, it "need not reimburse the encumbrancer or owner for any diminution in value of the real property caused by the absence of the goods removed or by any necessity of replacing them."[59] For example, suppose Secured Party has a perfected security interest in Grocer's walk-in freezer, which constitutes a fixture. Secured Party has priority over Bank, which holds a mortgage upon Grocer's store. Secured Party removes the fixture and sells it following Grocer's default. In the process of removing the freezer, Secured Party does $400 in physical damage to the store by tearing down a wall to gain access to the freezer. Further, Secured Party's removal of the freezer reduces the fair market value of the store by $4,000 (the cost to obtain and install a replacement freezer). Secured Party must reimburse Bank for the $400 in physical damage to the store premises but need not pay any sum to reimburse the Bank for the $4,000 reduction in the fair market value of the premises.

The rationale for this result should be clear. Article 9 typically grants secured parties priority as to fixtures if an adverse encumbrancer or owner has not relied on the presence of the fixtures. In this example, the fact that removal of the freezer reduced the fair market value of the premises by $4,000 should not seriously interfere with Bank's reasonable expectations, as Bank likely did not rely on having priority in the freezer. If Secured Party causes physical injury to the land in removing the freezer, however, there is a direct and substantial interference with Bank's expectations regarding the physical integrity of the mortgaged premises, and Secured Party should have to compensate

---

57. U.C.C. § 9-604(c).
58. U.C.C. § 9-604(d).
59. *Id.*

Bank for this interference.[60] The Code also provides that the owner or encumbrancer may refuse permission to remove a fixture until the secured party gives adequate security for the performance of this obligation.[61]

Sometimes an encumbrancer of land may foreclose its lien and force a sale of the land even though a secured party has priority with respect to fixtures. In this instance, the secured party retains the right to remove the fixtures, but can it leave the fixtures in place and instead claim an interest in the proceeds from the sale of the land? For example, suppose Bank holds a mortgage on Debtor's land and Secured Party has a perfected security interest in Debtor's fixtures that gives Secured Party priority over Bank. Debtor then defaults to Bank, which forecloses on Debtor's land, selling it to Buyer. Can Secured Party claim first priority in the sale proceeds? A leading case interpreting the 1972 text of Article 9, *Maplewood Bank & Trust v. Sears, Roebuck & Co.*,[62] held that the answer was no. The court held that a secured party's right to priority in fixtures was limited to their removal and that a secured party had no claim against the land itself—and thus no claim to the proceeds of the foreclosure sale. Instead, a secured party's priority in fixtures continued against the foreclosure-sale buyer.

Section 9-604(b) provides a way around the result in the *Maplewood* case[63] by providing that a party with a security interest in fixtures may choose to enforce its interest either under Article 9's enforcement provisions or under applicable state real estate law. If the secured party enforces its interest under real estate law, none of Article 9's enforcement provisions apply to its actions.[64] Thus, in the above hypothetical, if real estate law permitted Secured Party to join in Bank's foreclosure action and enforce its interest in that proceeding, Secured Party could claim first priority against the foreclosure-sale proceeds.[65]

---

60. If removal of a fixture would cause such massive harm as to be wasteful, a court might find that the goods are ordinary building materials and therefore no security interest continues to attach to them. *See* § 15.01, *supra*.

61. U.C.C. § 9-604(d). In *Berger v. Alexopoulos*, 280 A.D.2d 505, 721 N.Y.S.2d 81, 44 U.C.C. Rep. Serv. 2d 307 (2001), the owner of real property demanded rent and liability insurance as a condition to the secured party's removal of fixtures installed by the tenant/debtor. Because the owner was entitled only to compensation for any damages resulting from the removal, the court held that the owner's refusal to surrender the collateral constituted conversion.

62. 625 A.2d 537 (N.J. Super. Ct. App. Div. 1993).

63. *See* U.C.C. § 9-604, Comment 3.

64. U.C.C. § 9-604(b)(2).

65. If state law does not permit Secured Party to join in Bank's foreclosure action, then the purchaser at Bank's foreclosure sale takes title to the fixture subject to Secured Party's security interest, which Secured Party may enforce pursuant to Article 9. U.C.C. § 9-604(b)(1).

§ 15.05 Accessions — § 9-335

[A] Nature of the Interest

Accessions are analogous to fixtures, except that an accession is an item of personalty that is attached to another item of personalty rather than to real property. Accessions are "goods that are physically united with other goods in such a manner that the identity of the original goods is not lost."[66] In other words, an accession retains its identity and can be removed from the goods to which it is attached and sold separately. This distinguishes it from "commingled goods," which arise if an item of personalty becomes so incorporated into a larger whole (also personalty) that it loses its separate identity.[67]

Section 9-102(a)(1)'s definition of "accessions" differs somewhat from the common-law definition. At common law, an asset does not become an accession until it is so intertwined with the whole that, although it retains its separate identity, its removal would cause substantial harm to the whole.[68] Note that Section 9-102(a)(1)'s definition applies only to a dispute governed by Section 9-335, that is, a priority contest between a secured party claiming an interest in an accession and a third party claiming an interest in the whole. If the issue is simply whether a security agreement is sufficiently broad to grant the secured party an interest in a particular item that is somehow connected with a larger whole, the common-law definition of accession governs.

For example, if Secured Party has a security interest in Debtor's car, its interest extends to the motor because the motor, being integral to the functioning of the car, qualifies as a common-law accession. The security interest might not extend to a dashcam system that the Debtor installed in the car after buying the car; the dashcam likely would not constitute an accession as its removal would not cause substantial harm to the car as a whole or compromise its operability.[69] Thus, if Secured Party repossessed the car following Debtor's default and failed to remove the dashcam and return it to Debtor, Secured Party likely would be liable for conversion. As a result, a well-drafted security agreement will contain language that extends the security interest to all accessions and accessories, whenever acquired.

---

66. U.C.C. § 9-102(a)(1).

67. U.C.C. § 9-336(a). *See* § 15.06, *infra*.

68. *See generally* R. Brown, The Law of Personal Property §§ 6.1-6.7 (W. Raushenbush, ed. 3d ed. 1975).

69. Whether the dashcam device is a common-law accession turns, of course, on the manner and extent of its installation in the car. When a loan is secured by a manufactured home, disputes sometimes arise whether goods that have been installed in the manufactured home constitute accessions covered by a security interest in the manufactured home. *See, e.g., In re* Edwards, 94 U.C.C. Rep. Serv. 2d 607 (Bankr. E.D.N.C. 2017) (drapes, smoke detectors, and ceiling fans in mobile home were readily detachable and not accessions to the home).

[B] Priorities

Section 9-335 resolves the priority dispute that arises if a secured party has a security interest in an accession (as defined by the Code) and a third party claims a competing interest in the whole. Under Section 9-335(c), the Code's ordinary priority rules resolve this dispute, as demonstrated by the following examples:

- Debtor grants Bank a security interest in a new computer hard drive to be installed in Debtor's business computer. The computer is already subject to a perfected security interest in favor of Finance Company. If Bank's interest is a purchase-money security interest (i.e., if Debtor acquired the hard drive with money advanced by the Bank), Bank will take priority as to the hard drive over Finance Company's interest in the entire computer so long as Bank perfects its interest within the 20-day grace period after Debtor received possession of the hard drive.[70] If Bank fails to perfect its interest within this grace period, or if Bank's interest is not a purchase-money interest, Finance Company will take priority as to the installed hard drive based upon its prior-perfected security interest in the whole computer.[71]

- After installing the hard drive, Debtor sells the computer to Buyer. If Bank has perfected its security interest in the hard drive before the sale to Buyer, Bank's security interest in the hard drive will remain effective against Buyer. If, however, Buyer gave value and took possession of the computer without knowledge of Bank's security interest and before it was perfected, Buyer will take the computer free of Bank's interest in the hard drive.[72]

Section 9-335 provides a special priority rule for accessions to goods covered by certificate-of-title acts. Under Section 9-335(d), a security interest in an accession is subordinate to a security interest in the whole that is perfected under such an act.[73] Thus, suppose Debtor asks Seller to finance a new set of wheels for its car and agrees to grant a purchase-money security interest in the wheels. Bank has a security interest in the car that is perfected by compliance with the requirements of a certificate-of-title act. Under Section 9-335(d), Bank has priority over Seller with respect to the wheels, notwithstanding Article 9's traditional priority for a purchase-money secured party.[74]

---

70. U.C.C. §9-324(e). If Debtor's computer constitutes consumer goods, Bank's purchase-money security interest is automatically perfected upon attachment. U.C.C. §9-309(1).

71. U.C.C. §9-322(a)(1).

72. U.C.C. §9-317(b). If the security interest in the hard drive is a purchase-money security interest, however, Bank has a 20-day grace period in which to perfect its security interest and obtain relation-back priority over an intervening third party such as Buyer. U.C.C. §9-317(e).

73. U.C.C. §9-335(d) ("A security interest in an accession is subordinate to a security interest in the whole which is perfected by compliance with the requirements of a certificate-of-title statute under Section 9-311(d).").

74. *In re* Brady, 508 B.R. 736, 83 U.C.C. Rep. Serv. 2d 399 (Bankr. E.D. Wash. 2014). Seller could obtain priority over Bank with respect to the wheels if Seller and Bank entered into a subordination agreement. U.C.C. §9-339.

The issue of identifying accessions often arises in transactions involving manufactured home collateral. In most states, manufactured homes are covered by certificate-of-title acts.[75] If the secured party has a perfected, first-priority security interest in the home, it also has a perfected, first-priority security interest in any accessions to the home (such as the home's siding, tub, fireplace, and central air conditioning system).[76] That perfection would not extend, however, to goods that were not accessions to the home, such as drapes and appliances. As to such non-accessions, the manufactured-home secured party would have to perfect any security interest by filing a financing statement in the central filing office.[77]

§ 15.06 Commingled Goods— § 9-336

[A] Rights

Section 9-336 governs the effectiveness of a security interest in goods that have been "commingled," or "physically united with other goods in such a manner that [the goods'] identity is lost in a product or mass."[78] If a secured party's collateral becomes so commingled, its security interest attaches to the resulting product or mass.[79] Furthermore, if the secured party properly perfects its security interest in the goods prior to commingling, its resulting security interest in the product or mass is likewise perfected.[80]

For example, suppose Bank has a security interest in Debtor's flour and that Debtor later combines the flour with eggs, water, and sugar to make a cake. The flour loses its identity in the process of baking the cake, but this does not eliminate Bank's security interest. If Bank perfects its security interest in the flour and can prove that the flour went into the cake, it can claim a perfected security interest in the cake.[81]

Determining whether a security interest arises in a product or mass is not always easy. For example, suppose Supplier sells Debtor cattle feed on secured credit and Bank has a security interest in Debtor's cattle. If the cattle have consumed all the feed when Debtor defaults, can Supplier argue that it has an interest in the cattle as a "product

---

75. See §§ 4.02[F], 9.03, *supra*.

76. U.C.C. § 9-335(d); *In re* Sweeney, 556 B.R. 208 (Bankr. E.D.N.C. 2016).

77. See, e.g., Sweeney, 556 B.R. at 214–16 (secured party unperfected as to range, washer, dryer, and refrigerator which were not accessions); *In re* Edwards, 94 U.C.C. Rep. Serv. 2d 607 (Bankr. E.D.N.C. 2017) (secured party unperfected as to drapes, smoke detectors, ceiling fans, and small porch which were not accessions).

78. U.C.C. § 9-336(a).

79. U.C.C. § 9-336(c).

80. U.C.C. § 9-336(d).

81. Of course, if Debtor is a baker and Bank has a blanket lien on all of Debtor's inventory, now-owned and after-acquired, then Bank's security interest attaches directly to the cake (once-baked) in any event. Section 9-336 is only necessary in the circumstance in which Bank does not have any other basis under its security agreement for asserting an interest in the completed cake.

or mass" under Section 9-336? Caselaw has generally refused to allow feed suppliers to assert claims against cattle in these circumstances.[82] The theory behind these cases, however—that there is nothing left of the feed after the cattle have eaten it—seems a bit strained. The feed has clearly been converted into meat, and there is no logical reason why Section 9-336 should not apply. Nevertheless, a prudent feed supplier that wants an interest in the cattle as well as the feed should so specify in its security agreement.

[B] Priorities

One can easily resolve most priority problems involving commingled goods. With respect to the conflicting rights of lien creditors and buyers, Section 9-336 incorporates the Code's standard priority rules. Thus, a perfected security interest in a product or mass will have priority over the interest of a lien creditor or a buyer not in ordinary course of business, but a buyer in ordinary course takes free of the security interest.[83]

Any two or more conflicting perfected[84] security interests that arise solely under Section 9-336 rank equally in priority "in proportion to the value of the collateral at the time it became commingled goods."[85] For example, suppose Bank has a perfected security interest in Debtor's flour (worth $100) and Finance Company has a perfected security interest in Debtor's eggs (worth $200). Debtor commingles the flour and eggs to make cakes. Suppose further that after Debtor's default, the cakes are sold for only $150. From this $150, Bank will receive $50 and Finance Company $100.[86]

---

82. *See, e.g.*, First Nat'l Bank of Brush v. Bostron, 39 Colo. Ct. App. 107, 564 P.2d 964, 21 U.C.C. Rep. Serv. 1475 (1977); Farmers Coop. Elevator Co. v. Union State Bank, 409 N.W.2d 178, 4 U.C.C. Rep. Serv. 2d 1 (Iowa 1987); *In re* McDougall, 60 B.R. 635, 1 U.C.C. Rep. Serv. 2d 563 (Bankr. W.D. Pa. 1986); *In re* Pelton, 171 B.R. 641 (Bankr. W.D. Wis. 1994). The cases have also considered and rejected the argument that the cattle are "proceeds" of the feed.

83. U.C.C. § 9-336(e).

84. Not surprisingly, a perfected security interest in commingled goods takes priority over a conflicting unperfected security interest in the same goods. U.C.C. § 9-336(f)(1).

85. U.C.C. § 9-336(f)(2).

86. If there are multiple parties holding conflicting security interests in a single input, then Section 9-336 treats those parties as a single secured party for purposes of establishing their collective share, and then the Code's normal priority rules determine how to distribute that collective share among them. *See* U.C.C. § 9-336, Comment 6. For example, suppose Bank has a perfected first-priority security interest in Debtor's eggs (worth $200) to secure a debt of $150, Finance Company has a perfected second-priority security interest in the same eggs to secure a debt of $250, and First Savings has a perfected security interest in Debtor's flour (worth $400) to secure a debt of $500. Debtor commingles the eggs and flour to make cakes which sell for $750. Debtor then defaults to all three parties. For purposes of Section 9-336, Bank and Finance Company will be treated like a single secured party whose interest has equal priority with that of First Savings in proportion to the value of their respective inputs. Thus, First Savings would be entitled to collect $500 of the sale proceeds, and Bank and Finance Company will collectively have priority with respect to the other $250. As between Bank and Finance Company, priority with respect to that $250 will be based upon the first-to-file-or-perfect rule; thus, Bank will collect $150 of the proceeds in satisfaction of its debt, and Finance Company will receive the remaining $100. *See* U.C.C. § 9-336, Comment 6, Example 5.

Note, however, that this priority rule applies only if the conflicting security interests both arise under Section 9-336. That section's priority rule does not apply if one secured party claims a direct security interest in the commingled product or mass; in that case, the Code's standard priority rules apply. For example, suppose Bank has a perfected security interest in Debtor's flour and Finance Company has a perfected security interest in all of Debtor's now-owned and after-acquired inventory. Debtor commingles the flour with other ingredients to make cakes. If Finance Company files a financing statement covering the inventory before Bank files covering the flour, Finance Company has priority in the cakes under the first-to-file-or-perfect rule. Likewise, if Bank files against the flour before Finance Company files against the inventory, Bank has priority in the cakes to the extent of its security interest.[87]

---

87. U.C.C. § 9-336, Comment 7.

Chapter 16

Bankruptcy

Synopsis

§16.01 Background

[A] Shifting the Legal Landscape

All assertions of law made in this book thus far have presupposed that state law, particularly Article 9 of the U.C.C., controls. A bankruptcy filing fundamentally alters this assumption. When a debtor files for bankruptcy protection, a secured party's ability to enforce its security interest becomes subject to the substantive and procedural limitations imposed by federal bankruptcy law, which preempts relevant state law. Federal preclusion can dramatically change a creditor's rights under Article 9: in bankruptcy, a creditor may find its security interest avoided in its entirety if it was not properly perfected at the time of the bankruptcy filing. Bankruptcy is a common recourse for distressed debtors. Consequently, many of the most influential decisions interpreting and applying Article 9 arise in the federal bankruptcy courts. More importantly, a debtor's unilateral ability to initiate bankruptcy proceedings at virtually any time ensures that all secured transactions operate in the shadow of federal bankruptcy law. A thorough understanding of the law of secured transactions thus requires at least a basic understanding of bankruptcy law.

A variety of policies and concerns motivates our system of federal bankruptcy law. Bankruptcy began as a creditor's remedy and operated as such until the passage of the Bankruptcy Act in 1898, when debtors were first permitted to file their own voluntary petitions. Prior to the Bankruptcy Act, bankruptcy was viewed primarily as a method to ensure equitable distribution of an insolvent debtor's assets. Under state law models of collection, including the "first-in-time, first-in-right" structure of priority, creditors are incentivized to collect from a struggling debtor early to beat out potential competition. A debtor's financial distress can therefore trigger a "race to the courthouse" by its creditors. Those who are fastest to collect may recover in full, while latecomers may receive nothing. The rush to collect may be premature, insofar as it may force a quick liquidation of assets when time, planning, and some breathing space might otherwise have allowed the debtor to repay more of its debts. Thus, one of the primary objectives of bankruptcy law is to provide a comprehensive system of debt collection that can help either avoid or mitigate the adverse consequences of the race to the courthouse.

In bankruptcy, the debtor's financial affairs are administered in a collective proceeding rather than through the ad hoc collection efforts of individual creditors.[1] Within this collective proceeding, there is a strong emphasis on the equitable treatment of all creditors; bankruptcy law generally treats similarly situated creditors in a similar fashion and discourages attempts by creditors to opt out of the collective process. Bankruptcy also provides insolvent debtors with the opportunity to obtain a "fresh start" or to "reorganize" their financial affairs. Debtors may choose to liquidate their pre-bankruptcy assets or retain their assets and attempt to restructure and repay some or all of their pre-bankruptcy debts in a reorganization proceeding. Either way, federal bankruptcy laws will inform and may even subsume preexisting state law structures.

[B] The Bankruptcy Estate and Bankruptcy Jurisdiction

Whether the debtor is an individual or an organization, the filing of a bankruptcy petition immediately creates a bankruptcy estate. The bankruptcy estate comprises all of the debtor's "legal or equitable interests" in property at the moment of the petition, subject to a few limited statutory exceptions.[2] The bankruptcy estate includes property

---

1. Elizabeth Warren, *Bankruptcy Policy*, 54 U. Chi. L. Rev. 775 (1987).
2. 11 U.S.C. §541(a).

that is subject to a security interest even if the property has already been repossessed and is being held in anticipation of sale or disposition.[3] Secured property only ceases to be included in the debtor's bankruptcy estate if the creditor has completed an Article 9 disposition of the property before the filing, such that ownership has already passed to the foreclosure sale purchaser.[4]

The parameters of the bankruptcy estate inform the jurisdictional limits of the bankruptcy court. Under the Bankruptcy Code, the current version of bankruptcy law first enacted in 1978, bankruptcy courts are staffed by bankruptcy judges, who are appointed as judicial officers of the district court under Article I of the Constitution.[5] These bankruptcy judges lack the life tenure and salary protection afforded to district court judges under Article III of the Constitution and are instead appointed to 14-year terms.[6]

Bankruptcy judges may hear and determine cases arising under the Bankruptcy Code and "core proceedings" arising in or under the Code. Core proceedings are defined to include matters concerning the administration of the estate and claims against it, counterclaims against the estate, and other proceedings regarding the recovery of estate property, confirmation of bankruptcy plans, and similar topics.[7] Bankruptcy judges may also hear proceedings "related to" the case,[8] although in such proceedings the bankruptcy judge may only submit proposed findings of fact and conclusions of law to

---

3. 11 U.S.C. § 542(a); *see also* United States v. Whiting Pools, Inc., 462 U.S. 198, 209 (1983) ("[T]he reorganization estate includes property of the debtor that has been seized by a creditor prior to the filing of a petition for reorganization."); *In re* Moffett, 356 F.3d 518 (4th Cir. 2004) (vehicle that had been repossessed but not sold became part of bankruptcy estate); *In re* Estis, 311 B.R. 592 (Bankr. D. Kan. 2004) (same).

The U.S. Court of Appeals for the Eleventh Circuit raised some question about this issue, at least as applied to repossessed vehicles, in its decisions in *In re* Kalter, 292 F.3d 1350 (11th Cir. 2002) (interpreting Florida law), and *In re* Lewis, 137 F.3d 1280 (11th Cir. 1998) (interpreting Alabama law). In each of those cases, the secured party had not yet disposed of the repossessed vehicle prior to the bankruptcy petition but had applied for a title certificate. In each case, the court treated the secured party's conduct as having terminated the debtor's title to the vehicle and held that the debtor's unexercised right of redemption was merely an intangible interest insufficient to make the vehicle part of the bankruptcy estate.

The *Kalter* and *Lewis* decisions (both of which arose prior to the 1998 Official Text of Article 9) are poorly reasoned and patently incorrect. Furthermore, the 1998 Official Text added Section 9-619(c), which provides that "a transfer of the record or legal title to collateral to a secured party" in anticipation of an Article 9 sale is "not of itself a disposition of collateral" and thus would not extinguish the debtor's equitable interest in the vehicle. U.C.C. § 9-619(c). Following the enactment of Section 9-619(c), it is doubtful that any court would continue to follow the unfortunate decisions in *Kalter* and *Lewis*.

4. U.C.C. § 9-617(a)(1). In some cases, the trustee/DIP may even be able to set aside the prebankruptcy foreclosure sale as a fraudulent transfer, in which case the property would become part of the bankruptcy estate in spite of the disposition. *See* § 16.04[F][3], *infra*.

5. 28 U.S.C. § 152(a).

6. *Id*.

7. 28 U.S.C. § 157(b).

8. *Id*. § 157(c).

the district court.[9] The bankruptcy court has exclusive jurisdiction of "all the property, wherever located" of the debtor as of the commencement of the case.[10]

In recent years, the Supreme Court has grappled with the proper extent of a bankruptcy court's jurisdiction and attempted to delineate the authority of a bankruptcy judge. The Court has ruled that bankruptcy jurisdiction may be somewhat broader than "simple proceedings involving the property of the debtor or the estate,"[11] but there are ongoing arguments regarding its proper extent.[12] The Court has limited bankruptcy judges' statutory ability to issue final rulings in all core proceedings, concluding that a bankruptcy judge lacks constitutional authority to enter a final judgment on a state law counterclaim.[13]

[C] Bankruptcy Chapters and Bankruptcy Trustees

Although the bankruptcy judge oversees all bankruptcy cases, judicial involvement varies significantly depending on the type of bankruptcy being filed. The Bankruptcy Code divides bankruptcy law into nine separate "Chapters." Three of these Chapters (1, 3, and 5) contain general provisions that apply in all types of bankruptcy cases. The remaining Chapters govern the specific types of bankruptcy cases. Chapter 7 governs the liquidation of businesses and the "fresh start" for individual debtors.[14] Chapter 11 allows businesses and individuals to restructure pre-bankruptcy debts by proposing a custom plan of repayment.[15] Chapter 12 establishes specific rules for farmers and family fishermen seeking to reorganize.[16] Chapter 13 allows individual wage-earners

---

9. *Id.*

10. 28 U.S.C. § 1334(e).

11. Celotex Corp. v. Edwards, 514 U.S. 300, 308 (1995).

12. For example, many bankruptcy courts have approved bankruptcy plans that include injunctive releases protecting the assets of third parties against collection actions brought by a debtor's creditors, commonly called "third party releases." This practice, while common, is highly controversial. *See generally* Lindsey Simon, *Bankruptcy Grifters*, 131 Yale. L. J. 1154 (2022). Some commentators have argued strenuously that this practice runs afoul of the court's jurisdictional limitations. *See* Ralph Brubaker, *Bankruptcy Injunctions and Complex Litigation: A Critical Reappraisal of Non-Debtor Releases in Chapter 11 Reorganizations*, 1997 U. Ill. L. Rev. 959. As of the time of this printing, a case addressing the issue of third-party releases was pending before the Supreme Court. *See* Harrington v. Purdue Pharma L.P., No. 23-124 (2023).

13. Stern v. Marshall, 546 U.S.C. 462 (2011). This ruling inspired significant litigation, multiple law review articles, and considerable conjecture regarding the likely impact on bankruptcy jurisprudence. *See e.g.,* Mawerdi Hamid, *Constitutional Authority of Bankruptcy Judges: The Effects of* Stern v. Marshall *as Applied by the Courts of Appeals*, 27 Am. Bankr. Inst. L. Rev. 51 (2019) (tracing nearly 100 courts of appeals opinions dealing with *Stern*). But for the most part, judges have continued to hear all matters within the district court's bankruptcy jurisdiction regardless of their ability to enter final judgments, and the ruling has had minimal impact on the day-to-day function of most bankruptcy cases. *See, e.g.,* Douglas G. Baird, *Blue Collar Constitutional Law*, 86 Am. Bankr. L.J. 3 (2012).

14. 11 U.S.C. §§ 701-728.

15. *Id.* §§ 1101–1146. Although the majority of Chapter 11 cases involve debtors that are corporations, partnerships, or other business entities, the Supreme Court has held that individual debtors can use the provisions of Chapter 11. Toibb v. Radloff, 501 U.S. 157 (1991).

16. *Id.* §§ 1201–1231.

to restructure pre-bankruptcy debts and repay them using post-bankruptcy disposable income according to statutorily defined rules.[17] The two remaining chapters are Chapter 9,[18] which permits a municipality to restructure its debts, and Chapter 15,[19] which creates a structure for cross-border bankruptcies. This book focuses on those aspects of bankruptcy law that have noteworthy consequences for Article 9 secured transactions. These consequences are most frequently seen in cases filed under Chapters 7, 11, 12, and 13.[20]

In a Chapter 7 case, a bankruptcy trustee is automatically appointed by the court to manage the estate property. The Chapter 7 trustee is a private individual, typically an attorney or an accountant, drawn at random from a panel of Chapter 7 trustees established for that district. Chapter 7 trustees are selected, qualified, and trained by the U.S. Trustee, a division of the Department of Justice tasked with overseeing the administration of bankruptcy cases.

In Chapter 7, the estate assets are intended to be liquidated. However, individual debtors have the benefit of state and/or federal exemptions which allow the debtor to keep specific categories of property as part of the debtor's anticipated fresh start.[21] These exemptions do not affect a secured creditor's interest in estate property, although they may take precedence over nonconsensual liens, which will be "stripped" from exempt property in bankruptcy.[22] Business entities have no exemptions and no fresh start; all assets will be liquidated until there is no value remaining in the business entity. The Chapter 7 trustee will abandon property from which the trustee cannot extract value for creditors, including all exempt property, worthless property, and property that is fully encumbered by a security interest.[23] In addition to collecting and managing the estate property, the Chapter 7 trustee also investigates the debtor's financial affairs, sets aside improper pre-bankruptcy transfers by the debtor, liquidates valuable assets, and distributes the proceeds to those creditors entitled to payment under the Code's distributive scheme.[24]

In reorganization cases under Chapters 11, 12 and 13, the debtor typically stays in control of property of the estate. It is primarily the debtor's responsibility to propose a plan of repayment using income and assets generated after the filing. The reorganiz-

---

17. *Id.* §§ 1301–1330.

18. *Id.* §§ 901–946.

19. *Id.* §§ 1501–1532.

20. For further discussion of the general procedures of bankruptcy, see generally JEFFREY FERRI-ELL & EDWARD J. JANGER, UNDERSTANDING BANKRUPTCY (4th ed. 2019).

21. *See* 11 U.S.C. § 522(b). State law determines whether or not the federal bankruptcy exemptions are available to an individual debtor. If not, the debtor will only have the benefit of state exemption laws.

22. *See* 11 U.S.C. § 522(f); § 16.07, *infra*.

23. 11 U.S.C. § 554(a). When the trustee abandons property of the estate, title to that property is vested back into the debtor. Any creditor with a security interest in that property may then enforce that security interest, but only after first obtaining relief from the automatic stay as discussed in § 16.03[B], *infra*.

24. 11 U.S.C. § 704.

ing debtor can use estate property, including secured collateral, in its reorganization efforts. However, this use is subject to the supervision of the bankruptcy court.[25]

The trustee appointed in Chapter 12 or 13 does not collect and manage the property of the estate. Instead, the trustee reviews the debtor's proposed plan of repayment for adherence to statutory guidelines, investigates the bankrupt debtor's financial affairs, sets aside improper pre-bankruptcy transfers by the debtor, and collects the debtor's post-bankruptcy disposable net income under the terms of the plan that has been confirmed by the bankruptcy court. The trustee then uses this income to pay the claims of creditors.[26]

Trustees are not appointed as a matter of course in Chapter 11 cases.[27] In the typical Chapter 11 case, the Code authorizes the bankrupt debtor (called the debtor in possession, or DIP) to exercise the powers of a Chapter 11 trustee.[28] The powers of the Chapter 11 trustee are similar to those given trustees in the other bankruptcy chapters, except that the Chapter 11 trustee—or, more commonly, the DIP—is also responsible for filing a plan of reorganization to be confirmed by the court.[29]

In all cases, the trustee/DIP examines the claims of creditors for potential objections and enforces any legal claims the estate might have against creditors or other third parties. Pursuant to its avoiding powers, the trustee/DIP may invalidate certain pre-bankruptcy transfers, including unperfected security interests,[30] fraudulent transfers,[31] and security interests or other transfers that had the effect of preferring the Article 9 secured party over other pre-bankruptcy creditors.[32] These powers present the largest threat to an Article 9 secured party's ability to enforce its security interest. Much of the case law interpreting Article 9 arises when a bankruptcy trustee or DIP challenges a security interest.

25. *Id.* §§ 1107(a), 1203(a), 1303.

26. *Id.* § 1302(b). Functionally the same system applies in Chapter 12 cases. *Id.* § 1202(b).

27. A trustee may be appointed upon request of any party in interest for cause (including the debtor's dishonesty, fraud, or incompetence), or if the court concludes that appointment of a trustee is otherwise necessary to protect the estate or the interests of creditors or other interest holders (such as shareholders of a bankrupt corporation). *Id.* § 1104(a).

28. *Id.* § 1107(a).

29. *Id.* § 1106.

30. *Id.* § 544(a). *See* § 16.04[B], *infra.*

31. 11 U.S.C. §§ 544(b), 548. *See* § 16.04[F], *infra.*

32. 11 U.C.C. § 547. *See* § 16.04[E], *infra.* Although avoiding powers are not expressly given to a trustee in Chapter 13, most courts have concluded that the Chapter 13 trustee holds the authority to avoid actions and only relinquishes that authority to the Chapter 13 debtor under particular circumstances. *See, e.g., In re* Hamilton, 125 F.3d 292, 296 (5th Cir. 1997); § 16.04[A], *infra.*

§ 16.02 Contrasting Secured and
Unsecured Claims

[A] What Is a Claim?

When a debtor files for bankruptcy, it is generally because the debtor faces multiple financial obligations from various parties, and it cannot repay all of these obligations as they come due. Bankruptcy is thus a collective process to facilitate the recovery of claims against the estate in an orderly and equitable way. The Bankruptcy Code defines the term "claim" very broadly to incorporate any "right to payment, whether or not ... reduced to judgment, liquidated, unliquidated, fixed, contingent, matured, unmatured, disputed, undisputed, legal, equitable, secured, or unsecured."[33] Likewise, the Code broadly defines "creditor" to include any individual or entity that holds "a claim against the debtor" that arose prior to the bankruptcy petition.[34] By defining the terms "claim" and "creditor" so broadly, the Code makes it possible for the bankruptcy process to address and resolve all of the debtor's legal obligations arising out of its pre-bankruptcy activities.[35]

[B] The Allowance of Claims

Section 502 of the Bankruptcy Code distinguishes between allowed claims and disallowed claims. Under Section 502(a), claims are deemed allowed unless the trustee, the debtor, or some other party in interest raises a valid objection to the claim.[36] Once a proper party raises an objection to the claim, the court must conduct a hearing and determine the amount of the creditor's allowed claim.[37]

Bankruptcy law does not honor all pre-bankruptcy claims. Sometimes the rationale for disallowing a claim rests on nonbankruptcy law; for example, a "debt" evidenced by a forged promissory note is not enforced in bankruptcy.[38] In other cases, the rationale for disallowance is based on concerns of sound bankruptcy policy, such as the disallowance of claims for unmatured interest.[39] Bankruptcy law may also place a cap on the

---

33. 11 U.S.C. § 101(5)(A).

34. *Id.* § 101(10).

35. S. Rep. No. 989, 95th Cong., 2d Sess. 22 (1978).

36. 11 U.S.C. § 502(a) (claims deemed allowed unless party in interest objects).

37. *Id.* § 502(b) (if objection is filed, court must determine amount of allowed claim after notice and hearing). Section 502(b) elaborates on the circumstances upon which the court must disallow a creditor's claim; its full reach is beyond the scope of this book.

38. 11 U.S.C. § 502(b)(1).

39. *Id.* § 502(b)(2). For example, suppose Creditor asserts an otherwise valid claim for $1,000 for goods shipped to Debtor on open account, and Creditor's terms include an 18 percent interest charge on past due accounts. Section 502 allows the claim in the amount of $1,000, plus any interest that has accrued up to the date of the bankruptcy petition, but Section 502(b)(2) disallows the claim to the extent of any interest that otherwise would have accrued under nonbankruptcy law after the petition date. The Bankruptcy Code denies unmatured interest on unsecured claims as a matter of administra-

amount of claim allowed, as with damages for termination of a real property lease,[40] or of an employment contract.[41]

[C] Secured Claims, Unsecured Claims, and Valuation

The Bankruptcy Code further distinguishes between secured and unsecured claims. As a starting point, bankruptcy takes secured creditors as it finds them on the petition date; a security interest that is enforceable under nonbankruptcy law will also be respected in bankruptcy.[42] A creditor with a valid lien on certain of the debtor's assets, such as a mortgage or Article 9 security interest, is treated as the holder of a secured claim against those assets and retains its pre-bankruptcy priority for any distribution from those assets.[43] For example, if Bank holds a valid Article 9 security interest in Chapter 7 Debtor's inventory (worth $100,000) to secure a debt of $40,000, Bank will be repaid its $40,000 from the proceeds of the inventory before any administrative

---

tive convenience. Debtors typically do not have the assets to pay 100 percent of the principal balance of unsecured claims—much less any interest on those claims. By disallowing claims for unmatured interest, the Bankruptcy Code avoids the accrual of interest (and the inconvenience of recomputing claim balances) as the case proceeds. Vanston Bondholders' Protective Comm. v. Green, 329 U.S. 156 (1946); In re Brooks, 323 F.3d 676 (8th Cir. 2003); In re Hanna, 872 F.2d 829 (8th Cir. 1989).

Notwithstanding Section 502(b)(2), creditors holding oversecured claims (claims secured by property with a value exceeding the balance of the debt) can collect post-petition interest as part of their allowed claim, up to but not beyond the value of the collateral. 11 U.S.C. § 506(a)(1), (b). Interest on secured claims is discussed in further detail in § 16.03[B][1][a][ii], infra.

In recent years, courts have grappled with the enforceability of contractual provisions that require debtors to pay penalties when a loan ends prematurely through acceleration of repayment, as may occur in bankruptcy. These provisions were traditionally found in bond indentures but now also appear in connection with a wide variety of financing, including secured notes. These so-called "make-whole" clauses are seen by many as inappropriate efforts to collect unmatured interest in bankruptcy proceedings. Even in the context of oversecured claims, some argue that make-whole provisions should be disallowed. See, e.g., Bruce A. Markell, Dead Funds and Shipwrecks: Ultra Petroleum, 39 BANKR. L. LETTER, Apr. 2019. But see Douglas G. Baird, Making Sense of Make-Wholes, 94 AM. BANKR. L.J. 567 (2020) (arguing that the provisions should be understood as prepetition claims that are routinely allowed). Several bankruptcy courts have upheld creditors' claims to this compensation, even for unsecured claims. See, e.g., In re Ultra Petroleum Corp., 624 B.R. 178, 193–95 (Bankr. S.D.T.X. 2020); In re Hertz Corp., 637 B.R. 781, 790–92 (Bankr. D. Del. 2021). Compare In re Mallinckrodt PLC, no. 20-bk-12522 (Bankr. D. Del. Mar. 2, 2022).

40. 11 U.S.C. § 502(b)(6).

41. Id. § 502(b)(7).

42. This general statement is subject to two caveats regarding its scope. First, while the secured party's lien itself is respected, the bankruptcy petition stays the secured party's nonbankruptcy remedies to enforce that lien (such as foreclosure) during the pendency of bankruptcy, as discussed in § 16.03[A], infra. Second, in certain circumstances, the Code gives the trustee or the debtor the power to avoid a creditor's security interest, either in whole or in part, in order to advance one or more of the Code's underlying policy objectives. Section 16.04, infra, discusses these "avoiding powers," also termed "avoidance powers."

43. 11 U.S.C. § 506(a)(1).

expenses or general creditors will be paid.[44] In contrast, the holders of unsecured claims—general creditors without any pre-bankruptcy lien against specific assets of the debtor—receive payment only on a pro rata basis to the extent that assets remain after payment of secured claims and the expenses of bankruptcy administration.[45]

In some cases, however, a creditor will hold an undersecured claim: a claim that is secured by a lien on assets of the debtor that have a value less than the total balance of the creditor's allowed claim. Suppose Bank holds a valid Article 9 security interest in Chapter 7 Debtor's inventory (worth $40,000) to secure a debt of $100,000. The Bank-ruptcy Code will bifurcate Bank's claim, treating it as if it were two separate claims: a secured claim equal to the value of the collateral and an unsecured claim to the extent of the deficiency balance of Bank's claim.[46] In this example, Bank would thus have a secured claim of $40,000 and an unsecured claim of $60,000.[47]

Because the status of a creditor as fully secured or undersecured hinges on the underlying value of the collateral securing the debt, few issues have generated more controversy in bankruptcy than the proper method for determining the value of a secured party's collateral. An item of collateral might bring different prices if sold in different contexts. For example, a car sold at a foreclosure sale on the courthouse steps might bring a $10,000 sale price. The same car might bring a price of $11,000 if sold

---

44. The trustee could, however, first deduct the "reasonable, necessary costs and expenses" of preserving and disposing of the inventory to the extent those costs and expenses provided a benefit to Bank. *Id.* § 506(c).

45. *Id.* §§ 726(a), 507(b).

46. Section 506(a)(1) literally states that an allowed claim secured by a valid lien on certain prop-erty is secured to the extent of "the value of such creditor's interest in the estate's interest in such property." In interpreting this section, the Supreme Court has equated the quoted language with "the value of the collateral." United Savings Ass'n of Texas v. Timbers of Inwood Forest Assocs., Ltd., 484 U.S. 365 (1988).

47. In this hypothetical, the most likely scenario is that the Chapter 7 trustee will abandon the property to the debtor. The Bank will then request relief from the automatic stay to recover against its collateral, which will likely be granted. The Bank can then repossess the inventory, conduct an Article 9 sale, and apply the proceeds of the sale to Bank's debt. The unsecured portion of Bank's claim will be discharged in bankruptcy following any pro rata distribution to unsecured creditors. In limited circumstances, Chapter 7 debtors may attempt to retain an overencumbered asset, such as a house or a valuable piece of art or jewelry, for nonmonetary reasons. The Code permits a debtor to redeem personal property by paying the value of the secured claim, even if it is less than the total amount of the debt. *See* § 16.08, *infra.* A debtor may also reaffirm its debt to the secured creditor, waiving its right to a discharge as consideration for the creditor's waiver of its immediate right to foreclose on the collateral. *See* § 16.09, *infra.*

In Chapter 11 cases only, the Code gives the undersecured creditor an option. It can (i) allow its claim to be bifurcated under Section 506(a)(1) or (ii) elect to have its entire claim treated as secured under Section 1111(b), even though Section 506(a)(1) would otherwise bifurcate its claim. 11 U.S.C. § 1111(b). In the example given in the text, if Bank exercises its section 1111(b) election, Bank would have a secured claim for $100,000 and no unsecured claim at all. As a result of this election, Bank would have no right to receive any pro rata distributions to unsecured creditors.

In some Chapter 13 cases, a debtor cannot use Section 506(a) to bifurcate the claim of an under-secured creditor. The primary assets to which this limitation applies are motor vehicles. For further discussion of this limitation, see § 16.10, *infra.*

in a dealer auction, or a price of $13,000 if sold on a retail auto sales lot. Which price reflects the car's "value" for purposes of bankruptcy valuation?

Valuation of secured collateral is one of many determinations to be made by the bankruptcy judge, guided by Section 506 of the Code. Section 506(a)(1) provides a flexible case-by-case standard under which the court should determine the value of collateral "in light of the purpose of the valuation and of the proposed disposition or use of such property...."[48] This standard suggests that the court's determination of the collateral's "market value" is a function of both the debtor's proposed use of the collateral and the procedural context of the bankruptcy case.[49] For example, if a secured party is seeking relief from the automatic stay to be permitted to foreclose on the collateral, Section 506(a)(1) suggests that the court should value the collateral using the price the collateral would bring in a commercially reasonable foreclosure sale.[50]

By contrast, if a Chapter 11 debtor proposes to retain the collateral under its plan, a court evaluating the debtor's plan should value the collateral based on its "replacement value," that is, the price that it would cost the debtor to purchase similar collateral in a market transaction. Section 506(a)(2) mandates valuation based on replacement value for individual Chapter 7 and Chapter 13 debtors, regardless of the purpose for the valuation.[51] Replacement value is defined as the price a retail merchant would charge for the property, considering its age and condition, without deduction for costs of sale or marketing.[52] In amending Section 506 to include subsection (a)(2), Congress established different standards for valuation in business cases and individual cases.[53]

§ 16.03 The Automatic Stay

[A] Nature and Scope

Outside of bankruptcy, creditors can resort to any collection remedies available under state law upon the debtor's default. The filing of a bankruptcy petition, however, automatically triggers the stay authorized by Section 362(a), which enjoins creditors from exercising their ordinary remedies to enforce or collect debts that arose prior to

---

48. 11 U.S.C. § 506(a).

49. For a thoughtful treatment of valuation issues in bankruptcy, see Robert M. Lawless & Stephen P. Ferris, *Economics and the Rhetoric of Valuation*, 5 J. BANKR. L. & PRAC. 3 (1995).

50. *See* § 16.03[B] (valuation in context of motions for relief from automatic stay), *infra*.

51. This provision codifies the Supreme Court's decision in *Associates Commercial Corp. v. Rash*, 520 U.S. 953 (1997) (replacement-value measure appropriate in context of Chapter 13 debtor's proposal to retain collateral over objection of secured party).

52. 11 U.S.C. § 506(a)(2). For further discussion of the impact of Section 506(a)(2) in the Chapter 7 context, see § 16.08 (valuation in context of Chapter 7 debtor's redemption of collateral), *infra*.

53. *See* Stacy L. Molison, *A Look at Disparate Approaches to Valuation under Section 506 and Its Relationship to Section 1325*, 15 AM. BANKR. L. REV. 659, 668 (2007) (noting that individual Chapter 11 cases are covered under the business standard).

the bankruptcy petition.[54] Under Section 362(a), the filing of a bankruptcy petition means that a creditor may not legally engage in any of the following customary collection activities: filing suit to collect a pre-bankruptcy debt;[55] prosecuting a previously filed suit to collect a pre-bankruptcy debt;[56] enforcing a judgment obtained prior to bankruptcy;[57] attaching, levying upon, or repossessing property of the bankruptcy estate;[58] obtaining, perfecting, or enforcing a lien or security interest in property of the debtor or the bankruptcy estate;[59] or taking any other action "to collect, assess, or recover" a pre-bankruptcy debt, including setting off a mutual debt owed to the debtor.[60] Section 362(a) defines the scope of the stay in such broad and sweeping terms that dunning letters, phone calls to the debtor, and even polite requests for payment must stop once the debtor files its bankruptcy petition. Creditors "may continue to breathe, eat and sleep and are free to dream about the debtor"[61] but cannot take any action to collect unless that action falls within the limited and exclusive set of exceptions specified in Section 362(b).[62]

Creditor actions taken in violation of the automatic stay are void and may open the creditor to sanctions.[63] A creditor cannot argue that its actions should be given effect because it lacked notice or knowledge of the debtor's bankruptcy filing; actions

---

54. 11 U.S.C. § 362(a). The stay is self-executing; it arises automatically upon the filing of the bankruptcy petition, without any action by the debtor or the bankruptcy court.

55. *Id.* § 362(a)(1).

56. *Id.*

57. *Id.* § 362(a)(2).

58. *Id.* § 362(a)(3).

59. *Id.* § 362(a)(4), (5).

60. *Id.* § 362(a)(6), (7). The Supreme Court has held, however, that while a bank may not effect a set-off of the debtor's bank account without obtaining relief from the stay, a bank can place an "administrative freeze" on a debtor's bank account, thereby preventing any disbursements from the account, without violating the stay. Citizens Bank of Md. v. Strumpf, 516 U.S. 16 (1995).

61. 1 DAVID G. EPSTEIN, STEVE H. NICKLES & JAMES J. WHITE, BANKRUPTCY § 3-1, at 79 (West Prac. ed. 1992).

62. Section 362(b) allows the commencement or continuation of certain actions to establish or enforce the debtor's noncommercial obligations. *See* 11 U.S.C. § 362(b)(1) (criminal proceedings against debtor), (2) (actions to establish paternity or orders for alimony, maintenance or support), (4) (actions by governmental units to enforce police or regulatory power), (9) (governmental tax audits and issuance of tax deficiency notices). Section 362(b)(10) permits a landlord of nonresidential land to repossess the land from the debtor if the lease has expired. Finally, Section 362(b)(3) permits a secured party to perfect a lien against property of the estate (such as by filing an Article 9 financing statement) after the petition date, notwithstanding the stay prohibitions in Section 362(a)(4)–(5), in two limited circumstances that will be discussed in conjunction with the trustee's avoiding powers in § 16.04[B] and [E], *infra*.

63. *In re* Nat'l Century Fin. Enters., Inc., 423 F.3d 567 (6th Cir. 2005) (post-petition action to collect debtor's accounts receivable); 40235 Washington Street Corp. v. Lusardi, 329 F.3d 1076 (9th Cir. 2003) (post-petition tax sale); Easley v. Pettibone Michigan Corp., 990 F.2d 905 (6th Cir. 1993) (post-petition filing of lawsuit against debtor); *In re* Schwartz, 954 F.2d 569 (9th Cir. 1992) (post-petition IRS tax assessment); *In re* Ward, 837 F.2d 124 (3d Cir. 1988) (post-petition sheriff's foreclosure sale); *In re* Mitchell, 279 B.R. 839 (9th Cir. Bankr. 2002) (post-petition foreclosure of debtor's residence); *In re* Prine, 222 B.R. 610 (Bankr. N.D. Iowa 1997) (post-petition notation of secured party's lien on title certificate).

that violate the stay are void even if the creditor was unaware of the bankruptcy filing. Creditors that knowingly violate the stay face serious financial consequences. Under Section 362(h), an individual that suffers injury as a result of a willful violation of the stay can recover actual damages (including costs and attorneys' fees).[64] In addition, Section 362(h) authorizes the award of punitive damages for willful stay violations that involve egregious or outrageous conduct.[65] Unless the bankruptcy court terminates or modifies the effectiveness of the stay, it remains in effect as to the debtor until the bankruptcy case is closed or dismissed, or until the debtor receives its discharge, whichever occurs first.[66] Further, the stay remains in effect to enjoin actions against any asset that is property of the bankruptcy estate for as long as that asset remains a part of the bankruptcy estate.[67]

By halting all external collection efforts, the stay requires creditors to resolve their claims against the debtor through the collective bankruptcy process under the supervision of the bankruptcy court. The injunctive nature of the stay thus helps to promote

---

64. 11 U.S.C. § 362(h). On its face, Section 362(h) limits the availability of damages to an "individual" injured by a willful stay violation. The majority of circuit courts have interpreted this provision literally and refused to award damages or fees to corporate debtors. *In re* Spookyworld, Inc., 346 F.3d 1 (1st Cir. 2003); *In re* Just Brakes Corp. Sys., Inc., 108 F.3d 881 (8th Cir. 1997); Jove Engineering, Inc. v. I.R.S., 92 F.3d 1539 (11th Cir. 1996); *In re* Goodman, 991 F.2d 613 (9th Cir. 1993); *In re* Chateaugay Corp., 920 F.2d 183 (2d Cir. 1990). A few courts, however, have held that Section 362(h)'s reference to "individual" debtors was likely a drafting error by Congress and awarded damages or fees to corporate debtors. *In re* Atlantic Bus. & Community Corp., 901 F.2d 325 (3d Cir. 1990); Budget Serv. Co. v. Better Homes of Va., Inc., 804 F.2d 289 (4th Cir. 1986). *See also* St. Paul Fire & Marine Ins. Co. v. Labuzan, 579 F.3d 533 (5th Cir. 2009) (holding that principals had constitutional and prudential standing to pursue damages for stay violations, but only as creditors, not as owners/equity holders). Courts have also disagreed as to whether the trustee can recover damages and fees under Section 362(h). *Compare In re* Pace, 67 F.3d 187 (9th Cir. 1995) (no; trustee not an "individual") *with In re* Garofalo's Finer Foods, Inc., 186 B.R. 414 (N.D. Ill. 1995) (yes; trustee is an "individual"). Even if the trustee cannot recover damages and fees under Section 362(h), however, the court retains discretion to award the trustee costs and attorneys' fees under its power to sanction contempt, as articulated in 11 U.S.C. § 105(a). *In re* Pace, 67 F.3d 187; *In re* Lickman, 297 B.R. 162 (Bankr. M.D. Fla. 2003).

65. *See, e.g., In re* Wagner, 74 B.R. 898 (Bankr. E.D. Pa. 1987) (secured party burst into debtor's home, extinguished lights, held finger to debtor's head, and threatened to "blow [debtor's] brains out" unless debtor repaid debt). Such egregious examples are easy cases, but some bankruptcy courts have also awarded punitive damages for creditor activity that posed no physical threats. *See, e.g., In re* Shade, 261 B.R. 213 (Bankr. C.D. Ill. 2001) (secured party representative accosted debtor in courthouse following initial meeting of creditors and repeatedly demanded payment of secured party's claim, reducing debtor to tears; court awarded $9,000 in punitive damages); *In re* Cepero, 226 B.R. 595 (Bankr. S.D. Ohio 1998) (secured party disposed of repossessed automobile after receiving repeated phone calls advising that debtor had filed bankruptcy petition and requesting return of the automobile; court awarded $12,000 in punitive damages); *In re* Miller, 200 B.R. 415 (Bankr. M.D. Fla. 1996) (creditor continued sending dunning letters and phone calls to couple following Chapter 7 petition in effort to collect $770 claim; court awarded $10,000 in punitive damages).

66. 11 U.S.C. § 362(c)(2).

67. *Id.* § 362(c)(1). During the case, property of the estate remains in the estate unless it is liquidated or is abandoned under Section 554, or unless the debtor can and does claim the property as exempt under Section 522. In reorganization cases, confirmation of a plan of reorganization vests title to property of the estate in the reorganized debtor. *Id.* §§ 1141(b) (Chapter 11); 1227(b) (Chapter 12); 1327(b) (Chapter 13).

the key objectives of the bankruptcy process: to provide the debtor with a "breathing spell" during which the debtor can arrange a plan for its reorganization or its orderly liquidation without undue pressure or harassment from creditors,[68] and to preserve the assets of the bankruptcy estate for equitable distribution to similarly situated creditors.[69]

[B] Relief from Stay

The broad, encompassing, and self-executing nature of the stay in bankruptcy is intentionally over-inclusive in scope. Congress anticipated situations where an exception to the stay might be warranted and accordingly drafted provisions through which a creditor might move the bankruptcy court to "lift" the automatic stay. If the motion to lift the stay is granted, the creditor is permitted to engage in otherwise lawful collection efforts despite the ongoing bankruptcy.[70] The Bankruptcy Code sets forth two standards for relief from the stay that are relevant to Article 9 secured parties: Section 361(d)(1), which entitles a creditor to relief for "cause," and Section 362(d)(2), which entitles a creditor to relief if the debtor has no equity in the collateral and the collateral is not necessary for the debtor's effective reorganization.[71]

[1] Relief for "Cause"—11 U.S.C. § 362(d)(1)

Section 362(d)(1) provides that the court shall grant a creditor relief from the stay if that creditor demonstrates "cause, including the lack of adequate protection of an interest in property" held by that creditor.[72]

[a] Lack of Adequate Protection

The most frequently litigated ground in lifting the automatic stay for "cause" involves an allegation by a creditor that its interest in the debtor's property is not being "adequately protected." Motions raising these allegations are invariably brought by credi-

---

68. H.R. Rep. No. 595, 95th Cong., 1st Sess. 340 (1977).

69. *In re* Richardson Builders, Inc., 123 B.R. 736, 738 (Bankr. W.D. Va. 1990).

70. Section 362(d) specifies four types of relief that the bankruptcy court might order. First, the court could *terminate* the stay, permitting a creditor to begin or resume its collection efforts, but without validating any prior actions taken in violation of the stay. Second, the court could *annul* the stay, thereby validating any prior actions taken in violation of the stay. Third, the court could *modify* the stay, permitting a creditor to take a particular action but otherwise leaving the stay in place with respect to other actions (e.g., allowing the creditor to reduce an unliquidated claim to judgment in state court but not allowing any execution upon that judgment). Fourth, the court could *condition* the continued effectiveness of the stay upon some action by the trustee or the debtor (e.g., allowing the stay to remain in effect upon the condition that the debtor file its reorganization plan within 30 days).

71. 11 U.S.C. § 362(d). Section 362(d) also provides two other grounds for relief from the stay applicable to real estate mortgagees. Section 362(d)(3) permits relief from the stay to certain real estate mortgagees in cases involving "single asset real estate." Section 362(d)(4) permits relief from the stay to real estate mortgagees in cases in which the debtor's petition is part of a scheme to hinder, delay, or defraud creditors that involves either transfer of the mortgaged property without the mortgagee's consent or repetitive bankruptcy petitions.

72. *Id.* § 362(d)(1).

tors holding an enforceable interest in specific assets of the debtor, such as Article 9 secured parties. They typically involve claims that the property value is being damaged or depreciated and seek relief that would allow either immediate repossession or other compensation to offset the loss in property value.

[i] Value Preservation

Outside of bankruptcy, a secured party could repossess its collateral from the debtor after default, liquidate the collateral in compliance with applicable law, recover the collateral's value as of the date of the sale, and apply that amount to the underlying debt. By preventing the creditor from repossessing and selling the collateral, and by allowing the trustee or DIP to retain and use the collateral,[73] the stay imposes on the secured party a risk that its collateral may depreciate during the pendency of the bankruptcy case. This depreciation could result from ordinary fluctuations in the value of the collateral,[74] from use of the collateral that physically exhausts its economic value,[75] or from damage to or destruction of the collateral in an uninsured casualty. This risk of depreciation during bankruptcy poses a serious threat to the secured party. For example, assume Bank holds a valid lien on Debtor's car to secure a $5,000 debt. Debtor files a Chapter 11 petition, and on the petition date, the car's value is $5,000. During the Debtor's bankruptcy, however, the debtor's continued operation of the car will cause it to depreciate. This depreciation would be of no consequence if Debtor could repay Bank the full $5,000 balance of the debt, but as Debtor is insolvent, full repayment is unlikely. Debtor could remain in Chapter 11 for an extended period, fail to reorganize successfully, and then convert to a Chapter 7 liquidation. Assume for this example that Debtor has stayed in Chapter 11 for a full year before converting to Chapter 7, and that during this time the car's depreciation can be measured at $150 per month. After 12 months, the car's value would have depreciated by $1,800, so that by the time of the liquidation, the car would bring a sale price of only $3,200. Debtor's post-petition use of the car thus raises the threat that Bank will recover only a portion of its original claim, whereas if Bank had repossessed the car at the beginning of the case it would have recovered in full. In other words, Debtor's use of the car in this example means that Bank's security interest in the car is not adequately protected.

Congress provided a mechanism for a secured party such as Bank to protect itself from the risk of depreciation during the pendency of bankruptcy. Bank can request that the bankruptcy court terminate the stay and allow Bank to foreclose on its security interest immediately, or condition any continuation of the stay on Debtor's providing

---

73. Under Section 363(d), the trustee generally may use property of the estate in the ordinary course of business, without notice or hearing. The debtor in possession in a Chapter 11 case, or the debtor in a Chapter 12 or 13 case, also has the powers of a trustee under Section 363(d). *Id.* §§ 1107(a), 1203, 1303.

74. For example, inventory might decrease in value due to functional or stylistic obsolescence.

75. For example, by driving a car 2,000 miles per month during the pendency of the bankruptcy, Debtor would exhaust some portion of the car's useful life.

"adequate protection" of Bank's security interest.[76] Once Bank makes this request,[77] Debtor must either provide Bank with adequate protection of its security interest or surrender the collateral to Bank; if Debtor does neither, the bankruptcy court will lift the stay and permit Bank to pursue its nonbankruptcy remedies.

Adequate protection is a term of art in bankruptcy. Adequate protection may be any action that eliminates the risk that continuation of the stay will impose a depreciation loss upon the secured party.[78] It is perhaps easiest to think of adequate protection as being similar to "insurance" against depreciation in the collateral: the trustee/DIP must ensure that the value of the secured party's collateral (either the original collateral or some substitute collateral) is preserved or that the secured party is compensated for any depreciation that occurs. Section 361 provides an illustrative list of the ways in which the trustee/DIP might provide adequate protection:

- *Cash payments.* If the estate has sufficient unencumbered funds, the trustee/DIP can make cash payments to the secured party in an amount necessary to offset the expected depreciation in the collateral's value. The secured party would apply these payments to reduce the debt, thereby maintaining the value of the collateral relative to the underlying debt.[79]

- *Replacement lien.* If the estate has equity in another asset and the equity in that asset exceeds the anticipated depreciation of the collateral, the trustee/DIP can grant the secured party a lien on that other asset.[80]

- *The "Indubitable Equivalent."* The trustee/DIP can provide any other form of relief that will provide the secured party with the "indubitable equivalent" of its interest in the collateral.[81]

The term "indubitable equivalent" is vague, but courts have largely treated the phrase as self-explanatory.[82] Courts typically reference this provision when finding that

---

76. Although Section 363(d) authorizes the trustee to use a secured party's collateral in the ordinary course of business, Section 363(e) provides that, upon the secured party's request, the court may prohibit or condition the trustee's use of the collateral "as is necessary to provide adequate protection" of the secured party's interest in the collateral.

77. This request is typically made by way of a pleading filed with the bankruptcy court and titled either "Motion to Lift Stay" or "Motion for Adequate Protection."

78. For example, if the debtor has allowed casualty insurance on the collateral to lapse, adequate protection requires that the trustee/DIP insure the collateral up to its then-current value, and failure to do so justifies relief from the automatic stay. *In re* Jones, 189 B.R. 13 (Bankr. E.D. Okla. 1995); *In re* Hancock, 126 B.R. 270 (Bankr. E.D. Tex. 1991); *In re* Scott Segal Farms, Inc., 31 B.R. 377 (Bankr. S.D. Fla. 1983).

79. 11 U.S.C. § 361(1).

80. *Id.* § 361(2).

81. *Id.* § 361(3).

82. The phrase "indubitable equivalent" comes from an opinion by Judge Learned Hand in *In re Murel Holding Corp.*, 75 F.2d 941 (2d Cir. 1935), in which he used the term "most indubitable equivalence" in attempting to explain the parameters of the term "adequate protection" as it was used under the Bankruptcy Act of 1898. The phrase is also used in the context of a "cramdown" plan confirmation in Chapter 11. *See* 11 U.S.C. § 1129(b)(2)(A)(iii).

an "equity cushion" constitutes adequate protection. An equity cushion exists when secured collateral has surplus value (i.e., equity) in the collateral over and above the balance of the debt. For example, assume Bank holds a security interest in Debtor's car to secure repayment of a debt in the amount of $5,000. If Debtor's car had a value of $9,000 on the petition date, Bank would have a $4,000 equity cushion (the car's excess value relative to the $5,000 debt). Even if Debtor remained in bankruptcy for a full year and the car depreciated by $150 per month throughout that period, Bank would still remain fully secured at the end of that time. The depreciation would eat up $1,800 of Bank's equity cushion but would not threaten Bank's ability to be repaid in full from the value of the car.[83] In this scenario, the court should refuse to grant Bank relief from the stay because the equity cushion provides adequate protection for Bank's security interest.[84] The equity cushion is in the very collateral securing the Bank's interest; thus, it is the "indubitable equivalent" mandated by statute.

[ii] Opportunity Costs

When the debtor files for bankruptcy, it typically ceases making payments on its debts. The consequence is that any creditor holding a claim against the debtor is not collecting the interest that would otherwise accrue under the pre-bankruptcy agreement and applicable nonbankruptcy law. Outside of bankruptcy, of course, a secured party could repossess its collateral following default, liquidate the collateral, apply the proceeds to the debt, and then reinvest those proceeds in some alternative investment opportunity that would produce a return; for example, it could re-loan the proceeds to a solvent borrower capable of paying interest. By preventing the secured party from pursuing this course of action, the stay imposes a lost opportunity cost on the secured party. Further, bankruptcy law generally compounds this burden by disallowing claims for unmatured interest, as mentioned earlier.[85]

---

83. This statement assumes that the debtor continues to maintain adequate insurance on the car to protect against a casualty loss. If the debtor failed to maintain adequate insurance on the car, the secured party would lack adequate protection and could obtain relief from the automatic stay. *See, e.g., In re* Paradise Boat Leasing Corp., 2 B.R. 482 (Bankr. D.V.I. 1979).

84. *In re* Mellor, 734 F.2d 1396 (9th Cir. 1984); *In re* Colonial Ctr., Inc., 156 B.R. 452 (Bankr. E.D. Pa. 1993); *In re* Shaw Industries, Inc., 300 B.R. 861 (Bankr. W.D. Pa. 2003); *In re* Steffens, 275 B.R. 570 (Bankr. D. Colo. 2002). Over time, of course, depreciation of the collateral would eventually consume the equity cushion. Once the equity cushion is consumed and the secured party is no longer oversecured, the secured party could again request adequate protection of its interest. Thereafter, the trustee/DIP would have to provide adequate protection sufficient to satisfy Sections 361–363. Occasionally, creditors have argued that the trustee/DIP must adequately protect the equity cushion itself, that is, that the court must preserve the equity cushion at its bargained-for size. One could argue that, as an economic matter, the creditor that bargained for the security of an equity cushion may have agreed to accept a lower interest rate or may have made other concessions in return such that protection of the equity cushion is necessary to provide the creditor with the assurance of its bargain. Courts, however, have generally rejected arguments that the trustee/DIP must provide adequate protection of the equity cushion itself. *See, e.g., In re* Hanna, 912 F.2d 945 (8th Cir. 1990); *In re* Senior Care Props., Inc., 137 B.R. 527 (Bankr. N.D. Fla. 1992); *In re* Lane, 108 B.R. 6 (Bankr. D. Mass. 1989).

85. *See* § 16.02[B], *supra.*

For some secured creditors, Section 506(b) of the Bankruptcy Code partially mitigates this effect of the automatic stay. Section 506(b) provides that an *oversecured* creditor, a creditor with collateral that has a value exceeding the balance of its allowed claim, may collect interest on its secured claim, up to the total value of the collateral.[86] But what about undersecured creditors? A significant number of bankruptcy court decisions held that undersecured creditors should also receive post-petition interest, insofar as the automatic stay was preventing them from liquidating the collateral following default and reinvesting the proceeds in some alternative interest-bearing investment.[87] When the issue finally reached the Supreme Court in *United Savings Association of Texas v. Timbers of Inwood Forest Associates, Ltd.*,[88] it concluded that undersecured creditors were *not* entitled to interest during the pendency of the stay under the guise of "adequate protection."[89]

Commentators have criticized the *Timbers* decision both for its economic premises and its method of statutory interpretation,[90] but the Court's subsequent bankruptcy decisions have never questioned it. Accordingly, *Timbers* stands for the proposition that the trustee/DIP must provide "adequate protection" only in cases where the risk of depreciation in the value of the collateral poses a threat to the secured party's overall secured position.

[b] Other Cause for Relief

Section 362(d)(1) does not limit "cause" for relief from the automatic stay to those circumstances presenting lack of adequate protection. Instead, the bankruptcy court has the discretion to grant relief from the stay in other circumstances where the harm caused by the stay outweighs the benefit to the estate. Courts have terminated the stay upon concluding that a debtor had filed its bankruptcy petition in bad faith or in a clear attempt to abuse the bankruptcy process. An illustrative example is *In re Dixie Broadcasting, Inc.*,[91] in which the debtor had entered into a contract to sell a radio station but later reneged when it received a better offer from another prospective purchaser. When the contract vendee sued for specific performance, the debtor filed a Chapter 11 petition to prevent the state court from ordering specific performance. The court granted the vendee's motion to lift the stay, and the Eleventh Circuit affirmed, stating that "[t]he Bankruptcy Code is not intended to insulate financially secure sellers or buyers from

---

86. 11 U.S.C. § 506(b). If the trustee/DIP does not pay this interest to the oversecured creditor during the pendency of the bankruptcy stay, the unpaid interest accrues and is added to the creditor's secured claim.

87. *See, e.g., In re* American Mariner Indus., Inc., 734 F.2d 426 (9th Cir. 1984) (collecting cases).

88. 484 U.S. 365 (1988).

89. *Id.* at 372–73 (citations omitted).

90. Douglas G. Baird, The Elements of Bankruptcy 204 (rev. ed. 1993) ("[o]ne can look at *Timbers* as essentially requiring Bank to make a forced, interest-free loan for the duration of the bankruptcy"); David Gray Carlson, *Adequate Protection Payments and the Surrender of Cash Collateral in Chapter 11 Reorganizations*, 15 Cardozo L. Rev. 1357, 1359 (1994) (arguing that *Timbers* "denies that time exists").

91. 871 F.2d 1023 (11th Cir. 1989).

the bargains they strike."[92] Likewise, courts have lifted the stay against pending litigation based on the conclusion that the litigation would be more appropriately resolved in a forum other than the bankruptcy court.[93]

[2] Relief under 11 U.S.C. § 362(d)(2)

Under Section 362(d)(2), a secured party can obtain relief from the stay in order to repossess and foreclose upon its collateral if "the debtor does not have an equity" in the collateral and the collateral "is not necessary to an effective reorganization."[94] If both elements are present, relief from the stay is both necessary and appropriate; under such circumstances, neither the debtor nor general creditors will benefit if the collateral remains property of the estate.

[a] Does Debtor Have Equity in the Collateral?

For purposes of Section 362(d)(2), the debtor has no "equity" in an asset if the sum of all encumbrances on that asset exceeds the value of the asset.[95] To make this determination, of course, the bankruptcy court must determine the value of the collateral. The Bankruptcy Code does not specify a particular method of appraisal. Typically, the interested parties (usually the party seeking relief from stay and the trustee/DIP) present evidence regarding the value of the collateral, sometimes in the form of expert testimony. The bankruptcy court considers this evidence and makes a determination of the collateral's value "in light of the purpose of the valuation and of the collateral's proposed disposition or use,"[96] with the burden of persuasion placed upon the party seeking relief from the stay.[97] If the court's valuation shows the debtor does have equity in the collateral, the secured party's motion for relief from the stay under Section 362(d)(2) must be denied—as it should be, because the purpose of the stay is to protect that equity for the benefit of general creditors and for the debtor's potential reorganization.

Courts have disagreed as to the proper method of valuing collateral. Perhaps the best example of the divergent judicial views has involved the valuation of vehicles. To

---

92. *Id.* at 1028.

93. For example, the Fourth Circuit has suggested that the court can consider lifting the stay when the issues involved in pending litigation involve only state law such that the expertise of the bankruptcy court is unnecessary, and when modifying the stay to permit litigation to proceed in state court would promote judicial economy. *In re* Robbins, 964 F.2d 342 (4th Cir. 1992). *See also In re* MacDonald, 755 F.2d 715 (9th Cir. 1985) (bankruptcy court lifted stay to permit pursuit of state court spousal-support modification, in deference to state court expertise regarding family law matters); Garland Coal & Mining Co. v. United Mine Workers of Am., 778 F.2d 1297 (8th Cir. 1985) (bankruptcy courts ordinarily should lift stay to allow resolution of labor disputes through arbitration).

94. 11 U.S.C. § 362(d)(2). In a liquidation proceeding under Chapter 7, the debtor is not contemplating any reorganization; thus, only the first ground (lack of equity) is relevant.

95. *In re* Indian Palms Assocs., Ltd., 61 F.3d 197 (3d Cir. 1995); *In re* Sutton, 904 F.2d 327 (5th Cir. 1990); Stewart v. Gurley, 745 F.2d 1194 (9th Cir.1984); *In re* Hurst, 212 B.R. 890 (Bankr. W.D. Tenn. 1997).

96. 11 U.S.C. § 506(a)(1).

97. *Id.* § 362(g)(1); *In re* Dandridge, 221 B.R. 741 (Bankr. W.D. Tenn. 1998); *In re* Food Barn Stores, Inc., 159 B.R. 264 (Bankr. W.D. Mo. 1993).

illustrate the potential for different approaches, suppose Debtor owns an automobile subject to a properly perfected security interest in favor of Bank, securing Debtor's obligation to Bank in the amount of $10,000. Debtor files a Chapter 13 petition and wants to retain the automobile. This particular make and model of automobile has a "Blue Book" retail value of $12,000 and a "Blue Book" wholesale value of $9,900. In the context of a motion to lift the stay, should the court value Debtor's automobile at its retail value (leaving Debtor with equity in the automobile) or at its wholesale value (leaving Debtor with no equity)?[98]

Prior to 1997, courts generally followed one of three approaches to this question. A significant number of courts held that if a debtor proposed to retain an automobile as a part of its reorganization, the court should value the auto at its "going concern" or "retail" value.[99] Many other courts held that the court should value the automobile at its "wholesale" or "liquidation" value, on the theory that such a valuation more readily reflects the amount that a secured party like Bank would obtain if it foreclosed upon the automobile.[100] Yet other courts took a third, intermediate approach, holding that courts should value the automobile at the average of its retail and wholesale values.[101]

In 1997, the U.S. Supreme Court addressed this issue in *Associates Commercial Corp. v. Rash*.[102] In *Rash*, the debtor proposed to retain a tractor-trailer truck to use in his Chapter 13 reorganization efforts. The Fifth Circuit affirmed the bankruptcy court's valuation of the truck at its "net foreclosure value" (i.e., its liquidation value) rather than its "going concern" value.[103] By an 8–1 margin, the Supreme Court reversed and remanded, holding that when the debtor proposed to retain the collateral in a Chapter 13 case, Section 506(a) required the court to value the collateral at its "replacement value," that is, "the price a willing buyer in the debtor's trade, business, or situation would pay to obtain like property from a willing seller."[104] Justice Ginsburg's opinion suggests that this replacement-value measure is appropriate based on the risks presented to the secured party when the debtor proposes to retain the collateral:

> When a debtor surrenders the property, a creditor obtains it immediately, and is free to sell it and reinvest the proceeds.... If a debtor keeps the property and continues to use it, the creditor obtains at once neither the property nor its value and is exposed to double risks: The debtor may again default and the

98. It is more accurate to ask which measure should be the *starting point* for the court's valuation. Obviously, if the automobile is in below-average condition and in need of repair, the court should accordingly reduce the value below its Blue Book value. In contrast, if the automobile has low mileage and is generally in excellent condition, the court should increase the value above its Blue Book value.

99. *E.g., In re* Trimble, 50 F.3d 530 (8th Cir. 1995) (value of automobile properly based on retail value, without deduction for costs of sale).

100. *E.g., In re* Mitchell, 954 F.2d 557 (9th Cir. 1992).

101. *E.g., In re* Hoskins, 102 F.3d 311 (7th Cir. 1996).

102. 520 U.S. 953 (1997).

103. *In re* Rash, 90 F.3d 1036, 1044 (5th Cir. en banc 1996) ("[T]he creditor's interest is in the nature of a security interest, giving the creditor the right to repossess and sell the collateral and nothing more.... [T]he valuation should start with what the creditor could realize by exercising that right.").

104. *Rash*, 520 U.S. at 960.

property may deteriorate from extended use. Adjustments in the interest rate and secured creditor demands for more "adequate protection" do not fully offset these risks. Of prime significance, the replacement-value standard accurately gauges the debtor's "use" of the property.... The debtor in this case elected to use the collateral to generate an income stream. That actual use, rather than a foreclosure sale that will not take place, is the proper guide under a prescription hinged to the property's "disposition or use."[105]

Just as soon as the Supreme Court "clarified" this issue by adopting the replacement-value standard, however, the Court immediately complicated it again in a footnote, stating "[w]hether replacement value is the equivalent of retail value, wholesale value, or some other value will depend on the type of debtor and the nature of the property."[106] The Court also noted that even where retail value is the appropriate starting point for valuation, the court could make an appropriate downward adjustment to the value to account for the fact that the typical retail price would include some items (like warranties and reconditioning expenses) that "the debtor does not receive when he retains his vehicle."[107]

Courts have struggled to interpret the Supreme Court's footnote and (perhaps unsurprisingly) continued to reach different results. In the aftermath of *Rash*, many courts concluded that the "starting point" for valuing vehicles is the midpoint between the retail and wholesale Blue Book values.[108] A number of decisions, however, rejected this view as inconsistent with *Rash*'s admonition that valuation must occur on a case-by-case basis.[109] Many of these decisions have instead concluded that when the debtor proposes to retain the vehicle, the "replacement value" generally means retail Blue Book value, with a downward adjustment for items such as warranty or reconditioning costs.[110]

In 2005, Congress sought to clarify matters by adding Section 506(a)(2), which applies in cases involving individual debtors in Chapter 7 or Chapter 13. Under this section, debtors' property must be valued at its replacement value as of the petition date, without deduction for costs of sale or marketing.[111] If the individual Chapter 7 or 13 debtor acquired the property for personal, family, or household purposes, "replace-

---

105. *Id.* at 963 (citations and footnotes omitted).

106. *Id.* at 965 n.6.

107. *Id.*

108. *In re* Marquez, 270 B.R. 761 (Bankr. D. Ariz. 2001); *In re* Oglesby, 221 B.R. 515 (Bankr. D. Colo. 1998); *In re* Younger, 216 B.R. 649 (Bankr. W.D. Okla. 1998); *In re* Franklin, 213 B.R. 781 (Bankr. N.D. Fla. 1997).

109. Evabank v. Baxter, 278 B.R. 867 (N.D. Ala. 2002); *In re* Gonzalez, 295 B.R. 584 (Bankr. N.D. Ill. 2003).

110. Most courts have calculated the downward adjustment based upon the specific facts of the case. *See, e.g., In re* Gonzalez, 295 B.R. 584 (Bankr. N.D. Ill. 2003); *In re* Dziendziel, 295 B.R. 184 (Bankr. W.D.N.Y. 2003). Others have simply made a percentage deduction. *See, e.g., In re* Renzelman, 227 B.R. 740 (Bankr. W.D. Mo. 1998) (5 percent reduction appropriate to account for warranties, reconditioning, cleaning, detailing, dealer preparation, and other services not provided when debtor simply retains its vehicle).

111. 11 U.S.C. § 506(a)(2).

ment value" means the price that a retail merchant would charge for property in like condition.[112] In cases involving Chapter 11 debtors, Chapter 12 debtors, or Chapter 7 debtors other than individuals, valuation would continue to follow the case-by-case, context-driven approach suggested in Section 506(a)(1).

[b] Is the Collateral Necessary for Debtor's Reorganization?

If the court's valuation reflects that the debtor has no equity in the collateral, the court must grant relief from the stay unless the debtor can prove that the collateral is "necessary for an effective reorganization."[113] To carry the burden of persuasion on this point,[114] the debtor must prove two things. First, the debtor must prove that the particular item of collateral is "necessary" to the debtor's reorganization effort. The court must consider the particular asset's necessity in light of the kind of debtor involved and the kind of reorganization the debtor contemplates.[115] For example, assume that Waters' Edge, Inc., sells clothing in its own stores and by mail order and that it is attempting to reorganize in Chapter 11. If Waters' Edge contemplates a reorganization plan whereby it will continue to sell its merchandise in its own retail stores, a court would consider the debtor's trade fixtures (clothing racks, display shelving, counters, cash registers, etc.) to be "necessary" to the debtor's contemplated reorganization. If Waters' Edge plans to close its retail stores and sell only by mail order, however, the court would be more likely to consider the trade fixtures unnecessary to the debtor's reorganization.

Second, the debtor must prove that an "effective reorganization" is possible. As the Supreme Court noted in the *Timbers* decision, this requirement means that "there must be a 'reasonable possibility of a successful reorganization within a reasonable time.'"[116] If the debtor cannot prove that it is likely to reorganize successfully or within a reasonable period of time, the court should lift the stay; further reorganization efforts by the debtor under such circumstances will waste estate resources that could otherwise go to satisfy the claims of creditors. As a practical matter, the debtor's burden of proof on this point becomes progressively harder to meet the longer the debtor remains in bankruptcy. As one court has explained:

> [I]n the initial stages of a Chapter 11 proceeding, the debtor should be granted significant leeway in attempting to establish that successful reorganization is a reasonable possibility. However, as the case progresses, so too does the debtor's

---

112. *Id.*

113. *Id.* § 362(d)(2). Obviously, Chapter 7 cases contemplate liquidation of the debtor's property rather than reorganization of the debtor's financial affairs. Accordingly, in a Chapter 7 case, the court should grant a motion for relief from the stay if the debtor has no equity in the property.

114. *Id.* (party opposing relief from stay has burden of proof on all issues other than issue of debtor's equity in property); *In re* Food Barn Stores, Inc., 159 B.R. 264 (Bankr. W.D. Mo. 1993).

115. *See In re* Fields, 127 B.R. 150, 154 (Bankr. W.D. Tex. 1991).

116. 484 U.S. 365, 376 (1988) (quoting the Fifth Circuit's *en banc* opinion in the *Timbers* case). Although the quoted statement was dicta in the *Timbers* case, bankruptcy courts in subsequent cases have followed this standard uniformly.

burden of proving that successful reorganization may be reasonably expected.... [T]he test should be viewed as a continuum with the scales tipping in favor of the debtor in the early stages and the burden of proof becoming greater in the later stages.[117]

[3] Procedural Issues and Burden of Proof

A secured party seeking relief from the stay must file a motion with the bankruptcy court requesting that the court lift the stay. In exceptional circumstances, the court can order relief from the stay without notice if the party seeking relief would be "irreparably damaged" by the delay occasioned by notice and a hearing.[118] Under Section 362(e)(1), the court must act on the motion within 30 days; if not, the moving party automatically receives the requested relief.[119] Section 362(e)(2) extends this period to 60 days if the debtor is an individual and the case is filed under Chapter 7, 11, or 13.[120] During this 30-day (or 60-day) period, the court typically conducts a preliminary hearing, after which it either (a) enters an order granting or denying the requested relief or (b) continues the stay temporarily, pending a later final hearing and determination of the motion.[121] If the court continues the stay pending a final hearing under Section 362(e)(1), it must conclude that final hearing within 30 days of the preliminary hearing unless the court extends the 30-day period with the consent of the parties or based upon "compelling circumstances."[122] For individual debtors under Section 362(e)(2), the court may only extend the 60-day period if all parties in interest agree or "for such *specific* time as the court finds is required for good cause," and the court must make specific factual findings justifying the extension.[123]

The moving party bears the burden of persuasion on the issue of the debtor's equity in the property.[124] Accordingly, a secured party seeking relief from the stay under Section 362(d)(2) bears the burden of persuasion as to the value of the collateral. The party opposing relief from the stay (typically the trustee/DIP) bears the burden of persuasion on all other issues, including the existence of adequate protection (or other "cause") and the debtor's prospects for reorganization within a reasonable time.[125]

117. *In re* Ashgrove Apts. of DeKalb Cty., Ltd., 121 B.R. 752, 756 (Bankr. S.D. Ohio 1990).
118. 11 U.S.C. § 362(f).
119. *Id.* § 362(e)(1).
120. *Id.* § 362(e)(2).
121. *Id.* § 362(e)(1).
122. *Id.*
123. *Id.* § 362(e)(2) (emphasis added).
124. *Id.* § 362(g)(1); *In re* Dandridge, 221 B.R. 741 (Bankr. W.D. Tenn. 1998); *In re* Food Barn Stores, Inc., 159 B.R. 264 (Bankr. W.D. Mo. 1993).
125. 11 U.S.C. § 362(g)(2); *In re* Food Barn Stores, Inc., 159 B.R. 264 (Bankr. W.D. Mo. 1993).

§ 16.04 The Trustee's Avoidance Powers

[A] Background

The Bankruptcy Code authorizes a series of *avoiding powers*: causes of action that allow the bankruptcy trustee (or the debtor in reorganization proceedings)[126] to avoid, or nullify, certain dispositions of property by the debtor or obligations incurred by the debtor prior to or during bankruptcy. The avoiding powers include:

- the "strong-arm" power to avoid unperfected security interests and other transfers made or obligations incurred by the debtor that could have been avoided by judgment lien creditors (or bona fide purchasers in the case of land) under state law;[127]

- the power to avoid transfers made or obligations incurred by the debtor that could have been avoided by an actual unsecured creditor under applicable non-bankruptcy law;[128]

- the power to avoid certain statutory liens against the debtor's property;[129]

- the power to avoid preferential transfers that occurred within 90 days prior to bankruptcy (or within one year, if the preferred creditor was an "insider");[130]

- the power to avoid fraudulent transfers made or obligations incurred within two years prior to bankruptcy;[131]

---

126. In a Chapter 11 or Chapter 12 case, the debtor in possession receives the powers of a trustee, including the avoiding powers. 11 U.S.C. §§ 1107(a), 1203. The Code does not expressly delegate the avoiding powers to a Chapter 13 debtor. *Id.* § 1303. The legislative history, indicates that "[Section 1303] does not imply that the debtor does not also possess other powers concurrently with the trustee," 124 Cong. Rec. 32,409 (floor statement of Rep. Edwards), and a number of courts have concluded that a Chapter 13 debtor can exercise the avoiding powers. *See, e.g., In re* Fitzgerald, 237 B.R. 252 (Bankr. D. Conn. 1999); *In re* Hernandez, 150 B.R. 29 (Bankr. S.D. Tex. 1993); *In re* Pinkstaff, 121 B.R. 596 (Bankr. D. Or. 1990); *In re* Robinson, 80 B.R. 455 (Bankr. N.D. Ill. 1987). The trend in recent decisions, however, suggests growing doubt that a Chapter 13 debtor can exercise the avoiding powers. *See, e.g., In re* Hansen, 332 B.R. 8 (10th Cir. Bankr. 2005); *In re* Stangel, 219 F.3d 498 (5th Cir. 2000); *In re* Merrifield, 214 B.R. 362 (8th Cir. Bankr. 1997); *In re* Salaymeh, 361 B.R. 822, 826 (Bankr. S.D. Tex. 2007); *In re* Richardson, 311 B.R. 302 (Bankr. S.D. Fla. 2004); *In re* Montoya, 285 B.R. 490 (Bankr. D.N.M. 2002); *In re* Miller, 251 B.R. 770 (Bankr. D. Mass. 2000).

127. 11 U.S.C. § 544(a).

128. *Id.* § 544(b)(1). As described below, this section permits the pursuit of fraudulent-transfer actions under state law, which typically have a longer lookback period than the bankruptcy provision authorizing avoidance of fraudulent transfers. *See, e.g.,* Picard v. Bernard L. Madoff Inv. Sec. LLC (*In re* Sec. Inv. Prot. Corp.), 650 B.R. 524, 547 (Bankr. S.D.N.Y. 2023) (applying New York law granting a look-back period of six years or two years from the time the fraud was discovered); § 16.04[F], *infra*.

129. 11 U.S.C. § 545.

130. *Id.* § 547.

131. *Id.* § 548.

- the power to avoid unauthorized post-petition transfers of property of the estate;[132] and

- the power to avoid certain rights of set-off against the debtor.[133]

The trustee's avoiding powers generally enable the trustee to preserve the estate by ameliorating the harm caused by actions of creditors or the debtor just prior to or in anticipation of bankruptcy. They further empower the trustee to police opportunistic behavior by creditors prior to or in anticipation of bankruptcy in the interest of ensuring equitable treatment. The following sections discuss the avoiding powers individually, describing both the scope and the limitations of each.

[B] Strong-Arm Power—11 U.S.C. § 544(a)

[1] The Trustee as Hypothetical Lien Creditor versus the Unperfected Secured Party

Section 544(a)(1) provides that the trustee can avoid any transfer made or obligation incurred by the debtor that a judgment lien creditor could have avoided under nonbankruptcy law as of the date of the bankruptcy petition.[134] This "strong-arm"

---

132. *Id.* § 549(a). The purpose of Section 549 is the preservation of the estate. Once the debtor is in bankruptcy, estate property can be transferred only as authorized by the express terms of the Bankruptcy Code or by the order of the bankruptcy court. The trustee's power to avoid unauthorized post-petition transfers of estate property is subject to certain exceptions (listed in §§ 549(b) and (c)) that are beyond the scope of this book.

133. Generally speaking, a creditor can offset a mutual debt it owes to the debtor if each party's debt arose prior to the petition date and the creditor would have a right of set-off under nonbankruptcy law (such as a bank's right to exercise a set-off against the debtor's funds on deposit with the bank). The trustee can prevent a creditor from exercising its set-off right, however, to the extent any of the following is true: (1) the creditor holds a disallowed claim; (2) the creditor acquired its claim from a third party after the petition date; (3) the creditor acquired its claim from a third party during the 90 days prior to bankruptcy and while the debtor was insolvent; or (4) the creditor incurred its debt during the 90 days prior to bankruptcy, while the debtor was insolvent, for the purpose of acquiring a right to set-off. 11 U.S.C. § 553(a). For example, if Bank had accepted $15,000 of deposits by Debtor during the week prior to Debtor's bankruptcy, while Debtor was insolvent, Bank could not use those deposits to offset Debtor's $15,000 unsecured debt to Bank. *In re* United Scis. of Am., Inc., 893 F.2d 720 (5th Cir. 1990). In addition, the trustee can set aside any set-off that a creditor exercised during the 90 days prior to bankruptcy to the extent that the set-off had the effect of improving the creditor's position. 11 U.S.C. § 553(b).

134. 11 U.S.C. § 544(a)(1). In addition to granting the trustee the status of hypothetical judgment lien creditor, Section 544(a) grants the trustee the status of two other hypothetical persons. Section 544(a)(2) endows the trustee with the powers of a hypothetical creditor that obtained an execution upon the debtor that was returned unsatisfied. Section 544(a)(2) only has significance in those states where an unsatisfied execution confers special rights of avoidance on the execution creditor, and thus this provision is rarely used. Section 544(a)(3) bestows on the trustee the status of a hypothetical bona fide purchaser of the debtor's land (other than fixtures). Section 544(a)(3) would thus permit the trustee to avoid an unrecorded mortgage against the debtor's land. Giving the trustee the status of a bona fide purchaser is necessary to achieve this result because, under most state recording statutes, unrecorded mortgages are effective against judgment lien creditors; thus, the trustee could not avoid an unrecorded mortgage under Section 544(a)(1). Because Section 544(a)(2) is rarely used and Sec-

power primarily allows the trustee to avoid security interests that are unperfected as of the petition date.[135]

The trustee can avoid these interests through a two-step process that implicates legal provisions in Article 9 and the Bankruptcy Code. For example, suppose Bank obtains

---

tion 544(a)(3) deals with land, the text focuses exclusively on Section 544(a)(1) and the trustee as a hypothetical judgment lien creditor.

Because fixtures may be perfected under both Article 9 and real estate law, it is more difficult for the trustee to use strong-arm powers against an interest in fixtures. For example, consider the transaction in *In re Gregory*, 316 B.R. 82 (Bankr. W.D. Mich. 2004). A Chapter 7 debtor had granted a mortgage on its land that also covered "all fixtures now or hereafter a part of the property." A manufactured home installed on the land constituted a fixture under Michigan law. The mortgage was properly recorded in the county land records, but the mortgage lender did not have its encumbrance noted on the manufactured home's certificate of title. After the debtor's Chapter 7 petition, the trustee raised a strong-arm challenge to the mortgagee's lien on the manufactured home. The trustee argued that because the mortgagee failed to perfect its interest in the home by compliance with the requirements of a certificate-of-title act, the trustee could avoid the mortgagee's "unperfected" lien on the manufactured home under Section 544(a)(1). The court rejected this argument, noting that the mortgage lender did not take an Article 9 security interest in fixtures but instead took a valid mortgage lien (which attached to the manufactured home because the home was a fixture) and properly perfected that mortgage lien by recording the mortgage on the land records.

135. If a secured party perfected its security interest by filing a financing statement that is still effective on the petition date, the trustee cannot avoid the secured party's interest using the strong-arm clause even if the financing statement subsequently lapses during the bankruptcy case. Under U.C.C. § 9-515(c), the lapse of a financing statement causes the security interest to become unperfected and, furthermore, is deemed never to have been perfected against a "purchaser of the collateral for value." The trustee is not considered a purchaser of the collateral but instead has the status of a lien creditor. Although the lapse in the financing statement makes the security interest unperfected against future lien creditors, the trustee cannot retroactively invalidate the secured party's perfection on the petition date under the strong-arm clause and Section 9-515(c).

At least one court has held that lapse does not alter a creditor's senior position over junior creditors if the debtor is in bankruptcy, because liens are fixed as of the petition date. *See In re* Essex Const., LLC, 591 B.R. 630, 632 (Bankr. D. Md. 2018). This opinion seems clearly wrong. As observed by the court, federal bankruptcy law recognizes property interests under state law "[u]nless some federal interest requires a different result[.]" *Id.* at 634 (quoting Butner v. United States, 440 U.S. 48, 55 (1979)). In *Essex*, it was stipulated that the lapse of the senior creditor's financing statement would have rendered it subordinate to the junior creditor under state law. *Id.* Creditors can avoid lapse by filing a continuation statement, even in bankruptcy proceedings. *See* 11 U.S.C. § 362(b)(3) (the automatic stay does not apply to the filing of a continuation statement). Accordingly, there is no need to "freeze" the position of secured creditors during the administration of a bankruptcy case. *See In re* 800 Bourbon St., LLC, 541 B.R. 616, 626 (Bankr. E.D. La. 2015).

Courts have found that lapse of temporary perfection after the bankruptcy petition can render a secured creditor unperfected and vulnerable to avoidance of its security interest under the strong-arm clause. For example, suppose Secured Party holds an automatically perfected PMSI in Debtor's television (which constitutes consumer goods) and that, five days prior to the petition date, Debtor exchanges the television for a piece of equipment used in Debtor's business. On the petition date, Secured Party's proceeds interest in the equipment is temporarily perfected under U.C.C. § 9-315(c), but that perfection will lapse on the 21st day following the exchange unless Secured Party takes sufficient steps to perfect its interest in the equipment as proceeds under U.C.C. § 9-315(d). If Secured Party fails to file a financing statement or otherwise perfect its interest in the equipment within that period, its perfection will lapse and its interest in the equipment may be avoided. *See, e.g., In re* Reliance Equities, Inc., 966 F.2d 1338 (10th Cir. 1992); *In re* Schwinn Cycling and Fitness, Inc., 313 B.R. 473 (D. Colo. 2004).

a security interest in Debtor's inventory (worth $100,000) to secure a debt of $100,000, but Bank fails to file a financing statement covering the inventory. If Debtor files for bankruptcy, Section 544(a)(1) arms the trustee with all of the rights and powers of a judgment lien creditor as of the petition date (Step 1), thereby allowing the trustee to assert any rights that such a creditor could have asserted under nonbankruptcy law. In turn, U.C.C. § 9-317(a) provides that a lien creditor takes priority over an unperfected security interest. Therefore, the trustee/DIP can assert its status as a lien creditor under state law to avoid Bank's unperfected security interest (Step 2). The consequences of this avoidance are twofold. First, the trustee can liquidate the inventory and use the proceeds to pay administrative expenses and unsecured creditors rather than having to abandon the inventory to Bank or distribute the sale proceeds to Bank in reduction of Bank's claim against Debtor. Second, while Debtor's underlying obligation to Bank remains enforceable, Bank's claim is treated as unsecured, significantly reducing Bank's recovery on its claim.

Note that Section 544(a)(1) clothes the trustee with the status of a judgment lien creditor *even if no such creditor actually existed on the petition date*. The trustee has the status of the "hypothetical lien creditor" regardless of whether any of the debtor's actual creditors had acquired judgment liens prior to bankruptcy. To illustrate, suppose that in the above hypothetical none of Debtor's general creditors had reduced their claims to judgment and levied upon Debtor's assets prior to bankruptcy. Outside of bankruptcy, Bank's unperfected security interest would still have been effective against Debtor's other creditors, and Bank would have recovered its claim in full.[136] Debtor's bankruptcy filing, however, permits the trustee to assert the status of a lien creditor, thereby enabling the trustee to avoid Bank's unperfected security interest.[137] In this way, the bankruptcy trustee/DIP may police "secret liens" even though such unperfected liens are still enforceable against general creditors under nonbankruptcy law.[138]

Note that Section 544(a) allows the trustee/DIP to exercise the strong-arm power to avoid an unperfected security interest without regard to any knowledge that the trustee, the debtor, or any creditor might have about that security interest.[139] For example, suppose Bank holds an unrecorded mortgage on Debtor's land, but the trustee knows of the Bank's mortgage. The trustee's knowledge of Bank's unrecorded interest

---

136. U.C.C. § 9-201(a).

137. *Id.* § 9-317(a)(2); *In re* Airadigm Communications, Inc., 519 F.3d 640 (7th Cir. 2008); *In re* Merritt Dredging Co., Inc., 839 F.2d 203 (4th Cir. 1988); *In re* Kors, Inc., 819 F.2d 19 (2d Cir. 1987); *In re* Pasteurized Eggs Corp., 296 B.R. 283 (D.N.H. 2003); *In re* Szwyd, 394 B.R. 230 (Bankr. D. Mass. 2008); *In re* Hurst, 308 B.R. 298 (Bankr. S.D. Ohio 2004); *In re* Morgan, 291 B.R. 795 (Bankr. E.D. Tenn. 2003); *In re* Advance Insulation & Supply, Inc., 176 B.R. 390 (Bankr. D. Md. 1994), *aff'd*, 176 B.R. 401 (D. Md. 1995). *But see In re* Lynum, 246 B.R. 537 (Bankr. E.D. Ky. 2000) (while bankruptcy trustee could avoid unperfected security interest, trustee could not avoid properly perfected security interest held by another creditor, regardless of when the respective interests were obtained).

138. U.C.C. § 9-201(a).

139. *In re* Kitchin Equip. Co., 960 F.2d 1242 (4th Cir. 1992); McEvoy v. Ron Watkins, Inc., 105 B.R. 362 (N.D. Tex. 1987); *In re* Chama, Inc., 265 B.R. 662 (Bankr. D. Del. 2000); *In re* Williams, 124 B.R. 311 (Bankr. C.D. Cal. 1991).

does *not* deprive it of the ability to assert its strong-arm powers under Section 544(a). Section 544(a) makes the trustee's knowledge irrelevant; the strong-arm power bestows the status of a lien creditor without knowledge of Bank's security interest *even if no such creditor actually existed as of the petition date.* Because such a bona fide purchaser of the land would have prevailed over Bank's unrecorded mortgage, the trustee/DIP can avoid Bank's mortgage despite its actual knowledge.

[2] Relation-Back Priority—11 U.S.C. § 546(b)

Recall that state law grants some creditors a window of time in which to perfect a security interest while retaining priority based on relation-back rules. For example, suppose Debtor purchases a drill press from Seller, which takes a purchase-money security interest (PMSI) in the press. Seller has the benefit of a 20-day grace period in which to perfect its PMSI and still prevail against intervening lien creditors.[140] Now suppose that Debtor files a bankruptcy petition but that Seller subsequently files a financing statement in the appropriate filing office within the 20-day window.

If one looked solely at the language of Section 544(a)(1), Trustee in Debtor's bankruptcy would be able to avoid Seller's security interest on the ground that Seller had not perfected that interest prior to Debtor's bankruptcy filing. Outside of bankruptcy, however, Seller's PMSI would have taken priority over the claim of an intervening lien creditor because Seller perfected its PMSI by filing within the grace period specified in U.C.C. § 9-317(e). Given the rationale of the strong-arm clause, Trustee logically should stand in the same position as a lien creditor would have stood under nonbankruptcy law. To accomplish this result, Congress limited the trustee's strong-arm power in Section 546(b), thereby making the power subject to any provisions of nonbankruptcy law (such as Article 9's grace period for perfecting PMSIs) that permit relation-back priority over intervening third parties.[141] Because Seller perfected its PMSI within the grace period specified in Article 9, Trustee cannot avoid Seller's PMSI under the strong-arm clause.

Full understanding of this example requires additional consideration of Section 362 and the effect of the automatic stay. As discussed previously,[142] the filing of the bankruptcy petition operates to stay "any act to … perfect … any lien against property of the estate."[143] On its face, the stay would seem to prevent Seller's post-petition financing statement from having any legal effect to perfect Seller's PMSI. But Section 362(b)(3) provides an exception in this particular circumstance, allowing a creditor to undertake "any act to perfect … an interest in property to the extent that the trustee's

---

140. U.C.C. § 9-317(e). *See also* § 10.04, *supra.*

141. 11 U.S.C. § 546(b)(1)(A) (the avoiding powers are subject to "any generally applicable law that permits perfection of an interest in property to be effective against an entity that acquires rights in such property before the date of perfection"). Note that Section 546(b) does not itself authorize relation-back priority for any secured party but only recognizes and incorporates provisions of nonbankruptcy law that provide for relation-back priority over third parties that claim intervening interests.

142. *See* § 16.03[A], *supra.*

143. 11 U.S.C. § 362(a)(4).

rights and powers are subject to perfection under section 546(b)....."[144] This exception permits a secured party in Seller's position to file its financing statement without violating the automatic stay so long as the secured party acts to perfect its interest within the applicable state-law grace period.[145] Further, the exception applies only to permit the secured party's *perfection* of the interest; the stay remains effective to prevent any action to *enforce* the lien unless the court orders relief from the stay.

[C] Subrogation to State-Law Avoidance Powers of an Unsecured Creditor—11 U.S.C. § 544(b)(1)

Section 544(b)(1) authorizes the trustee to avoid "any transfer of an interest of the debtor in property or any obligation incurred by the debtor that is voidable under applicable law by a creditor holding an unsecured claim[.]"[146] This provision allows the trustee to assert any state-law avoidance claim that one of the debtor's *actual* unsecured creditors could have asserted. Unlike the strong-arm clause, Section 544(b)(1) does not endow the trustee with the status of a "hypothetical" creditor. To assert an avoidance claim under Section 544(b)(1), the trustee must identify an actual, honest-to-goodness unsecured creditor of the debtor that could have asserted the power to avoid the particular transfer under state law.[147] If the trustee can identify such a creditor, Section 544(b)(1) subrogates the trustee to the rights of that creditor and permits the trustee to assert this claim on behalf of the estate.[148]

Trustees/DIPs have asserted Section 544(b)(1) avoidance claims in two primary situations. The first involves transfers that are fraudulent under applicable state fraudulent-transfer law; these transfers are treated in greater detail in conjunction with the discussion of Section 548 of the Bankruptcy Code.[149] The second involves bulk-sale transfers that do not comply with applicable state law governing bulk sales. In a jurisdiction in which U.C.C. Article 6 still governs bulk sales,[150] Section 544(b)(1) allows the trustee to set aside a bulk sale under Article 6 if it can identify a particular creditor that did not receive notice of the sale as required by that article.[151]

---

144. *Id.* § 362(b)(3).

145. *In re* Aulicino, 400 B.R. 175 (Bankr. E.D. Pa. 2008); Ivester v. Miller, 398 B.R. 408 (Bankr. M.D.N.C. 2008); *In re* Cont'l Country Club, Inc., 64 B.R. 177 (Bankr. M.D. Fla. 1986).

146. 11 U.S.C. § 544(b)(1).

147. *See, e.g., In re* Wingspread Corp., 178 B.R. 938, 945 (Bankr. S.D.N.Y. 1995).

148. The trustee may avoid the transfer under Section 544(b)(1) in its entirety, regardless of the size of the actual unsecured creditor's claim. *In re* Coleman, 426 F.3d 719 (4th Cir. 2005); *In re* Acequia, Inc., 34 F.3d 800 (9th Cir. 1994); *In re* Agric. Res. & Tech. Group, Inc., 916 F.2d 528 (9th Cir. 1990); *In re* DLC, Ltd., 295 B.R. 593 (8th Cir. Bankr. 2003).

149. *See* § 16.04[F][4], *infra*.

150. The Code's sponsors have recommended repeal of Article 6. Nevertheless, the article remains in effect in a few states.

151. *In re* Villa Roel, Inc., 57 B.R. 835 (Bankr. D.D.C. 1985).

[D] Power to Avoid Statutory Liens

Statutory liens are liens that arise as a matter of nonbankruptcy law "solely by force of a statute on specified circumstances or conditions."[152] Statutory liens often reflect a legislative judgment that particular types of creditors (such as mechanics who service automobiles) deserve special protection from the risk of nonpayment. Generally speaking, bankruptcy law respects statutory liens arising under nonbankruptcy law, and the trustee/DIP cannot avoid statutory liens that validly arose prior to the petition date.

Section 545, however, allows the trustee/DIP to avoid a statutory lien against an asset of the debtor in three limited circumstances. First, Section 545(1) permits the trustee/DIP to avoid a statutory lien against any asset if that lien took effect only because the debtor became insolvent or filed for bankruptcy.[153] This provision is necessary to preserve the efficacy of federal bankruptcy law; otherwise, states could establish statutory "insolvency" liens that would circumvent the Bankruptcy Code's priority scheme for distribution to creditors. Second, Section 545(2) permits the trustee/DIP to avoid a statutory lien against any asset if the lien could not have been enforced against a bona fide purchaser of the asset outside of bankruptcy.[154] For example, Section 545(2) allows the trustee to avoid a federal tax lien against a debtor's assets if the IRS has not filed a notice of tax lien as of the petition date.[155] This provision allows the trustee/DIP to avoid secret statutory liens to the same extent as they would be avoidable by an innocent purchaser under nonbankruptcy law. Finally, Sections 545(3) and 545(4) permit the trustee/DIP to avoid any common-law or statutory landlord's lien for unpaid rent.[156] A pertinent example involves a landlord's statutory lien on farm products for unpaid rent on leased crop land. This lien is an agricultural lien governed by Article 9 once it arises,[157] but it is not consensual in nature and accordingly is subject to avoidance under Sections 545(3) and 545(4).[158]

[E] Power to Avoid Preferential Transfers— 11 U.S.C. § 547

[1] Background

Suppose Debtor has two creditors, A and B, to which Debtor owes $100 each. Suppose further that Debtor has only $100 in assets and uses those assets to make full payment to A before declaring bankruptcy. A receives payment in full, B receives

---

152. 11 U.S.C. § 101(53). *See* Chapter 13, *supra.*

153. 11 U.S.C. § 545(1).

154. *Id.* § 545(2).

155. *In re* J.B. Winchells, Inc., 106 B.R. 384 (Bankr. E.D. Pa. 1989).

156. 11 U.S.C. § 545(3), (4). Note that Section 545 does not authorize the trustee to avoid a lien for rent for which the lienor contractually bargained; such a lien is a security interest, not a statutory lien. Dallas v. S.A.G., Inc., 836 F.2d 1307 (11th Cir. 1988).

157. Agricultural liens are discussed in § 13.02, *supra.*

158. *See, e.g., In re* Harrell, 55 B.R. 203 (Bankr. E.D.N.C. 1985).

nothing. One might say that Debtor has "preferred" A to B, or that A has received a "preferential" payment. Outside of bankruptcy, commercial law generally does not care about preferential transfers and leaves creditors like A and B to their own collection efforts. If Debtor pays A in full (whether voluntarily or in response to A's demands) and pays B nothing, that is B's problem; B could have prevented this result by pursuing its remedies more promptly or by being more insistent in its collection efforts.

Bankruptcy law does care about such transfers, however, because one of the goals of bankruptcy is to provide a collective debt-resolution process that distributes Debtor's assets in a way that treats similarly situated creditors alike. In the above example, before the payment, A and B were similarly situated general creditors; in a Chapter 7 liquidation, each creditor would have received $50 on its claim. By choosing to pay A in full and B nothing, Debtor circumvents bankruptcy's distributive scheme to the detriment of B.

Transfers can have preferential effect regardless of the debtor's motive or the impetus for the transfer. For example, suppose the payment of $100 to A had occurred involuntarily as a result of an execution sale of Debtor's property. The payment still has precisely the same effect as a voluntary payment by Debtor; if the execution had never occurred, both A and B would have received $50 in a Chapter 7 liquidation. The intent of either the transferring debtor or the receiving creditor is irrelevant in a preferential transfer action.

[2] Proving the Elements of a Preference

The trustee can avoid any transfer of an interest in the debtor's property that meets all of the following characteristics specified in Section 547(b):

- *The transfer must have been made to a creditor or must have benefitted a creditor.*[159] The word "benefit" refers to a pecuniary advantage, such as the payment of a claim or the grant of a security interest, and generally excludes an intangible improvement of position.[160] If the transfer does not benefit a creditor (e.g., the debtor makes a gift of valuable property to a friend), preference law does not apply to that transfer.[161]

- *The transfer must have been made on account of an antecedent debt, that is, a liability that the debtor incurred before the debtor made the transfer.*[162] Preference law focuses only upon those transfers that enable a creditor to collect a preexisting debt or render a preexisting debt more secure. Thus, if Debtor grants Bank a security interest in a car to secure a simultaneous $2,000 loan to Debtor by

---

159. 11 U.S.C. § 547(b)(1).

160. *See, e.g., In re* Erin Food Servs., Inc., 980 F.2d 792, 800–01 (1st Cir. 1992).

161. In some cases, gift transfers by the debtor prior to bankruptcy may be avoidable as fraudulent transfers under Section 548 of the Bankruptcy Code. *See* § 16.04[F][2], *infra.*

162. 11 U.S.C. § 547(b)(2).

Bank,[163] there is no preference. In contrast, if Debtor grants Bank a security interest in a car to secure an otherwise unsecured $2,000 loan made by Bank to Debtor two months earlier, Debtor has transferred an interest in its property on account of an antecedent debt.

- *The debtor must have been insolvent when the transfer took place.*[164] Preference law is not concerned with avoiding transfers that occurred while the debtor was solvent. If a debtor is solvent, it can repay all of its obligations, and thus any transfer by the debtor could not have had the effect of preferring the recipient to the detriment of other creditors. Section 547(f) provides that in any action to avoid a preferential transfer, the debtor is presumed to have been insolvent during the 90 days prior to the filing of the bankruptcy petition.[165] As a consequence of this presumption, the recipient of the allegedly preferential transfer bears the burden of coming forward with evidence to demonstrate that the debtor was solvent at the time of the transfer.

- *The transfer must have taken place within 90 days prior to the filing of the bankruptcy petition (or within one year prior to the petition in the case of a transfer to an "insider").*[166] In addition to the goal of promoting equality among creditors, another goal of preference law is to discourage creditors from "opting out" of the collective bankruptcy process by trying to collect or secure their pre-bankruptcy claims during the debtor's "slide into bankruptcy."[167] Rather than adopting a subjective standard that would evaluate the creditor's intent in receiving a preference, Congress opted for a bright-line preference period. Transfers that occur within the 90 days before a filing are conclusively suspect as potential preferences even if the creditor had no idea of the debtor's financial difficulties. In contrast, the trustee cannot reach transfers that occurred more than 90 days prior

---

163. As a practical matter, a truly simultaneous transfer is unlikely. Even when Buyer pays cash to Seller to purchase goods over the counter, Buyer's payment typically occurs at least a few seconds after Buyer's obligation to pay for the goods arises. Technically speaking, even a delay of one second between the arising of Buyer's obligation and Buyer's transfer would mean that the transfer occurred on account of an antecedent debt, a result that would stretch the trustee's preference-avoiding power well past the bounds of reason. As a practical matter, courts have not interpreted the term "antecedent" so restrictively as to set aside payments made in cash sales. Furthermore, as discussed § 16.04[E][4][a], *infra*, Section 547(c)(1) provides an exception that prevents the trustee from recovering transfers such as cash sales that involve "substantially contemporaneous" exchanges for new value. Thus, in many cases, Section 547(c)(1) would mitigate the effect of a court's decision to adopt an overly technical interpretation of Section 547(b)(2).

164. 11 U.S.C. § 547(b)(3). The Bankruptcy Code applies a "balance sheet" test for insolvency; the debtor is "insolvent" if the sum of its debts exceeds the value of its assets. *Id.* § 101(32).

165. *Id.* § 547(f). This presumption is motivated primarily by efficiency. In most bankruptcy cases, the debtor will have been insolvent for some time prior to filing its bankruptcy petition, and thus it would serve no real purpose to force the trustee to spend the time and resources necessary to reconstruct the debtor's records to prove that the debtor was insolvent at the time of the allegedly preferential transfer.

166. *Id.* § 547(b)(4).

167. H.R. Rep. No. 595, 95th Cong., 1st Sess. 177–78 (1977).

to bankruptcy even if the benefitted creditor fully expected the debtor to seek bankruptcy protection in the near future. Note that the Code expands the preference period to one year if the transferee is an "insider."[168] Because "insiders" have a close relationship with the debtor, they could possess inside information about the debtor's financial circumstances and could possibly exercise control over the debtor's financial decisions (such as when to seek bankruptcy protection). To prevent insiders from using this information or control to manipulate the timing of preferential transfers,[169] the Bankruptcy Code expands the preference period to one year for transfers that benefit insiders.

- *Finally, the transfer must have actually improved the creditor's position.*[170] Section 547(b) only reaches those transfers that enabled the recipient to recover more than the recipient would have recovered through liquidation alone. To apply Section 547(b), the court must determine what amount the creditor would have received in a Chapter 7 liquidation case *if the alleged preferential transfer had not been made.* If the creditor actually received more than that "hypothetical liquidation" amount, then the transfer had the effect of improving the creditor's position.

The following four variations on a common hypothetical demonstrate the proper application of section 547(b):

Hypothetical 1. Debtor makes full repayment of a $10,000 unsecured loan from Bank and files its bankruptcy petition 20 days later. If Debtor had not made the repayment, Bank would have received only a partial distribution on its claim in a Chapter 7 liquidation.[171] By receiving payment in full prior to bankruptcy, Bank has improved its position to the detriment of Debtor's other general creditors and may be liable in a preference avoidance action.

---

168. 11 U.S.C. § 101(31) provides a list of characteristics that make a transferee an "insider." An insider can be a relative, an officer or director of a corporation, or a partner of a partnership—in other words, someone who has a sufficiently close relationship with the debtor that they can be presumed to be in a position to possess information about the debtor's financial condition, or to possess control over the debtor's financial decisionmaking. Note, however, that if the trustee attempts to recover an allegedly preferential transfer from an insider and that transfer occurred more than 90 days prior to the petition date, the trustee is *not* entitled to the presumption that the debtor was insolvent at the time of the transfer. The presumption of insolvency in Section 547(f) is strictly limited to the 90 days immediately prior to the petition date.

169. For example, suppose X is president and sole shareholder of Debtor, and that X had loaned $10,000 to Debtor. As an insider, X is in a position to cause Debtor to repay its debt to X and also cause Debtor not to file bankruptcy until 91 days later, which is after the general preference period would have passed.

170. 11 U.S.C. § 547(b)(5).

171. This statement assumes that Debtor is insolvent at the time of the bankruptcy petition. A creditor targeted by a preference action may offer proof of the Debtor's solvency at the time of the transfer as a defense. *In re* Keplinger, 284 B.R. 344 (N.D.N.Y. 2002); *In re* Milwaukee Cheese Wis., Inc., 164 B.R. 297 (Bankr. E.D. Wis. 1993); *In re* Lease-A-Fleet, Inc., 141 B.R. 853 (Bankr. E.D. Pa. 1992).

Hypothetical 2. Debtor makes full repayment of a $10,000 loan secured by Debtor's inventory, which has a value of $30,000. Because Bank held a fully secured claim, Bank would have received full payment on its claim in a Chapter 7 liquidation case; the repayment did not improve Bank's position. For this reason, courts have held that payment to a fully secured creditor is not an avoidable preference.[172]

Hypothetical 3. Debtor makes full repayment of a $10,000 loan secured by Debtor's inventory, which has a value of $5,000. At the time it received payment, Bank held an undersecured claim. Had Bank not received the payment and had Debtor filed a Chapter 7 petition, Section 506(a)(1) would have bifurcated Bank's claim into a secured claim of $5,000 and an unsecured claim of $5,000. In that hypothetical Chapter 7 liquidation, Bank would have received full payment of its secured claim but less than full payment on its unsecured claim. Therefore, Debtor's payment to Bank improved its position and can be avoided as a preference.[173]

Hypothetical 4. Debtor borrows $10,000 on an unsecured basis from Bank. Debtor subsequently experiences financial difficulties and is rendered insolvent. Debtor then grants Bank a security interest on the $10,000 loan. Debtor files for bankruptcy within 90 days of granting the security interest. Because the security interest made Bank better off than it would have been as an unsecured creditor in liquidation proceedings, the security interest would be avoidable as a preference.[174]

[3] Determining When the Transfer Occurred

A transfer cannot constitute a preference unless it occurred on account of an antecedent debt and within the applicable preference period. Given these standards, the trustee must establish the date on which a transfer took place to establish that the transfer satisfies Section 547(b). Section 547(e) deems any allegedly preferential payment to have been made when the payment legally took effect between the parties

---

172. *In re* EDC, Inc., 930 F.2d 1275 (7th Cir. 1991); Braniff Airways, Inc. v. Exxon Co., U.S.A., 814 F.2d 1030 (5th Cir. 1987); *In re* Pineview Care Ctr., Inc., 142 B.R. 677 (Bankr. D.N.J. 1992), *aff'd*, 152 B.R. 703 (D.N.J. 1993). If the bankruptcy trustee is able to avoid Bank's security interest, then Bank will be treated as an unsecured creditor, and the $10,000 payment will have improved Bank's position. *In re* Adams, 102 B.R. 271 (Bankr. M.D. Ga. 1989).

173. *In re* Smith's Home Furnishings, Inc., 265 F.3d 959 (9th Cir. 2001); *In re* Air Conditioning, Inc., of Stuart, 845 F.2d 293 (11th Cir. 1988); *In re* Telesphere Comms., Inc., 229 B.R. 173 (Bankr. N.D. Ill. 1999); *see also* 4 COLLIER ON BANKRUPTCY ¶ 547.08, at 547–47 to 547–48 ("[p]ayments to a partially secured creditor from property not covered by its lien ... have a preferential effect, because in a chapter 7 liquidation, that creditor would receive a distribution for its lien in addition to the payments already received").

174. The result is the same if the Bank were to obtain a nonconsensual lien during the preference period. *See, e.g., In re* Imagine Fulfillment Servs., LLC, 489 B.R. 136 (Bankr. C.D. Cal. 2013).

under nonbankruptcy law.[175] Thus, a $10,000 payment to Bank by Debtor on December 4 would be deemed to have occurred on December 4 for purposes of Section 547(b).[176]

The granting of a security interest by the debtor to secure a previously unsecured debt can also constitute a preferential transfer. Section 547(e) provides an intricate timing rule that dates the security interest based upon when it was perfected. Section 547 deems a security interest to have been granted when it legally took effect between the parties under nonbankruptcy law (e.g., for a security interest in personal property, when that interest attached under U.C.C. §9-203), but only if the secured party perfected[177] that security interest at that time or within 30[178] days thereafter.[179] If the creditor perfects the security interest but delays in doing so for more than 30 days following attachment, the security interest will be deemed to have been granted on the date that the creditor actually perfected that interest.[180] If the creditor has not perfected its security interest by the later of the petition date or the end of the 30-day period

---

175. 11 U.S.C. §547(e)(2)(A).

176. One caveat is appropriate here. If a debtor makes a payment to a creditor using a check, the Supreme Court has held that a transfer under Section 547(b) does not occur when the debtor delivers the check to the creditor; rather, a transfer occurs only when the check is *actually paid* by the drawee bank. Barnhill v. Johnson, 503 U.S. 393 (1992).

177. A transfer of an interest in personal property or fixtures is perfected for purposes of preference law "when a creditor on a simple contract cannot acquire a judicial lien that is superior to the interest of the transferee." 11 U.S.C. §547(e)(1)(B). Under Article 9, of course, a lien creditor generally cannot acquire rights superior to the holder of a validly perfected Article 9 security interest. U.C.C. §9-317(a)(2). Thus, if a security interest was validly perfected under Article 9, it is perfected for purposes of section 547. *See, e.g., In re* North, 310 B.R. 152 (Bankr. D. Ariz. 2004) (secured party applied for certificate of title reflecting its interest more than 90 days prior to bankruptcy, but certificate was actually issued less than 90 days prior to bankruptcy; because filing of proper application was sufficient for perfection under state law, transfer of security interest did not occur within preference period).

178. 11 U.S.C. §547(e)(2)(A). A prior version of Section 547(e)(2)(A) provided only a ten-day period. This created substantial problems because the ten-day period did not match the 20-day grace period available to purchase-money secured parties under Article 9, nor the 30-day grace period available in some states to creditors taking a security interest in titled vehicles. *See, e.g.,* Fidelity Fin. Servs., Inc. v. Fink, 522 U.S. 211 (1998) (lender's security interest in automobile avoidable as preference where lender delayed in perfection for 21 days after security interest attached, even though applicable law allowed lender 30 days to perfect and obtain relation-back priority over intervening judicial liens). Section 547(e)(2)(A)'s expansion of the period to 30 days resolves these problems, as 30 days is equal to or longer than virtually all relation-back priority rules applicable under state law.

179. 11 U.S.C. §547(e)(2)(A). If the debtor files for bankruptcy before this period elapses, the secured party can still act to perfect its security interest for purposes of Section 547 without violating the automatic stay, as long as the secured party acts before the end of the applicable period. 11 U.S.C. §§362(b)(3), 547(e)(2)(A). Thus, if Debtor granted Bank a non-purchase-money security interest on June 1 and filed a bankruptcy petition on June 3, Bank could file its financing statement (and thereby perfect its security interest for purposes of Section 547) up to and including July 1 without violating the automatic stay. Caution: *This timing rule is relevant only for purposes of Section 547.* In the above example, Bank's security interest would still have been unperfected under Article 9 as of the petition date, and thus the trustee could avoid that security interest under the strong-arm power. *See* §16.04[B][1], *supra; In re* Planned Protective Servs., Inc., 130 B.R. 94 (Bankr. C.D. Cal. 1991).

180. 11 U.S.C. §547(e)(2)(B).

following attachment, the security interest will be deemed to have been granted on the date of the bankruptcy petition.[181]

The following example demonstrates Section 547(e)'s timing rule. Suppose Debtor borrows $20,000 from Bank on June 1 and simultaneously grants Bank a security interest in certain equipment to secure repayment of the debt. Debtor then files for bankruptcy on July 10. If Bank filed a proper financing statement in the correct office on or before July 1, the security interest will be deemed to have been granted on June 1, meaning that the creation of the security interest was not a transfer on account of an antecedent debt, and thus the trustee cannot avoid the security interest as a preference. But if Bank did not file its financing statement until July 5, the security interest will be deemed to have been granted on that date. Because the debt arose on June 1, the security interest will be considered a transfer on account of an antecedent debt for purposes of Section 547(b). If Bank never filed its financing statement or took possession of the collateral, the security interest will be deemed to have been granted on July 10 (the petition date) and thus will be a transfer on account of an antecedent debt.

The rationale for this timing provision lies in the fact that delayed perfection of a security interest creates an ostensible-ownership or "secret-lien" problem. As explained previously, this secret-lien problem can mislead the debtor's creditors or other third parties into believing that encumbered assets are not encumbered.[182] Further, because an unperfected security interest is not effective against lien creditors such as the trustee, one might characterize delayed perfection of a security interest prior to bankruptcy as a last-minute attempt by a creditor to improve its position in anticipation of bankruptcy.[183]

Section 547(e) provides another timing rule that applies primarily in cases of security interests covering after-acquired property. Suppose that on June 1, Debtor borrows $100,000 from Bank, which takes and properly perfects a security interest in Debtor's ten machines under a security agreement that also covers after-acquired equipment. Suppose further that Debtor files for bankruptcy on December 1, that Debtor acquired two additional machines on November 1, that the value of all 12 machines is $80,000, and that Debtor still owes Bank $100,000. The trustee cannot avoid Bank's security interest in the original ten machines as a preference. Because the security interest in those ten machines is deemed to have been granted on June 1 (when the security interest was perfected), two of the necessary elements of a preference are missing: the debtor did not create the security interest in the original ten machines on account of an antecedent debt, nor did the debtor create this interest within the 90-day avoidance period. Preference law, however, treats the security interest in the two after-acquired machines differently. Under Section 547(e)(3), the security interest in those

---

181. *Id.* § 547(e)(2)(C).

182. 1 David G. Epstein, Steve H. Nickles, & James J. White, Bankruptcy, § 6-11, at 542 (West Pract. ed. 1992).

183. *Id.*

two machines is deemed to have been granted on November 1, when Debtor acquired them.[184] As a result, the security interest in the two machines acquired on November 1 is an avoidable preference: there was a transfer of a security interest in Debtor's property (the two machines), to a creditor (Bank), on account of an antecedent debt (a transfer deemed to have occurred on November 1, on account of a debt that arose on June 1), within the 90 days prior to bankruptcy (30 days prior to the bankruptcy filing on December 1), and while Debtor was insolvent (recall that Debtor is presumed to have been insolvent during the 90 days prior to bankruptcy). Finally, the transfer made Bank better off by reducing Bank's unsecured claim. With the transfer, the Bank has a security interest in 12 machines (worth $80,000) to secure a $100,000 claim; without the transfer, the Bank would have had a security interest in only 10 machines (worth less than $80,000, assuming the two additional machines have some economic value) to secure a $100,000 claim.

Section 547(e)(3) obviously places the bankruptcy trustee in a better position than a lien creditor would occupy outside of bankruptcy under Article 9. Outside of bankruptcy, a lien creditor could not avoid a properly perfected security interest against after-acquired collateral.[185] But this provision makes sense in light of the objectives of preference law. In this example, Debtor took funds that would have been unencumbered property of the estate and used them to purchase goods that improved the position of a partially unsecured creditor just prior to bankruptcy. In substance, this action had the same effect as if Debtor had taken the same dollars and instead used them to pay an unsecured creditor, which would have been an obvious preference.

[4] Exceptions to the Trustee's Preference Avoidance Power

Section 547(b) casts a broad net designed to catch all transfers that have a preferential effect. Because Congress drafted it so broadly, Section 547(b) catches many legitimate transfers that Congress did not wish to deter. To protect these benign transfers from the trustee's preference avoiding powers, Congress provided a series of exceptions in Section 547(c). Insofar as they permit some types of preferential transfers to stand, these exceptions can serve to undermine the equal distribution goals motivating preference law.[186]

---

184. 11 U.S.C. § 547(e)(3) ("For purposes of this section, a transfer is not made until the debtor has acquired rights in the property transferred.").

185. *See* U.C.C. § 9-317(a)(2).

186. *See* Brook E. Gotberg, *Conflicting Preferences in Business Bankruptcy: The Need for Different Rules in Different Chapters*, 100 Iowa L. Rev. 51, 66 (2014).

[a] Substantially Contemporaneous Exchanges for New Value

Suppose that on June 1, Debtor purchases a machine from Seller, paying with a check. The following day, Seller presents the check for payment to the drawee bank, and the bank pays the check. Because payment by check is technically a credit transaction, the transfer of Debtor's funds to Seller does not occur until the drawee bank actually paid the check on June 2, meaning that a very technical read of the statute could find a preferential transfer, as the Seller received a payment on account of an antecedent debt (the debt incurred on June 1).[187] To prevent this result, Congress provided that the trustee cannot avoid a transfer that was "intended by the debtor and the creditor ... to be a contemporaneous exchange for new value given to the debtor" as long as the transfer was "in fact a substantially contemporaneous exchange."[188]

Although the legislative history of Section 547(c)(1) suggests that Congress was primarily concerned with the "payment by check" scenario, the language of the provision is not so limited. For example, suppose that while shopping in a rural area 45 miles from home, Debtor locates and decides to purchase a rare antique vase for $5,000. Seller is only willing to accept cash or check, so Debtor calls Bank (where Debtor is a favored customer) and asks Bank for a $5,000 loan to be immediately deposited into Debtor's account to cover Debtor's check to Seller. Bank agrees to make the loan so long as Debtor will grant Bank a security interest in Debtor's equipment; Bank and Debtor agree that Debtor will come to the Bank when Debtor returns later that day to sign the necessary documents to reflect Bank's security interest. Later that day, Debtor indeed signs a security agreement with Bank, and Bank properly perfects its security interest by filing. Even if Debtor files for bankruptcy within 90 days, Trustee cannot avoid Bank's security interest. Although Debtor's obligation to Bank arose before Bank's security interest attached (and therefore was an antecedent debt), the parties intended the security interest to be a contemporaneous exchange for new value (the $5,000 loan) given to Debtor by Bank, and the transfer was in fact *substantially* contemporaneous. Under the circumstances surrounding this transaction, the delay of a few hours does not justify allowing the trustee to recover a windfall at Bank's expense.[189]

---

187. Until the drawee bank pays the check, Seller has essentially extended credit to Debtor. Accordingly, there is a transfer of Debtor's property (payment of the check), to a creditor (Seller), on account of an antecedent debt (the check was paid on June 2 on account of a debt incurred on June 1), during the 90-day avoidance period (during which Debtor is presumed to have been insolvent), and the transfer enabled Seller to receive payment in full (better treatment than it would have received as an unsecured creditor in a Chapter 7 liquidation).

188. 11 U.S.C. § 547(c)(1).

189. Caselaw clearly establishes that contemporaneity is a question of fact that courts must determine on the merits of each case. Thus, establishing strict timetables is hazardous; nevertheless, courts generally have concluded that delays of one week or less have satisfied Section 547(c)(1)'s "substantially contemporaneous" requirement. Dean v. Davis, 242 U.S. 438 (1917) (mortgage executed to secure loan made one week earlier considered substantially contemporaneous); *In re* Quade, 108 B.R. 681 (Bankr. N.D. Iowa 1989) (substitution of collateral substantially contemporaneous even though substitution delayed by six days). *Compare In re* Holder, 892 F.2d 29 (4th Cir. 1989) (perfection of a

Note that Section 547(c)(1) requires that the parties must have intended that the transfer constitute a contemporaneous exchange for new value.[190] If this intent is not present at the time the debtor's obligation arises, the subsequent transfer does not qualify for the protection of Section 547(c)(1), no matter how small the delay.[191]

[b] "Ordinary-Course" Payments

A wide variety of pre-petition payments constitute preferences under the standard set forth in Section 547(b). For example, utility payments, payments on installment debt, and timely payments for inventory or equipment purchased on open account may all satisfy the definition of an avoidable preference. Congress felt that widespread avoidance of such routine payments would be too disruptive of daily commercial activity. Further, Congress worried that widespread avoidance of such routine payments could discourage a financially distressed debtor's primary creditors from extending further credit, thereby exacerbating the debtor's financial difficulties and perhaps even increasing the likelihood of the debtor's bankruptcy.[192]

To avoid such effects, Congress enacted Section 547(c)(2), which provides an exception for "ordinary course" payments. Section 547(c)(2) provides that the trustee cannot recover any transfer in payment of a debt incurred by the debtor in the ordinary course of business or financial affairs of the debtor and the transferee so long as *either* (A) the payment was made in the ordinary course of business or financial affairs of the debtor and the transferee, *or* (B) the payment was made according to ordinary business terms.[193]

---

security interest 19 days after attachment is not substantially contemporaneous); *In re* Lopez, 265 B.R. 570 (Bankr. N.D. Ohio 2001) (perfection of a security interest 45 days after attachment is not substantially contemporaneous); *In re* Petrewsky, 147 B.R. 27 (Bankr. S.D. Ohio 1992) (a transfer of security interest that occurred more than ten days before perfection is not substantially contemporaneous).

190. "New value" is defined to include money, money's worth in goods, services, or new credit, and the release of an otherwise unavoidable lien against the debtor's property. 11 U.S.C. § 547(a)(2); *In re* Robinson Bros. Drilling, Inc., 877 F.2d 32 (10th Cir. 1989) (even though satisfaction of debt was not new value, release of lien against debtor's assets was new value). "New value" does not include satisfaction of an antecedent unsecured debt. *In re* Chase & Sanborn Corp., 904 F.2d 588 (11th Cir. 1990) (such an argument would render Section 547 a "tautological nullity"); *In re* Jotan, Inc., 264 B.R. 735 (Bankr. M.D. Fla. 2001). Further, "new value" does not include the mere substitution of a new unsecured obligation in place of the original obligation, *In re* Wellington Constr. Corp., 82 B.R. 424 (Bankr. N.D. Miss. 1987), or mere forbearance in the collection of a debt. *In re* Air Conditioning, Inc., of Stuart, 845 F.2d 293 (11th Cir. 1988); *In re* RDM Sports Group, Inc., 250 B.R. 805 (Bankr. N.D. Ga. 2000).

191. *In re* Jolly N, Inc., 122 B.R. 897 (Bankr. D.N.J. 1991). This "intent" requirement derives from the Supreme Court's decision in *National City Bank of New York v. Hotchkiss*, 231 U.S. 50 (1913). *Hotchkiss* involved a bank that made an unsecured loan to the debtor but then, later that day, demanded collateral. The debtor complied with the bank's request by pledging valuable securities. In the debtor's subsequent bankruptcy, the Court affirmed the trial court's conclusion that the pledge was a preferential transfer.

192. *See* Vern Countryman, *The Concept of a Voidable Preference in Bankruptcy*, 38 VAND. L. REV. 713 (1985).

193. 11 U.S.C. § 547(c)(2).

If the debtor incurred the debt or the creditor extended the credit under atypical circumstances, Section 547(c)(2) cannot protect payments on that debt.[194] Likewise, Section 547(c)(2) is unlikely to protect payments that are made involuntarily via levy or garnishment,[195] nor will it protect payments that are unusually large relative to the regular periodic payment amount.[196]

By its terms, the "ordinary-course" exception is limited to payments; the granting of a security interest could not qualify for protection from avoidance under Section 547(c)(2) even if the debtor and creditor routinely enter into security agreements in the ordinary course of their financial dealings.[197]

[c] Security Interests Granted in Conjunction with Enabling Loans

The typical PMSI transaction does not result in an illegitimate preferential transfer to a creditor; after all, the granting of a PMSI enables the debtor to acquire additional property, thereby expanding the size of the debtor's estate. The timing of certain enabling loan transactions, however, can result in security interests that technically satisfy each element for a preferential transfer under Section 547(b).[198] For example, suppose that on June 1, Debtor borrows $40,000 from Bank to purchase a new drill press that Debtor plans to acquire later in June when Debtor expands its operations. Contemporaneously with the loan, Debtor signs a security agreement and financing

---

194. *In re* Energy Co-op, Inc., 832 F.2d 997 (7th Cir. 1987) (payment made to settle breach of contract claim not made in ordinary course); *In re* Indus. & Mun. Engineering, Inc., 127 B.R. 848 (Bankr. C.D. Ill. 1990) (payment made to settle lawsuit not made in ordinary course).

Prior to 1984, Section 547(c)(2) provided that payments could not qualify for protection unless they were made within 45 days of the date the debt arose. Under that provision, payments on long-term debt could not qualify for ordinary-course protection. In 1984, Congress removed the 45-day limitation, and this triggered a debate in the courts regarding whether payments on long-term debt could qualify for protection as ordinary-course transfers. In *Union Bank v. Wolas*, 502 U.S. 151 (1991), the Supreme Court held that payments on long-term debt can qualify for protection under Section 547(c)(2).

195. *See* WJM, Inc. v. Massachusetts Dep't of Pub. Welfare, 840 F.2d 996 (1st Cir. 1988). If the debtor makes a payment without judicial process in response to creditor demands for payment, however, the debtor's payment is still within the "ordinary course" if the creditor's collection effort (e.g., dunning letters or phone calls) is not unusual. *See, e.g., In re* L. Bee Furniture Co., 203 B.R. 778 (Bankr. M.D. Fla. 1996).

196. *See In re* Healthco Int'l, Inc., 132 F.3d 104 (1st Cir. 1997); *In re* McElroy, 228 B.R. 791 (Bankr. M.D. Fla. 1999); *In re* Roemig, 123 B.R. 405 (Bankr. D.N.M. 1991).

197. *See In re* Blackburn, 90 B.R. 569 (Bankr. M.D. Ga. 1987).

198. Not all enabling loan transactions will need to be saved by Section 547(c)(3). In fact, most purchase-money secured transactions will not even run afoul of Section 547(b) in the first place. For example, suppose Consumer buys a TV set from Retailer under an installment contract by which Retailer retains a PMSI. In this situation, Consumer would not be granting the PMSI on account of an antecedent debt but rather on account of a contemporaneous debt. As a result, the trustee could not avoid the security interest under Section 547(b), and Retailer would not have to rely upon the Section 547(c)(3) exception. As explained in the text, Section 547(c)(3) primarily protects the enabling lender in cases where attachment is delayed after the purchase-money debt arises.

statement describing the drill press, and Bank files the financing statement. Debtor purchases the drill press on June 19 and then files for bankruptcy protection on August 1. Under these circumstances, Bank's PMSI is a transfer that satisfies each element of Section 547(b): it is a transfer to a creditor (Bank), on account of an antecedent debt (the PMSI does not attach until June 19 when Debtor acquires rights in the drill press, whereas Debtor incurred the debt on June 1), during the 90 days prior to bankruptcy, while Debtor is presumed to have been insolvent, and the PMSI makes Bank better off than it would have been as an unsecured creditor in a Chapter 7 liquidation. However, the transfer is not of a kind that should be avoided under preference law, because Bank's PMSI enabled Debtor to acquire a valuable asset. Allowing Trustee to avoid Bank's PMSI would bestow a windfall on Debtor's other creditors to the detriment of Bank solely because attachment was delayed until Debtor acquired the drill press.

To prevent this result, Section 547(c)(3) provides that the trustee/DIP cannot avoid a security interest to the extent that it meets the following standards:

- the security interest covers new value given at or after the signing of a security agreement describing the collateral;
- the new value was given by or on behalf of the secured party;
- the new value enabled the debtor to acquire the collateral and was in fact used by the debtor to acquire the collateral; and
- the security interest was perfected on or before 30 days after the debtor took possession of the collateral.[199]

Note that Section 547(c)(3) does not protect PMSIs from avoidance when perfection has been delayed. Returning to the above example, suppose Debtor had purchased the drill press on June 19, but Bank had not filed its financing statement to perfect its PMSI until July 25 (more than 30 days after Debtor took possession of the drill press). Because of this excessive delay in perfection, Bank's PMSI would not qualify for protection under Section 547(c)(3) and trustee could avoid the PMSI as a preference.[200]

[d] Transfers Ameliorating an Earlier Preference

Suppose Debtor is a financially distressed baker seeking additional flour from Supplier. Supplier refuses to consider supplying any more flour to Debtor unless Debtor pays 50 percent of its existing account balance of $12,000. In response to this statement, Debtor pays $6,000 to Supplier. Four days later, Supplier agrees to and does ship

---

199. 11 U.S.C. § 547(c)(3).

200. In this example, Bank might then attempt to argue that the PMSI should be treated as a contemporaneous exchange for new value under Section 547(c)(1). Such an argument, however, will almost certainly fail. Most courts have concluded that Section 547(c)(1) does not apply to purchase-money or "enabling loan" transactions. *In re* Locklin, 101 F.3d 435 (5th Cir. 1996); *In re* Tressler, 771 F.2d 791 (3d Cir. 1985). Likewise, a delay in perfection beyond the 30-day period provided in Section 547(e)(2)(A) would likely defeat any argument that the PMSI was a substantially contemporaneous transfer for new value. *In re* Holder, 892 F.2d 29 (4th Cir. 1989). *See* note 189, *supra*, and accompanying text.

Debtor an additional $2,500 worth of flour. Debtor cannot extract itself from financial difficulty, however, and files for bankruptcy three weeks later. Debtor's payment to Supplier constitutes a preference under Section 547(b); Supplier cannot claim the payment was a contemporaneous exchange for new value or an ordinary course transfer. Nevertheless, Supplier subsequently ameliorated the effect of this payment by extending new credit that enabled Debtor to acquire additional assets. Avoiding the full $6,000 payment in similar situations might discourage creditors such as Supplier from extending additional unsecured credit to distressed debtors, which in turn could compromise the ability of debtors to resolve their financial affairs and avoid bankruptcy.[201]

To account for such "post-preference" extensions of new value, Section 547(c)(4) provides that the trustee cannot recover an otherwise preferential transfer to the extent that, after the transfer, the preferred creditor gave new value to or for the benefit of the debtor (A) not secured by an otherwise unavoidable security interest and (B) on account of which new value the debtor did not make an otherwise unavoidable transfer to or for the benefit of the creditor.[202] The language of Section 547(c)(4) is not a model of clarity, but the idea behind it is simple: the trustee should not be able to avoid a preferential transfer to the extent that the benefitted creditor subsequently extends new value or credit that ameliorates the effect of the earlier preference. In the above example, Supplier's extension of $2,500 of unsecured credit ameliorated the effect of the earlier $6,000 preferential payment; thus, trustee can only recover $3,500 from Supplier.[203] New value or credit may take the form of goods or services. If Debtor pays $10,000 owed to its lawyer on the 80th day prior to Debtor's bankruptcy petition, Trustee cannot recover this payment if Debtor's lawyer provided an additional $10,000 worth of uncompensated services between the time of the payment and the time of the bankruptcy petition.[204]

As noted above, the new value ameliorating an earlier preference must be unsecured. If Supplier in the earlier hypothetical had taken a PMSI when it sold Debtor the $2,500 of additional flour, Section 547(c)(4) would not protect Supplier, and the trustee could avoid the $6,000 payment in full.[205] As noted by one court, "[a] key justification for the new value exception is that while the payment of preferences to the creditor diminished the estate, other creditors are not really worse off since the subsequent advance of new value replenishes the estate."[206] New value encumbered by a security

---

201. *See In re* New York City Shoes, Inc., 880 F.2d 679 (3d Cir. 1989); *In re* IRFM, Inc., 144 B.R. 886 (Bankr. C.D. Cal. 1992), *aff'd*, 52 F.3d 228 (9th Cir. 1995).

202. 11 U.S.C. § 547(c)(4); *In re* Micro Innovations Corp., 185 F.3d 329 (5th Cir. 1999).

203. What if Supplier had shipped the flour before Debtor had repaid half of its account balance? The net effect of this transaction on Debtor's balance sheet would have been the same; in this situation, however, the advance of new credit would not ameliorate a prior preference, and thus Section 547(c)(4) would not protect Supplier. *In re* McLaughlin, 183 B.R. 171 (Bankr. W.D. Wis. 1995).

204. *In re* Sounds Distrib., Inc., 80 B.R. 749 (Bankr. W.D. Pa. 1987).

205. 11 U.S.C. § 547(c)(4)(A); *In re* Micro Innovations Corp., 185 F.3d 329 (5th Cir. 1999); *In re* Toyota of Jefferson, Inc., 14 F.3d 1088 (5th Cir. 1994).

206. *In re* Micro Innovations Corp., 185 F.3d 329, 336 (5th Cir. 1999).

interest does not replenish the estate in the same way and therefore falls outside the new value exception.

[e] Floating Liens in Inventory and Receivables

In a floating-lien transaction covering inventory or payment rights such as accounts, the parties understand that the secured party will advance credit to the debtor as the debtor acquires inventory or generates accounts and that the debtor will correspondingly repay some or all of that credit as the debtor sells inventory or collects accounts. This process of borrowing and repaying continues on a revolving basis, with the secured party's possessing a lien on the collateral the debtor owns at any point in time. As the debtor acquires new inventory or generates new accounts, they are added to the "pool" of collateral over which the secured party's lien "floats."

Section 547(e)(3)'s timing rule presents a problem to secured parties with floating liens. Under Section 547(e)(3), the "transfer" of a security interest in any particular item of collateral does not occur until the debtor acquires rights in that item of collateral. For purposes of preference law, therefore, each time the debtor acquires a new item of inventory, the debtor's inventory lender receives a "transfer" of a security interest in that item of inventory. Because the security interest in this new item of inventory secures the balance of the debtor's previously incurred loan, the transfer occurs on account of an "antecedent" debt. As a result, the security interest in any item of inventory acquired during the 90 days prior to bankruptcy qualifies as a potentially preferential transfer under Section 547(b) unless the secured party was already fully secured at the time the debtor acquired that item of inventory.

This timing problem is exacerbated by the fact that, for many debtors, their inventory or accounts "turn over" (i.e., their inventory is sold or their accounts are collected and then replaced with new inventory or new accounts) every 90 days, if not more frequently. For example, suppose Debtor files for bankruptcy protection on June 1, owing Bank $100,000 secured by a floating lien on Debtor's inventory, which is worth $80,000. Further, suppose that each item of Debtor's inventory as of the petition date has been acquired during the previous 30 days. Under these circumstances, Bank's security interest in Debtor's entire inventory technically constitutes a preference under Section 547(b). Unless bankruptcy law provides some measure of protection, the trustee could avoid Bank's entire floating lien.

Such a result would undermine the use of inventory or accounts as collateral. Floating liens generally provide a convenient and efficient means for businesses to finance business inventory or receivables and do not inherently offend any policies underlying preference law. Accordingly, the law protects floating liens in inventory and receivables from blanket avoidance in Section 547(c)(5).[207]

---

207. Section 547(a)(1) defines the terms "inventory" and "receivable" more broadly than the corresponding Article 9 categories "inventory" and "account." For purposes of Section 547, "inventory" includes farm products held for sale or lease, and "receivable" includes any right to payment (thus

A floating lien may still be subject to some preference avoidance, however. Purchases of new inventory can create a recoverable preferential benefit if they serve to improve the secured creditor's position within the 90 days before bankruptcy. For example, an undersecured creditor with a floating lien may bring pressure on the debtor to acquire additional collateral to bolster the creditor's overall secured position. To the extent that the debtor acquires this additional collateral with assets that would otherwise have remained available for payment to general creditors, the acquisition of the additional collateral bestows a recoverable preferential benefit upon the creditor. Section 547(c)(5) permits the trustee to avoid a floating lien in inventory or receivables to the extent that the "transfers" (i.e., the attachment of the secured party's lien when the debtor acquires additional inventory or receivables) resulted in an improvement of the creditor's overall secured position to the detriment of unsecured creditors during the last 90 days prior to bankruptcy (or one year, in the case of an insider creditor).

To determine the amount that the trustee can avoid, Section 547(c)(5) applies a "net improvement" test that requires the following calculations:

- Step One: Determine the debtor's outstanding loan balance on the 90th day prior to the debtor's bankruptcy filing and the value of the collateral on that same day.[208]

- Step Two: Determine the debtor's outstanding loan balance on the petition date and the value of the collateral on that same date.

- Step Three: Compare the creditor's overall secured position (i.e., the value of its collateral less the outstanding loan balance) on the 90th day prior to bankruptcy with the creditor's overall position on the petition date.

If the creditor held a fully secured claim on the 90th day prior to bankruptcy, the creditor's overall secured position cannot be improved to the detriment of unsecured creditors, and the trustee cannot avoid the creditor's floating lien to any extent. But if the creditor was undersecured on the 90th day prior to bankruptcy and that shortfall has been reduced by the petition date, the debtor's acquisition of additional inventory or receivables has improved the creditor's position, and the trustee can avoid the creditor's floating lien to the extent of the improvement.[209]

The improvement in position must arise "to the prejudice of other creditors holding unsecured claims."[210] This requirement means that the debtor must have used otherwise unencumbered assets to acquire additional collateral that improved the creditor's position. If the creditor's position is improved because the debtor's inventory simply

including Article 9 accounts, chattel paper, payment intangibles, and rights to payment under instruments). The use of accounts in the examples in the text is illustrative.

208. 11 U.S.C. § 547(c)(5)(A)(i). If the creditor is an insider, the relevant date would be the date one year prior to debtor's bankruptcy. *Id.* § 547(c)(5)(A)(ii). If the creditor's first extension of credit to the debtor occurred within 90 days prior to bankruptcy, the relevant date would be the date of the creditor's first extension of credit to the debtor. *Id.* § 547(c)(5)(B).

209. *In re* Wesley Indus., Inc., 30 F.3d 1438 (11th Cir. 1994); *In re* Ebbler Furniture & Appliances, Inc., 804 F.2d 87 (7th Cir. 1986).

210. 11 U.S.C. § 547(c)(5).

appreciated in value, this improvement did not reduce the value of the debtor's estate to the prejudice of unsecured creditors, and the trustee cannot avoid the creditor's lien on account of that improvement.

To make the necessary calculations under Section 547(c)(5), the court must determine the appropriate value of the collateral as of the relevant measuring dates. The trustee and the creditor will often disagree, however, on the proper valuation of the collateral. Because there is no avoidable improvement in position if the creditor held a fully secured claim on the 90th day prior to bankruptcy, the trustee will seek to value the collateral at its lowest possible value (e.g., its liquidation or foreclosure sale value). In contrast, the creditor will seek to value the collateral at its highest possible value (e.g., the retail value of inventory or the face amount of receivables). As with valuation in other contexts, courts have developed no hard-and-fast rules for the appropriate valuation of inventory for purposes of Section 547(c)(5); instead, courts conduct this valuation on a case-by-case basis, taking into account the likely manner of the use or disposition of the collateral. For example, in *In re Clark Pipe and Supply Co., Inc.,*[211] the evidence reflected that the debtor was in the process of liquidating its assets throughout the 90-day period prior to bankruptcy. Based upon this evidence, the Fifth Circuit concluded that the inventory properly was valued at its liquidation value.[212] In contrast, if a Chapter 11 debtor is seeking to operate and reorganize its retail department store operations, the court might more properly value the debtor's inventory using a "going concern" or "replacement value" measure.[213]

[f] Statutory Liens

If a creditor obtains a valid statutory lien under nonbankruptcy law during the 90 days immediately prior to bankruptcy, the attachment of that lien satisfies the standards for a preferential transfer in Section 547(b). The trustee/DIP cannot use Section 547 to avoid a statutory lien, however; Section 547(c)(6) provides that Section 545 is the exclusive statutory authority by which the trustee/DIP can avoid a statutory lien.[214]

[g] Statutory Floor for Consumer Transfers

If the debtor is an individual with primarily consumer debts, Section 547(c)(8) provides that the trustee cannot recover any transfer in which the total value of the property transferred was less than $600.[215] Section 547(c)(8) does not apply, and so

---

211. 893 F.2d 693 (5th Cir. 1990).

212. *Id.* (appropriate measure of collateral value is net amount creditor could have received if/when it could have repossessed and sold inventory).

213. The Supreme Court's decision in *Associates Commercial Corp. v. Rash*, discussed in § 16.03[B][2][a], *supra*, focused on the valuation of vehicles in Chapter 13 in the context of lifting the automatic stay. However, the Court's interpretation of Section 506(a) suggests that a replacement-value approach would be required whenever a debtor seeks to use the collateral in its reorganization efforts.

214. 11 U.S.C. § 547(c)(6). *See* § 16.04[D], *supra.*

215. 11 U.S.C. § 547(c)(8). A number of courts have concluded that multiple transfers to the same creditor can be aggregated and avoided if the total of those transfers exceeds $600. *See, e.g., In re*

does not exempt any portion of a preferential transfer from avoidance, if the total value of the property transferred exceeds $600.[216]

[h] Statutory Floor for Non-Consumer Transfers

If the debtor does not have primarily consumer debts, Section 547(c)(9) provides that the trustee cannot recover any transfer in which the total value of the property transferred was less than $7,575.[217] As with the floor in Section 547(c)(8), courts decline to extend this provision to any transfer in which the value of the property transferred is $7,575 or more.[218] In other words, creditors cannot use this provision to protect the first $7,575 of a larger preferential transfer.[219]

[5] Preference Actions as Nuisance Litigation

As part of the Small Business Reorganization Act of 2019 (SBRA), Congress amended Section 547 to permit a trustee to avoid preferential transfers only "based on reasonable due diligence in the circumstances of the case and taking into account a party's known or reasonably knowable affirmative defenses."[220] Because creditors may innocently receive preferential transfers, avoidance actions are often perceived to be unfair.[221] Creditors have been known to describe preference actions as "nothing more than nuisance litigation,"[222] a charge that holds additional weight in light of the frequency with which preference actions are settled rather than litigated.[223]

Courts have queried whether the SBRA amendment introduces a new element required for pleading a preference claim, but most have found it unnecessary to resolve the issue because the additional pleading requirements are minimal and

---

Hailes, 77 F.3d 873 (5th Cir. 1996); *In re* Djerf, 188 B.R. 586 (Bankr. D. Minn. 1995); *In re* Alarcon, 186 B.R. 135 (Bankr. D.N.M. 1995).

216. Creditors have attempted to argue that Section 547(c)(8) should protect the first $600 of a transfer from avoidance, but courts have rejected these arguments. *In re* Via, 107 B.R. 91 (Bankr. W.D. Va. 1989); *In re* Vickery, 63 B.R. 222 (Bankr. E.D. Tenn. 1986).

217. This amount is effective as of April 1, 2022, and is automatically adjusted at three-year intervals based on the Consumer Price Index. 11 U.S.C. § 104(a).

218. *See, e.g., In re* Bay Area Glass, Inc., 454 B.R. 86 (B.A.P. 9th Cir. 2011).

219. *Id.* at 90.

220. *See* Small Business Reorganization Act of 2019, Pub. L. No. 116-54, § 3, 133 Stat. 1079, 1085 (codified at 11 U.S.C. §§ 1181–1195 and scattered sections of 11 U.S.C. and 28 U.S.C.).

221. *See generally* Brook E. Gotberg, *Conflicting Preferences in Business Bankruptcy: The Need for Different Rules in Different Chapters*, 100 IOWA L. REV. 51, 53–60 (2014).

222. Statement of David Pollack, *ABI Commission to Study the Reform of Chapter 11*, AM. BANKR. INST. (June 4, 2013), http://commission.abi.org/sites/default/files/statements/04jun2013/ABI_Field_Hearing_Transcript_6-04-13_Final.doc.

223. *See generally* Brook E. Gotberg, *Optimal Deterrence and the Preference Gap*, 2018 BYU L. REV. 559, 576.

typically satisfied.[224] It remains to be seen whether the amendment will bring about observable changes to preference litigation.[225]

Separately, within the SBRA, Congress amended the venue provisions associated with adversary proceedings, which are separate lawsuits conducted within a bankruptcy case to resolve disputed claims like avoidable preferences.[226] The amended statute requires that actions seeking less than $15,000 of consumer debt, or less than $25,000 in non-consumer debt, can only be brought in the district court for the district in which the defendant resides.[227] This restriction is said to apply to all proceedings "arising in or related to" a bankruptcy case.[228] Very few courts have addressed the issue, but notable decisions have concluded that the new limitation does not apply to preference actions, which "arise under" the Bankruptcy Code.[229]

[F] Power to Avoid Fraudulent Transfers

[1] Intentionally Fraudulent Transfers— 11 U.S.C. § 548(a)(1)(A)

Sometimes debtors deliberately seek to frustrate the legitimate collection efforts of their creditors by giving property (or transferring it for insufficient consideration) to friends or relatives. Since the Statute of 13 Elizabeth in 1570, the common law has allowed creditors harmed by intentionally fraudulent transfers to invalidate such transfers. Today, both the Uniform Fraudulent Conveyance Act (UFCA) and the Uniform Voidable Transfer Act (UVTA) contain provisions that permit creditors to avoid transfers made by the debtor with the intent to hinder, delay, or defraud creditors.[230] Because these transfers would disadvantage an insolvent debtor's unsecured creditors, Section 548(a)(1)(A) of the Bankruptcy Code permits the trustee/DIP to bring an action to avoid intentionally fraudulent transfers made by the debtor within the two-year period prior to bankruptcy.[231]

---

224. *See, e.g., In re* Center City Healthcare, LLC, 641 B.R. 793, 801–02 (Bankr. D. Del. 2022); *In re* Pinktoe Tarantula Ltd., 2023 WL 2960894 (Bankr. D. Del. Apr. 14, 2023) (collecting cases).

225. *See* Brook E. Gotberg, *Poking at Preference Actions: SBRA Amendments Signal the Need for Change*, 28 ABI L. REV. 285, 295 (2020) (anticipating that the amendment is unlikely to alter practices or reduce the number of preference actions brought).

226. *See* FED. R. BANKR. P. 7001 (defining the ten types of adversary proceedings).

227. 28 U.S.C. § 1409(b).

228. *Id.*

229. *See In re* Insys Theraputics, Inc., 2021 WL 3508612 (Bankr. D. Del. June 17, 2021).

230. UFCA § 7, UVTA § 4(a)(1). The UVTA is the more recent of the two model fraudulent-transfer statutes and was designed to modernize and replace the UFCA. Prior to 2014, the UVTA was known as the Uniform Fraudulent Transfer Act (UFTA). The Uniform Law Commission reasoned that "[t]he original title was a misleading description because fraud has never been a necessary element of a claim under the Act[.]" Uniform Law Commission, *Voidable Transaction Act Amendments – A Summary* (2014).

231. 11 U.S.C. § 548(a)(1)(A).

[2] Constructively Fraudulent Transfers— 11 U.S.C. § 548(a)(1)(B)

More frequently, a financially distressed debtor makes a transfer by gift or for insufficient consideration without any specific intent to hinder, delay, or defraud creditors. The debtor's pure motives provide cold comfort to creditors for whom the transfer has the same effect: assets that might have satisfied creditor claims have instead gone to other parties for less than fair market value, thereby depleting the assets available for unpaid creditors. In recognition of the fact that such transfers tend to have the same impact as intentionally fraudulent transfers, the common law has long deemed such transfers by insolvent debtors to be avoidable as *constructively* fraudulent transfers. Both the UFCA and the UVTA allow creditors to avoid constructively fraudulent transfers,[232] and the Bankruptcy Code provides a similar rule in Section 548(a)(1)(B). This section permits the trustee/DIP to avoid any transfer of the debtor's property or any obligation incurred by the debtor, if:

- the transfer was made or the obligation was incurred within two years prior to the debtor's bankruptcy;
- the debtor received less than a "reasonably equivalent value" in exchange; and
- one or more of the following are true:
  - the debtor was insolvent at the time the transfer was made or obligation was incurred, or was rendered insolvent as a result of the transfer;
  - the debtor was engaging in business or a transaction with "unreasonably small capital";
  - the debtor intended to incur or expected to incur debts beyond its ability to repay; or
  - the debtor made the transfer or incurred the obligation to or for the benefit of an insider under an employment contract and not in the ordinary course of business.[233]

Thus, if Debtor sells equipment worth $100,000 to Buyer for a price of $50,000, thereby rendering Debtor insolvent, and Debtor files for bankruptcy within two years of the sale, Trustee can establish that the transfer was constructively fraudulent under Section 548(a)(1)(B). Trustee can thus recover the equipment from Buyer even if Buyer acted in good faith and without knowledge that the transfer was voidable.[234]

Because of the harshness of this result for Buyer, the Bankruptcy Code provides some protection for good-faith purchasers and their subsequent transferees. If Buyer purchased the equipment in good faith, it will receive a lien on the equipment to secure

---

232. UFCA § 4, UVTA § 4(a)(2).
233. 11 U.S.C. § 548(a)(1)(B).
234. *Id.* § 550(a)(1).

repayment of the $50,000 that Buyer paid to Debtor.[235] Further, if Buyer has already conveyed the equipment to Third Party by the time Trustee discovers the fraudulent sale to Buyer, Trustee cannot recover the equipment from Third Party if Third Party took the property for value, in good faith, and without knowledge of the fact that Buyer's purchase from Debtor violated Section 548(a).[236]

Generally, Section 548(a)(1)(b) presents few significant threats to the typical secured party (except in the context of a pre-bankruptcy foreclosure sale, which will be discussed shortly). The trustee cannot avoid pre-petition payments by the debtor on the debt as constructively fraudulent transfers because the debtor receives equivalent value (satisfaction of the debt) in exchange for the payments.[237] Likewise, because Section 548 defines "value" to include "securing... [an] antecedent debt,"[238] the trustee/DIP cannot use Section 548 to avoid a security interest just because the debtor granted that interest to secure a previously unsecured obligation of the debtor.[239] In contrast, if the debtor granted a security interest in its property to secure the debt of an unrelated person, the debtor would not have received any value in exchange. Under those circumstances, the trustee could avoid the security interest as a fraudulent transfer if the debtor was insolvent at the time or was rendered insolvent as a result of granting the security interest.[240]

[3] Pre-Bankruptcy Foreclosure Sales as Fraudulent Transfers

A trustee might attempt to invoke Section 548 to set aside a pre-bankruptcy foreclosure sale as a constructively fraudulent transfer. As discussed in Chapter 18, *infra*, foreclosure sales sometimes bring notoriously low prices. Foreclosure sales often occur

---

235. *Id.* § 548(c) ("a transferee ... that takes for value and in good faith has a lien ... to the extent that such transferee ... gave value to the debtor in exchange for such transfer...."); Stratton v. Equitable Bank, N.A., 104 B.R. 713 (D. Md. 1989), *aff'd*, 912 F.2d 464 (4th Cir. 1990).

236. 11 U.S.C. § 550(b). This can lead to litigation on the question of whether a transferee is an immediate or mediate recipient of the transfer. *See, e.g., In re* Video Depot, Ltd., 127 F.3d 1195 (9th Cir. 1997). The good-faith defense available to mediate transferees may also apply in cases where the transfer being avoided is a preference. *See In re* Global Protection USA, Inc., 546 B.R. 586, 620 (Bankr. D.N.J. 2016).

237. Section 548(d)(2)(A) expressly defines "value" to include "satisfaction ... of a present or antecedent debt."

238. 11 U.S.C. § 548(d)(2)(A).

239. *See In re* Anand, 210 B.R. 456 (Bankr. N.D. Ill. 1997); *In re* Countdown of Conn., Inc., 115 B.R. 18 (Bankr. D. Conn. 1990).

240. For purposes of determining whether the debtor is insolvent under Section 548(a)(2), the court must take into account both the debtor's fixed liabilities and its contingent liabilities. In valuing the debtor's contingent liabilities (e.g., the debtor's liability on a guaranty of another's obligation), the court must take into account the probability that the contingency will occur. Covey v. Commercial Nat'l Bank of Peoria, 960 F.2d 657 (7th Cir. 1992). Thus, if Debtor grants a security interest in its equipment to Bank to secure the obligation of Third Party, the court, in valuing the contingent liability created by Debtor's granting of the security interest, must take into account the likelihood of default by Third Party.

quickly and with less advertising than arms-length sales. As a consequence, foreclosure sales often yield few bidders and can result in bargain prices.

For example, suppose that after default by Debtor, Bank repossesses Debtor's inventory pursuant to its security agreement and conducts a public sale at which Buyer purchases all of the inventory for a total price of $50,000. Suppose further that the inventory had a wholesale value of $90,000 if bought and sold in the ordinary course of business. If Debtor then files for bankruptcy, Trustee might attempt to invalidate the foreclosure sale as a constructively fraudulent transfer. While avoidance of the sale would benefit Debtor's other creditors, there are countervailing policy concerns that argue against this outcome. To the extent trustees can collaterally attack foreclosure sales based upon low sale prices, this practice could have the undesirable effect of discouraging or "chilling" bidding at foreclosure sales, which in turn could further depress foreclosure sale prices.[241]

Foreclosure sales like the one described above are constructively fraudulent transfers under the clear language of the statute. There is a transfer of Debtor's property (the sale of the inventory) while Debtor was insolvent, and Debtor appears to have received less than "reasonably equivalent value" in exchange—Debtor received only $50,000 in exchange for inventory with a significantly higher market value.[242] Assuming that Debtor was insolvent at the time of the foreclosure sale,[243] the foreclosure sale seems to fit the standard established in Section 548(a)(1)(B). Further, avoidance of such sales fulfills the central purpose of the statute; if Trustee can unwind the sale and subsequently liquidate the inventory at its fair wholesale value, Trustee can capture $40,000 of additional value for the benefit of general creditors.

The question of whether the trustee can avoid a pre-bankruptcy foreclosure sale that generated a price below fair market value raged through bankruptcy courts until the Supreme Court purported to resolve the debate in *BFP v. Resolution Trust Corporation*.[244] The foreclosure sale at issue in *BFP* involved the debtor's house, which had an alleged fair market value of $725,000 but which sold at a pre-bankruptcy foreclosure for only $433,000. The trustee argued that the sale was constructively fraudulent because it yielded only 57% of the home's fair market value.[245] The purchaser argued,

---

241. This same "chilling effect" explains the rationale behind Article 9's rather strong finality rules that permit collateral attack against Article 9 foreclosure sales in only very limited circumstances. *See* § 18.02[E], *infra*.

242. The cash Buyer pays for the inventory will actually go to Bank, the creditor conducting the sale. Bank will then reduce the amount of Debtor's obligation by the same amount, less reasonable expenses incurred to repossess and dispose of the collateral. *See* § 18.02[D], *infra*.

243. The trustee bears the burden of proving that the transfer was fraudulent, *In re* Colonial Realty Co., 226 B.R. 513 (Bankr. D. Conn. 1998), and thus must prove that the debtor was insolvent at the time of the transfer or was rendered insolvent as a result. *In re* North Am. Dealer Group, Inc., 62 B.R. 423 (Bankr. E.D.N.Y. 1986). Section 548 does not create a presumption of insolvency similar to the one that exists in preference actions under Section 547.

244. 511 U.S. 531 (1994).

245. The trustee's argument relied on a rule that derived from the opinion in *Durrett v. Washington National Insurance Co.*, 621 F.2d 201 (5th Cir. 1980), in which the court suggested that any sale for less

however, that the purchase price received at a regularly conducted, noncollusive fore-closure sale should be deemed "reasonably equivalent value."[246] Unlike the UVTA, which contains express language adopting such a conclusive presumption,[247] Section 548(a)(1)(B) contains no language purporting to define the term "reasonably equivalent value," nor does it establish any presumption regarding its meaning. Nevertheless, the purchaser urged the Court to find that this conclusive presumption was implicit in Section 548(a)(1)(B).

In a 5–4 decision, the Court held that the trustee cannot use Section 548 to set aside a regularly conducted, noncollusive foreclosure sale of land, regardless of the fact that the sale generated a price far below an ordinary market sale price.[248] Justice Scalia concluded that the term "reasonably equivalent value" as used in Section 548(a)(1)(B) did not mean "fair market value" in the context of a foreclosure sale:

> The language [of Section 548(a)(1)(B)] requires judicial inquiry into whether the foreclosed property was sold for a price that approximated its worth at the time of sale. An appraiser's reconstruction of "fair market value" could show what similar property would be worth if it did not have to be sold within the time and manner strictures of state-prescribed foreclosure. But property that must be sold within those strictures is simply worth less. No one would pay as much to own such property as he would pay to own real estate that could be sold at leisure and pursuant to normal marketing techniques.[249]

Justice Scalia concluded that state foreclosure and fraudulent-transfer laws have never authorized the setting aside of a foreclosure sale solely because the sale generated an inadequate price. Given this long history of state laws designed to promote finality in foreclosure sales, Justice Scalia concluded that the words "reasonably equivalent value" in Section 548(a)(1)(B) do not reflect a clear legislative intent to displace state

---

than 70 percent of the property's fair market value was presumptively constructively fraudulent. Prior to *BFP*, a significant number of bankruptcy courts had adopted this rule of thumb, which became known as the "*Durrett*" rule. *See, e.g., In re* Littleton, 888 F.2d 90 (11th Cir. 1989). *See also* William H. Henning, *An Analysis of* Durrett *and Its Impact on Real and Personal Property Foreclosures: Some Proposed Modifications*, 63 N.C. L. Rev. 257 (1985).

246. Prior to *BFP*, two Circuits adopted the rule advocated by the purchaser. *In re* Winshall Set-tlor's Trust, 758 F.2d 1136 (6th Cir. 1985); *In re* Madrid, 21 B.R. 424 (9th Cir. Bankr. 1982), *aff'd on other grounds*, 725 F.2d 1197 (9th Cir. 1984).

247. UVTA § 3(b) ("[A] person gives reasonably equivalent value if the person acquires an interest of the debtor in an asset pursuant to a regularly conducted, noncollusive foreclosure sale or execution of a power of sale for the acquisition or disposition of the interest of the debtor upon default under a mortgage, deed of trust, or security agreement."). The UFCA uses the term "fair consideration" instead of "reasonably equivalent value," UFCA § 3, and its definition of "fair consideration" contains no presumption comparable to the one found in UVTA § 3(b).

248. *BFP*, 511 U.S. at 545.

249. *Id.* at 538–39. Commentators have strongly criticized Scalia's statement that property being sold at foreclosure is "worth less" than it would be if sold at arm's-length, on the ground that Scalia is conflating the terms "value" and "price." The fact that a foreclosure sale brings a lower price does not mean that the property is intrinsically worth less. Robert M. Lawless & Stephen P. Ferris, *Economics and the Rhetoric of Valuation*, 5 J. Bankr. L. & Prac. 3 (1995).

foreclosure law and permit bankruptcy trustees to set aside foreclosure sales based solely upon low sale prices.[250] Accordingly, the majority concluded that "a fair and proper price, or a 'reasonably equivalent value,' for foreclosed property, is the price in fact received at the foreclosure sale, so long as all the requirements of the State's foreclosure law have been complied with."[251]

Thus, the trustee/DIP cannot use Section 548(a)(1)(B) to attack a pre-bankruptcy foreclosure sale of land unless there is some irregularity in the conduct of the sale.[252] The Court explicitly limited the *BFP* decision to private foreclosures of land, purporting to leave open the question of whether Section 548(a)(1)(B) applies to other forced sales (such as tax sales or Article 9 sales).[253] The rationale of *BFP* would suggest that the trustee could not set aside such foreclosure sales, but a split has arisen on this point, particularly in the context of tax foreclosures. Some jurisdictions apply the logic of *BFP* to tax sales,[254] while others do not.[255] The rationale of *BFP* would suggest that the trustee could not set aside a sale in which the secured party complied with all the requirements of Article 9 and conducted a commercially reasonable sale, regardless of the sale price.[256] In contrast, if the secured party failed to comply with the requirements of Article 9 and conducted a commercially unreasonable sale, a bankruptcy court might permit the trustee to assert Section 548(a)(1)(B) if the sale resulted in a manifestly low price relative to the collateral's fair market value.[257] However, courts may differ in their willingness to extend *BFP* in the context of an Article 9 sale.

---

250. *BFP*, 511 U.S. at 538–45.

251. *Id.* at 545.

252. *Id.* at 545–46 ("Any irregularity in the conduct of the sale that would permit judicial invalidation of the sale under applicable state law deprives the sale price of its conclusive force under [Section 548(a)(1)(B)], and the transfer may be avoided if the price received was not reasonably equivalent to the property's actual value at the time of the sale.").

253. *Id.* at 537 n.3.

254. *See, e.g., In re* Tracht Gut, LLC, 836 F.3d 1146, 1149 (9th Cir. 2016) (the price received at a tax sale conducted in accordance with state law conclusively establishes reasonably equivalent value under the logic of *BFP*); *In re* Grandote Country Club Co., Ltd., 252 F.3d 1146, 1152 (10th Cir. 2001) (same); Matter of T.F. Stone Co., Inc., 72 F.3d 466, 471 (5th Cir. 1995).

255. *See, e.g.,* Gunsalus v. Cnty. of Ontario, New York, 37 F.4th 859, 865 (2d Cir. 2022) (ruling that *BFP* is limited in scope and does not control tax sales); *In re* Smith, 811 F.3d 228, 237 (7th Cir. 2016) (same). The discrepancy in case decisions is attributable to the variances in state tax lien enforcement. In some states, tax lien enforcement occurs through an execution sale at public auction comparable to a judicial mortgage foreclosure sale. In these states, because a tax sale should produce robust public bidding, the logic of *BFP* should control. By contrast, in other states, tax lien enforcement does not require a public auction sale; a private investor could pay off the amount of the property owner's unpaid taxes and eventually obtain a tax deed to the property without a public sale. In those states, applying the logic of *BFP* to protect the investor's "bargain price" makes no sense.

256. U.C.C. §9-617(b). *See* §18.02[E], *infra*.

257. Even this conclusion is subject to doubt, however, as Article 9 typically does not allow the debtor to invalidate even a commercially unreasonable sale. *See* U.C.C. §9-617(b) (good-faith transferee at Article 9 foreclosure sale receives debtor's rights in collateral even if secured party fails to comply with Article 9 sale requirements).

[4] Avoiding Fraudulent Transfers under State Law— 11 U.S.C. § 544(b)(1)

Section 544(b)(1) allows the trustee to set aside any transfer of the debtor's property that an actual unsecured creditor could have avoided under state law.[258] As discussed earlier, state fraudulent-transfer laws (either the UVTA, the UFCA, or some statutory descendant of the Statute of 13 Elizabeth) permit unsecured creditors to set aside both intentionally and constructively fraudulent transfers. Thus, assuming the trustee can identify an actual unsecured creditor of the debtor that is capable of asserting a state-law fraudulent-transfer claim, the trustee could use Section 544(b) to assert that claim on behalf of the estate.

Because the applicable standards for establishing a fraudulent transfer are essentially the same under Section 548(a) and most applicable state fraudulent-transfer laws, the trustee will choose to proceed under Section 544(b) only if the transfer occurred more than two years prior to bankruptcy (and thus outside the two-year reach-back period of Section 548). State law may provide aggrieved creditors with a longer reach-back period for avoiding fraudulent transfers. For example, the UVTA generally allows creditors a period of four years in which to seek avoidance of a fraudulent transfer.[259]

§ 16.05 The Trustee's Right to Assert the Debtor's Defenses—11 U.S.C. § 558

Under Section 558, the trustee can assert on behalf of the estate "any defense available to the debtor as against any entity other than the estate."[260] This would include any defense against a secured creditor's claim. Accordingly, although Section 558 technically is not an avoiding power, the trustee can use it to similar effect. First, the trustee can use Section 558 to reduce or eliminate a creditor's security for its claim to the extent the debtor had a valid defense to the claim. For example, suppose Bank claims a pre-petition security interest against all of Debtor's inventory, but Debtor did not properly authenticate the security agreement. Under section 558, the trustee could assert that Bank failed to satisfy the requirements for attachment and thus acquired no valid security interest in Debtor's inventory.[261]

Alternatively, the trustee may use Section 558 to attack the enforceability of the creditor's underlying claim. For example, suppose Shark claims a security interest in Debtor's jewelry to secure a debt incurred when Shark made Debtor a loan at usurious interest rates. If the jurisdiction's usury law would have permitted Debtor to avoid the

---

258. *See* § 16.04[C], *supra*.

259. UVTA § 9(a), (b).

260. 11 U.S.C. § 558.

261. In this scenario, Bank would also be vulnerable to an avoidance action under Section 544(a)(1), insofar as an unattached interest would be avoidable by the trustee acting as a hypothetical lien creditor. § 16.04[B], *supra*.

obligation to repay some or all of the principal or interest of this loan, the trustee may assert that usury law as a defense to Shark's claim, thereby reducing the debt and the lien that secures it.[262]

In asserting the debtor's defenses under Section 558, the trustee stands no better and no worse than the debtor stood as of the bankruptcy petition date. Any attempted waiver of defenses by the debtor after the bankruptcy petition is filed has no legal effect; Section 558 makes clear that the debtor's attempted post-petition waiver of defenses "does not bind the estate."[263] In contrast, if the debtor had waived the defense in question prior to the petition date and the waiver was enforceable under nonbankruptcy law, the trustee would be bound by the waiver and could not assert that defense under Section 558.[264]

§ 16.06 Security Interests in After-Acquired Property—11 U.S.C. § 552

[A] The General Rule Cutting Off Liens against After-Acquired Property— 11 U.S.C. § 552(a)

Businesses commonly finance their activities by granting lenders floating liens that cover all presently owned and after-acquired collateral of a particular type, such as inventory and/or accounts receivable. Outside of bankruptcy, the debtor cannot avoid an enforceable and properly perfected floating lien; each time the debtor acquires new assets of the type covered by the floating lien, the floating lien automatically attaches to those assets and will continue to cover all new assets of that type until the debtor satisfies the underlying obligation.

In the interests of facilitating debtor reorganization, the Code cuts off a floating lien to open additional financing opportunities. Section 552(a) provides that "property acquired by the estate or by the debtor after the commencement of the case [i.e., the petition date] is not subject to any lien resulting from any security agreement entered into by the debtor before the commencement of the case."[265] This means that collateral acquired post-petition is available to secure new loans. For example, suppose Bank holds a perfected floating lien on Debtor's inventory and accounts. Debtor needs additional credit to reorganize successfully, but Bank does not wish to provide further financing to Debtor. Finance Company is willing to provide Debtor with a credit line, but only if Finance Company can be assured of a first-priority lien on Debtor's new inventory and accounts. Pursuant to Section 552(a), Debtor is afforded the ability to

---

262. *In re* McCorhill Pub., Inc., 86 B.R. 783 (Bankr. S.D.N.Y. 1988).
263. 11 U.S.C. § 558.
264. *In re* Wey, 827 F.2d 140 (7th Cir. 1987).
265. 11 U.S.C. § 552(a).

negotiate for post-petition credit to be secured by assets acquired post-petition without being limited by the terms of pre-petition floating liens.[266]

Note that Section 552(a) has no effect on the creditor's security interest to the extent it had attached to property acquired by the debtor *prior to the petition date*; Section 552(a) only cuts off the *prospective effect* of a creditor's floating lien as of the petition date. A useful way to recall the effect of Section 552(a) is to analogize it to the chalk line that police draw around the body of an accident or murder victim. Bankruptcy declares Debtor "dead" in a financial sense, and Section 552(a) draws a chalk line around Debtor's "body" (i.e., Debtor's pre-petition property). If Bank has a validly perfected and otherwise unavoidable security interest against any of the property within that chalk line (such as Debtor's pre-petition inventory), Bank maintains its security interest in that property, notwithstanding Debtor's bankruptcy. But if Debtor in reorganizing acquires new inventory after the petition date, Section 552(a) provides that Bank's security interest does not attach to that new inventory even if Bank's pre-petition security agreement contained an after-acquired property clause that would have been enforceable outside of bankruptcy. The new inventory would remain "outside the chalk line," and Debtor could use it freely in its reorganization efforts.

[B] Proceeds of Pre-Petition Collateral— 11 U.S.C. § 552(b)(1)

The Code differentiates between (a) after-acquired property of the debtor and (b) proceeds of pre-petition collateral that the debtor receives post-petition. Although a pre-petition security interest is cut off as to after-acquired property, a pre-petition security interest continues in the proceeds of pre-petition collateral. For example, suppose that on the petition date, Debtor owns 100 units of inventory subject to Bank's validly perfected pre-petition security interest. Two weeks after bankruptcy, Debtor sells those 100 units for a total of $10,000. Outside of bankruptcy, Bank would have a validly perfected security interest in the $10,000 because it is identifiable proceeds of collateral in which Bank had a perfected security interest.[267] The Bankruptcy Code preserves this result in Section 552(b)(1), which provides that if a pre-petition security interest encumbers both pre-petition collateral and its proceeds, any proceeds of that pre-petition collateral remain subject to the security interest, even if the debtor receives them after the petition date.[268] In the above example, Bank's pre-petition security interest

266. *In re* Bumper Sales, Inc., 907 F.2d 1430 (4th Cir. 1990); *In re* Photo Promotion Assocs., Inc., 53 B.R. 759 (Bankr. S.D.N.Y. 1985).

267. U.C.C. § 9-315(a), (c), (d).

268. 11 U.S.C. § 552(b)(1); *In re* Bumper Sales, Inc., 907 F.2d 1430 (4th Cir. 1990). The language of Section 552(b)(1) covers not only "proceeds" of pre-petition collateral but also "profits," "products," or "offspring" of pre-petition collateral. Smith v. Dairymen, Inc., 790 F.2d 1107 (4th Cir. 1986) (creditor with pre-petition lien on cows and milk entitled to lien on post-petition milk); *In re* Wobig, 73 B.R. 292 (Bankr. D. Neb. 1987) (creditor with pre-petition lien on sows and offspring entitled to lien on feeder pigs born after bankruptcy petition). Section 552(b)(2) provides similar protection for post-petition

had validly attached to Debtor's pre-petition inventory, and Bank's security interest in that inventory automatically continued into identifiable proceeds.[269] Bank thus would continue to hold an enforceable security interest in the $10,000 of inventory proceeds, notwithstanding Section 552(a).

This outcome reflects sound policy. Bank's pre-petition security interest in the 100 units of inventory, which is not affected by Section 552(a), is worthless if Debtor can liquidate those units of inventory and use the proceeds without regard to Bank's lien. To provide meaningful protection for Bank's security interest in pre-petition collateral, bankruptcy must protect not only Bank's interest in the collateral but also the proceeds of that collateral.

Now consider a more complicated scenario in which Debtor files for bankruptcy holding 100 units of inventory subject to Bank's validly perfected pre-petition floating lien. Two weeks after the petition date, Debtor sells all 100 units of inventory for $10,000 and uses that cash to purchase 100 new units of inventory from suppliers. Bank cannot claim a direct security interest in the new inventory by virtue of the after-acquired property clause in its pre-petition security agreement; as discussed above, Section 552(a) cuts off the prospective effect of that clause. The new inventory, however, constitutes identifiable second-generation proceeds of the pre-petition inventory.[270] Can Bank successfully claim a security interest in the new inventory as proceeds of the pre-petition inventory under Section 552(b)? As the Fourth Circuit noted in *In re Bumper Sales, Inc.*,[271] the answer is yes. In *Bumper Sales*, the secured party held a validly perfected pre-petition floating lien against the debtor's inventory and accounts. The debtor continued operating in bankruptcy for nearly six months before the secured party asked the court for adequate protection of its security interest. During that period, the debtor's inventory and accounts turned over at least twice so that, by the time of the secured party's motion, all of the debtor's existing inventory and accounts had been received or generated after the petition date. Accordingly, the debtor argued that Section 552(a) had extinguished the secured party's lien altogether. The Fourth Circuit disagreed, holding that the new inventory was identifiable second-generation proceeds of the pre-petition inventory, and thus the secured party's lien remained effective under section 552(b)(1).[272]

The secured creditor in *Bumper Sales* was extraordinarily lucky. Because the debtor in the case stipulated that it had acquired all of the post-petition inventory using the

"rents" of pre-petition collateral. Note, however, that a secured party will not have an automatic security interest in an asset that is not proceeds. Proceeds are discussed in § 2.03, *supra*.

269. Recall that proceeds coverage is automatic under Article 9 unless the security agreement provides otherwise. U.C.C. §§ 9-203(f), 9-315(a). *See* § 2.04[B], *supra*.

270. Recall that proceeds of proceeds constitute "proceeds," U.C.C. § 9-102(a)(64), and thus the security interest in the original collateral continues in such proceeds so long as they are "identifiable," that is, so long as they can be traced back to the original collateral. *Id.* § 9-315(a), (b).

271. 907 F.2d 1430 (4th Cir. 1990).

272. *Bumper Sales*, 907 F.2d at 1439; *see also In re* Package Design & Supply Co., Inc., 217 B.R. 422 (Bankr. W.D.N.Y. 1998); *In re* Sherwood Ford, Inc., 125 B.R. 957 (Bankr. D. Md. 1991).

proceeds of pre-petition inventory and accounts, the secured party did not have to trace the post-petition inventory precisely back to the pre-petition inventory. As a result, the Fourth Circuit had no choice but to conclude that the new inventory was identifiable proceeds of the pre-petition inventory. A prudent secured party should not count on being so fortunate. As under Article 9, a secured party only obtains a security interest in *identifiable* (i.e., traceable) proceeds.[273] If the *Bumper Sales* debtor had commingled any of the proceeds of pre-petition inventory with other operating funds and had then used those commingled funds to purchase new inventory during bankruptcy, the secured party would have had a difficult (and perhaps impossible) tracing burden and thus might have lost its security interest altogether under Section 552(a).

The secured party in *Bumper Sales* should have filed a motion for adequate protection as soon as the debtor filed its bankruptcy petition.[274] This motion should have sought an order requiring the debtor to sequester all proceeds of the secured party's collateral in a separate account containing only proceeds, thus enabling the secured party to trace the proceeds of its collateral with ease and preserving the secured party's ability to invoke the protection of Section 552(b)(1). Alternatively, the motion should have asked the court to condition the debtor's use of the proceeds by allowing such use only if the debtor granted the secured party a replacement lien on post-petition inventory and accounts.[275]

§ 16.07 The Debtor's Right to Claim Exempt Property

[A] State and Federal Exemptions

The common law generally permits a creditor to enforce a judgment against any assets of the debtor that the creditor can locate. This general rule, however, is subject in every jurisdiction to constitutional or statutory *exemption* provisions, which allow an individual debtor to declare certain assets (or a portion of the debtor's equity in certain assets) to be exempt from seizure and sale by creditors. The goal of exemption laws is to avoid leaving an individual debtor destitute as a result of creditor collection activity. By providing the financially distressed debtor with some minimum amount of assets free of creditor claims, exemption laws enable the debtor to gain the financial foothold necessary to make a fresh financial start.[276]

---

273. U.C.C. § 9-315(a)–(b).

274. *See* § 16.03[B], *supra*.

275. Placing such a condition on cash proceeds of collateral—so-called "cash collateral"—is common. The Bankruptcy Code prohibits the use of cash collateral unless the creditor consents or the court enters an order permitting use. *See* 11 U.S.C. § 363(c)(2).

276. William J. Woodward, *Exemptions, Opting Out, and Bankruptcy Reform*, 43 OHIO ST. L.J. 335 (1982).

Bankruptcy law incorporates the idea of exemptions for individual debtors. Section 522(d) provides a list of exemptions accorded to an individual debtor as a matter of bankruptcy law. These include, *inter alia*, $27,900 of equity in the debtor's residence, $4,450 of equity in one motor vehicle, $700 of equity in each item of the debtor's household goods (up to a total of $14,875), $1,875 of equity in the debtor's jewelry, and $2,800 of equity in the debtor's professional books or tools.[277] Under Section 522(b), an individual debtor may declare certain assets as exempt from the claims of creditors pursuant to the foregoing federal exemptions or may choose instead the exemptions available in the debtor's jurisdiction under nonbankruptcy law,[278] unless the debtor is located in a state that has opted to require debtors to rely only on nonbankruptcy exemption laws.[279]

The debtor must file a list of the property that it claims as exempt with the court with the petition or within 15 days thereafter.[280] The trustee and any creditor may then object and challenge any particular claim of exemption. Absent timely objection,[281] the property is exempted as claimed.[282] Following a timely objection, the court must determine whether the debtor is entitled to the claimed exemption, with the objecting party bearing the burden of persuasion.[283] If the debtor is entitled to exempt an asset in its entirety (e.g., if the state's exemption law entitles the debtor to claim $2,000 of equity in one vehicle, and the debtor's car is worth only $1,500), the asset is abandoned by the trustee and returned to the debtor. If the asset is only partially exempt, the estate is entitled to the nonexempt portion of the asset; the trustee thus retains possession of the asset, and the debtor instead receives payment equal to the value of the exemption out of the proceeds of the asset.[284]

---

277. 11 U.S.C. § 522(d). These amounts are effective as of April 1, 2022, and they are automatically adjusted at three-year intervals based upon the Consumer Price Index. *Id.* § 104(a).

278. *Id.* § 522(b)(1).

279. *Id.* § 522(b)(2). Most states have opted out of the federal bankruptcy exemptions contained in Section 522(d). Consequently, in most states, debtors may only claim state law exemptions, both in and out of bankruptcy.

280. 11 U.S.C. § 522(*l*); Bankr. Rules 1007, 4003(a).

281. Generally, the trustee or any creditor must file any objection within 30 days after the initial meeting of creditors, unless the court grants additional time for objections. Bankr. Rule 4003(b).

282. The Supreme Court has held that a Chapter 7 trustee cannot contest the validity of a debtor's claimed exemption after the 30-day objection period expires, even if debtor had no colorable basis for claiming the exemption. Taylor v. Freeland & Kronz, 503 U.S. 638 (1992).

283. Bankr. Rule 4003(c).

284. *In re* Salzer, 52 F.3d 708 (7th Cir. 1995); *In re* Hyman, 123 B.R. 342 (9th Cir. Bankr. 1991), *aff'd*, 967 F.2d 1316 (9th Cir. 1992).

[B] The Debtor's Power to Avoid Liens against Exempt Property

Consider the consequences to Debtor's exemption in an automobile posed by three different liens: a voluntary security interest granted to Bank to secure a $5,000 loan, an mechanic's lien held by Garage for unpaid repairs totaling $2,000, and an execution lien for a $10,000 judgment in favor of Plaintiff. If the applicable exemption law permits Debtor to exempt $4,000 of equity in one vehicle, to what extent do these liens affect Debtor's ability to claim the car as exempt property?

A debtor's ability to claim exemptions is of no concern to a voluntary secured creditor like Bank. Exemptions generally are not effective against the holder of a valid security interest; as a practical matter, the granting of a consensual security interest in an asset is tantamount to a waiver of the right to assert the exemption against the secured party. This remains true in bankruptcy; as long as a security interest is valid and not otherwise avoidable in bankruptcy, the debtor's exemption rights are generally subordinate to the secured party's interest.[285] The same principle holds true for statutory lienholders like Garage: statutory liens generally take priority over the debtor's exemptions, on the theory that the debtor's assertion of the exemption would compromise the legislature's decision to accord special protection to the statutory lienholder. In contrast, exemptions can be enforced against judicial liens that arise through execution, levy, or the like—the very processes against which exemptions seek to protect debtors.[286]

Under Section 522(f)(1)(A) of the Bankruptcy Code, the debtor can avoid a judicial lien against an asset "to the extent that such lien impairs an exemption to which the debtor would have been entitled,"[287] in other words, to the extent that the debtor would have been entitled to claim the asset as exempt under applicable exemption law but for the effect of the judicial lien.[288] Of the three liens described above, Debtor cannot avoid the liens of either Bank or Garage, regardless of the car's value. But Debtor can avoid Plaintiff's execution lien under Section 522(f)(1)(A) to the extent that Plaintiff's lien impairs Debtor's ability to claim an exemption in the car. If the car is worth $4,000 or less, any enforcement of Plaintiff's execution lien against the car would impair Debtor's

---

285. 11 U.S.C. § 522(c)(2); H.R. Rep. No. 595, 95th Cong., 1st Sess. 361 (1977). This means, of course, that if the lien is so large that no equity is left in the property, the debtor effectively loses the exemption altogether.

286. See § 12.02, supra.

287. 11 U.S.C. § 522(f)(1)(A). By its language, Section 522(f)(1) allows the debtor to avoid "the fixing ... [of a lien upon] an interest of the debtor in property." The Supreme Court has interpreted this language to mean that a debtor can avoid an exemption-impairing judicial lien against an asset that the debtor owned before the judicial lien arose, but not a judicial lien that arose before the debtor owned the asset or simultaneously with debtor's acquisition of the asset. Farrey v. Sanderfoot, 500 U.S. 291 (1991) (in divorce settlement, debtor received ex-wife's share of family home, subject to judicial lien in favor of ex-wife to secure debtor's monetary payment obligations; debtor could not avoid ex-wife's lien because it arose simultaneously to his acquisition of ex-wife's share of the home).

288. Owen v. Owen, 500 U.S. 305 (1991).

ability to claim the $4,000 exemption, and the lien could be avoided in its entirety.[289] If the car was worth $5,000, Debtor could not avoid Plaintiff's lien altogether, but could avoid the lien to the extent of the Debtor's exempt portion of the equity in the car. The lien would remain effective, however, against the nonexempt portion of Debtor's equity in the car ($1,000).

The Code provides one significant exception to the general rule that exemptions are not effective to defeat the rights of a secured party. Under Section 522(f)(1)(B), the debtor may avoid a *nonpossessory, non-purchase-money* security interest to the extent it would impair the debtor's ability to claim an exemption in any of the following assets belonging to the debtor or a dependent:

- household furnishings, household goods, clothes, appliances, books, animals, crops, musical instruments, or jewelry, so long as these assets are held for personal, family, or household use;
- implements, professional books, or tools of the trade; or
- professionally prescribed health aids.[290]

Section 522(f)(1)(B) permits the debtor to avoid exemption-impairing liens against these types of assets even if the debtor had earlier signed a waiver of its exemptions.[291] Congress feared that creditors lending money to consumer debtors were taking security interests in household goods and requiring debtors to waive the right to claim those goods as exempt. Creditors could then use threats of repossession as a means of coercing debtors into making payments they could not otherwise afford to make.[292] Although assets like household furnishings, tools of the trade, or health aids generally have high replacement costs, they tend to have low resale values. Accordingly, creditors would be unlikely to recover much from repossession but could nevertheless achieve

---

289. Under Section 522(f)(2), a lien "impairs" an exemption to the extent that the value of the property is less than the sum of (a) the lien, (b) all other unavoidable liens on the asset, and (c) the allowed amount of the exemption. Assume that Bank's $5,000 loan, Garage's $2,000 lien and Plaintiff's $10,000 lien have all encumbered Debtor's car. In that case, Plaintiff's lien impairs Debtor's exemption and is fully avoidable if the car is valued at less than $11,000.

290. 11 U.S.C. § 522(f)(1)(B). Courts have disagreed as to whether a debtor may use Section 522(f)(1)(B) to avoid an exemption-impairing lien on livestock such as dairy cattle. *Compare In re Patterson*, 825 F.2d 1140 (7th Cir. 1987) (dairy cattle are "animals"; do not constitute "tools of the trade"; and lien in animals cannot be avoided unless animals held for personal, household, or family purposes) *with In re Parrotte*, 22 F.3d 472 (2d Cir. 1994) (livestock constituted tools of debtor's trade) *and In re Heape*, 886 F.2d 280 (10th Cir. 1989) (same). The debtor cannot avoid a security interest in household furnishings if the debtor acquired them primarily for business or commercial purposes. *See, e.g., In re* Reid, 757 F.2d 230 (10th Cir. 1985) (paintings acquired by debtor in satisfaction of business debt and pledged as collateral for business loan).

Although Section 522(f)(1)(B) allows the debtor to avoid the identified exemption-impairing liens, Section 522(f)(3) imposes a maximum dollar limit with respect to certain items. Under Section 522(f)(3), a debtor who takes the applicable state law exemptions cannot avoid a lien against implements, professional books, tools of the trade, farm animals, or crops to the extent that the value of such items exceeds $7,575.

291. 11 U.S.C. § 522(f)(1)(B).

292. H.R. Rep. No. 595, 95th Cong., 1st Sess. 127 (1977).

an *in terrorem* effect by way of the security interest. By allowing the debtor to preserve exemption rights in these assets despite a waiver of exemptions, Section 522(f)(1)(B) prevents this sort of creditor overreaching.[293]

The debtor may not use Section 522(f)(1)(B) to avoid an exemption-impairing possessory security interest. According to the courts, whether the security interest is "nonpossessory" for purposes of Section 522(f)(1)(B) depends on the intent of the parties at the time the security interest attached. If the parties structured the transaction as a pledge, with the secured party's holding the collateral, the security interest is not avoidable under Section 522(f)(1)(B) even if it impairs the debtor's right to claim that item as exempt. In contrast, if the debtor retained possession prior to default, the security interest is nonpossessory even if the secured party rightfully took possession of the collateral prior to bankruptcy to enforce its lien.[294] Likewise, to the extent a lien qualifies as a PMSI under state law, the debtor may not use Section 522(f)(1)(B) to avoid the lien.[295] This limitation reflects the solicitude that commercial law typically provides to purchase-money creditors.

Section 522(f)(1)(B) has generated a significant amount of litigation regarding whether the purchase-money character of a security interest survives the debtor's refinancing of the debt. For example, suppose Debtor purchases a television set from Seller, which retains a PMSI to secure the set's purchase price of $800, and Seller subsequently assigns its interest to Finance Company. Suppose further that nine months later, after paying off one-half of the price of the set, Debtor signs a new promissory note to Finance Company in the amount of $1,000, representing both the refinancing of the $400 balance of the original contract and a new loan to Debtor of $600. Debtor then goes bankrupt without repaying anything to Finance Company, seeks to retain the television set as exempt, and further seeks to avoid Finance Company's security interest as an exemption-impairing lien. A significant minority of courts have held that Debtor's refinancing of the original debt "transforms" the PMSI into a non-purchase-money security interest avoidable under Section 522(f)(1)(B).[296] Most of these courts have reasoned that refinancing a purchase-money debt extinguishes the original debt and replaces it with a new obligation secured by a lien that cannot qualify as a PMSI because the debtor already owned the collateral at the time of the refinancing.[297] In

---

293. 11 U.S.C. § 522(f)(1)(B) is not the only federal law that prevents such creditor behavior. Federal Trade Commission and Federal Reserve Board regulations prohibit non-purchase-money security interests in a consumer's household goods. *See, e.g.,* 16 C.F.R. § 444.2(4) (FTC); 12 C.F.R. § 227.13(d) (FRB).

294. *In re* Vann, 177 B.R. 704 (D. Kan. 1995); *In re* Schultz, 101 B.R. 68 (Bankr. N.D. Iowa 1989).

295. 11 U.S.C. § 522(f)(1); U.C.C. § 9-103.

296. This is often called the "transformation" rule. *See In re* Matthews, 724 F.2d 798 (9th Cir. 1984).

297. A few courts have reasoned, incorrectly, that a security interest cannot constitute a PMSI under Article 9 if it secures more than the purchase price. *E.g., In re* Jones, 5 B.R. 655 (Bankr. M.D.N.C. 1980); *In re* Scott, 5 B.R. 37 (Bankr. M.D. Pa. 1980). This interpretation is at odds with the language of Article 9 — which provides that a security interest is a PMSI "to the extent that" it secures the purchase price or an enabling loan, U.C.C. § 9-103(b) — and has been rejected by most courts. *E.g.,* Geist v.

contrast, the majority of courts have adopted the view that Debtor's refinancing does not *automatically* destroy the purchase-money character of Finance Company's lien.[298]

Under the majority view, Finance Company's security interest would have a dual status: it would be a PMSI to the extent that it secures the unpaid balance attributable to the television set ($400), and a non-purchase-money security interest to the extent of the remaining loan balance ($600). Debtor thus could not avoid Finance Company's lien to the extent the lien secures the $400 balance attributable to the television, but Debtor could use Section 522(f)(1)(B) to avoid the lien to the extent it secures the remaining loan balance.[299]

§ 16.08 The Chapter 7 Debtor's Right of Redemption — 11 U.S.C. § 722

A debtor in default may wish to retain the collateral despite the secured creditor's right to repossess and sell it. Retention is possible even after default if the debtor can redeem the property.[300] Outside of bankruptcy, a debtor in default can avoid foreclosure of a valid security interest through redemption only by paying the full amount of the debt (plus accrued but unpaid interest and reasonable costs of collection).[301] This requirement may render it impossible for a debtor in difficult financial circumstances to retain possession of encumbered property, especially property in which the debtor has no equity.

In a Chapter 7 case, however, bankruptcy law gives certain individual debtors the ability to redeem the collateral from a lien at a bargain price: the amount of the creditor's allowed secured claim. In the case of an undersecured claim, this enables the debtor to redeem the collateral by paying the value of the collateral rather than the full balance of the debt. To qualify for a right of redemption under Section 722 of the Bankruptcy Code:

Converse Cnty. Bank, 79 B.R. 939 (D. Wyo. 1987); *In re* Russell, 29 B.R. 270 (Bankr. W.D. Okla. 1983); *In re* Conn, 16 B.R. 454 (Bankr. W.D. Ky. 1982).

298. *E.g.*, Pristas v. Landaus of Plymouth, Inc., 742 F.2d 797 (3d Cir. 1984); *In re* K & P Logging, Inc. 272 B.R. 867 (Bankr. D.S.C. 2001); *In re* McAllister, 267 B.R. 614 (Bankr. N.D. Iowa 2001). Note that Article 9 generally provides that a PMSI does not lose its status as a PMSI merely because "the purchase-money obligation has been renewed, refinanced, consolidated, or restructured." U.C.C. § 9-103(f)(3). By its terms, Section 9-103(f) applies only to non-consumer-goods transactions. Courts are explicitly directed to draw no inference from the rule found in Section 9-103(f) in consumer-goods transactions. *See* U.C.C. § 9-103(h). This leaves open the possibility that a court might still apply the transformation rule in such transactions.

299. *In re* Parsley, 104 B.R. 72 (Bankr. S.D. Ind. 1988). Note that a creditor such as Finance Company must prove the extent to which its security interest qualifies for purchase-money status, and the creditor's failure to meet this burden would enable the debtor to avoid the security interest altogether under Section 522(f)(2). Geist v. Converse Cnty. Bank, 79 B.R. 939 (D. Wyo. 1987).

300. U.C.C. § 9-623.

301. *Id.* § 9-623(b).

- The creditor's lien must secure a dischargeable consumer debt.[302]

- The collateral to be redeemed must be tangible personal property intended primarily for personal, family or household use—"consumer goods" as defined by U.C.C. Article 9.[303]

- The collateral to be redeemed must be exempted under section 522 or must have been abandoned by the trustee under section 554.[304] The debtor cannot redeem collateral that could be sold for the benefit of general creditors.

- The debtor must have filed a timely statement of its intention to redeem the collateral. The debtor must file this statement with the clerk of the bankruptcy court within thirty days following the petition date or, if the initial meeting of creditors takes place during that thirty days,[305] by the date of such meeting.[306]

- The debtor must actually complete the redemption within 30 days after the initial meeting of creditors (or within such additional period as the court shall grant for cause).[307] The debtor must make a lump-sum payment to the creditor equal to the amount of the creditor's allowed secured claim.[308]

Before the debtor may exercise its redemption right under Section 722, the court must value the creditor's secured claim under Section 506(a). Valuations for redemption purposes typically involve two principal issues, both of which are resolved by Section 506(a)(2). The first issue is the timing (i.e., the effective date) of the valuation: should the collateral be valued as of the petition date or the date on which the debtor actually redeems the collateral (by which time the collateral's value might have either appreciated or, perhaps more likely, depreciated)? Section 506(a)(2) provides that in a Chapter 7 or 13 case involving an individual debtor, the collateral is to be valued as of

---

302. *In re* Runski, 102 F.3d 744 (4th Cir. 1996) (debtor may not use Section 722 to redeem collateral that secures a business indebtedness); *In re* Pipes, 78 B.R. 981 (Bankr. W.D. Mo. 1987) (same). Certain debts—for example, liability for child-support obligations, liability for willful or malicious injury, or liability for death or personal injury caused by drunk driving—cannot be discharged in bankruptcy. 11 U.S.C. § 523(a).

303. U.C.C. § 9-102(a)(23). *See also In re* Runski, 102 F.3d 744 (4th Cir. 1996); *In re* Pipes, 78 B.R. 981 (Bankr. W.D. Mo. 1987).

304. *See, e.g., In re* Fitzgerald, 20 B.R. 27 (Bankr. N.D.N.Y. 1982); *In re* Zaicek, 29 B.R. 31 (Bankr. W.D. Ky. 1983).

305. Every bankruptcy case has an initial meeting of creditors conducted pursuant to 11 U.S.C. § 341. At this meeting, the trustee and creditors may question the debtor under oath about the debtor's assets and financial affairs. 11 U.S.C. § 343.

306. *Id.* § 521(a)(2). If the debtor fails to redeem the property within the 30-day period following the first meeting of creditors, the automatic stay terminates with respect to the property. *Id.* § 521(a)(6).

307. *Id.* § 521(a)(2)(B).

308. *Id.* § 722 (payment must be "in full"); In re Edwards, 901 F.2d 1383 (7th Cir. 1990); *In re* Bell, 700 F.2d 1053 (6th Cir. 1983). If the debtor wants to retain possession of the collateral and make installment payments to the creditor, the debtor has other alternatives for doing so, including (a) reaffirmation of the debt under Section 524(c), *see* § 16.09, *infra*, and (b) filing a Chapter 13 petition and providing for installment payments to the creditor as part of the Chapter 13 plan. *See In re* Tucker, 158 B.R. 150 (Bankr. W.D. Mo. 1993) (debtor must redeem in lump-sum rather than installments).

the petition date and not the redemption date.[309] The rationale for this choice is that outside of bankruptcy, the creditor could have repossessed the collateral and resold it under Article 9 with little delay and without the consequence of the automatic stay. Thus, a petition-date valuation would more closely approximate the creditor's alternative foreclosure remedy.

The second issue concerns the measure of value that courts should use for redemption purposes. Section 506(a)(2) resolves this issue by stating that collateral must be redeemed based upon its "replacement value," meaning "the price a retail merchant would charge for property of that kind considering the age and condition of the property."[310] This measure of value prevents a consumer debtor from redeeming the collateral at a price lower than the consumer debtor would have been required to pay in the retail market for a comparable replacement asset.

§ 16.09 Reaffirmation by the Debtor— 11 U.S.C. § 524(c)

[A] Reaffirmation Agreements

When redemption is not feasible, the Bankruptcy Code provides the debtor with another option for retaining encumbered property: reaffirmation of the debt. Under limited circumstances, Section 524(c) allows a debtor in bankruptcy to make a new contract with a creditor under which it agrees to repay a pre-petition debt even though bankruptcy would otherwise discharge that debt. For example, suppose Debtor owes Bank $5,000, secured by a consensual lien on Debtor's car. The car is worth only $4,000, and the Chapter 7 trustee has abandoned the car to Debtor. Debtor needs the car to get to and from work and desperately wants to retain possession of it. Unfortunately, Debtor does not have $4,000 in cash with which to redeem the car from Bank's lien under Section 722, nor can Debtor obtain credit to acquire a comparable car. Bank is willing, however, to allow Debtor to retain possession of the car if Debtor will reaffirm its obligation to Bank (i.e., if Debtor promises to resume and continue making monthly payments on the full $5,000 balance of the debt). Section 524(c) permits Debtor to enter into a reaffirmation agreement with Bank that will permit Debtor to retain possession of the encumbered collateral.[311]

Although the Bankruptcy Code permits reaffirmation agreements, it does not encourage them. Discharge of indebtedness is one of the primary benefits that bankruptcy provides the individual debtor, and reaffirming a dischargeable debt often may not be in a debtor's best economic interest. Indeed, Congress feared that many reaf-

---

309. 11 U.S.C. § 506(a)(2).

310. *Id.*

311. Reaffirmation under Section 524 is not limited to secured debts; theoretically, a debtor could choose to reaffirm an unsecured debt. In this text, discussion of reaffirmation is limited to its application to secured debts.

firmations were not economically sensible and resulted from threats or overreaching by creditors (e.g., "Reaffirm this debt or we'll make sure that you never get credit from us or anybody else again.").[312] In an attempt to reduce the frequency of unwarranted reaffirmations, Congress provided a series of prerequisites in Section 524(c) that must be satisfied before a creditor may legally enforce a reaffirmation agreement:

- The debtor and creditor must enter into the reaffirmation agreement before discharge.[313]

- At or before the time the debtor signs the agreement, the debtor must receive a set of disclosures advising the debtor of the amount of the reaffirmed debt, the pertinent credit terms, the debtor's right to rescind the agreement, and the fact that the debtor is not required to enter into a reaffirmation agreement (among other things).[314]

- The reaffirmation agreement must be filed with the bankruptcy court.[315]

- If the debtor is *not* represented by an attorney at the time the agreement is negotiated, the bankruptcy court must approve the agreement. To ensure that the debtor fully understands the consequence of the agreement, the Code requires the debtor to appear in person before the court. At the hearing, the bankruptcy judge must inform the debtor that the debtor is not required to enter into a reaffirmation agreement and must explain the legal effect and consequences of entering into and defaulting under a reaffirmation agreement.[316] The court cannot enforce the agreement unless the court determines that the agreement is in the "best interest of the debtor" and will not pose "undue hardship" to the debtor or a dependent.[317]

- If the debtor *is* represented by an attorney at the time the agreement is negotiated, that attorney must file an affidavit with the bankruptcy court declaring that the debtor entered into the reaffirmation agreement voluntarily and with full information, that the agreement does not impose an undue hardship on the debtor or a dependent, and that the attorney fully advised the debtor of the consequences of entering into and defaulting under a reaffirmation agreement.[318]

---

312. H.R. Rep. No. 595, 95th Cong., 1st Sess. 162–64 (1977).

313. 11 U.S.C. § 524(c)(1); *In re* Kinion, 207 F.3d 751 (5th Cir. 2000). The Bankruptcy Code enjoins any act to collect on a discharged debt. 11 U.S.C. § 524(a)(2); *In re* Bennett, 298 F.3d 1059 (9th Cir. 2002); *In re* Zarro, 268 B.R. 715 (Bankr. S.D.N.Y. 2001); *In re* Smurzynski, 72 B.R. 368 (Bankr. N.D. Ill. 1987).

314. 11 U.S.C. § 524(k).

315. *Id.* § 524(c)(3).

316. *Id.* § 524(d)(1).

317. *Id.* § 524(c)(6)(A), (d)(2). This determination is not required if the debtor is seeking to reaffirm a consumer debt secured by real estate. *Id.* § 524(c)(6)(B), (d)(2). A debtor's apparent inability to make the payments specified in the reaffirmation agreement may be grounds for disapproving the agreement as not being in the debtor's best interest. *In re* Stillwell, 348 B.R. 578 (Bankr. N.D. Okla. 2006); *In re* Melendez, 224 B.R. 252 (Bankr. D. Mass. 1998).

318. 11 U.S.C. § 524(c)(3)(A)–(C).

The rationale for this provision is that if the debtor entered into the agreement with the advice of a competent attorney, the agreement probably reflects the debtor's best interests and thus should be freely enforced without the need for court approval.[319]

- The agreement must be enforceable under applicable nonbankruptcy law.[320]

- Bankruptcy law permits the debtor to rescind a reaffirmation agreement that the debtor subsequently decides would be an imprudent decision. The debtor may rescind a reaffirmation agreement any time prior to discharge or within 60 days after the reaffirmation agreement has been filed with the court, whichever is later.[321]

Whereas redemption under Section 722 is nonconsensual, reaffirmation under Section 524(c) obviously requires an agreement between the debtor and the secured creditor.[322] Neither party can legally compel the other to accept reaffirmation. Thus, it is important to appreciate the circumstances under which a debtor is likely to reaffirm a secured debt. For example, consider the hypothetical introduced at the beginning of this section, in which Debtor wishes to retain possession of its car, which has an estimated value of $4,000, but does not have the $4,000 cash necessary to redeem the vehicle from Bank's $5,000 loan. If Debtor is in Chapter 7 liquidation, both Debtor and Bank (which holds an undersecured claim) have an incentive to reaffirm the debt. Reaffirmation is the only statutory means by which Debtor can retain the car, and it is Bank's only means of ensuring repayment beyond the value of the car. If Debtor simply surrendered the car, Bank would receive $4,000 (less expenses of sale) from the car, but little or nothing on its unsecured deficiency claim.[323]

---

319. This requirement was added in 1984. Prior to 1984, the court had to approve *all* reaffirmation agreements, regardless of whether the debtor had the benefit of counsel. One might argue that a sophisticated debtor who enters a reaffirmation agreement with the advice of counsel should be held to the agreement regardless of whether the agreement meets the other requirements of Section 524(c). Courts have rejected this argument, however. *See In re* Getzoff, 180 B.R. 572 (9th Cir. Bankr. 1995).

320. 11 U.S.C. § 524(c). Nonbankruptcy law may provide the debtor with defenses to the enforcement of the reaffirmation agreement such as unconscionability, fraud, or duress.

321. *Id.* § 524(c)(4).

322. If the debtor wishes to reaffirm a secured debt in order to retain the collateral, Section 521 requires the debtor to file a statement of its intent with the clerk of the bankruptcy court within 30 days following the petition date (or, if the initial meeting of creditors takes place during that 30 days, by the date of such meeting). *Id.* § 521(a)(2)(A). Further, section 521 obligates the debtor to carry out its intent and enter into a reaffirmation agreement within thirty days following its statement of intent. *Id.* § 521(a)(2)(B).

323. While reaffirmation is not limited to Chapter 7, debtors in Chapter 11, 12, or 13 cases do not need reaffirmation to retain possession of collateral; those Chapters permit a debtor to retain possession of collateral while repaying undersecured pre-petition claims under a reorganization plan. *But see* § 16.10 (discussing inability of Chapter 13 debtors to modify certain claims secured by automobiles), *infra*.

[B] Retention of Collateral without Either Redemption or Reaffirmation

Continuing with the previous hypothetical, what if Debtor can neither redeem the car nor negotiate an acceptable reaffirmation agreement with Bank? Does Debtor have any other alternative for retaining possession of the car? If Debtor was in default at the time of its petition, the answer is no. But if Debtor was not in default at the time of its petition, the answer is less clear. Some have argued that if Debtor keeps making its monthly payments in a timely fashion and Bank keeps accepting them, Debtor can retain possession of the car without having to redeem it or enter into a reaffirmation agreement—a practice often called a "ride-through." Courts have split on whether the Bankruptcy Code permits this practice.

Prior to 2005, when the Bankruptcy Code was amended,[324] many courts allowed debtors to retain possession of collateral as long as they continued making timely installment payments under the original contract.[325] The debtor was permitted to "ride through" the bankruptcy filing without surrendering, redeeming, or reaffirming, while still receiving protection from the automatic stay and discharge injunction. Other courts read the statute as restricting the debtor's choices to redemption, reaffirmation, or surrender of the collateral and would permit creditors to repossess even if the debtor was current on payments.[326]

The 2005 amendments kept the relevant language regarding a debtor's responsibility to file a statement of intention to redeem, reaffirm, or surrender the collateral in place. However, it also added Section 362(h)(1), which provides that if the debtor fails to file or perform its statement of intention on a timely basis, the automatic stay is lifted and the property ceases to be property of the bankruptcy estate.[327] Immediately following this amendment, commentators and several courts concluded that Section 362(h)(1) abolishes "ride through."[328] However, in the years since, many courts that previously recognized "ride through" have continued to do so.[329] Courts may uphold a debtor's ability to "ride through" when:

---

324. Bankruptcy Abuse Prevention and Consumer Protection Act of 2005, Pub. L. No. 109-8, 119 Stat. 23 (BAPCPA).

325. 11 U.S.C. § 521(a)(2). *See, e.g., In re* Boodrow, 126 F.3d 43 (2d Cir. 1997); *In re* Belanger, 962 F.2d 345, 347 (4th Cir. 1992); *In re* Parker, 139 F.3d 668 (9th Cir. 1998); Lowry Fed. Credit Union v. West, 882 F.2d 1543 (10th Cir. 1989).

326. *See, e.g., In re* Burr, 160 F.3d 843 (1st Cir. 1998); *In re* Johnson, 89 F.3d 249 (5th Cir. 1996); *In re* Edwards, 901 F.2d 1383 (7th Cir. 1990); *In re* Taylor, 3 F.3d 1512 (11th Cir. 1993).

327. 11 U.S.C. § 362(h)(1). The trustee can file a motion seeking turnover of the collateral on the ground that it is "of consequential value or benefit to the estate." If the court agrees after notice and a hearing, the court can order the debtor to turn the collateral over to the trustee and, if so, the automatic stay remains intact. *Id.* § 362(h)(2).

328. *See, e.g.,* Philip R. Principe, *Did BAPCPA Eliminate the "Fourth Option" for Individual Debtors' Secured Personal Property?,* 24 AM. BANKR. INST. J. 6, 48–49 (Oct. 2005); *In re* Jones, 591 F.3d 308, 311 (4th Cir. 2010); *In re* Steinhaus, 349 B.R. 694, 703 (Bankr. D. Idaho 2006); *In re* Norton, 347 B.R. 291, 299 (Bankr. E.D. Tenn. 2006).

329. *See* S. Marc Buchman, *Ride-Through is Dead! Long Live Ride-Through!,* ABI J. 20 (July 2022).

(1) the debtor filed a statement of intent to reaffirm the debt, but the court failed to approve the agreement under Section 524(c)(6);[330]

(2) the debtor filed a statement of intent to reaffirm the debt, but counsel failed to submit the affidavit necessary under Section 524(c)(3),[331] or

(3) state law would prevent enforcement of an *ipso facto* clause that declares the debtor in default by virtue of the bankruptcy filing, despite the debtor's being current on the debt, or there is no such clause in the contract.[332]

The rationale for denying creditors the right to repossess in these cases is that the debtor has taken all necessary steps under the Bankruptcy Code, and therefore the creditor has no remedy.[333] Based on this reasoning, a creditor that continues to accept regular installment payments on the debt during the pendency of bankruptcy may risk losing the right to object to the debtor's attempt to retain possession without redemption or reaffirmation. The lifting of the automatic stay would clearly permit the secured party to foreclose on the collateral, but only if the debtor is in default. If a secured party has continued to accept monthly payments post-petition, a court might well conclude that the creditor had waived its ability to claim a default by virtue of the bankruptcy filing.[334]

§ 16.10 "Cramdown" in Chapter 13 and the "Negative Equity" Dilemma

[A] Introduction

In a Chapter 13 proceeding, the Bankruptcy Code generally permits the debtor to modify the terms of a secured creditor's claim,[335] even over that creditor's objection, as long as the debtor's treatment of that claim satisfies the plan confirmation standards set forth in Section 1325.[336] Modification of a secured claim over the objection of the

---

330. *See, e.g.,* Coastal Fed. Credit Union v. Hardiman, 398 B.R. 161, 186–87 (E.D.N.C. 2008); *In re* Blakeley, 363 B.R. 225, 230 (Bankr. D. Utah 2007); *In re* Moustafi, 371 B.R. 434, 439 (Bankr. D. Ariz. 2007).

331. *See, e.g., In re* Rhodes, 635 B.R. 849, 854 (Bankr. S.D. Cal. 2021).

332. *See, e.g., In re* Frazier, 599 B.R. 275, 280–81 (Bankr. D.S.C. 2019); *In re* Baker, 390 B.R. 524, 531 (Bankr. D. Del. 2008).

333. *See, e.g., In re* Blakeley, 363 B.R. 225, 230 (Bankr. D. Utah 2007) ("Having entered into the reaffirmation agreement 13 days after the first meeting of creditors, Debtor fully complied with the requirement under § 521(a)(6), and the remedy found under § 521(a)(6) is inapplicable to this Debtor.").

334. *See, e.g.,* 4 COLLIER ON BANKRUPTCY ¶ 521.14[5], at 521–52 (16th ed. Supp. 2009).

335. 11 U.S.C. § 1322(b)(2) (Chapter 13 plan may "modify the rights of holders of secured claims, other than a claim secured only by a security interest in real property that is the debtor's principal residence.").

336. The confirmation standards require that with respect to a secured claim, the debtor's plan must either (a) be accepted by the secured creditor, (b) provide for the surrender of the collateral to the secured creditor, or (c) provide that the secured creditor will retain its lien in the collateral and that the secured creditor receive payments during the plan that have a present value, as of the plan's effective date, equal to or greater than the value of the collateral. If the plan provides for periodic payments,

creditor is known as "cramdown," and it is best demonstrated by an example. Suppose that five years ago, Debtor borrowed $10,000 from Bank and granted Bank a security interest in Debtor's sailboat. Now Debtor has filed a Chapter 13 petition, still owing Bank $10,000. On the petition date, Debtor's sailboat is worth only $7,000. Debtor proposes a plan under which Debtor will (a) retain the sailboat, (b) pay off Bank's secured claim by repaying $7,000 with interest at the prevailing market interest rate in equal monthly installments over three years, and (c) pay 10 percent of its unsecured claims (including Bank's $3,000 unsecured claim).

Even if Bank objects to this plan, Debtor nevertheless may be able to have it confirmed. As explained earlier in this chapter, Section 506(b) of the Bankruptcy Code bifurcates Bank's claim into a secured claim for $7,000 (the value of the sailboat) and an unsecured claim for $3,000.[337] Under Chapter 13, Debtor can retain the sailboat over Bank's objection as long as (a) Bank retains its lien on the sailboat, (b) Debtor's plan agrees to pay Bank, on account of its secured claim, payments that have a present value equal to or greater than $7,000,[338] and (c) Debtor's plan agrees to pay Bank, on account of its unsecured claim, an amount no less than Bank would have received if Debtor's assets had been liquidated in Chapter 7.[339] In this way, Chapter 13 generally permits a debtor to "write-down" an undersecured claim to the current value of the collateral.[340]

[B] Section 1325(a)(5) and the "Hanging Paragraph"

Suppose that Jones buys a new Honda automobile for $25,000, financing the entire purchase price through credit extended by Honda Motor Credit (which takes a PMSI in the car). Suppose further that Jones makes payments for a year, reducing the balance of the debt to approximately $21,000, before defaulting. At the time of the default the value of Jones's car is only $16,000. This reduced value does not mean, of course, that Jones failed to care for the car adequately; often, early in the life of a new car, its market value will decline by an amount that exceeds the buyer's principal repayments during that same period. Nevertheless, because Jones has defaulted after only one year, Honda

---

these payments must be in equal monthly installments. Further, if the collateral is personal property, periodic payments must be sufficient to provide the secured party with adequate protection of its interest in the collateral during the plan period. 11 U.S.C. § 1325(a)(5); JEFF FERRIELL & EDWARD J. JANGER, UNDERSTANDING BANKRUPTCY § 18.08[F], at 672–680 (4th ed. 2019).

337. *See* note 46, *supra*, and accompanying text.

338. 11 U.S.C. § 1325(a)(5)(B).

339. *Id.* § 1325(a)(4).

340. Chapter 13 thus provides the debtor with an ability comparable to the Chapter 7 debtor's right to redeem certain personal property collateral under Section 722 at a redemption price equal to the then-current value of the collateral. *See* § 16.08, *supra*. However, two major exceptions affect the Chapter 13 debtor's right to modify secured claims. First, as explained in note 333, *supra*, a Chapter 13 debtor may not modify a claim that is secured only by real estate that is the debtor's principal residence. Second, as explained in the following text, a Chapter 13 debtor may not bifurcate certain claims secured by a PMSI in a motor vehicle.

Motor Credit is undersecured, and a foreclosure sale would not bring a price sufficient to satisfy the balance of the debt.

Prior to 2005, the Bankruptcy Code's general Chapter 13 modification rules (discussed in the preceding subsection) applied to secured car loans. Thus, if Jones had filed a Chapter 13 petition prior to 2005, the modification rules would have permitted Jones to "write down" the principal amount owed on the car loan to $16,000 (the then-market value of the car), even over the objection of Honda Motor Credit, and to pay the remainder of Honda's claim (the unsecured portion) at only a fractional dividend.

Automobile lenders complained vociferously throughout the 1990s that allowing such "write-downs" to Chapter 13 debtors constituted bad policy. Lenders argued that they had to pass the costs of "cramdown" losses through to all automobile buyers in the form of higher interest rates and loan fees, thus making automobile credit less accessible and perhaps depressing the market for automobile sales. In 2005, Congress amended Section 1325(a), adding a paragraph at the end of that section that has come to be known as the "hanging paragraph" because the paragraph is not numbered and is not connected to the prior numbered paragraph. The hanging paragraph provides as follows:

> For purposes of [§ 1325(a)(5)], section 506 shall not apply to a claim described in that paragraph if the creditor has a purchase money security interest securing the debt that is the subject of the claim, the debt was incurred within the 910-day [period] preceding the date of the filing of the petition, and the collateral for that debt consists of a motor vehicle ... acquired for the personal use of the debtor....[341]

Under the hanging paragraph, if Jones now filed a Chapter 13 petition within the first 910 days after purchasing the car, Section 506 would not apply to bifurcate Honda Motor Credit's claim. As a result, notwithstanding the current value of the car, Honda Motor Credit would have a secured claim for $21,000. Therefore, Jones could not retain the car in Chapter 13 unless Jones's plan provided payments to Honda Motor Credit that have a present value of at least $21,000.

[C] The Hanging Paragraph and the "Negative Equity" Conundrum

Now consider the prior discussion in the context of a different hypothetical. Suppose that three years ago, Davis purchased a new Honda in which Honda Motor Credit (HMC) took a PMSI to secure the unpaid purchase price of $25,000. Davis drove the car for two years, making timely monthly payments that reduced the balance owed to HMC to $18,000. One year ago, Davis traded in the Honda for a new Acura, with the

---

341. 11 U.S.C. § 1325(a). Why 910 days? Presumably the number reflects a rational legislative judgment that if the debtor has been paying on a car loan for two and one-half years already, the principal balance of the loan is more likely to have been reduced by an amount exceeding the depreciation in the car's value over that same period.

agreed purchase price of the Acura being $35,000. At that time, the Acura dealer gave Davis a trade-in credit of $14,000 (based on the then-value of the Honda) and agreed to finance the purchase through Acura Financial Services (AFS). Davis thus signed a contract requiring her to pay $39,000 to AFS—the $35,000 price of the Acura, minus Davis's trade-in allowance, plus the unpaid balance of the debt to HMC[342]—and granting AFS a security interest in the Acura. Davis made timely payments on the Acura for the past year, reducing the balance to $34,000, but has now defaulted and filed a Chapter 13 petition. On the petition date, the Acura's value is $24,000. Can Davis use Chapter 13 to write-down the outstanding balance due on the Acura, or does the hanging paragraph prevent her from doing so?

The hanging paragraph provides that Davis cannot use Chapter 13 to bifurcate the claim of AFS if AFS holds a PMSI. But Davis might argue that a portion of the obligation owed to AFS does not reflect the cash price of the current collateral (the Acura) but instead reflects the "negative equity" Davis had on her trade-in vehicle (the Honda), that is, the difference between the balance due to HMC at the time Davis traded-in the Honda and the Honda's value at that time (on the facts used in the problem, $4,000). On this view, Davis might argue that to the extent of this "negative equity" on the Honda trade-in, the security interest of AFS in the Acura is not a PMSI. If that view is correct, Davis could use Chapter 13 to bifurcate AFS's claim into a secured claim for $30,000 and an unsecured claim for $4,000.[343] By contrast, if that view is incorrect, bifurcation is not permitted and AFS would hold a secured claim for $34,000.

While the appropriate interpretation of the hanging paragraph is a question of federal law, courts have consistently looked to the text and comments of U.C.C. § 9-103 for guidance as to the meaning of "purchase-money security interest."[344] Article 9 defines "purchase-money obligation" as "an obligation ... incurred as *all or part of the price of the collateral* or for *value given to enable the debtor to acquire rights in or use of the collateral* if the value is in fact so used."[345] So is the "price" of the Acura limited to its cash price, or does it include the "negative equity" advanced by AFS to clear the title to Davis's trade-in vehicle?

---

342. This amount was added to the debt to allow the Acura dealer to pay off the balance owed to Honda Motor Credit so that the Acura dealer can obtain a clear title to the Honda (and thus be in a position to re-sell the Honda to a new buyer).

343. This explanation assumes that the court applies the "dual-status" rule under which the same security interest can constitute both a PMSI (to the extent of the price of the collateral) and a non-purchase-money security interest (to the extent of other obligations). See § 16.07, *supra*. In consumer-goods transactions, however, Article 9 does not mandate application of the dual-status rule but instead "leave[s] to the court the determination of the proper rules." U.C.C. § 9-103(h). This discretion would permit a court to apply the "transformation" rule, under which a security interest would lose its purchase-money character completely if the collateral secures an obligation other than its purchase price. See § 16.07, *supra*. If a court applied the transformation rule in this problem, the hanging paragraph would not apply at all; Davis could bifurcate AFS's claim into a secured claim for $24,000 (the value of the Acura) and an unsecured claim for $10,000.

344. *Cf.* United States v. Butner, 440 U.S. 48 (1979) (in bankruptcy, property interests are usually defined by reference to state law).

345. U.C.C. § 9-103(a)(2) (emphasis added).

The official comments to Section 9-103 provide a helpful clue:

> As used in subsection (a)(2), the definition of "purchase-money obligation," the "price" of collateral or the "value given to enable" includes obligations for expenses incurred in connection with acquiring rights in the collateral, sales taxes, duties, finance charges, interest, freight charges, costs of storage in transit, demurrage, administrative charges, expenses of collection and enforcement, attorney's fees, and other similar obligations.[346]

Based upon this language, courts in the Second, Fourth, Fifth, Sixth, Seventh, Eighth, Tenth, and Eleventh Circuits have held that the debtor's negative equity in a trade-in vehicle does constitute part of the purchase price of the replacement vehicle.[347] Representative of these decisions is *In re Mierkowski*,[348] in which the Eighth Circuit (in a majority decision) reasoned as follows:

> Comment 3 lists a wide range of obligations that can be part of a vehicle's "price," indicating that "price" should be broadly interpreted. The [debtor's] negative-equity obligation is sufficiently similar to those listed in Comment 3, so as to be within the "other similar obligations" part of the definition of "price." Since the parties here agreed to include the negative equity as part of the total sale price of the new vehicle, the negative equity was "an integral part of" and "inextricably intertwined" with the sales transaction. The negative-equity financing of the trade-in and the new-car purchase were a "package deal." Therefore, there was a "close nexus" between the acquisition of the new vehicle and the negative equity financing.
>
> The amount financed to pay off the negative equity in the trade-in is "part of the price" of the new car, so it is a purchase-money obligation. The new car is purchase-money collateral securing the purchase-money obligation. Thus, [the secured party] has a PMSI securing the negative-equity financing.[349]

Under this view, AFS's security interest in the Acura would constitute a PMSI to the full extent of the balance of the debt (including Davis's negative equity in the Honda trade-in). Thus, under the hanging paragraph, Davis could not use Chapter 13 to bifurcate AFS's claim based upon the market value of the Acura.

As a policy matter, one might defend this result as consistent with the view that Congress adopted the hanging paragraph in response to what it viewed as abuse of Chapter 13 cramdown by automobile buyers. The issue has generated substantial controversy, however. Several of the federal appellate decisions (including *Mierkowski*) have produced strong dissents, and the Ninth Circuit reached a contrary ruling in *In re*

---

346. U.C.C. § 9-103, Comment 3.

347. *In re* Peaslee, 547 F.3d 177 (2d Cir. 2008); *In re* Graupner, 537 F.3d 1295 (11th Cir. 2008); *In re* Price, 562 F.3d 618 (4th Cir. 2009); *In re* Dale, 582 F.3d 568 (5th Cir. 2009); *In re* Mierkowski, 580 F.3d 740 (8th Cir. 2009); *In re* Ford, 574 F.3d 1279 (10th Cir. 2009); *In re* Westfall, 599 F.3d 498 (6th Cir. 2010); *In re* Howard, 597 F.3d 852 (7th Cir. 2010).

348. 580 F.3d 740 (8th Cir. 2009).

349. *Mierkowski*, 580 F.3d at 742–43 (citations omitted).

Penrod,[350] which held that negative equity in a trade-in vehicle constituted antecedent debt, not an "expense[] incurred in connection with acquiring rights in the collateral" within the meaning of Comment 3 to Section 9-103.[351] The dissenting opinion in *Mierkowski* elaborates the rationale for this contrary view:

> [N]egative equity is not part of the price or a cost directly related to purchasing a new vehicle or which *necessarily* arises when purchasing a new vehicle. A new vehicle may be purchased without financing negative equity but cannot be purchased without paying the tax, title, license, etc. Admittedly, in today's market an agreement to finance negative equity is frequently part of the transaction, but our focus is on the "price" of the vehicle, not the transaction.... The fact that financing negative equity has become a customary industry practice ... does not alter the fact that negative equity does not fall within Article 9's definition of "price" or "value given." Money or value given to pay off the negative equity in a trade-in vehicle is not, in the strictest sense, given to acquire rights in the secured collateral. Neither does the negative equity represent any part of the price of the vehicle or associated costs arising directly from the sale.... Negative equity is an antecedent unsecured debt and cannot be transformed into a purchase money obligation secured by a PMSI by rolling it into the loan used to finance the actual price and costs directly related to purchasing the vehicle....
>
> ... Article 9's definition of "purchase money obligation" intends a causal connection between the value given and the acquisition of rights to the collateral. If a creditor loans money to allow a consumer to purchase a vehicle, the value given must be used to acquire the vehicle, not to pay off existing debt. Value given to finance negative equity is not directly related to acquiring the collateral, even if without such financing the transaction would not come to fruition.[352]

The Ninth Circuit has continued to stand alone in rejecting negative equity as falling under the hanging paragraph of Section 1325(a). It remains to be seen if and how Congress or the Supreme Court will resolve the circuit split.[353]

---

350. 611 F.3d 1158 (9th Cir. 2010).

351. *Penrod*, 611 F.3d at 1162–63.

352. *Mierkowski*, 580 F.3d at 746–47 (Bye, J., dissenting) (emphasis in original).

353. The First and Third Circuits have not yet ruled on the issue. Bankruptcy courts in the Third Circuit are split. *Compare In re* Mancini, 390 B.R. 796 (Bankr. M.D. Penn. 2008) (creditor does not have PMSI in negative equity) *with In re* Knepper, 405 B.R. 568 (Bankr. W.D. Penn. 2009) (negative equity is included in lender's PMSI in new vehicle). The one published ruling on the matter in the First Circuit has sided with the Ninth Circuit's view. *See In re* Look, 383 B.R. 210 (Bankr. D. Me. 2008) (negative equity was not included in the price of new vehicle).

Part V

Default

Chapter 17

Default and Its Consequences

Synopsis

§ 17.01 Importance of the Concept of Default

A security interest becomes enforceable when it attaches to the debtor's rights in the collateral.[1] Enforceability means that when "default" occurs,[2] the secured party legally may pursue the remedies set forth in the security agreement and in Article 9.[3] A default is thus critical to the availability of those remedies.[4]

---

1. U.C.C. § 9-203(a).

2. "Default" typically involves an action or failure to act by the obligor on the debt, such as a failure to make timely payment. In some cases, however, the obligor is not the owner of the collateral (or the "debtor," as Article 9 defines the term in Section 9-102(a)(28)(A)). In those cases, a default may involve an action or failure to act by the debtor, such as a sale of the collateral in violation of the security agreement. In most cases, the obligor and the debtor are the same person. For ease of reading, the text often uses the customary term "debtor's default" or "default by the debtor" rather than the more cumbersome "default by the debtor or obligor."

3. U.C.C. § 9-601(a).

4. A secured party that wrongfully repossesses collateral, whether intentionally or in the mistaken belief that a default has occurred, potentially faces significant liability. See, e.g., Ansley v. Conseco Fin. Serv. Corp., 49 U.C.C. Rep. Serv. 2d 955 (Mich. Ct. App. 2002) (creditor liable in conversion when creditor provided no proof that it held security interest in mobile home or that debtor was in default on payment obligations). Repossession in the absence of default typically constitutes a conversion that entitles the debtor to a credit equal to the fair market value of the collateral at the time of the repossession. Further, as conversion is an intentional tort, wrongful repossession also exposes the secured party to the risk of punitive damages. Damages for wrongful repossession are discussed in § 19.01[B], *infra*.

The U.C.C. does not define default, leaving that to the agreement of the parties and to the common law. Most of the cases holding the debtor in default as a matter of common law involve a failure to make a payment when due.[5] While an occasional case holds that some other event constitutes a common-law default,[6] the prudent secured party will not rely solely on the common law for sufficient protection. Every well-drafted security agreement contains a section setting forth the various events (often called "events of default") that will constitute a default under the agreement. The parties should tailor the list of events of default to fit the context of their transaction, but common events of default include the following:

- failure to make a payment when due;[7]

- breach of any obligation imposed on the debtor under another contract between the debtor and the secured party;

- materially false representations by the debtor in financial statements or other information furnished to the secured party in connection with any transaction between the parties;

- breach of any warranty made by the debtor to the secured party, such as a warranty that the debtor has unencumbered title to the collateral;

- breach of any promise made to the secured party by the debtor, such as a promise to use the collateral in a certain manner, keep the collateral in a certain location, insure the collateral, or permit inspection of the collateral or of the debtor's records;

- sale or other disposition of the collateral, or any attempt to sell or dispose of it, without the secured party's written consent (except for ordinary-course sales of inventory);[8]

- creation of a competing lien on the collateral, whether the lien arises voluntarily as a result of the debtor's agreement (i.e., a competing security interest) or involuntarily as a result of a rule of law (e.g., an artisan's lien, tax lien, or judgment lien);

---

5. *See, e.g.,* Cofield v. Randolph Cnty. Comm'n, 90 F.3d 468, 30 U.C.C. Rep. Serv. 2d 374 (11th Cir. 1996).

6. *See, e.g.,* Kahwaty v. Potter, 128 Wash. App. 1004, 57 U.C.C. Rep. Serv. 2d 1000 (2005) (not reported in P.3d) (failure to insure collateral constituted default).

7. Sometimes the loan documents may specify that payment is due by a particular date, but the security agreement provides the obligor with a "grace period" after the due date for payment before a default can arise. Where such a grace period exists, no default can exist to permit the secured party's exercise of default remedies until the grace period expires. *See, e.g.,* Mitchell v. Auto Mart, LLC, 2022 WL 2818346 (D. Nev. 2022) (upholding Fair Debt Collection Practices Act complaint against repo company that repossessed debtor's car prior to expiration of 30-day grace period in security agreement).

8. *See, e.g.,* Seifert v. U.S. Bank, 2022 WL 1311177 (E.D. Cal. 2022) (even if debtors were current in payments on recreational vehicle loan, security agreement obligated them to keep RV in their possession and not to attempt to sell it without secured party's written permission, which debtors violated by transferring possession to a broker for sale).

- death or bankruptcy of the debtor;[9]

- dissolution, termination, insolvency, or failure of the debtor's business; or an assignment for the benefit of creditors, receivership, or other state debtor/creditor relief proceeding;

- theft, loss, or substantial damage to or destruction of the collateral;

- failure to account properly for proceeds of the collateral; and

- any event that causes the secured party to feel insecure, such as a decline in the debtor's business fortunes or a depletion in the value of the collateral.[10]

The preceding list is not exclusive, and a secured party may define other events as defaults depending on the nature of the transaction.[11] In many commercial financing arrangements, for example, the secured party will require the debtor to maintain at all times collateral valued at a stipulated level in relation to the loan balance (the loan-to-value ratio),[12] and failure to maintain the necessary ratio will constitute an event of default. For another example, suppose Secured Party sells goods to Debtor on credit, retaining a purchase-money security interest in them. If the goods prove to be defective in breach of warranty, Debtor may unilaterally reduce its payments, relying on an Article 2 provision that permits a buyer to notify a seller of breach and then deduct all or part of the damages from that portion of the price that is still due.[13] Secured Party, of course, will insist that Debtor's payment obligation is independent of the warranty obligation. A clause making any attempt at set-off an event of default, regardless of motivation, will achieve this result. A competent transactional attorney must have a solid understanding of the transaction at issue and a good imagination to anticipate foreseeable risks and draft a document that protects the secured party against those risks. The security agreement should include, as a default, anything that foreseeably could impair the debtor's ability to pay or the secured party's interest in the collateral.

---

9. While security agreements customarily specify that the debtor's bankruptcy constitutes a default, these "ipso facto" clauses are generally not enforceable in bankruptcy. *See* Jeffrey Ferriell & Edward J. Janger, Understanding Bankruptcy § 9.03[F] (4th ed. 2019).

10. The secured party may declare a default and accelerate the maturity of the debt on grounds of insecurity only if the agreement explicitly so provides and the secured party "in good faith believes that the prospect of payment or performance is impaired." U.C.C. § 1-309. The debtor bears the burden of establishing the secured party's lack of good faith. *Id.* For further discussion, see § 17.01[B], *infra.*

11. State statutes sometimes limit the permissible events of default in consumer contracts, and a secured party's remedies under Article 9 are subject to such statutes. U.C.C. § 9-201(b), (c). For example, Mo. Rev. Stat. § 408.552 provides that in certain credit transactions, primarily consumer in nature, an agreement concerning default "is enforceable only to the extent that: (1) The borrower fails to make a payment as required by agreement; or (2) The lender's prospect of payment, performance, or ability to realize upon the collateral is significantly impaired; the burden of establishing significant impairment is on the lender."

12. *See* § 3.04[B], *supra.*

13. U.C.C. § 2-717.

[A] Waiver of Default

The fact that a default occurs does not mean that the secured party *must* foreclose on its collateral. In some instances, the security agreement may grant the secured party a remedy that is not as drastic as foreclosure. For example, if the debtor fails to keep the collateral insured, the security agreement may provide that the secured party may purchase insurance and add its cost to the principal balance of the obligation.[14] Even in the event of a default in payment, the secured party typically will attempt to work with the debtor to resolve the problem without having to resort to foreclosure. For example, suppose the debtor makes a late payment. Rather than declaring a default and accelerating the loan, the secured party may admonish the debtor, extend the time for the debtor to make the payment, or just do nothing. After all, foreclosure is an expensive process that may not satisfy the debt in full; further, if carried out improperly, foreclosure can expose the secured party to liability. In short, the secured party may choose to waive the default or otherwise forbear from exercising its default remedies.

While this attitude of leniency and compromise is one that courts should encourage, numerous court decisions have held that waiver of a default may compromise the secured party's ability to enforce its rights in the event of a future default. For example, suppose Debtor makes one late payment which Secured Party accepts. Suppose further that Debtor is late making its payment the following month, at which time Secured Party refuses the payment, accelerates the debt, and repossesses the collateral. Debtor may argue that the waiver in the first instance operated also as a waiver in the second instance, thereby obligating Secured Party to accept the untimely payment rather than declare a default. Based on the weight of authority, with just one prior waiver, a court probably will not accept Debtor's argument.[15] If Secured Party has accepted late payments from Debtor on several previous occasions, however, Debtor's argument becomes much stronger. For example, the secured party in *Slusser v. Wyrick*[16] repeatedly accepted payments as many as 15 days late from a debtor that had purchased an automobile on a retail installment contract, yet it later repossessed the automobile only three days after the due date of a payment. The court affirmed a judgment that the secured party had wrongfully repossessed the automobile, stating:

> The record in this case reveals, however, that appellant repeatedly accepted appellees' untimely (late) installment payments. Under these facts, a majority of those courts which have considered the issue have interpreted [Article 9] to impose a duty on the creditor to notify the debtor that strict compliance with the time for payment will henceforth be required in order to avert repossession. Stated in other words, the acceptance of late payments by a creditor who

---

14. A secured party in possession of the collateral has the right to purchase insurance and add it to the debt, even without a clause in the security agreement authorizing it to do so. *See* U.C.C. §9-207(b)(1).

15. *See, e.g.*, Page v. JP Morgan Chase Bank, N.A., 605 Fed. Appx. 272 (5th Cir. 2015) (applying Texas law); Ash v. Peoples Bank of Greensboro, 500 So. 2d 5, 3 U.C.C. Rep. Serv. 2d 426 (Ala. 1986).

16. 28 Ohio App. 3d 96, 502 N.E.2d 259 (1986).

has the statutory or contractual right to repossess the collateral estops the creditor from lawfully repossessing said collateral without notice after subsequent late payment default.[17]

If the debtor attempts to resist foreclosure by arguing that the secured party's prior conduct has waived its enforcement rights, the secured party may attempt to rely on an "anti-waiver clause" (assuming its security agreement contained such a clause). An anti-waiver clause, which is a boilerplate provision contained in most security agreements, typically provides roughly as follows:

> All rights, powers, and remedies of Secured Party hereunder or under any other obligation are cumulative and not alternative and shall not be exhausted by any single assertion thereof. The failure of Secured Party to exercise any such right, power or remedy will not be deemed a waiver thereof nor preclude any further or additional exercise of such right, power or remedy, now or in the future, upon any obligation of Debtor. The waiver of any default hereunder shall not be a waiver of any subsequent default.

Parties asserting anti-waiver clauses have met with mixed success in court decisions. In some cases, courts have held that the inclusion of an anti-waiver clause in the security agreement did not preclude a conclusion that the creditor had nevertheless waived its ability to declare a default based on untimely performance. Many such courts have relied on a "course-of-performance" argument.[18] For example, the secured party in *Moe v. John Deere Co.*[19] accepted a series of late payments and then declared a default without notifying the debtor that it had decided to enforce all future payment due dates in a strict fashion. The court held that the secured party had engaged in a course

---

17. *Slusser*, 28 Ohio App. 3d at 97, 502 N.E.2d 259 at 260 (citations omitted). *Accord* Found. Prop. Inv, LLC v. CTP, LLC, 286 Kan. 597, 186 P.3d 766 (2008); Cobb v. Midwest Recovery Bureau Co., 295 N.W.2d 232, 28 U.C.C. Rep. Serv. 941 (Minn. 1980); Nevada Nat'l Bank v. Huff, 94 Nev. 506, 582 P.2d 364 (1978).

In *Cobb*, the Minnesota Supreme Court held that "the repeated acceptance of late payments by a creditor who has the contractual right to repossess the property imposes a duty on the creditor to notify the debtor that strict compliance with the contract terms will be required before the creditor can lawfully repossess the collateral." *Cobb*, 295 N.W.2d at 237. But a recent federal court decision in Minnesota calls into doubt whether a debtor could bring a federal Fair Debt Collection Practices Act action against a secured party for failure to send the notice ostensibly required by *Cobb*. In *Freeman v. Ally Financial, Inc.*, 528 F. Supp. 3d 1038, 104 U.C.C. Rep. Serv. 2d 492 (D. Minn. 2021), the debtor brought such an action, but the creditor argued that Minnesota's Credit Agreement Statute, MINN. STAT. § 513.33 (which prohibits an action on a credit agreement unless the agreement is in writing), precluded the debtor's action. The court held that the debtor's FDCPA claim depended on proof of an unwritten agreement between the debtor and the secured party regarding late payments and thus was barred by Section 513.33. *Freeman*, 528 F. Supp. 3d at 1045–46.

18. U.C.C. § 1-303(a). Waiver by estoppel can also arise based on a course of dealing established during past loan transactions between the parties. U.C.C. § 1-303(b). *See, e.g.*, J.R. Hale Contracting Co. v. United N.M. Bank, 799 P.2d 581, 13 U.C.C. Rep. Serv. 2d 53 (N.M. 1990).

19. 516 N.W.2d 332, 25 U.C.C. Rep. Serv. 2d 997 (S.D. 1994).

of performance that estopped it from insisting on timely payment or relying on the anti-waiver provision in the security agreement.[20]

Nevertheless, the weight of recent authority has upheld the enforceability of an anti-waiver provision. *Minor v. Chase Auto Finance Corp.*[21] is representative:

> [I]f a contract includes non-waiver and no-unwritten-modification clauses, the creditor, in accepting late payments, does not waive its right under the contract to declare default of the debt, and need not give notice that it will enforce that right in the event of future late payments....
>
> [A] rule providing that non-waiver clauses could themselves be waived by the acceptance of late payments is "illogical, since the very conduct which the [non-waiver] clause is designed to permit[,] acceptance of the late payment[,] is turned around to constitute waiver of the clause permitting the conduct."[22]

The *Minor* court concluded that the parties' agreement as to the non-waiver clause placed the secured party in the position of one who had never accepted a late payment (and thus had not waived its ability to insist upon timely payment).[23] However, because of the lack of judicial consensus on whether a non-waiver clause can itself be waived, a creditor should not rely solely on an anti-waiver clause absent clear judicial authority in the applicable jurisdiction. Instead, a creditor that chooses to forbear in the face of a default should always communicate to the debtor, in a record, that the creditor's forbearance does not constitute a waiver of the creditor's right to insist that the debtor make timely performance of its future obligations.

While the waiver-by-estoppel argument has some appeal in consumer cases, it loses some of its force in commercial contracts.[24] After all, a commercial debtor is probably well aware of the fact that it is making its payments late, and it may well be relying on the fact that it is more trouble for the secured party to foreclose on the loan than it is to continue to accept late payments. As a result, many courts have refused to apply

---

20. *Moe*, 516 N.W.2d at 338. *See also* Smith v. General Fin. Corp. of Ga., 243 Ga. 500, 255 S.E.2d 14 (1979) (evidence of seller's acceptance of repeated late and irregular payments raised jury question whether seller had waived the contract's anti-waiver provision); Battista v. Savings Bank of Balt., 67 Md. App. 257, 507 A.2d 203 (1986) (same). The *Moe* court noted that the secured party could revoke its waiver by notifying the debtor that it would insist upon timely payments in the future. U.C.C. § 2-209(5) permits revocation of a waiver affecting the executory portion of a sales contract unless revocation would be unjust because of reliance on the waiver.

21. 372 S.W.3d 762, 72 U.C.C. Rep. Serv. 2d 610 (Ark. 2010).

22. *Minor*, 372 S.W.3d at 767–68, 72 U.C.C. Rep. Serv. 2d at 615, 617 (quoting Van Bibber v. Norris, 275 Ind. 555, 419 N.E.2d 115 (1981)). *See also* Wells Fargo Bank v. Smith, 2013 WL 5230615 (Ohio Ct. App. 2013) (not reported in N.E.2d).

23. *Minor*, 372 S.W.3d at 768, 72 U.C.C. Rep. Serv. 2d at 617. *See also* Lewis v. Nat'l City Bank, 814 F. Supp. 696, 21 U.C.C. Rep. Serv. 2d 380 (N.D. Ill. 1993), *aff'd*, 23 F.3d 410 (7th Cir. 1994); Van Bibber v. Norris, 275 Ind. 555, 419 N.E.2d 115 (1981); Ford Motor Credit Co. v. Ryan, 72 U.C.C. Rep. Serv. 2d 977 (Ohio Ct. App. 2010).

24. *See, e.g.*, B.P.G. Autoland Jeep-Eagle, Inc. v. Chrysler Credit Corp., 799 F. Supp. 1250, 19 U.C.C. Rep. Serv. 2d 649 (D. Mass. 1992).

the waiver doctrine in the commercial context, especially if the security agreement contained an anti-waiver provision.[25]

As discussed previously,[26] any repossession when there is no default constitutes a conversion. Thus, a secured party that repossesses the collateral, only to have the debtor successfully raise the defense of waiver by estoppel, is liable for conversion. If the creditor has simply tired of accepting late payments and chosen to accelerate the debt, however, courts have shown the creditor more leniency than in cases of knowing conversion. For example, the court in *Cobb v. Midwest Recovery Bureau Co.*,[27] while holding that the secured party's repossession was wrongful because the secured party failed to notify the debtor that it would insist on timely payments in the future, refused to allow punitive damages against the secured party. Courts have not been equally forgiving when the secured party pursues its default remedies following an express waiver of default. For example, in *Alaska Statebank v. Fairco*,[28] the secured party told the defaulting debtor that it would not foreclose until after the holidays. When it later reneged and repossessed its collateral, effectively shutting down the debtor's business before it could reap the benefits of the holiday season, the court approved an award of punitive damages.

[B] Acceleration Clauses and Insecurity Clauses

If default occurs, the secured party may invoke the remedies provided in Article 9 as well as any remedies included in the security agreement. The agreement typically will contain an acceleration clause which, when invoked, renders the entire outstanding debt presently due and payable. The secured party will then repossess the collateral and proceed with foreclosure.[29]

If the secured party accelerates the maturity of the debt following one of the standard events of default, there is relatively little controversy. For example, suppose Secured Party accelerates the maturity of the debt after Debtor misses two monthly payments

---

25. *See, e.g.,* Bank of Am., N.A. v. New Eng. Quality Serv., Inc., 790 Fed. Appx. 314 (2d Cir. 2019); Lewis v. Nat'l City Bank, 814 F. Supp. 696, 21 U.C.C. Rep. Serv. 2d 380 (N.D. Ill. 1993), *aff'd*, 23 F.3d 410 (7th Cir. 1994); First Nat'l Bank of Omaha v. Centennial Park, LLC, 303 P.3d 705 (Kan. Ct. App. 2013) (mortgage lender's right to accelerate after default not waived by acceptance of late payment where note contained unambiguous anti-waiver clause). *See also* Shields Ltd. P'ship v. Bradberry, 526 S.W.3d 471 (Tex. 2017) (commercial landlord did not waive non-waiver clause in commercial lease by accepting late rental payments because clause specifically precluded acceptance of late rental payments as a waiver of landlord's enforcement rights). Watkins Dev., LLC v. Jackson Redev. Auth., 283 So. 3d 170 (Miss. 2019) (commercial landlord's initial forbearance did not estop it from terminating lease for failure to meet deadline for tenant improvements where lease contained anti-waiver clause).

26. *See* note 4, *supra.*

27. 295 N.W.2d 232, 28 U.C.C. Rep. Serv. 941 (Minn. 1980).

28. 674 P.2d 288, 37 U.C.C. Rep. Serv. 1782 (Alaska 1983).

29. The secured party need not accelerate prior to foreclosure, but if it fails to accelerate, it cannot retain from the foreclosure sale any proceeds in excess of the amount due and unpaid at that time. Thus, it is exceptionally rare for a secured party to foreclose without first accelerating the maturity of the debt.

and fails to keep the collateral insured. Debtor may attempt to argue that acceleration is improper because Debtor's net worth is large enough to ensure that Secured Party will eventually collect full payment of the debt. Nevertheless, if the security agreement provides that nonpayment and failure to insure are events of default, Debtor's argument will fail.[30]

Problems can arise, however, if the secured party accelerates[31] based upon an "insecurity clause," that is, a clause that entitles the secured party to accelerate either "at will" or when it "deems itself insecure." The U.C.C. permits acceleration based on an insecurity clause only if the secured party "in good faith believes that the prospect of payment or performance is impaired."[32] Even though the debtor bears the burden of establishing lack of good faith,[33] numerous lenders have incurred liability under this standard. Much

---

30. The general obligation of good faith in the enforcement of a security agreement, *see* U.C.C. § 1-304, does not mean that a secured party can pursue its remedies only when its likelihood of payment or its security is threatened. The weight of authority holds that the specific provisions of Section 1-309, which require likelihood of nonpayment or a threat to the creditor's security before the creditor may accelerate "at will" or for "insecurity," do not apply following a traditional objective event of default defined in the security agreement. *See, e.g.,* Bowen v. Danna, 637 S.W.2d 560, 34 U.C.C. Rep. Serv. 1095 (Ark. 1982). There is one noteworthy case to the contrary, *see* Brown v. AVEMCO Inv. Corp., 603 F.2d 1367 (9th Cir. 1979) (acceleration of debt and repossession and sale of plane, based upon debtor's lease and sale of plane, lacked good faith when plane's purchasers were prepared to redeem the plane, and thus secured party had no reason to believe its prospect of payment was impaired), but there is little doubt that the case is wrongly decided.

Thus, although the general duty of good faith always governs the secured party's actions, a court is not likely to hold that a secured party violated that duty by accelerating due to an event that the parties agreed would constitute a default. Acceleration based on such a default would be permissible unless the court concluded that the secured party was using the event of default as a pretext and was, in truth, accelerating the loan due to personal animus or some other illegitimate reason. *See* R. Wilson Freyermuth, *Enforcement of Acceleration Provisions and the Rhetoric of Good Faith,* 1998 BYU L. Rev. 1035.

31. Although most of the cases involve attempts to accelerate, the problems described in this section also arise when the secured party requires the debtor to provide additional collateral pursuant to a clause that allows the secured party to make such a demand, either at will or when the secured party deems itself insecure. U.C.C. § 1-309.

32. *Id.* Section 1-309 applies only to acceleration of a debt that is otherwise due on a future date. The section does not apply to a "demand note," which is a note under which full payment is not due on a specific future date but instead on the creditor's demand. *Id.,* Comment 1; Reger Dev., LLC v. Nat'l City Bank, 592 F.3d 759 (7th Cir. 2010) (applying Illinois law); In re Lehman Bros. Holdings Inc., 541 B.R. 551 (S.D.N.Y. 2015) (applying New York law).

Disputes can potentially turn on the specific language of an insecurity clause. For example, in *Hussein v. UBS Bank USA,* 446 P.3d 96 (Utah Ct. App. 2019), the loan documents permitted UBS (the secured party) to accelerate the debt if it "deems itself *or its security interest in the Collateral* insecure" (emphasis added). The collateral included more than 2 million shares of Quality Systems, Inc. (QSI), which began rapidly declining in value, reducing the value of the collateral by more than $20 million. UBS wanted to liquidate the shares, but the debtor did not wish to do so because of an ongoing proxy contest for control of QSI. UBS nevertheless sold the shares, at which point the debtor sued for breach of the loan agreement, arguing that UBS could not reasonably have deemed itself insecure because the debtor's assets exceeded the unpaid loan amount. The court rejected this claim, holding that UBS could have felt its collateral was insecure (based on the drop in QSI's market value) and thus properly accelerated on that basis even if it did not feel insecure as to repayment of the loans.

33. *Id.* The effect is to create a presumption of good faith in the secured party's favor.

of the litigation in these cases has turned on whether a lender's good faith is evaluated using a subjective or an objective standard. The Code's original definition of "good faith" invoked a purely subjective test—whether the secured party is honest in its belief that its prospect of payment or performance is impaired.[34] Under the purely subjective good-faith standard, an honest lender invoking an insecurity clause would be immune from liability even if most lenders would not have accelerated under the same circumstances. Indeed, under the subjective standard, some courts treated secured parties as acting in good faith even though they relied upon incorrect information and further inquiry would have revealed the true facts.[35] However, the Uniform Commercial Code revision process has resulted in a systematic redefinition of "good faith" to include both "honesty in fact" and "the observance of reasonable commercial standards of fair dealing."[36] Under this approach, a lender's decision to invoke an insecurity clause will also be evaluated based upon whether a reasonable secured party might have chosen to act similarly based upon the same circumstances.[37] Generally speaking, lenders have not fared well in litigation, and an entire field of "lender liability" cases has developed in which courts have imposed substantial damages for conduct that may well have been subjectively honest.[38] While many of these cases involved unsecured loans, their analysis of the problems associated with acceleration is relevant to enforcement of secured loans as well.

---

34. U.C.C. § 1-201(19) (1972 text).

35. *See, e.g.,* Van Horn v. Van De Wol, Inc., 6 Wash. App. 959, 497 P.2d 252, 10 U.C.C. Rep. Serv. 1143 (Wash. App. 1972) (negligence in failing to investigate further is irrelevant to determination of good faith).

36. U.C.C. § 1-201(b)(20).

37. Even under the Code's original subjective definition of good faith, numerous courts held that a lender's decision to invoke an insecurity clause lacked good faith under circumstances when a reasonable lender would not have taken such action. For example, in *Sheppard Federal Credit Union v. Palmer*, 408 F.2d 1369, 6 U.C.C. Rep. Serv. 30 (5th Cir. 1969), the secured party, a credit union located on an Air Force base, accelerated and repossessed a vehicle because the debtor (an officer) was leaving the Air Force. The secured party accelerated even though every indication suggested that the debtor would quickly find other suitable employment, and the debtor in fact did obtain other employment. The court, citing Professor Gilmore's authoritative treatise *Security Interests in Personal Property*, held that the secured party had acted in bad faith because it did not have an objective basis for believing that its debt was insecure. *See also* Bank of China v. L.V.P. Assocs., LLC, 2021 WL 6139750 (N.J. Super. Ct. App. Div. 2021) (not reported in A.3d) (determining whether "material adverse change" existed to justify acceleration involves objective determination of what a reasonable creditor would view as material); Bay Venture Elyria, LLC v. Advanced Plastics Reclaiming, LLC, 82 U.C.C. Rep. Serv. 2d 264 (N.D. Ohio 2013) (not reported in F. Supp. 2d); Blaine v. General Motors Acceptance Corp., 82 Misc. 2d 653, 370 N.Y.S.2d 323, 17 U.C.C. Rep. Serv. 641 (Cnty. Ct. 1975) (applying objective standard to uphold creditor's acceleration for insecurity where creditor acted following debtor's arrest for drug transportation, based upon threat of forfeiture of collateral); Clayton v. Crossroads Equip. Co., 655 P.2d 1125, 34 U.C.C. Rep. Serv. 1448 (Utah 1982) (applying objective standard to impose liability on accelerating creditor that had received information indicating that debtor's financial condition had deteriorated).

38. The seminal case in this area is *K.M.C. Co. v. Irving Trust Co.*, 757 F.2d 752 (6th Cir. 1985), in which the creditor refused to extend the debtor additional credit under an outstanding line of credit.

§ 17.02 Remedies Available upon Default

[A] Types of Remedies

If the debtor is in default, the secured party can avail itself of a variety of remedies. Because Article 9 sets forth the core remedies, the security agreement need not reiterate them, although the typical security agreement does precisely that. The Code's remedial scheme permits the secured party to take possession of the collateral (through self-help if it can be done without breach of the peace, but otherwise through judicial action) and then dispose of it and apply the proceeds toward the underlying obligation.[39] This process is the right of *foreclosure*.

Most security agreements establish remedies that go well beyond what the Code provides. The most important remedy not provided by operation of law, as discussed in the preceding section, is the right to accelerate the debt. In addition, most well-drafted security agreements provide for some (or all) of the following remedies:

- the right to require the debtor to provide additional collateral;[40]

- the right to recover attorneys' fees and costs of collection;

- the right to remedy a default (e.g., to purchase insurance for uninsured collateral or to pay off a competing lien) and add the cost of doing so to the principal balance of the debt;[41]

- the right to require that the debtor assemble the collateral and make it available to the secured party at a place designated by the secured party (so long as it is reasonably convenient to the debtor);[42] and

- the right of the secured party to use collateral other than consumer goods pending its disposition.[43]

---

39. If the collateral is intangible and not capable of repossession, Article 9 provides alternative methods for realizing its value. *See* § 18.03, *infra*.

40. When linked to an insecurity clause, the provisions of U.C.C. § 1-309 apply to this right. *See* § 17.01[B], *supra*.

41. *See, e.g.,* Foster v. Parker Comm. Credit Union, 915 N.W.2d 730 (Table) (Wis. Ct. App. 2018) (secured party permitted to obtain and bill debtors for retroactive gap insurance for period of time debtors failed to maintain continuous insurance coverage).

42. U.C.C. § 9-609(c) explicitly authorizes this remedy, but only if the security agreement so provides. The value of this remedy lies in its *in terrorem* effect, although at least one court has issued a mandatory injunction requiring that the debtor comply with a mandatory assembly clause. *See* Clark Equip. Co. v. Armstrong Equip. Co., 431 F.2d 54, 7 U.C.C. Rep. Serv. 1249 (5th Cir. 1970).

43. U.C.C. § 9-207(b)(4) provides this remedy. A secured party in possession of collateral has a statutory right to use or operate it for the purpose of preserving its value even if this right is not included in the security agreement. But if the secured party wishes to use the collateral to produce revenue, such as by leasing it to generate rent, the security agreement must permit this remedy, or the secured party must get a court order authorizing such use. For a case in which the secured party leased an aircraft to produce significant revenue pending disposition, see Contrail Leasing Partners, Ltd. v. Consolidated Airways, Inc., 742 F.2d 1095, 39 U.C.C. Rep. Serv. 9 (7th Cir. 1984). *See also In re* MJK Clearing, Inc., 286 B.R. 862, 48 U.C.C. Rep. Serv. 2d 1244 (Bankr. D. Minn. 2002) (security agreement gave pledgee right to commingle money given as collateral or to repledge it in other transactions).

The security agreement may specify additional remedies depending on the context of the transaction or the law of the jurisdiction. In Missouri, for example, a secured party may include a clause in its security agreement allowing it to sell collateral upon 15 days' notice following replevin[44] by the sheriff even though the court has not rendered a final judgment awarding possession to the secured party.[45]

A secured party need not pursue its remedies as an Article 9 secured party at all. It can instead sue to obtain an *in personam* judgment on the debt and then use the jurisdiction's ordinary judicial procedures available to any judgment creditor.[46] In other words, the secured party can obtain a writ of execution pursuant to which the sheriff can levy on and sell *any* nonexempt assets of the debtor, real or personal. These assets can include, but are not limited to, the collateral.[47] This procedure provides a potential advantage for the secured party. Because the sheriff conducts the sale following procedures approved under non-Code state law, the secured party is insulated from liability based on a defect in the sale process.[48] Further, the secured party does not lose its Article 9 priority by proceeding in this fashion as any lien on the collateral created by the levy relates back to the date on which the secured party perfected its security interest (or, if earlier, the date on which it filed its financing statement).[49]

---

44. Replevin is a judicial action in which the collateral is seized by the sheriff and then the court determines which party has the superior right of possession. If the debtor is in default, the secured party is statutorily entitled to possession, U.C.C. § 9-609(a), and will ultimately obtain a judgment of possession from the court. The debtor, however, must have the opportunity to answer, and if the debtor does so, the issue must proceed to trial. In the meantime, the sheriff holds the asset *in custodia legis*.

45. *See* B-W Acceptance Corp. v. Alexander, 494 S.W.2d 75 (Mo. 1973).

46. U.C.C. § 9-601(a)(1) permits the secured party to reduce its claim to judgment, foreclose, or otherwise enforce the security agreement by any available judicial procedure. *See, e.g.,* VFS Financing, Inc. v. Shilo Mgmt. Corp., 372 P.3d 582, 89 U.C.C. Rep. Serv. 2d 600 (Or. Ct. App. 2016) (secured party can pursue judgment on note and guaranty without moving forward with sale of collateral); Spellman v. Independent Bankers' Bank of Fla., 161 So.3d 505, 84 U.C.C. Rep. Serv. 2d 333 (Fla. Dist. Ct. App. 2014) (creditor could repossess collateral while concurrently pursuing a money judgment for full amount due); Okefenokee Aircraft, Inc. v. PrimeSouth Bank, 676 S.E.2d 394, 68 U.C.C. Rep. Serv. 2d 576 (Ga. Ct. App. 2009) (secured creditor may seek money judgment on loan balance without first having to dispose of collateral); Financial Pacific Leasing, L.L.C. v. Freeman, 2001 Wash. App. 2350, 46 U.C.C. Rep. Serv. 2d 610 (2001) (contrary to debtor's assertion, secured party was not required to make effort to repossess collateral before bringing claim for judgment).

47. *See* § 14.02, *supra.*

48. *See, e.g.,* Timothy R. Zinnecker, *The Default Provisions of Revised Article 9,* 54 Bus. Lawyer 1113, 1116 (1999); Dakota Bank & Trust Co. v. Reed, 402 N.W.2d 887, 3 U.C.C. Rep. Serv. 2d 1976 (N.D. 1987). By contrast, if the secured party conducts an Article 9 foreclosure sale, the secured party faces liability if it conducts a commercially unreasonable sale that causes injury to the debtor. U.C.C. §§ 9-610(b), 9-625(b).

49. U.C.C. § 9-601(e). Conceptually, the sheriff's levy and sale is a foreclosure of the original security interest. U.C.C. § 9-601(f). In most states, levy creates a lien that runs in favor of the judgment creditor. *See* § 14.02, *supra.* In the case of a secured party, this lien is not important unless the secured party failed to perfect its security interest. The fact that the sheriff's sale is a foreclosure of the original security interest offers protection against a claim that the levy and sale amount to a preferential transfer that is avoidable in bankruptcy. *See* § 16.04[E], *supra.*

Serious drawbacks, however, accompany a decision to sue on the debt without first proceeding to repossess and foreclose on the collateral. Unless the secured party has some basis for pre-judgment attachment,[50] it must wait until final judgment before it can obtain a writ of execution. During this interim period, the collateral—which is still in the hands of the debtor—may diminish in value or disappear, threatening the secured party's prospects for eventual recovery. Further, because most sheriff's sales are auction sales for ready cash, they typically bring very low prices, perhaps much lower than a secured party might obtain in an arms-length private sale under Article 9. This latter disadvantage is offset by the fact that the secured party can bid at the sheriff's sale,[51] and, because the amount bid by the purchaser at the sheriff's sale is applied to reduce the judgment debt (after the costs of the sheriff's sale are paid), the secured party can "credit bid" up to the amount of its judgment without producing any cash. In other words, if the judgment is for $10,000 and the secured party is the successful bidder at $7,000, its judgment will simply be reduced to $3,000. The secured party then becomes the owner of the asset and can resell it in a more favorable market without having to worry about Article 9's procedural requirements for foreclosure sales.[52]

The Code creates one additional remedy worth a brief mention. If the secured party has taken a security interest in both real and personal property as part of the same transaction,[53] it may be convenient to sell them together. Indeed, it may be financially advantageous to sell a business that owns the real property on which it operates as a going concern rather than in a piecemeal fashion. In such cases, the Code provides that "a secured party may proceed ... as to both the personal property and the real property in accordance with the rights with respect to the real property, in which case the other provisions of [Article 9, Part 6] do not apply."[54] This means that the secured party can sell the personal property as a part of the real property foreclosure, in which case it need not also comply with the procedural rules governing Article 9 foreclosure sales.

---

50. Although the grounds for attachment vary from state to state, the secured party typically must allege some type of fraud or evasion of process to obtain pre-judgment attachment. A writ of attachment, when issued, orders the sheriff to seize assets of the debtor (including the collateral) and to hold them pending the outcome of the litigation. If the secured party ultimately obtains a judgment, the assets can be sold under a writ of execution.

51. U.C.C. § 9-601(f). Similarly, the secured party can bid at its own Article 9 foreclosure sale if that sale is a public auction sale. See § 18.02[C], infra.

52. Sometimes a judgment creditor may acquire the property at an execution sale via credit bid and then later sell the property at a profit. When this occurs, the judgment debtor may attempt to set aside the execution sale based upon the inadequacy of the sale price. Courts generally will not set aside an execution sale based upon inadequacy of the sale price alone, absent some irregularity in the execution sale procedure. See, e.g., Miebach v. Colasurdo, 102 Wash. 2d 170, 685 P.2d 1074 (1974). Likewise, the Uniform Voidable Transactions Act (formerly the Uniform Fraudulent Transfer Act) provides that a below-market-value execution sale price will not render the execution sale a fraudulent conveyance if the sale was "regularly conducted" and "noncollusive." UVTA §§ 3(b), 4(a)(2).

53. This is common in commercial mortgage loans. For example, a commercial loan secured by a hotel might include both the land and hotel building (realty) as well as all of the equipment, furniture, and intangibles used in operating the hotel (personalty).

54. U.C.C. § 9-604(a)(2).

Alternatively, the secured party can proceed under Article 9 with respect to the personal property without prejudicing any rights that it has with respect to the real property.[55]

[B] Cumulation of Remedies

Article 9 provides that the remedies available to the secured party—those available under the Code, the security agreement, and non-Code state law—are cumulative.[56] The secured party thus may exercise the various remedies simultaneously and need not make an election among them. The secured party can sue to obtain an *in personam* judgment without losing its right to repossess the collateral at a later date and commence an Article 9 foreclosure.[57] It can go through the Article 9 foreclosure process and then sue to obtain a judgment for any remaining deficiency.[58] It can first pursue guarantors and then proceed against the collateral, or vice-versa.[59] It can exercise its common-law right of set-off against a bank account of the debtor and later proceed against the rest of its collateral.[60] Perhaps the most extreme instance of the application of the cumulative remedies doctrine *is Kennedy v. Bank of Ephraim*,[61] in which the secured party held as collateral a certificate of deposit that it had issued to the debtor. Rather than cashing out the certificate, the secured party sued the debtor for an *in personam* judgment and then proceeded to levy against real estate owned by the debtor. The court held that the secured party was free to follow this rather unusual course under the cumulative-remedies doctrine.

The doctrine has some limitations. A few states have special consumer legislation that requires the secured party to make an election of remedies.[62] In addition, a few

---

55. U.C.C. § 9-604(a)(1); *In re* Kearns, 314 B.R. 819, 544 U.C.C. Rep. Serv. 2d 958 (Bankr. 9th Cir. 2004) (secured creditor did not forfeit its mortgage lien on the borrowers' real property by foreclosing on its security interest in the borrowers' automobile that secured the same loan).

56. U.C.C. § 9-601(c).

57. *See, e.g.*, VFS Financing, Inc. v. Shilo Mgmt. Corp., 372 P.3d 582, 89 U.C.C. Rep. Serv. 2d 600 (Or. Ct. App. 2016); Spellman v. Indep. Bankers' Bank of Fla., 161 So.3d 505, 84 U.C.C. Rep. Serv. 2d 333 (Fla. Dist. Ct. App. 2014); Okefenokee Aircraft, Inc. v. PrimeSouth Bank, 296 Ga. App. 782, 676 S.E.2d 576 (2009); Center Capital Corp. v. Marlin Air, Inc., 66 U.C.C. Rep. Serv. 2d 139 (E.D. Mich. 2008); *In re* Plante, 66 U.C.C. Rep. Serv. 2d 384 (Bankr. D. Idaho 2008).

58. The secured party's right to a deficiency judgment may be precluded or limited because of its misconduct during the foreclosure process. *See* § 19.02, *infra*.

59. If the secured party is going to defer action against guarantors, it should advise them that, by doing so, it is not abandoning its rights against them. Although such notice ought not be necessary under the doctrine of cumulative remedies, courts are solicitous of guarantors. Failure to give notice exposes a secured party to the argument that it abandoned its rights against a guarantor. *Cf.* ESL Fed. Credit Union v. Bovee, 56 U.C.C. Rep. Serv. 2d 517 (N.Y. Sup. Ct. 2005) (denying summary judgment against guarantor where secured creditor returned repossessed vehicle and released its security interest upon debtor's cure of default, without obtaining guarantor's consent).

60. *See, e.g.*, Jensen v. State Bank of Allison, 518 F.2d 1, 17 U.C.C. Rep. Serv. 286 (8th Cir. 1975).

61. 594 P.2d 881, 26 U.C.C. Rep. Serv. 558 (Utah 1979).

62. See, for example, California's Unruh Act, CAL. CIV. CODE § 1801 *et seq.* (West 1985), pursuant to which parties enforcing retail installment sales contracts must make a binding election to pursue either the collateral or an *in personam* judgment. Some states also have a "one-action" rule

courts have held that a secured party may not simultaneously pursue two remedies against the debtor. The leading case to this effect is *Ayares-Eisenberg Perrine Datsun, Inc. v. Sun Bank of Miami*,[63] in which the court concluded that simultaneously maintaining an action for an *in personam* judgment and foreclosing against the collateral amounted to harassment of the debtor. Although Article 9 does not entirely displace common-law limitations on harassment of debtors,[64] it is difficult to understand why it is harassment for a secured party to do simultaneously what it could legitimately do sequentially, and a contrary (and appropriate) result was reached in *Glamorgan Coal Corp. v. Bowen*.[65] The secured party has an obligation to proceed in good faith, and compliance with this duty should provide sufficient protection against debtor harassment.

In some circumstances, to protect the rights of another creditor, a court may require a secured party to exhaust the value of specific collateral before proceeding against other assets. This concept, called "equitable marshaling," arises when two potential assets are available for satisfaction of competing creditors' claims, but only one of the creditors has access to both funds. For example, suppose both First Bank and Second Bank have perfected security interests in Debtor's equipment, with First Bank having priority. First Bank also has a mortgage on Debtor's real estate, but Second Bank does not. Under the doctrine of marshaling, a court may require First Bank to foreclose against the real estate before it can enforce its security interest in the equipment, thereby maximizing Second Bank's chances of being repaid out of the proceeds of the equipment.[66] The marshaling doctrine is designed to protect competing creditors, and it cannot be used by the debtor or guarantors to undercut the cumulative-remedies doctrine. In other words, a guarantor cannot insist that a secured party proceed against the collateral before attempting to enforce the guaranty.

---

that prevents a creditor from simultaneously suing on the debt secured by real estate and enforcing a security interest in collateral securing that debt. *See, e.g.*, Cal. Civ. Code § 726; N.Y. Real Prop. Act. & Proc. L. § 1301. A one-action rule, however, would not prevent a creditor holding multiple items of collateral from simultaneously foreclosing on them. *See, e.g.*, Nebari Nat. Resources Credit Fund I, LP v. Speyside Holdings LLC, 74 Misc. 3d 1217(A), 161 N.Y.S.3d 756 (Table) (Sup. Ct. 2022) (creditor foreclosing on mortgage could simultaneously foreclose on personal property collateral without violating New York one-action rule because foreclosure against personal property collateral was not an "action" on the debt).

63. 455 So. 2d 525, 39 U.C.C. Rep. Serv. 360 (Fla. App. 1984).

64. U.C.C. § 1-103(b) ("Unless displaced by the particular provisions of [the Uniform Commercial Code], the principles of law and equity ... supplement its provisions.").

65. 742 F. Supp. 308, 13 U.C.C. Rep. Serv. 2d 596 (W.D. Va. 1990).

66. One of the leading cases on equitable marshaling is *Shedoudy v. Surgical Supply Co.*, 100 Cal. App. 3d 730, 161 Cal. Rptr. 164, 28 U.C.C. Rep. Serv. 1181 (1980). For a more robust discussion of marshaling, see Grant S. Nelson, Dale A. Whitman, Ann M. Burkhart & R. Wilson Freyermuth, Real Estate Finance Law § 10.9 (6th ed. 2015).

Chapter 18

The Foreclosure Process

Synopsis

§ 18.01 Repossession—§ 9-609

Once default occurs,[1] a secured party may take possession of the collateral,[2] dispose of it,[3] and apply the proceeds of that disposition to the balance of the debt.[4] To facilitate this objective, Article 9 permits a secured party to "require the debtor to assemble the collateral and make it available to the secured party at a place to be designated by the secured party which is reasonably convenient to both parties."[5] Frequently, however, the debtor does not cooperate and voluntarily relinquish the collateral. In such cases, the secured party must choose between using judicial process to recover possession of the collateral or trying to recover possession by "self-help" (i.e., outside the judicial process). Article 9 permits the secured party to use self-help to repossess the collateral if it can do so without "breach of the peace."[6] If the secured party cannot repossess the collateral without breaching the peace, it may not use self-help and must instead repossess by judicial action.[7]

---

1. As discussed in Chapter 17, a secured party can repossess and sell collateral only after a default. Absent default, repossession and disposition of the collateral constitutes conversion. *See, e.g.,* Ansley v. Conseco Fin. Serv. Corp., 49 U.C.C. Rep. Serv. 2d 955 (Mich. Ct. App. 2002).

2. U.C.C. § 9-609(a)(1).

3. U.C.C. § 9-610(a).

4. U.C.C. § 9-615(a).

5. U.C.C. § 9-609(c).

6. U.C.C. § 9-609(b). A secured party that breaches the peace during an attempted self-help repossession exposes itself to considerable liability, including the possibility of punitive damages. For example, in *Big Three Motors, Inc. v. Rutherford,* 432 So. 2d 483, 36 U.C.C. Rep. Serv. 338 (Ala. 1983), the secured party's agents forced the debtor's car off the highway and insisted that she return to their office, where they seized her car. Not surprisingly, the jury treated the seizure as a conversion and assessed significant punitive damages. The scope of a secured party's liability for conversion and/or failure to satisfy its obligations under Article 9 is discussed further in Chapter 19, *infra.*

Few repossessions are as dramatic as the one in *Rutherford,* but self-help repossession inherently involves the risk of a breach of the peace that could result in liability. Furthermore, a secured party cannot avoid potential liability merely by hiring an independent contractor to repossess the collateral. Virtually all courts have held that repossession is a nondelegable duty and that the secured party is liable if an independent contractor breaches the peace in carrying out the repossession. *See, e.g.,* Droge v. AAAA Two Star Towing, Inc., 468 P.3d 862 (Nev. Ct. App. 2020); Daniel v. Morris, 181 So. 3d 1195 (Fla. Dist. Ct. App. 2015); Binion v. Fletcher Jones of Chicago, Ltd., 83 U.C.C. Rep. Serv. 2d 1055 (Ill. Ct. App. 2014); Aviles v. Wayside Auto Body, Inc., 49 F. Supp. 3d 216 (D. Conn. 2014); Merrell v. Consumer Portfolio Servs., 62 U.C.C. Rep. Serv. 2d 49 (W.D. Mo. 2007); Mbank, El Paso, N.A. v. Sanchez, 836 S.W.2d 151, 17 U.C.C. Rep. Serv. 2d 1358 (Tex. 1992). Likewise, the fact that a repo agent acts on behalf of the secured party in repossessing collateral does not insulate the repo agent from liability for its own tortious acts in effecting repossession. *See, e.g.,* Magley v. M & W Inc., 926 N.W.2d 1, 96 U.C.C. Rep. Serv. 2d 384 (Mich. Ct. App. 2018).

7. Louisiana does not permit a secured party to exercise self-help repossession if the debtor does not voluntarily surrender the collateral. LA. STAT. ANN. tit. 10, § 9-609. Likewise, the Wisconsin Consumer Transactions Act provides that a merchant may not "take possession of collateral ... by means other than legal process" unless the debtor surrenders the collateral. WIS. STAT. ANN. § 425.206(1)(a). The Wisconsin statute creates a narrow exception for motor vehicles, but even then a secured party cannot use self-help to repossess without first giving the debtor notice by mail of the default, which notice must inform the debtor that it has 15 days in which to demand in writing that the secured party proceed with any repossession through judicial process. *Id.* § 425.205(1g).

[A] Self-Help

The theoretical justification for self-help repossession is economic efficiency. A secured party incurs costs in recovering possession of its collateral by way of judicial action. These include the costs of filing a civil action, including attorneys' fees if the secured party proceeds with the assistance of counsel, as well as the "lost-opportunity" costs the secured party suffers because the judicial process delays it in enforcing its security interest. If the secured party incurs these costs but cannot recover them from either the obligor or the collateral,[8] it may simply "pass along" that cost to all borrowers in the form of higher interest rates. Theoretically, the availability of peaceful self-help repossession, which permits the secured party to repossess and sell its collateral without incurring these costs, should reduce the cost of borrowing.

Attempts to exercise self-help repossession, however, sometimes present the risk of confrontation and violence. Because of the risk of injury to the debtor, the secured party, and possibly even innocent bystanders, Article 9 attempts to avoid these potential costs by permitting the secured party to use self-help only if it will not constitute a breach of the peace.

[1] "Breach of the Peace"

Article 9 does not define the term "breach of the peace," but the Code drafters were aware of its meaning based on pre-Code caselaw.[9] Whether a secured party has breached the peace necessarily depends on the factual context of the dispute. Nevertheless, some general guidelines have developed from repeatedly recurring situations in the case law.

If the debtor consents to the repossession, the secured party is free to proceed by self-help.[10] Likewise, if the debtor is not present and the secured party is repossessing

---

8. Most security agreements provide that the obligor is personally liable for the secured party's costs of repossession and enforcement and that the collateral also secures the repayment of any such expenses incurred by the secured party. Article 9 permits the secured party to recover the reasonable expenses of repossession and disposition out of the proceeds of the disposition (including attorneys' fees where the security agreement so provides). U.C.C. § 9-615(a)(1). Nevertheless, disposition of the collateral may not generate sufficient proceeds to allow the secured party to recover the expenses of disposition, and the obligor may lack sufficient nonexempt assets with which to satisfy its liability for those expenses.

9. See, e.g., Girard v. Anderson, 219 Iowa 142, 257 N.W. 400 (1934) (leading pre-Code case holding that secured party's unauthorized entry into debtor's business premises to repossess collateral amounted to breach of the peace, notwithstanding contract provision that permitted forcible entry).

10. See, e.g., McGrady v. Nissan Motor Acceptance Corp., 40 F. Supp. 2d 1323, 41 U.C.C. Rep. Serv. 2d 986 (M.D. Ala. 1998) (no breach of peace based simply on debtor's allegation that she felt under duress and was crying when she nevertheless consented to repossession).

A secured party is probably on safe ground if the debtor is not present and someone other than the debtor consents to the repossession. See, e.g., Cornelius v. Bank of Nova Scotia, 93 U.C.C. Rep. Serv. 2d 409 (V.I. 2017) (debtor's employer consented to repossession of van from debtor's workplace); Komar Indus., Inc. v. Thompson, Hine & Flory, LLP, 60 U.C.C. Rep. Serv. 2d 929 (Ohio Comm. Pl. 2005) (consent by landlord of leased premises where collateral was located and premises were apparently aban-

the collateral from a public location (for example, if the collateral is an automobile and the secured party is repossessing it from a public street or a parking lot), the repossession does not breach the peace.[11] If the debtor is present and protests the secured party's attempt to repossess the collateral, however, the prudent secured party will cease its self-help efforts. The weight of authority establishes that if the secured party continues with its self-help repossession after the debtor has raised an objection, it has breached the peace, *even if actual violence does not result.*[12] Courts have interpreted the breach-of-the-peace standard to forbid self-help in circumstances that pose a reasonable possibility that violence may result and concluded that the debtor's protest is sufficient to alert the secured party as to the risk of violence if the secured party continues to use self-help.

The debtor's timely objection effectively forces the secured party to use the judicial process to repossess the collateral.[13] Although this approach adds to the cost of repossession and creates some delay in the secured party's enforcement of its remedies,

---

doned); Cottam v. Heppner, 777 P.2d 468, 9 U.C.C. Rep. Serv. 2d 805 (Utah 1989) (third-party consent to removal of debtor's cattle from third-party's corral). However, because of potential exposure to civil or even criminal liability, a secured party should not enter a closed area to remove collateral based on the consent of a small child or someone obviously lacking in mental capacity. Society recognizes a strong interest in protecting these classes of individuals from dealings with strangers.

11. *See, e.g.*, Rivera v. Dealer Funding, LLC, 178 F. Supp. 3d 727 (E.D. Pa. 2016). Even so, a repossession that does not breach the peace might violate other consumer protection laws. For example, the Wisconsin Supreme Court held that a repo agent that repossessed a car from an open ground-floor garage in a multi-story, multi-tenant apartment building violated the state's Consumer Transactions Act because the Act prevents repossession by "enter[ing] a dwelling used by the customer" without their consent—and in the Court's judgment, the garage was part of the dwelling because it was in the same building! Duncan v. Asset Recovery Specialists, Inc., 968 N.W.2d 661 (Wis. 2022).

12. *See, e.g.*, Bank v. Huizar, 178 N.E.3d 326 (Ind. Ct. App. 2021); Noel v. PACCAR Fin. Corp., 568 F. Supp. 3d 558 (D. Md. 2021); McLinn v. Thomas County Sheriff's Dep't, 535 F. Supp. 3d 1087 (D. Kan. 2021); Goodwin v. His Choice Towing & Recovery LLC, 2019 WL 7944075 (N.D. Ga. 2019) (objection by debtor's spouse); Doucette v. Belmont Sav. Bank, 34 Mass. L. Rptr. 183 (Mass. Super. Ct. 2017); Morris v. First Nat'l Bank & Trust Co. of Ravenna, 21 Ohio St. 2d 25, 254 N.E.2d 683, 7 U.C.C. Rep. Serv. 131 (Ohio 1970); Dixon v. Ford Motor Credit Co., 72 Ill. App. 3d 983, 391 N.E.2d 493 (Ill. Ct. App. 1970); Hester v. Bandy, 627 So. 2d 833, 24 U.C.C. Rep. Serv. 2d 1344 (Miss. 1993).

As a practical matter, most of these decisions involved an objection by a debtor who was present at the time of the attempted repossession. By contrast, can a debtor "pre-empt" a creditor's self-help repossession effort by sending a letter stating the debtor's objection to any such efforts? Absent a statutory provision like the Wisconsin statute described in note 7, *supra*, the likely answer is no. *See* Valentino v. Glendale Nissan, Inc., 740 N.E.2d 538, 43 U.C.C. Rep. Serv. 2d 680 (Ill. Ct. App. 2000) (despite letter sent in advance indicating debtor objection to any repossession attempt, no breach of peace when secured party repossessed car in debtor's absence). Similarly, where a secured party had ceased a prior repossession effort in the face of the debtor's objection, the secured party did not breach the peace by carrying out a self-help repossession without incident more than one month later. *See, e.g.*, Wade v. Ford Motor Credit, 668 P.2d 183 (Kan. Ct. App. 1983). *But see* Russell v. Santander Consumer USA, Inc., 2020 WL 4251757 (E.D. Wis. 2020) (second repossession attempt a mere 30 minutes following debtor's objection to first attempt held to be continuation of first attempt and breach of the peace).

13. As explained in note 12, *supra*, the debtor's timely objection forces the secured party to stop the repossession attempt in question, but the Code does not prevent the secured party from later attempting another self-help repossession effort after an appropriate delay. But if the debtor repeatedly

most judicial actions to repossess collateral are routine, and the costs are not excessive. Further, the secured party may recover the costs of judicial repossession following the disposition of the collateral (including the secured party's attorneys' fees, if the security agreement so provides).[14] As a result, cases taking a broad view of breach of the peace reflect an implicit conclusion that the societal benefit of requiring judicial process in the face of the debtor's protest (i.e., the avoidance of violent confrontation and the risk of potential injury) outweighs the additional costs of collection.

Some decisions have upheld a secured party's use of self-help repossession, even in the face of a debtor's protest, when no actual violence ensued. For example, in *Chrysler Credit Corp. v. Koontz*,[15] the secured party sent its "repo" agent to the debtor's home, where the agent proceeded to take possession of a car in the debtor's front yard. The debtor came racing out of the house in his underwear, shouting "Don't take it," but the agent ignored the debtor and took the car. The court reasoned that, even though actual violence is not necessary to establish a breach of the peace, some language or conduct must bring home to the repossessor the fact that violence is imminent. The court thus held that no breach of the peace occurred because the debtor had not held a weapon, clenched his fists, or even argued toe-to-toe with the repossessor.[16]

Decisions such as *Koontz* reflect poor public policy. Assessing the volatility of a debtor's protest is difficult, particularly after the fact, when the parties and other witnesses may have different perceptions about "how vehemently" the debtor protested. The debtor's protests alone should have alerted the agent to the possibility of violence. Further, to the extent courts expect judicial decisions to influence future conduct, the holding in *Koontz* encourages the very behavior that the breach-of-the-peace standard seeks to avoid. Based on this decision, an attorney advising a client who is in default and fears repossession would have to suggest that the client express himself vehemently—perhaps even by threatening physical violence—to stop the repossession. This approach, however, would simply exacerbate the risk of violence and increase the likelihood that self-help repossession would result in injury to the debtor or bystanders. Although the *Koontz* court stressed the efficiency of self-help, efficiency is an insufficient rationale for a decision that increases the risk that repossessions will turn violent.

The facts of *Koontz* also raise a question of whether a secured party can enter the debtor's premises to repossess the collateral. The Restatement (Second) of Torts

---

and successfully raises an objection in the face of each self-help repossession effort, the secured party is practically forced to resort to judicial process.

14. U.C.C. § 9-615(a)(1).

15. 277 Ill. App. 3d 1078, 661 N.E.2d 1171, 29 U.C.C. Rep. Serv. 2d 1 (Ill. Ct. App. 1996).

16. Other comparably poor decisions include *Garcia v. Dezba Asset Recovery, Inc.*, 2023 WL 2691756 (S.D.N.Y. 2023) ("[T]o constitute a breach of the peace, something more than possession over an objection is needed.... [I]f a mere objection constitutes a breach of the peace, a car could essentially never be repossessed for nonpayment when the person in possession is present.") and *Clarin v. Minnesota Repossessors, Inc.*, 198 F.3d 661 (8th Cir. 1999) (applying Minnesota law) (repossession in face of debtor's objection not a breach of the peace where repossession took place in public parking lot and repo agent gave debtor the opportunity to contact the secured party and the police prior to completing repossession).

provides that "[o]ne is privileged to enter land in the possession of another, at a reasonable time and in a reasonable manner, for the purpose of removing a chattel to the immediate possession of which the actor is entitled…."[17] Consistent with this principle, most courts have held that the secured party has a limited privilege against trespass liability and can make minimally intrusive incursions onto the debtor's land to repossess collateral.[18] For example, numerous decisions allow the secured party to go onto the debtor's driveway or yard to remove an asset in plain sight.[19] Most courts, however, have refused to extend the privilege to assets located in an enclosed space such as the debtor's home or garage, where the debtor presumably has a greater expectation of privacy from unwanted intrusions. Several decisions permitting the removal of assets from the debtor's land stress that the repossession occurred without the secured party's entering any "gates, doors or other barricades."[20] A secured

---

17. Restatement (Second) of Torts § 198.

18. A prudent secured party must nevertheless exercise great care in entering onto the debtor's land. For example, in *Thrash v. Credit Acceptance Corp.*, 821 So. 2d 968, 48 U.C.C. Rep. Serv. 2d 1224 (Ala. 2001), agents of the secured party repossessed a car from the debtor's driveway by placing clear dishwashing soap on the driveway to provide a lubricant to drag the car from the driveway into the street. The agents then left the scene without removing the fluid from the driveway or warning the debtor of its presence, and the debtor later slipped on the fluid and injured his back. The court held that the secured party breached the peace by creating a hazard that posed a substantial risk of injury.

19. *See, e.g.*, Callaway v. Whittenton, 892 So. 2d 852, 52 U.C.C. Rep. Serv. 2d 525 (Ala. 2003) (secured party entitled to enter debtor's front yard to repossess debtor's vehicle); Giles v. First Va. Credit Serv., Inc., 46 U.C.C. Rep. Serv. 2d 913 (N.C. Ct. App. 2002) (no breach of peace due to removal of automobile from debtor's driveway without entry to any enclosed area); Oaklawn Bank v. Baldwin, 709 S.W.2d 91, 1 U.C.C. Rep. Serv. 2d 596 (Ark. 1986) (removing car from debtor's driveway did not breach peace); Raffa v. Dania Bank, 321 So. 2d 83, 18 U.C.C. Rep. Serv. 263 (Fla. Dist. Ct. App. 1975) (car partially under carport in debtor's driveway removed without breach of the peace).

Comment d to Section 198 of the Restatement (Second) of Torts suggests that a secured party must make demand upon the debtor for turnover of the collateral before entering onto the debtor's premises to effect a repossession: "Ordinarily a demand on the possessor, either to deliver the chattel at the border of the land or to permit the actor to go on the land and get it, is required before an entry can reasonably be made." In most cases, however, a prudent secured party will send a written notice to the debtor following the debtor's default, notifying the debtor that a default exists and demanding that the debtor turn over the collateral.

20. *See, e.g.*, Oaklawn Bank v. Baldwin, 709 S.W.2d 91, 1 U.C.C. Rep. Serv. 2d 596 (Ark. 1986); Ragde v. Peoples Bank, 53 Wash. App. 173, 767 P.2d 949, 7 U.C.C. Rep. Serv. 2d 1314 (1989). Most courts have supported the repossessing creditor with respect to collateral located in an open garage. *See, e.g.*, Pierce v. Leasing Int'l, Inc., 142 Ga. App. 371, 235 S.E.2d 752, 22 U.C.C. Rep. Serv. 269 (1977). However, most courts have held that unauthorized forced entry into a closed or locked garage constitutes a breach of the peace (or at least states a claim sufficient to survive summary judgment). *See, e.g.*, Gerbasi v. NU Era Towing & Serv., Inc., 443 F. Supp. 3d 411 (W.D.N.Y. 2020); Freeman v. Ally Fin. Inc., 528 F. Supp. 3d 1038, 104 U.C.C. Rep. Serv. 2d 492 (D. Minn. 2021); McDonald v. Nicholas Fin., Inc., 2013 WL 12380630 (N.D. Ga. 2013); Johnson v. Americredit Fin. Servs., Inc., 69 U.C.C. Rep. Serv. 2d 861 (M.D. Tenn. 2009). By contrast, where a secured party had obtained a judicial replevin order, a third-party repo agent's breaking of a locked gate to effect the repossession was held not to constitute a breach of the peace. *See* Carter v. First Nat'l Bank of Crossett, 552 S.W.3d 40 (Ark. Ct. App. 2018). *See also* First Nat'l Bank of Black Hills v. Beug, 400 N.W.2d 893, 3 U.C.C. Rep. Serv. 2d 856 (S.D. 1987) (even if breach of the peace occurred during court-ordered repossession, secured party was not responsible for resulting damages).

party that chooses to enter a restricted space risks the assessment of punitive damages and, in extreme cases, criminal sanctions for trespass or for breaking and entering.[21] For example, in *Bloomquist v. First National Bank of Elk River*,[22] the secured party removed a pane of glass and entered the debtor's place of business to remove collateral. The court held that this was a breach of the peace and sustained an award of punitive damages.

When repossessing collateral from land owned by a third person, the secured party should exercise caution even if the collateral is in plain sight. Even though the debtor may have impliedly consented to minimal intrusions onto its own land, no comparable basis supports a conclusion that a third party has done so. Although the cases in this area are mixed, the action is risky;[23] as a result, a prudent secured party should obtain the third party's consent to enter the land before effecting a repossession.

Another common theme in the cases is the secured party's use of trickery to effect the repossession. Several decisions have held that bringing along a uniformed off-duty police officer to make it appear that the secured party is carrying out the repossession under color of law amounts to "constructive force" and thus breaches the peace.[24] These cases rest on the rationale that the debtor has the right to protest (and thus require the secured party to repossess by judicial process) and that the presence of a police officer discourages the debtor from asserting this right—after all, most persons are strongly disinclined to resist the efforts of a police officer apparently acting within his or her authority. Yet courts occasionally have upheld other types of trickery. For example, in *Thompson v. Ford Motor Credit Co.*,[25] the court upheld the secured party's repossession from a parking garage even though the secured party falsely told the garage operator that it had the debtor's express permission to take the car. The court suggested that no breach of the peace occurred because the trickery did not prevent the debtor from asserting a legal right, nor did it increase the risk that the repossession would turn violent.

---

21. For further discussion of remedies for creditor misconduct, see § 19.01[B], *infra*.

22. 378 N.W.2d 81, 42 U.C.C. Rep. Serv. 37 (Minn. Ct. App. 1985).

23. *See, e.g.*, Census Fed. Credit Union v. Wann, 403 N.E.2d 348, 28 U.C.C. Rep. Serv. 1207 (Ind. Ct. App. 1980) (removal from apartment building's parking lot did not breach peace); Salisbury Livestock Co. v. Colorado Central Credit Union, 793 P.2d 470, 12 U.C.C. Rep. Serv. 2d 894 (Wyo. 1990) (court reversed directed verdict in favor of secured party and remanded for trial, holding that reasonable juror could conclude that removal of collateral from land of third party breached the peace).

24. *See, e.g.*, McLinn v. Thomas Cnty. Sheriff's Dep't, 535 F. Supp. 3d 1087 (D. Kan. 2021); Murray v. Poani, 980 N.E.2d 1275 (Ill. Ct. App. 2012); Walker v. Walthall, 588 P.2d 863, 25 U.C.C. Rep. Serv. 918 (Ariz. Ct. App. 1978); First & Farmers Bank of Somerset v. Henderson, 763 S.W.2d 137, 7 U.C.C. Rep. Serv. 2d 1305 (Ky. Ct. App. 1988); Stone Machinery Co. v. Kessler, 463 P.2d 651, 7 U.C.C. Rep. Serv. 135 (Wash. Ct. App. 1970). *But see In re* 53 Foot Trawler Pegasus, 67 U.C.C. Rep. Serv. 2d 839 (M.D. Fla. 2008) (no constructive breach of the peace where secured party was accompanied by nonuniformed police officer and debtor did not realize he was a police officer until after secured party had completed the repossession).

25. 550 F.2d 256, 21 U.C.C. Rep. Serv. 907 (5th Cir. 1977).

The reader should take the foregoing comments as generalizations. The cases are extremely fact-specific and colorful, and authority can be found on both sides of almost every issue.[26] In the face of this uncertainty, a creditor might be tempted to provide in the security agreement its own definition of breach of the peace. After all, the Code generally permits the parties to specify the standards by which the fulfillment of their rights and duties are to be measured as long as those standards are "not manifestly unreasonable."[27] Nevertheless, given the strong policy in favor of deterring violence, the Code makes clear that a security agreement may not authorize a secured party to engage in conduct that would otherwise constitute a breach of the peace.[28]

[2] Disabling the Collateral

If the collateral is large or heavy equipment, repossession and storage prior to disposition may be prohibitively expensive. Accordingly, after default, Section 9-609(a) allows a secured party to "render equipment unusable and dispose of collateral on a debtor's premises."[29] This disablement remedy would allow a secured party with a security interest in a machine to remove key components, thereby preventing the debtor from using the machine prior to disposition, and to sell the machine in place on the debtor's premises. Traditionally, this provision has been of limited use, and secured parties rarely rely on it. First, if the secured party removes a part from the collateral but leaves the debtor in possession, the debtor may be able to replace the part and continue using the collateral. Second, selling the collateral on the debtor's premises makes little sense without the debtor's cooperation because the buyer will have to take possession of the collateral from the debtor—and will likely have to resort to judicial process if the debtor is not cooperative. This complication is likely to drive down the price that a buyer will pay for the collateral.

Section 9-609(a)'s disablement remedy was created at a time when "disablement" required the secured party to act against the collateral in a direct and proximate way, that is, by physically removing parts from the collateral or by immobilizing the collateral to prevent its use (such as by placing a boot on a vehicle). Today, however, electronic technology allows a secured party to disable many items of collateral remotely. For example, a secured party with a security interest in an automobile might require a debtor to install a "kill-switch" device that would permit the secured party to disable the car remotely using GPS technology if the debtor defaulted.[30]

---

26. For a comprehensive discussion of case law on the subject, see Jean Braucher, *The Repo Code: A Study of Adjustment to Uncertainty in Commercial Law*, 74 WASH. U. L.Q. 549 (1997). *See also* Ryan McRobert, *Defining "Breach of the Peace" in Self-Help Repossessions*, 87 WASH. L. REV. 569 (2012).

27. U.C.C. § 9-603(a).

28. U.C.C. § 9-603(b).

29. U.C.C. § 9-609(a)(2).

30. If self-driving vehicles should become the norm, a secured party might repossess the car remotely by instructing the car to drive itself to an impound lot or other location directed by the secured party.

Nothing in Article 9 explicitly prohibits remote disablement of collateral, and the Code generally allows the parties to a security agreement to define the secured party's post-default remedies by agreement.[31] Nevertheless, the agreed standards measuring the secured party's compliance with its duties must not be "manifestly unreasonable."[32] Further, the disablement remedy remains subject to the requirement that the secured party may not breach the peace and to the secured party's general obligation to act in good faith in the enforcement of its remedies.[33] The breach-of-the-peace standard, which is relevant if disablement would require physical contact with the collateral, seems irrelevant as a limit on remote disablement (which will occur without physical confrontation). The duty of good faith would, at a minimum, require pre-default disclosure by the secured party that the collateral contains some type of payment assurance technology that would allow the secured party to disable the collateral remotely.[34] But the more difficult question arises after default. If the debtor defaults, can the secured party remotely disable the collateral—either at all, or without first giving the debtor prior notice and some opportunity to cure? And should the rules differ in consumer and business transactions?

Obviously, a security agreement can explicitly prohibit remote disablement or can create a requirement that exercise of that remedy requires post-default notice and opportunity to cure. But Article 9, Part 6, contains no such limits, and the act of disablement is not itself a "disposition" (which would require notification)[35] because it neither dispossesses the debtor of the collateral nor extinguishes the debtor's right of redemption. Still, the remote disabling of a vehicle could have profound consequences for the debtor, for example, preventing the debtor from reaching its place of employment or, in a worst-case scenario, preventing the debtor from taking an injured child to the hospital for emergency treatment.[36]

A few states have adopted non-uniform Article 9 amendments to address remote disabling of collateral. Connecticut's amendment requires post-default notice to the debtor prior to exercising electronic self-help[37] and prohibits the secured party from

---

31. U.C.C. § 9-601(a) ("After default, a secured party has the rights provided in this part and, except as otherwise provided in Section 9-602, those provided by the agreement of the parties.").

32. U.C.C. § 9-603(a).

33. U.C.C. § 1-304.

34. Manufacturers of payment assurance devices established a trade association (the Payment Assurance Technology Association) to establish standards for the use of such devices. These standards require association members to commit to disclose the existence of the device and its purpose (i.e., to facilitate remote disabling of the collateral). The standards are discussed in Juliet M. Moringiello, *Automating Repossession*, 22 NEV. L.J. 563 (2022).

35. U.C.C. § 9-611(b).

36. Some creditors use remote disablement not as a step in a post-default disposition process but rather to pressure the debtor to make a payment. For example, after disabling a vehicle, automobile financers routinely send a text message to the debtor, providing a phone number to call to make a payment, and functionality is restored as soon as the debtor makes the payment. In this scenario, the secured party's conduct does not breach the peace but may still raise potential concerns over placing the debtor or third parties in danger.

37. CONN. GEN. STAT. § 42a-9-609(d)(2).

using electronic self-help if it "has reason to know that its use will result in substantial injury or harm to the public health or safety or grave harm to the public interest substantially affecting third parties not involved in the dispute."[38] Colorado has adopted a provision that limits the disablement remedy to situations where the collateral is equipment,[39] meaning that remote disablement is not available where the collateral is consumer goods. Other states regulate the issue through consumer finance statutes regulating motor vehicle sales finance or through unfair trade practices statutes.[40] Because technology will continue to evolve, statutory regulation of the use of remote-disabling technology is likely to remain a moving target in the near and intermediate term.[41]

[B] Judicial Action

If a debtor does not surrender the collateral and the secured party cannot peacefully repossess it, the secured party must resort to a judicial action to recover possession. An action in replevin[42] typically commences with the secured party's filing a petition asking the court to find that its right to possession is superior to that of the debtor.[43] The secured party typically also asks for a writ of replevin, which is a court order directing the sheriff to take possession of the collateral. Because the sheriff handles the repossession under color of law, the risk of a violent confrontation is dramatically reduced; if violence does result, the sheriff is the appropriate person to deal with it. In many jurisdictions, the sheriff turns the property over to the secured party for safekeeping while the action is pending; in others, the sheriff retains possession of the property during

---

38. CONN. GEN. STAT. § 42a-9-609(d)(5). This limitation is itself unclear. Obviously, it would appear to prevent a secured party from disabling a vehicle that was currently in motion (as that would pose a threat to the safety of persons in nearby vehicles). It might also apply to prevent a secured party from remotely disabling an ambulance or medical equipment being used in a doctor's office or hospital. But it is hard to see how the ordinary disabling of a consumer's car, even if doing so could place a passenger in the car in danger, would threaten "public health or safety."

39. COLO. REV. STAT. ANN. § 4-9-609(a)(2) ("After default, a secured party ... [w]ithout removal, may render equipment unusable....").

40. A discussion of California, Nevada, New Jersey, and New York legislation can be found in Moringiello, note 34, *supra*, at 587–90.

41. As yet, there is scant judicial authority on the limits of remote disablement under Article 9. To date, most judicial decisions have focused instead on whether a creditor's use of remote-disabling technology following a debtor's bankruptcy filing constituted the exercise of control over the collateral in violation of the automatic stay. *Compare, e.g., In re* Franklin, 614 B.R. 534 (Bankr. M.D.N.C. 2020) *and In re* Hampton, 319 B.R. 163 (Bankr. E.D. Ark. 2005) (stay violation), *with In re* Grisard-Van Roey, 373 B.R. 441 (Bankr. D.S.C. 2007) (no stay violation). For further discussion, see § 16.03, *supra*.

42. Replevin has been superseded in some jurisdictions by a statutory cause of action called "claim and delivery."

43. The secured party's right to possession must be predicated on a default. See U.C.C. § 9-609 and the discussion of default in Chapter 17, *supra*. *See also* Christie's Inc. v. Davis, 49 U.C.C. Rep. Serv. 2d 684 (S.D.N.Y. 2002) (debtor's default and secured party's immediate right to foreclose entitled secured party to replevin despite debtor's speculation that secured party would act in a commercially unreasonable manner in disposing of collateral).

the pendency of the action. Once the secured party obtains a final judgment awarding it permanent possession of the collateral,[44] it may proceed with its Article 9 disposition.

Because replevin requires the involvement of a public official, replevin actions involve state action and must satisfy the Constitution's mandate that deprivation of property requires due process of law. In a series of cases that began with *Fuentes v. Shevin*[45] and culminated with *North Georgia Finishing, Inc. v. Di-Chem, Inc.*,[46] the Supreme Court defined the type of notice and hearing necessary to satisfy the due process standard. In *Fuentes*, the Court held that, in consumer transactions, a public official could not seize assets of the debtor unless the debtor received notice and an opportunity for a pre-seizure hearing for the purpose of contesting the validity of the creditor's claim. The most important of the cases is *Mitchell v. W.T. Grant Co.*,[47] in which the Court backed off somewhat from its holding in *Fuentes*. The *Mitchell* decision allows seizure without prior notice and an opportunity for a pre-seizure hearing, so long as the replevin process contains the following safeguards:

- a judge (rather than a clerk) must sign the writ of replevin;
- the creditor must file an affidavit in support of its petition that contains specific factual allegations supporting its claim for possession;
- the debtor must have a right to a hearing soon after the seizure at which the debtor has the opportunity to show that it will probably prevail on the merits and that therefore the writ should be dissolved and the property returned;
- the debtor must have an alternative right to regain possession by posting a bond; and
- the creditor must post a bond indemnifying the debtor against loss.

If these procedures are in place, the court may issue a writ of replevin on an *ex parte* basis.

Replevin involves costs that a secured party can avoid using self-help repossession.[48] In addition to costs and attorneys' fees, the secured party must post a bond to indemnify the debtor for its damages in the event the secured party's action proves wrongful.[49] Replevin also involves procedural delays because the debtor must receive time to answer the petition. In most cases, however, the costs and delays are minimal

---

44. Originally, a replevin action resulted only in a judgment for possession of the collateral, but many modern versions allow for an alternative judgment for the value of the collateral.

45. 407 U.S. 67, *reh'g denied*, 409 U.S. 902 (1972).

46. 419 U.S. 601 (1975) (extending the holding in *Mitchell*, note 47, *infra*, to non-consumer transactions).

47. 416 U.S. 600 (1974).

48. The secured party can include in its security agreement a clause allowing it to add to the indebtedness its attorneys' fees and legal expenses (to the extent that such clauses are enforceable under state law). U.C.C. §9-615(a)(1).

49. The typical case involving damages is one in which the debtor convinces the court that there has been no default and thus that the repossession was wrongful.

because the debtor fails to answer the petition and the secured party obtains a default judgment.

§ 18.02 Disposition of Collateral— §§ 9-610–9-615

Once a secured party has possession of collateral, through self-help or judicial action, it can proceed with its foreclosure. A foreclosure sale transfers to the buyer the debtor's rights in the collateral.[50] The secured party usually will dispose of the collateral by sale, following procedures set forth in Article 9.[51] While disposition can consist of a lease of goods or a license of a general intangible rather than a sale,[52] virtually all

---

50. U.C.C. § 9-617(a)(1). The correct view is that the secured party's repossession does not cause the debtor's title to pass to the secured creditor; title remains in the debtor until the secured party disposes of the collateral or satisfies the procedures to accept the collateral in full or partial satisfaction of the secured obligation (strict foreclosure). *See* U.C.C. § 9-622(a)(2); Motors Acceptance Corp. v. Rozier, 597 S.E.2d 367, 54 U.C.C. Rep. Serv. 2d 31 (Ga. 2004). In a misinterpretation of state law and Article 9, federal courts in the Eleventh Circuit have held that where the secured party had repossessed (but not sold) the collateral prior to the debtor's bankruptcy, the collateral was no longer property of the bankruptcy estate. *See, e.g., In re* Kalter, 292 F.3d 1350, 48 U.C.C. Rep. Serv. 2d 411 (11th Cir. 2002) (interpreting Florida law); *In re* Lewis, 137 F.3d 1280, 35 U.C.C. Rep. Serv. 2d 740 (11th Cir. 1998) (interpreting Alabama law). To the extent these decisions indicate that mere repossession terminates the debtor's title to the collateral, they are inconsistent with Sections 9-617(a)(1) and 9-622(a)(2) and thus plainly incorrect. For the correct analysis, see *In re* Moffett, 288 B.R. 721, 48 U.C.C. Rep. Serv. 2d 740 (Bankr. E.D. Va. 2002), *aff'd*, 289 B.R. 55, 49 U.C.C. Rep. Serv. 2d 1341 (E.D. Va. 2003), *aff'd*, 356 F.3d 518 (4th Cir. 2004); *In re* Robinson, 285 B.R. 732, 49 U.C.C. Rep. Serv. 2d 327 (Bankr. W.D. Okla. 2002).

51. The alternative is strict foreclosure (retention of title to the collateral by the secured party in lieu of sale), discussed in § 18.04, *infra*.

52. *See, e.g.*, Canadian Community Bank v. Ascher Findley Co., 229 Cal. App. 3d 1139, 280 Cal. Rptr. 521, 14 U.C.C. Rep. Serv. 2d 958 (1991). Another variant, involving neither sale nor lease, arises if the collateral is a certificate of deposit issued by the secured party. The secured party can simply cancel the CD and retain its proceeds in satisfaction of the debt, a procedure that is akin to exercising the common law right of set-off. Because the CD is worth a fixed amount of money, a sale is not needed to maximize its market value. *See, e.g.*, Smith v. Mark Twain Nat'l Bank, 805 F.2d 278, 2 U.C.C. Rep. Serv. 2d 1059 (8th Cir. 1986). Similarly, if insured collateral is totally destroyed by the debtor, the secured party should be free simply to convey the debtor's title to the insurer in exchange for a settlement check.

If the collateral is shares of stock and after default the secured party has the shares reissued in the name of the secured party, no disposition has occurred unless and until the secured party transfers ownership of the collateral for value. *See, e.g.*, Spellman v. Indep. Bankers' Bank of Fla., 161 So.3d 505, 84 U.C.C. Rep. Serv. 2d 333 (Fla. Ct. App. 2014); Sports Courts of Omaha, Ltd. v. Brower, 534 N.W.2d 317, 26 U.C.C. Rep. Serv. 2d 1272 (Neb. 1995).

secured parties hold foreclosure sales. A foreclosure sale of goods is subject to the provisions of Article 2, and Article 2A is applicable if the disposition is by lease.[53]

Before exploring Article 9's specific procedures, it is important to understand their underlying philosophy. The drafters hoped that Article 9 dispositions would produce higher prices than those typically obtained in real estate foreclosures. They were keenly aware that the procedures traditionally governing real estate foreclosures tend to produce prices below fair market value. Specifically, real estate foreclosures are almost invariably conducted by auction rather than by placement with a qualified broker. Further, bidders must typically pay cash when the hammer falls, which reduces the pool of potential buyers. Lastly, many states grant the debtor a right to redeem the land after the foreclosure sale, which further discourages potential bidders.

By contrast, Article 9 does not permit post-disposition redemption,[54] and its procedures governing disposition are deliberately flexible. The secured party can dispose of the collateral by any commercially reasonable method and can do so for cash or on credit.[55] Article 9 does not require a secured party to obtain an asset's fair market value, but by requiring the secured party to dispose of the asset in a commercially reasonable manner, it encourages the adoption of procedures designed to achieve that goal.

[A] The Standard of Commercial Reasonableness

Section 9-610(b) requires that every aspect of a secured party's disposition of collateral—including the manner, method, time, place and other terms—be "commercially reasonable."[56] The advantage of this flexible standard is that it encourages secured

---

53. U.C.C. § 9-610, Comment 11. Article 9 provides that a sale or other disposition by the secured party "includes the warranties relating to title, possession, quiet enjoyment, and the like which by operation of law accompany a voluntary disposition" of such goods, unless the secured party effectively disclaims such warranties. U.C.C. § 9-610(d). The secured party may disclaim any such warranties by means of "a record evidencing the contract for disposition and including an express disclaimer or modification" of the warranties. U.C.C. § 9-610(e). A record will constitute a sufficient disclaimer if it indicates "[t]here is no warranty relating to title, possession, quiet enjoyment, or the like" or uses similar language. U.C.C. § 9-610(f). By contrast, a general disclaimer providing that the secured party was making "no warranties" with respect to the collateral was held to be insufficient to disclaim the implied warranty of title. See, e.g., Ulbrich v. Groth, 78 A.3d 76, 82 U.C.C. Rep. Serv. 2d 77 (Conn. 2013). See also Moutopoulis v. 2075-2081 Wallace Ave. Owners Corp., 47 Misc. 3d 1049, 10 N.Y.S.3d 823 (Civ. Ct. 2015) (secured party that disposed of shares in two cooperative apartment units made no implied warranty about the title of the cooperative, as distinguished from the shares, and had disclaimed any warranty; thus, high bidder that refused to consummate purchase of units was not entitled to return of earnest money deposits).

54. Article 9 does provide a pre-disposition right of redemption. See U.C.C. § 9-623, discussed in § 18.05, infra.

55. U.C.C. § 9-610(b). This provision also allows a secured party to dispose of the collateral as a unit or to break it down into parcels that are disposed of separately.

56. Students sometimes conflate "commercial reasonableness" and "good faith." A secured party must always act in good faith in enforcing its security interest, that is, the secured party must act honestly in fact and must observe reasonable commercial standards of fair dealing. U.C.C. §§ 1-201(b)(20), 1-304. However, commercial reasonableness is a higher standard than good faith. While a secured

parties[57] to adopt procedures[58] designed to bring a fair price for the collateral.[59] The disadvantage (at least from a creditor's perspective) is that it allows courts to use 20/20 hindsight to second-guess virtually every step that a creditor has taken in disposing of collateral. Courts have examined numerous factors, such as whether the secured party chose an adequate method of disposition given the nature of the collateral, whether the secured party properly advertised the disposition, whether the secured party conducted the disposition at a reasonable time (both in absolute terms and in relation to the date on which the advertising appeared), and whether the terms of the disposition were reasonable.

---

party's failure to act in good faith may provide evidence that a sale lacked commercial reasonableness, the fact that a secured party disposed of collateral in good faith does not establish that the disposition was commercially reasonable. *See* Hicklin v. Onyx Acceptance Corp., 970 A.2d 244, 68 U.C.C. Rep. Serv. 2d 413 (Del. 2009).

57. The commercial reasonableness requirement does not apply to a disposition conducted by the debtor unless the secured party is controlling the debtor's actions. *See, e.g.,* MB Fin. Bank v. Jacobs, 96 U.C.C. Rep. Serv. 2d 685 (Ill. Ct. App. 2018) (where collateral was sold by management company hired by an assignee for the benefit of creditors, and assignee was agent of debtor and not secured party, no requirement that sale be commercially reasonable); Bremer Bank v. Matejcek, 916 N.W.2d 688, 96 U.C.C. Rep. Serv. 2d 158 (Minn. Ct. App. 2018) (where secured party merely consented to sale by debtor, no requirement that sale be commercially reasonable).

58. Although Article 9 does not permit a contractual waiver of a secured party's duty to dispose of collateral in a commercially reasonable fashion, U.C.C. § 9-602(7); General Elec. Capital Corp. v. FPL Serv. Corp., 986 F. Supp. 2d 1029, 82 U.C.C. Rep. Serv. 2d 191 (N.D. Iowa 2013), it does permit the parties to agree on the standards measuring the fulfillment of that obligation if those standards are not manifestly unreasonable. U.C.C. § 9-603(a). *See* HSBC Bank USA v. Econ. Steel, Inc., 747 N.Y.S.2d 661, 48 U.C.C. Rep. Serv. 2d 1494 (App. Div. 2002) (debtor precluded from complaining that sale was commercially unreasonable when parties had agreed that specified auctioneer would sell collateral). *But see* Baird Credit Corp. v. Seher, 50 U.C.C. Rep. Serv. 2d 591 (N.D. Ill. 2003) (although security agreement gave creditor sole option to decide whether to liquidate collateral on default, creditor's discretion controlled by duty of good faith).

Landlords sometimes obtain a security interest in goods to secure a tenant's unpaid rental obligation. If the tenant leaves those goods in the premises after termination of the lease, in some states the landlord may be able to dispose of them without compliance with Article 9's requirements if the goods are deemed abandoned to the landlord under the provisions of the lease and applicable law other than Article 9. *See, e.g.,* 3455 LLC v. ND Props., Inc., 2014 WL 3845696 (N.D. Ga. 2014).

59. *See, e.g.,* Robb v. Bond Purchase, L.L.C., 580 S.W.3d 70 (Mo. Ct. App. 2019) (sale of stock not commercially reasonable when secured party ran ads in publications customarily advertising real estate foreclosures, secured party never provided the corporation or its other shareholders notice of the sale or offered them the shares in a private sale, secured party modified the terms of the sale on the day prior to sale, and majority owner of secured party allowed friend to buy the stock at a price lower than what the owner had previously offered); Comerica Bank v. Mann, 13 F. Supp. 3d 1262 (N.D. Ga. 2013) (sale of 82-foot luxury yacht not commercially reasonable when lender did not market yacht in European market which was stronger for yachts of that design, advertised yacht as "bank repo," and sold to buyer for $300,000 less than next lowest offer lender had received); R & J of Tennessee, Inc. v. Blankenship-Melton Real Estate, Inc., 166 S.W.3d 195, 55 U.C.C. Rep. Serv. 2d 278 (Tenn. Ct. App. 2004) (sale of truck, tractor, and mobile home not commercially reasonable when secured party waited over seven months to conduct the sale, allowed debtor to use the collateral during this period, did not advertise the sale in a newspaper, did not use the services of an appraiser or experienced auctioneer, and was the only bidder at the sale).

[1] Duty to Publicize

One of the most important elements of a commercially reasonable disposition, and one not mentioned directly in the Code, is the duty to publicize it adequately. Compliance with this duty requires the secured party (a) to ensure that the advertising is sufficient to reach the proper audience for the collateral involved, (b) to provide sufficient time following the advertising for potential buyers to respond before the disposition occurs, (c) to disclose in the advertising adequate and accurate information about the collateral and the disposition, and (d) to make the collateral available for inspection by potential buyers prior to the disposition.

The most important of these issues is whether the advertising was sufficient to reach potential buyers for the type of asset involved. With highly specialized collateral, targeted advertising may be needed, perhaps even in publications or trade magazines that have a nationwide circulation. For example, *Contrail Leasing Partners, Ltd. v. Consolidated Airways, Inc.*[60] involved the foreclosure sale of a corporate jet. The court held that the secured party's advertising, which consisted of one small ad in a trade publication, was not commercially reasonable. The court suggested that the secured party should have run a more conspicuous ad and should have placed that ad in additional trade journals to expose the collateral to buyers likely to be interested in a corporate jet. Likewise, in *Comerica Bank v. Mann*,[61] the court held that the secured party's disposition of an 82-foot luxury yacht was commercially unreasonable, noting specifically that the secured party failed to take reasonable measures to market the yacht in Europe (where the market for yachts of that design was stronger at the time of sale) and that the secured party decision to advertise the yacht as a "bank repo" likely chilled bidding. These decisions suggest that a secured party must explore the potential market so that its advertising will be effective,[62] and a prudent secured party disposing of specialized collateral might well consult a broker or dealer of such goods to help design its approach to advertising. Courts often cite the secured party's retention of a broker or auction marketing firm with particularized expertise in the type of collateral as evidence to support the commercial reasonableness of the sale.[63]

---

60. 742 F.2d 1095, 39 U.C.C. Rep. Serv. 9 (7th Cir. 1983).

61. 13 F. Supp. 3d 1262 (N.D. Ga. 2013)

62. *See also, e.g.*, Comm. Credit Group, Inc. v. Barber, 682 S.E.2d 760, 69 U.C.C. Rep. Serv. 2d 968 (N.C. Ct. App. 2009) (time and manner of advertisements for public auction sale of heavy-duty waste recycler was not commercially reasonable where, despite limited pool of likely interested bidders for the collateral, secured party ran only two advertisements in general circulation newspapers unlikely to be seen by prospective bidders and ran them during Christmas holidays); Key Bank of Maine v. Dunbar, 28 U.C.C. Rep. Serv. 2d 398 (E.D. Pa. 1995) (failure to take time necessary to explore and reach potential market for boat rendered sale commercially unreasonable); Chavers v. Frazier, 93 B.R. 366 (Bankr. M.D. Tenn. 1989) (sale of jet plane commercially unreasonable due to advertising that ran too briefly and used text that suggested a distress sale); Smith v. Daniels, 634 S.W.2d 276, 34 U.C.C. Rep. Serv. 355 (Tenn. Ct. App. 1982) (advertising in county paper and calling local dealers was unreasonable for amusement equipment which was normally sold by advertising in major cities, in trade magazines, and by sending flyers to dealers).

63. *See, e.g.*, 395 Lampe, LLC v. Kawish, LLC, 89 U.C.C. Rep. Serv. 2d 460 (W.D. Wash. 2016) (sale conducted by largest auction marketing firm in Pacific Northwest preceded by newspaper advertising

Advertising must do more than merely reach the proper audience. It must also accurately describe the collateral,[64] and it must give correct information regarding the mechanics of the disposition.[65] Courts have also held that the advertising must give sufficient information to allow prospective buyers to inspect the collateral prior to the disposition.[66]

[2] Disposition within a Reasonable Time

For most transactions, the Code does not specify the time period within which a secured party must dispose of collateral after default, other than to state that the time of the disposition must be commercially reasonable.[67] In other words, a secured party must not act precipitously and dispose of the collateral before its advertising has had time to be effective, nor can it delay so long that the collateral depreciates significantly in value. The cases exploring this issue are highly fact-specific.[68] For example, courts

---

as well as direct marketing to 150 targeted prospects identified by marketing firm); Icon Agent, LLC v. Kanza Constr., Inc., 364 P.3d 579 (Table), 88 U.C.C. Rep. Serv. 2d 825 (Kan. Ct. App. 2016) (sale of railroad construction equipment conducted by world's largest industrial auction company which marketed sale through large database of buyers of rail and heavy equipment). *See also* Bank of Am. v. Dello Russo, 610 F. Appx. 848 (11th Cir. 2015); Key Equip. Fin. v. Southwest Contracting, Inc., 87 U.C.C. Rep. Serv. 2d 647 (D. Colo. 2015).

64. *See, e.g.*, ROC-Century Assoc. v. Giunta, 658 A.2d 223, 27 U.C.C. Rep. Serv. 2d 1091 (Me. 1995) (sale of partnership interest unreasonable because advertising mischaracterized nature of rights being sold); Comm. Credit Group, Inc. v. Barber, 682 S.E.2d 760, 69 U.C.C. Rep. Serv. 2d 968 (N.C. Ct. App. 2009) (sale of inoperable goods covered by a manufacturer's warranty was commercially unreasonable where advertisement indicated that sale would be "as is" where warranty could have defrayed some or all costs of repair).

65. *See, e.g.*, In re Inofin, Inc., 455 B.R. 19, 75 U.C.C. Rep. Serv. 2d 269 (Bankr. D. Mass. 2011) (notice of sale indicated wrong sales date until corrected notice was sent only two days prior to sale); Comm. Credit Group, Inc. v. Barber, 682 S.E.2d 760, 69 U.C.C. Rep. Serv. 2d 968 (N.C. Ct. App. 2009) (advertisement indicated that buyer would have to pay full sale price in cash although security agreement specified that sale would be 25 percent cash downpayment with balance due within 24 hours following the sale);Weiss v. Northwest Acceptance Corp., 274 Or. 343, 546 P.2d 1065, 19 U.C.C. Rep. Serv. 348 (1976) (advertising inaccurately stated that cash would be required).

66. *See, e.g.*, Kobuk Eng'g & Contracting Servs., Inc. v. Superior Tank & Constr. Co.-Alaska, Inc., 568 P.2d 1007, 22 U.C.C. Rep. Serv. 854 (Alaska 1977); Connex Press, Inc. v. Int'l Airmotive, Inc., 436 F. Supp. 51, 22 U.C.C. Rep. Serv. 1310 (D.D.C. 1977).

67. In fact, in most circumstances, Article 9 does not mandate that the secured party dispose of the collateral after default. U.C.C. § 9-610(a) (secured party "may" dispose of the collateral after default). Article 9 imposes a mandatory disposition requirement only if the collateral is consumer goods and if more than 60 percent of the cash price (in the case of a PMSI) or the principal amount of the secured obligation (in the case of a non-PMSI) has been paid. U.C.C. § 9-620(e). The general lack of a mandatory disposition requirement is explained by the fact that Article 9 permits the secured party to propose to retain the collateral in full or partial satisfaction of the secured obligation (strict foreclosure). *See* § 18.04, *infra*.

68. For example, even if a foreclosure sale results in a reduced sale price due in part to a secured party's delay in the foreclosure, other factors may justify a conclusion that the secured party's conduct was commercially reasonable. *See, e.g.*, Layne v. Bank One, Ky., N.A., 395 F.3d 271, 55 U.C.C. Rep. Serv. 2d 704 (6th Cir. 2005) (secured party's sale of stock that declined significantly in value when "tech bubble" burst in 2001 nevertheless commercially reasonable despite delay, where debtors were negotiating with secured party to provide additional collateral to avoid sale). Alternatively, a four-year

obviously allow a longer time period if the collateral is a motor vehicle than if it is perishable food. The conduct of a secured party during this time period is also relevant. A creditor that is "sitting on its hands" will evoke less sympathy than one that takes time to fix the collateral to enhance its value or to conduct a widespread advertising campaign to attract additional bidders.[69] Cases involving a secured party's delay in disposing of the collateral often emphasize such factors as the length of the delay, whether the collateral is depreciating, the extent to which the secured party bears responsibility for the delay, and the extent of the secured party's marketing efforts during the delay.[70]

---

delay was held to render the secured party's sale commercially unreasonable to the extent the delay injured a secondary obligor whose exposure increased because the secured obligation continued to accrue interest during the delay prior to sale. Jefferson Loan Co., Inc. v. Session, 397 N.J. Super. 520, 938 A.2d 169, 64 U.C.C. Rep. Serv. 2d 817 (App. Ct. 2008).

69. One situation that has generated controversy involves foreclosures on mezzanine loans. In a mezzanine loan, the borrower is an entity that owns a commercial real estate project; however, the collateral is not the real estate itself (which would require the grant of a mortgage) but the ownership interests in the borrower entity. If the borrower entity defaults, the secured party could dispose of the ownership interests (which are usually general intangibles) in an Article 9 foreclosure sale. Assuming that the loan is secured by the assignment of a controlling portion of the ownership interests, the buyer of these ownership interests at the mezzanine foreclosure could then exercise control over the real estate without having to go to the relatively more significant time and expense of conducting a mortgage foreclosure. (By contrast, in judicial foreclosure states, it might take a mortgage lender many months or even years to complete a foreclosure of the real estate after default.)

Theoretically, an Article 9 foreclosure sale in a non-consumer transaction could happen in as few as ten days, U.C.C. § 9-612(b), but sales of real property typically do not occur that quickly given the due diligence customarily involved in real property sale transactions. (This provides a partial explanation for the much longer pre-sale notice periods required in real property foreclosure, even in states that allow for nonjudicial foreclosure of mortgages and deeds of trust.) Thus, one might argue that it would be commercially unreasonable for a secured party to foreclose an equity pledge in a mezzanine loan without providing a longer notice period prior to sale, given that the sale of the ownership interests is tantamount to a sale of control of the real estate. In *Atlas MF Mezzanine Borrower LLC v. Macquarie Texas Loan Holder LLC*, 199 A.D.3d 439, 158 N.Y.S.3d 19 (2021), the court held that the auction of an equity pledge was commercially reasonable even though there were just under two months between default and sale, given that the secured party sent targeted e-mail marketing to 8,400 potential investors, created of an online data room to facilitate due diligence by potential bidders, and ran advertisements of the sale in the *Real Estate Alert* and the *Wall Street Journal*.

70. *Compare In re* Estate of Nardoni, 86 U.C.C. Rep. Serv. 2d 295 (Ill. Ct. App. 2015) (after default, bank received certificates in its own name for pledged stock but refused for three years either to sell the stock or permit debtor to sell it; bank's actions commercially unreasonable) *and* Jefferson Loan Co. v. Session, 938 A.2d 169, 64 U.C.C. Rep. Serv. 2d 817 (N.J. Sup. Ct. App. Div. 2008) (four-year delay between repossession and disposition of vehicle while interest continued to accrue on debt held commercially unreasonable) *with* Breckenridge v. Nissan Motor Acceptance Corp., 98 U.C.C. Rep. Serv. 2d 872 (E.D. Mich. 2019) (ten-month delay in disposing of vehicle not commercially unreasonable, where ambiguity about vehicle's mileage delayed secured party's ability to obtain an accurate title certificate for the vehicle) *and* 395 Lampe, LLC v. Kawish, LLC, 89 U.C.C. Rep. Serv. 2d 460 (W.D. Wash. 2016) (three-year delay in sale of collateral not unreasonable where collateral generated income during the delay in excess of accruing interest and delay was largely attributable to litigation by the debtor). *See also* Dow Chemical Employees' Credit Union v. Geiling, 95 U.C.C. Rep. Serv. 2d 1268 (Mich. Ct. App. 2018) (two-year delay in sale of boat was commercially reasonable given evidence of secured party's active efforts to market the boat during that period).

Prior to the enactment of revised Article 9, some decisions penalized secured parties for unreasonable delay in disposition using a doctrine known as "constructive strict foreclosure." Strict foreclosure is a voluntary mechanism initiated by a secured party that intends to retain the collateral, including any equity to which the debtor (or a junior secured party) might otherwise be entitled, in lieu of a normal foreclosure disposition of the collateral.[71] Although Article 9 has always required that the secured party send an effective notification of its intent to pursue strict foreclosure, some courts nevertheless treated the secured party's unreasonable delay in disposing of the collateral as being the "constructive" equivalent of notice of the secured party's intent to retain the collateral.[72] Revised Article 9 abolished the doctrine of constructive strict foreclosure.[73] Instead, it makes clear that unreasonable delay in disposition renders the secured party liable for any damages caused by the delay.[74]

There is one situation in which Article 9 provides a specific period for the disposition of collateral. If the collateral is consumer goods and the debtor has repaid 60 percent of the loan (or, in a purchase-money transaction, 60 percent of the cash price),[75] the debtor likely has built up some equity in the collateral. Article 9 does not allow the secured party in such cases to initiate a strict foreclosure.[76] Instead, it requires the secured party to dispose of the collateral within 90 days after taking possession, unless "the debtor and all secondary obligors have agreed [to a longer period] in an agreement to that effect entered into and signed after default."[77]

---

71. If there is equity in the collateral, the debtor or junior secured party can object to strict foreclosure and force a disposition. In the absence of a timely objection, title to the collateral vests in the secured party. Strict foreclosure generally results in the full satisfaction of the debtor's obligation even if the value of the collateral is less than the outstanding balance of that obligation, but Article 9 does permit the secured party and the debtor to agree to a stipulated deficiency amount and thereby use strict foreclosure in partial satisfaction of the debtor's obligation (except in consumer transactions). U.C.C. § 9-620(a). Strict foreclosure is discussed in greater detail in § 18.04, *infra*.

72. *See, e.g.*, Haufler v. Ardinger, 28 U.C.C. Rep. Serv. 893 (Mass. Ct. App. 1979).

73. U.C.C. § 9-620(b). *See also* U.C.C. § 9-620, Comment 5. For further discussion of strict foreclosure, see § 18.04, *infra*.

74. U.C.C. § 9-625(b).

75. Article 9 differentiates between purchase-money and other transactions. U.C.C. § 9-620(e). In a typical non-purchase-money transaction, the debtor takes out a loan against consumer goods that he or she already owns, and determining whether 60 percent of the principal amount of the loan has been repaid is a straightforward matter. In a purchase-money transaction, the 60-percent threshold is applied to the "cash price," and that price is not necessarily the amount financed. It is instead the amount that the seller would have charged if the asset had been sold for cash rather than on credit. If, for example, the seller's price for a car is $20,000 and the buyer makes a $2,000 down payment and finances $18,000 (with the seller or with a lender), the secured party may not use strict foreclosure after the debtor has paid a total of $12,000 (60 percent of the cash price of $20,000). The debtor gets credit for the down payment, and thus the rule is triggered when the debtor has reduced the principal by an additional $10,000.

76. *See* § 18.04, *infra*.

77. U.C.C. § 9-620(f)(2). The section permits waiver of the 90-day period by agreement to accommodate circumstances in which a disposition within 90 days might be unreasonable. For example, suppose Secured Party repossesses a pleasure boat from Debtor in Wisconsin on December 1. It would make little sense for Secured Party to sell the boat in Wisconsin during the dead of winter or to spend

[3] The Method of Disposition: Public versus Private

A secured party can dispose of the collateral at either a public or private disposition so long as the method chosen is commercially reasonable.[78] The distinction between public and private dispositions is relevant to the following issues: (1) whether the method chosen is commercially reasonable; (2) what information the required notice should contain; and (3) whether the secured party may purchase the collateral. This section discusses the first issue.[79]

As a rule, a public disposition means a disposition by auction sale, and a private disposition refers to any other type of disposition. Although the Code does not define the term "public disposition," the Comments to Section 9-610 provide that a "public disposition" is "one at which the price is determined after the public has had a meaningful opportunity for competitive bidding."[80] This provision suggests that the auction must be open to the general public.[81] This issue has arisen in cases involving "dealer's auctions," which are auctions open only to dealers in assets of that type. The typical dealer's auction involves automobiles. Most courts have concluded that such dispositions are private because they are not open to the general public,[82] but this result is debatable.

---

the funds necessary move the boat to Florida where it might sell during that 90-day period. In such a case, the parties could agree that the Secured Party could simply wait until spring to sell the boat.

78. U.C.C. § 9-610(b). *See also* Colonial Pac. Leas. Corp. v. N & N Partners, LLC, 981 F. Supp. 2d 1345 (N.D. Ga. 2013) ("Debtors do not have the right to have their collateral sold by public sale except as provided for by law.").

79. Notice is discussed in § 18.02[B], *infra*, and a secured party's right to buy at its own sale is discussed in § 18.02[C], *infra*.

80. U.C.C. § 9-610, Comment 7.

81. In *Gardner v. Ally Financial Inc.*, 61 A.3d 817 (Md. 2013), the Maryland courts addressed when an auction sale was a "public sale" within the meaning of the state's Closed End Credit Act. The debtors objected to the secured party's effort to characterize the sales of repossessed cars as "public sales," where attendance was limited to those who paid a refundable $1,000 cash deposit. The court held that a public sale must be "open" and "transparent" (as a protection against collusive or unfair practices) and that the admission fee "obscured transparency because bidders and interested parties would have had to accumulate and part with money, at least temporarily, in order to merely observe the auction." *Id.* at 828. Accordingly, the court held that the admission fee prevented the sale from constituting a "public auction" under the state statute. *Id.*

82. *See, e.g.*, Central Trust Bank v. Branch, 651 S.W.3d 826, 108 U.C.C. Rep. Serv. 2d 975 (Mo. 2022) (auction limited to auto dealers licensed in Missouri); John Deery Motors, Inc. v. Steinbronn, 383 N.W.2d 553, 42 U.C.C. Rep. Serv. 1855 (Iowa 1986) (auction limited to automobile dealers); Morrell Emp. Credit Union v. Uselton, 28 U.C.C. Rep. Serv. 269 (Tenn. Ct. App. 1979) (auction limited to credit union members). *See also* RESTATEMENT OF SECURITY § 48, Comment c (indicating that a public sale must be open to the public).

The cases that find such dispositions to be private generally turn on whether the notice sent to the debtor was sufficient. Typically, a secured party will have sent a notice that states the date of the auction but not the time and place. This notice would be sufficient for a private disposition, but not for a public disposition. U.C.C. § 9-613(1)(E). Because the debtor likely will not be eligible to bid at an auction limited to dealers, it may be that a private-sale type of notice is sufficient, and thus the decisions can be explained as an attempt by the courts to protect secured parties that have sent such notices. Nevertheless, on balance, commercial policy would better serve debtors' interests if it characterized dealer's auctions as public dispositions. Requiring that a secured party state the date and time of an auction in its notice is not particularly burdensome.

By holding that a dealer's auction is private, the courts prevent the secured party from bidding at such sales.[83] If the auction is competitive, the debtor is better served by letting the secured party bid against other prospective buyers.[84] The hallmark of a public disposition should be its competitive nature, not whether the public is invited.

Some courts have recognized this, particularly in cases where the debtor may wish to have its business sold as a going concern. In this situation, the debtor and the secured party may negotiate a potential price for the secured party to purchase the collateral as part of a sale process in which the debtor is also seeking third-party purchasers for the debtor's assets. For example, in *Edgewater Growth Capital Partners LP v. H.I.G. Capital, Inc.*,[85] the debtor negotiated a foreclosure agreement with the senior secured party under which the debtor could hold an auction for its assets after a "market check," during which private equity investors and other stakeholders could organize bids for the company's assets (and which permitted the debtor's board to withdraw from the foreclosure agreement and sell the collateral to a third party instead, if that third party made a superior bid). When this market check failed to produce a buyer, an affiliate of the senior secured party made the only bid for the assets at the auction. Following the sale, the private equity investors objected that the sale was unreasonable as a private sale at which an affiliate of the secured party had purchased the collateral. The court rejected this argument:

> If a court deemed a sale "private" whenever a debtor-company negotiates substantial contractual concessions from the foreclosing party in order to give the debtor *more* of a chance to find another buyer, but the secured lender ends up buying it, it would create counterproductive incentives for secured creditors exercising their rights under the Uniform Commercial Code to the detriment of debtor. Rather than encouraging secured creditors to work with debtors to give debtors a meaningful opportunity to market the collateral for sale effectively, it would encourage creditors to go it alone. In the context of selling a company, it would be especially counterproductive because the debtor (the company itself) has access to confidential information and its officers and directors are also in the best position to market the company for sale, or at the very least, advise the secured lender on how to market the company. Therefore ... as the Code itself intimates in the comment describing what makes a sale public, negotiated agreements between secured creditors and debtors that

---

83. A secured party cannot purchase the collateral at a private disposition unless the collateral is of a type customarily sold in a "recognized market" or is of a type for which there exist "widely distributed standard price quotations." U.C.C. § 9-610(c)(2). Comment 9 to Section 9-610 defines a "recognized market" as "one in which the items sold are fungible and prices are not subject to individual negotiation." Because a dealer's auction is not a "recognized market," the secured party cannot bid at a dealer's auction if that auction is a private disposition.

84. A debtor might also argue that a disposition by dealer's auction ought not be approved because it resulted in a wholesale price being paid for the collateral rather than a retail price. This issue is discussed in § 18.02[A][5], *infra*.

85. 68 A.3d 197 (Del. Ch. Ct. 2013).

provide a structure for marketing an asset for sale do not necessarily make a sale private. Instead, what matters is whether the end result of whatever process the secured lenders used gave third parties a "meaningful opportunity" to bid for the collateral.[86]

The court ultimately concluded that the sale process—which lasted nearly three months and in which a broker contacted 67 potential buyers and provided 36 potential bidders with confidential information regarding the debtor—was both public and commercially reasonable even though the process ultimately produced no bids to supplant the secured party's "stalking horse" price.

At some auctions, very few parties, and sometimes, only the secured party, shows up to bid. The lack of competitive bidding may result in a disposition of the collateral for a fraction of its value. Because the price received on disposition provides the basis to establish the amount of any deficiency, an obligor may attempt to argue that a low price demonstrates that the disposition was not commercially reasonable. The paucity of bidders and/or a low price, standing alone, should *not* lead to the conclusion that a disposition was commercially unreasonable. Instead, the proper inquiry is whether the *procedures* adopted by the secured party were reasonably designed to result in a competitive auction.[87] A paucity of bidders and/or a low price may serve as a red flag that justifies further investigation of the circumstances surrounding the auction. For example, the fact that the secured party was the only bidder may suggest inadequate advertising, that an auction was not a commercially reasonable method of disposition, or that the time selected for the auction was not commercially reasonable. Although courts should be suspicious in such cases and investigate such auctions with care, the facts may indicate that the secured party acted in all respects in a commercially reasonable manner and that the lack of bidders or low sale price was happenstance or explainable by other factors.[88] In such a case, the court should not penalize the secured

---

86. *H.I.G. Capital*, 68 A.3d at 213–14 (emphasis in original).

87. *See, e.g.*, Gardner v. Ally Fin., Inc., 61 A.3d 817 (Md. 2013); Vornado PS, L.L.C. v. Primestone Investment Partners, L.P., 821 A.2d 296, 49 U.C.C. Rep. Serv. 2d 1348 (Del. Ct. Ch. 2002) (secured party's decision to conduct public disposition was not commercially unreasonable when secured party was one of the most interested and able potential buyers of the collateral, and private disposition would have eliminated secured party as potential buyer).

88. *See, e.g.*, Airpro Mobile Air, LLC v. Prosperity Bank, 631 S.W.3d 346, 101 U.C.C. Rep. Serv. 2d 1403 (Tex. Ct. App. 2020) (secured party ultimately sold collateral without inspecting, managing, marketing, or appraising it, but had made repeated efforts to do so, all of which were frustrated by debtor's landlord who had possession of the collateral, claimed priority in it, and refused to cooperate in secured party's sales efforts; court held that secured party's disposition was commercially reasonable in light of landlord's interference); *In re* Adobe Trucking, Inc., 551 F. Appx. 167 (5th Cir. 2014) (debtor cannot establish unreasonableness of sale due to secured party's failure to make the collateral available for inspection given debtor's refusal to surrender the collateral, identify its location, or otherwise cooperate with secured party's marketing efforts); Regal Fin. Co., Ltd. v. Tex Star Motors, Inc., 355 S.W.3d 595 (Tex. 2010) (creditor's sale of 906 repossessed vehicles to auto wholesalers was commercially reasonable when creditor hired experienced auto sales professional to evaluate and sell each vehicle after soliciting at least two bids on each, even though volume of repossessed vehicles and their poor condition meant that some vehicles were sold without having received two bids).

party for going ahead with the auction.[89] Nevertheless, a secured party whose auction attracts disappointingly few bidders should consider abandoning the effort and starting over with a private disposition. In so doing, it should take care to re-notify all parties entitled to notice and to tailor its advertising to its newly selected method.[90]

Although a secured party should be permitted significant latitude in choosing the method of disposition, its range of discretion has limits. *United States v. Willis*[91] is a classic case disapproving of a public disposition. The secured party was aware of two offers to purchase the collateral privately but chose to go ahead with an auction that resulted in a price only one-fifth the amount expressed in the private offers. The court properly held that the secured party's decision to dispose of the collateral at auction was commercially unreasonable.[92] The comments to Section 9-610 support the result in *Willis*, stating that Section 9-610 "encourages private dispositions on the assumption that they frequently will result in higher realization on collateral for the benefit of all concerned."[93]

Of course, the arguments set forth above apply equally if the results of a private disposition prove disappointing. This fact may suggest that the collateral was of a type that should have been disposed of at auction. For example, in some parts of the country, livestock may bring higher prices at auctions than in private dispositions.

Some secured parties may choose to dispose of repossessed collateral through an internet auction site. The rapid increase in online auction sales volume provides evidence supporting the view that disposition by online auction can be commercially reasonable, particularly to the extent that it exposes the collateral to a vastly increased

89. *See, e.g., In re* Zsa Zsa, Ltd., 352 F. Supp. 665, 11 U.C.C. Rep. Serv. 1116 (S.D.N.Y. 1972), *aff'd*, 475 F.2d 1393 (2d Cir. 1973) (secured party did not bid, but sale at 10 percent of market value to sole bidder upheld). *See also* U.C.C. § 9-627(a) (fact that secured party could have obtained better price by disposition at different time or in different manner is not, by itself, sufficient to establish that disposition was commercially unreasonable).

90. *See, e.g.,* Gateway Aviation, Inc. v. Cessna Aircraft Co., 577 S.W.2d 860, 25 U.C.C. Rep. Serv. 901 (Mo. Ct. App. 1978) (debtor entitled to notice of private disposition when secured party shifted to that method, even though notice of abandoned public disposition had been sent). *See also* § 18.02[B][2] and [3], *infra*.

91. 593 F.2d 247, 25 U.C.C. Rep. Serv. 1178 (6th Cir. 1979).

92. *See also* United States v. Terrey, 554 F.2d 685, 21 U.C.C. Rep. Serv. 1488 (5th Cir. 1977) (sale of assets of electric sign-manufacturing enterprise at auction was commercially unreasonable). However, the debtor cannot dictate the secured party's method of disposition. For example, the debtor in *U.S. Bancorp Equip. Fin., Inc. v. Ameriquest Holdings LLC*, 55 U.C.C. Rep. Serv. 2d 423 (D. Minn. 2004), had purchased commercial aircraft via secured financing and leased those aircraft to commercial airlines. The debtor went into default after the economic impact of the 9/11 tragedy resulted in the cancellation of these leases. The debtor argued that the secured party's auction sale of the planes was commercially unreasonable because the secured party refused to follow the debtor's suggestion of leasing the planes to foreign carriers. The court rejected this argument, noting that nothing in Article 9 required the secured party to agree to lease the planes to foreign carriers.

93. U.C.C. § 9-610, Comment 2. *See, e.g.,* Automotive Fin. Corp. v. Smart Auto Ctr., Inc., 334 F.3d 685, 51 U.C.C. Rep. Serv. 2d 297 (7th Cir. 2003) (because odometer and title problems on vehicles from Canada would have required them to be sold "mileage unknown," which would likely have produced low auction prices, secured party's private disposition to dealer experienced in handling Canadian vehicles with unknown mileage was commercially reasonable).

universe of potential buyers. Prior to 2010, some commentators argued that Article 9's textual silence as to disposition by online auction created uncertainty that discouraged secured parties from using online auctions and stifled the growth of online auction markets.[94] In response to these concerns, the Comments were amended in 2010 to support both public and private dispositions over the internet if commercially reasonable.[95] Further, Article 9 provides a solution for any remaining uncertainty regarding internet dispositions by authorizing the secured party and the debtor to agree as to the manner by which the secured party may comply with its duty to dispose of the collateral in a commercially reasonable fashion.[96] If a security agreement expressly permits the secured party to dispose of the collateral by online auction, that agreement should be enforceable unless the collateral is of a type entirely unsuited for such an auction sale.[97]

[4] Is There a Duty to "Fix Up" the Collateral?

A secured party is under a duty to use reasonable care in the "custody and preservation of collateral" in its possession.[98] Does this obligation, however, include a duty to "fix up" the collateral so that it will command a higher price? Certainly, policy reasons support imposing at least minimal responsibilities on the secured party. For example, a car dealer that is going to sell a repossessed car from its lot at retail should at least clean the car so that it is attractive to customers. Perhaps the dealer should even have to send the car to its body shop (if it has one) to knock out minor collision damage, or to its service department for a minor tune-up so that the car runs smoothly. Of course, the decision whether to commit major resources to repairing an item should be solely within the discretion of the secured party.

Article 9 does not expressly impose even a minimal duty to "fix up" collateral but instead leaves such decisions to the discretion of a secured party.[99] A few decisions,

---

94. *See* Stephen S. Gilstrap, Comment, *Refreshing the Page on Online Collateral Auctions*, 120 YALE L.J. 679 (2010); Michael Korybut, *Article 9's Incorporation Strategy and Novel, New Markets for Collateral: A Theory of Non-Adoption*, 55 BUFF. L. REV. 137, 156–57 (2007).

95. U.C.C. § 9-610, Comment 2. The location of the sale for purposes of the required pre-sale notification would be the Uniform Resource Locator (URL). U.C.C. § 9-613, Comment 2.

96. U.C.C. § 9-603(a) ("The parties may determine by agreement the standards measuring the fulfillment of the rights of a debtor or obligor and the duties of a secured party ... if the standards are not manifestly unreasonable.").

97. Richard H. Nowka, *eBay Auctions of Repossessed Motor Vehicles—A Template for Commercial Reasonableness under Revised Article 9*, 31 SO. ILL. U. L.J. 281, 308-17 (2007). An additional uncertainty regards whether an internet auction sale is a "public disposition" or a "private disposition," as discussed in the text accompanying note 82, *supra*. On the one hand, because such auctions typically are open only to persons registered on the auction site, one might argue such a sale is a private disposition (analogous to a dealer's auction) at which the secured party could not purchase the collateral under Section 9-610(c). On the other hand, to the extent that anyone can register on the site, the better view would treat the online auction sale as a public sale at which the secured party could bid.

98. U.C.C. § 9-207(a). This provision is equally applicable to possessory security interests in the absence of default.

99. Article 9 states explicitly that the secured party can dispose of the collateral in its existing condition or after any commercially reasonable preparation or processing. U.C.C. § 9-610(a). Further, the Code states that the secured party "may" make use of the collateral for the purpose of preserving

however, have relied on the general concept of commercial reasonableness in imposing a minimal fix-up duty.[100] For example, in *Harley-Davidson Credit Corp. v. Galvin*,[101] the secured party repossessed and sold a plane that had been vandalized while in the secured party's possession: its avionics had been removed, preventing the plane from being flown. While the secured party did sell the plane through a dealer specializing in repossessed aircraft, it did so without fixing the damage, and at least one prospective purchaser had insisted upon replacement of the avionics as a condition of the purchase. The secured party moved for summary judgment that the sale was commercially reasonable given the involvement of the dealer, but the court rejected this argument, noting that the secured party had failed to demonstrate that it was commercially reasonable to sell the aircraft without repair.[102]

[5] Price as an Indicator of Commercial Unreasonableness

A low price may suggest that a secured party did not properly advertise the disposition, that its method of disposition was unreasonable, or that it conducted the disposition at an unreasonable time. However, a low price standing alone, uncoupled from any of these procedural flaws, is not sufficient to render the sale unreasonable or invalidate a disposition.[103] The standard of commercial reasonableness requires that

---

its value. U.C.C. § 9-207(b)(4). However, the Comments make clear that the secured party's discretion is not unbounded, providing that "[a]lthough courts should not be quick to impose a duty of preparation or processing on the secured party, [Section 9-610(a)] does not grant the secured party the right to dispose of the collateral in its then condition in *all* circumstances." U.C.C. § 9-610, Comment 4 (emphasis in original).

100. *See, e.g.,* Whitney Nat'l Bank v. Air Ambulance by B & C Flight Mgmt., Inc., 516 F. Supp. 2d 802 (S.D. Tex. 2007) (noting that a creditor "might have a duty to prepare the collateral if that preparation is part of the usual practice" in the sale of comparable goods); Weiss v. Northwest Acceptance Corp., 274 Or. 343, 546 P.2d 1065, 19 U.C.C. Rep. Serv. 348 (1976). *But see* C.I.T. Corp. v. Duncan Grading & Constr., Inc., 739 F.2d 359, 38 U.C.C. Rep. Serv. 1821 (8th Cir. 1984) (secured party not under duty to clean up construction equipment prior to sale). The Code, to some extent, discourages secured parties from fixing up their collateral. After all, if a decision to invest in the collateral is not commercially reasonable, the secured party will be unable to recoup its investment from the proceeds of disposition. *See* U.C.C. § 9-615(a)(1). Courts have somewhat ameliorated this constraint by showing general leniency in allowing secured parties to recover the expenses of preparing collateral for disposition. See discussion in § 18.02[D], *infra.*

101. 807 F.3d 407, 88 U.C.C. Rep. Serv. 2d 424 (1st Cir. 2015).

102. *Id.* Such decisions establish sound policy, as a court should not ratify a secured party's decision to drag a filthy car straight to the auction block without a detour through the carwash, or its decision to sell an otherwise operable car without tires.

103. Gardner v. Ally Fin. Inc., 61 A.3d 817 (Md. 2013) ("[T]he primary focus of commercial reasonableness is not the *proceeds* received from the sale but rather the *procedures* employed for the sale."); Hicklin v. Onyx Acceptance Corp., 970 A.2d 244, 68 U.C.C. Rep. Serv. 2d 413 (Del. 2009) ("It is improper to reason backwards from price alone to determine the commercial reasonableness of the overall sale process."). The Code explicitly states that the fact that the secured party could have obtained a better price by following other procedures is not *of itself* sufficient to hold that a disposition was commercially unreasonable. U.C.C. § 9-627(a). *See also* General Elec. Capital Corp. v. Stelmach Constr. Co., 45 U.C.C. Rep. Serv. 2d 675 (D. Kan. 2001) (sales price substantially below valuation of debtor's expert did not render sale commercially unreasonable when secured party followed reasonable sale procedures directed toward enhancing sale price); *In re* Zsa Zsa, Ltd., 352 F. Supp. 665,

the secured party adopt procedures *designed*, not *guaranteed*, to produce a reasonable price. Nevertheless, low prices cause courts to scrutinize closely the secured party's disposition efforts.[104]

Suppose a secured party chooses to sell the collateral at wholesale. Can the debtor successfully claim that the sale was commercially unreasonable because the secured party made no attempt to obtain a retail price?[105] The court in *Ford Motor Credit Co. v. Jackson*[106] answered this question in the affirmative. In *Jackson*, the secured party, a dealership that owned both retail and wholesale outlets, held a truck as collateral and chose to sell it at wholesale. The court noted that the truck did not need repairs to prepare it for retail sale and that the secured party received only about one-half the price it would have obtained through a retail sale. These factors persuaded the court that the decision to sell at wholesale rendered the foreclosure commercially unreasonable.

Despite their superficial appeal, decisions like *Jackson* are incorrect. First, they are contrary to the express language of the Code. Article 9 provides that "[a] disposition of collateral is made in a commercially reasonable manner if the disposition is made: (1) in the usual manner on any recognized market; (2) at the price current in any recognized market at the time of the disposition; or (3) *otherwise in conformity with reasonable commercial practices among dealers in the type of property that was the subject of the disposition*."[107] Further, the fact that the secured party may have obtained a higher

---

11 U.C.C. Rep. Serv. 1116 (S.D.N.Y. 1972), *aff'd*, 475 F.2d 1393 (2d Cir. 1973) (sale at 10 percent of market value to sole bidder upheld). *But see* F.D.I.C. v. Herald Square Fabrics Corp., 81 A.D.2d 168, 439 N.Y.S.2d 944, 32 U.C.C. Rep. Serv. 558 (N.Y. Sup. Ct. 1981) (low price alone proved commercial unreasonableness of sale).

As noted in § 18.02[E], *infra*, even if a sale failed to comply with Article 9's commercial reasonableness requirement, this does not inherently invalidate the sale. The sale nevertheless would remain valid to pass the debtor's interest to a good-faith purchaser for value, U.C.C. § 9-617(b), and the debtor's recourse would be limited to damages (or the reduction of the obligor's liability on the debt).

104. Whitney Nat'l Bank v. Air Ambulance by B & C Flight Mgmt., Inc., 516 F. Supp. 2d 802 (S.D. Tex. 2007). *See, e.g.*, Coxall v. Clover Comm. Corp., 4 Misc. 3d 654, 781 N.Y.S.2d 567, 54 U.C.C. Rep. Serv. 2d 5 (N.Y. City Civ. Ct. 2004) (foreclosure sale brought a price only 18.5 percent of car's original purchase price four months earlier, and court noted that "marked discrepancies between the disposal and sale prices signal a need for closer scrutiny, especially where … the possibilities for self-dealing are substantial…."); SNCB Corp. Fin., Ltd. v. Shuster, 877 F. Supp. 820, 26 U.C.C. Rep. Serv. 2d 953 (S.D.N.Y. 1994) (low price caused court to scrutinize procedures closely, but sale upheld as commercially reasonable). *See also* U.C.C. § 9-610, Comment 10.

105. *Compare In re* Estate of Sagmiller, 615 N.W.2d 567, 44 U.C.C. Rep. Serv. 2d 309 (N.D. 2000) *and* Ford Motor Credit Co. v. Mathis, 660 So.2d 1273, 27 U.C.C. Rep. Serv. 2d 1448 (Miss. 1995) (use of dealer-only auction sale was commercially reasonable) *with* Action Mgmt., Inc. v. Gross, 44 U.C.C. Rep. Serv. 2d 623 (Pa. Ct. Com. Pl. 2001) (sale at wholesale auction in absence of any prior attempts to sell vehicle held commercially unreasonable). *See also In re* Severance Truck Line, Inc. 35 B.R. 332, 37 U.C.C. Rep. Serv. 1021 (Bankr. M.D. Fla. 1983) (sale of repossessed truck at wholesale price to repossessing creditor was not commercially reasonable).

106. 466 N.E.2d 330, 39 U.C.C. Rep. Serv. 743 (Ill. Ct. App. 1984).

107. U.C.C. § 9-627(b) (emphasis added). This provision does not mean, however, that any "dealer's auction" sale will automatically satisfy the Section 9-627(b) safe harbor; dealer's auctions may differ in important ways from auction to auction. *See, e.g.*, Hicklin v. Onyx Acceptance Corp., 970 A.2d 244, 68 U.C.C. Rep. Serv. 2d 413 (Del. 2009) ("The sale of a car to the highest bidder at a poorly

price at a retail sale does not mean that the retail price is more "fair" or "reasonable." Retail sales often involve higher costs (e.g., retail sales commissions), and the price received at a retail sale reflects those increased costs. Further, by selling at retail, the secured party may lose a sale that it otherwise would have made (i.e., the secured party might have sold another unit from its own inventory to the same customer). Judge Posner gave perhaps the best analysis of the issue in *Contrail Leasing Partners, Ltd. v. Consolidated Airways, Inc.*,[108] when he stated:

> [A]n ironclad rule against selling collateral at wholesale rather than retail would make no sense. Although retail prices tend to be higher than wholesale prices, this is because it costs more to sell at retail. Not only can there be, therefore, no presumption that the net gains to the seller are different at the two levels, but economic theory implies that returns at the two levels will tend toward equality, since until they are equalized dealers will have incentives to enter at the level where the higher returns are being earned and by entering will bid those returns down.[109]

[B] Notification of Disposition

Unless they receive notice of a proposed disposition, persons with an interest in the collateral may be unable to protect their interests. Sufficient prior notice of a disposition may permit these persons to find financing to redeem the collateral,[110] to seek injunctive relief if there is any valid basis to challenge the secured party's conduct,[111] or to attract additional bidders to the disposition (which should help to maximize the price and thus limit the size of any deficiency). To ensure that affected persons have an adequate opportunity to protect their interests from foreclosure, Article 9 generally requires the foreclosing secured party to send a notification, prior to disposition, to certain persons most likely to be affected by that disposition.

The most common issues arising with respect to notification are (1) the persons entitled to notification, (2) the extent of notice required prior to disposition, (3) the contents of the notification, and (4) the circumstances which excuse notification altogether. The following subsections discuss these issues.

---

publicized, sparsely attended, and inconveniently located auction would not be meaningful; but a sale to the highest bidder at a highly-publicized, well-attended auction run by a highly-regarded auctioneer in a convenient location would be."). As explained in § 19.02, *infra*, if the secured party is seeking a deficiency judgment and the obligor alleges that the secured party did not dispose of the collateral in a commercially reasonable fashion, the secured party has the burden of establishing that its disposition was commercially reasonable in all respects.

108. 742 F.2d 1095, 39 U.C.C. Rep. Serv. 9 (7th Cir. 1983).

109. 742 F.2d at 1101, 39 U.C.C. Rep. Serv. at 17.

110. U.C.C. § 9-623.

111. Any person entitled to notification may want to police the disposition to make certain that it is carried out in a commercially reasonable manner. Injunctive relief in furtherance of this goal may be obtained under U.C.C. § 9-625(a). *See* Chapter 19, *infra*.

[1] Persons Entitled to Notification

Article 9 requires that a secured party send a pre-disposition notification to the "debtor" and "any secondary obligor."[112] In this context, the distinction between the terms "debtor" and "obligor" is relevant. The Code defines the term "obligor" to include the person that "owes payment or other performance of the obligation" being secured.[113] A "debtor" is "a person having an interest, other than a security interest or other lien, in the collateral, whether or not the person is an obligor."[114] The term "secondary obligor" describes a person that is a surety for the secured obligation.[115] By its terms, Article 9 thus requires a secured party to notify the person who supplied the collateral (the "debtor") and any surety for the debt (the "secondary obligor"), but it does not require the secured party to notify the primary obligor unless that person is also a debtor.

For example, suppose Henning borrows $1,000 from Bank, Gotberg grants a security interest in her automobile to secure Henning's obligation (but does not co-sign Henning's promissory note or otherwise guarantee the obligation), and Freyermuth agrees to be a surety for the obligation. If Henning defaults and Bank repossesses the car from Gotberg, to whom must Bank send a pre-disposition notification? Under Section 9-611(b), Bank must notify Gotberg (the debtor) and Freyermuth (a secondary obligor) but has no obligation to notify Henning, who is the primary obligor but not a debtor.[116] The rationale is that a notification to Gotberg (who, as debtor, will have a strong incentive to police the disposition to protect her equity in the collateral) and Freyermuth (who, as secondary obligor, will have a strong incentive to police the disposition to minimize the amount of his liability) should be sufficient to protect Henning, who, after all, must pay the full amount of the obligation to Bank (absent misconduct by the Bank). Nevertheless, for prudential reasons, Bank will probably send Henning a notification of the disposition anyway, whether out of courtesy, because the security agreement independently obligated the Bank to do so, or in hope that Henning may make additional efforts to satisfy the debt prior to the disposition.

The Code does not require that an entitled person *receive* the notification, only that the secured party send it. This distinction is consistent with the Code's definition of "notify," which states that "[a] person 'notifies' or 'gives' a notice or notification to another person by taking such steps as may be reasonably required to inform the other person in ordinary course *whether or not the other person actually comes to know of it*."[117] Thus, in most cases, the secured party need only place the notification

112. U.C.C. §9-611(c)(1), (2).
113. U.C.C. §9-102(a)(59).
114. U.C.C. §9-102(a)(28)(A).
115. U.C.C. §9-102(a)(72) ("'Secondary obligor' means an obligor to the extent that: (A) the obligor's obligation is secondary; or (B) the obligor has a right of recourse with respect to an obligation secured by collateral against the debtor, another obligor, or property of either.").
116. *See* U.C.C. §9-611, Comment 3.
117. U.C.C. §1-202(d) (emphasis added). *See also* McGrady v. Nissan Motor Acceptance Corp., 40 F. Supp. 2d 1323, 41 U.C.C. Rep. Serv. 2d 986 (M.D. Ala. 1998) (no evidence that notification containing proper name and address had been sent improperly despite nonreceipt by debtor).

in the mail, properly addressed and with proper postage, to comply with the Code's requirements.[118] As the Tennessee Supreme Court explained in *Auto Credit of Nashville v. Wimmer*:

> To require every creditor to verify receipt of notification in every situation would place an unreasonable burden on them, making secured transactions in this state unduly cumbersome. It is quite conceivable that many debtors, when faced with the notification sent by certified mail, may refuse delivery, thus prolonging the time the creditor must wait to sell the collateral, causing additional costs to accrue to the creditor. Even without such affirmative acts by the debtor, any number of situations may arise which prevent actual receipt of written notification: debtors move, mail gets lost, or someone other than the debtor may receive the letter then misplace it.[119]

Several caveats, however, are in order. If a secured party *knows* that an entitled person has moved and is aware of the new address, some courts have held that the secured party must send a notification to that address.[120] If the secured party knows that an entitled person has moved but does not have the new address, some courts have imposed a duty to take minimal steps to locate and notify the entitled person, such as looking in a city directory or contacting a known relative or business associate of the person.[121]

---

118. If a debtor has multiple addresses, a prudent secured party will send a copy of the notification to each address. Likewise, if the secured party knows that an attorney represents the debtor, the secured party should also send the notification to the debtor's attorney. *See, e.g.,* Greenpoint Credit, L.L.C. v. Murphy, 57 U.C.C. Rep. Serv. 2d 747 (Ky. Ct. App. 2005) (secured party repossessed mobile home and sent notification of sale to vacated address at which home had been located but failed to send notification to the debtor's attorney despite knowing that the debtor was represented; notification held inadequate).

119. 231 S.W.3d 896, 902–03, 63 U.C.C. Rep. Serv. 2d 626 (Tenn. 2007). Nevertheless, prudent secured parties frequently attempt to verify receipt of the notification. As an evidentiary matter, proof that the debtor received the notification is likely to preclude any later dispute regarding whether the secured party sent the notification.

120. *See, e.g., In re* Carter, 511 F.2d 1203, 16 U.C.C. Rep. Serv. 874 (9th Cir. 1975). Out of caution, the secured party should also send a notification to the address specified in the agreement.

121. *See, e.g.,* Mallicoat v. Volunteer Fin. & Loan Corp., 57 Tenn. App. 106, 415 S.W.2d 347, 3 U.C.C. Rep. Serv. 1035 (1966) (secured party that received notification back from post office marked "undeliverable" had duty to try to locate debtor). The comments to Section 9-611 suggest that a secured party that sends a notification and later learns that the intended recipient did not receive it *may* have to attempt to locate the person and send another notification. *See* U.C.C. §9-611, Comment 6 (leaving to "judicial resolution" whether requirement of reasonable notification requires "second try" by secured party). A "second try" is particularly advisable when the address used for the first notification is no longer correct and the secured party can easily identify a new address for the debtor (or can give the notification to the debtor's counsel). *See, e.g.,* Textron Fin. Corp. v. Lentine Marine Inc., 630 F. Supp. 1352, 68 U.C.C. Rep. Serv. 2d 923 (S.D. Fla. 2009) (summary judgment denied to secured party which knew notifications were returned undeliverable and which made no effort to further steps to notify debtor or its counsel). By contrast, if the address used remains correct, and the debtor has simply refused to accept the previous notification, no "second try" is required. Panora State Bank v. Dickinson, 713 N.W.2d 247, 58 U.C.C. Rep. Serv. 2d 726 (Iowa App. 2006).

A secured party should make certain that each entitled person is sent a copy of the notification.[122] If, for example, the debtors are husband and wife, the secured party should send a separate notification to each. If the notification is sent to "Mr. and Mrs." and the couple has separated, the secured party's notification to the debtor that no longer lives at the address may be insufficient.[123] The problem is not that the notification was sent to the wrong address—the secured party may rely on the debtor's original address if it has not been notified of a different address—but rather that the secured party cannot depend on the debtor's still living at the address to forward the information to the other debtor.

If the collateral is consumer goods, a secured party does not have to notify anyone other than the debtor and any secondary obligor. For all other types of collateral, however, a foreclosing secured party may have to notify other persons. Junior secured parties, for example, have a significant interest in obtaining notice of a senior secured party's disposition because it will extinguish the junior security interest.[124] Further, a junior secured party has an interest in generating a surplus at the disposition because the Code allows it to have that surplus applied to the junior secured debt.[125] Alternatively, a junior might want to redeem the collateral by paying off the senior and adding its expenditure to the principal obligation.[126]

Section 9-616(b) contains a requirement that a secured party in a consumer-goods transaction must send the obligor(s) an explanation of how the secured party calculated the surplus or deficiency following the sale. In *Central Trust Bank v. Branch*, 651 S.W.3d 826, 108 U.C.C. Rep. Serv. 2d 975 (Mo. 2022), the secured party sent such an explanation to the obligor, but delivery was unsuccessful; the obligor later challenged the secured party's attempt to collect a deficiency on the ground that the secured party made no "second try" to send the required explanation. The court rejected this argument, noting that there was no need for a second try to send a post-sale explanation (given that the debtor's right of redemption has already been extinguished) but that consistent with § 9-611, Comment 6, the "second try" might be warranted when sending a pre-sale notification. *Id.* at 831.

122. Under U.C.C. § 1-202(f), a notification sent to an organization is effective "from the time it is brought to the attention of the individual conducting that transaction and, in any event, from the time it would have been brought to the individual's attention if the organization had exercised due diligence." "Organization" is broadly defined to include any legal person other than an individual, U.C.C. § 1-201(b)(25), and the term "person" includes essentially all forms of business entities. U.C.C. § 1-201(b)(27).

123. *See, e.g.*, Huntington Nat'l Bank of Wash. Court House v. Stockwell, 10 Ohio App. 3d 30, 460 N.E.2d 303, 37 U.C.C. Rep. Serv. 1799 (Ct. App. 1983). If the couple resides together, most courts have found that a notification to one spouse is notification to the other. In *In re De Pasquale*, 166 B.R. 663, 23 U.C.C. Rep. Serv. 2d 1022 (Bankr. N.D. Ill. 1994), the court justified this result on the basis that the other spouse was aware of the notification.

124. U.C.C. § 9-617(a)(3). The title of the buyer at the foreclosure sale is discussed in § 18.02[E], *infra.*

125. The junior must notify the senior in a record that it wants to share in the surplus before distribution of the proceeds of sale is complete. U.C.C. § 9-615(a)(3). See discussion in § 18.02[D], *infra.* In addition, notification to the senior will entitle the junior to damages if the senior's sale is commercially unreasonable and would, if properly conducted, have generated a surplus. U.C.C. § 9-625(b).

126. A competing secured party (junior or senior) may avoid a foreclosure sale by redeeming the collateral. U.C.C. § 9-623.

Article 9 accordingly requires the foreclosing secured party to search the Article 9 filing records and provide a pre-sale notification to any other secured party or lien-holder that, as of ten days prior to the date of the notification, holds an interest in the same collateral that is perfected either by filing or by notation on a certificate of title.[127] The drafters imposed this search duty on the foreclosing secured party because "[m]any of the problems arising from dispositions of collateral encumbered by multiple security interests can be ameliorated or solved by informing all secured parties of an intended disposition and affording them the opportunity to work with one another."[128] Article 9 provides a "safe-harbor" rule to help the foreclosing secured party satisfy its search obligations.[129]

Furthermore, Article 9 requires a foreclosing secured party to send a notification to any other secured party or lienholder (such as the holder of a judgment lien) that has previously advised the foreclosing secured party, via a signed notification, that it claims an interest in the collateral.[130] Although the drafters intended this notification provision primarily to benefit junior interests, a senior secured party that learns that a junior has acquired an interest in its collateral may also take advantage of the provision.[131] By advising the junior of its interest, the senior gains some protection if the debtor defaults to the junior and the junior commences foreclosure proceedings. Although the junior's disposition will not extinguish the senior's interest,[132] the senior will want to know of

---

127. U.C.C. § 9-611(c)(3)(B), (C).

128. U.C.C. § 9-611, Comment 4.

129. U.C.C. § 9-611(e). To qualify for this safe harbor, a foreclosing secured party should file a "request for information" with the filing officer, seeking information about all financing statements indexed under the debtor's name. The request must be filed not less than 20 days nor more than 30 days prior to the notification date. The notification date is the earlier of the date the secured party sends the notification to the debtor and any secondary obligor or obtains waivers from such persons. U.C.C. § 9-611(a). After filing its request, the foreclosing secured party should receive from the filing officer copies of all effective financing statements indexed under the name of the debtor. The foreclosing secured party may then provide the necessary notification to any secured party that has filed a financing statement describing the collateral. If the foreclosing secured party provides a notification to every person revealed by a timely request for information, or if it files a timely request but does not receive a response from the filing officer, it is deemed to have satisfied the "search-and-notify" obligation imposed by § 9-611(c)(3)(B).

130. U.C.C. § 9-611(c)(3)(A). This provision allows a judgment lienholder to take steps to ensure the receipt of notification of a senior creditor's disposition of the collateral. Typically, the existence of a judgment lien against personal property would not appear in the UCC filing records (and thus the "search-and-notify" obligation would not protect the typical judgment lienholder).

131. In most such cases, the senior will have the option of declaring a default and proceeding to foreclose on the collateral. Most security agreements make the creation of a competing security interest an event of default.

132. See discussion in § 18.02[D], *infra*. Even if the buyer at a foreclosure sale is a buyer in ordinary course of business (which will likely be the case if the secured party is a seller that puts the collateral back into its inventory for resale), the buyer cannot take advantage of U.C.C. § 9-320(a) because the senior's security interest will not have been created by the buyer's immediate seller (the junior secured party). Accordingly, the buyer at the foreclosure sale is at risk of having the collateral repossessed from it by the senior if the debtor is in default to the senior. Because the buyer may then have to redeem the collateral to protect its interest, it should pay no more at the junior's sale than the fair market value

it.[133] This awareness will permit the senior to redeem the collateral from the junior prior to disposition or to take steps to have the foreclosure buyer redeem the collateral to avoid repossession by the senior. Another option (though seldom exercised) is for the senior to repossess the collateral from the junior before the junior's disposition.[134] As between the two secured parties, the senior has the superior possessory interest if default has occurred; by taking over the process and conducting its own disposition, the senior gains a significant level of protection.

There is a party not mentioned in the Code that must also be notified of a disposition by sale. If the United States government has filed a notice of tax lien more than 30 days before a foreclosure sale, its lien will survive that sale, even if that lien is junior to the secured party's interest, unless the secured party provides proper notice to the IRS at least 25 days prior to the sale.[135]

In limited circumstances, a person may be a debtor, secondary obligor, or other person entitled to notice and yet may be unknown to (and undiscoverable by) the foreclosing secured party. For example, suppose Freyermuth holds a perfected security interest in Henning's equipment and repossesses it following default. Unknown to Freyermuth, however, Henning had sold the equipment two days earlier to Gotberg, who had not yet taken delivery of the equipment. Also unknown to Freyermuth, Gotberg had granted a security interest in the equipment to Bank, which filed a financing statement covering the collateral that named Gotberg as debtor. Technically, Gotberg is now a debtor with respect to the collateral (even though Gotberg is not an obligor)—but requiring Freyermuth to notify Gotberg and Bank of the sale would pose an impossible search burden on Freyermuth. In this context, Article 9 excuses Freyermuth from providing notification to either Gotberg or Bank; notification to Henning alone is legally sufficient.[136]

---

of the collateral less the amount of the senior's debt. Also, the buyer at the junior's sale should notify the senior of its interest to prevent the senior from making post-sale advances to the debtor that would increase the senior's interest in the collateral. *See* U.C.C. §9-323(d). Nothing the buyer can do will prevent the secured party from obtaining priority for advances made pursuant to a commitment entered without knowledge of the buyer's interest. *See* U.C.C. §9-323(e). A secured party's priority rights against a buyer with respect to future advances is discussed generally in §11.03[A][3], *supra*.

133. The fact that the senior's interest survives foreclosure is of little use if its collateral has been sold to a third party that disappeared with it.

134. *See, e.g.,* American Heritage & Trust Co. v. O. & E., Inc., 576 P.2d 566, 23 U.C.C. Rep. Serv. 1034 (Colo. Ct. App. 1978).

135. 26 U.S.C. §7425(b). The government has a post-sale right of redemption for real property, but not for personalty. *See* 26 U.S.C. §7425(d). Tax liens are discussed generally in Chapter 14, *supra*.

136. U.C.C. §9-605(1), (2). If Freyermuth became aware of the transfer to Gotberg prior to the sale and also became aware of Gotberg's address (or some other means of communicating with her), Freyermuth would then have to notify both Gotberg and Bank.

[2] Time Period for Notification

Section 9-611(b) requires that a secured party send a "reasonable signed notification" of the disposition.[137] The secured party must send the notification so that a party receiving it in due course will have a reasonable opportunity, prior to disposition, to exercise its redemption rights or take other steps reasonably calculated to protect its interests.[138] Article 9 provides the foreclosing secured party with an express "safe harbor" in non-consumer transactions if the secured party sends the notification no later than ten days prior to the disposition.[139] This does not suggest that the secured party *must* send notification ten days prior to disposition. At least one court has approved of a notification that gave the debtor only three business days prior to a sale,[140] and the comments to Section 9-612 clearly indicate that the ten-day provision is a "safe harbor" and not a "minimum requirement."[141] A notification period of less than ten days is dangerous, however; even a notification sent a week before the disposition has occasionally been attacked because a weekend or holiday cut down on the amount of time available to the recipient to protect its interest.[142]

A careful secured party should never encounter a problem. Although a debtor or secondary obligor cannot waive the right to notice prior to default, a security agreement can establish the standards by which to measure the secured party's fulfillment of its duties if the standards selected are not "manifestly unreasonable."[143] Further, should a secured party or the debtor find a buyer willing to pay a fair price but not willing to wait for the necessary time to expire, the debtor can facilitate a sale by waiving its right to notification.[144]

[3] Form and Content of Notification

Article 9 requires a secured party to send a "signed" notification,[145] which effectively requires that it send the notification in a "record," that is, either as a writing or

---

137. U.C.C. §9-611(b).

138. U.C.C. §9-612, Comment 2.

139. U.C.C. §9-612(b).

140. *See, e.g.,* Citizens State Bank v. Sparks, 276 N.W.2d 661, 26 U.C.C. Rep. Serv. 589 (Neb. 1979).

141. U.C.C. §9-612, Comment 3.

142. *See, e.g.,* Levers v. Rio King Land & Inv. Co., 560 P.2d 917, 21 U.C.C. Rep. Serv. 344 (Nev. 1977).

143. U.C.C. §9-603(a). A security agreement specifying that notice will be deemed sufficient if it is sent a certain number of days before the disposition should insulate the secured party as long as it subsequently complies with the terms of the agreement.

144. The right to notice may be waived after default in a signed record. See U.C.C. §9-624(a) and the discussion in §18.02[B][4], *infra.* A secured party that wants to facilitate an early disposition should obtain waivers of the right to redemption as well as the right to pre-disposition notice. *See* §18.05, *infra.*

145. U.C.C. §9-611(c).

as information that is "stored in an electronic or other medium and is retrievable in perceivable form."[146] An oral notification will not suffice.[147]

As discussed earlier, reasonable notification allows the recipient to protect its interest by redeeming the collateral, attending the disposition (or causing others to attend) and bidding the price up to a fair level, or policing the disposition to make certain that it comports with the requirement of commercial reasonableness. Prior versions of Article 9 provided minimal guidance regarding the contents of a "reasonable" notification. Revised Article 9 addressed this shortcoming by providing the secured party with a safe-harbor rule applicable to most foreclosures. Except in the case of a consumer-goods transaction,[148] a secured party's notification is sufficient if it:

- describes the debtor and the secured party;
- describes the collateral that is the subject of the intended disposition;
- states the method of the intended disposition;
- states that the debtor is entitled to an accounting of the unpaid indebtedness and states the charge, if any, for such an accounting; and
- states the time and place of a public disposition or the time after which the secured party may dispose of the collateral privately.[149]

A secured party does not have to provide the notification in the exact words that appear in the statute.[150] Furthermore, a court may conclude that a secured party's notification is "reasonable" under the circumstances even if it lacks one or more of the elements listed in the safe-harbor provision.[151] Nevertheless, a secured party would be wise to track the suggested language closely.

---

146. U.C.C. § 9-102(a)(70).

147. *See* U.C.C. § 9-611, Comment 5. As a matter of policy, the preclusion of oral notification is questionable if such notification is commercially reasonable under the circumstances. As a best practice, however, any secured party should send a record because the secured party will ordinarily bear the burden of proving compliance with the notification requirement, *see, e.g.,* Boatmen's Bank v. Dahmer, 716 S.W.2d 876, 2 U.C.C. Rep. Serv. 2d 754 (Mo. Ct. App. 1986), and a record greatly simplifies that task.

148. U.C.C. § 9-102(a)(24). Recall that revised Article 9 distinguishes between a "consumer transaction" and a "consumer-goods transaction." For discussion of the distinction, see § 1.04[A][1], *supra.*

149. U.C.C. § 9-613(1). Where the notification of a public sale indicates the time and place and the sale takes place at that time, the notification is not insufficient merely because the agreement with the transferee created by the sale is consummated later. *See, e.g.,* Mountaineer Inv. LLC v. Heath, 165 Wash. App. 1008, 76 U.C.C. Rep. Serv. 2d 196 (2011) (notification of public sale of mobile home not insufficient merely because sale did not close until a month later, given that sale commenced at date and time specified in the notification).

150. *See* U.C.C. § 9-613(4) ("A particular phrasing of the notification is not required."). For example, a notification that does not state the debtor was entitled to an accounting of the unpaid debt is nevertheless sufficient if the notification actually provides such an accounting. *See* Connex Credit Union v. Thibodeau, 266 A.3d 930, 106 U.C.C. Rep. Serv. 2d 627 (Conn. Ct. App. 2021); McDonald v. Wells Fargo Bank, N.A., 374 F. Supp. 3d 462, 98 U.C.C. Rep. Serv. 2d 780 (W.D. Pa. 2019).

151. U.C.C. § 9-613(2). For convenience, Article 9 also provides a suggested form that, if complied with, satisfies the reasonable-notification requirement. U.C.C. § 9-613(5).

In a consumer-goods transaction, the five elements indicated above are *mandatory*.[152] Furthermore, a notice in a consumer-goods transaction must also include the following:

- a description of any liability that the recipient may have for a deficiency judgment following disposition;

- a telephone number from which the recipient may obtain information about the amount that must be paid to redeem the collateral; and

- a telephone number or mailing address from which the recipient may obtain information concerning the disposition of the collateral and the obligation secured.[153]

Again, although no particular phrasing is required, a prudent secured party should track the language of the statute as closely as possible. For convenience, the revisions also provide a suggested safe-harbor form, written in "plain English," that (if complied with) satisfies the reasonable-notification requirement.[154]

Secured parties should take special care to comply with these requirements. Although a creditor could argue that less-than-perfect compliance does not render a notification unreasonable,[155] courts have shown a willingness to construe the statutory requirements strictly. For example, in *Gateway Aviation, Inc. v. Cessna Aircraft Co.*,[156] the secured party sent proper notification of an auction but withdrew the collateral when the bidding proved disappointing and instead sought a private buyer. The secured party later found a person who purchased the collateral for several thousand dollars more than the top bid at the auction. In an action for a deficiency, the court held

---

152. There is no good-faith defense if the secured party's notification fails to contain these mandatory disclosures. *See, e.g., In re* Schwalb, 347 B.R. 726, 60 U.C.C. Rep. Serv. 2d 755 (Bankr. D. Nev. 2006); *see also* Coxall v. Clover Comm. Corp., 4 Misc. 3d 654, 781 N.Y.S.2d 567, 54 U.C.C. Rep. Serv. 2d 5 (N.Y. City Civ. Ct. 2004) (letters to debtor insufficient because they did not indicate debtor had the right to an accounting or the charge, if any, for an accounting).

153. U.C.C. §9-614(1). *See also In re* Downing, 286 B.R. 900, 49 U.C.C. Rep. Serv. 2d 983 (Bankr. W.D. Mo. 2002) (notification that provided "You are notified that [secured party] intends to sell the vehicle as allowed under state law, but no sooner than 10 days after the date of this letter" held insufficient because it failed to notify debtor that secured party intended private disposition, that debtor had right to accounting, and that debtor would be liable for any deficiency following disposition).

154. U.C.C. §9-614(3).

155. *See* U.C.C. §9-613(2) (finder of fact may conclude that a notification is reasonable under the circumstances even if it lacks some of the information specified in the "safe harbor" provision). For example, in *Caterpillar Financial Services Corp. v. Get 'Er Done Drilling, Inc.*, 286 A.3d 302, 109 U.C.C. Rep. Serv. 2d 444 (Pa. Super. Ct. 2022), the notification indicated that a public internet auction would begin and end on November 2, but the auction actually began on October 12 and concluded on October 26. At first blush, this error seems prejudicial in that the premature sale could compromise the debtor's ability to redeem the collateral; in other words, the debtor reasonably would have thought it had until November 2 to redeem the collateral based on the notification, when in fact the sale's conclusion on October 26 extinguished that redemption right. The court nevertheless held that the notification was reasonable because the error did not prejudice the debtor, who had not read the notification and had no funds with which to redeem the collateral.

156. 577 S.W.2d 860, 25 U.C.C. Rep. Serv. 901 (Mo. Ct. App. 1978).

that the private disposition was defective because the secured party had failed properly to notify the debtor.[157]

A secured party may include additional information in its notification, beyond the stated requirements of the Code, if the additional information is not seriously misleading.[158] For example, a notification may be defective if the secured party overstates the amount of the debt and thereby discourages the debtor from exercising its redemption right.[159] If the notification contains errors in required or additional information that are not misleading or prejudicial to the debtor, however, courts should be careful not to penalize the secured party, especially in transactions not involving consumers.

Article 9 holds the secured party to a slightly higher standard in consumer-goods transactions. Errors in the information required by Section 9-614(1) render the notification defective.[160] Assuming that the secured party has used the safe-harbor form specified in section 9-614(3), errors in additional information that the secured party chooses to provide will not render the notification defective unless that information is misleading with respect to the recipient's rights under Article 9.[161]

---

157. Although harsh, the result in *Gateway Aviation* can be justified. The debtor should have had an opportunity to police the private disposition to make certain that it was conducted fairly; further, with additional notification of the private disposition, the debtor might have come up with the money to redeem the collateral after the date of the auction but before the private disposition occurred. *See also* VFS Leasing v. Bric Constructors, LLC, 2012 WL 2499518 (Tenn. Ct. App. 2012) (denying summary judgment to secured party that sent proper notification of its planned private sale but later shifted to public sale without providing further notification of the time and place of the public auction). *But see* Drewry v. Starr Motors, Inc. 65 U.C.C. Rep. Serv. 2d 905 (E.D. Va. 2008) (on facts analogous to those in *Gateway Aviation*, held that secured party was not required to provide second notice prior to subsequent private sale).

158. U.C.C. § 9-613(3)(B).

159. *See, e.g.*, Wilmington Trust Co. v. Conner, 415 A.2d 773, 28 U.C.C. Rep. Serv. 900 (Del. 1980); Travis v. Blvd. Bank, 880 F. Supp. 1226, 28 U.C.C. Rep. Serv. 2d 410 (N.D. Ill. 1995). Whether the notification must advise the debtor of redemption rights is discussed in § 18.05, *infra*.

160. Section 9-613(3)(B) provides that minor and not seriously misleading errors in the required information do not defeat the sufficiency of the notification, but Section 9-614 provides no such flexibility; the Comments make clear that errors (even minor, not misleading ones) in Section 9-614(1)'s required information will defeat the effectiveness of the Section 9-614 notification. U.C.C. § 9-614, Comments 2 & 3. For an example, consider *Williams v. American Honda Finance Corp.*, 98 N.E.3d 169, 95 U.C.C. Rep. Serv. 2d 1241 (Mass. 2018), where the secured party sent a pre-sale notification advising the obligor that the deficiency would be based on the foreclosure sale price. The court held the notification insufficient because other applicable law required deficiency judgments in consumer credit transactions to be calculated by reference to fair market value. *See also* Piazza v. Santander Consumer USA, Inc., 2020 WL 1190825 (D. Mass. 2020) (notification comparable to the one in *Williams* was not made sufficient by inserting the words "subject to applicable law" as it was not clear debtors would understand that applicable law required the deficiency to be calculated by reference to fair market value).

161. U.C.C. § 9-614(5). Overly rigorous policing of the foreclosure process (in this and other contexts) by the courts could have the unintended effect of causing more secured parties to have their collateral sold through a judicial proceeding. This approach could have the perverse effect of reducing the amounts realized through foreclosure, thereby increasing the deficiencies borne by debtors.

[4] When Notification Is Excused

A secured party need not send a pre-disposition notification if (1) the collateral is perishable, (2) the collateral threatens to decline speedily in value, (3) the collateral is of a type customarily sold on a recognized market, or (4) there is an effective waiver of the right to notification.[162]

The rationale for the first exception is obvious. If the collateral is a crop of harvested tomatoes sitting in a truck in the heat of summer when repossession occurs, the secured party should not have to send notification. The collateral is perishable, and the debtor will suffer positive harm if the secured party waits until it has complied with a notification requirement. Cases involving truly perishable assets are rare, however, and secured parties have had little success in attempting to use this provision. Several reported cases involve cattle, which must be fed and watered or they will perish, and the courts are nearly uniform in holding that a secured party disposing of cattle must send a notification.[163] This result is appropriate because the cattle should not depreciate in value if they receive appropriate care, and the secured party has the statutory responsibility to provide that care following repossession.[164]

The most common examples of collateral that threatens to decline speedily in value are stocks and commodities. In *Moutray v. Perry State Bank*,[165] the secured party failed to send notification prior to disposition of the debtor's milo crop, but the court held that notification was excused because the evidence showed that the market for milo was likely to drop precipitously.

In contrast, in *Chittenden Trust Co. v. Andre Noel Sports*,[166] the secured party failed to send a notification prior to its disposition of high-fashion ski and sports apparel. The court properly refused to excuse the failure because the ski season had ended long before the disposition had occurred.[167] Had repossession occurred just before the end of the season, however, the secured party might have prevailed by convincing the court that such seasonal goods had to be disposed of immediately to obtain a fair price.

Courts have limited the third exception, collateral customarily sold on a recognized market, to assets that are sold without negotiation.[168] If, for example, the collateral con-

---

162. U.C.C. §§ 9-611(d), 9-624(a).

163. *See, e.g.*, Boatmen's Bank of Nev. v. Dahmer, 716 S.W.2d 876, 2 U.C.C. Rep. Serv. 2d 754 (Mo. Ct. App. 1986). *Cf.* City Bank & Trust Co. v. Van Andel, 220 Neb. 152, 368 N.W.2d 789, 41 U.C.C. Rep. Serv. 282 (1985) (whether cattle were perishable was question of fact for jury).

164. U.C.C. § 9-207(a).

165. 748 S.W.2d 749, 7 U.C.C. Rep. Serv. 2d 1340 (Mo. Ct. App. 1988).

166. 159 Vt. 387, 621 A.2d 215, 20 U.C.C. Rep. Serv. 2d 710 (1992).

167. Had repossession occurred just before the end of the ski season, the secured party might have tried to convince the court that such seasonal goods had to be disposed of immediately to obtain a fair price. As a best practice, however, no responsible secured party should dispose of non-depreciating collateral without giving a pre-sale notification (or obtaining a valid post-default waiver of that requirement from the debtor and any other party entitled to notification). *See* note 173, *infra*.

168. U.C.C. § 9-610, Comment 9.

sists of shares of a commonly traded stock, no plausible rationale supports requiring notification.[169] If the debtor has the money to redeem the stock, the same money will buy an equivalent number of shares on the market. Furthermore, the debtor does not need to police the sale of a commonly traded stock for fairness. If the secured party sells the stock for its prevailing market price, the sale is, by definition, commercially reasonable; if it is not sold for that price, the secured party's misconduct sticks out like a sore thumb.[170]

Secured parties have sometimes tried to use this exception in connection with the disposition of a used car or similar asset that has a "Blue Book" price quotation. The courts have almost universally (and appropriately) rejected such arguments.[171] While shares of a company's common stock are fungible, used cars are not—their value varies based on condition, mileage, and other factors. Blue Book quotes simply provide a starting point for negotiating a price. With other assets, the issue is murkier. For example, even with a prevailing market price for cattle, they may be sold at auction by competitive bidding in a particular area. In such cases, whether the collateral falls within the exception is an issue of fact for the jury.[172]

Finally, a person entitled to notification can waive the requirement after default by a signed agreement.[173] An entitled person may not waive the notification requirement in advance,[174] but allowing waiver once default occurs makes sense. If the secured party finds a potential buyer that is willing to pay a reasonable price for the collateral but is unwilling to wait while the secured party notifies the debtor and a commercially reasonable time passes, it may be in everyone's interest to waive the notification requirement so that the secured party can proceed with the disposition. After default occurs, it is less likely that a waiver is the product of overreaching by the secured party.

---

169. *See, e.g.,* Finch v. Auburn Nat'l Bank of Auburn, 646 So. 2d 64, 25 U.C.C. Rep. Serv. 2d 1300 (Ala. Ct. App. 1995) (notification not required for stock traded on Midwest Stock Exchange). *See also* Ross v. Rothstein, 92 F. Supp. 3d 1041 (D. Kan. 2015) (failure to notify debtor prior to disposition excused where collateral was stock sold on recognized market).

170. The same rationale underlies the policy permitting the secured party to buy such assets at a private disposition. U.C.C. § 9-610(c)(2). See discussion in § 18.02[C], *infra.*

171. *See, e.g.,* Beneficial Fin. Co. of Black Hawk Cnty. v. Reed, 212 N.W.2d 454, 13 U.C.C. Rep. Serv. 974 (Iowa 1973). This phrase ("type sold on a recognized market") is discussed further in the context of the secured party's right to purchase the collateral at a private disposition. See discussion in § 18.02[C], *infra.*

172. *See, e.g.,* Havins v. First Nat'l Bank of Paducah, 919 S.W.2d 177, 29 U.C.C. Rep. Serv. 2d 1053 (Tex. Ct. App. 1996) (cattle auction); Aspen Enters., Inc. v. Bodge, 37 Cal. App. 4th 1811, 44 Cal. Rptr. 2d 763, 27 U.C.C. Rep. Serv. 2d 681 (1995) (used tires).

173. U.C.C. § 9-624(a).

174. U.C.C. § 9-602(7).

[C] Whether Secured Party Can Purchase at Disposition

A secured party is free to purchase the collateral at a public disposition. It may not do so at a private disposition unless the collateral is of a type customarily sold on a "recognized market" or is the subject of "widely distributed standard price quotations."[175] This distinction between public and private dispositions is sound. A public disposition features competitive bidding,[176] and as a matter of policy and fairness the secured party should be able to join the competition. The debtor and other interested persons can only benefit from the participation of an extra bidder. In contrast, private dispositions provide too great an opportunity and temptation for secured parties to purchase the collateral and then later resell it for their own account at a higher price. If the collateral is something like a commonly traded stock or a commodity that sells without negotiation on a recognized market, however, nothing should prevent the secured party from buying at a private disposition. If the secured party pays less than the prevailing price, the debtor can easily prove that the transaction was not commercially reasonable.[177]

The more difficult problem involves the meaning of the phrase "widely distributed standard price quotations." Because the Code uses the companion phrase "customarily sold on a recognized market" to describe one of the situations that excuses notice, the additional phrase "widely distributed standard price quotations," which the Code does not use in the notice context, arguably refers to something other than a disposition on a recognized market. But what? The most obvious example would be the used-car type of situation, where the asset is the subject of Blue Book price quotations. Several decisions suggest the secured party should not be allowed to purchase such assets privately because the Blue Book price is only the starting point for negotiations; the actual price paid depends on the individual characteristics of the particular asset.[178] A few decisions, however, rule to the contrary.[179]

Although the language of the Code invites courts to allow a secured party to purchase Blue Book assets privately, policy considerations dictate otherwise. Such an interpretation would allow a secured party to "cherry pick," that is, to buy those assets that are in better-than-average condition for their Blue Book price and then resell them at a higher price. Because the price at the foreclosure disposition establishes the amount of the debtor's deficiency, such a result would be patently unfair. Courts should

---

175. U.C.C. § 9-610(c).

176. Whether auctions that are not open qualify as public dispositions so that a secured party can compete is discussed in § 18.02[A][3], *supra*.

177. *See* § 18.02[B][4], *supra*.

178. *See, e.g.*, Northern Comm. Co. v. Cobb, 778 P.2d 205, 10 U.C.C. Rep. Serv. 2d 197 (Alaska 1989) (construction equipment did not fit within exception even though nationally published retail and wholesale prices were available); M.P. Crum Co. v. First Southwest Sav. & Loan Ass'n, 704 S.W.2d 925, 1 U.C.C. Rep. Serv. 2d 332 (Tex. Ct. App. 1986) (disposition of home mortgages).

179. *See, e.g.*, Dischner v. United Bank Alaska, 631 P.2d 107, 33 U.C.C. Rep. Serv. 796 (Alaska 1981). *Cf.* L.C. Arthur Trucking, Inc. v. Evans, 13 U.C.C. Rep. Serv. 2d 623 (Va. Cir. Ct. 1990) (tractor-trailer was of type customarily sold in recognized market).

discourage this type of activity even if it means effectively collapsing the definition of "standard price quotations" into that used for "recognized markets."

[D] Application of Proceeds of Disposition

Article 9 establishes a four-step process to govern how a foreclosing secured party must distribute the proceeds of its disposition of the collateral. First, the secured party may reimburse itself for the reasonable expenses incurred to repossess and dispose of the collateral.[180] The secured party may also recover its attorneys' fees and other legal expenses from the proceeds of the collateral if the security agreement so provides and the law of the jurisdiction does not otherwise preclude such recovery.[181] Second, the foreclosing secured party must apply the proceeds to the balance of the secured indebtedness being foreclosed upon.[182] Third, if additional proceeds still remain, the foreclosing secured party must apply them to the claims of junior secured parties or other junior lienholders that have provided the foreclosing secured party with a timely demand for payment.[183] Fourth, the secured party must turn over any remaining surplus to the debtor.[184]

If the proceeds of a secured party's disposition are insufficient to satisfy the secured obligation, the obligor is liable for any deficiency.[185] Generally, the amount of the deficiency is measured by the difference between the amount of the secured obligation and the net proceeds received on disposition (i.e., the disposition price less expenses of sale). If the secured party's disposition of the collateral was commercially reasonable, the price received on disposition establishes the amount of the deficiency even if the price was less than the collateral's actual fair market value. While Article 9's

---

180. U.C.C. § 9-615(a)(1). These expenses include the following: the cost of repossession; the cost of holding or storing the collateral pending disposition; the cost of preparing the collateral for disposition, including any commercially reasonable expenses incurred in fixing the collateral so that it commands a higher price (see discussion in § 18.02[A][4], *supra*); and the cost of conducting the disposition, including any reasonable auctioneer's charges. Courts have also allowed the secured party to recover expenses incurred in paying off other liens to clear the title to the collateral prior to disposition. *See, e.g.*, Contrail Leasing Partners, Ltd. v. Consol. Airways, Inc., 742 F.2d 1095, 39 U.C.C. Rep. Serv. 9 (7th Cir. 1983).

181. U.C.C. § 9-615(a)(1).

182. U.C.C. § 9-615(a)(2).

183. U.C.C. § 9-615(a)(3). To be entitled to payment, any subordinate party must make a signed demand before the foreclosing secured party has completed distribution of the proceeds. If the foreclosing secured party requests reasonable proof of the junior's claimant's interest and the junior claimant fails to provide it, the foreclosing secured party can ignore the demand. U.C.C. § 9-615(b).

184. U.C.C. § 9-615(d)(1). The debtor's right to a surplus cannot be waived. U.C.C. 9-602(5); Kapor v. RJC Invest., Inc., 434 P.3d 869, 97 U.C.C. Rep. Serv. 2d 1168 (Mont. 2019) (secured party obligated to account to debtor for surplus proceeds of sale of manufactured home even though debtor had voluntarily vacated the home and signed a document purporting to release all rights in the home).

The statement in the text assumes that the security interest secures an indebtedness. If the secured party is a buyer of accounts, chattel paper, payment intangibles, or promissory notes, it owns the equity and need not account to the debtor for it.

185. U.C.C. § 9-615(d)(2).

requirements are designed to produce a disposition that will generate a fair price for the collateral, compliance with those requirements does not guarantee that the secured party will receive such a price. By itself, a low price is not sufficient to establish that the disposition was unreasonable.[186]

In one situation, however, a low disposition price may result in a limitation on a secured party's deficiency rights. This situation arises if the secured party, a person related to the secured party, or a secondary obligor acquires the collateral at the disposition for a price that is "significantly below" the price that the secured party would have received in a commercially reasonable sale to an unrelated third party. In such a case, Section 9-615(f) provides that a surplus or deficiency will be calculated based on the price that the secured party would have received in such a sale rather than the price it actually received.[187] As the Comments indicate, this section tries to address the risk that a secured party might acquire the collateral at foreclosure for a bargain price and thereby capture an unjustifiable share of the debtor's equity in the collateral or inflate the amount of the obligor's deficiency.[188]

As noted above, Section 9-615 authorizes the foreclosing secured party to apply proceeds to the claims of junior lienholders that have made a timely and effective demand for the distribution of surplus proceeds. Occasionally, courts have become confused regarding the proper distribution of proceeds under a disposition conducted by a *junior* secured party when a *senior* secured party asserts a claim to them. Suppose Henning owns equipment subject to two security interests held by Gotberg and Freyermuth, respectively, with Gotberg holding the senior interest. Henning defaults to Freyermuth, and Freyermuth repossesses the equipment and conducts an auction sale. Does Gotberg have a superior claim to the proceeds from the auction?

The correct answer is no. When a secured party takes a security interest in an asset owned by the debtor, its interest in the asset is limited. The debtor retains its property interest in the collateral and, in a nonpossessory security arrangement, the right of possession. Should default and repossession occur, the debtor retains a right of redemption. Most importantly, the debtor has a right to any equity that it has built up in the collateral—a right that is vindicated in foreclosure proceedings by the secured party's duty to turn over to the debtor any surplus proceeds. Thus, when a junior secured party like Freyermuth acquires an interest in collateral already subject to a senior's lien, the junior's security interest technically does not interfere with the existing rights of the senior. Conceptually, the junior's interest is best understood as attaching only to the debtor's equity in the collateral. Even if the senior's security agreement makes

---

186. *See* § 18.02[A][5], *supra*. A secured party's liability for failing to dispose of collateral in a commercially reasonable manner, and the effect of such a disposition on a secured party's ability to recover a deficiency judgment, is addressed in §§ 19.01[B][2] and 19.02, *infra*.

187. U.C.C. § 9-615(f).

188. U.C.C. § 9-615, Comment 6 ("[This section] recognizes that when the foreclosing secured party or a related party is the transferee of the collateral, the secured party sometimes lacks the incentive to maximize the proceeds of the disposition. As a consequence, the disposition may comply with the procedural requirements of [Article 9] ... but nevertheless fetch a low price.").

it an event of default for the debtor to alienate that equity, the debtor has the *power* to do so.[189] Thus, although Freyermuth has a right to repossess the equipment and foreclose on it, all he can dispose of is his right to Henning's equity (and Henning's title and right to possession). As a result, the person who purchases the equipment at the foreclosure takes it subject to Gotberg's senior security interest and is at risk of having Gotberg repossess the equipment if Henning also defaults to Gotberg.[190] Conceptually, the proceeds of Freyermuth's disposition are not "proceeds" of Gotberg's security interest because the disposition did not transfer the rights to which Gotberg's security interest attached. As a result, Article 9 does not entitle Gotberg to participate in the distribution of the proceeds of Freyermuth's disposition.[191] To reach them, Gotberg must employ an extra-Code process such as garnishment.

Not every court has understood this point. According to some courts, Freyermuth's failure to turn the proceeds over to Gotberg on demand would constitute a conversion.[192] The decisions are incorrect; requiring the foreclosing junior to turn over the proceeds of its disposition to the senior is inconsistent with both the derivative rights principle that provides a conceptual underpinning for Article 9 and the express language of Section 9-615(a), which does not provide for application of proceeds of disposition to the claims of senior secured parties. In the above hypothetical, Gotberg's security interest remains intact, and she can continue to look to the equipment for satisfaction.

Article 9 places an additional duty on a foreclosing secured party in a consumer-goods transaction.[193] If disposition produces a surplus to which the debtor is entitled, the secured party must provide the debtor with a written explanation of how the secured party calculated that surplus. Likewise, if the disposition leaves a deficiency for which a consumer obligor is liable, the secured party ordinarily must provide the obligor with a written[194] explanation of how it calculated the deficiency.[195] The secured

189. U.C.C. § 9-401(b).

190. *See* related discussion in § 18.02[B][1], *supra*. Because the Code authorizes the junior's disposition, the buyer is not a converter. It becomes liable for conversion, however, if it later resists the senior's proper demand to turn over possession. Because security agreements often define repossession as an event of default, the prospect of the debtor's default to the senior is high.

191. *See, e.g.*, Continental Bank of Buffalo Grove, N.A. v. Krebs, 184 Ill. App. 3d 693, 540 N.E.2d 1023, 10 U.C.C. Rep. Serv. 2d 246 (1989).

192. *See, e.g.*, Consolidated Equip. Sales, Inc. v. First State Bank & Trust Co. of Guthrie, 627 P.2d 432, 31 U.C.C. Rep. Serv. 677 (Okla. 1981); Delaware Truck Sales, Inc. v. Wilson, 618 A.2d 303, 20 U.C.C. Rep. Serv. 2d 1420 (N.J. 1993).

193. For a definition of the term "consumer-goods transaction" and how that term differs from the term "consumer transaction," see § 1.04[A], *supra*.

194. The term "writing" rather than "record" is used, meaning that the explanation must be provided in tangible form. U.C.C. § 1-201(b)(43).

195. U.C.C. § 9-616(b). The "explanation" must be a writing that states the amount of the surplus or deficiency, explains how the secured party calculated it, states whether "future debits, credits, charges ... and expenses may affect the amount of the surplus or deficiency," and provides a phone number or mailing address from which the recipient can obtain additional information about the transaction. U.C.C. § 9-616(a)(1). Further, Section 9-616(c) requires that the explanation is sufficient only if it includes the following information in the following order: the aggregate amount of the secured obligation(s); the amount of proceeds of the disposition; the aggregate amount of the secured

party must provide the explanation at or before the time when it accounts for any surplus or makes its first written demand for payment of the deficiency.[196] A debtor or consumer obligor does not have to wait until the secured party makes a written demand for payment to receive an explanation of how the secured party calculated the surplus or deficiency. Instead, Section 9-616 authorizes the debtor or consumer obligor, after disposition of the collateral, to make a signed request to receive an explanation. Within 14 days after such a request, the secured party must either provide an explanation[197] or a record waiving its right to pursue a deficiency judgment.[198]

[E] Property Rights of Transferee at Disposition

If a secured party disposes of collateral after default to a transferee that pays value, the disposition transfers the debtor's rights in the collateral to the transferee,[199] thereby extinguishing the right of redemption (which exists only until the time of disposition).[200] The disposition also discharges both the security interest being foreclosed and any subordinate liens or security interests.[201] This discharge is an application of the doctrine of derivative rights, pursuant to which a transferee acquires whatever rights were held by its transferor. If a senior secured party transfers collateral to a buyer at foreclosure, the buyer acquires the senior's rights and this results in the extinguishment of junior liens.[202] The buyer, however, takes subject to any liens that are senior to the interest of the foreclosing secured party. A foreclosure buyer thus should pay no more than the fair market value of the collateral (if unencumbered) less the balance of any debts secured by senior liens.

---

obligation(s) after the application of the proceeds; the amount and types of expenses of repossession and disposition; the amounts of credits (if any) to which any obligor is known to be entitled; and the amount of the surplus or deficiency. No particular phrasing is required, and an explanation substantially complying with the requirements is sufficient even if it contains minor errors that are not seriously misleading. U.C.C. § 9-616(d); McDonald v. Wells Fargo Bank, N.A., 374 F. Supp. 3d 462, 98 U.C.C. Rep. Serv. 2d 780 (W.D. Pa. 2019).

In *Central Trust Bank v. Branch*, 651 S.W.3d 826, 108 U.C.C. Rep. Serv. 2d 975 (Mo. 2022), the secured party sent a Section 9-616 explanation to the obligor, but delivery was unsuccessful. The obligor later challenged the secured party's attempt to collect a deficiency on the ground that the secured party made no "second try" to send the required explanation. The court rejected this argument, noting that the Code did not obligate the secured party to make a second try (unlike the pre-sale notification requirement where a "second try" may be necessary). *Id.* at 831.

196. U.C.C. § 9-616(b)(1)(A).

197. U.C.C. § 9-616(b)(1)(B).

198. U.C.C. § 9-616(b)(2).

199. U.C.C. § 9-617(a)(1).

200. U.C.C. § 9-623(b).

201. U.C.C. § 9-617(a)(2), (3).

202. The junior secured party's right to notification of the disposition so that it can protect its interests is discussed in § 18.02[B][1], *supra*, and the junior's right to participate in the distribution of the proceeds is discussed in § 18.02[D], *supra*.

A good-faith transferee for value at a foreclosure disposition acquires these rights even if the secured party has breached the peace in its repossession efforts, conducted a commercially unreasonable disposition, or failed to give all necessary notifications. In other words, the secured party's failure to comply with its responsibilities under Article 9 does not give the debtor a basis for collateral attack of the disposition through judicial proceedings. The debtor's remedy is against the foreclosing secured party, not the transferee.[203] This rule promotes the finality of rights acquired through foreclosure—and thereby (hopefully) encourages widespread participation in foreclosure dispositions.

Under limited circumstances, however, Article 9 permits an adversely affected person to seek judicial invalidation of a secured party's disposition of collateral. Section 9-617(b) provides that the transferee does not acquire "clear title" (i.e., the debtor's rights in the collateral, free of the interest foreclosed and subordinate interests) if the transferee did not act in "good faith."[204] "Good faith" means both honesty in fact and the observance of reasonable commercial standards of fair dealing.[205] A transferee that lacks good faith takes the collateral subject to the debtor's rights in it as well as the security interest of the foreclosing party and all other security interests or liens.[206] Thus, if the transferee lacks good faith, a person with redemption rights may still redeem the collateral by satisfying the debt.[207]

A transferee lacks good faith if it knows of defects in the disposition, or acts in collusion with the secured party or other bidders.[208] Suppose Debtor owes Secured Party $9,500, secured by a security interest in Debtor's car. Secured Party repossesses Debtor's car following default and schedules an auction. Gotberg wants to purchase the car for $10,000 but lacks the cash needed to participate in the auction. Gotberg approaches Secured Party, and they agree that if Secured Party purchases the car at the auction, Secured Party will in turn sell the car to Gotberg for $10,000 and will extend her $8,000 in credit to complete the purchase. Secured Party conducts the auction and purchases the car for a high bid of $9,000. In this circumstance, by virtue of Secured Party's collusion with Gotberg, the disposition did not extinguish Debtor's interest in the car. Debtor could bring an action against Secured Party and either redeem the car by satisfying the debt or require Secured Party to conduct a new disposition.[209]

---

203. Chapter 19 provides further discussion of the remedies for creditor misbehavior.
204. U.C.C. § 9-617(b).
205. U.C.C. § 1-201(b)(20).
206. U.C.C. § 9-617(c).
207. U.C.C. § 9-623(b); Atlas MF Mezzanine Borrower, LLC v. Macquarie Texas Loan Holder LLC, 174 A.D.3d 150, 105 N.Y.S.3d 59 (2019). In other words, the disposition transaction cannot be fully unwound—the bad-faith transferee does take the debtor's possessory rights in the collateral, but the debtor retains the right to redeem those rights.
208. U.C.C. § 9-617, Comment 3.
209. Injunctive relief to force a secured party to conduct a commercially reasonable disposition is available under U.C.C. § 9-625(a). A properly conducted second disposition would not excuse the secured party from any liability that it might have incurred as a result of its first disposition.

Recent U.C.C. revisions have expanded the duty of good faith beyond its original and purely subjective "honesty-in-fact" definition, and this expansion poses a risk that it may have an unintended chilling effect on prospective bidders. Under former law, buyers at auctions had no duty to investigate the secured party's compliance with the requirements of Article 9 or to inquire into the circumstances surrounding the disposition.[210] This approach made sense because the Code's duty of good faith then required only "honesty in fact."[211] But because good faith now incorporates "the observance of reasonable commercial standards of fair dealing,"[212] must an auction buyer conduct an inquiry into the character of the disposition? It is doubtful that the drafters so intended—and such an inquiry could easily discourage bidding, leading to lower auction prices and correspondingly higher deficiency judgments. Nevertheless, courts have often demonstrated a willingness to apply the duty of good faith in sweeping terms when presented with compelling facts.

Even unsecured parties (or in the event of an insolvent debtor, a trustee in bankruptcy as the debtor's representative) may be able to set aside a disposition if it constitutes a fraudulent conveyance.[213] Courts will typically order in such cases restitution of the purchase price to the buyer as a condition to granting relief.[214]

---

210. U.C.C. § 9-504, Comment 4 (1972 text).

211. U.C.C. § 1-201(19) (1972 text).

212. U.C.C. § 1-201(b)(20).

213. If the trustee sets aside the disposition and is then able to avoid the security interest, it can make a distribution to unsecured creditors. *See, e.g.,* Sheffield Progressive, Inc. v. Kingston Tool Co., 10 Mass. App. Ct. 47, 405 N.E.2d 985, 29 U.C.C. Rep. Serv. 292 (1980). *Cf.* Bezanson v. Fleet Bank-NH, 29 F.3d 16, 24 U.C.C. Rep. Serv. 2d 399 (1st Cir. 1994) (facts suggested fraudulent conveyance, but debtor's action was brought against secured party for holding commercially unreasonable disposition that failed to produce surplus). The subject of fraudulent conveyances in bankruptcy is discussed in detail in § 16.04[F], *supra.*

214. If the secured party is joined in the action, the court should order it to make the restitutionary payment. If it is not joined, the party setting aside the disposition should be entitled to restitution from the secured party for the payment made to the buyer.

A foreclosing secured party might also have liability to the buyer based on breach of a warranty. Under Article 9, a foreclosure disposition includes any warranty of title or quiet enjoyment that is implied by other law governing the transaction, unless the secured party disclaims the warranty as provided by the other law or by Section 9-610(e) and (f). *See* U.C.C. §§ 2-312 (warranty of title in sale of goods), 2A-211 (warranty against interference in lease of goods). The secured party may also be liable for breach of an express warranty made in connection with the disposition (U.C.C. §§ 2-313, 2A-210), and for breach of an implied warranty of merchantability if it is a merchant with respect to goods of that kind (U.C.C. §§ 2-314, 2A-212).

§ 18.03 Foreclosure on Rights to Payment and Other Intangible Assets—§ 9-607

If a foreclosure involves collateral representing rights to payment (e.g., accounts, chattel paper, payment intangibles, and promissory notes), a secured party may choose to take steps that are inapplicable to foreclosure against other types of assets. The secured party must first choose whether to sell the collateral as a package to a factor[215] or attempt to collect from the various account debtors and persons obligated on promissory notes.[216] If the secured party sells the collateral to a factor *en masse*, the normal provisions governing Article 9 foreclosures govern the sale.

The secured party might instead choose to enforce the obligations of account debtors and other persons obligated on collateral.[217] If it selects this option, it has the right to notify each account debtor and other person obligated on collateral to make payment to it or for its benefit.[218]

After receiving a notification that its payment obligation has been assigned and an instruction to pay the secured party, an account debtor can obtain a discharge of the payment obligation only by paying the secured party.[219] To illustrate, suppose Buyer purchases goods on unsecured credit from Seller (thereby creating an account) and Seller grants Bank a security interest in all its present and after-acquired accounts as collateral for a loan. If Seller defaults, Bank can notify Buyer (and other account debtors[220]) in a signed record[221] that its payment obligation has been assigned and that it must make future payments to Bank. This does not impose on Buyer a legal obligation to pay Bank, but if Buyer continues to pay Seller after receiving the notification, it

---

215. The term "factor" describes a person that buys payment rights, whether at foreclosure or otherwise. *See* § 3.04[A], *supra*. After making its purchase, the factor will collect from the individual account debtors or obligors on promissory notes. Having bought the assets outright, the factor will not be under a duty to remit any surplus to the debtor. Any surplus value should have been realized through the secured party's commercially reasonable disposition to the factor.

216. U.C.C. § 9-102(a)(3). The term "account debtor" does not include a person obligated on a negotiable instrument even if the instrument is part of chattel paper. *Id.*

217. U.C.C. § 9-607(a)(3). The term "account debtor" means a person obligated on an account (including a controllable account), chattel paper (unless the obligation to pay that is part of the chattel paper is evidenced by a negotiable instrument), or a payment intangible (including a controllable payment intangible). U.C.C. § 9-102(a)(3). The phrase "person obligated on the collateral" refers to a person obligated on another type of collateral, such as a promissory note.

218. U.C.C. § 9-607(a)(1).

219. U.C.C. § 9-406(a).

220. In *Whitney Bank v. SMI Companies Global, Inc.*, 949 F.3d 196 (5th Cir. 2020), the bank had a security interest in all of the debtor's accounts, and when the loan matured, it sent a notice to all of the debtor's customers to pay their accounts directly to the bank even though some of those customers did not owe any obligation to the debtor at the time. The debtor sued the bank for tortious interference with business relations, arguing that the Code did not authorize the bank to notify and demand money from customers who owed the debtor nothing. The court rejected the claim.

221. U.C.C. § 9-406(a). The notification may be sent by either the assignor (the Article 9 debtor that granted the security interest) or the assignee (the secured party). *Id.* The contents of the notification are set forth in U.C.C. § 9-406(b).

will not receive a discharge for the payments.[222] For example, suppose, after receipt of notification, Buyer continues to make payments to Seller. It will not receive a discharge for the payments, and Bank can recover the amount of the payments from Buyer, leaving Buyer to seek restitution from Seller. Buyer may ask for reasonable proof that the assignment occurred and may continue to receive a discharge by paying Seller until reasonable proof is provided.[223]

If the record evidencing the transaction between Buyer and Seller had been in electronic form and had specified that Buyer would pay the person in control of the record, Seller's right to receive payment would be a controllable account.[224] The rules for collection are similar to the rules for ordinary accounts, but Bank would need to have control of the controllable electronic record evidencing the controllable account to be entitled to payment.[225] Once Buyer receives a notification in a signed record that its payment obligation has been transferred and that it must make future payments to Bank, it can no longer obtain a discharge by paying Seller.[226] In addition to the information required in a notification related to the assignment of an ordinary account, the notification to an account debtor on a controllable account must "[identify] the transferee, in any reasonable way, including by name, identifying number, cryptographic key, office, or account number; and [provide] a commercially reasonable method by which the account debtor is to pay the transferee."[227] As with an ordinary account, Buyer may ask for reasonable proof that the transfer occurred and may continue to receive a discharge by paying Seller until reasonable proof is provided. The notification is ineffective unless Seller and Buyer have agreed in a signed record on a commercially reasonable method by which reasonable proof that control has been transferred may be furnished.[228]

Article 9 also permits a secured party to notify account debtors prior to default that the right to payment has been assigned and that payment should be made to the secured party.[229] Certain transactions, known as "notification-financing transactions," follow this pattern.[230] In those transactions, if there is a default by the debtor, the secured party will already have notified the account debtors and other persons obligated on collateral to make payment to it, and thus no further notification will be necessary.[231]

---

222. U.C.C. § 9-406(a).

223. U.C.C. § 9-406(c).

224. U.C.C. § 9-102(a)(27A). The same rules apply in the case of a controllable payment intangible. U.C.C. § 9-102(a)(27B).

225. U.C.C. § 12-106(a)(1).

226. U.C.C. § 12-106(c).

227. U.C.C. § 12-106(b)(4), (5).

228. U.C.C. § 12-106(d)(1).

229. U.C.C. § 9-607(a)(1).

230. The payments received by the secured party in a notification-financing transaction are applied to reduce the secured obligation.

231. *See* Xynergy Healthcare Cap. II LLC v. Mun. of San Juan, 2021 WL 2769818 (D.P.R. 2021) (notification instructing municipal account debtor to pay assignee was effective even though sent a few days before security agreement was signed).

In addition to having the right to enforce the obligations of an account debtor or other person obligated on collateral, the secured party "may exercise the rights of the debtor ... with respect to any property that secures the obligations of the account debtor or other person obligated on the collateral."[232] For example, suppose Buyer purchases a machine from Seller on secured credit and grants Seller a security interest in the machine (thus creating chattel paper), and Seller grants Bank a security interest in all its present and after-acquired chattel paper as collateral for a loan. If Seller defaults on its obligation to repay the loan, Bank may collect from Buyer using the procedures detailed above. If Buyer, in turn, defaults on its obligation to pay for the machine, Bank can exercise Seller's rights under its security agreement with Buyer and foreclose on the machine.[233] Bank cannot foreclose on the machine merely because Seller has defaulted; Buyer must also have defaulted on its obligation for foreclosure of the machine to be justified. In both collecting from an account debtor or other person obligated on collateral and in exercising rights against property that secures the account debtor's or other person's obligation, Bank is stepping into Seller's shoes, and its enforcement rights are limited to those that could have been exercised by its debtor.

Article 3 governs the mechanics of collection from a person obligated on a negotiable instrument. Just as a secured party needs control of the controllable electronic record evidencing a controllable account (or controllable payment intangible) to collect from the account debtor, so a secured party needs possession of a negotiable instrument to collect from a person obligated on the instrument.[234] The secured party will have an easier time of collection if it is a holder of the instrument; to achieve that status, it will have the debtor indorse the instrument to it and will take possession of it. Having the status of holder is a necessary first step for the secured party if it later needs to assert that it is a "holder in due course" entitled to collect the instrument free from the claims of third parties and defenses of the person obligated on the instrument.

A secured party that is a lender against accounts, chattel paper, payment intangibles, or promissory notes must collect from the account debtors or other persons obligated on collateral in a commercially reasonable manner. The secured party thus must exercise reasonable judgment in deciding whether to expend resources in pursuit of financially strapped account debtors and other persons obligated on collateral, and it must act reasonably in compromising claims against account debtors and other per-

---

232. U.C.C. § 9-607(a)(3).

233. Similarly, if a secured party's collateral for a loan to a debtor is a promissory note on which a third party is liable, made payable to the order of the debtor, the secured party can collect from the third party (who is obligated on the collateral) if the debtor defaults and can foreclose on the machine if the third party defaults.

234. A person obligated on an instrument obtains a discharge only by paying a person entitled to enforce the instrument. U.C.C. § 3-602(a). By definition, a holder is a person entitled to enforce. U.C.C. § 3-301(i).

sons obligated on collateral who assert defenses or counterclaims that might have been valid if the debtor had attempted to collect.[235]

By contrast, if a secured party is a buyer of (rather than a lender against) accounts, chattel paper, payment intangibles, or promissory notes in a transaction within the scope of Article 9, it ordinarily need not worry about collecting in a commercially reasonable manner because the obligor[236] will not be liable for any deficiency and the secured party need not account for any surplus.[237] However, its security agreement with the debtor (seller of the payment rights) will typically give it a right of recourse or charge-back in the event an account debtor or other person obligated on collateral asserts a contract defense or counterclaim. If a secured party has such a right, its collection efforts must be commercially reasonable,[238] and it must be able to defend any compromise it makes with an account debtor or other person obligated on collateral as a commercially reasonable exercise of judgment.

Section 9-607 also governs the secured party's right to foreclose if the collateral is a deposit account. The secured party's ability to foreclose easily against a deposit account hinges on its having perfected its security interest by control.[239] If the secured party is the bank at which the account is maintained, the secured party can apply the sums in the deposit account to the secured obligation.[240] If the secured party has perfected by control by becoming the customer of the depositary bank or through a control agreement, the secured party can direct the depositary bank to pay the deposited funds to the secured party.[241]

---

235. The most common example would be a breach of warranty claim against the debtor. For example, suppose Henning purchased equipment on account from Seller/Debtor, which assigned the account to Bank. Bank will take the account subject to any claim Henning might have that the equipment breached any express or implied warranties of quality or fitness unless Henning has entered into an enforceable agreement not to assert claims against any assignee of Seller/Debtor. U.C.C. § 9-404(a). In attempting to collect the account from Henning, Bank may enforce Henning's agreement to waive claims and defenses to defeat any breach of warranty claim, if Bank took its assignment of the account for value, in good faith, and without notice of any such claim. U.C.C. § 9-403(a).

236. The "obligor" in a secured transaction must be distinguished from "a person obligated on collateral. To illustrate, if Merchant grants a security interest in its promissory notes to Bank, Merchant is the debtor and the obligor, and the makers of the promissory note are persons obligated on the collateral.

237. If a secured party buys accounts, chattel paper, payment intangibles, or promissory notes outright, there is no underlying obligation; thus, concepts like deficiency and surplus are inapt, and the debtor is neither entitled to a surplus nor is the obligor liable for any deficiency unless the security agreement provides otherwise. U.C.C. § 9-608(b), Comment 3.

238. U.C.C. § 9-607(c).

239. See, e.g., Davis Forestry Prods., Inc. v. DownEast Power Co., LLC, 12 A.3d 1180, 73 U.C.C. Rep. Serv. 2d 415 (Me. 2011) (party holding security interest in deposit account that has not been perfected by control has no independent ability to access the funds or protect interest against third-party liens or attachments without judicial action).

240. U.C.C. § 9-607(a)(4) (secured party perfected by control under Section 9-104(a)(1)).

241. U.C.C. § 9-607(a)(5) (secured party perfected by control agreement under Section 9-104(a)(2) or by becoming bank's customer as to the account under Section 9-104(a)(3)).

A secured party contemplating a security interest in an ordinary general intangible, health-care insurance receivable, or promissory note or general intangible that will secure an obligation should carefully read the contract between the debtor and the account debtor or the promissory note. A term in the agreement or note that is effective under law other than Article 9 and "prohibits, restricts, or requires the consent of"[242] the account debtor or person obligated on the note to a transfer of rights in the asset has a limited but critically important effect. The term is ineffective to prevent the attachment and perfection of a security interest in the asset,[243] but it is effective to prevent enforcement.[244] For example, suppose Henning purchases a license for business software from Macrosoft, which license is nontransferable by its terms without the prior consent of Macrosoft. Henning later grants a security interest in all of his general intangibles to Bank. Bank can obtain and perfect a security interest in the software notwithstanding the no-transfer provision; nevertheless, Bank cannot enforce the security interest without the prior consent of Macrosoft. Thus, Bank is unable to enforce its security interest against Henning's computers (without risking liability to Macrosoft for conversion) without first removing the software.[245] Similar contract terms[246] that relate to accounts other than health-care-insurance receivables, chattel paper, or promissory notes or payment intangibles that secure obligations are entirely ineffective; that is, a security interest can attach, be perfected, and be enforced notwithstanding the terms and laws.[247]

The example in the previous paragraph involving software is one example of a general intangible, but there are many others.[248] Some are payment intangibles, including controllable payment intangibles, and the procedures described above for collecting from an account debtor on an account apply to collecting from an account debtor on a payment intangible. As with the software example, the secured party will need the consent of a third party to effectively transfer the debtor's rights by foreclosure if there is an anti-assignment term or law. For another example, if a secured party has a security interest in a debtor's right to be a franchisee and, after default, wishes to sell

---

242. U.C.C. § 9-408(a), (b) (inapplicability of section's rules to promissory notes and payment intangibles that secure obligations).

243. U.C.C. § 9-408(a)(i). The term is also ineffective to the extent it provides that a transfer of rights in the general intangible "[gives] rise to a default, breach, right of recoupment, claim, defense, termination, right of termination, or remedy" under the general intangible. U.C.C. § 9-408(a)(ii).

244. U.C.C. § 9-408(d). The rules that apply to contract terms and terms in promissory notes also apply to laws having the same effect. U.C.C. § 9-408(c).

245. Similarly, a term in a franchise agreement that prohibits transfer of the right to be a franchisee will not prevent attachment and perfection of a security interest in the right, but it will prevent enforcement of the security interest without the consent of the franchisor.

246. As with general intangibles and related assets discussed above, the rules that apply to contract terms and terms in notes also apply to laws having the same effect. U.C.C. § 9-406(f).

247. U.C.C. § 9-406(d) (contract terms overridden), (e) (inapplicability of section's rules to sales of promissory notes and payment intangibles).

248. See discussion in § 1.04[B][6], supra.

that right at a disposition sale, the buyer at the sale will ordinarily have to meet with the franchisor's approval.[249]

§ 18.04 Strict Foreclosure— §§ 9-620–9-622

Strict foreclosure is an Article 9 remedy that can, in appropriate circumstances, benefit both the secured party and the debtor. A strict foreclosure is essentially a trade under which the secured party acquires the debtor's rights in the collateral without having to go through the normal disposition processes (with the procedural hassles that accompany those processes and the potential liability for failing to comply with them).[250] In exchange, the underlying obligation of the debtor (or some portion of that

---

249. Some franchise agreements preclude assignment entirely, and similar problems arise with licenses such as software and government licenses. Under Article 9, the fact that a franchise or license agreement, or a law governing a franchise agreement or rights under a license, prohibits the debtor from creating a security interest in the franchise or license (or makes such a transfer an event of default) does not prevent the security interest from having legal effect. U.C.C. § 9-408(a) (contract restrictions on transfer), (c) (legal restrictions on transfer). Likewise, the fact that a statute or other rule of law purports to prohibit or restrict the debtor from creating a security interest in a license or permit or requires government consent for such a transfer does not prevent the security interest from taking effect. U.C.C. § 9-408(c).

250. The normal processes are discussed in § 18.02, *supra*.

Students sometimes think that when a pawnbroker exercises its right to keep pawned goods when the borrower who pawned them does not timely repay the pawnbroker, the pawnbroker is exercising Article 9 strict foreclosure, but that is not correct. A pawn transaction strongly resembles a possessory security interest, but pawn transactions in most states are heavily regulated by statutes other than Article 9. *See, e.g.*, Mo. Rev. Stat. §§ 367.011–376.060. For example, assume that Henning needs $200 cash and obtains it by pawning a watch with a Missouri pawnbroker. The pawn agreement specifies that Henning can recover the watch by repaying the $200 plus the agreed pawn service charge by March 1 (the maturity date), and it also specifies that (i) Henning has no legal obligation to redeem the watch and (ii) absent redemption, the watch will be forfeited to the pawnbroker 60 days after March 1. Under Missouri's pawnbroker statute, if Henning owned the watch prior to pawning it, the pawnbroker's only recourse against Henning is against the watch (i.e., the pawnbroker could not get a personal judgment against Henning on the pawn loan). Mo. Rev. Stat. § 367.044(2). If Henning does not timely repay the loan by March 1 or repay it within a 60-day redemption period after March 1, title to the watch passes to the pawnbroker "without foreclosure, and the right of redemption by the borrower shall be forever barred." *See, e.g.*, Mo. Rev. Stat. § 367.040(1). Title passes by virtue of the pawnbroker statute, however, and not by Article 9 strict foreclosure.

In some cases, a pawnbroker might make a loan that does not actually qualify as a loan covered by the pawnbroker statute, and in that case the pawnbroker's rights in the pawned property would be governed by Article 9. For example, in *In re Hambright*, 635 B.R. 614 (Bankr. N.D. Ala. 2022), the owner of a car obtained a loan from a pawnbroker and delivered to the pawnbroker the title certificate for the car, but the owner kept possession of the car and continued to drive it. When the loan was not timely repaid, the pawnbroker argued that it had title to the car under Alabama's pawnbroker statute. The court disagreed, holding that the transaction was not a pawn transaction covered by the statute because the debtor had possession of the car; thus, the pawnbroker still had a security interest in the car that had to be foreclosed under Article 9.

obligation) is extinguished.[251] The secured party is then free to do as it wishes with the collateral, without regard to the provisions that govern Article 9 dispositions.[252]

A secured party initiates a strict foreclosure by making a "proposal," which the Code defines as "a record signed by a secured party which includes the terms on which the secured party is willing to accept collateral in full or partial satisfaction of the obligation it secures."[253] The secured party must provide a notification of the proposal to all persons who would have been entitled to notification prior to a disposition.[254] The decision to seek strict foreclosure rests with the secured party; the debtor cannot force the secured party to use the procedure.

If a secured party receives a timely signed notification of objection from any recipient of its proposal, or from any other person holding a subordinate interest in the collateral, the secured party cannot use strict foreclosure.[255] A person entitled to notification of the secured party's proposal must notify the secured party of an objection

---

251. In this regard, strict foreclosure under Article 9 is analogous to the mortgagor's execution and delivery of a "deed in lieu of foreclosure" under the law of real estate mortgages.

Under Article 9 as originally promulgated, strict foreclosure resulted in the *complete* satisfaction of the debtor's obligation; the Code did not authorize strict foreclosure in *partial* satisfaction of the debt. *See* U.C.C. § 9-505(2) (1972 text) (secured party may retain collateral "in satisfaction of the obligation); U.C.C. § 9-505, Comment 1 (1972 text) (strict foreclosure involves "abandoning any claim for a deficiency"). This position was subject to criticism on the ground that the parties should be free to stipulate to a "fair price" for the collateral in lieu of foreclosure—and thereby stipulate to a deficiency if the stipulation occurs after default. Article 9 now permits partial strict foreclosure only in non-consumer transactions. U.C.C. § 9-620(a), (g).

252. Because strict foreclosure is voluntary on the debtor's part, it constitutes a sale to the secured party. If it is a sale of payment rights subject to Article 9, the secured party whose interest in the collateral was formerly to secure an obligation becomes a secured party in the sense of having an ownership interest in the payment rights. The secured party must perfect this interest to be protected from potential third-party claims, but this does not present a serious problem because a filing that perfected its interest as to accounts or chattel paper prior to strict foreclosure will remain effective; further, the security interest is automatically perfected in the case of payment intangibles and promissory notes. U.C.C. § 9-320, Comment 10.

253. U.C.C. § 9-102(a)(66). Courts have required that the notice clearly indicate the creditor's intention to retain the collateral in satisfaction of the debt. *See, e.g.,* Ainslie v. Inman, 577 S.E.2d 246, 49 U.C.C. Rep. Serv. 2d 1319 (Va. 2003) (letter notifying debtor that creditor was "taking possession of and foreclosing upon" collateral insufficient notice that creditor intended to retain collateral in full satisfaction of debt); Hansford v. Burns, 241 Ga. App. 407, 40 U.C.C. Rep. Serv. 2d 592 (1999) (letter indicating creditor was "taking back the collateral" insufficient to indicate proposal to retain collateral in satisfaction of debt).

254. U.C.C. § 9-621(a). The question of which persons are entitled to receive notice prior to disposition is discussed in § 18.02[B][1], *supra*. *See also, e.g.,* 111 West 57th Inv. LLC v. 111 W57 Mezz Inv. LLC, 192 A.D.3d 618, 146 N.Y.S.3d 95 (2021) (member of LLC was not entitled to notice or opportunity to object to strict foreclosure of LLC's property based merely on LLC membership); digiGAN, Inc. v. iValidate, Inc., 52 U.C.C. Rep. Serv. 2d 1022 (S.D.N.Y. 2004) (secured party's failure to send strict foreclosure proposal to person to whom debtor had already sold the collateral did not defeat effectiveness of secured party's proposal when buyer had not provided secured party with a signed notification of its claim of interest in the collateral). Note that a secured party need only notify a secondary obligor if the secured party is proposing partial strict foreclosure. U.C.C. § 9-621(b).

255. U.C.C. § 9-620(a)(2).

within 20 days after notification of the proposal was sent to the objecting person.[256] Any other person (such as a creditor that holds a subordinate judgment lien but that has not sent the secured party a signed notification of its interest in the collateral) may notify the secured party of an objection within 20 days of the last notification given by the secured party or, if no notifications are given, before the debtor consents to the proposal.

For example, suppose Henning owns an automobile subject to a first-priority security interest in favor of Freyermuth, a second-priority security interest in favor of Gotberg, and a judgment lien in favor of Dean. On February 1, Henning defaults to Freyermuth. On February 2, Freyermuth proposes in a signed record to accept the car in full satisfaction of Henning's obligation, sending notification of the proposal to Henning. Freyermuth sends notification of the proposal to Gotberg on February 5. Henning may object to Freyermuth's proposal until February 22. Gotberg and Dean may object to the proposal until February 25. Even if Henning and Gotberg consent to the proposal, Freyermuth may not use strict foreclosure if Dean provides a timely objection.

If a secured party does not receive a timely objection to its proposal, the debtor's rights in the collateral become vested in the secured party, and the secured party's interest is extinguished (along with any subordinate security interests or liens).[257] Further, the debt is discharged to the extent specified in the proposal. Thus, following a partial strict foreclosure, the secured party may seek to recover the stipulated deficiency from any obligor via judicial action.[258]

Obviously, a debtor should object to a strict foreclosure proposal if it believes that a normal disposition would generate a surplus. Because a successful strict foreclosure will also extinguish the lien of a junior secured party or lienholder, the holder of a junior interest should also object if a normal disposition could reasonably produce a surplus over the balance of the lien being foreclosed.

The Code precludes a secured party from initiating strict foreclosure in certain cases involving consumer goods. The provision presumes that if the debtor has repaid 60 percent of the loan in a non-purchase-money transaction or 60 percent of the cash price in a purchase-money transaction, the debtor likely has acquired sufficient equity to justify disposition of the collateral to preserve that equity for the debtor's benefit.[259]

---

256. U.C.C. § 9-620(d)(1).

257. U.C.C. § 9-622(a). Strict foreclosure extinguishes subordinate interests even if the secured party fails to comply with its notification requirements. U.C.C. § 9-622(b). Any person that was entitled to notification but did not receive it may recover any damages caused by the secured party's noncompliance. U.C.C. § 9-625(b).

258. U.C.C. § 9-622(a)(1). Partial strict foreclosure is not available in consumer transactions. U.C.C. § 9-620(g). Further, the comments make clear that a secured party's proposal of partial strict foreclosure must specify the amount of the secured obligation to be satisfied, or at least a means of calculating that amount. See U.C.C. § 9-620, Comment 4. Finally, a debtor may not be deemed to have consented to partial strict foreclosure by silence; instead, the debtor must accept the proposal in a record signed after default. U.C.C. § 9-620(c)(1).

259. U.C.C. § 9-620(e). See also § 18.02[B][2], supra.

A debtor that believes that this assumption is false and would prefer a strict foreclosure may waive this compulsory-disposition requirement after default.[260]

As originally promulgated, Article 9 required a secured party to have possession of the collateral before it could propose strict foreclosure.[261] Because no convincing rationale justified this requirement, Article 9 now permits the secured party to propose strict foreclosure even prior to taking possession.[262] If the collateral is consumer goods, however, a debtor may not give effective consent to a secured party's proposal while the collateral remains in the debtor's possession.[263]

The Code imposes on the secured party a duty of good faith in the enforcement of any of its remedies.[264] As the comments make clear, this duty applies to a secured party's proposal of strict foreclosure.[265] Suppose that the collateral for a debt vastly exceeded the amount of the unpaid debt (e.g., suppose Henning owes Freyermuth $1,000, secured by a security interest in a $50,000 corporate bond). Can the secured party propose to accept the collateral in full satisfaction of the obligation, hoping that the debtor will inadvertently fail to object on a timely basis and thus allowing the secured party to capture that equity for itself? One may argue that under these circumstances, the secured party's proposal lacks good faith and is not effective. However, the Comments state that determinations about the existence of good faith are contextual and that the mere existence of equity in the collateral does not equate to a lack of good faith.[266] For example, in *McDonald v. Yarchenko*,[267] the secured party proposed to retain the collateral (the debtor's one-sixth interest in an LLC) in satisfaction of a $12,000 debt even though the collateral was worth at least $400,000 and possibly as much as $1.6 million. After failing to timely object, the debtor later argued that the proposal lacked good faith and was thus ineffective. The court rejected this argument, noting that the discrepancy did not establish bad faith (after all, the debtor could simply have objected to the proposal!).[268]

In some situations, secured parties have entered into workout agreements with debtors under which the secured party took title to some (but not all) of the collateral, with the agreement's providing that the secured party would become the owner of the remaining collateral automatically if the debtor failed to repay the remaining debt in a timely fashion. For example, *Fagen, Inc. v. Exergy Development Group of Idaho,*

260. U.C.C. § 9-624(b).

261. U.C.C. § 9-505(2) (1972 text).

262. U.C.C. § 9-620, Comment 7.

263. U.C.C. § 9-620(a)(3).

264. U.C.C. § 1-304.

265. U.C.C. § 9-620, Comment 11.

266. *Id.* ("[I]n the normal case proposals and acceptances should not be second-guessed on the basis of the 'value' of the collateral involved. Disputes about valuation or even a clear excess of collateral value over the amount of obligations satisfied do not necessarily demonstrate the absence of good faith.").

267. 81 U.C.C. Rep. Serv. 2d 165 (D. Or. 2013).

268. *Id. See also* Eddy v. Glen Devore Personal Trust, 131 Wash. App. 1015 (2006) (not reported in P.3d) (strict foreclosure on $90,000 promissory note to satisfy $5,000 debt was not unconscionable).

L.L.C.,[269] involved a workout agreement under which the secured party purchased 99 of the debtor's 100 membership units in a subsidiary and retained a security interest in one remaining unit. After the debtor's subsequent default under the workout agreement, the secured party claimed ownership of the 100th unit pursuant to a clause providing for the automatic transfer of that unit upon default. The court correctly held that the secured party violated its duties under Article 9, Part 6, by relying on the automatic transfer clause, which was not sufficient to effectuate a strict foreclosure of the 100th unit.

§ 18.05 Redemption—§ 9-623

Under Section 9-623, a right of redemption extends to "[the] debtor, any secondary obligor, or any other secured party or lienholder."[270] The latter category includes both senior or subordinate security interests as well as judicial and other liens.[271]

The U.C.C. does not allow post-disposition redemption;[272] therefore, the redeeming person must exercise its right before the secured party has disposed of the collateral, entered into a contract for its disposition, or acquired the debtor's rights by strict foreclosure.[273] To redeem, the person must tender "fulfillment of all obligations secured by the collateral" (including expenses reasonably incurred by the secured party in repossessing the collateral and preparing it for disposition)[274] and, to the extent provided in the agreement and not prohibited by law, the secured party's reasonable attorneys' fees and legal expenses.[275] The fact that the redeeming person must satisfy the entire indebtedness plus costs makes the redemption provision of limited usefulness to debtors in financial distress. The reality is that the right is more helpful to other secured parties than it is to debtors.

One of the major purposes underlying the Code's notice requirements is protection of the right of redemption. While commercial debtors and other secured parties are likely to realize that a foreclosure disposition will terminate their redemption rights, consumer debtors are less likely to know this. Accordingly, the secured party in a consumer-goods transaction must include in the pre-disposition notification a

---

269. 90 U.C.C. Rep. Serv. 2d 810 (D. Minn. 2016).

270. U.C.C. § 9-623(a).

271. U.C.C. § 9-623, Comment 2.

272. The right to redeem the collateral following a bad-faith disposition is discussed in § 18.02[E], *supra*.

273. U.C.C. § 9-623(c). *See, e.g.*, South Bay Bank N.A. v. Oates, 47 U.C.C. Rep. Serv. 2d 422 (Cal. Ct. App. 2001) (junior secured party cannot redeem collateral after senior secured party has retained collateral in satisfaction of obligation).

274. U.C.C. § 9-623(b)(1). *See, e.g.*, Automotive Fin. Corp. v. Smart Auto Ctr., Inc., 334 F.3d 685, 51 U.C.C. Rep. Serv. 2d 297 (7th Cir. 2003) (because exercise of redemption right requires full payment of all monetary obligations due, secured party did not have to return possession of collateral based upon debtor's offer to enter new agreement extending time for payment).

275. U.C.C. § 9-623(b)(2).

telephone number from which the recipient may obtain information from the secured party regarding the amount necessary to redeem the collateral.[276] Even if not required to do so, many secured parties routinely advise debtors of their redemption rights, but doing so can create a trap for the careless creditor. In several cases, secured parties have provided inaccurate redemption information, and courts have responded by concluding that the inaccuracy rendered the entire notice invalid. In *Moore v. Fidelity Financial Services, Inc.*,[277] for example, the secured party sent the debtor a notice of private disposition that properly indicated the date *after which* the collateral would be sold. Unfortunately for the secured party, the notice went on to state that the collateral could be redeemed *until the specified date*. The correct rule is that the debtor can redeem until the disposition actually occurs or the secured party enters into a contract to dispose of the collateral; thus, the court felt that the notice could have misled the debtor into believing that he had less time to redeem than he actually had. This type of scrutiny by courts is understandable, as inaccurate information regarding redemption may have the effect of discouraging entitled persons from seeking redemption. As a result, a creditor that chooses (or is required) to advise entitled persons of the right of redemption must be sure to do so in an accurate manner.[278]

Generally speaking, a person with a right of redemption may waive that right after default in a signed agreement.[279] The only reason for doing so would be to facilitate an early disposition of the collateral, and a secured party seeking a waiver of the right of redemption should make certain that the waiver also covers the debtor's right to be notified of the disposition.[280] Article 9 does not permit waiver of the right to redemption in a consumer-goods transaction.[281]

---

276. U.C.C. § 9-614(1).

277. 869 F. Supp. 557, 25 U.C.C. Rep. Serv. 2d 1306 (N.D. Ill. 1994).

278. *See also* DiDominico v. First Nat'l Bank of Md., 57 Md. App. 62, 468 A.2d 1046, 37 U.C.C. Rep. Serv. 1427 (1984) (notice inaccurately informed debtor that redemption was limited to 15 days).

279. The right of redemption cannot be waived prior to default. *See* U.C.C. § 9-602(11). *See also* Data Security, Inc. v. Plessman, 1 Neb. App. 659, 510 N.W.2d 361, 23 U.C.C. Rep. Serv. 2d 989 (1993).

280. The right to notice may also be waived after default in a signed agreement. *See* U.C.C. § 9-624(a), (b). A secured party that wants to consummate a quick disposition should seek a waiver of both the right to notice and the right to redemption.

281. U.C.C. § 9-624(c).

Chapter 19

The Consequences of Creditor Misbehavior

Synopsis

§ 19.01 Overview

Chapter 18 dealt primarily with the rights and duties of secured parties during the foreclosure process. This chapter focuses on the consequences that may befall a secured party that fails to comply with the Code's requirements. Creditor misbehavior takes many forms, among them:

- repossessing collateral when no default has occurred;[1]

- repossessing collateral in a manner that constitutes a breach of the peace;[2]

- failing to take one or more of the many steps necessary to ensure a commercially reasonable disposition of the collateral;[3]

---

1. *See* Chapter 17, *supra.*
2. *See* § 18.01[A][1], *supra.*
3. *See* § 18.02[A], *supra.*

- failing to give proper notice of disposition (sometimes characterized as an aspect of commercial reasonableness);[4]

- buying improperly at a private disposition;[5]

- failing to allow redemption;[6]

- failing to use reasonable care to preserve collateral in its possession;[7]

- failing to file a termination statement or to relinquish control when required by the Code;[8] and

- failing to respond to the debtor's request for a statement confirming the balance of the indebtedness or identifying the collateral.[9]

The most common complaints allege a failure to conduct a commercially reasonable disposition and/or a failure to give proper notice. If a secured party fails to conform its conduct to the Code's requirements, Article 9 provides a variety of pre-disposition and post-disposition remedies to aggrieved persons.[10]

[A] Pre-Disposition Remedies

If a secured party is about to conduct a sale in a commercially unreasonable manner, for example, if it gave notification of its intention to sell the collateral at an auction sale at 2:00 a.m. on a Sunday morning, the debtor, a secondary obligor, or a junior lienholder might wish to obtain a court order requiring the secured party to conduct the sale in a commercially reasonable manner. If a secured party plans to proceed in a manner that is inconsistent with the Code's duties of good faith and commercial reasonableness, an injunctive remedy may be useful if it can be implemented before the secured party can complete a commercially unreasonable disposition. Section 9-625(a) therefore provides that "[i]f it is established that a secured party is not proceeding in accordance with [Article 9], a court may order or restrain collection, enforcement, or

---

4. *See* § 18.02[B], *supra.*
5. *See* § 18.02[C], *supra.*
6. *See* § 18.05, *supra.*
7. *See* § 19.01[B][3], *infra.*
8. *See* § 19.01[B][4], *infra.*
9. *See* § 19.01[B][5], *infra.*
10. Article 9 does not expressly limit the persons who may sue for relief for a secured party's failure to comply with Part 6 of Article 9. In the typical situation, only the debtor, an obligor, or a junior lienholder would suffer harm from the secured party's conduct. *See, e.g.,* Abele Tractor & Equip. Co., Inc. v. Schaeffer, 137 N.Y.S.3d 174, 188 A.D.3d 1500 (2020) (would-be buyer of titled construction vehicle was not "debtor" and did not have standing to pursue claims against creditor for violations of Article 9, Part 6, where buyer did not exercise dominion and control over vehicle and acknowledged that title and possession would pass only on buyer's making full payment); Robertson v. Horton Bros. Recovery, Inc., 56 U.C.C. Rep. Serv. 2d 925 (D. Del. 2005) (family members of debtor who did not demonstrate that they helped debtor purchase her car or that they held a property interest in the car did not have standing to pursue claim for damages allegedly suffered due to secured party's attempted repossession of the car).

disposition of collateral on appropriate terms and conditions."[11] An injunctive pre-disposition remedy may be useful in the following situations:

- if a secured party is planning a commercially unreasonable disposition, such as a public auction of an asset that is so specialized that only a private sale will suffice, a court may issue a mandatory injunction requiring the secured party to conduct the sale in accordance with terms and conditions dictated by the judge;

- if a secured party has failed to give proper notification prior to an anticipated disposition, a court can issue a temporary restraining order prohibiting dispo-sition for a time that is sufficient to allow an aggrieved party either to redeem or to prepare to protect its interests;[12] and

- if a secured party's repossession is wrongful because there is no default, the debtor should be able to recover the collateral through a replevin action.

In the first two situations,[13] a question arises whether the party seeking relief must demonstrate the ordinary equitable requirements for obtaining injunctive relief, most notably, the requirement of showing irreparable injury if the relief is not granted.[14] Because most secured parties are financially solvent (and thus capable of paying any damages awarded), the cases are rare in which the party seeking relief can make such a showing. Although the courts have split on the point, some authority supports the proposition that the party seeking relief need not meet the normal conditions for ob-taining injunctive relief if the relief is authorized by statute.[15] Because of the importance that the drafters placed on the pre-disposition remedies and the limited intrusiveness of those remedies, the better-reasoned position is that the Code displaces the condi-tions normally found in equity.[16]

If a defaulting debtor complains that the secured party breached the peace in repos-sessing the collateral, replevin should not be available to the debtor;[17] the secured party still has the superior possessory interest, even if it gained possession in an inappropri-

---

11. U.C.C. § 9-625(a).

12. Another situation might involve an attempt by a lienholder to enjoin a foreclosure sale by a secured party who claims priority, under circumstances where the objecting lienholder has asserted a colorable claim to subordinate the foreclosing party's security interest. See Nelson v. Project Spokane, LLC, 2020 WL 3470311 (D. Mont. 2020) (enjoining ostensible senior secured party from foreclosing on collateral until junior's subordination claim was resolved on the merits).

13. In the third situation, the laws governing replevin actions typically specify the type of showing that the party seeking relief must make and the security it must provide.

14. See generally DAN B. DOBBS & CAPRICE L. ROBERTS, THE LAW OF REMEDIES § 2.9(2), at 168 (3d ed. 2018). The other common requirements are that the party seeking relief post security for any harm caused by the court's order and demonstrate a probability of success on the merits. Id. § 2.11(2), at 190.

15. Id. § 2.10, at 182–86 (tendency is for courts to view statutory authorization of injunctive relief as substitute for irreparable injury rule).

16. See U.C.C. § 1-103(b) (unless displaced by specific Code provisions, Code is supplemented by principles of law and equity).

17. See, e.g., Clark v. Assoc. Comm. Corp., 820 F. Supp. 562, 21 U.C.C. Rep. Serv. 2d 860 (D. Kan. 1993) (temporary restraining order pending replevin inappropriate where debtor was in default but repossession breached the peace).

ate manner. Returning the collateral to the debtor will not cure the default, and the secured party could simply repossess it again. In such a circumstance, damages are sufficient to compensate the debtor for any injury it suffers.

[B] Monetary Damages

What theories support a monetary recovery if a secured party engages in creditor misconduct? The answer depends on the type of misconduct involved.

[1] Wrongful Repossession

Section 9-625(b) provides that a secured party is liable for damages "in the amount of any loss caused by a failure to comply with this Article." This language authorizes the court to award damages in an amount sufficient to place the injured party in the position it would have occupied had no violation occurred.

Section 9-625(b)'s provision for damages, however, does not displace the injured party's remedies under tort law.[18] If a secured party repossesses collateral in the mistaken belief that the debtor has defaulted, the debtor may seek recovery of the goods *in specie* and sue for the tort of trespass to chattels. In such an action, the debtor may recover possession of the collateral as well as damages for any harm done to the collateral and for the loss of its use while the collateral was in the secured party's possession.[19] Alternatively, if the debtor does not want the collateral returned *in specie*, the debtor may allow the secured party to retain it and instead assert a claim for the intentional tort of conversion.[20] The standard measure of damages for conversion is the fair market value of the asset at the time of the conversion.[21] For example, suppose Freyermuth holds a security interest in Henning's automobile to secure a personal loan to Henning in the amount of $10,000. Because he incorrectly (but in good faith) believes Henning is in default, Freyermuth repossesses the car and conducts a commercially reasonable sale at which Gotberg purchases the car for $8,000, or $3,000 less than its actual fair market value of $11,000. Henning could sue to set aside the foreclosure sale and

---

18. Droge v. AAAA Two Star Towing, Inc., 468 P.3d 862, 102 U.C.C. Rep. Serv. 2d 177 (Nev. Ct. App. 2020) (Section 9-625(b) is not an exclusive remedy).

19. *See* RESTATEMENT (SECOND) OF TORTS § 222, Comment a.

20. *See, e.g.*, Warren v. Ford Motor Credit Co., 693 F.2d 1373, 35 U.C.C. Rep. Serv. 306 (11th Cir. 1982); Chen v. Profit Sharing Plan of Donald H. Bohne, DDS, P.A., 456 S.E.2d 237 (Ga. App. 1995). Similarly, a subordinate creditor that takes possession of property in which a secured party has a superior security interest following default is also liable in conversion if the subordinate creditor refuses to turn over the collateral to the senior secured party. *See, e.g.*, Fleet Capital Corp. v. Yamaha Motor Corp., U.S.A., 2002 U.S. Dist. LEXIS 18115, 48 U.C.C. Rep. Serv. 2d 1137 (S.D.N.Y. 2002); Guaranty State Bank & Trust Co. v. Van Diest Supply Co., 55 P.3d 357, 48 U.C.C. Rep. Serv. 2d 1197 (Kan. Ct. App. 2002).

21. *See, e.g.*, Fleet Capital Corp. v. Yamaha Motor Corp., U.S.A., 48 U.C.C. Rep. Serv. 2d 1137 (S.D.N.Y. 2002); Chemlease Worldwide, Inc. v. Brace, Inc., 338 N.W.2d 428, 37 U.C.C. Rep. Serv. 647 (Minn. 1983); RESTATEMENT (SECOND) OF TORTS § 222A, Comment c (providing for recovery of "full value" of converted asset).

recover the automobile from Gotberg,[22] and he could also sue Freyermuth for damages for any harm done to the automobile and for the loss of the automobile's use following repossession (e.g., the amount required to lease a comparable vehicle during the period Henning was out of possession). Alternatively, Henning could simply choose to sue Freyermuth for damages for conversion and could recover damages from Freyermuth in the amount of $1,000, which is the $11,000 fair market value of the automobile[23] less the $10,000 balance owed to Freyermuth.[24]

Even though conversion is an intentional tort, courts typically refuse to allow a jury to impose punitive damages if a secured party has acted in the mistaken but good-faith belief that a default has occurred.[25] Although the standards vary somewhat from state to state, an award of punitive damages typically requires some type of egregious conduct by the secured party—either actual malicious conduct or what courts have often called "constructive malice." Constructive malice typically consists of conduct that is reckless or grossly negligent. A case that comes close to the line is *Mitchell v. Ford Motor Credit Co.*,[26] in which the court approved an award of punitive damages following a wrongful repossession. The court concluded that the secured party was guilty of gross negligence because its records were in such a shambles that such incidents were bound to occur.

A debtor that claims wrongful repossession because the secured party committed a breach of the peace does not have a right to return of the goods *in specie*;[27] in such cases, the debtor may recover only monetary damages. In determining the theoretical basis for assessing damages, most courts simply treat the situation as analogous to a wrongful repossession without default and hold the secured party liable in conversion.[28] This approach is entirely appropriate and has the advantage of providing a uniform approach to all aspects of wrongful repossession. Courts may award punitive damages in cases of egregious conduct by the secured party.

---

22. Absent default, a secured party cannot pass the debtor's rights in the collateral to a transferee. U.C.C. § 9-617(a).

23. While the $8,000 price received by Freyermuth at the otherwise commercially reasonable sale would be some evidence of the car's fair market value, it is not conclusive in that regard. *See* § 18.02, *supra*.

24. In contrast, if the fair market value of the car had been only $9,000, Henning could raise the claim for conversion as a counterclaim to an action by Freyermuth for a deficiency judgment. *See* § 19.02, *infra*.

25. *See, e.g.*, Oaklawn Bank v. Baldwin, 709 S.W.2d 91, 1 U.C.C. Rep. Serv. 2d 596 (Ark. 1986).

26. 688 P.2d 42, 38 U.C.C. Rep. Serv. 1812 (Okla. 1984).

27. *See, e.g.*, Clark v. Associates Commercial Corp., 820 F. Supp. 562, 21 U.C.C. Rep. Serv. 2d 860 (D. Kan. 1993).

28. *See, e.g.*, Davis v. Complete Auto Recovery Servs., Inc., 2022 WL 17038956 (4th Cir. 2022); Kinetics Tech. Int'l Corp. v. Fourth Nat'l Bank of Tulsa, 705 F.2d 396, 36 U.C.C. Rep. Serv. 292 (10th Cir. 1983); Henderson v. Security Nat'l Bank, 72 Cal. App. 3d 764, 140 Cal. Rptr. 388, 22 U.C.C. Rep. Serv. 846 (1977). *But see* Nez v. Forney, 783 P.2d 471, 10 U.C.C. Rep. Serv. 2d 289 (N.M. 1989) (debtor's action for wrongful repossession sounded in contract).

A related situation occurs when a secured party refuses to accept a tender of the proper amount necessary to redeem the collateral.[29] In this situation, courts have appropriately recognized a cause of action for conversion because the secured party is in the same position it would have occupied had it repossessed in the absence of a default. Similarly, damages based on conversion are appropriate if a secured party miscalculates the amount necessary to redeem and demands an amount larger than the outstanding balance of the secured obligation.[30]

Depending on the nature of a secured party's conduct, liability may accrue for torts other than conversion, and the secured party might even face criminal sanctions in extreme cases. The cases are replete with instances of overbearing creditors that wrongfully entered another person's property or roughed up someone who resisted repossession. On the civil side, this conduct may constitute trespass, assault, battery, or intentional infliction of emotional distress, or perhaps a violation of the federal Fair Debt Collection Practices Act.[31] On the criminal side, the secured party may be guilty of trespass, breach of the peace, assault, or battery. A debtor injured by a wrongful repossession could seek to recover damages under Section 9-625(b) and could recover the amount necessary to place the debtor in the position it would have occupied had no violation occurred.[32] Section 9-625(b) does not preclude the debtor, however, from claiming a different measure of damages under tort law.[33]

For example, suppose Freyermuth holds a security interest in Henning's car and repossesses the car following Henning's default, but he does so by self-help despite Henning's strong verbal objection and attempted physical resistance, thereby breaching the peace under the law of the jurisdiction. Assume that this conduct enables Freyermuth to obtain possession of the car one month sooner than he would have obtained it in a judicial proceeding. At the time of the repossession, Henning owes Freyermuth $10,000 and the car's fair market value is $15,000. Freyermuth proceeds to conduct a commercially reasonable foreclosure sale at which Gotberg purchases the car for $10,000. On what theories can Henning recover damages, and in what amount?

---

29. Redemption is discussed in § 18.05, *supra*.

30. *See, e.g.*, Owens v. Auto. Recovery Bureau, Inc., 544 S.W.2d 26, 20 U.C.C. Rep. Serv. 820 (Mo. Ct. App. 1976).

31. The FDCPA provides that a debt collector may not use "unfair or unconscionable means" to collect a debt, including taking or threatening to repossess by self-help if "(A) there is no present right to possession of the property claimed as collateral through an enforceable security interest; (B) there is no present intention to take possession of the property; or (C) the property is exempt by law from such dispossession or disablement." 15 U.S.C. § 1692f(6).

32. *See* U.C.C. § 1-305(a); *see also* U.C.C. § 9-625, Comment 3.

33. U.C.C. § 9-625, Comment 3. *See also* U.C.C. § 1-103(b) (unless specifically displaced, principles of law and equity supplement the Code's provisions); Droge v. AAAA Two Star Towing, Inc., 468 P.3d 862, 102 U.C.C. Rep. Serv. 2d 177 (Nev. Ct. App. 2020) (Section 9-625(b) is not an exclusive remedy); Osborne v. Minn. Recovery Bureau, Inc., 59 U.C.C. Rep. Serv. 2d 879 (D. Minn. 2006) (Section 9-625(b) allows recovery for emotional distress damages resulting from altercation arising during repossession attempt).

If Henning chooses to proceed under Section 9-625, the appropriate measure of damages will be the amount reasonably calculated to put Henning in the position he would have occupied had Freyermuth complied with Article 9 and sought judicial repossession (i.e., Henning would have had possession and use of the car for another month). Thus, under Section 9-625, Henning could recover the value of one month's use of the car, which may be no more than a few hundred dollars. As a result, Henning will likely raise a conversion claim instead, for which he could recover damages in the amount of $5,000 (the car's fair market value less the balance of the debt owed to Freyermuth). In contrast, if the fair market value of the car had been only $10,000 at the time of repossession, Henning might instead choose to proceed under Section 9-625(b). Under either approach, the court could award punitive damages, if appropriate, for Freyermuth's decision to proceed with self-help despite Henning's verbal objection and attempted physical resistance.[34]

[2] Wrongful Disposition of the Collateral

If an aggrieved person seeks damages for a secured party's conduct in disposing of collateral, Section 9-625(b) authorizes the aggrieved person to recover the damages that flow from the secured party's wrongful conduct.[35] In measuring the aggrieved person's damages, one must look to the Code's general damages provision, which states that the remedies provided by the Code "must be liberally administered to the end that the aggrieved party may be put in as good a position as if the other party had fully performed but neither consequential or special damages nor penal damages may be had except as specifically provided in [the Uniform Commercial Code] or by other rule of law."[36] If the aggrieved person seeks damages under this provision, recovery of consequential damages (such as damages for emotional distress) is limited by the high foreseeability standards of general contract law. Furthermore, the aggrieved party typically cannot recover punitive damages unless it can state a tort claim for trespass, conversion, intentional infliction of emotional distress, or the like.

As noted above, the fact that Section 9-625(b)'s damages provision sounds in contract does not mean that it displaces the availability of conversion (or another tort theory) as an alternative remedy. Sound policy reasons justify permitting recovery using a conversion measure in certain situations, especially in cases where the misconduct involves a failure to give proper notification to the debtor. Debtors rarely redeem collateral or take steps to protect their interests at foreclosure sales; thus, a failure to give notification is not likely to have an impact on the price received at the sale. Allowing only Section 9-625(b) as a basis for recovery would yield no damages in such circumstances. Such a result would provide secured parties with relatively little incentive

---

34. The Code does not generally permit punitive damages, but it permits a court to award punitive damages if another rule of law (such as the law of conversion) so authorizes. U.C.C. § 1-305(a). The Comments to Section 9-625 make clear that underlying principles of tort law, such as the law of conversion, supplement the remedies provided in Section 9-625. U.C.C. § 9-625, Comment 3.

35. U.C.C. § 9-625(b).

36. U.C.C. § 1-305(a). *See also* U.C.C. § 9-625, Comment 3.

to comply with their obligations under Article 9.[37] Allowing debtors the alternative remedy of conversion in appropriate cases, however, presents secured parties with the more meaningful risk that a court might award damages and thus may have a more significant *in terrorem* effect.[38]

Schrock v. Citizens Valley Bank,[39] in which the secured party conducted a commercially unreasonable auction sale, illustrates the difference between damages based on conversion and damages based on the Code's remedial provision. The auction produced only $143,000, but expert testimony indicated that a commercially reasonable auction would have produced $170,000, or roughly 85 percent of the collateral's $200,000 fair market value. Using the Code's remedial provision, the court should place the debtor "in as good a position as if the [secured] party had fully performed," and full performance in this context means a commercially reasonable auction. Thus, assuming that the debt in *Schrock* was $150,000, the Code's remedial scheme would entitle the debtor to recover damages of $20,000, that is, the surplus that would have been produced by a commercially reasonable sale. In conversion, however, the debtor could recover damages of $50,000, that is, the fair market value of the collateral less the balance of the secured debt.[40]

[3] Failure to Use Reasonable Care Regarding Collateral in Secured Party's Possession

Article 9 obligates a secured party to use reasonable care in the custody and preservation of collateral in its possession.[41] If the secured party fails to satisfy this obligation, an aggrieved person may recover damages for "any loss" caused by such failure.[42]

---

37. Even if it does not lead to measurable damages, failure to give notice can have a profound effect on the secured party's right to a deficiency judgment. *See* § 19.02, *infra*.

38. *But see* Caterpillar Fin. Servs. Corp. v. Get 'Er Done Drilling, Inc., 286 A.3d 302, 109 U.C.C. Rep. Serv. 2d 444 (Pa. Super. Ct. 2022) (defaulting debtor that could not redeem collateral stated no conversion action against secured party for including erroneous date in notification of sale); Kennedy v. Fournie, 898 S.W.2d 672, 26 U.C.C. Rep. Serv. 2d 640 (Mo. Ct. App. 1995) (debtor was not entitled to conversion damages for failure to give proper notification because secured party was entitled to possession and debtor made no attempt to redeem the collateral).

39. 621 P.2d 96, 30 U.C.C. Rep. Serv. 1169 (Or. Ct. App. 1980).

40. The effect of such misconduct on a secured party's claim for a deficiency is discussed in § 19.02, *infra*.

41. U.C.C. § 9-207(a). The debtor and secured party may define in the security agreement what constitutes "reasonable care," unless the standards are "manifestly unreasonable." U.C.C. § 9-603(a). *See, e.g.,* Grimes v. Auto Venture Acceptance, 2023 WL 2817487 (Ky. Ct. App. 2023) (where security agreement provided that debtor assumed responsibility for personal property left in a vehicle that was repossessed and stored in a reasonably safe place, clause was effective to waive any negligence by secured party that stored the car in a fenced lot surrounded with razor wire and a "No trespassing" sign indicating the lot was subject to video surveillance).

42. U.C.C. § 9-625(b).

[4] Failure to File or Send Termination Statement

The Code permits a debtor to demand that a secured party provide a termination statement terminating the effectiveness of a financing statement if no obligation remains outstanding and the secured party has no commitment to make subsequent advances, incur obligations, or otherwise give value to be secured by the collateral described in that financing statement. Upon proper demand, the secured party must comply within 20 days.[43] If the collateral is consumer goods, the Code obligates the secured party to file such a termination statement within one month after satisfaction of the secured obligation even if the debtor does not request a termination statement.[44] If the secured party fails to satisfy its obligation in a timely fashion, the secured party is liable for a statutory penalty in the amount of $500 *plus* any loss caused by its failure.[45]

[5] Filing of Unauthorized Financing Statement

A secured party may file a financing statement or amend a filed financing statement only if Section 9-509(a) permits the secured party to do so.[46] The filing of an unauthorized financing statement can have a detrimental impact on the debtor's ability to obtain future credit using property covered by the unauthorized financing statement.[47] As a result, Section 9-625(b) permits a debtor injured by an unauthorized financing statement to recover damages for any loss resulting from the unauthorized financing statement.[48] In addition, Section 9-625(e)(3) allows the person identified in the unau-

---

43. U.C.C. § 9-513(c). *See* § 5.06[C], *supra*.

44. U.C.C. § 9-513(a).

45. U.C.C. § 9-625(e)(4). Similarly, a secured party that fails to relinquish control as required by Section 9-208 or 9-209 is liable for any loss caused plus the statutory penalty. U.C.C. § 9-625(e)(1), (2).

46. A secured party can file an initial financing statement if (a) the debtor has authorized the filing in a signed record, U.C.C. § 9-509(a)(1); (b) the debtor has signed a security agreement that describes the collateral indicated in the financing statement, U.C.C. § 9-509(b)(1); or (c) the debtor has acquired the collateral subject to secured party's already-existing security interest, U.C.C. § 9-509(c).

47. The problem of unauthorized financing statements typically arises in one of two contexts. The first involves the "spite" filing, where a disgruntled person simply files a financing statement to spite or harass the person identified as the debtor even though that person owes the filer no secured obligation. The injured person can file an information statement explaining the problem, U.C.C. § 9-515(a), or a termination statement, U.C.C. § 9-515(d)(2). Article 9 does not provide a mechanism that allows the filing office to remove the financing statement, although some states have adopted nonuniform provisions allowing the removal of a financing statement by administrative action.

The second involves the unauthorized "overbroad" filing, where the filer has a security interest in certain assets but files a financing statement covering more assets than the actual collateral (e.g., the secured party has a security interest in the debtor's "equipment" but files a financing statement covering "all of the debtor's personal property"). Because a secured party cannot justify filing an overbroad financing statement based solely on the debtor's execution of the security agreement, U.C.C. § 9-509(b)(1), an overbroad financing statement is not permitted unless the debtor explicitly authorizes that filing in a signed record. *Id.* § 9-509(a)(1).

48. This recovery could include, for example, damages resulting from the loss of favorable financing terms because the would-be lender refused to close the loan due to the presence of the unauthorized financing statement.

thorized financing statement as the debtor to recover a statutory penalty in the amount of $500.[49]

[6] Failure to Provide Statement of Account or List of Collateral

Article 9 permits a debtor to request that the secured party issue a statement setting forth or confirming the outstanding balance of the debtor's unpaid obligation to the secured party. In addition, Article 9 permits the debtor to request that the secured party approve or correct a list of the secured party's collateral.[50] Such statements are of some use to the debtor in obtaining subsequent financing or in refinancing the secured obligations, as future potential secured parties likely will seek to confirm the extent of encumbrances against the debtor's assets.[51] Article 9 obligates the secured party to respond to the debtor's request within 14 days;[52] if the secured party fails to comply, it is liable for any resulting loss, which may include the debtor's inability to obtain alternative financing or the increased costs of such financing.[53] Furthermore, in the event the secured party fails to comply with such a request without reasonable cause, it is also liable for statutory damages of $500 (in addition to actual damages).[54]

---

49. U.C.C. § 9-625(e)(3); McDaniel v. 162 Columbia Heights Housing Corps., 21 Misc. 3d 244, 863 N.Y.S.2d 346, 66 U.C.C. Rep. Serv. 2d 508 (Sup. Ct. 2008); Padilla v. Ghuman, 183 P.3d 653, 66 U.C.C. Rep. Serv. 2d 472 (Colo. Ct. App. 2007).

50. U.C.C. § 9-210(b).

51. The impact of the Code's first-to-file-or-perfect rule for conflicting security interests in the same collateral (as explained in Chapter 10) may render these statements of somewhat limited use to future secured parties. For example, suppose Bank is considering a loan to Debtor secured by all of Debtor's equipment (which has a value of $50,000). In investigating Debtor's creditworthiness, Bank discovers an existing filed financing statement in favor of Finance Company, covering the Debtor's equipment. Bank requires Debtor to ask Finance Company to confirm the balance of the secured obligations under Section 9-210, and Finance Company confirms that the balance of the debt is only $500. As explained in Chapter 10, Bank cannot assume that it can safely make the loan based on the confirmation that Debtor has $49,500 of equity in the equipment. If Bank made the loan to Debtor, nothing would prevent Finance Company from later making another loan to Debtor secured by the Debtor's equipment (as long as its financing statement covering equipment remained effective to perfect that interest). Under Section 9-322(a)(1), Finance Company would have priority as to the equipment to the full extent of those additional loans. As a result, Bank cannot ensure its desired priority if it relies solely on Finance Company's confirmation to the debtor of the balance of the secured obligations.

52. U.C.C. § 9-210(b).

53. U.C.C. § 9-625(b).

54. U.C.C. § 9-625(f). If the secured party never claimed any interest in the collateral or the obligations referenced in the request, it has reasonable cause for its failure to comply. *Id.*

§ 19.02 Secured Party's Right to Deficiency Judgment

Claims of creditor misconduct commonly arise when a secured party conducts a foreclosure that fails to satisfy the secured obligation and thereafter seeks a judgment for the remaining deficiency. The secured party's right to recover a deficiency arises from Section 9-615(d), which provides that "the secured party shall account to and pay a debtor for any surplus" following disposition and that "the obligor is liable for any deficiency."[55] The secured party's failure to observe Article 9's disposition rules, however, renders it liable for any resulting loss under Section 9-625(b). To what extent does the secured party's failure to observe Article 9's disposition rules affect its right to collect its deficiency judgment?

To understand Article 9's treatment of this question, first consider the way courts approached it prior to Article 9's revisions in 1998. Suppose that Debtor owes Bank $225,000 secured by a security interest in Debtor's equipment. Debtor defaults, and Bank conducts a commercially unreasonable auction sale that yields a price of $150,000. Further, suppose that a reasonable auction sale would have produced a price of $175,000 and that the equipment could have sold for as much as $185,000 if it could have been sold in an arms-length transaction (i.e., not in the context of a foreclosure auction). Finally, suppose Bank attempts to sue Debtor to collect a deficiency judgment of $75,000, and Debtor objects that Bank's sale was commercially unreasonable.

Prior to 1998, courts took one of three approaches to such a dispute. The first approach, sometimes called the "set-off" approach, applied a straightforward reading of the text of the prior version of Article 9: the secured party could recover the amount of the deficiency reduced by any actual losses attributable to its misconduct. Courts following this approach would calculate independently the amount due to each party and then "net out" the results, leaving a judgment in favor of one of the litigants.[56] Under this approach, a secured party's misbehavior neither barred a deficiency nor created a presumption of harm. The secured party bore the burden of proving the facts that supported its claim, and the obligor carried the burden of proving that the misconduct had caused it to suffer a loss. In the above hypothetical, Bank would have a claim for a $75,000 deficiency, calculated as its debt ($225,000) less the proceeds of its sale ($150,000). In turn, if Debtor raised a successful counterclaim based on Article 9's remedial provision, Debtor would recover damages of $25,000, the amount that Bank would have received had it conducted a commercially reasonable sale ($175,000) less the actual sale proceeds ($150,000). When the claims are netted out, Bank would recover a judgment for $50,000. If Debtor instead raised a successful counterclaim

---

55. U.C.C. § 9-615(d). If the issue of a deficiency arises following a secured party's collection or enforcement of rights to payment, Section 9-608(a)(4) provides a similar rule.

56. *See, e.g.,* Boender v. Chicago N. Clubhouse Ass'n, Inc., 608 N.E.2d 207, 20 U.C.C. Rep. Serv. 2d 687 (Ill. Ct. App. 1992).

based on the tort theory of conversion,[57] it would recover damages of $35,000, the collateral's fair market value ($185,000) less the actual disposition price ($150,000). Thus, after netting the claims, Bank would recover a deficiency judgment for $40,000.[58]

The "set-off" approach was both straightforward and consistent with the text of prior Article 9, but few courts adopted it. Many state courts instead adopted the "absolute-bar" rule, under which a secured party that violated its obligations in disposing of the collateral could not recover a deficiency judgment *regardless of the collateral's actual value*. Applying the absolute-bar approach to the above hypothetical, once Debtor proved that Bank's sale was commercially unreasonable, Debtor would be entitled to summary judgment against Bank on Bank's action for a deficiency judgment—even though a commercially reasonable sale would have produced a bona fide deficiency of $50,000![59]

Some courts took a third approach, rejecting the absolute-bar rule because (i) it had no support in the text of Article 9, (ii) it created undeserved windfalls for debtors in cases such as the above hypothetical, and (iii) such a punitive sanction was disproportionate given the relatively nebulous "commercially reasonable" standard that Article 9 imposes on secured parties.[60] These courts adopted a rule known as the "rebuttable presumption" rule. Under this rule, once an obligor demonstrated that the secured

---

57. See discussion in § 19.02[B], *infra*.

58. If the value of Debtor's counterclaim exceeded the value of Bank's claim, using whatever measure the court deemed appropriate, Debtor would be entitled to an affirmative recovery for the excess.

59. *See, e.g.*, In re Kelaidis, 276 B.R. 266, 47 U.C.C. Rep. Serv. 2d 823 (10th Cir. Bankr. 2002) (noting Utah courts' consistent application of absolute-bar rule). For a compilation of cases applying the absolute-bar rule, see Robert M. Lloyd, *The Absolute Bar Rule in UCC Foreclosure Cases: A Prescription for Waste*, 40 UCLA L. Rev. 695 (1993).

60. *See, e.g.*, Baragas v. Coupland State Bank, 46 U.C.C. Rep. Serv. 2d 565 (Tex. Ct. App. 2001) (despite failure to give proper notice of public auction, court upheld deficiency judgment against guarantors because most of sale proceeds had derived from private sales with proper notice, guarantors did not show that public sale was commercially unreasonable, and barring deficiency would give guarantors windfall).

In the hypothetical in the text, for example, Bank will expect a significant deficiency (somewhere around $50,000). Bank thus has a significant incentive to conduct a sale that will preserve its right to enforce that deficiency. But Bank will be hard-pressed to know exactly when it has done "enough" to make its sale "commercially reasonable." For example, how many advertisements should it run? Three? Six? Twelve? On the one hand, we presumably want Bank to run an additional advertisement if it will attract more bidders and produce a higher sale price. On the other hand, because Bank will add these expenses of sale to the balance of the debt, U.C.C. § 9-615(a)(1), such expenses will increase Debtor's deficiency if they do not actually produce a higher sale price.

The problem is that Bank has no way to know exactly when an additional advertisement will (or will not) produce more bidders, and thus the absolute-bar rule may in fact encourage secured parties to run extra (and potentially ineffective) advertisements, thereby driving up deficiency judgments, just to protect its right to collect a deficiency judgment (i.e., to protect against the risk that a court might say, after the fact, "you should have run more advertisements"). Thus, some have argued that the absolute-bar rule, although a boon to the individual entitled to raise it, was not in the best interests of debtors as a class. *See* Robert M. Lloyd, *The Absolute Bar Rule in UCC Foreclosure Cases: A Prescription for Waste*, 40 UCLA L. Rev. 695 (1993).

party violated Article 9's requirements in disposing of the collateral, the court drew a presumption that the collateral's value equaled the outstanding debt.[61] In other words, the court established a presumption that a proper disposition would have generated sale proceeds exactly sufficient to satisfy the debt. This presumption placed on the secured party the burden of going forward with evidence to the contrary; that is, to recover a deficiency, the secured party had to produce evidence that even a sale in full compliance with Article 9's requirements would still have resulted in a deficiency. If the secured party could not rebut the presumption, it could not recover a deficiency judgment. If the secured party did successfully rebut the presumption, it could recover a deficiency measured by the difference between the unpaid debt and the amount that would have resulted from a commercially reasonable disposition (unless, of course, the obligor successfully refuted the secured party's evidence). The obligor bore the ultimate burden of persuasion on the issue of loss.

In the above hypothetical, the rebuttable presumption rule would have given Debtor the benefit of a presumption that the collateral was worth $225,000 (the full amount of the debt). Bank would have to produce evidence to rebut the presumption and demonstrate that a commercially reasonable auction still would have resulted in a deficiency. Thus, assuming Bank produced sufficient credible evidence that a commercially reasonable sale would have produced a price of $175,000, Bank could recover a deficiency judgment in the amount of $50,000.[62]

Based on widespread criticism of the absolute-bar rule, the 1998 Article 9 revisions expressly adopted the rebuttable presumption rule *for all non-consumer transactions.* If a secured party seeks a deficiency judgment, it does not have to establish compliance with the Code's requirements as part of its prima facie case.[63] If the debtor or a secondary obligor raises the secured party's noncompliance as an issue, the secured party must prove that the disposition complied with the Code's requirements.[64] If the secured party fails to carry this burden, then a presumption arises that a disposition in compliance with the Code's requirements would have produced a price sufficient to satisfy the outstanding debt.[65] The secured party may not recover a deficiency unless it proves that a disposition in compliance with the Code's requirements would have produced a price less than the balance of the debt. If the secured party carries this burden, it may

---

61. *Cf.* Lease Resolution Corp. v. Aut-A-Wash, Inc., 59 Mass. App. 1107, 52 U.C.C. Rep. Serv. 2d 534 (2003) (rebuttable presumption approach inapplicable where evidence showed that secured party gave proper notice and complied with all other provisions of Article 9).

62. If the obligor proceeded on a conversion theory, the secured party would have to produce evidence tending to prove that the fair market value of the collateral was less than the amount of the debt. Thus, if Bank produced sufficient credible evidence that the fair market value of the collateral was only $185,000, Bank could recover a $40,000 deficiency judgment.

63. U.C.C. § 9-626(a)(1).

64. U.C.C. § 9-626(a)(2).

65. U.C.C. § 9-626(a)(4).

recover a judgment equal to the amount of the secured obligation less the amount that would have been received in a commercially reasonable disposition.[66]

In *consumer transactions*, however, Article 9 does not provide a specific rule to govern the consequences of a secured party's noncompliance. Section 9-626(b) provides that Article 9 "is intended to leave to the court the determination of the proper rules in consumer transactions" and permits courts in consumer transactions "to apply established approaches."[67] In consumer transactions, courts thus retain the discretion to apply any of the three approaches taken by courts prior to 1998—including the absolute-bar rule. Not surprisingly, some courts in states that had applied the absolute-bar rule prior to 1998 have continued to apply that rule in consumer transactions.[68]

§ 19.03 The Consumer Penalty— § 9-625(c)

Article 9 contains a provision often called the "consumer penalty." If a secured party fails to comply with Article 9 in disposing of consumer goods,[69] Section 9-625(c) permits the debtor or a secondary obligor to recover "in any event an amount not less than the credit service charge plus 10 percent of the principal amount of the debt or the time price differential plus 10 percent of the cash price."[70] Because Section 9-625(b)'s basic remedies provision is subject to Section 9-625(c), which establishes an amount recoverable "in any event," one should read the consumer penalty as a substitute for ordinary monetary damages. If the consumer cannot establish loss in the ordinary manner or the amount of that loss is less than the consumer penalty, the consumer may recover the penalty *rather than* ordinary damages. In other words, the consumer cannot recover both actual damages and the full amount of the consumer penalty.[71]

---

66. U.C.C. § 9-626(a)(3). *See, e.g., In re* Knight, 544 B.R. 141 (Bankr. E.D. Ark. 2016); *In re* Sandpoint Cattle Co., LLC, 83 U.C.C. Rep. Serv. 2d 863 (D. Neb. 2014); *In re* MarMc Transp., Inc., 469 B.R. 84, 76 U.C.C. Rep. Serv. 2d 862 (Bankr. D. Wyo. 2012).

67. U.C.C. § 9-626(b).

68. *See, e.g.,* Hicklin v. Onyx Acceptance Corp., 970 A.2d 244, 68 U.C.C. Rep. Serv. 2d 413 (Del. 2009); Missouri State Credit Union v. Wilson, 176 S.W.3d 182, 61 U.C.C. Rep. Serv. 2d 558 (Mo. Ct. App. 2005) (applied absolute bar rule without discussing section 9-626(b)); Coxall v. Clover Comm. Corp., 4 Misc. 3d 654, 781 N.Y.S.2d 567, 54 U.C.C. Rep. Serv. 2d 5 (N.Y. City Civ. Ct. 2004). *But see* Folks v. Tuscaloosa County Credit Union, 989 So. 2d 531, 64 U.C.C. Rep. Serv. 2d 957 (Ala. Ct. App. 2007) (applying "set-off" rule in consumer transaction, as previously established in pre-revision Alabama decisions).

69. The penalty applies if the collateral is consumer goods even if the transaction is not a consumer-goods transaction. The caption to Section 9-625(c) as originally drafted mistakenly referred to a consumer-goods transaction. The 2010 amendments corrected this error.

70. U.C.C. § 9-625(c)(2); *see, e.g.,* Coxall v. Clover Comm. Corp., 4 Misc. 3d 654, 781 N.Y.S.2d 567, 54 U.C.C. Rep. Serv. 2d 5 (N.Y. City Civ. Ct. 2004) (consumer debtor entitled to statutory damage recovery of $1,846.24). Other aggrieved parties (such as a junior secured party) may recover damages under Section 9-625(b) but may not rely upon the consumer penalty.

71. Chisolm v. TranSouth Fin. Corp., 194 F.R.D. 538, 42 U.C.C. Rep. Serv. 2d 332 (E.D. Va. 2000) (actual damages or statutory damages are recoverable, but not both). In this regard, the consumer

Calculating the amount of the consumer penalty can be tricky because of the two basic formulas. Understanding which formula to use requires an appreciation of the difference between a *credit service charge* (the equivalent of interest on a loan) and a *time-price differential*. At the time the Code was first adopted, several jurisdictions had statutes or constitutional provisions establishing restrictive usury laws. For example, suppose that a state's law allowed for a maximum interest rate of 10 percent. If a debtor went to a bank to borrow money to buy a car, the bank could not charge interest at a higher rate. Though these restrictions were popular in many states, they had a negative impact on some sectors of the economy in those states. For example, if a national automotive concern that sold cars to consumers on secured credit could not obtain a competitive interest rate in a particular state, it might choose to do business in another state. Recognizing this economic reality, some courts devised the fiction of the time-price differential. In a state with a 10 percent usury limit, if a seller was willing to sell an asset for $10,000 today but required the buyer to pay a credit price of $11,500 in installments over the course of a year, these courts reasoned that the $1,500 difference was not "interest" and thus not subject to the usury laws; it was instead a "time-price differential." In other words, the time-price differential was simply a means to avoid the impact of the usury laws.

The following hypothetical situations illustrate the differences in the two formulas. Suppose Henning, a consumer, decides to purchase a car priced at $25,000. He intends to pay $5,000 down and finance $20,000 and has a choice of having Dealer or Bank handle the financing. If Henning borrows $20,000 from Bank to be repaid over four years and the total interest Bank will receive over the life of the loan is $4,000, the consumer penalty that Bank must pay if it engages in misconduct will be $6,000, that is, the sum of $2,000 (10 percent of the principal amount of the debt) and $4,000 (the credit service charge). If he had decided to finance the $20,000 with Dealer and had agreed to repay a total of $24,000 over four years, the consumer penalty would be $4,000 (the time-price differential) plus 10 percent of the cash price. But would the "cash price" be the cash amount that Henning had to pay Dealer to buy the car without any financing ($25,000) or the amount financed ($20,000)? It is tempting to say that $20,000 is the proper amount because it equates the penalties for sellers and lenders. The problem is that the Code also uses the term "cash price" in its strict foreclosure provision,[72] and in that context, it almost certainly means the full price that would have been paid on the date of sale (in the example, $25,000).[73]

---

penalty functions somewhat like a liquidated damages provision, even though the "penalty" concept and the "liquidated damages" concept are antithetical in contract law. The term "consumer penalty" is thus something of a misnomer.

72. U.C.C. § 9-620(e).

73. The purpose of the limitation on strict foreclosure is to protect the debtor's equity, while the purpose of the consumer penalty is (at least in part) to penalize creditor misbehavior. Thus, one might argue that it is appropriate to assign different meanings to the same term in these different contexts. This argument is subject to criticism, however, as the consumer penalty also serves to protect the equity of consumer debtors generally, by encouraging creditors to conduct reasonable sales.

After grasping the basic formula, one can apply the consumer penalty in a relatively straightforward fashion. For example, suppose that in the above hypothetical, Henning chose to finance the car from Bank. Suppose further that Bank conducts a commercially unreasonable sale, bringing a price of $8,000 and leaving a deficiency of $8,000. As discussed above, Bank would incur a $6,000 penalty because of its misconduct. If Bank cannot overcome the presumption that the car was worth the same amount as the debt, Bank cannot recover a deficiency judgment. Should Henning also be allowed to obtain a judgment for the $6,000 consumer penalty? The answer should be no. The effect of the presumption is to establish the loss flowing from the misconduct; on our facts, the loss is presumed to be $8,000. Because the consumer penalty is an alternative to damages, allowing Henning to recover it would violate the spirit of the Code.[74]

In this regard, remember that Article 9 permits courts to apply the absolute-bar rule to prohibit a deficiency judgment if a secured party has conducted a commercially unreasonable disposition in a consumer transaction. Can a consumer debtor both avoid a deficiency judgment entirely under the absolute bar rule *and* recover the consumer penalty? The answer should be no, as this would appear to add a penalty on top of a penalty. The debtor should have to elect between the absolute-bar rule and the result that would be reached by netting out the deficiency against the consumer penalty.[75] Unfortunately, a few decisions, such as *Wilmington Trust Co. v. Conner*,[76] have permitted consumer debtors to apply both the absolute-bar rule and the consumer penalty. Even more unfortunately, the drafters of revised Article 9 expressly refused to reject cases like *Conner*; the Comments to Section 9-625 merely state that the Code "leaves the treatment of statutory damages as it was under former Article 9."[77] Although the drafters presumably did not intend this language to reflect their approval of cases like *Conner*, some courts may use the Comments to justify allowing debtors in consumer-goods transactions to recover both actual damages and the consumer penalty (or to assert the benefit of the absolute-bar rule and still recover the consumer penalty).

---

74. If Bank's unreasonable sale produced a price of $11,000, leaving a deficiency of $5,000, and Bank could not overcome the presumption, Henning would have a choice of taking the presumed $5,000 in damages (wiping out the deficiency) or the $6,000 consumer penalty. Obviously, Henning would select the consumer penalty, but the court should net this out against the full deficiency. In other words, Henning should recover $1,000.

75. For a case that gets the issue right, see First City Bank-Farmers Branch v. Guex, 659 S.W.2d 734, 37 U.C.C. Rep. Serv. 1008 (Tex. Ct. App. 1983).

76. 415 A.2d 773, 28 U.C.C. Rep. Serv. 900 (Del. 1980). *See also, e.g.,* Coxall v. Clover Comm. Corp., 4 Misc. 3d 654, 781 N.Y.S.2d 567, 54 U.C.C. Rep. Serv. 2d 5 (N.Y. City Civ. Ct. 2004); *In re* Angel, 142 B.R. 194 (Bankr. S.D. Ohio 1992).

77. U.C.C. § 9-625, Comment 4.

Table of Cases

Table of Statutes

Code of Federal Regulations

Internal Revenue Code

Uniform Fraudulent Conveyance Act

Uniform Voidable Transfer Act

Index

[References are to sections.]